Brian [illegible]
March 2013

for
Tamara Petkevich
see page 204 in
"The Besieged"

MEMOIR OF A GULAG ACTRESS

TAMARA

PETKEVICH

Memoir

OF A GULAG ACTRESS

Translated by Yasha Klots and Ross Ufberg

Foreword by Joshua Rubenstein

NORTHERN ILLINOIS UNIVERSITY PRESS / DeKalb

Published by the Northern Illinois University Press, DeKalb, Illinois 60115

Manufactured in the United States using postconsumer-recycled, acid-free paper.

Design by Julia Fauci

Library of Congress Cataloging-in-Publication Data

Petkevich, T. V. (Tamara Vladimirovna)

[Zhizn'—sapozhok neparnyi. English]

Memoir of a Gulag actress / Tamara Petkevich ; translated by Yasha Klots and Ross Ufberg ; foreword by Joshua Rubenstein.

p. cm.

Includes index.

ISBN 978-0-87580-428-6 (clothbound : alk. paper)

1. Petkevich, T. V. (Tamara Vladimirovna) 2. Political persecution—Soviet Union—History. 3. Women political prisoners—Soviet Union—Biography. 4. Political prisoners—Soviet Union—Biography. 5. Actresses—Soviet Union—Biography. 6. Concentration camp theater—Soviet Union—History. 7. Soviet Union—History—1925–1953—Biography. 8. Kommunisticheskaia partiia Sovetskogo Soiuza—Purges. 9. Glavnoe upravlenie ispravitel'no-trudovykh lagerei OGPU—History. 10. Soviet Union—Politics and government—1936–1953. I. Title.

DK268.P44A3 2010

365'.45092—dc22

[B]

2010014125

Frontispiece spread: A road through the snow in the Komi Republic. 1943–1950

CONTENTS

FOREWORD

JOSHUA RUBENSTEIN

More than a half century since the death of Joseph Stalin in 1953 and nearly two decades since the collapse of the Soviet Union itself, the memoirs of onetime political prisoners—the survivors of the Gulag—still have the power to shock us. *Memoir of a Gulag Actress* is no exception. Tamara Petkevich spent seven years in different hard-labor camps, first in Kirghizia and then in the Komi Republic. She worked in the forests, felling trees and sawing lumber. She worked in a gravel pit. She collected hemp stalks for the production of fibers, the raw material for rope and sacking that was needed at the front during World War II. This was all exhausting and physically dangerous work. The prisoners lacked proper equipment and adequate food and clothing. Like many others, she suffered from scurvy, in spite of the "vitamin allowance" handed to the prisoners that included a "decoction of spruce and pine needles." Her symptoms disfigured her. "It began with purple spots over the legs and then grew into pus sores, then finally open ulcers." But she survived, in part because she was young and otherwise healthy, but mostly because her medical training and natural acting talents landed her safer work as a camp nurse and as an actress in a traveling theatrical troupe involving prisoners.

Born in Petrograd in 1920, young Tamara grew up in a family of idealistic communists. Her parents had fought in the Civil War, determined to prevent the restoration of the autocratic monarchy and to establish a just society based on the egalitarian teachings of Karl Marx. Her father was especially strict; he had little patience for his mother-in-law's stubborn interest in Russian Orthodoxy and objected whenever Tamara or either of her two sisters was taken to church. As *Memoir of a Gulag Actress* makes clear, the Bolsheviks were determined to remake society, to carry out a social revolution as thoroughgoing as the political revolution they had engineered. Tamara's father exemplified this single-minded determination. He was quick to use a leather whip on his daughters when they misbehaved, and proud of his service to the Party. None of this saved him.

One of the virtues of *Memoir of a Gulag Actress* is how Petkevich recalls the 1920s, the initial decade of Bolshevik rule, as both a time of naïve idealism and a time when her French teacher was exiled, church property confiscated, and the process of dekulakization unfolded in the countryside, leaving millions uprooted or dead. Eventually, her father, too, became a victim, first assigned to supervising the harvesting of peat and then arrested and condemned to oblivion like so many others. His arrest led to her family's impoverishment. At one time they had enjoyed a spacious apartment with a housekeeper. Now they were relatives of an "Enemy of the People," compelled to move to miserable quarters, shunned by onetime friends and neighbors and resigned to endless waiting in dispiriting lines in front of prison information bureaus. Families like themselves, in a scene made immortal by the poet Anna Akhmatova, beseeched callous officials for news, *any news*, about the fate of their loved ones, then handed in packets of food or money in case they were still alive.

As Petkevich's story takes us through four decades of Soviet life, we feel the steel ring of history clamp around her neck. She cannot separate her father's fate from the atmosphere of dread that engulfed the country in the late 1930s when the purge trials of veteran Bolsheviks, including several close associates of Lenin himself, provoked indignation and confusion with their accusations of betrayal and treason. She was a teenager at the time and shared the widespread wonderment over what compelled the defendants to behave as they did, to confess to outlandish crimes that could only lead to the scaffold.

The war compounded the general suffering. Her mother and one of her sisters died of starvation during the Siege of Leningrad. Petkevich herself, living in Frunze where she had moved to marry a young man she had met in a line of prisoners' relatives, was arrested in early 1943. The Soviet Union remained at war, with the Germans and against its own people. She was stunned by the experience of interrogation and the outlandish accusations rained down on her. Before her arrest, she never thought of the NKVD without a sense of alarm. Now she was in its clutches. The interrogations exhausted her. They asked her about gatherings with friends in Leningrad where they "read unauthorized poems by Akhmatova and Esenin," decadent poets in the eyes of the regime. She and her friends "held anti-Soviet discussions." She denied the accusations, but like all such accused, understanding that the secret police had already rummaged through her life, she could not help but imagine who had informed on her. "Viewing my own past through the prism of others' denunciations led me to madness." In the end, she faced a three-part indictment: belonging to a Leningrad terrorist center; counterrevolutionary propaganda; and anti-Semitism. The last accusation underscored the preposterous nature of the case; it was in 1943, following the turning point in the war when the Red Army defeated the Wehrmacht at Stalingrad and at Kursk, that the regime began a systematic campaign to limit the number of visible Jews in the country's premiere cultural institutions like museums, intellectual journals and the Bolshoi Opera.

For the next seven years Tamara endured the harsh isolation, difficult work and humiliation of being a woman political prisoner, a *zek*, in the Gulag. Much will seem familiar to people who have read the works of Eugeniya Ginzburg. But several aspects of Petkevich's story stand out.

First, she was not a politically engaged woman, and we can only conclude that it was her father's arrest when she was still a teenager in high school that led to the regime's interest in her and her eventual arrest. Second, her story relates how Stalinism, whether you were a prisoner or "at liberty," subverted human relations. Tamara was seduced by an unscrupulous doctor, Filipp Bakharev. He saved her life by helping to transfer her to work in a prison medical clinic. But he also fathered her child and later, after her release, maneuvered with his mistress to prevent Tamara from gaining custody of her son. Only an inhuman system would deny a former prisoner the right to raise her own child. The thread of this story runs through much of the book. It is told in great psychological detail, with portraits of Filipp and the friends who tried to help her.

Much of the literary power of *Memoir of a Gulag Actress* lies in Petkevich's vivid recall of the people in her life: her first husband, Erik, and their lives together in Frunze where she joined a family that failed to accept her; Aleksandr Osipovich Gavronsky, a renowned theater director, who leads the prisoner troupe and adopts her as if she were his daughter; her lover, Nikolai Danilovich—"tall, slim, handsome, elegant and professional"—an actor whose devotion sustains her; and her sister, Valentina, whom she locates upon her release. Their individual destinies, in the camps or "at liberty," reflect the full pathos of Stalin's miserable kingdom.

Finally, incidents of human decency will startle readers. In *The Gulag Archipelago*, Aleksandr Solzhenitsyn wrote that "the line separating good and evil passes not through states, nor between classes, nor between political parties either—but right through every human heart—and through all human hearts." Petkevich experienced unexpected kindness, from a school headmistress, prison guards, from prisoners who had initially scorned her, even from an officer in the Ministry of the Interior who looked into her case at a time when, following her release, she was being hounded to become an informer. When she entered the MGB public reception room in Moscow, she assumed she was giving up her life one more time. But instead, the officer reviewed her case dispassionately, one might be tempted to say professionally, and sent her on her way.

During her years as a prisoner, her relations with free workers who sometimes worked alongside her presaged the difficulties she experienced in the Big Zone. Some were considerate, others were suspicious and afraid. Most everyone thought former prisoners could only emerge "broken" from the camps and even decades later *zeks* were widely regarded as a "nuisance." Tamara feared that she would "never be able to wash off this stain," that "the line between people and enemies of the people remained insurmountable."

But she did overcome these obstacles and fashioned a new and inspiring life in the theater. For many years, she assumed that her experiences in the Gulag "belonged to a dark past that would trouble very few people today." But when her book first appeared in Russia in 1993, it provoked an intense reaction. "A tornado of human feelings," she remembered in a magazine interview at the time. "I suddenly understood that there were an enormous number of crippled destinies around me. Before that, I understood that there were many, but I did not know that even today there remains such human pain, pain that has not grown silent or disappeared." Under Nikita Khrushchev in the 1950s and 1960s, Soviet society was initially introduced to memoirs of the Gulag and other accounts of the Stalinist terror. Later, under Brezhnev, such memoirs and historical accounts had to circulate unofficially, in *samizdat*, in order to thwart the regime's heavy-handed censorship. It was only under Mikhail Gorbachev in the late 1980s that official censorship was entirely relaxed, and a great many works by both Soviet and Western authors became freely available in the former Soviet Union. So it is a testament to the power of *Memoir of a Gulag Actress*—to the vivid, human dimensions of her experience—that a memoir like this could still evoke such passions in a society grown weary of its tormented past.

TRANSLATORS' NOTE

YASHA KLOTS AND ROSS UFBERG

Since 1993 when Tamara Petkevich's memoir was first published, it has become one of Russia's most admired and widely read books about the Gulag. It would be a gross oversimplification, however, to reduce the value of the book to this topic alone. Although it came out long after Ginzburg's and Solzhenitsyn's pioneering works on the same subject, Petkevich's book has attracted a tremendous number of contemporary readers because its subtle psychological insight into events of the past resonates in the present and, we believe, will not fade away in the future; because it is, above all, a story told from a deeply personal perspective, rich in nuance and photographic detail. What makes Petkevich's book unique in the genre of Gulag memoirs is its acute focus on the individual rather than the collective, and the resulting novelistic tension that underpins the author's artistic vision, which extends beyond mere testimony. This is what we have tried to retain above all in our translation. It is for this reason that our foremost goal as translators has been to perpetuate the gripping flow, along with the historical significance, of Tamara Petkevich's text—at times, at the expense of word-for-word faithfulness to the original.

Our first task was to find a suitable English title. In Russian, the book is called *Zhizn'—sapozhok neparny* (literally, "Life Is an Unpaired Boot"), a line taken from the poem "Molodost'" ("Youth") by Marina Tsvetaeva, with only the first word changed: Tsvetaeva's "youth" extends to "life." We have chosen, with the consent of the author, to retitle the book as *Memoir of a Gulag Actress.*

Because of the inherent differences in the very structures of the two languages, translating from Russian into English usually results in a "trimming" of the original. For example, while it is normal for a Russian sentence to accommodate multiple subordinate clauses, English syntax calls for a more laconic rendition (hence, an original Russian sentence would often be split in parts). As we worked on the translation, we found it an especial challenge to replicate the expressivity of some of the Russian constructions, syntax in general and even punctuation, with which the original abounds (intonation, rhetorical questions, exclamations and exclamation marks, etc.). The passive and so-called impersonal forms natural to Russian grammar—and, arguably, reflecting the motif of losing one's sense of individuality in the depersonalizing conditions of hard-labor camps—have sometimes also been a stumbling block and called for a more neutral yet also more natural rendition in idiomatic English. At the same time, we tried to preserve the local color, as well as the sociolinguistic and geographical realia, of the original, often opting for a mere transliteration of words with no direct equivalents in the English language (e.g., *subbotnik, burzhuyka, desyatina, Solovki*, etc.). Unless they are explained in the main text, the reader can look them up in the Glossary. For the same reason, we preferred a literal translation of some of the expressions emblematic of the Soviet era and of the Gulag in particular. For example, we kept the phraseology "to sit out one's prison term," since we found it to be stronger and more adequate to the reality described in the book than the English equivalent "to serve one's time." The original construction well reflects the tendency of prison culture to alter the traditional understanding of things, sometimes achieving an inverse proportionality between the planes of content and expression for, ironically, the verb "to sit" hardly goes along with the kinds of physical work that prisoners in the Gulag had to perform (felling trees, digging mines, etc.). Of course, "to sit in prison" also reflects the condition of being immobilized, that is to say, removed from the enthusiastic atmosphere of building socialism and working for the Soviet society as a free person.

In general, with the goal of keeping the stylistic lucidity and the plot of Petkevich's memoir clear and accessible for the English reader, we have slightly redacted the original and shaped it to a narrower, more plot-bound narrative. The original text is replete with letters and epistolary poems sent to the author by people who played an important role in her life, including those from Aleksandr Gavronsky, Tamara Petkevich's friend and mentor, under whose guidance she began acting on the stages of the camp in the northern Komi Republic. Constrained by the necessity to abridge the Russian original to a still rather generous length, in most cases we opted to incorporate these texts into the main body of the narrative by paraphrasing their content so as not to give up the role that they play in the story. In the same manner, consistent with our goal of maintaining an uninterrupted narrative flow, we have assimilated most of the author's notes, originally published at the end of some chapters (7, 12 and 13), which we felt belonged to the book's main story line. We have not, however, left out any personal names or historical references. These decisions were made in consultation with the author.

Translating this memoir, we employed a collaborative method for the advantage of a dual perspective on our respective native languages and cultures, English and Russian. We hope that our efforts do justice to Tamara Petkevich's story.

TRANSLITERATION

A modified version of the Chicago Style transliteration system is used throughout for all proper names, titles, toponyms and other non-translated words, with the exception of those that have traditionally been spelled otherwise in the English language (Tchaikovsky, Rachmaninoff, etc.).

ACKNOWLEDGMENTS

Above all, we would like to express our deepest gratitude to the author, Tamara Vladislavovna Petkevich, for writing this book. For several years, since we first opened *Zhizn'—sapozhok neparny*, it has been a part of our lives; working on the English translation was a task of great magnitude, an experience that has left an indelible trace on us. We are grateful to Tamara Vladislavovna for her moral support, enthusiasm and patience.

Tamara Vladislavovna's book would never have appeared in print were it not for the help of many people, including Andrew Sharp, whose generosity made the first Russian publication possible. He was also Yasha Klots's first collaborator on the English translation. We thank him for the precious work he did.

We are grateful to Valentina Yarovaya, who introduced us to this book and supported the idea of translating it into English.

We would like to thank our colleagues, friends and family, whose unflagging enthusiasm about the book has been a support throughout our work: Professor Katerina Clark of Yale University for offering a special course on autobiography and Gulag memoirs; Professors Vladimir Alexandrov (Yale University) and Brian Baer (Kent State University) for their guidance on the translation sample and publication proposal; Professors John Bartle (Hamilton College) and Maxim D. Shrayer (Boston College) for their insights into literary translation in general, and ours in particular; Dina Odnopozova, the first reader of our entire manuscript, whose useful comments and warm understanding were especially important to us then and before; Melissa Smith, Constantine Rusanov, Tatiana Filimonova, Svetlana Adamova-Sussman and Harris Sussman, Trevor Jockims, Natasa Milas, Rossen Djagalov, Emil Niculescu, Roman Utkin and Ashley Cleek—for their help with the earlier drafts; Professor and poet Tomas Venclova (Yale University) and his wife, Tatiana, for many warm words about the book and its author; Professor Michael Connolly (Boston College) and Natalya Ashimbaeva (Dostoevsky Museum) for the summer program in St. Petersburg in 2004, when Yasha Klots first met with Tamara Petkevich; Alla Klots, Ksenia Glotova, Nora Gortcheva, Amanda Russell and Natalya Klimenchenko for their help with preparing the manuscript for submission; Amy Farranto, our editor at Northern Illinois University Press, for all her efforts to bring the manuscript to publication; finally, our friends and families (Bob and Laney Ufberg et alia; Natalya Yakhlakova, Leonid and Olga Klots, Jesse and Nina Izenberg; the late Al and Leah Ufberg, who wanted nothing more than to see this project come to fruition) for their sincere and encouraging interest in our work.

We are grateful to the European Studies Council (Yale University), the Gilder Lehrman Center for the Study of Slavery, Resistance and Abolition (Yale University) and the U.S. Fulbright Program in Russia for supporting our project.

MEMOIR OF A GULAG ACTRESS

Chapter 1

And no rosy childhood…

ANNA AKHMATOVA

Early nineteen-twenties. Petrograd.

Everything falling apart, everything coming together.

The Revolution, the Civil War, everything that shook our society's foundations, tearing apart people's deepest convictions—all this happened during the time of my parents' youth.

They met at the front during the Civil War. My mother, Efrosinya Fyodorovna, a Russian, had just graduated from the gymnasium. Like many young women her age, she believed in the revolution and went to the front. There she became a typist at the headquarters where my father was Commissar.

My father, Vladislav Iosifovich, of Polish descent, was born in Riga. He reached the age of conscription just before the First World War and was drafted into the army. It was probably there that his worldview was shaped. Father's support of the revolution was considered and deliberate. In 1918, he joined the Russian Bolshevik Communist Party.

A photo he gave my mother, dated February 1919, is inscribed, Remember Vileyka, Mozyr, Gomel, Bobruysk—presumably places where their division had fought. I can't say how it was that they both were taken prisoner by Petlura. I do know, however, that they were condemned to face the firing squad but somehow managed to escape. I also know that my father suffered severe shellshock.

My parents married after the war. I was born in 1920. That same year they came to Petrograd and moved into a rather unusual building. At the turn of the century the Emir of Bukhara and his agents erected a number of buildings in the area of the city called the Petrograd Side. These were expensive rental apartments that were soon occupied by well-to-do members of the public: prominent engineers, doctors and officials. Between 1918 and 1920 many of them fled abroad. They left in great haste, taking only their valuables and clothing and leaving behind their furniture, kitchenware, pots and pans. The superintendents locked up the apartments to keep everything intact should the owners return, but the new Soviet government established co-operatives and collectivized these residences. Father belonged to one such co-op and was offered an apartment in one of the "Emirate" houses on the Embankment of the Karpovka River, No. 30.

The building, crowned by a tower, was adorned by ornamental pillars. The plaster eagles, chimeras and lions that reposed on either side of the entrance seemed positioned to ward off evil powers. The balconies of our apartment rested upon the muscular shoulders of three Atlases whose bowed heads gazed blankly down at the street through empty eyes of chalk. These giants collapsed following the German bombardments of 1942, but the balconies survived.

It was a quiet corner of the city out of reach of public transport. Looking out of the window for an hour you'd see five or so passers-by. The river was muddy and sleepy. The wooden railings along its banks were falling down and the slopes were littered with bricks and broken glass and overgrown with red and white clover, giant burdocks and dandelions. Still, if you clambered down, you might manage to catch a beautiful dragonfly or butterfly.

On the opposite bank of the Karpovka, across from our house, was a monastery. Gathered there, kneeling in prayer, the faithful paid homage to the remains of Saint John of Kronshtadt. Nuns hurried back and forth.

The most crowded spot was by the beerhouse where Kamennoostrovsky Prospect crossed the river. In the window, red papier-mâché crayfish lay on a small plate edged with green peas. In gusts of warm air, men barely able to stand would stumble out into the cold of the street. At twilight, an old poor fiddler would settle himself down on the sidewalk opposite the beerhouse and play the same wistful tune. My mother would give me a coin, which I tossed onto the shabby velvet lining of his violin case. Moving on, I would look back over my shoulder to see if anyone else would throw something in.

Mother told me about the fashionably dressed folk who used to roller skate at the rink, which was now a rubbish-covered heap of rocks. Later it became the site of the Lensovet Palace of Culture.

The flood of 1924 furthered the decrepitude. Returning home from our *dacha,* kneeling on my seat in the tramcar, I stared through the window at the piles of dislodged wooden paving blocks.

"Are they repairing the road?" I asked Mama.

"No, darling, it's a flood. Everything here was flooded with water and the wooden blocks floated to the surface."

There appeared a wooden bench in our apartment: my father had floated home on it. Soon someone drew a white line on the façade of our building with the inscription: *WATER LEVEL DURING THE FLOOD, 1924.* Together with other little girls I would measure myself; the line was well above my head.

Our six-room apartment was filled with a gloomy order. There was a hall with alcoves, a dining room, Papa's study, the living room, the nursery and the kitchen, next to which was another room for the servant. I must have been left home alone quite often as I distinctly remember wandering aimlessly through the apartment's dense silence. Of all the rooms, Papa's study was the most mysterious. The snouts of wooden lions with jaws wide open protruded from the backs of carved oak chairs, elbow-rests of the armchairs and the drawers of my father's bureau. I cautiously stretched out my finger toward them. No, they didn't bite.

Who owned this apartment previously? Who lived here before us? My parents didn't know… What was ours, what belonged to someone else… This was something I never found out.

In the early twenties we lived in these spacious quarters as a foursome: Mama, Papa, our housemaid and me. My mother, beautiful and feminine, had a gentle nature. She didn't work but busied herself with running our household and taking care of me. My father, a strong and passionate man, was consumed by the idea of rebuilding the world. With fanatical devotion, he went to work wherever he was called. In those years he was the director of the Gold Trust of Petrograd. He came home from work late and was hardly ever around.

On Sundays we received guests, mainly my parents' friends from the front. Father's uncompromising integrity further strengthened the respect he had gained during the war. Even now, he was most often addressed not by his first name and patronymic, but as "Commissar." They would say, "Commissar, what do you think?" or "Commissar, explain this to us…" The guests would gather in Papa's study, reminiscing about the old days, debating and smoking.

I listened with rapt attention to Papa's story about how, when he and his soldiers had just come to a halt, lit a campfire and cooked their *kasha,* a ragged little girl of about ten appeared out of the woods. Spellbound by the sight of the soldiers eating, she began to repeat rapidly and stubbornly: "Ah wohnee, ah wohnee!" Eventually they understood: "I won't eat." But when they finally offered her a bowl of *kasha*, she ate it up in an instant.

By listening in on the many grown-up conversations, I learned that poverty would soon be a thing of the past. All people would live equally well. Houses would be constructed in a whole new manner, with rooftops covered in rich soil for planting trees and flowers. There would be plenty of public swimming pools. Food would be prepared in fully mechanized kitchens so that housewives would no longer have to cook. Children would never go barefoot or hungry, and their parents would never again know worry. With plenty of time to relax after work, they would regularly take their children to the cinema, which would, of course, be free. Best of all, though, would be the kindergartens, filled with luxuriant potted plants and aquariums swarming with exotic fish.

For a time our apartment became a veritable model home. "German communists have arrived. I've invited them over," Father would announce to Mama. Or, "A delegation from Bulgaria is here. They are coming to see us." Or, "On Sunday we've got to hold a reception for our Spanish comrades…" Well-dressed dignitaries, accompanied by their interpreters, would tour our apartment, stay for dinner and ply us with questions. During the early years of Soviet power our life must have been exemplary of the way things were meant to be: orderly, stately, plentiful.

I wasn't terribly interested in such matters, however. My attention was taken up with internal family conflicts, of which no one else around seemed aware. My parents quarreled a lot, but they quarreled without shouting. Prolonged disputes would end in an oppressive silence. Perched behind the wrought-iron railing of our balcony, I would watch them pace back and forth along the riverbank. My only desire was that they would make up with one another.

It is likely that my parents argued not just about problems in their relationship but also over me and how to bring me up. One Christmas, the custodian delivered a fir tree, which Mama set about decorating. Catching her at this, Papa declared harshly:

"As a communist, I will not allow a Christmas tree in our home!"

"But the child needs it," Mama protested.

"Let her grow up without all these lights and this Christmas-tree nonsense!"

The tree remained abandoned in a corner of the dining room.

Grandma Darya's arrival brought some warmth and humor into our house. I would eagerly devour her stories about the rivalry between the old

Prince Diamond and the young Prince Bell, about the land flowing with milk and honey or Cinderella. She quickly taught me to play cards and just as quickly took me to church. A row immediately ensued.

"Don't you dare take the child to church!" raged Papa.

After the dreadful rebuke, Grandma told me calmly:

"No one can live without God. We'll go to church anyway, but in secret."

Our secret was soon discovered. Grandma left, and I began to realize what people meant when they said Papa had a "difficult nature."

"When I was his typist, if I didn't show up on time at some railway station or other," my mother told her girlfriend about their wartime past, "he would dispatch the transport without allowing anyone to come and get me. I'd have to dash to catch up with the train. Then I would get a scolding. And what a scolding, let me tell you! I knew no peace from his rebukes and faultfinding..."

Mama confessed to one of her girlfriends how awfully afraid she had been of the strict Commissar, and how stunned she was when he suddenly declared his love.

I empathized closely with Mama, but, surreptitiously observing Papa, I also found his character intriguing. "It must be just as difficult for him," I thought to myself.

I would rejoice when we had a "Surprise Sunday." On those Sunday mornings, a delicious odor would waft from the kitchen: Papa was baking bread rolls! They would come out fluffy and fragrant. Papa would undergo some sort of transformation and become barely recognizable. He would tease me kindly and joke with Mama, and she would shine with happiness. How fervently I wished those days would last forever!

While dreaming of the well-being of all the world's children, of the magnificent kindergartens of the future, my parents were bringing up their own child in a most peculiar way. They dressed me well. I recall the beautiful hair ribbons and a white dress with blue roses they gave me one birthday. Once a governess appeared in our home to look after me, but she actually impressed me much less than the furniture she installed in the nursery: a sofa, a dresser and a folding screen covered with a cream-colored damask, embroidered with exotic flowers and parrots. The governess didn't stay long, though. The next in a series of housemaids soon took her place. However, I was still often left to my own devices. Understanding little of what was happening around me and even less of myself, I was making sense of the world on my own, like a creature of the wild. Estranged from my parents' lives, I often lacked the courage to ask them about something more than once.

"Bring me some newspapers!" Mama called to me from another room.

"How many is 'some'?"

Mama became angry:

"What a stubborn little girl you are!"

I knew: one, two, ten, but still had no idea exactly how many "some" was; I dragged in all the newspapers I could find.

I am struggling to remember what I used to be punished for, but I cannot, as if those memories have been sealed off by some distant elemental fear. I didn't steal, lie or swear. Did I gallop wildly about the apartment? Maybe. Scrape my knees while playing outside in the street? Well, yes. Was I naughty? Perhaps. There must have been some grounds for my punishment.

A braided leather whip hung from the headboard of my parents' nickel-plated bed. When I stayed home alone and touched it, it didn't frighten me at all…

It was always unexpected when Papa would grab the lash and start beating me, ferociously and without mercy. My howls only urged him on. I would scream, wriggling in his tight grip. "Daddy, dear, don't, please…!" But "dear Daddy" would sullenly continue thrashing me, across the shoulders, back and bottom, arms and legs. Turning white with tears, I would hear my own cries as if they were hovering somewhere outside my body, but he wouldn't stop.

With every whipping I learned to handle the pain better, to scream less loudly and not to be so quick to apologize. I was indeed becoming a "stubborn little girl," although I blindly feared my father just as much as before.

If I didn't beg for forgiveness I would be made to stand in the corner. Evening would pass into night; my parents would turn off the lights and go to bed. Tears and sobs would subside, street sounds would die down and my soul would empty and dry out. I no longer felt like saying "Forgive me, dear Daddy." The world around me seemed dreadful and brutal. My imagination would split in two. The darkness in the corner of the wardrobe would start glowing, and the castle of Prince Diamond from Grandma Darya's tales would arise in silvery radiance. Real mice scratched under the floorboards, the real clock struck twelve, and Cinderella, running away from the ball, lost her glass slipper.

Unable to bear it any longer, Mama would jump out of bed.

"Come, my sweet! Tell Papa you are sorry and you can go to sleep."

I would finally mumble: "I'm sorry, Daddy." They'd let me go and I would fall into a deep sleep.

I used to have a recurring dream, in which I'd see an odd symbol that looked like a hieroglyph, resembling a six-armed Cyrillic letter crossed with another sign similar to the Greek letter Phi. As if it had lungs capable of inhaling and exhaling, the symbol would steadily expand until its exterior was almost bursting, before shrinking again. The vision would take over my whole being. I'd try to get rid of it, fighting it off, and wake in panic. Perhaps it was a sign of Fate, which I remembered but, at the time, couldn't decipher.

Sometimes I dreamed my mother was dead. In fear, I would jump out of bed and run on tiptoe to my parents' bedroom to make sure Mama was breathing. After that I wouldn't be able to get back to sleep for a long time. The street lamp outside my window would start swinging, the parquet floor would crackle or the wardrobe door would creak. Eerie sounds of iron groaning and clanking in the wind, the squeaking of rusted, half-detached cellar and pantry doors would drift from the nearby wasteland. No, I wasn't scared, but I was lonely, and the feeling that nobody needed me was more intense at night than in the daytime.

One floor above ours lived the family of Doctor D. The father was a physician, the mother a biologist. Their two children, Lyolya and Vova, were both my age. Sometimes the brother and sister would come to play with me but more often it was I who asked for permission to go to their place. "Don't stay longer than an hour," Mama would answer.

There wasn't much furniture in Dr. D.'s apartment. The parquet floors were so polished they shined; the rooms were airy and light. A microscope stood on their mother's desk. Everything in their home interested me very much. After Vova and Lyolya's parents returned from work, the entire family would sit down to dinner. Their father would ask, "So, how was your day?" The children would answer, weaving together both the important and trivial events of the day. I found this display of adult interest in childish concerns astonishing.

"Why didn't Father love me?" I once dared ask a relative when I was already a grown-up.

"What do you mean, he didn't love you?" she said, staring at me in surprise. "He loved you very much!"

Then what was the matter? Did I fail to remind him of that proud little girl from his rougher past, who said "Ah wohnee" instead of "I am hungry"? Since childhood, I had heard my parents' friends say: "Remarkable people like Vladislav Iosifovich simply do not exist anymore!" I sensed that Papa was not in any way an evil person, and the reasons he would so mercilessly flog his uncomprehending little girl were bound to have been complex. It might have been the result of his wartime shellshock. Maybe he was giving vent to the long-standing brutality of the Civil War. No one can explain it to me now, and it still haunts me. What was it all for?

There is, however, one thing I can't be mistaken about: I was born at the wrong time.

EVERY CHILD HAS HIS OWN SECRET FEAR. Mine was the orphanage. The very word filled me with dread. I would freeze, stock-still, at the sight of the children from the building across the street being led out two-by-two, all dressed in loose gray sateen jackets and gray cloth caps. Submissively they filed past on their way to the bathhouse, or just for a walk. In autumn they would return from an outing to the woods each carrying a single maple leaf; in winter, a bunch of fir twigs.

Once, after being punished by Mama, my fear of the orphanage grew into sheer horror. In order to get a cup out of the sideboard I had to pull up a chair to climb on: it was the only way I could reach the top cupboard where the cups were kept. But it was much quicker to balance with one foot on the key that stuck out of the lower door. Then I could reach the cup in a flash. The key snapped under my weight and I tumbled to the floor, smashing the cup. Mama came running in and saw what had happened.

"What's this mess you are making?" she yelled. "Get out of this house at once! Get dressed! You're going to the orphanage!"

I couldn't believe my ears.

"Out, off to the orphanage!"

She wouldn't calm down. She dragged me over to the sideboard where she cut off a crust of bread and handed it to me. "This will do for the time being. Get dressed and go to the orphans!" Her hand pointed to the door.

I trembled.

Of course, no one actually drove me out of the house. As a six-year-old I was still incapable of discerning where "Mama" ended and a woman with her own store of misfortune and sorrow began. But from that moment I could no longer believe in Mama's unconditional love, which up till then had been the mainstay of my life. A feeling of insecurity arose, which was to haunt me for decades.

Once Mama decided to send me to a class led by the "Frenchwoman." In fact, she turned out to be a Russian; her name was Ekaterina Ivanovna. She was married to the tsarist General Balanin, who had joined the Soviet side during the Civil War. French wasn't the only thing she taught us. Ten or eleven of us children learned to write, count, glue colored paper onto cardboard, construct small boxes. We were taught how to curtsey and how to converse politely. There were Christmas parties every year without fail, to which the parents were also invited. It was there that I played my first role in a staging of Krylov's fable *The Mouse and the Rat.* But no one could understand why, after memorizing the mouse's lines, I suddenly refused to put on the loose gray overalls that had been sewn especially for my role. I couldn't bring myself to confess: the costume reminded me of the jackets worn by the orphans.

Petrograd-Leningrad, the Embankment of the Karpovka River, No. 30, where the Petkevich family lived in 1920–1930.

(above) Father, Vladislav Iosifovich Petkevich. 1918.

(right) Father and mother, with their three daughters: Renata, Valentina, and Tamara. 1933–1934.

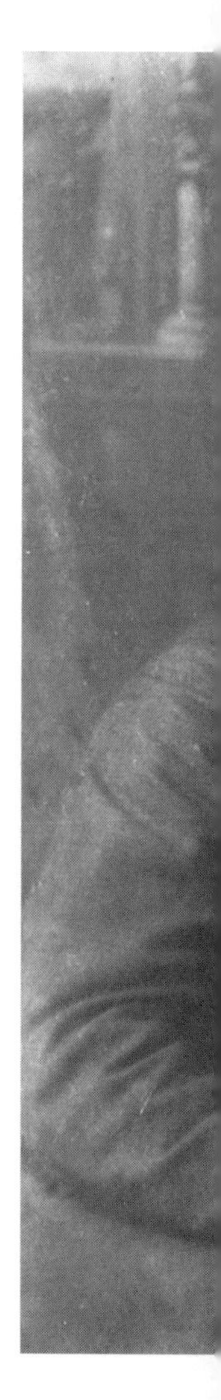

(above) With friends after graduating from school: David Neiman, Nina Izenberg, Raya Shard, Liza Rayskina, Zinaida Bodrova, and Tamara. 1939–1940.

(left) Graduation day. School No. 4, Vasilievsky Island, Leningrad. 1938.

Tamara Petkevich after her father's arrest. 1937.

Tamara Petkevich. 1940.

The French group didn't last long. Its end was marked with my first hearing of a phrase, which at the time carried no meaning for me: "They were exiled." I only knew that these people still existed but, for some reason, were very far away.

IN SUMMER MAMA AND I went to Byelorussia. Once, the two of us stayed at the Puchkovo estate. The place was derelict and devastated. There was not another soul around. The nearest village, Popadino, was one and a half *versts* away.

I clearly remember our journey there: we passed through a forest and fields, and then the landscape led us into an alley with a neat, well-paved road. There was a garden on our right and when we turned left we saw a white stone house, connected by avenues of jasmine and lilac to another house, this one made of wood, with terraces.

We settled ourselves into one of the intact rooms in the stone house. It had resonant floors, cracked mirrored doors and a circular staircase leading to the attic. The house was surrounded by flowerbeds of pink and white daisies, and behind it a fruit orchard stretched for an entire *verst*.

We would rise early. Mama would give me a pair of scissors to cut the roses. The rose garden, a mass of bushes covered in white, scarlet, tea-colored and almost black blooms, was behind a fence across the road. The dew still lying on the grass and leaves kept everything cool. The thorns scratched my hands and pricked my fingers, as if defending the flowers, which I nonetheless snipped off.

The morning sun wouldn't be hot yet. Dragonflies hung suspended on their glassy blue wings. Wasps and bees buzzed and birds gaily chirped their tunes. This abandoned garden seemed remote from the human world. Like a living organism, it let me feel its dispositions, protests and defenselessness. It was here I learned the meaning of freedom, what was dawn and what was dusk.

Years later I found out that before the revolution the estate of Puchkovo had belonged to a landowner who had been the director of the Maly Theater in St. Petersburg. People said that the overseer of the Puchkovo estate was a monster but the owner himself was good and kind. He would often come to his estate with a gypsy actress who was his lover.

The landowner had one peculiar whim: every year all the furniture at the estate had to be replaced. One year it would be Karelian birch, the next year—mahogany, then—walnut. He would give orders that the old furniture be hauled up to the attic. During the revolution the owner escaped abroad, and the peasants from the surrounding villages helped themselves to his furniture.

Mother and I spent only one summer in Puchkovo. After that we would go to the neighboring village of Popadino, where two of Grandma Darya's brothers, Uncle Grisha and Uncle Kolya, lived.

Grandma Darya had four brothers. When their father died, each of them inherited nine *desyatinas* of land. Two of the brothers disposed of their inheritances and soon left the village, but the other two decided to stay. Their houses stood next door to each other, separated by a fence. Both uncles had cows and other livestock. They sowed and harvested their own grain. The vegetable garden and orchard yielded vegetables, berries and apples.

The day here began at sunrise. The women herded the mooing cows out of the dairy after they milked them. To the sound of twinkling bells, shepherds led their flocks to pasture. After breakfast everyone headed into the field and I, too, would go with them in the chilly morning air.

On the Day of Ivan Kupala, girls would weave two wreaths, toss them into the lake and wait to see whether the water would unite or separate them. If the wreaths came together, there would be a marriage that year. The festivities would get into full swing toward nightfall. It was believed that whoever saw the first blooming of the ferns would find a treasure. Scared of stepping on a frog, frightened by the dampness and pitch-darkness, I plunged into the depths of the forest without looking back. Returning to the clearing I found a huge bonfire in full blaze. The adults were taking a running start to jump over the fire, their piercing cries flying off somewhere into the ether.

In the company of children my age as well as adults, immersed in the friendly atmosphere of physical labor and ritual, I was rescued from my loneliness. I was paid the same amount of attention as everyone else, fed like all the rest and joked with everyone.

Then suddenly everything changed in the village of Popadino. The idyllic world was split apart when the word "gold" swept in from somewhere.

The events wouldn't have troubled me had my Father not been involved.

The government requisitioned all the Church's gold. The nearest town with a church was Nevel, and in our village people told with fear and anger how all the gold and silver implements had been removed. "It's a sin!" they whispered, fearfully crossing themselves, "God will punish this blasphemy!" The requisitioners were called "Antichrists." Among them was my Father, whose job was to make an inventory of the confiscated property. Not understanding what Antichrist meant, I watched with a mixture of fear and curiosity as Father, calm and evidently confident in his actions, returned along the country road, followed by the malicious stares of the locals.

Later, in 1929, two more words invaded my childish consciousness:

"dekulakization" and "exile." The latter, already associated with my teacher, Ekaterina Ivanovna, now created an almost visible image in my mind.

In the family album there were photographs of Uncle Kolya's two eldest daughters, Maria and Nina. They were pictured separately, each in a wedding veil and gown, bridegrooms standing alongside them. But there were also other, faded snapshots from Yakutia and Solovki, taken some years later. I couldn't believe that the two pretty brides and the women in the rough amateur shots could be the same girls. The adults explained that they had changed so much because one of them now had tuberculosis and the other a heart disease. Maria's husband's family had been dekulakized and exiled to Yakutia. The second sister, Nina, had married an employee of the State Secret Service, the OGPU, and settled in Moscow. Maria's husband escaped from exile and returned to live with his sister-in-law. The neighbors denounced them, reporting that someone was hiding out at the home of an OGPU employee. Nina and her husband were exiled to Solovki.

Events developed quickly. Dekulakization reached Popadino. There was a brief argument over which class the head of each family belonged to: the *kulaks,* the rich peasants, or the *srednyaks,* the middle-class peasants. Uncle Kolya, who owned more land because his older brother's portion had been allotted to him, and who took on hired labor during the high season, was the first to be dekulakized. Uncle Grisha, in whose house we lived during our last summer there, was right after him. Both of them were exiled. Each had six children. The ones who weren't old enough to live independently were dispatched to children's homes for labor training. The others ended up who knows where.

In this way whole families were expelled from Popadino. The fragrant, delicious, routine and sensible order of village life, so capable of settling and reviving the human soul, was being erased from the face of the earth.

Much was changing in the city as well. In 1926 and 1927, quiet Petrograd was rapidly transformed into overpopulated Leningrad. People streamed in from villages and smaller cities. The so-called process of "densification" had begun: families with housing warrants were moved into our six-room apartment until soon we were left with only two rooms to ourselves.

Each of the new tenants installed their own table in the kitchen, which became the center of life and turned into a loud and talkative place, the primus and kerosene stoves humming with steady fire and emitting fumes. At first it seemed these people would only stay for a while, but soon I understood they were there forever. Our apartment had become a communal apartment, a *kommunalka,* like every other.

IN 1927 AN IMPORTANT EVENT OCCURRED in our family: my sister was born. I had to spend a few days with my father's relatives. When I returned home, I found my newborn sister asleep in a sandalwood trunk. As she gazed up at the ceiling, I tried to move into her line of vision. Mama wanted to call her Galina, but Papa objected; her name was Valentina.

Three years later, in the same Karpovka apartment, another sister was born—Renata, or Renochka. Our family life became more hectic and cramped, but also somehow cozier. My parents finally sorted out their relationship and stopped quarreling. Papa would come home from work just as late as before, but on those rare evenings when he was around I noticed he was more tender with my little sisters than with me.

Suddenly, Papa disappeared.

Some man on the street had "identified" him as a tsarist officer, and Papa was arrested. He was put in prison on Shpalernaya Street. A few days later Mama and I went to visit him. It took about a month to clear up the mistake, but after he was released Papa was transferred to another job.

Soon he was sent on a dekulakization mission in Siberia. People gossiped that the class struggle in the villages had grown into a real battle: "The *kulaks* will kill you while your back is turned, they burn people alive." It was at the very peak of such frightful conversations that Father left.

Letters from him came rarely. Mama was worried, and so were friends who came to visit us. I was shocked to see the photo that Papa sent us from Siberia. He looked unrecognizable. He had grown a beard and seemed tormented, emaciated and withdrawn.

After about a year, Papa returned home a different person. From bits of sentences and mainly from some of his seemingly illogical actions I was able to conclude that during that year he had lived a complex inner life, torn between the demands of the Party and mere humanity. I don't know what he came to understand in Siberia, but when he came back, he obtained a residence permit for two of Uncle Grisha's sons from Popadino to move in with us, after their families had been dekulakized.

Time and again the word "purge" would appear in my parent's conversations until it became a fixed addition to their vocabulary. Periodically, one or another Party member would be "purged," which led to much discussion at home. The Party would occasionally, and more frequently as time progressed, do checkups on people, which were meant to verify their social background, including whether they might have relatives living abroad. Many of these checkups ended in their being purged from the Party. To the latter question, of relatives abroad, Papa naturally answered yes, since his mother and sisters still lived in Riga.

Father's relationships with his wartime friends changed too. Marked inequalities in their stations began to manifest themselves. Tikhonov and Krasovsky would come to see us wearing the same old shabby wartime overcoats, but the visits of one friend named Shlemovich, who had been transferred to Moscow to work for the Kremlin, were real festivities. He would bring delicious things that none of us had ever seen before: imported persimmons, caviar, hams. Promising to arrange everything for Papa, Shlemovich tried to convince him to move to Moscow too, but Father categorically refused: "I won't leave Leningrad. Our current hardship is only temporary and I have to stay here to help the people."

WE MOVED TO ANOTHER APARTMENT on Vasilievsky Island. It was much worse than our previous place on the Karpovka, but at least here we could live by ourselves. The apartment was on the first floor, with windows facing north, which made it dark and gloomy. But my sisters and I liked to play in the courtyard, hiding behind the huge piles of logs.

I was almost eleven when I went to a new school on Sredny Prospect, School No. 4, which I liked much better than my old one on the corner of Leo Tolstoy Square and Bolshoy Prospect. Studying suddenly became interesting. I was especially interested in botany, physics and chemistry.

Food and clothing became scarcer and scarcer. Although my father earned four hundred rubles and was affiliated with a privileged grocery distributor called Red Star, which was closed to the public, my parents struggled to maintain the family budget. Mama stitched underwear and tarpaulin gloves for workers on her Singer sewing machine. I remember it as an extraordinary event when once I visited Papa at work and he took me to the cafeteria, where they had mashed potatoes and meat.

Once Father returned from a trip bringing two live geese with him. We kept them in a shed for several days and then moved them to the bathroom. My girlfriends from school came over. I was dying to show them our "zoo." A few days later, when a list granting cafeteria privileges to certain selected students was announced, one of my classmates raised her hand: "Petkevich doesn't need cafeteria privileges. She has geese at home!"

At home I found an old bundle of magazines with photographs of the First World War: freshly dug pits and dead soldiers who had not yet been thrown in; impenetrable mud, through which tired warriors dragged themselves, and more graves and still more corpses. I asked Mama:

"Mama, what's the most frightening thing in the world?"

I was sure she would say war, but putting down her sewing Mama answered in a quiet voice: "Hunger, my child!"

I didn't yet know what hunger really was.

Father's social status changed rapidly. Mama said he had his own view on certain issues, which he didn't hesitate to express, and so he fell out of favor.

There was an expression "to dispatch someone on a shock mission," which meant to send a capable leader to accomplish an important and exigent task. Following the Party policy, they started dispatching my Father here and there to carry out various projects.

Leningrad was in need of fuel. All around the city, in the marshlands, there were deposits of peat, which had to be exploited. Father was made director of the Andogostroy Peat Works, near the town of Cherepovets.

I remember the first summer of Father's out-of-town service. We accompanied him to the new place. On a moonlit, resonant June night, I watched the wide wooden ferry making its way through a shroud of mist to moor on the bank of the Suda River. The ferry carried us to the other side.

When I saw the place where we had to live, I was confused. It was a single room divided in half by a calico curtain. Mama burst out laughing and said she liked it here. At once I liked everything here too, especially Mama's laughter and Father's grateful smile.

Lumber floated down the Andoga River. The enormous rafts loaded with tree trunks would jam up, then just as soon they would be swiftly carried down the river again. The river, covered by this floating blanket of wood, frightened me. There were so many times I saw snakes in the lumber clearings, so many times a thunder storm started when I was in the middle of the forest! But my love for the forest bordered on obsession, and the forest spared me.

Meanwhile, a difficult problem hit our family. My middle sister, Valechka, developed tuberculosis as a result of the pneumonia she caught back when we still lived in our cold apartment on the Karpovka. Better nutrition was the only thing that could help her recover. After giving it serious thought, my parents decided to get Grandma Darya to come to take care of me in Leningrad so that I could continue my studies; as for themselves, they would go with the two younger girls to Papa's next mission, a small worksite near the town of Tikhvin, where they would settle in a village and buy a cow to nourish my sisters on milk and butter.

This meant a radical change in my life.

Everyone left. Grandma Darya and I stayed by ourselves in Leningrad. I was left to my own devices more than ever before. I plunged myself into the world of books and devoured them one after another. I read absolutely everything—from a volume of Andersen's fairy tales, which my father had given to me for getting good marks in school, to the Grimm Brothers, to the classics, to the most dubious dime-store novels that had somehow found their way into our house. Immersed into the imaginary world of truth and fantasy, I found it so much more vivid than the real world around me that I hurried to be done with homework as soon as possible so I could get back to reading.

ON DECEMBER 1, 1934, the day when the secretary general of the Communist Party in Leningrad, S. M. Kirov, was murdered, Father was at home. Without saying a word to anyone, he sat behind the table, his head resting on his arms. I was sent off to buy a newspaper.

Dry snow was falling. On the corner of First Line and Sredny Prospect, near the newsstand, there was a long line of people standing silent close to each other, waiting for the evening newspapers. When I returned, Father was still sitting in the same position. His confusion and the obvious earnestness of his sentiment flavored this event with a sinister significance.

The newspaper didn't clarify a thing: who killed Kirov, and why? The name of the assassin, a certain Nikolaev, which appeared out of nowhere later on, didn't explain much either.

Early next morning, when I arrived at school—it was still dark and the electric lights were turned on—we were lined up single-file and taken to bid farewell to the secretary general. We joined the endless stream of mourners and silently filed past the coffin. Dim light, the shuffling of feet, funeral music, and—whether I saw it later in a dream or it just seemed to me at that time, there, at the top of the gallery—Stalin's face, looming and disappearing again.

It was the first political murder that my fourteen-year-old memory could register.

My eagerness to be agreeable and useful to my Motherland was an elevated feeling. At the Komsomol District Committee of Vasilievsky Island, at my induction examination, I answered all of the questions capably and articulately, including those about the current state of international affairs; I even managed to remember the names of all the People's Commissars. I was solemnly inducted as a member of the Komsomol and received a Komsomol card.

The fervency of youth, the arrogant enthusiasm of ideas, the faith in the triumph of universal justice, so often the subject of Father's speeches,—it all became very important to me. On the eve of the November holidays, in 1936, I was issued a special pass to the old Smolny Cathedral: I was honored to watch the parade from the special tribune. My whole family was extremely excited. The parade and the demonstration entered my memory as a symbol of power, that of the consentient and cheerful unity of the people.

The Spanish Civil War made the discussion of politics our daily "spiritual bread." Like a living flame, the war burned through the geographical map, riveting people's hearts and thoughts. The name of Dolores Ibarruri, who had said: "Better to die on one's feet than live on one's knees!" made an impression on us all. I believed that "No pasarán!" could prevent any kind of injustice and I kept up with current events. Our men—ideals, heroes—were setting off for Spain, and I was simply in love with them. I considered my admiration for the volunteers who left for the war as my personal affiliation with these historical events.

Many Leningrad families took in dark-haired boys and girls from Spain. People seemed to be a single family. Victory on the Popular Front was not far off.

The ideas of international unity that Father cultivated in me, the belief that there should be no room for any falsehood in life—these notions complemented each other. I was thrilled by the thought that even today, not only during the legendary times of Joan of Arc, one was still capable of heroic deeds, that one could fight and even die for the ideals of liberty and brotherhood. It was Spain that brought together dream and reality.

The anticipation of victory, however, was gradually losing its resilience. People no longer discussed the events as fervently and loudly as before, and soon the conversations faded away completely. It was as if a splinter had been left in our hearts for years. Still, the war in faraway Spain helped me adopt a much broader insight and interest in everything that was going on in my own country.

The radio and the newspapers were an unquestionable authority. One's belief in what was said in a newspaper was about as firm as one's unconditional faith in truth and justice, and it was only through these two virtues that one's life could be measured.

Yet my perception of social life would sometimes become overcast.

I was sick and wasn't allowed to go to the May Day parade. Seeing how upset I was, Mama conceded and allowed me to stand by the gate in our yard. Festively decorated trucks with mock-ups, banners and portraits of the leaders drove past. Demonstrators sang and marched along with the orchestra. Leaflets were dropped from airplanes. I picked one from the ground: *WHOEVER IS NOT WITH US IS AGAINST US.* Standing as I was, apart from the crowd marching by, I suddenly felt that this slogan was talking to me. It seemed to be blaming me for not joining in without knowing the reasons why. My high spirits immediately evaporated.

Like every Komsomol member, I was a mentor for a group of young pioneers. Once, when I came to meet with them, I saw that my place was occupied by a girl from another class.

"I am their leader now!" she said boldly.

I turned around and left, bursting into tears when I got home. "Who had appointed her? Why haven't they talked to me, why didn't they let me know?"

I told Father about what had happened, but instead of consoling me, he started reproaching me:

"Who gave you the right to leave the group with a stranger? What if she was an enemy? It was your duty to find out what had happened. You should have fought!"

I must have felt that my father was right, but the concept of "fighting the enemy" somehow seemed out of place. In my mind, one could fight for victory in Spain, but not in your own school, in front of your own group of students…

I GREW USED TO LIVING WITH GRANDMA. I loved her very much, even though sometimes I acted up and annoyed her with my moods, claiming: "Do as I want, or I will not eat anything for lunch!" or "Let me go play outside, or I won't touch my dinner!" When my parents sent us foodstuffs, whether it was cottage cheese, sour cream or butter, it never occurred to me what price they had to pay to get it. I would immediately call my girlfriends over, and they would gobble up everything that my grandma had hoped to make last for at least a couple of weeks.

I was sixteen when dancing was finally allowed at school parties. One day it was announced that there would not only be dancing but also a whole masquerade. My classmate and I volunteered to go to the theater workshops and seek out costumes. With unspeakable enthusiasm I burrowed in the storeroom, picking out the most exotic things: a harlequin outfit, traditional Russian costumes with *kokoshniks,* as well as Gypsy and Spanish clothing. For myself I chose a Polish costume: a blue-velvet *kazakin* trimmed with fur and a white velvet skirt embroidered with silver. We were delayed at the theater registering our receipts, and when I finally got home there was only half an hour left before the masquerade.

As I stormed into the apartment, I bumped into Mama and yelled:

"Quick! Get me something to eat!"

Hearing this, Father thundered:

"How dare you speak to your mother in that tone? How dare you demand anything?"

Once again he was right. I begged Mother to forgive me, but Father was in a bad mood.

"You are not going anywhere! No masquerade!"

"Papa, forgive me, I was wrong. Let me go, please!"

"No."

That was it. I knew very well how firm my father was on his word.

I tried to explain that I was the only one at school who knew how to unpack the sacks with the costumes, but my argument seemed to have no effect on him.

"Call them over the phone and explain."

My little sisters wept too, and even Mother pleaded for me. Nothing helped. The masquerade must have already been in full swing, but I was locked up at home, flooding my room with tears. My sisters reported that our uncle had resolved to talk to Father as a sort of delegate on my behalf. It was already late in the evening when he managed to change Father's mind. I was allowed to leave, but the fight had exhausted me so much that I no longer wanted to go.

"How am I supposed to go there now, when my eyes are red from crying?"

My sisters quickly found a solution. They had overheard Mama mentioning a masquerade mask, so they dashed away and returned with a gasmask, sure it was precisely the mask in question. But even this couldn't cheer me up, and I remembered my first masquerade very vaguely, though I never forgot how happy my sisters became when I was finally forgiven and allowed to go.

Once in winter I was visiting my parents in Tikhvin. Father came to pick me up from the station in a low wide sleigh. On the way home we made a long detour through the forest. The ruby sun was setting and the silent forest buried under snow was unbelievably beautiful. I imagined that Father had decided to present me with this beauty as if hoping I would forgive him for his cruelty. For the rest of my life I kept returning again and again to the memory of our silent journey, the resonant scraping of the sleigh blades on the forest floor, the frost and the red shimmering woods illuminated by the sunset.

When my parents lived in the Tikhvin region, I only visited them during my summer and winter school breaks, but when Father was transferred to the nearby Irinovka, I went there every weekend. There our family was allocated a separate house, almost a farmstead, about three *versts* away from the train station. The place was secluded and picturesque. We called it a villa.

In winter my sisters and I would dash downhill in a sleigh at breathtaking speed. I would ski down the hill, climb back up and slide down again, giving no thought to fear or precaution. When summer came, I learned to ride a horse. It was sheer bliss to dash across the meadow on horseback in the face of the whistling wind.

There, for the first time in my life, I had a separate bedroom. In the daytime it was flooded with sunlight, at night the room was bathed in gentle moonlight. I read and reread *War and Peace,* delved into Spielhagen, James Oliver Curwood and Eugenie Marlitt. My life consisted of moonlit evenings, scents and reveries, images from books.

The old house belonged to a priest. My girlfriend Nastenka also lived there. There was a unique old library. Nastenka and I picked books on dream interpretations and palmistry. We would open the window and struggle to hold back the branches of a lilac tree, which streamed into the room and lashed us on the arms when we sat on the windowsill to read.

Our entire family participated in the *subbotniks* held regularly at the construction sites. And when a fire alarm sounded, even children had to run to help extinguish the peat fire. Personal honesty was above everything, and my parents were very serious about it. My mother mended her old dresses and sewed clothes for me out of them, while my own clothes were used to make frocks for Valechka and Renochka.

It was strange to see Mama milking the cow or mixing bran in a bucket. Not too long ago, a group of intelligent and educated men from Leningrad had sung her serenades! Now the role of "princess" had become a thing of her past and was replaced by that of a farm worker.

My father also changed. His voice became raspy. Unhealthy hollows formed under his eyes. In his tarpaulin overcoat and top boots he would set out for the construction site and stay there until late at night. Something or somebody would always wake him up in the middle of the night, whether to unload a cargo train or meet the trucks arriving to collect the peat. Papa would get up and disappear into the dark. I don't remember him ever having a vacation. Nor can I recall him laughing. A former commissar and passionate debater, in Irinovka he turned increasingly grim. He would bring over his coworkers, just as exhausted and careworn as he was, and they would sit at the table, always with a bottle of vodka. More and more often I started seeing my father drunk.

Just as before, I wasn't allowed to poke my nose into my parents' problems, but Father's drinking was so out of keeping with his ideals and cast of mind that once I dared ask Mama:

"Why has Papa started drinking?"

She spoke of his accursed job. As director, it was his responsibility to seek out whatever was necessary for construction: lumber, bricks, iron, transport.

To find common language with the authorities on whom much depended, he had to drink with them. There seemed to be no other way to go about it, so daily drinking was inevitable.

I could see he was ruining himself. But one day my pity for him was erased by a heretofore unfamiliar feeling of hatred.

It was a white night in June. We were returning home in a horse-drawn carriage from my father's friends. My sisters snuggled together, sleeping. I, too, was dozing to the sound of the horse's clip-clop. I could hear my parents quarreling. I knew Papa had drunk a lot and I tried not to notice his cursing. All of a sudden he gave my mother a hefty blow and knocked her out of the moving carriage. With a wild roar I jumped out and ran toward her. Father pulled on the reins. The horse stopped. Jumping to her feet, Mama grabbed my sisters.

The whole thing lasted no more than a few seconds.

I clambered up from the ground and saw Father. His face was unrecognizable, transformed by anger. He whipped the horse and the carriage, wildly zigzagging on only two wheels, lurched forward onto a bridge. There were no siderails. The wheels on the right hung in mid-air above the void. I can't imagine what prevented the carriage from tumbling down into the river, but Father didn't even notice what happened. He thundered across the bridge and whirled away.

Mother and I made sure we weren't injured. We finally managed to calm down my two howling sisters and began walking home. Never before had I seen my father raise his hand to my mother.

At home the lights were on. Father was storming about the room like a beast. He was looking for his wallet, which he couldn't find anywhere. Mama knew that the wallet contained a thick roll of public funds. Terrified of what the consequences would be for losing it, she looked at me sternly and said:

"Go! Look all along the road. You have to find it. Do you understand? You have to find it!"

It was four in the morning. I walked out of our house and dragged myself along the road toward the settlement, carefully examining the curbs. I had walked a couple of *versts* when I finally saw Father's wallet lying in a ditch.

Birds twittered. The first rays of sunlight were illuminating the birch trunks.

I entered the house and hurled the wallet onto the table. Father didn't thank me.

"Where's Mama?" he asked me angrily.

I knew exactly where Mama usually hid when he came home drunk. But I answered defiantly:

"She's gone!"

My tone threw him into a rage.

"Tell me right now! Where is she?"

Beside myself with anger, I yelled in his face:

"I won't tell you!"

He came after me. I was terrified. His eyes were bloodshot, his fingers clenched into a fist. But at that moment I, too, became a clod of burning hatred, and without shielding myself, I didn't take a single step back. I knew I wouldn't let him hit me. I looked straight into his eyes.

He hissed through his teeth:

"Go away! I'll kill you!"

"Kill me!" I heard myself yell out. "Kill me!!"

Father stumbled, became flabby, and sat down.

After that night he promised to stop drinking. He was true to his word: I never saw him drunk or even tipsy after that. He did, indeed, have a strong character.

I was stunned by my own outburst of hatred. Where had that feeling come from? Guilt and shame gnawed at me. I longed to be recognized by my father, but our relationship was doomed, and it was I who suffered from it. Had I asked him: "Papa, why are you never interested in what's at the bottom of my heart?" I know what he would have said: "Do well what you ought to do, and this will tell everyone what kind of person you are. It's not that difficult."

AMONG MY FATHER'S COWORKERS there were a few who always went with him when he was transferred from one construction site to another. One of them, Mikhail Ivanovich Kazakov, an engineer, was a frequent guest at our home.

One evening in Irinovka, while the guests were loudly discussing something in the kitchen, he knocked on the door to my room.

"I ran away from them," he said.

The window was open. It was a warm moonlit August night. His coming didn't disturb me, though it seemed unusual. He was a kind man. He told me how sad he was because of the difference in our ages: he was already thirty-five and I was still so young. And then he kissed me.

Now I had my own secret. I didn't tell anyone about this kiss.

Iosif Antonovich Kurchevsky, another friend of Papa's, persuaded him to move to the Nazievsk peat works near the Zhikharyovo train station. In comparison with the other towns we'd lived in, this village seemed much more civilized. There were two-storey buildings, a stadium, a tennis court and a club. Many young people worked on the construction projects there, and as soon as we arrived I found myself in the company of recent graduates of various Leningrad universities. A group of joyful friends would meet me at the station when I came to visit my parents on Saturdays, and even Papa put up with the fact that I was now always surrounded by young men.

Each of us tried to compose a poem, a satirical essay, or retell an amusing story in front of the group. There was the feeling of a competition between us. When Ch.'s turn came, his story intrigued us more than anybody else's.

"A Soviet specialist, on a business trip to London, upon walking through a certain square, noticed how a woman in black, standing by the walls of the cathedral, started toward him at a quick pace. After throwing a small note at his feet, she disappeared. Hesitantly, the engineer picked up the note, tried to read it by the light of the street lamp, but saw that it was written in a language he couldn't recognize.

"In the morning, arriving at the Soviet Embassy, he told them what had happened and showed them the letter. They took away the note, but within a few minutes, instead of giving him a translation, they ordered: 'In an hour a ship will depart for the Soviet Union from the port. You must be on that ship.' He tried to protest, citing the fact that his work wasn't yet finished, but they wouldn't listen to him. An order is an order. However, they gave him back the note.

"Depressed by the absurd circumstances surrounding his departure, the Soviet citizen was standing on the deck of the ship when a forceful gale started up. The crew was ordered to dump all extra cargo into the sea. With all hands on deck, the engineer conspicuously worked alongside the crew. When the storm quieted down, they informed the captain about the courageous passenger; the captain invited him into his cabin. At the peak of the conversation, feeling he could confide in the captain's friendly tone, our specialist related to him the story with the note, guessing that the captain knew several languages and would be able to translate the mysterious letter. However, after reading it, the captain's face was transformed, he ordered his crew to lock the engineer in the hold of the ship, and to keep him there until they entered Soviet waters.

"The despondent engineer still had the chance to show the note to his wife when he got home. She was a teacher of foreign languages. After the first few minutes of their meeting, he told her the story of his misadventures, expecting, finally, an answer to all of the mysteries that had ensued. But after glancing at the note, his wife, without offering an explanation, told him to leave the house immediately and never to come back.

"The despairing engineer seized on one final opportunity: the State Translation Bureau, who would simply be obliged to translate the letter. However, when he arrived at the office and reached into his pocket for the note, it wasn't there."

We listened in complete rapture. We simply couldn't accept such an ending. We all demanded that Ch. unravel the mystery, but no matter how we begged him to reveal what had been written on the note, he wouldn't budge.

The next day, when I ran into Ch., he told me that if I really wanted to know what was written on the note, he would write it out for me under one condition: I had to find a way to translate it myself. He gave me the note. I unfolded it. It wasn't German. It wasn't French. It wasn't English. How was I to translate it?

The game continued.

Ilya Granovsky, a boy in our class, studied Esperanto. I gave him the note. Frowning, Ilya told me that it was a declaration of love.

MEANWHILE, THE NEWSPAPERS and the radio reported newly discovered political conspiracies: notable political leaders, who only recently had ruled the country, staged railway accidents, caused mishaps in the coal mines, poisoned food supplies, and so on. The "chiefs" were proven to be the "enemies."

Although the political arena, where such incomprehensible and sinister events unraveled, seemed distant, if not entirely disconnected, from real life, the word "enemy" had drawn near to our own family. We learned that one of my parents' comrades from the front was arrested in Moscow. It was Shlemovich, the one who had worked at the Kremlin and used to bring us delicacies back in Leningrad. It was his wife who wrote about his arrest to my parents. They were going to send him a parcel but it turned out his wife didn't indicate the address, and so my parents had to wait.

I saw how dispirited my father was. More and more often we would hear about the arrests of our acquaintances, neighbors or father's coworkers. Without saying it aloud, people confessed to each other in secret that they couldn't fall asleep at night, that they froze in apprehensive fear when they'd hear the gritting sound of a car slowing down outside their house.

Men in gabardine overcoats, often with a dog on a leash, strutted about Leningrad. They were a special type of people. All of them had something in common, most clearly seen in their brusque and unhurried gait, as if they truly enjoyed every single step they made and felt no need to hide this from anyone.

I would chat over the phone with my friends about such topics as homework, cinema, young men and so on. But once there was a phone call of a different type. Grandma called me to the phone. A voice asked:

"Tamara Vladislavovna?"

No one had ever called me by my name and patronymic before.

"Yes," I answered.

"Hello. This is one of your parents' friends."

"Hello. What is your name?"

"You don't know me."

"I know all my parents' friends."

"Not me. How are your parents?"

"They're well, thank you."

"And you are still living in the same house, aren't you?"

"Have you been to our place, then?"

"More than once. The bed in the big room is on the right hand side, same as the buffet by the wall. The mirror is in the window corner. Am I right?"

"Yes. But if you've been to our place, then I must certainly know you."

"My name is Mikhail Mikhaylovich."

"And your last name?"

"I'll tell you when we meet."

"Do you want to visit us? But my parents now live in Zhikharyovo."

"I know, I know. No, I'd like you to come straightaway to the corner of First Line and the Embankment. I'll be waiting for you there."

"What for?"

"I have to give you something for your father. You're going to visit him over the weekend, aren't you?"

"Yes. Could you bring it to us at home?"

"Please come to the place I indicated. I'll be waiting for you there in fifteen minutes."

He hung up. I had never heard my parents mention the name Mikhail Mikhaylovich. Still, I thought I had no right not to go: he wanted to pass something on to my father.

A friend of mine was visiting me, and I asked her to come with me.

The corner of First Line and the Embankment was a popular meeting point. When we came, there were a few people milling around. I remembered that he said he would come up to me himself. We waited. No one approached.

As we turned to go, someone called me:

"Tamara Vladislavovna, may I speak with you for a moment?"

I saw a well-groomed man of about forty. He wore an expensive overcoat of thick wool and smelled of cologne.

"Why have you brought your friend along?"

"Why? Shouldn't I have?"

"Of course, you shouldn't have! You should've come alone."

"What was it that you wanted to pass along to my father?"

"I better give it to you next time."

I returned home perplexed. The meeting, in spite of the man's seeming respectability, left me with an unpleasant feeling.

On Saturday I traveled to Zhikharyovo and told Mother about the phone call and the meeting. She tried to remember a Mikhail Mikhaylovich among their former acquaintances, but there was no one with that name.

A month later the alleged friend of my parents rang again. Again he wouldn't tell me what his last name was, but I insisted. It was Serebryakov.

"How are things at home?" he began.

"Good. I asked my mother about you. She doesn't remember you."

"We'll talk about that later. Now there is something more important. Are you planning on going to Zhikharyovo this weekend?"

"Yes."

"You shouldn't go."

"What? Why not?"

"Nothing special. Don't worry."

"Has something happened?"

"No, nothing. I'm only asking you to stay in Leningrad. That's all."

I was already afraid of him. I was afraid of his name, his innuendos, his evasive phrases.

On Saturday I went to see my family as usual. When I arrived, I told Mother everything. She would know better than I when to tell Father about all this. I spent the entire day at home, not even stepping outside for a moment, and when the phone rang I asked Mother to say I wasn't there.

That evening Father had to go to the warehouse to meet new workers coming from far away. I asked him to take me along; I had to tell him about Serebryakov.

In his work boots and canvas overcoat, Father strode ahead. I could hardly keep up with him. The new workers got off the train at the station and Father gave a speech of welcome. In spite of the pouring rain, the brass band played a march. It was already dark when we walked back home. The lights from the construction site flickered through the sheets of rain.

"Papa," I began. "Some strange man called a couple of times. He says he's your friend. I don't know what he wants, but he told me not to travel here today."

"That must be one of your young admirers, pulling your leg."

"No! I saw him! He is old, he..."

"Nonsense!"

He simply didn't believe me and didn't want to talk about it. Yet again, another conversation between us that just couldn't be.

At 10 p.m. I had to travel back to Leningrad. My friends accompanied me to the station. Mother came too.

Boarding the train, I glanced back to wave good-bye to them one more time when I suddenly saw Serebryakov coming out of the station building and walking toward the train with a dog. Mother noticed my horror, turned around and also saw him. He boarded one of the front cars. The train started to move. My only comfort was that Mother had seen him. I was afraid to sit in the half-empty car, knowing that the strange man was on the train, too. He might have not been an enemy, but he was not a friend either, to be sure. I kept staring at the door, waiting for him to come in with his dog.

It wasn't until the Leningrad platform that he approached me.

"Fine, now I know you are not to be trusted. You are not a serious person."

He walked past me.

I didn't answer. I had no idea what to say. His words stayed in my memory, sickening and unsettling.

A COUPLE OF DAYS LATER Iosif Antonovich Kurchevsky, the director of the works, was arrested. Father was so shaken at his friend's arrest that he couldn't talk to anyone. Without delay Father was thrown out of the Party, on the grounds that he had once written a recommendation for Kurchevsky, who was now an "Enemy of the People." Papa was demoted from the position of deputy works director to leader of the transportation division.

Mother told me that Father didn't close his eyes for three nights and kept repeating only one phrase: "What right do the three of them have to expel me from the Party?" The procedure of Father's expulsion was carried out not by a general assembly, but simply by three people from the Politburo.

Mother wept.

"They're going to arrest you too, Vladek!"

Father screamed in fury:

"What for? What can they arrest me for? Don't talk nonsense! How dare you say such a thing out loud?"

On Friday, November 22, 1937, Mother came from Zhikharyovo to Leningrad to collect some things we planned to take back together on Saturday. That night she stayed with me and Grandma. But when I came home from school the next day, she wasn't there.

"Where is Mama?" I asked Grandma.

"Sit down and eat," she said, crying.

"Where is Mama?"

"Sit down and eat," she repeated.

A neighbor, who was renting a room from my parents, came in.

"Tamara, you are a grown-up girl," he said. "You must be brave. Last night they arrested your father."

I couldn't yet comprehend what had happened to us; I could hear the two words, "father" and "arrested," but they only reverberated in my ears, rattling and muffling everything else.

The telephone operator at Zhikharyovo had called Mother and told her that they had come in the night to arrest Father, that there was a search in the house, and that, as the witnesses said, Papa's hair had turned white in the course of a few minutes. As they led him away, my little sisters ran after him to the railway station. They were shooed away, but the girls didn't know where to go and kept running after Father, weeping. The telephone operator said she had taken them in to look after them until morning.

After the phone call Mother dashed to the railway station to catch the first train to Zhikharyovo. I grabbed the things she left behind and ran after her.

In the city tram people were chatting with each other as usual. Everything around me suddenly seemed strange, as if from a different life.

In the train I climbed to the upper bunk to avoid speaking to anyone and stared through the window at the falling snow. I imagined Papa, two armed men escorting him; he must have stumbled and sunk into the snow, the two men pushing him forward. I couldn't get rid of the picture, nor could I digest it: my father walking silently under escort in an unknown direction. I suddenly realized that deep in my heart I loved my strict and honest father.

Lost in thought, I almost missed the Zhikharyovo station. I managed to jump off the train but forgot all my belongings in the car.

At home everything was in chaos after the search. My sisters stared blankly into the corner from their seats. Mother lay on the bed, indifferent to the disorder around her. She asked me to heat the room and prepare something to eat. I wanted to go see the telephone operator, but Mother stopped me.

"Don't! She asked us not to visit her. She had to go to the next station to make the phone call."

I understood everything without further questions. Papa was gone. The world in which we had lived was no more. And yet there was no other world.

It was November 23, 1937. With one blow we found ourselves in complete isolation. The gates of our house had been marked with the sign of extermination. Nothing from now on could ever reverse it.

We couldn't decide what to do first. Mama kept weeping and I could see she was incapable of making any decisions.

The next day I said in an uncertain voice that maybe we had to move back to Leningrad.

"Yes," she answered meekly.

It became clear: I had to take responsibility for the family, no matter that I was totally unprepared for this.

We began packing. Our things had to be taken to the station. Mother telephoned some people at the construction site and asked if they could send a car. But they refused to help the wife of an arrested man, their former boss. The two of us had to carry all our belongings on our backs.

I still imagined my friends would hurry to help us, but the settlement seemed deserted. People who knew us watched us through their windows, but no one came out of their houses.

As we were carrying our sewing machine we finally saw somebody coming in our direction. It was Mikhail Ivanovich Kazakov, the man who once knocked on my door on that moonlit August night in Irinovka, the man with whom I shared my first secret kiss. He paid a dear price for this stirring of his soul: in a few days he was thrown out of the Party on the grounds of "being connected with the family of an 'Enemy of the People.'"

We moved back to Leningrad. We had to support Father. We had to start looking for him in the city prisons.

But how was one to go about such a task? Where was one supposed to turn for help?

Chapter 2

From the day of Father's arrest I became known as a "Daughter of an Enemy of the People." It was the first political label fastened to me by Time. At school the teachers no longer called on me to speak but, instead, always seemed to find some pretext or other for me to sit in the back row.

Papa's arrest meant we had to make a lot of urgent decisions, particularly for me to get a job. I abandoned my studies and instead spent time combing the "Help Wanted" ads posted throughout the city. A mosaic workshop that paid a stipend to its apprentices seemed the best option.

With a heavy heart I went to school to collect my documents.

After the headmistress, Nina Vasilyevna Zapolskaya, had heard me through, she closed the staffroom door and said in a quiet, decisive voice: "I won't let you go. Whatever happens, Tamara, you've got to finish school and you've only got half a year left. If you need to earn some money, I'll find private students for you to tutor."

Nina Vasilyevna kept her word, and so the most important thing now seemed settled. The catch, however, was that *everything* was "most important": searching for my father, looking after my mother's health, taking care of my sisters, struggling to balance school and work… Life had begun in earnest.

Two weeks after Father's arrest I was summoned to the bureau of the Komsomol committee.

A long table stood draped with red bunting at one end of the room, beneath portraits of Stalin and Ezhov. Restless specks of dust danced in a slanting shaft of sunlight. The new Komsomol organizer and members of the bureau got straight down to business. They said I had always been a model member of the Komsomol and therefore they wanted to help me; however, in this moment of truth, everything depended on me alone. In order to make it clear to everyone that in my "new circumstances" my commitment as a loyal Soviet citizen remained as firm as ever, I had to publicly denounce that Enemy of the People, my father. Such was the duty of every honest person, and there could be no compromise.

"My father is innocent!" I protested. My faith in Father precluded even the faintest suspicion that he could be guilty.

"How do you know that? Who gave you the right to vouch for your father?"

"The right? No one gave me the right—I know it myself! He's innocent!"

"Prove it!"

I could speak about how hard he worked, about his unselfish devotion, about how important it was for him that children were brought up to be just and fair. But prove it? I decided that this conversation must have been designed to intimidate or test me, for who could take seriously a demand to denounce their own father?

A couple of days later a general Komsomol meeting was announced. One of the points on the agenda was me.

Again I couldn't believe what I was hearing. The chairman reported in a hard voice about a certain Petkevich, Daughter of an Enemy of the People, a girl for whom the authority of the organs of the NKVD apparently meant nothing. She didn't believe that her father had been arrested for any good reason and refused to denounce him. In this manner she had placed herself outside the Komsomol.

"Who is for Petkevich being expelled from the Komsomol?"

A forest of hands went up. Only two abstained: Ilya Granovsky, the cream of the crop of the school, and a boy from a parallel class.

The decision was formulated to expel Petkevich from the Komsomol: 1) on account of a lack of political vigilance (since among her own family members she failed to recognize an Enemy of the People); 2) for slandering the organs of the NKVD (since her belief in her father's innocence meant that she questioned the actions of the People's Commissar of Internal Affairs); and 3)... for some reason the third point completely slipped my memory.

It still seemed that at any second someone would come and reverse all of this. I waited for it to happen. In any case, the supervisory division of the Komsomol, the Komsomol District Committee, would surely be outraged by the decision to expel me. At least this was what I assumed when summoned there soon after.

"The decision is ratified. You are no longer a member of the Komsomol. Place your membership card on the table," they announced coldly.

I took my card out of my handbag and left it on the secretary's desk.

The next day I felt sick, and for several weeks afterward I stayed in bed. Our house reeked of medicines and herbal decoctions. The doctors said I'd had a nervous breakdown.

No one rang our doorbell. We were excluded from the world and the normal flow of life. Privation had barged its way into our house like an efficient, merciless surgeon and we had no choice but to come to terms with it.

AS SOON AS WE ARRIVED IN LENINGRAD we set about looking for Papa. Someone advised us to go to the transit prison. Mother looked at me helplessly, and I realized I would have to go there by myself.

Father's name did not appear on the lists. Nor could they find his name at the Kresty prison, the Crosses. There I met women who explained that first I had to register my inquiry at the Bolshoy Dom, the Big House, on Liteyny Prospect.

It was a "big house" indeed, especially by the standards of the day. A gray, solidly constructed modernist building, it was designed to impose an aura of invincible power.

The transit prison, the Kresty and the Bolshoy Dom gave me a new view of the city. Until then I was only familiar with its monuments and palaces, its tram and bus routes. Another life opened up to me. Prisons, barred windows, the despairing faces of the people I stood in line with… It was as if I had come to an edge, beyond which lay the end of the world. But my father was over there somewhere and I had to help him, at any cost.

The gigantic colonnaded hall of the information bureau at the Bolshoy Dom took my breath away. It was like a railway station crammed with people. I couldn't tell whether it was a chaotic crowd or a hopelessly long line. If it was a line, where did it end? Despite the general hubbub, the people standing near me were silent, their eyes fixed desperately on a spot somewhere in front of them. Instantly I was swept up in the all-pervasive sense of agitation. My eyes saw and my skin felt what my mind had not yet realized. So great seemed the destructive power of the anguish rising from this mass of people that I wondered why the walls of the building did not come crashing down around us.

Utterly downcast, with no clue where to go or what to do, I finally managed to make my way to the back of the line.

Deep within this womb, strangers confided to one another in whispers about how it all had happened:

"They rang the doorbell, came right in, said—"

"They started rummaging through the bedding, books, letters, turning everything upside-down—"

"They finished the search, led him away—"

A woman standing nearby was recounting how her husband had sat up nights on end listening to every sound. Then suddenly he became strangely calm, only begging her again and again not to lose heart, smiling oddly at her and cheering her up.

"And my husband kept on repeating: 'Believe me! Do you hear? You have to believe me—I'm not guilty of anything! You must make it clear to the children that their father is innocent. It's very important. That's all I ask of you!'" said another.

A third joined in: "And my husband screamed: 'Who gave you the right? It's a misunderstanding! You wouldn't dare arrest an innocent man!'"

Suddenly someone asked in a low, demented voice:

"Do you think they are being tortured? I've heard they beat them brutally; one man had all his ribs broken."

An elderly woman and her grown-up son stood next to me at the end of the line.

"Who are you here for?" the young man asked me.

"My father. And you?"

"My father, too."

Questions followed: when was my father arrested? How big was our family?

"What's your name?" my new acquaintances asked me.

I told them. "And you?" I asked.

"My name's Erik. And this is my mother, Barbara Ionovna."

Every two minutes a bell rang shrilly above one of the doors of this hellish hole, to signal that the next in line should come in. At the information desk things moved quickly. Question, answer, and the little window would slam shut. From there a door led directly into the street. But the line seemed interminable. On that first day we came nowhere near the front. The mother and son offered to hold a place for me the following morning.

The next day a baldheaded man in the information window asked me:

"Name?"

"Petkevich, Vladislav Iosifovich."

"In the prison on Shpalernaya."

And the wooden hatch banged shut.

In the Bolshoy Dom I learned we could give thirty rubles to a prisoner once a month on a day corresponding to the first letter of the prisoner's last name. It turned out that Erik's father's last name also began with "P."

At Shpalernaya we received further information:

"'P'? The second of every month."

In 1937 and 1938, second-hand stores in Leningrad resembled dumping grounds for expensive antiques: carpets, paintings, chandeliers, silver, crystal, furs, clothing… One such place on Nevsky Prospect, near the General Staff Building, took up the entire ground floor of a large, gray, neo-Gothic structure. Mother and I had to stand in line for a long time to sell a pair of monogrammed plates and some crystal goblets that we'd thus far managed to hang on to. We also took some things to a pawnshop, where money was paid right away. In this way we were able to support Father, as well as have something for ourselves to live on.

On December 2, the day we were to hand over the money for Papa, we got up at 5 a.m., well before dawn. My little sisters woke up and cried as they fearfully watched Mama wrap me in a warm shawl and force me to put on my thick felt boots. On that dark, stinging morning I boarded the tram for the first ride of my premature adulthood.

On Shpalernaya Street I saw people darting in and out of the entryway of a small building adjacent to the prison. The registration point was on the third-floor landing. More than two hundred people were trying to force their way up the stairs. Awakened by the noise, the outraged tenants were opening their doors and swearing indignantly, turning the "guests" out into the street. When people heard that the tenants were going to call the yard-keeper and the police, they went to look for another entryway, but soon they were driven out of there in exactly the same way. Nor could they stand in front of the prison gates, which kept opening to swallow more and more Black Marias, the prison wagons making their deliveries.

We shivered in the cold until eight o'clock, when finally we were allowed inside. People fell silent and formed a line. When my turn came, I handed over Father's thirty rubles through a little window, though I found it hard to imagine a kiosk in the prison corridors where he would be able to buy anything for himself.

My new acquaintances and I agreed to meet at the Public Prosecutor's Office. We planned to make an appointment with Pozern, one of the lawyers, but in a couple of days a newspaper article appeared branding him an Enemy of the People. We were advised to go see Zakovsky, then Goglidze, but soon they, too, were denounced as Enemies. The name-carnage continued. Instead of being given actual appointments with a prosecutor, we were instructed to put our requests in writing.

Once, in the reception area of the Prosecutor's office, while everyone was intently filling out forms, a man stood up and addressed us all in a loud, fervent voice, saying that we were witnessing crimes committed against old Bolsheviks and good people in general, that if we simply waited in vain for something to happen without doing anything about it, everyone would be exterminated. We listened avidly, but also with fear. No one arrested or even interrupted him. He made a passionate political speech, thrillingly courageous. However, his words seemed somehow... exaggerated. The new regime consisted of the same class of workers and peasants which had suffered so much in its own historical time, and it was inconceivable that they could now turn around and harm their own people.

AS WE VISITED all sorts of information desks and public bureaus, Erik told me about his life as a third-year student at the Medical Institute and his dreams of becoming a surgeon.

Once he asked:

"What will become of us?"

"What do you mean?" I asked cautiously.

"You know what I mean: the families of the arrested get deported."

"Where to? Why?"

"Because we are relatives of Enemies of the People. Where? Anywhere, as long as it's far enough away from here."

It was the first time I'd heard this. It must have been an exaggeration. It couldn't be! I decided not to say anything to my mother.

I kept going to school, but by now my life was almost entirely spent shuffling between various bureaus, from one waiting room to another. Valechka and Renochka were studying. Mama was ill. She constantly cried, and I didn't let her go anywhere.

One evening, Krasovsky, Father's devoted comrade from the front, showed up at our door. He hadn't seen our father for a long time and had come to pay him a visit. It was dark and gloomy in our house. We hardly had any food. When Mama told him that Father was in prison, Krasovsky howled and fell to his knees before Father's portrait on the wall. In a loud and terrible voice he cried, "Commissar! Our dear old Commissar! What've they done? If they've arrested *you*... What is going on in the world? What are they doing to you there?"

I never imagined a man could sob so violently. Father's former life, which had hitherto been foreign and quite boring to me, suddenly appeared important and extraordinary. Krasovsky's words, "What are they doing to you there?" immediately plunged me into remembering what I had heard in the Bolshoy Dom. I pictured to myself the insufferable; I suddenly believed in the existence of this world's dark side, in the reality of dungeons where inconceivable, unbearable pain was inflicted.

Krasovsky went out to get a bottle of liquor. He sat up with Mother late into the night. They talked about Father, their youth and the war.

On January 2, 1938, I once again went to Shpalernaya to hand over the thirty rubles for Father. I was stunned to see how much shorter the line had become in just a month.

"Transported," people muttered, one after another, as they came back from the little window.

New expressions appeared. Unthinkable fear emanated from phrases such as "The troika passed sentence" and "Transported."

Through the open window I, too, was told:

"Petkevich? Transported."

Erik was told the same thing. Transported? A long journey? Where? For how long? I saw Father's terrified eyes before me. Was he led out through this gate? At night? Was he shoved onto a wagon, and then a train?

Erik accompanied me to the tram stop. He gave me a letter but asked me not to read it until I got home.

When I opened it, I read:

> It is unfortunate that I have to tell you this at a time of such great tragedy but we do not know what will become of us tomorrow. Perhaps we will be both exiled, and you'll go someplace, my family will go someplace else. I have to tell you that I cannot live without you. I love you.

My consciousness had to stretch itself to encompass the meaning of his words, for I felt nothing remotely similar for him. The letter complicated everything, and anyway it seemed to me somewhat false, so I decided not to answer.

Soon afterward Erik phoned. He realized his declaration must have upset me and asked me to forget about it. "We have to remain friends," he said.

I HAD TO GO TO THE BOLSHOY DOM AGAIN. It was the only place I could find out how long the troika had sentenced my father for and where he had been sent.

By now I had grown used to the place and was able to distinguish individuals from the faceless crowd. Never before had I seen so many splendid women gathered together in one place! A portraitist could've had a field day, with so many beautiful bearings and faces to choose from. Their dignity, their grace and charm, acquired over generations of good breeding, were now overshadowed by anguish and suffering, but these women didn't collapse in hysterics. Even here they were elegantly dressed and coiffed. They still knew how to weather events with poise.

Once one of them spoke to me:

"Who are you here for, child?"

"My father."

"I'm here for my husband."

She spoke the word "husband" melodiously, as if to reveal how beautiful love's secrets could be. She asked about my family. I opened up to her without questioning why it was so easy. I told her things I had not told anyone, such as how I would never forgive those who had disavowed us in Zhikharyovo when we were leaving for Leningrad, or those who had voted to throw me out of the Komsomol. She listened intently, then replied softly and sadly, without condemnation:

"Remember, child: one must never be too quick to draw conclusions."

I always remembered these words and more than once in my life this beautiful, pensive woman's advice proved useful. The beauty of her face, her eyes of steel-blue and almond, her hair tied into a bun, her refined speech and her words themselves lived on in me as the last vestige of a vanished culture.

"I have no doubt I'll be exiled," she said to me in farewell, "but you are still so very young, I hope you'll be spared."

"An acquaintance of mine," said someone, "a very beautiful and unusually brave woman, managed, if it's possible to imagine, to obtain the services of a public prosecutor. In his office he had a sofa for female visitors. He assured her that her husband would be set free. Of course, nothing like that ever happened. Now he himself is under investigation."

Trying to dispel their grief, many people harbored a sliver of naïve trust in these assurances. Many tried to explain things logically, considering their case some sort of mistake. But someone or other would always dispel such illusions, remarking bitterly:

"God! Don't you see, this whole thing has been designed to wipe out the intelligentsia?"

I was seventeen. It was too early for me to believe the story of the prosecutor and the beautiful lady or the shrewd conjecture about deliberate repressions.

My turn came to inquire after Father. As always, as soon as I stood in front of the information window, I got a lump in my throat, and it took me some time before I was able to utter Papa's name.

"Ten years. Magadan," came the answer. "Without the right to correspondence."

Thus determined the troika.

On the way home I kept thinking that the news would kill Mama. I made up my mind not to tell her at once, but when I saw her eyes looking straight into my soul, I told her everything. From that moment a new common language of frankness was established between the two of us.

Rumor had it that when a prison transport arrived at its destination, a more accurate address would be provided.

My last visit to the Bolshoy Dom was marked by an event that made an indelible impression on me. All of a sudden the incessant din of voices fell away. Silence spread out from within the hall, all sounds ceased and agitation drew in. Like many others, I didn't immediately grasp what happened next. From the side doors, twelve or fifteen shaven-headed men filed out, clutching bundles in their hands. The dense crowd had its own instincts: a corridor was immediately formed for them.

Suddenly the man at the head of the file stopped and called in a rasping voice:

"Mothers! Wives! Daughters! Listen to us! You're not here in vain! You have to plead! Write to everyone! See, we are the first ones set free through your persistence! Dear women, fight for the truth! Don't give up!"

My God, what a hullabaloo ensued! They'd released them! Everything was exploding. The information bureau of the NKVD turned into a noisy, feverish battlefield. Loud sobs, cries and an avalanche of questions. "Where have you come from? From the transports? From prison? How long have you been inside? How do they feed people there? How many have been freed?"

Then came relief: of course, this was precisely why we were waiting there! And how could one not believe in this? The nightmare was over! It was all a misunderstanding! They were letting them go!

The administration of the Bolshoy Dom was already restoring order and shoving the men out, but the women kept clinging to them with questions, drowning each other out. Exultation reigned. Reborn hope stirred the nerves, people seemed drunk on this good news. How desperately they wanted to believe what they'd just seen and heard, rather than what had already been fated!

Not everyone, though, gave in to the delirium. Many calmed down at once. Although my thoughts were dancing and my imagination was stirred, I, too, was left with mixed feelings. Still, I ran home with the news: "I saw it, they're setting them free!"

We drank tea, made plans: Papa was coming back, his health would have to be properly attended to. Leaving Leningrad was now out of the question.

How unfortunate that they had already sent him off on a transport; it would certainly delay his return, for it was a long way...

But Papa didn't come back.

The file of men I'd seen in the hall of the Bolshoy Dom must have just been a small group released by accident, or else it could've all been staged, a provocation, as some suggested.

Verst after *verst,* special trains with prisoners clattered on toward the eastern edge of the Soviet Union, to the ocean, to the Bay of Nagaevo, to death. The unpaid labor was already bringing the government a lot of revenue. It was a profitable business.

Papa's address was Magadan. That was all. As for the stipulation, "without the right to correspondence," we took it literally.

I thought about him constantly. True, he used to punish me, and I still didn't know what fatherly tenderness was, yet I became inextricably linked to him, firmly and forever.

Father's arrest left us with unanswerable questions: why did life treat him and so many like him in this way? His worldview was born out of sympathy for the "oppressed and poverty-stricken Russia." All his life he selflessly aspired to serve the shining ideal of a new and upright society. But whenever blind phrases like "I'm a communist!" got in the way of traditional moral values, Father was always able to pull back and follow his conscience, in spite of the risks.

His uncompromising exactitude was depressing. There was little warmth at home: tenderness was considered excessive and superfluous. Falsehood was the greatest evil of all, something we were organically averse to, regardless of the circumstances. Not a single kopeck was to be earned in addition to our salary. Trivial conversations were never held in our house; no rubbish was to be spoken, not a single frivolous word.

Father was handsome when young, but when he came back from the collectivization mission in Siberia he was worn out and emaciated. Then, as he traveled from one construction site to another, he grew hardened and worn out. By the time of his arrest he was already in poor health. Now I imagined my father as I had never actually seen him: cut off from the hectic pace of life, discouraged and bitter. What was he thinking as they led him away? Later I was to understand not with my brain but with the very cells of my body just how he must have endured his lot.

ERIK'S FATHER had also been given ten years, also Magadan, also "without the right to correspondence."

We'd hardly had time to digest the news when Erik phoned:

"A notification came today. We're being exiled. They've given us three days to vacate our apartment."

My immediate thought was that it would be the same for us. Exile meant darkness, virtual death. Mother was reaching for the phone to speak to Barbara Ionovna, but I talked her out of it, since I could only imagine what it was like at their place now. Erik asked me to come over the next morning.

Their dimly lit well-furnished apartment was in chaos. Things were being collected together, tied up and prepared for sale. Without shedding a tear, Barbara Ionovna was dismantling with her own hands the household she had put together over decades.

Erik and I dragged their possessions from one store to another: the overfilled pawnshops were no longer accepting goods from families sentenced to exile.

As apartments were being vacated, people were waiting to take them over. More often than not, they were investigators and NKVD officials, and it was not unusual for a good apartment to serve as grounds for exiling an arrested man's family.

Erik's family hadn't been told where they were going. They would only find out their destination in Moscow.

In three days, Erik and his mother were to depart. My mother asked me to take her along to see them off. I was afraid she wouldn't be able to bear the scene of farewell between Barbara Ionovna and her elder son, who for some reason had been spared.

Several people came to the train station. Erik had the idea that once they got to Moscow they would be able to get the exile order repealed. He wouldn't let me take a step away from him and begged me to vow that I would answer his letters. Just before the train departed he said again, "I'll love you forever, whatever happens to me!"

Barbara Ionovna cried only at the last moment. Everything seemed dreamlike and surreal.

The train pulled out. The people who had come to say good-bye to Erik were already walking away from the platform, chatting and even laughing, as if to say, "Life goes on."

ANY DAY NOW we expected to be notified of exile, but notification never came. We began to think we had been spared, though we could never be sure. Balancing these two feelings became the norm.

After Papa's arrest our circle of friends fell apart. Many of my parents' acquaintances were arrested, their families exiled. Others expressed their sympathy and looked after us for a while, but they, too, had their own problems. After I was expelled from the Komsomol, I lost most of my friends. There was a period when we lived as if in a sheer vacuum.

Then we had a visitor.

I spent the night before our graduation exam at the house of my girlfriend Nina, one of the few who had remained faithful to me. Early in the morning Valechka came running to see me.

"Come quickly, something has happened!"

She ran off without telling me what it was.

My mother looked very excited:

"A stranger is here! He wants to see you. Something tells me he's come from Father!"

In the room sat a man of indeterminate age in a badly worn suit, and with such a pale, pasty face that he seemed mortally ill. I introduced myself. He asked me which grade I was in, if my mother was working, how we lived and on what.

I knew the man wasn't asking these questions out of idle curiosity. I continued answering so he wouldn't leave. For breakfast we had only pearl barley soup. Mama heated it up and we sat down to eat together at the table. Only then did the man slip his hand into his pocket and pull out a letter. The envelope was signed with Father's handwriting… and the letter was addressed to me. "My dear daughter, I am writing to you because I am sure Mama has been exiled with the little ones, but I think you may have been allowed to finish school…"

Father wrote that he was completely innocent, asked where Mother was and whether she was in good health, how my sisters were doing and how we were all managing to live. As for himself, he wrote he was working in a bay on the Sea of Okhotsk, up to his knees in water. A hundred rubles were enclosed in the envelope.

Mother and I shivered. We found out nothing about Papa's living conditions, the state of his health or where he got the money, and we deluged the man with questions.

"I don't know him. I've never seen him," he interrupted us.

We were bewildered.

Then our visitor recounted something we could not imagine. He explained that in the camp where my father was living, hardly anyone knew each other's last names, since the prisoners had only numbers sewn on their camp jackets. Only those who shared a barracks could know more of each other. At night the barracks were locked.

"How is it possible that you brought us a letter from Father without knowing him?" we asked the man.

He said there was a "waiting list" for prisoners sentenced "with no right to correspondence." Anyone who was released, by the rules of the prisoner code of honor, had to take a few letters from those staying behind. It was my father's turn when our guest was set free.

"Are you from Leningrad? Do you live here?"

"No, I'm from Central Russia."

"Then… you've come all the way to Leningrad just to bring us a letter from Father?"

"One could say that."

Expressions of delight seemed inappropriate. We had to do something for him. But what?

Mama and I ran him a bath, made up our best bed and invited him to stay as our guest for a few days. Then I rushed off to buy tickets to the theater. I picked my favorite place, the Alexandrinsky.

Seated in the comfortable dark-red velvet seats, we saw *Talent and Admiration.* I noticed our guest wasn't especially impressed by the play but was very pleased by the atmosphere. He relaxed and rested, yet at the same time seemed somewhere very far away.

Getting ready to leave, he noticed our torment and offered to try to find a bargeman and persuade him to take a letter to Father. At day's end, he came home with news that the bargeman had agreed. Mother and I set about writing an endless letter, in which we tried to convince Father that nothing was wrong with us, that we all still lived together in Leningrad and that we couldn't wait until he came back.

Did our letter ever reach Father? Of course not: that would be too much to expect. We never again heard anything from Papa or had any news of him.

Twenty-seven years later Valechka made an inquiry about Papa. We finally got an answer:

> DEATH CERTIFICATE P-B #293408
>
> Citizen Petkevich, Vladislav Iosifovich, died February 10, 1942. Age: 66 years. Cause of Death: Liver abscess. Corresponding entry (#2) in the official register of deaths on June 29, 1956.
>
> Died in—city, settlement—
>
> Registered in Mginsk District Registry Office of the Leningrad Oblast.
>
> Issued June 29, 1956.
>
> Head of Registry Office Bureau (Signature)

The official who signed the certificate hadn't even bothered getting my father's age correct. If Father had really died in 1942, he would have been only fifty-two. The indifference of the hand which wrote that document also counts as history.

My father died abandoned, in utter loneliness and obscurity. The place where he died is unknown—there is a dash on the form. The whereabouts of the mass grave in which he was buried remained a state secret. And the sinister date of his death, February 1942, was a time destined to take on an awful significance in our family history.

The assurance of the leaders that "the son is not responsible for his father" was familiar from the time of collectivization, when the children of dekulakized farmers were exiled to homes for juvenile delinquents in Yakutia and Solovki, and anyone who was spared could not gain admission to any institute or university in the country. In 1937–1938, this saying took on a second life: the children of Enemies of the People were usually exiled.

We seemed to be an exception, and people kept telling us we should be grateful.

"It's because I have three children," my mother would answer, looking for an explanation.

"So what? Wives with as many as six children have been exiled," they would correct her.

Toward the end of 1938, when the dark word "arrest" was heard slightly less often, I was unexpectedly called to the Komsomol District Committee of Vasilievsky Island, the same place where they had taken away my Komsomol membership card. This time, without any explanation or apology, they casually told me I could have my card back.

Just like that! I still remembered the weeks of my sickness. I never stopped regarding my father as completely innocent. On his camp jacket a number was sewn; he worked knee-deep in water. Nothing stirred up inside me in response to their cold offer. I told them I didn't need it and walked out.

All my friends were appalled. Without exception they called me dumb, proud, arrogant and snobbish. Particularly hurtful was their "logical deduction" that the Komsomol was right to expel me.

Perhaps that was the time when a special "dossier" on me was opened.

THE MONEY I EARNED in my after-hours tutoring, in addition to what we managed to sell, still wasn't enough to support a family of five including my grandmother, who was now also living with us.

Chance came to our rescue.

Whenever Father used to go away, Mother would rent out one of our two rooms to the D. family. After Father's arrest, the D.s retained the room. They had a daughter my age, and a friend of theirs was teaching her the craft of batik, in return for a small fee.

One day an imposing woman knocked on our door asking to use the phone. About thirty years old, green-eyed, she was wearing a brightly colored shawl. She noticed that I couldn't take my eyes off it and suggested, "Tamarochka, how about I also teach you batik?"

Mama and I thanked her but politely declined the offer.

"For free, of course," she swiftly added.

Sympathy and help finally entered our house in the guise of this artist, Elizaveta Egorovna, who later became my friend. She confessed her interest in me was aroused by "the rule of opposites": the D.s had told her about our living conditions and described me as a mediocre and uninteresting girl. They were right: I had become a shapeless thing of whims and emotions, without a sign of talent or potential for accomplishment.

At first I worked as an assistant at her house. Working in an atelier, Lily (as people called her) also took private commissions. Among her clients were famous Leningrad ballerinas and high-society women who dressed only in the latest fashion. Before long I passed the exam in the atelier and became an independent worker, able to work from home. From the atelier I got stretchers, glue, aniline dyes and parachute silk for making patterned kerchiefs, and soon I was taking one order after another. My sister Valechka also enjoyed the new trade: she helped me devotedly, and her naïve admiration would often inspire me to new compositions. My earnings turned out to be quite decent, and now it seemed we could manage.

My high school graduation was fast approaching. Lily suggested we buy some inexpensive fabric, stretch it in a frame and design a pattern. Mother found a piece of black velvet for finishing touches, and before long the dress for my graduation party was ready.

I thought I'd never forgive the forest of hands raised to expel me from the Komsomol, but youth forgets quickly. I was one of the prettiest girls at school, my yearning for friendship was as strong as ever, and by graduation time I had forgotten those offenses. We were all looking forward to our new lives; events of the past dissolved in nervous but happy anticipation of the future.

When the party began, my classmate Ilya Granovsky led me to the window. Trams jingled in the street. He said that the next morning would be the worst of his life because he wouldn't be going to school and would therefore be deprived of seeing me. "I don't suppose you'd want to keep seeing me when there is no more school, would you?" he said.

Another boy was jealously watching us. A third was already on his way over to ask me to dance.

After we received our diplomas, the teachers wished us good luck and happiness. Their tone was friendlier and less pedagogic than usual. Our literature teacher recited poetry and it was as if we were seeing him for the first time. Many years later we found out that he was among the first to die in the Siege of Leningrad, but we remembered him just the way he was at our graduation party—unruly and surprising. Our strict math teacher was suddenly more approachable, and our charming teacher of physics announced that "of all the girls in this class, Tamara will be the first to get married." It turned out that everyone else believed this too, which deeply offended and perplexed me.

The night was full of sad and joyful words, waltzes and polkas, declarations and embarrassments, gratitude and a barely conscious sense of guilt, which life itself was to perpetuate in the ensuing decades for those of us who survived.

"What institute are you applying to?" we kept asking one another. My dream was to enter the English Department at the Institute of Foreign Languages; I was tempted by the idea of translating books. Still, I didn't really want to become a teacher, and in reality, after graduating from the Institute, that's what most people ended up doing.

I discussed my plans with Mother, and she agreed, but only if I studied during the day and worked in the evenings, figuring that a stipend combined with a job would be enough to cover our needs.

Not long after, I passed the entrance examinations to the First State Institute of Foreign Languages.

The dormitories of the erstwhile finishing school resonated with the romantic spirit of a bygone era, of the whispered secrets of its former boarders. I adored the building, the garden stretching down to the Neva, the dilapidated wall in the garden, the gorgeous girls with whom I had taken the exam, my new status as a student, the tramlines that led across the Palace Bridge to the Institute. Every time I crossed that bridge I would look out the tram window to see what color the sky was above the Peter and Paul Fortress and the Winter Palace, and whether the Admiralty Spire gleamed brightly or merely shimmered in the sun. I was eighteen. In spite of everything, I fell in love with life and started to believe in it once again.

Soon after the entrance examinations, Mama talked me into visiting my uncle who lived near Tikhvin, where my father used to work. I remembered the place for its glorious twilights, brimming with life. The lilac thickets and the rye meadows swirled in the breeze as birds sang and the evening fog descended.

When my uncle met me at the train station, he told me, in an ironic tone, that someone had been expecting me.

The settlement had grown much bigger. The pine trees hadn't been cut down yet, and the place looked like a resort. It was Papa who had given this place its start, and even though he wasn't here now, life really did go on.

"It's up to you," my uncle joked, "to accept the invitation, or to decline it: Juzef and his mother have invited us for *pirogi*."

"Accept!" I ordered.

Youth demanded romantic adventures, and this was to be my first.

A magnificent dinner was spread out on the table. Juzef, my father's former colleague, was gazing at me as devotedly as ever. His mother and sister were both very kind to me. Outside the window, a thunderstorm broke out. The lightning poeticized the party. Juzef played the violin but the music was muffled by the thunder.

A week later Juzef proposed to me. His proposal was most properly made. I declined. Everything was as I had intended: the suitor was desperate, my heart was sinking. Pity, mixed with guilt and extreme curiosity, made me leave the house. A window was lit in the administration building. I took my shoes off so the floorboards wouldn't creak and ran up to the second floor. Through a half-open door I saw Juzef sitting motionless, absorbed in his thoughts. My curiosity satisfied, I ran away. A few minutes later, he came to see me in astonishment, saying he had just had a hallucination: he thought he saw me in a white dress outside his door in the administration building, but the following moment I had disappeared.

When I returned to Leningrad and opened the door of our apartment, Mama exclaimed, "God! I've been going crazy. I sent you there before I remembered about Juzef!"

Every word or phrase Mama uttered revealed something new to me about her.

We were doing the laundry. Bent over a wooden trough and unable to see Mama through the clouds of steam, I was singing. Suddenly she came closer, kissed me and said, "Thank you for singing!" There was humility, gratitude and God only knows what else in that phrase! I stopped singing; my heart began to ache. I had no idea what Mama felt deep down. At one moment she would give up all routine, almost making me feel like the head of our family, while at the next moment she would demand total obedience of me.

It wasn't until about a year and a half after Papa's arrest that Mama managed to regain some balance. She said she was going to find work. Indeed she did find some job or other but just for a short while, and it only foreshadowed the deeper spiritual deterioration to come.

ERIK AND BARBARA IONOVNA had been exiled to Frunze, the capital of Kirghizia. Letters from them came one after another. They didn't know how long their exile would last. An undergraduate medical student, Erik could only work as a sanitary inspector, but he also worked at an outpatients' clinic for a quarter of the normal wage. They missed Leningrad. Erik described Kirghizia—the Central Asian climate, their daily life. They were renting a room in a house with a clay floor and had to fetch water from a well.

In every letter, Erik wrote that he loved me. I answered his letters but avoided responding to his feelings. My own soul was racked with guilt because I was able to study while he had been deprived of such an opportunity.

With time I gathered a close circle of friends. Friendship gave me the feeling that I was participating in real life. Our studies, common interests and the secrets we entrusted to one another gradually helped me develop my independence.

I had known David N. since we were little. We used to live in the same building and studied in the same class at school. In the difficult times he hadn't betrayed me. Now he said he was in love with me. He used to throw flowers through my window; he would find out from Mother what I needed the most and buy it for me as a birthday present; he would bring a watermelon or chocolate to our place and even asked his mother to sew me a dress.

Most of my girlfriends were fellow students in the English Department. My best friend, Nina, lived with her mother. Her father had another family but loved his daughter and often visited her. He had left Nina a rich home library, which apart from the classics also included books on theosophy. We avidly read Solovyov and Krzhizhanovskaya and were fascinated by the idea of reincarnation. Nina's harmonious relationship with her mother amazed me. It resembled a friendship between two girlfriends rather than the relationship between a mother and daughter. Nina spoke in a soft voice and never said anything superfluous. I wasn't surprised when after many years she and her mother became deeply religious: how else could one satisfy such a deep and inquisitive spirit?

Liza R., thin and dark-eyed, brisk and temperamental, fell in love easily, and always with very handsome young men. All her romantic events lived their own lives within her, and they would always start with various sounds and fragrances: the squeak of tires, wet asphalt, moonlight flooding the road, the wafting smell of cherry trees in blossom. Only after such an introduction would a man appear in Liza's stories, which were always full of impressive nuance.

She was one of many children. Her mother was a despotic woman for whom money was the most important thing in life. She had stuffed Liza full of prejudices; "forbidden" was the operative word in their household. Liza's mother implanted in her daughter such an aversion toward any sort of visceral impulse that Liza's life became a constant struggle between emotions and various kinds of interdictions. Longing to break free from her mother's overbearing care, Liza avidly absorbed the world around her.

The interesting, observant and skeptical Raya Sh. was the most intelligent, serious and ironic of us all; her jokes were often sad and bitter. It seemed that some burden, which we didn't understand at the time, already loomed over her life.

In our circle we had two boys with the same first name: one was called White Kirill, the other—Black Kirill. Both were studying at the Hydrographic Institute. White Kirill was the heart of our group. He would always spice up our conversation with English words. Black Kirill was his opposite: quiet, prudent and reserved. He was educated, but very full of himself.

There was also Kolya G., the artist Makovsky's grandson, who lived three houses away from ours in a splendid apartment with stucco ceilings. In his room, huge windows with marble windowsills overlooked the Neva. There was a grand piano and both Kirills played it well. Kolya's apartment became our usual gathering place. We listened to Scriabin, Chopin and Schubert, read Esenin, Akhmatova and Severyanin. We talked about books, argued over the existence of God and sprinkled our conversations with the aphorisms of Oscar Wilde.

From time to time new people would show up. I was quite embarrassed when a student of the French Department, Roksana Siobori, came up to me at the Institute and said she was going to transfer to our department just to see me on a regular basis. I murmured back something polite, but she was quite insistent and asked if she could come to visit me at home.

As soon as my acquaintanceship with someone or other became somewhat closer, I immediately warned the person that my father had been arrested. When I told this to Roksana, her reaction was especially sympathetic.

Once, when Roksana was visiting us and stayed till late at night, she suddenly felt sick. We let her stay over, but in the next few days she didn't get any better. So she stayed with us for about two weeks. Mother and I looked after her, and soon she became almost a member of our family.

Roksana was in her fifth year at the French Department, seven years older than me. She had a conspicuous appearance, unattractive and thin, with a fringe of dark hair on her forehead and a protruding lower jaw. Despite the age difference, we talked with enthusiasm about everything in the world. My other girlfriends had families, but she was all alone.

Our friendship was complicated because the rest of my friends categorically disliked her. I fought for her, asking to bring her over. Grudgingly they would agree.

Roksana said very little about herself, but once she told me about Yavorsky, the man she loved. She said she'd like to have my opinion of him and one day she brought him along. He was an interesting man with blue eyes and grayish hair. The guest scrutinized our group and looked through the collection of postcards of a Parisian salon, of which Kolya G. was very proud.

"I didn't like him," I told Roksana later.

"One simply cannot dislike a man like him!" she answered roughly. "If you're trying to tell me he left you indifferent, I don't believe you. You're not open with me! You've got so many admirers and you're trying to convince me you like none of them?"

"I really don't!" I answered.

Roksana burst out, "You've got a whole swarm of boys running after you, and you don't want any of them! Do you really think if Yavorsky doesn't like me I won't find another boyfriend? Well, you're wrong: I've had plenty of love adventures. Sometimes it happens like this: he picks me up in his car late at night and takes me to his place; he kneels before me and kisses the hem of my shabby skirt. Yes, yes, kisses it!"

Roksana's speech was full of strange and dramatic challenges, and it revealed her hostility toward me; I was struck by the unusual tone of her monologue. Night, a car, he kneels down and kisses the hem of her skirt... It was hard to say why, but I unconditionally believed in the faithfulness of her portrayal of this scene, not knowing back then how important it was to take notice of what left you perplexed by an obscure subtext, in which more truth was buried than in the literal meaning of words.

IT WAS TOO OFTEN that, facing the casuistry of the time, I proved to be unsophisticated and blind.

Serebryakov, whose name I directly associated with Papa's arrest, regularly reminded us of himself. Every now and then I heard his smarmy and murmuring baritone with its baffling questions in the telephone receiver. As soon as I realized it was he who was calling, my heart would sink, and I could never find the right words to answer him.

Several years before, when Papa was still in the Shpalernaya Prison, Serebryakov rang, asking if I would like to see my father. That was during the time when I paced back and forth along the prison walls, hoping that the window of Father's cell might overlook the street and that he might see me.

"Yes," I answered. I was near to fainting.

"Great! I knew you'd say so. Wait in front of your house and take your passport with you. I'll be there soon."

Passport? I knew one wasn't supposed to entrust his passport to a stranger, but Serebryakov had introduced himself as Father's friend, and while there was no evidence to prove it, the word "friend" nevertheless colored his name. Though it was a question of seeing Papa, I still hesitated. I didn't know whether I could trust this man.

Even earlier, shortly after Father was arrested, Serebryakov had told me:

"When they searched your house, they confiscated your father's photo from the front room and a copy of *The History of the Party* by Knorin."

Mother checked. It was true. Who was he?

I walked out of the house but didn't take the passport with me.

"What do you need my passport for?"

"Don't you trust me?"

"I do," I said, not wanting to upset him.

"Then what's the matter?"

I stood silent. Serebryakov waited and then said:

"Well, it looks like you don't really want to see your father."

I tried to think logically. I had never heard of anyone being allowed a visitor in prison. If Serebryakov could really arrange a secret visit, why would he need my passport? But the next moment I thought: what if such considerations are only an excuse to justify my own cowardice and weak character? What if I might really be allowed to see Father? Couldn't Serebryakov have a plan of his own that he had to keep secret from me?

Some time before Papa's arrest Serebryakov had told me not to go to Zhikharyovo but I didn't listen. After that, at the Moscow Railway Station, he exposed my unreliability and said: "Now I know you're not to be trusted." He had applied a subtle psychological technique. Since then I'd been trying to rehabilitate myself in his eyes, trying to prove that in fact I was a reliable person and could be trusted. Now that Papa had already been transported to Magadan, Serebryakov still rang regularly, offering favors.

"I have to talk to you right away. Come to the gate. I'll be right there."

He appeared with a fashionably dressed man.

"Allow me to introduce Mr. Richmond."

Richmond held out his hand to me. Everything inside me shrank. Contact with a foreigner in 1938 was dangerous, especially when it was considered maintaining "connections abroad" just to correspond with our relatives in Riga.

"Tamara Vladislavovna, I know how difficult your situation is now. Mr. Richmond has to learn Russian. He'll pay you well. You need money, don't you?"

The foreigner was smiling as if he could only vaguely guess what we were talking about. I felt it was all staged, but who was the author of this performance? I refused with thanks, saying I wasn't in a position to accept the offer.

I didn't tell my mother everything about Serebryakov. For example, I never mentioned the incident with the passport. The episode with Mr. Richmond surpassed everything that had come before. I was at a loss. The very thought of further phone calls made me shiver. I had to confide in someone, but who could I tell?

The only thing my friends knew about Serebryakov was that he was some strange acquaintance of my father's. None of them could answer my question about who he really was. The fact that my father had been arrested separated me from everyone and everything. Finally I made up my mind.

I deeply respected the former Komsomol organizer of our school, David Samuilovich Kh., and decided to draw him into my confidence, still not entirely sure I was doing the right thing. David Samuilovich said I should not refuse to meet with Serebryakov, but that I should also instantly inform him about every meeting.

I didn't have to wait long before the next "urgently important" call. I managed to let David Samuilovich know by phone and by the time I was to meet Serebryakov he was already there.

This time Serebryakov invited me to the cinema.

When we arrived at the "Barrikada" movie theater, the film had already begun. Serebryakov bent down in front of the cashier's window and, it seemed, I saw him make a gesture I had heard about: the NKVD people loosened the lapel of their jackets when they needed a "green light."

The film was called *Komsomolsk*. The heroine, played by the actress Makarova, was chasing a spy along the Amur River. "Could you do such a thing?" asked Serebryakov. I didn't know what to say. But why was he asking me this in such a blunt and insulting manner?

I felt calmer only when I saw David Samuilovich on the same bus on the way home. But calmness was precisely what Serebryakov didn't want me to feel.

"I hope you didn't catch a cold last night on the Neva," he mentioned casually the next day.

At around two in the morning I had indeed gone down to the Neva, together with a neighbor. There was a flood, and because we lived on the ground floor I wanted to check how high the water had risen. There were only two or three people on the embankment, but Serebryakov certainly wasn't among them. I became very frightened.

"The green dress suits you," he continued.

I had worn a green dress when I visited friends a couple of days before. What did this all mean?

David Samuilovich said he needed a few days. I could scarcely wait until he called.

"So who is he? What does he want?"

"Calm down!" answered David Samuilovich. "He won't bother you again."

"But who is he? Who is he?" I asked impatiently.

"I told you all you need to know. Don't worry about anything else."

It was clear he knew something but didn't want to tell me. Someone must have forbidden him to do so.

Serebryakov didn't disappear, however. Under all possible pretexts he would continually remind me of himself, although there was some break after David Samuilovich got involved.

AN OLD FRIEND from my childhood on the Karpovka reappeared in my life. After we moved to Vasilievsky Island I lost track of Vova and his sister. After eight years, he suddenly came to see me. Noisy, full of enthusiasm and bursting with self-confidence, he was now a student at the Medical Institute.

In the white nights we raced our bicycles along the empty streets and embankments or went for walks across the Tuchkov Bridge. Our walks were always spontaneous and full of joy.

Many students in their third year at our institute were sent abroad for further training. Those returning from America shared their impressions, students coming back from Paris told frivolous anecdotes, but none of them actually spoke in any meaningful way about their stay there. Many students naturally had great expectations and anticipated outstanding career opportunities. There were rumors that a few young men who studied with us were being groomed for diplomatic activity. This was the case for a number of girls, too.

I had no such expectations because my personal file was unclean. My stained biography guaranteed that there would be no pleasant surprises for me in my future. Besides, I didn't have enough ambition and didn't do well enough in my studies. After classes my friends from the Institute would go home and do their homework, and I had to run to the atelier to make batik. (A law was unexpectedly passed that forbade working from home.)

Lily introduced me to her friends, mainly dramatists and journalists. I liked to visit their houses where the wonderful tradition of gathering for dinner and sharing impressions of recent concerts and performances was preserved. Later, as I walked around the city, I would often recognize the faces on posters announcing various musical or theatrical performances.

Platon Romanovich, one of Lily's friends, lived in Moscow. He was thirty-two and worked in the People's Commissariat for Film, where he was responsible for exchange with other cinema houses abroad.

"Come, let's go to 'Passage'! We'll get you a new pair of shoes," he once announced. "Passage" was a fancy department store and I felt that a kind and generous person had knocked on the door of my life, but although his care touched me, I declined the offer. I answered his love with friendship. Fate would devise a very strange time and place for us to meet again.

I was drawn to people my own age. To fall in love? To marry? Of course, all that was waiting for me. Three of my girlfriends had already been in love for a long time. My dear friend Nina was ecstatic and thanked God for the love she was living through.

"You can't imagine how happy I am!" she would say furtively, her eyes filled with tears. Even without words it was not hard to see how thrilled she was.

"My J. is getting ready for an expedition to the North Pole. If only we could go together, he and I!" dreamily said the clever and elegant Raya.

"Ser-yo-zha! Ser-yo-zha!" sang the enamoured Liza.

We trusted each other endlessly. We knew everything not only about each other but also about each other's mothers and sisters. We phoned and saw each other daily. Our house, too, was always full of people, and everyone felt open and relaxed.

But then more and more often one of us wouldn't show up, and then another would be absent, and even when they tried to explain, the reasons sounded obscure.

Liza, who was always forthright and honest, was the first to bring up the subject.

"Swear you won't tell anyone! I've been summoned."

"Where?"

"To the Bolshoy Dom. They were asking about all of us. About you, too."
"What?"
"They weren't especially interested in you, though. They only said: 'This girl's attitude is clear. Her father's been arrested. She can't be held in good faith in the Soviet regime…' Why are you so shocked? They asked about everyone!"
"And you?"
"Well, at first I was terribly frightened. But the man there was really nice, a real gentleman. He took my coat and offered me a seat. It was nice to feel they trusted me. They asked about Raya."
"They? How many were there?"
"Two."
"What did they want to know about Raya?"
"They said: 'You're all so poor and badly dressed, but your girlfriend Raya wears a real fur coat. Have you ever wondered where she might have gotten it? Her mother doesn't earn much.'"
"What does a fur coat have to do with them?"
"But it's true, isn't it: where did she get her fur coat? She told us something about her uncle. Maybe he bought it for her. We haven't really given it any thought, have we?"
Liza's story left me horrified. Something told me she wasn't at all disturbed by the summons. On the contrary, she seemed proud of herself. It filled her with significance and endowed her life with additional meaning. That we were slowly being infected by this spreading scourge of mutual mistrust, however peripherally for now, she didn't realize.
Next was David.
"Don't get upset, Tomochka. I was summoned to the Bolshoy Dom. They wanted to know what we do when we meet, what we talk about and why we meet at your place or at Kolya's. I played dumb and said we simply meet there, that's all."
No one else said anything. I could only guess whether the two Kirills, Raya, Kolya or Nina were summoned too. Could it be that they kept silent because they'd been ordered to? I didn't dare ask them. Keeping silent meant one didn't want to discuss the topic. But I was grateful to Liza and David for their frankness.
We still hadn't found out anything more about Father. It was incomprehensible why Serebryakov kept looming around me, or why the Komsomol organizer refused to tell me who Serebryakov really was. Liza's story revealed what the organs thought about me and my family. The phrase kept

flashing through my mind: "This girl's attitude is clear. Her father's been arrested. She can't be held in good faith in the Soviet regime..." I understood the meaning behind it: they'd put the label "REJECTED" on me.

NO ONE SPOKE about the summonses anymore. We kept meeting, although not as frequently as we used to.

Once, after we had all gathered at Kolya's, he invited me to his father's room. He said he had something important to tell me. He lit an antique lamp designed to look like a bonfire and sat me down in a cozy armchair. He gathered up his courage and said:

"I love you. Be my wife!"

His words complicated our relationship. Now that I had to say no, some uneasiness grew between us. But the difficult refusal was nevertheless uttered, and we went back to the living room, where White Kirill was playing the piano.

Suddenly a strange noise was heard from the street. At first no one paid attention, but it grew louder and louder. Along First Line of Vasilievsky Island soldiers were marching, disassembled mess halls and tanks drove past. We sat on the marble windowsill and looked at the procession, but there was no end to it. More and more people were coming out of their houses into the street. A huge crowd formed. One of the boys, uncertain, uttered the word "war," as if both asking a question and answering one at the same time.

The next morning we heard on the radio that the Finnish War had begun.

In a few days both Kirills were drafted into a ski battalion. Kolya G. went to the front as a volunteer. When we went to the Military Commissariat to say good-bye to the boys, they weren't boastful and jocular as usual but looked strange and haggard. Their families cried. It was incredible to think that either, or both, of them might be killed.

I reproached myself for turning Kolya down. At home everyone felt sorry for him and looked at me narrowly, as if to say, "You drove him to volunteer for the front!"

Leningrad sank into darkness. Blue lamps burned on the lampposts and in the doorways, but they could scarcely illuminate the sidewalks. It was a severe winter. The streets looked strange without electrical light. Buildings of varying height and architectural form loomed in the moonlight as one bulk of stone, some unnatural conglomeration of half-populated apartments.

The Mannerheim Line, not far from Leningrad, turned out to be an invincible obstacle. It was rumored that the Finns were full of hatred and fought violently. People said they jumped down from trees onto our soldiers, camouflaged in white overalls, and finished them off like savages, cutting strips of skin from their backs or gouging out their eyes. Even those who were wounded and lay on the surgical tables in our hospitals would sometimes manage to stab our doctors in the stomach.

But then came a letter from Kirill, in which he described the seizure of Vyborg and how the soldiers of our Red Army looted people's houses, smashed furniture and broke mirrors.

When the war was over and we heard that our troops were coming home, we all ran out to the same old First Line on Vasilievsky Island. The triumphant residents emptied the shops, buying up cigarettes and chocolate to throw to the soldiers of the Red Army as they passed through the streets. But the soldiers seemed reluctant to share the joy of the victory. Sitting in the open trucks, they looked so exhausted and worn out that the triumphant clamor soon died away.

Our boys came back alive. White Kirill was wounded in the leg. Soon he married my former classmate. It was all the more unexpected when Kolya G., who only shortly before had sworn eternal love to me, also announced his marriage. A gentle and placid woman came to him from Byelorussia, and they started their life together.

WHENEVER PLATON ROMANOVICH came to Leningrad from Moscow he would try to persuade me to go with him to a theater, operetta or restaurant.

"What? You've never been to a restaurant?" he asked, amazed. "Then we're going to the Evropeysky."

Platon Romanovich brought along a redheaded friend.

"Let me introduce Syoma, my old chap."

The glittering hall of the Evropeysky restaurant, the ceremonious atmosphere, the zeal of electric lights, perfectly starched tablecloths, marble columns, glasses shimmering with different colors… all this awoke in me an unaccustomed feeling and made me want to walk differently, to dress differently.

When waiters came for our order, Platon Romanovich asked what I would like to have, but I couldn't utter a single word. My companions realized I needed to be left alone for a while.

As I grew more used to the new surroundings, I noticed a large wheat-haired man walk in. He strolled to the middle of the hall, leaned melancholically against a column and allowed his gaze to glide over the people sitting at the tables. It was Yakhontov, a famous recital artist whom I first saw on stage, in Leningrad, when I was in the eighth grade.

Our eyes met and the next moment I saw him coming toward our table, looking straight at me as he approached. As if in a dream I heard Platon Romanovich exclaim:

"Volodya! You're also here in Leningrad? Sit with us!"

Yakhontov hardly answered the greeting, disregarding the ritual of introductions. He gently took a chair and placed it somewhat behind mine. He leaned toward me and, with gusto, launched upon an amusing anecdote.

Platon Romanovich was pouring wine and they were already chatting among themselves, but I still remained intoxicated by the atmosphere of the elevated world in which I had appeared so strangely and unexpectedly. Without participating in their conversation, I was guessing whether the handsome actor would leave or stay.

The men accompanied me home. Yakhontov recited Mayakovsky.

"What do you think of him?" he asked.

"I don't understand Mayakovsky," I answered like a model schoolgirl.

"That's something we'll have to discuss tomorrow at noon, by the Bronze Horseman." As we were parting, Yakhontov added, "And those two gentlemen… they didn't realize they should have left us alone long before!"

Puzzled if he meant it seriously, as if in delirium, I hopped over puddles as I ran through our courtyard and into the house.

"Mama, Mama! Yakhontov asked me to go on a date with him, tomorrow at noon!"

I didn't get a wink of sleep that night. The next morning I decided to skip my lectures at the Institute and set off at twelve to the prearranged meeting point.

The city was shrouded in a thick milky fog. Its hazy swells engulfed the Senate building and the monument of Peter the Great and devoured the vast expanse over the Neva. Fog drowned the silhouettes of people and muffled the honking of vehicles.

We stood in front of each other. The next moment he was already reciting Pushkin's poem. I realized that the most important person in the world for Yakhontov was himself. The city of Peter the Great and I were merely an audience. But wasn't that enough? We walked arm in arm along the banks of the river, reciting poetry in the murky shadow of the Bronze Horseman.

There were posters hanging throughout the city, announcing Yakhontov's role in *Romeo and Juliet* at the Leningrad City Philharmonic that very evening.

"There will be two seats reserved in your name," he told me.

Who could I take with me? Whoever would be quietest, would say nothing, would merely exist.

To find myself in the performance hall of the Philharmonic—a crystal-colored fairy tale—leaning my elbows against the ivory armrests for me was already a miracle. But finally to understand, hearing that strong voice, that it was addressing *me*—I simply lost my head.

During the entr'acte my girlfriend and I didn't even go out to the foyer. Everybody glanced at me with curiosity. My girlfriend was able to utter only exclamations. And I sat still, afraid to make a move, afraid to scare off this miracle that was occurring with me at its center.

"Why didn't you stop in to see me? Why didn't you wait for me?" asked Yakhontov on the telephone the next day. "I'll be waiting for you in the lobby of my hotel at three. Why are you silent?"

I was hesitant. I understood: his hotel room, face-to-face, alone. But something inside of me told me to meet him: "Go on," it seemed to say. "I'll save you."

Hypnotized by this extraordinary set of occurrences, I went. Yakhontov was waiting downstairs in the lobby. We went up to his room. He called down and ordered wine and fruit. Again he recited Mayakovsky, saying it was impossible not to love the poet. He asked what was wrong, poured us champagne, cut an apple, plucked grapes for me. I was thinking about how wonderful it was going to be to tell about this, and how terrible it would be if he now decided to move closer… which action, it stands to reason, seemed imminent. And so he did.

I was very far removed from such adult games. Rushing out of the hotel room I tried to see the situation from his point of view. It did sort of seem that I was acting deceptively: if I was only going to run from his advances, why did I come in the first place?

Soon Yakhontov was going back to Moscow. He asked me to write to him. I never would have remembered the content of my naïve letters to him had he not telephoned me and told me what had impressed him in them. He said he had always looked for them first amongst the pile of letters he received.

ONCE MY MOTHER ASKED ME:

"Tamarochka, would you mind if a man came over to visit us?"

"Why?" I asked with cold suspicion.

Mother fell silent. She hoped her eldest daughter would understand and accept her right to have her own life and desires. But I crushed that hope. My mother was only thirty-nine. She and I could have become very close friends at that moment. But there was my father, somewhere in the Bay of Nagaevo, carting rocks, up to his waist in water. On his padded jacket a number was sewn. He was deprived of the right to write to us, and he wasn't allowed to receive letters from us either, let alone any sort of help.

Her despair became apparent when she began to buy wine and drink a glass or two by herself. Her eyes looked endlessly sad, shame and remorse tormented her as she drowned her sorrows in drink.

"Where is my dress, Mama?"

"It's... I sold it, child."

When I realized she wasn't joking I became horrified and furious. I threw a fit and threatened to move out. One day I really did move into the student dormitories, but when I stopped by our home and found Mother in bed with a compress on her head, my sisters sitting completely withdrawn into themselves, I came straight back.

"Mama, don't! Stop doing this to yourself!"

"Yes, I'll stop!"

But it all began again. She had withstood the front and imprisonment. Men adored her for her charm. When Father was no longer considered any good for Party work and was demoted, she calmly followed him from one construction site to another. But the year 1937 my dear Mama could not withstand.

Despite her "illness," which we tried to keep secret in every way, Mama remained the highest authority in our family. All our things had been sold. My sisters were growing and needed clothing. Mother would suddenly pull herself together and look for a job. She would work for three or four months before losing her will again.

Various epidemics were raging in Leningrad. I became ill and was put in a hospital, where I had to stay for quite a long time. The patients were telling each other how they went to see "such a young dying girl." Thinking I was a hopeless case, the doctor wanted to try out a new medicine on me. In the end this medicine worked. When I finally felt completely healthy, I asked him when they were going to release me.

"I am going on leave in five days. We'll discharge you then," he said.

In five days, before I was about to leave the hospital, he ordered:

"When you get your things back, get dressed and go straight to the gate. I'll be waiting for you there with a car."

I tried not to pay attention to the expressive glances of this thirty-six-year-old doctor, much less let him drive me home. When Valechka brought my clothes to the hospital, we walked to the tram stop and safely got home. Our apartment smelled of chicken broth, which by our standards was a princely meal. I was very moved by Mama's welcome.

Less than half an hour had passed before the doorbell rang, and the doctor stood in the doorway.

"May I come in? It's nothing really, but Tamara is still so weak... Why wouldn't she let me bring her home by car? Ah, you've got two more daughters? Life certainly doesn't go easy for you!"

The doctor enchanted my mother, our neighbors and even my aunt. He started visiting us regularly, and I began to loathe him. I couldn't understand what others saw in him. Everything about him seemed detestable.

"So what would Tamulenka like?" he once asked me in the third person.

"A box of sweets!" I exclaimed, just to annoy him.

Mother fell speechless as the next day he unpacked a box of sweets on the table.

Soon Doctor M. proposed to marry me. He had already written a dissertation, had his own *dacha* and an apartment with a grand piano. "Tamulenka and the kids will like studying music," he would say.

My girlfriends joked that one could certainly find happiness at a resort, but to find love in a hospital... None of them took such a potential bridegroom seriously. But when our "home council" gathered, things got more complicated. Although our neighbors weren't exactly my mother's close friends, they pitied her. My aunt, who also took part in the discussion, was but another witness of our daily hardships.

"Well, Tamara, you are the eldest, you've studied and finished school. Now your sisters have to be given a chance. One mustn't think only of oneself. He's a respectable man, and he loves you. What else do you want? Just look at your mother and your little sisters! You're about the age to marry anyway."

When I saw Mother's acquiescent look, I became even more confused: could she really want me to marry a man I did not love?

The very idea of marrying the doctor made me freeze. I stopped sleeping at night and no matter how hard I tried to find a way out, the thought that I'd rather jump into the Neva than marry M. was all I could come up with.

A serious conversation with Mother seemed to be looming, and I prepared myself for it. We were never alone together at home, so I asked her to go for a walk with me.

"Do you really want me to marry him?" I asked.

In my heart I had hoped she would assail me with the exclamation, "Are you crazy? How could you even think that?" But instead, she answered half-heartedly:

"If you don't love him, then no. Of course, I want you to be happy."

Mama's unwilling intonation betrayed her words. She had hoped to see her oldest daughter married to precisely a man like this. I thanked Mama, concealing from her what I had managed to read behind her words.

ONCE MY CLASSMATE from the Institute brought along two young men from her native town of Sevastopol. Both were called Misha and both studied at the Leningrad Marine Academy. Misha K., the older of the two, started coming to see us often. Not very talkative, on Sundays he would sit with us for a couple of hours and then ask if he could come again in a week. He definitely liked being at our place.

One day he arrived very downcast and asked if I could go for a walk with him.

The wind blew in our faces. We walked to the statues of Egyptian sphinxes opposite the Academy of Arts. Without any introduction Misha said:

"I've been offered a choice: you or the Academy."

At first it didn't even hurt a bit. Leaving myself behind, I hastily said:

"You've made the right choice, Misha. The Academy, of course!"

"You must understand: my mother has high hopes for me..."

"Right choice!" I repeated, already running away, first along the embankment, then along First Line toward our house, and past the house, farther and farther. I was hounded by a pain, a pain that seemed to be growing bigger and bigger. How did they find out in the Marine Academy that Misha was visiting us? Why couldn't anyone come to see us? Was I some kind of plague? Only two phrases flashed through my mind: "This girl's attitude..."; "You or the Academy..."

Soon a letter from Serebryakov came from the Crimea. There was nothing in it apart from greetings and reports on the weather. He just wanted to remind me of his existence.

In about two weeks my aunt told me that a man in a leather jacket had come and brought a freshly killed hare.

An hour later Serebryakov phoned:

"I went hunting and I've sent you a gift with my driver."

Again, I didn't know how to react, but my mother ripped the receiver out of my hand:

"We invite you to have roasted hare with us!" she blurted out.

Everything I had been previously telling Mama about Serebryakov didn't seem convincing enough to her. She wanted to make her own judgment of the mysterious man.

Serebryakov came with his "cousin," as he introduced a man with three stripes on the blue, turned-up collar of his uniform jacket. They brought a box of expensive chocolates and a bottle of champagne.

"You told my daughter you knew my husband, but I've never seen you before," my mother was already telling them.

It was in vain to expect any embarrassment. Serebryakov answered in an easy and friendly manner:

"Oh, yes, we mainly met in the service. But one time I really was at your place. You must've forgotten."

It was hard to imagine what we would speak about. Serebryakov began talking about hunting, about the courtship of the wood grouse, about how one had to wait with bated breath to catch sight of a gray hen, a duck or a hare.

In front of us sat a harmless man, enthusiastically describing the dawn and the forest. But my fear was growing stronger and stronger. It would've been much easier had he just said, "Yes, yes, we're watching, we're following you."

"What an unpleasant man! No, I've never seen him before," said my mother after he left. That was all she said.

I no longer confided in anyone. Even what happened shortly afterward I kept to myself.

One day as I was coming back home from the Institute by tram, I dropped a mitten on the floor. A man sitting next to me picked it up. Before I could thank him he whispered: "You mustn't be so absent-minded, Tamara Vladislavovna!" I was shocked. I'd never seen him before. He was addressing me by my first name and patronymic, just like Serebryakov. Who was he? In a moment his colorless face assumed a faraway look, as if it hadn't been him at all, as if his face was saying, "It wasn't me whose hollow whisper you've just heard." For a moment I even thought I imagined it, but then I realized: it was the agent's own whim; he decided to break protocol and allow himself this small pleasure just to see me flustered.

Not noble knights but spies migrated from books into my life! At night I started dreaming that I was being chased and baited liked a desperate animal.

DURING THE NOVEMBER HOLIDAYS my mood was lifted when I received several telegrams, one from Erik in Frunze, one from Yakhontov and another one from Platon Romanovich in Moscow. But when the following evening a money order came from Erik—"to cover your trip expenses"—my good mood vanished without a trace.

The money order was a disaster. Everything that concerned Erik, from our first meeting to his exile, was closely connected to my own family's misfortune and occupied a special place in my life. At first we wrote to each other as if trying to remain true to our obligations. For the past three years, Erik addressed me as "my only love, my dear," which even made our correspondence artistic. But now the money order was bound to change everything.

Erik's older brother, Valery, recently visited them in Frunze. When he came back, he told me: "The two of you should definitely get married. What are you waiting for? Erik is a popular man there." After that I stopped writing to Erik for a while. Now I had to react, to give a clear and prompt answer. Not having the right to travel, Erik was calling for me to come to him.

I couldn't imagine giving up my family, the Institute, my city.

"What should I tell him?" I asked Mother. But she left it up to me to decide.

Though I was very angry with Erik, I wrote: *COMING.*

There was one thing that assuaged my doubts: if I went to Frunze, I would be able to support my family. What I didn't know yet was how much I loved my poor mother, my sisters and my city.

When the decision was finally announced, an uproar ensued. My friends called me crazy, begged me to come back to my senses, to reconsider the decision and cancel the trip.

At the time I disliked everything that was "my own." My own outward appearance seemed alien to me, my work—mechanical and boring. I hated my own temperament and fear, my permanent and helpless waiting, as if expecting to be stricken by a blow from someone or other; I hated being pursued by state informers, being reproached by the people around me for refusing to marry the doctor. I lived with the feeling that Father's arrest had uprooted me from my place, that I was racing downhill in a sled at breakneck speed toward a predetermined point, and that my flight was influenced by a dark and evil will. I longed to jump out of the sled, to turn away from that ill-famed point of destination, to set my own will against that power, even despite common sense. I hadn't started to live yet! It was time for me to find out who I was. Did no one really need my imagination, the strength of my soul? What if someone needed me *there?* I tried to hack a window through my own self, and Erik's faithfulness and patience were showing through it from the other side. But I was also driven by a different force, whose essence never makes itself completely clear: Fate.

The only person who supported my decision to go to Frunze was Lily.

"Erik is young and handsome. It's truly amazing how much he loves you. But remember: the moment you see him you'll know right away if you should stay or not. It's going to be just one moment, but you'll feel it immediately. If he doesn't turn out to be the one, then telegraph me right away, and I'll send you money for the return trip."

Lily's words sat well with me. I believed her and calmed down a little.

Then, in the midst of the preparations, I lost confidence again. I suddenly realized I was parting with my mother and sisters and became very scared.

Everything was already happening by itself. I clung to Lily's words like a drowning man to his raft. She even collected a kind of dowry for me and said she would accompany me to Moscow. The day before our departure she booked a room in the Hotel National.

About thirty people or more stood on the platform by the train. I wasn't paying attention to anyone except my mother and sisters. It never occurred to me until this moment that my heart could feel such agonizing pain, such explosive sorrow. Mother and I looked at each other. Now we understood what we were never able to understand before.

"Mama, Valechka, Renochka! I don't want to go, I can't leave you! You're all I have! I don't know what I'm doing! I don't understand what's happening!"

The train started to move… I could no longer see Mama or my sisters… And only David, a true friend from my childhood, limping, ran and ran alongside the train car to the very end of the platform. At the last moment he shoved a small package into my hands. It was a brown leather handbag monogrammed FOR TOMOCHKA FROM DAVID. In the handbag I found fifty rubles and a note: *Dear Tomochka, why are you doing this?*

Beside myself, I stood on the platform of the train car and sobbed. The train gathered speed.

IN MOSCOW, Platon Romanovich came to meet me and Lily at the train station. His red-haired friend Syoma was with him. It was a bright and chilly November day. The room at the National was luxurious, with windows overlooking Manege Square and the Kremlin.

I'd never been in Moscow before. Double-decker buses drove through the streets. Crooked side streets, with wooden houses on both sides, seemed cozy; the names of the streets were lovely: Meshchanskaya, Arbat, Kalashny Ryad.

Lily and I were together, which made me feel less lonely. For a while I even forgot what the purpose of my journey was. But then a ticket to Frunze was booked. In two days I was to travel on.

One thing I wanted to avoid was having to give explanations. But Platon Romanovich insisted. When he heard where I was going and why, he didn't believe me.

"To go into exile of your own will? There have to be important reasons for a thing like that. You must be in love with him! If that's the case, I understand. But it's not, is it?"

"I don't know."

"But this is exactly what you have to know! My God! You don't love him! Just as you don't love me. So why not marry me? I love you. Listen to me, I love you!"

At that moment I made up my mind to move on without looking back, no matter how hard it might be. No reasonable arguments could stop me.

Lily and I went to see Red Square. The stars of the Kremlin were lit up in the early evening twilight. They seemed full of flame. The air was frosty.

We were walking slowly toward the Square when I suddenly saw Yakhontov, dressed in a warm winter coat, heading in our direction. I wasn't sure he'd recognize me, but I couldn't bring myself to call his name first. He saw me himself:

"You're in Moscow? And you didn't let me know?"

He happened to be free that evening. We went to the Square together, then went back to the hotel room and sat there for a while. Then he invited me to go for a walk.

After wandering through the city for several hours, we stopped for dinner at the restaurant in the Novomoskovskaya Hotel. I was again in a festive mood, just like back in Leningrad.

As we were leaving the restaurant, Yakhontov stopped me in the hallway and asked where I was going. I figured he was asking out of politeness, and I answered nonchalantly. But he listened to me attentively and suddenly grew concerned. With surprising care in his voice he said:

"You're making a mistake. You mustn't do this."

He became strangely serious:

"If there was someone who could send your mother five hundred rubles every month, would you stay?"

Though his question seemed odd, behind it I discerned generosity and a desire to help. It was good to feel that a question like this could still be asked.

And yet, both Platon Romanovich and Yakhontov were outside my destiny. I myself had to love. Only then would true life begin, no matter whether in the capital or in exile.

Platon Romanovich brought some food and chocolate to the station.

Lily cried:

"I want you to be happy! But if the slightest thing goes wrong, telegraph me immediately and come back!"

Once again, all that was happening around me seemed unreal. Choked by tears, I couldn't say anything intelligible. I only asked to send my regards to the people I had left behind at home.

The train set off. Surrendered to fate, I found my seat in the carriage. Before me lay a five-day journey.

Chapter 3

I was going to Central Asia, to a strange land and a strange town, to a family and above all to a man whom I scarcely knew. I tried to imagine what Erik and Barbara Ionovna would look like now, not as I'd seen them three years before at the Information Bureau of the Bolshoy Dom. Barbara Ionovna seemed to me the embodiment of the intelligentsia. As for Erik, I had built up an image of him from his letters, and even for my friends his name was synonymous with love and stability.

I had no doubt he loved me. Everything depended on me alone: would I be able to reciprocate his love? Would that mysterious feeling, which so many others had told me about, take hold of me when I saw him?

The Russian landscape receded, was left behind. Now the steppe began.

I spotted a camel out the window. It was monotonously chewing grass and seemed rather proud of itself. I excitedly told the rest of the passengers what I'd seen, but people glanced at me with indifference. No one was surprised by the exotic animal. I expected to see rare species of birds, but on the telegraph wires sat common sparrows. Crows, concerned with something or other, soared up off the ground.

Dispassionately and pedantically, time was converting hours into days.

Steppe turned into desert, where a sandstorm was raging. The sand got crammed into the window slits, into one's mouth, under the wheels of the train car. People said we'd soon arrive at the station Arys, from where one track would lead to Kazakhstan and the other to Kirghizia.

Vast plains were replaced by mountains, the spurs of the Tian Shan. Villages of clay-walled huts built in the shade of poplar trees grew denser and denser. Snowy mountain peaks loomed in the distance. Tunnels appeared more and more often. Breaking out into the open air, the train would run for a while in a canyon of greenish stone. I was impressed by the beautiful, alien landscape, by how peacefully the steppe expanse could coexist with the imposing mountains.

By the end of the fifth day, we arrived at the Pish-Kek station. Frunze was next.

The train pulled into the station, jolted one last time and stopped. My arms and legs were filled with heaviness, my head ringing. Erik's face appeared on the other side of the window. I recognized him instantly, although he was now a mature man. As if in a vacuum I heard his voice:

"Mama! She's here!"

He forced his way against the stream of exiting passengers and climbed into the car. We looked at each other briefly. A smile of unbridled joy lit up his face.

"Where is your suitcase?"

"Up there on the berth."

Barbara Ionovna wiped her tears, hugged me and sighed.

From the station Erik led me through the town's macadam side streets. He had picked a roundabout way specifically to give me an impression of the Kirghiz capital. The town resembled the bottom of a deep bowl framed with snow-capped mountains. Water murmured in irrigation ditches along the streets. Behind the poplars, which were losing their last leaves, clay huts stood close to each other. Donkeys and camels laden with heavy burdens walked beside buses and cars.

As we walked through the town, we exchanged a couple of meaningless phrases. It all seemed like a strange dream. Erik couldn't stop smiling, simultaneously expressing triumph and diffidence. His smile became my only support in this new world.

His family lived in an elongated, four-room house on Toktogul Street. The doors of all four rooms led to the front garden. We went into the living room. There sat Erik's elder brother, Valery, with his wife, Lina, and their little daughter, Tatochka. I didn't know they were also here. Erik had to hurry to work and asked Valery to take me to the clinic later, after I got some rest.

Questions followed:

"What's new in Leningrad? Have you heard anything about your father? Has anyone returned from exile? What are people saying?"

Barbara Ionovna was interested in everything, even though Valery and Lina had just arrived from Leningrad.

"Is it true they are going to remove the tramlines from Nevsky Prospect? Are the streetlights still the same?"

I was answering their questions, giving out the gifts I brought with me.

Valery hurried me:

"Come, come! I'll take you to Erik."

Agitated after the journey, without resting for a single minute, I set off to the clinic. A patient walked out from a room marked "Surgeon." There was no one else in the hall. Erik, in a white smock and cap, rose to meet us. Valery left. We were alone.

The noise of the entire world finally died down as I listened to his fervent words, reaching straight to my heart:

"I didn't believe you would come! Do you understand what your arrival means to me?"

Erik spoke about how he had waited and dreamed and how much he loved me. By now I already knew I wouldn't leave, because a blissful calm suddenly descended on me; because for the first time in my life I understood what it felt like to make another person happy. Was this the moment that Lily had told me about? Never before had I heard another's heart beating so close.

I moved into Erik's room, the furthest one at the back of the house. There was no electric light. After tea, when the entire family gathered at the table, Erik and I would go for a walk. To the sound of babbling water in the irrigation ditches, we walked along the unpaved streets, telling each other everything that had happened during the three years we'd been apart. The black soil under our feet felt soft. We walked as though one, our steps, our conversations, even our silences, perfectly synchronized. The sky above us was full of stars.

IT WAS 1940. Our wedding was scheduled for December 26.

Exiles lived without passports. They had to register with the police every ten days to provide evidence they had not fled from their prescribed place of residence. Since Erik had no passport, the office refused to register our marriage. With great difficulty we managed to obtain some provisional ID for Erik, where they stamped the marriage seal. The official ceremony was short and matter-of-fact. At home Barbara Ionovna and Valery congratulated us. And for some reason Lina hung a string of pretzels onto my neck.

Telegrams with congratulations came from Mother and my friends in Leningrad.

I was twenty, Erik was twenty-two. He had a winning smile, was tender and ingratiating. His movements were slightly lazy. Behind his charm hid some implicit strength of its own kind. Newly awakened love carried me into unknown festive lands. To wait for Erik, to listen to him, to recognize him by his footsteps, to read his every wish in his eyes, to surprise him with dozens of ideas and amusements, all this became the purpose of my life. I felt confident in the uniqueness of our relationship and handed over my very soul to him.

I easily coped with the daily routine: I fetched water from the well, scrubbed the earthen floor with pressed dung, brought food from the market for the whole family. I stencilled all possible fabrics and decorated our little home with a great many "carpets" and tablecloths. Folding gauze in two halves, I sewed bed-linen.

No matter where he'd been in the morning, Erik always rushed home for lunch. Sometimes it was only for five or ten minutes, "to check if it's really true that it's true." But if he didn't check in and see his mother during those hurried moments, Barbara Ionovna would get angry. I understood how she felt and scolded Erik.

A wonderful photograph of my mother-in-law hung on the wall over the old sofa in the family room: a young girl in a white dress with a white rose, on the day of her first ball. Barbara Ionovna often plunged herself into memories. She thought about her husband every day and hoped he was alive.

I'd had the impression that the lives of exiles were filled with the constant exchange of ideas and intellectual debates. I had hoped to meet intelligent people who would help me tame the chaos in my head, to pave my way toward clarity and maturity. But the exiles in Frunze lived quietly and were isolated from each other, although friendships did sprout up among them.

In the town I'd frequently ask Erik who this or that lady was. He would explain: the wife, daughter or sister of a diplomat, a military officer or tradesman. Women with beautiful faces and gorgeous figures walked along the streets among the local population. Some of them still looked after themselves, while others gradually let themselves go. Each individual, although just as dismayed as her neighbor, bore her cross differently. But however different their interests, goals and expectations might have been, all the exiles in Frunze considered themselves lucky because they had been exiled to a town.

"Just imagine, Tukhachevsky's ex-wife, the one he divorced ten years before his arrest," I heard once, "she was exiled to a *kishlak*. People said that at first she held herself together. But the locals always pointed at her. Then she lost control, began drinking and now she's completely fallen apart."

"Yesterday," replied another woman, "I got a letter from my girlfriend's daughter, also from a *kishlak*. She wrote that her mother couldn't bear it and hanged herself. The girl is now completely desperate and needs help. Of course, I could try to bring her here, to Frunze, but I am afraid."

Afraid! It turned out exile wasn't the end of the punishment. It could imply a number of secondary torments, such as the fear of internal exile throughout Kirghizia, which often proved to be the kiss of death. I had hoped to find myself among the intelligentsia and intellectuals, but what I actually saw was nothing but a bitter desire merely to survive.

Barbara Ionovna had her own small circle of friends. One of them, a very neat and fussy man, clung to his customary habits despite the routine of exile: he cooked for himself, laid the table in his hut, and tucked a snow-white serviette in his collar. Sitting at the dinner table in his tumbledown shack, he made a feast out of his loneliness. His hoping to shield himself from all his problems by maintaining an outer appearance of orderliness made him look tragic and pathetic.

Another of my mother-in-law's acquaintances struggled over the question of whether or not she should marry. It was surreal to see her grieve, and to hear other people echo her reasoning that it was useless for her to wait for her husband, who still had ten years of prison before him.

The name of Anna F., whose husband had also been sentenced to ten years of hard labor, was often mentioned in Erik's family. She seemed to be a close friend. Once she invited us to her place. When we arrived, she politely asked us to sit down at the table, but every now and then she'd walk out to the kitchen where she stood for a long time weeping. It seemed we came at a bad time and I couldn't understand why we didn't just leave at once. Barbara Ionovna explained she was crying because of her son; she said she'd tell me about it later, when we got home. I could feel that this thirty-year-old woman didn't like me. When we were finally leaving, she declared sarcastically she couldn't understand why in the world I had voluntarily come from Leningrad to Frunze. I was shocked by her tone but tried my best to hide the heavy feeling that arose in me toward her.

Most of all Barbara Ionovna spoke to me about her friend Olga Aleksandrovna P., a descendant of the Zamoiskis, a royal Polish family. Her husband, General P., defected to the Soviet side during the Civil War. Although he had a writ of protection from Lenin, he was nevertheless arrested and shot in 1937. His wife and son, a historian, were exiled. Olga Aleksandrovna was very educated; she knew five or six languages, was a good musician and in her own time was even one of Paderewski's favorite students. I couldn't wait to meet her, but when she finally came over, it was difficult to imagine that she was, in fact, royalty. Had I seen her on the street, not knowing who she was, I would've given her alms. She was an old woman in a shabby coat; her gray hair was tangled. But all her dignity and composure became obvious as soon as she started speaking. Later I would meet with her often, but every time she'd set about telling me her wonderful stories I had to adjust myself anew to the brilliance of her speech, to all her neatness and wittiness. She truly revived as she recalled her past. She spiced her stories with French words and phrases and had no doubts that the listener understood them.

She moved around the room, clumsily maneuvering between her bed and the table. Her place looked like a storehouse for rags. Everything there was in chaos. Dirty dishes towered on top of each other in a huge pile. She would pull out an old photo album from her suitcase. Looking through these pictures was like traveling back in time: a glaringly beautiful woman with a stately bearing stared out of these photographs. The splendor of her hair, her reserved smile, her charm and irresistibility, a sable tippet or fur shawl draped over her shoulders… It was all hers; this woman used to be her.

"You used to wear furs, Olga Aleksandrovna!" I exclaimed.

"Yes, I preferred furs to diamonds," she said, coming alive.

Life had reduced all her heraldic ancestral advantages to nought. Unfit for physical work, not knowing how to maintain the basic comforts of daily life, she lived apart from the reality of the exile world, though she never felt hapless or unfortunate. Her son always accompanied her, and wherever they went, they were absorbed in lively conversation. The external world didn't seem to matter. When I saw them sharing their thoughts, I understood how significant and rich their own world was.

Of all the local exiles I became the most friendly with Varvara Nikolaevna Krestinskaya. Her brother was the former People's Commissar for Foreign Affairs, who had served as the Russian ambassador first in Berlin and then in Paris. I was always happy to go for a walk with her. Wearing a spotless white blouse, she'd talk about the most actual and important matters of spiritual life.

From his father, a lawyer, Erik had inherited an interest in law. He bought a two-volume edition of *Cases and Protocols,* a collection of the interrogation proceedings of Pyatakov, Kamenev, Bukharin, Krestinsky and others. Erik would read the book aloud. Taken all together, the confessions of the defendants, who publicly declared their premeditated sabotage, drew my attention to the same fateful year, 1937. I struggled with the impending thought that their declarations must have been forced out of them by torture. If they were innocent, why would they confess to crimes they had not committed? Too much depended on the answer to that question.

"What do you think?" I once asked Erik, frightened.

"They used chemicals on them," he replied.

"What do you mean, 'chemicals'?" I was still quite far from understanding how dangerous such straightforward correlations could be.

I dared broach this topic in a conversation with Varvara Nikolaevna and asked her what she made of her brother's confessions.

"I don't read lies. I know my brother. He is innocent," she answered sharply.

I was burning with shame. I hoped for a legal explanation, but the real revelation lay elsewhere. Her firmly cast answer contained much more. To resist the general psychosis of accusations was not only a personal right of a relative or a friend, but in fact a duty. Varvara Nikolaevna confirmed what I myself had blindly sensed after Father's arrest.

ENGULFED BY MY FEELINGS for Erik and preoccupied with household duties, I didn't immediately notice that there appeared more and more a chill in my relationship with Erik's family. Barbara Ionovna was often short with me, while Lina was overtly inimical. They would speak in loud voices among themselves in their room, but as soon as I came in they would fall silent.

We always gathered together for lunch, with Barbara Ionovna sitting at the head of the table. She cut the meat in small portions and gave a piece to each of us, together with the soup. One day she left my plate empty. I wouldn't have thought much of it, but Erik looked at her furiously and demonstratively put his slice onto my plate. Something shameful was happening before the eyes of the entire family and I didn't know how to react.

Sometimes it was as if the mother and son spoke some foreign dialect, which could not be translated into the language of my own family.

"Erka! I could sell my overcoat to your Tamara, if you'd like."

"How much do you want?"

"Well, I've worn it quite a bit, but the wool is still decent."

Barbara Ionovna would name her price.

As I later found out, Valery, who worked as a junior investigator with the police, was permitted to remain in Leningrad because he had renounced his arrested father. That had saved him from exile, but he was fired soon after anyway. Confused and offended, instead of looking for a new job, he came straight to Frunze, not to visit, but to live, without any particular plans. The family held endless discussions on that subject, but I was never included in them. Frunze was teeming with exiles, and it was practically impossible to find any job. So the family of six lived solely off of Erik's wage.

I didn't have enough common sense to realize I was just an extra mouth to feed. I was the beggarly daughter-in-law, who had brought no wealth into the household and on top of everything only cared about her own folks at home. To help my mother, I tried to find occasional work, such as making various signs and graphics for the hospitals and ambulances. Erik would add a little from his second job, and so I would send Mother a small amount of money every month.

Back in 1937, Barbara Ionovna and Erik's exile seemed to be sheer disaster. And now, whenever Barbara Ionovna treated me with unfairness, I was always eager to attribute it to these circumstances. I was not in a position to blame her.

Once I gave her a photo of Erik and me. Underneath I wrote: *For dear Mama, from her two loving children.* Everything immediately became clear. She read the inscription and said:

"I'm a mother only to my son. I can have dozens of daughters like you."

I couldn't muster a single word in reply.

After a long hesitation I asked Erik if we shouldn't perhaps start eating separately. He was glad to hear that and told his mother he would still be giving them money, but from then on we would eat on our own.

Our landlady, who often saw me crying, offered to help me:

"I'll give you a frying pan, a teapot, and a few saucepans. You already have a primus stove, so now you can cook to your heart's content. And keep away from them!" she nodded in the direction of the family room.

Of course, I knew nothing about cooking. At the market I would eavesdrop on the conversations of housewives, pick one who seemed amiable and ask her bravely:

"Can you please tell me what I can make with a piece of meat like this? May I walk with you a little and maybe you could give me some advice? And after I roll the meat in flour, what should I do next? And how many onions should I add? And also, could you teach me how to cook *vareniki*... Do I need to add any sugar?"

Oh, the world was inhabited with good people! Equipped with countless recipes, I'd run home and "cook to my heart's content," proudly laying out the results on the table, thrilled to hear Erik say: "Delicious! I've never tasted anything better!"

My house, my Erik, his love and his unsophisticated stories! He would tell me about an owl who sat on an elm branch and watched me from the other side of the window every night as I fell asleep.

SPRING CAME, imperious and stormy. The sun soaked the earth and the trees with its warmth. The buds swelled and instantly burst open. From the mountains whirled roaring streams of muddy water, filling the irrigation ditches.

I was standing in the wind, hanging up the laundry to dry and joking with the landlady. I went back into the house to rinse the linen in the wash tub, and as I was walking out again, holding the basin in my hands, I heard a neighbor and the landlady gossiping:

"She's much better than that other plump one!"

"She was pretty high on herself…"

"And ugly, too…"

I must've gone crazy! My breath stopped from what I heard. It seemed unthinkable that Erik could have had another woman!

Not knowing how to approach him about this, I became more and more withdrawn. But the discoveries clung one to another.

I heard how Valery bawled out Erik in the garden:

"A fine fellow you are! Your Lyalya came here, strutted like a peacock and buzzed off again! Think it over and take good care of Tamara, you jackass!"

Near to fainting, I gathered all my courage and asked Erik who Lyalya was.

"What Lyalya? Who is Lyalya?"

"You know."

"I don't know anything. Who are you talking about?"

"About Lyalya, the girl who visited you here."

"What does that have to do with me? Who told you all this?"

"Tell me yourself."

"No one visited me here. I don't know what you're talking about."

I was hot and cold. He looked me right in the eyes and lied.

Lyalya was Erik's childhood friend. Barbara Ionovna had kept her pictures. The closer I scrutinized her cold face, the more pernicious the whole affair seemed to me.

Yes, Lyalya had been to Frunze. She stayed for a while, took a good look at how Erik's family lived and left, saying she wasn't born to be a Decembrist's wife. That phrase was in the family archive. But what was it with Erik? Whom did he invite first—her, me or maybe both of us at the same time? Did he write the same letters to us both? The one thing I longed to hear from Erik was that he loved only me. Instead he just plaintively begged me to forgive him. To maintain inner balance I eagerly sustained myself on his words about my uniqueness and my incomparability… and Erik was lavish with such praise.

As soon as Barbara Ionovna and Lina saw how affected I was by the news, they took advantage of the situation. One day, when I came home from town, I found an anonymous letter shoved under the door of our room. It had neither a name nor address. There were only a few words: *Erik always loved Lyalya only, and he still loves her. He married you because he wanted to take revenge on her after she turned him down.*

Anonymous letters weren't a novelty in my life, but it was beyond me to surmise that they could actually be written by a relative or, worse, by one's mother-in-law. The cruel, stinging power of this letter gripped my throat, as if with pliers. I gasped for breath. I wanted to run away at once without looking back.

Penniless, I rushed to the landlady and her husband. Shaking their heads, they counted out some money for my travel. I ran straight to the train station, but on the way I saw Erik coming back from work, walking in my direction.

"No!" he screamed. "I'll die, I'll throw myself under a train, I'll do something terrible! I can't live without you!"

He pleaded, begged, asked me to let him explain everything. The next moment he was already dragging his mother by the hand.

"Tell me right now, why did you do this?"

Barbara Ionovna was pale and trembling. She started yelling out accusations at her son, as if she now sought an ally in me.

"When he was twelve he stole some old gold coins from me and took them to a pawnshop! That's the kind of man he is! You don't know him! He is a liar!"

"What kind of nonsense are you talking about, Mama?" called Erik. "What's wrong with you? Stop it!"

Much had accumulated between mother and son over a long time, and now they were throwing this mixture of foulness and pettiness in each other's faces. The myth of Barbara Ionovna's belonging to the intelligentsia, the very idea of their whole family, crumbled into dust. Unable to witness this sickening scene, I ran into the garden.

Erik was calling me. From the place where I was hiding I could see how, without his glasses, he fumbled his way through the darkness with outstretched hands and peered into every corner. I suddenly felt how helpless, ashamed and confused he was. What was meant to have destroyed him in my eyes in reality awoke in me an unexpected fit of compassion.

From that day on, fearing I would pack up and leave, Erik often came home from work for a few minutes just to see if I was still there. His care became so immense that I took it for love again. In the end I believed he lied because he was afraid of losing me.

I went to the post office daily. My mother asked me in every letter if I was happy. Somehow she didn't seem to believe my effusive assurances. I received a great many letters from my friends: David, the two Kirills, Raya, Liza, Roksana, Lily. Raya's detailed letters helped me visualize what life was like back in Leningrad. As for Liza, her manner of writing was artfully sketchy, impressionistic. Nina's letters were deeply perspicacious, just as she had always been herself.

One day, when the clerk at the post office counter saw Erik standing at a respectful distance behind me, she called him and said there was something for him as well. He could do nothing but come straight to the counter and take the envelope.

"From whom?" I asked, chilled. It was a total novelty for me that apart from receiving mail at home he also collected letters from the post office.

Erik murmured something unintelligible and stuck the letter into his pocket.

"Show it to me!" I demanded rudely.

He became flustered, but wouldn't show me the letter.

"If you don't tell me who it's from," I persisted, "I'm leaving!"

He pulled the letter out of his pocket, ripped it up without opening it and threw it into a trash bin.

It was clear: Erik lived a double life; Lyalya wasn't just part of his past, but also part of his present.

My decision to leave was now irreversible. A ticket to Leningrad was purchased immediately.

Erik stood morbid on the platform. He swore he loved only me, begged me not to leave and promised never to cause me any distress again.

No longer sure I was doing the right thing, I kept second-guessing myself. Erik was chained to Frunze and couldn't travel. My departure devastated him. But my longing to see my mother and sisters caused almost physical pain. I promised I'd return in a couple of weeks.

When the train arrived in Orenburg and stopped, I suddenly heard someone in the car call my name:

"Is Petkevich here? Where is Petkevich? A telegram for Petkevich!"

It was from Erik: *Confirm you will be back or I will not live I love you.*

The telegraph office was next to the station. I rushed toward it along the ice-covered platform. The cold wind bit my face. I turned the corner and suddenly saw the town. Orenburg! The freedom of the steppes, a different century, Pushkin's Pugachev…

After the telegram, my journey became easier and more cheerful.

Three pilots, traveling in the same compartment, teased me: "Now we see! Just imagine what love can be like!"

"What's your main goal in life?" They wouldn't leave me alone.

I couldn't forget the scene at the post office. I remembered the scathing pain and the power with which I demanded that Erik give me the letter.

"My goal in life? To improve myself!" I answered bravely.

The pilots had a lot of fun at the expense of my answer. They themselves surely did not have to worry about such matters, since it came with their profession to handle both the elements and themselves.

The wheels clattered rhythmically. Villages and small stations flashed by in the window.

"See that station?" asked one of the pilots. "It's just one of many in our great country. It looks neat and tidy, just like a decent citizen… but for me it's still like I saw it during the Civil War: filthy, crammed with typhus victims and corpses."

After a long pause he continued thoughtfully, as if asking himself, "Are we really going to go through the same thing again?"

It was March 1941. Three months before the start of the war.

I ARRIVED IN LENINGRAD in the morning, without announcing to my friends or my family that I was coming: I wanted to hear their joyful cheer, to see their astonishment.

No sooner had I walked into the yard of our house than Valechka, seemingly preoccupied with some urgent business, hurried past without recognizing me. In the middle of the yard, in front of our entryway, stood a truck heavily loaded with our furniture and belongings. Mama and Renochka stood nearby throwing something on top of it. Confused, I went straight up to them, forgetting the carefully prepared words of greeting. Mother groaned loudly.

"What's the matter with you? Why are you so thin?"

I knew how much I had changed, but somehow I'd stopped thinking about it.

"What's going on?" I mumbled.

"We're moving."

There was nothing left to do but to go inside our apartment and say goodbye to the empty rooms. Our home no longer existed. With a sinking heart I climbed onto the truck and we drove off.

Unable to cope with poverty, Mother couldn't see a way out other than to swap our two rooms for one. Such a deal brought her some extra money. The new room was near the Vitebsk Railway Station, on the fourth floor, in a building with no elevator. The window looked out onto a wall.

Dispirited that Mother had made this decision without consulting with me, I plunged into feelings of my own failure and guilt. There was no time for me to talk about my own misfortunes, and it was good that we had to be constantly busy settling in.

My girlfriends could only see me happy and I had no right to look otherwise. When my arrival was finally disclosed—first by Roksana, then by the others—I had to pretend. They continued with their studies at the Institute. By now they were already in their third year. My friends reproached me for devoting so little time to them since I came to Leningrad. Everything, they said, had fallen apart without me. I greedily hearkened to their declarations about how they needed me, and this warmed my heart. I loved them all dearly.

I wanted to see Lily. I remembered her always being optimistic and enjoying life no matter what. When I called, a strange male voice answered the phone and said that Lily was very sick and that I couldn't come to see her. I asked who I was speaking to:

"Her husband," the voice answered.

After I introduced myself, I was allowed to stop by for half an hour.

A stately man opened the door.

Lily lay in bed, white as a ghost. She held out her hand to me. Her two sons sat at the table doing their homework. They jumped up to greet me, but their new father didn't allow them to break off from their studies. Lily's eloquent look and gestures made me realize she wasn't only unhappy but even afraid of this man. In the few moments that we were alone, she whispered:

"He's a real sadist! He's separated me from the children, he's so jealous of them!"

"How can he have such power over you?" I asked, knowing how much Lily cherished freedom.

"I don't know..."

I hoped to talk to her about my life in Frunze. After all, I was going to return... But I didn't need to explain anything. Lily only exclaimed:

"I see, I understand. I've given you such awful advice! You are unhappy. I can feel it. How dreadful!"

I sat beside her on the bed. We looked into each other's eyes and cried.

Half-forgotten and at first glance insignificant details of the past kept surfacing in my head. They grew like a snowball and eventually turned into a series of self-accusations. I remembered how once, a long time ago, before Papa's arrest, I was wiping dust from my parents' pictures that hung framed on the wall. Adjusting a lopsided picture of my mother, I noticed a portrait of an unfamiliar man behind it. It must've been a very old photograph from the time of my mother's youth. I instantly shoved it back. Her old secret was like a thorn in my heart. Now I understood that my poor mother knew no happiness. How could I have been so cruel to dare ask "Why?" when she sought my permission to invite a man to our house? It was unthinkable how much she endured before drowning herself in wine. I had imagined that, having married a man whom I loved, I would be able to support my family, but I crushed her hope and proved incapable of helping them.

One day, as I was leaving the apartment and locking the front door, somewhere below I heard my sisters coming home. Breaking into silky laughter, Renochka was telling Valya about some funny incident at school. They were cracking up so much they couldn't take a single step up the stairs. I stood frozen, leaning against the door, engulfed with fondness and love. My little sisters, my old home, my poor mother, bitter without Papa! My limitless love for my family was laced with feelings of guilt. The unsettled Leningrad life was the ingenious, intimate and sacred world that inwardly I relied on more than anything else.

The money from the house-swap could last for half a year, no more. Valechka was only in the sixth grade, Renochka in the third.

I decided to persuade Mama to move to Frunze with my sisters and live together. She was quiet for a while, then smiled.

"You think so? I've thought about it too."

She reproached me for not taking her along to the railway station when Erik and Barbara Ionovna were leaving Leningrad. At least that way she could've had some idea of their family. But the conversation, which I had been so afraid of, put everything in order.

"All right. Let the girls finish their school year. It's easier to move during the summer anyway."

Then Mama added:

"I hope everything will be all right with you by then."

"What do you mean, Mama?"

"You don't look happy..."

My mother's decision to move to Frunze relieved me of pain and assuaged my feelings of guilt. Now we could both exhale.

Telegrams that came from Erik were addressed not only to me but also to my mother. He asked me to come back as soon as possible. His impatience seemed persuasive to her.

Two and a half weeks flew by, and a ticket to Frunze was in my pocket. With the money from the house swap, Mother bought me a new pair of shoes and a dress. "I have no dowry for you, so at least take this."

It was an unacceptable squandering. I tried to refuse the new dress, but there appeared such a weary firmness and strength of will in Mother's tone that I, "poor and barefoot," finally accepted the gift.

Once again the station; again saying good-bye.

My dear Mama! Please forgive me for allowing this apartment swap to happen, for not buying *you* a dress and a new pair of shoes... Forgive me for everything... I told you nothing about my life because I didn't want you to be frightened, but we must live together!

The train had not yet reached the signal post when Mother's face, which I kept gazing at fixedly until the last moment, vanished from my memory. In a panic, I tried to bring it back from the abyss of darkness but couldn't. It was gone. Little by little my memory recaptured the familiar features, but the awful fear wouldn't leave me for a long time.

In Moscow, after registering my ticket to Frunze, I decided to phone Platon Romanovich. He came to the station, reproaching me for not telling him I'd been to Leningrad. He asked if I was happy and I assured him that I was. As we walked along the platform, he tried to hold my arm. I fended him off.

"Of course, the lady is married now! You are so —"

I thought he would strike me with some hurtful words out of his aggrieved male pride, but he finished his thought with sadness:

"— dear to me!"

His words were unexpected and generous.

"I want you to do something for me," he said as the train set off. "When you have a son, call him Seryozha. Will you promise? It's always been my dream to have a son called Seryozha."

FROM THE STATION Erik took me straight to a new room he had rented for us to live separately. The room was nice and in the center of town.

Another piece of fantastic news was awaiting me. The Kirghiz and the Russian theaters had their own workshops for designing backdrops, making sketches, sewing costumes and creating props. I was invited for an interview to join the workshops as a set designer. Work in a theater! Could I have ever even dreamed of such a thing?

I was interviewed by a very strange looking and unattractive artist, whose name was Trusova. She gave me a task and was satisfied with the result.

The job made me feel more independent. Most important, now I could send more money to my mother. Erik approved of, and was even happy about, the idea of her moving to Frunze. Mother and I agreed that by the end of the school year I would start looking for a place for my family to live.

Erik was unrecognizable, especially attentive and caring. He bought black silk fabric for me to make a dress out of and even found a dressmaker. It was the most beautiful dress I ever owned.

One day he came home from work very excited. Not knowing Erik was an exile, his new director decided to send him on a trip. Erik had to register with the police every ten days, but he had just gone there the day before, so we had enough time. The trip was to Osh. To get there one had to travel through Uzbekistan. Erik was stuck in Frunze and it was a great temptation to get out of town. I used a couple of days off from my future vacation time, and we set about preparing for our belated honeymoon.

We couldn't tear ourselves from the window: the train rolled through the steppes of Kirghizia, through tunnels, past the mountain ranges parallel to the railroad. The air smelled of dust and burned grass. In the Fergana Valley I mistook salt exuding through the soil for snow, which greatly amused our fellow passengers. In the mountains we saw volley fire and heard the loud roar of military maneuvers, which seemed discordant with the peaceful landscape. In the towns we would get out of the train and run to the bazaars where fruit was piled up right on the ground. In Tashkent we enjoyed the tiny narrow side streets, the ornaments, the fountains and the blooming roses. All of it made us feel like carefree vacationers.

In the mountain town of Osh the enervating heat was even harder to bear than on the train. Only evening brought some relief. We sat on the windowsill of our hotel room and listened to the brass band playing waltzes in the park. We prayed that no one would call on us, since only I was registered at the hotel, while Erik, who didn't have a passport, was staying there illegally.

Exile didn't prevent us from dreaming about the future. Erik worked in the clinic under the surgeon Tsarev, who would occasionally allow him to perform an operation. Surgery fascinated Erik most of all, and he talked about it all the time. Each time he bombarded me with some medical terminology, I had to stop him and ask him to explain what such terms as "anamnesis" or "histology" meant.

Gradually, the idea of finishing the Medical Institute took root in him and was put on our family agenda.

Erik didn't want to hear anything about any "Seryozha." He said it was a crime to even think of having a child in exile. "When it's all over, we will leave and start everything anew," was the refrain of every such conversation. Yet as I listened to him, I couldn't always follow. I had no aspirations for the future, and when I tried to imagine it nonetheless, my thoughts always seemed to be blocked by some sort of black curtain from going any further.

One day Erik asked if his mother could visit. "She wants to make up with you," he said.

I made a picnic in our garden and cooked stuffed cabbage rolls. Barbara Ionovna approached me hesitantly.

"Will you be able to forgive me, Tamara?"

"I've already done so," I replied.

In the meantime, the chickens pecked the cabbage rolls and nearly ate them all. The confusion lightened our reconciliation.

IF IT STARTED TO RAIN while Erik was still at work, I would rush to meet him, bringing his raincoat along and hiding myself under an umbrella. The alleys were deserted. Splashing through the puddles, I would recite a poem or replay the plots of some unfamiliar story in my mind. I would become transformed and imagine myself a queen, who granted pardons or saved her subjects. Some strange and passionate power imbibed me and carried me away, saturating me with a feeling of freedom and happiness.

I took a great interest in my work as a set designer. The workshops were located in a shady oak garden. The theater rehearsed *Coppelia.* We had to work till late at night, and Erik would often bring me dinner.

One day in the theater courtyard I saw Erik talking to the director of the Russian Drama Theater. I could hardly believe my eyes when the next day the director came to our workshop, approached me and said:

"Shame on you! What a strange position you've put me in! Smirnov-Sokolsky came here on tour and gave me a real scolding. 'How come Petkevich is not in your troupe?' he said. 'She is such a great actress.'"

It took me a while to appreciate the joke. Then the director asked:

"What if we try you in the role of Ksenia in *The Breach*?"

I'd seen the play long ago in one of the Leningrad theaters and was in love with the role!

I ran home and with a hammering heart told Erik about the offer.

"No, no! It's out of the question," he interrupted me without letting me finish. "Stage acting? You must be joking! It's thoughtless. We're in exile. Please. I beg you: put it out of your head."

His arguments were reasonable and full of common sense.

Yes, we were in exile, as obvious as that! I had to treasure the work I had. I was lucky even to have it, and of course, I had no right to fool around. To have something of my own, something just for myself—that was of little importance.

In the theater I got to know the Anisov family. An ex-impresario of the

Nizhny Novgorod Theater, Aleksandr Nikolaevich Anisov was then the director of the Russian Drama Theater. His wife, Maria Konstantinovna Butakova, was a pianist. The Anisovs were thirty-five years older than Erik and me, but I didn't feel the age difference. I became attached to these good and hospitable friends and enjoyed many comfortable evenings in their house. Maria Konstantinovna gave me a lot of the warmth and sympathy that I expected from Barbara Ionovna.

Before the premiere of *Coppelia* we were invited to the balcony to see the backdrop, stretched on the floor of the stage.

I climbed the stairs with Natalya Nikolaevna Trusova.

"How I dreamed of a night like this there, in the camp!" she suddenly said.

"Where?" I asked, confused.

Everyone respected her talent but considered her a bit crazy. Indeed, she was strange. Her hair was plaited in two thin pigtails and tied with red ribbons, and her face looked sad.

In 1927 her father was arrested as a landowner and vanished without a trace. Natalya Nikolaevna studied in the private art school of Baron Stieglitz. She was among the most gifted students and was sent to Italy to continue her education. There were numerous photographs of her by the sea, near monuments and sculptures, in front of various paintings, or sitting at the table with an Italian family and finishing a huge plate of spaghetti. It was impossible to associate the old woman she had become with the young girl with thick plaits and shining eyes who looked at me from these pictures.

She married soon after her return to the Soviet Union, but just a couple of months later she was arrested. During the interrogations they dragged her to nearby railroad tracks. The interrogator, always with a dog on a leash, would order her to walk straight ahead.

"Lie down on the tracks," he would command.

Lying on the rails she had to answer his questions. She would hear a train coming closer and closer and try to stand up, but the interrogator yelled: "Lie down!"

At those moments she thought she was losing her mind.

Sometimes the interrogator would set the dog on her. He wouldn't order the dog to let her go until the last moment, when Natalya Nikolaevna nearly lost consciousness.

She served the entire eight years of her sentence. Her husband, with whom she had lived together only for such a short time, waited for her, but two weeks after she returned home, he died in her arms.

"How are you able to carry on?" I asked, shattered.

"I have my small pleasures. When I wake up at night I can switch on the light and read a book. I can open the window and peer into the garden, look up at the stars, or drink a glass of compote, which I make for myself before going to bed. I know I am old, but sometimes I just forget about it. It's as if I hadn't lived during those years. I take the ribbons and weave them into my hair. People must be laughing at me… But it doesn't matter."

Many were curious as to what we could have in common. Natalya Nikolaevna and I went together to the *subbotniks* to dig the Grand Chuysk Canal; we worked side by side at the theater workshop. I often walked her home. and afterward I'd find myself thinking about her: "She must be making herself a glass of compote… Or maybe she's just sitting by the open window…" It seemed inconceivable what she had lived through, that in the twilight of one's life the "little pleasures" were reduced to an open window and a glass of compote. What special knowledge was held in that gaze up toward the starry sky? What must she feel while drinking her fruit beverage?

IT WAS THE MORNING of June 22, 1941.

The kitchen door was open. Through the hissing of the loudspeaker I heard: "…German troops… invaded…"

Everything presaged disaster. Here it was! I called Erik. He listened and said: "This is the end!"

My first thought was about Mama: she must immediately come here with my sisters! At breakneck speed I ran to the post office and wired her money for a train ticket, along with a telegram: *Come immediately.* There was a jostling crowd; everyone wanted to get in touch with their families.

And Erik? What would become of him?

A week passed. The German army, whose power was still impossible to imagine, was at the western border of our country. Brest and Minsk had already surrendered.

In the beginning of July all theater staff was gathered in the auditorium, where a loudspeaker was installed. Everyone waited to hear our leader's address.

"…Soldiers, mothers… Brothers and sisters!"

He had chosen the only possible tone: everyone and everything was called to fight.

A telegram came from Mother followed by a letter. She wrote she was drafted to dig trenches in Leningrad and therefore their arrival in Frunze had to be put off. It wasn't clear who was looking after my sisters; nor did the letter say how long her duty would continue.

No one knew if the exiles were going to be drafted, but in a couple of weeks Valery was conscripted. When we came to see him off, Barbara Ionovna lost her temper and yelled at Erik:

"It's nothing to you, of course!"

Evacuees started to arrive in Frunze. Our landlady took in a tenant, a refined lady who wore gold jewelry on her arms, around her neck and in her ears. Her elegance seemed to challenge the fate of both the exiles and those who had already tasted suffering in the war.

One day, walking through the town, I saw Yavorsky, that dubious suitor of my girlfriend Roksana from Leningrad. Our eyes met, but he didn't say anything. A thirty-five-year-old man had been evacuated while my mother had to dig trenches!

My mother wrote that she was being transferred to a different place. I implored her to hurry. In my prayers I tried to draw near her and managed to get as far as her heart, when I suddenly grasped something very personal about her: by digging the trenches, she was trying to atone for what she had missed out on during the previous wasted, idle years. I understood her reasoning but couldn't accept it.

The Badaev warehouses burned down in Leningrad.

At last a letter arrived, in which Mama wrote that they were leaving for Frunze in the next few days.

Soon I received letters from my friends too. The envelopes were postmarked from the most unexpected places. Liza wrote from Birobidzhan, Raya from the Novosibirsk region. Both described the toil of evacuation, their journeys on the train, life in their new surroundings. They all asked if it was possible to come to Frunze. Only Nina and her mother still remained in Leningrad. The two Kirills and Kolya G. were at the front. No one seemed to know anything about Roksana.

From the front came a letter from Platon Romanovich. It was full of questions about my life, about Mama and my sisters. He said I was the most precious person to him in the entire world and asked me to write to him.

Various administrations in Frunze set about organizing medical courses. The Supreme Council of Kirghizia offered Erik a position training nurses.

ONCE WE STAYED at Barbara Ionovna's so late we had to spend the night. Valery and Lina's daughter, Tatochka, was asleep in her cot. Lina lay down next to their other daughter. Barbara Ionovna settled herself on a couch. It was a humid moonlit night. The door to the garden was open. Overripe apples plopping to the ground reminded me of the peaceful summer months in Byelorussia, where my mother took me as a child. On such a night the war seemed a foul illusion.

We were still chatting when a car pulled up outside. Someone knocked on the door of the neighbors', who were also exiles. We heard the order "Open up!" There were voices and noise, then silence, then sobs. We could hear something falling to the floor.

We sat as if glued to our places and listened, knowing perfectly what these sounds meant. From the outside there was war; from within—unceasing arrests. The gears of the times were wildly spinning and it was impossible to stop them.

The neighbor was taken away. The next morning we found out that five more exiles had been arrested that night.

We were again afraid of nightfall, of the sound of cars braking in front of the house. I was permanently afraid for Erik. If he wasn't home from work on time, I'd run to his workplace, sure he had been arrested. If he wasn't there, I ran to Barbara Ionovna's, or to the nurses' training facility. Sometimes I would return home, not having found Erik anywhere. But then he would show up.

"Where were you? I've nearly gone mad!"

"I was at work."

"I've just been there. Why are you lying to me again? Why?"

"I'm sorry! It's nothing, of course. I just met Bragin and Vorobtsov and we went to their place. I won't do it again, I promise! Help me, keep teaching me!"

A weary feeling crept through me when I heard Erik's words. With a sense of inner devastation I once again ran out into the garden. And again, Erik followed insecurely, squinting shortsightedly, with his hands stretched out before him as he murmured: "My God, where are you?"

Once, when I was in the middle of cleaning the house, I heard the gate creak. Neither Erik nor the landlady was at home. I rushed outside. Four men were standing in our yard.

"Who are you looking for?"

They stood staring at me, not saying a word.

"What do you want?" I asked again.

"We've come for you," one of them finally said.

The blood in my veins ran cold. I almost fainted and leaned against the doorpost.

One of the men grinned:

"What are you so frightened of? You turned so pale… Innocent people don't have anything to fear. We just wanted to see your landlady. Is she home?"

After playing their joke, the four men turned and headed back to the gate. The one who jeered at me looked back one more time:

"You turned so pale, so pale... You must be up to something, no?"

Since my days in Leningrad I'd been trying to chase away the fear that had settled in my heart. Now it penetrated to my bones.

I had no word from Mother. I could no longer find peace anywhere.

WINTER BEGAN in November. Snow was falling, thick as a wall.

Erik and I were walking to the center of town when I noticed a placard leaning against the fence by the park. It was half-plastered with snow, and the writing was difficult to make out. I could only discern four letters: *YAKH.* I came closer and wiped off a layer of damp snow with my glove:

YAKHONTOV. NOVEMBER 28. THE PHILHARMONIC.

I couldn't believe my eyes. Here in Frunze? On his birthday?

Just as we arrived at the Philharmonic, a car pulled up to the entrance. Out stepped Yakhontov. He threw a glance around him and quickly moved toward the colonnade. He took a few steps and turned around:

"You?"

"Yes, it's me, Vladimir Nikolaevich."

I introduced him to my husband. Yakhontov turned to Erik:

"Promise you'll both come to see me after the performance. I have to be sure."

The hall was packed. Extra chairs were added to the rows. It was a mixed audience: locals, evacuees, exiles. The program for the evening was Dostoevsky; the piece was *Nastasya Filippovna.* As soon as Yakhontov appeared on the stage, people began applauding. He sat in an armchair by a small table, holding an imaginary book in his hands. What went on in the Frunze Philharmonic that night was nothing but magical. I listened to him, enraptured and enchanted. I don't know where I was during those three hours.

After the show I went to wish him a happy birthday.

"Oh, yes. I completely forgot! How did you remember?" he asked in amazement.

We must have talked about something, but what, exactly, escapes my memory. I'd seen many of his recitations based on Esenin, Mayakovsky, Pushkin and Shakespeare, and each time his voice produced something heretofore unfathomed.

The next day I shared my impressions with the Anisovs. They listened, smiling mysteriously, and then said there'd be a surprise that evening. The surprise was Yakhontov.

Aleksander Nikolaevich Anisov was Yakhontov's neighbor in Nizhny Novgorod. He had known Yakhontov since he was a little boy and called him Volodichka.

Maria Konstantinovna cooked a huge pan of onions in the oven. The men talked about the war. Yakhontov spoke about the Second Front; when I later recalled his words, I was amazed by his farsightedness. He was evacuated from Moscow on November 16, 1941. The hastiness and chaos of the evacuation, the fear, the masses of refugees had somehow affected his consciousness. He never tired of telling how they had to jump out of the bus and run across the fields to escape an air raid, or how they had to dive into a trench to hide from the bombs. It seemed he was hoping that someone would interrupt him and object: "You just had a stroke of bad luck. Everything went wrong on that particular day, but generally everything is under control." He had gotten used to being worshipped, and now, torn from his usual surroundings, he struggled to adjust to the new way people treated him. He spoke with an almost childish directness of how strikingly different the attitude of the hotel staff was toward him and Lyubov Orlova. They came to Frunze together and were both staying at the Hotel Kirghizstan.

From time to time I would run into Vladimir Nikolaevich in town. He would help me carry a pumpkin or a bag of potatoes home from the market. Along the way he would tell me stories, but it seemed he expected others to be interested in what he was telling me as well. A few curious individuals would always drag behind.

A couple of times he broke off our conversation to ask me:

"Turn around, but pretend it's nothing. Someone's watching me. Who is walking behind us?"

I would turn around. Behind us walked ordinary people.

He would tell me again:

"Look around, someone's following me!"

Once he asked me to come to his room in the hotel to pick up a manuscript.

I waited at the door.

"Come in!"

I hesitated, then entered. He took me by the arm and pulled me toward him.

"Can't you feel how much I need you, how important you are to me?!"

I ran away. Again I proved to be immature and naïve, but this time in a much more critical moment for him. His impulse was stirred by the stormy chaos and uncanny confusion in his soul, a torment that broke through so openly and violently. As an artist he felt the incurable sickness of the times especially deeply. It was from these depths that he stretched out his hands to me, begging for help.

IT WAS CLEAR BY NOW that because of the siege my family could not get out of Leningrad. They needed food and money. Even in Frunze, a loaf of bread cost a hundred and fifty rubles on the black market. After standing for hours at the flea market, I managed to sell my last dress and even my swimsuit. I imagined how I would come to Leningrad with a sack full of bread and preserves, and how we would make our way back to Frunze together, where I would help my family get back on their feet.

In those days I was haunted by a recurring dream: I was crawling through a cellar searching for my family, turning over people's bodies, all with morgue tags on their throats. There were so many of them, but I had only been allowed in for a few hours; I couldn't find Mama or my sisters anywhere. In the daytime, in the desperate hope of seeing my family, I began to examine the faces of the passers-by, in which I kept imagining Valechka's features.

I decided to travel to Leningrad and told Erik about my plans, but it wasn't until I went to the war commissariat that he started worrying. The war commissariat, however, didn't deal with such matters, and I was redirected to the political administration office. After two weeks I received a denial.

I ran to the post office several times a day. Finally they handed me a letter postmarked Leningrad. I grabbed it and ran out into the street.

I ripped open the envelope. Inside was a note in semiliterate handwriting:

> Tamara, you must know the truth. Your mother died of starvation. I myself can hardly move. There was no one to bury her. We could only drag her out to the staircase. Valya and Rena are in the hospital. Evdokia Vasilyevna.

Terrified, I cried endlessly, wildly. The pain was unbearable, appalling. Mama died of hunger... My mother's body had been thrown out onto the landing of the same staircase where I had once stood and listened to my sisters' laughter.

As if from some place far away I heard Erik's voice: "Stop. It's embarrassing..." But I couldn't. I ran away from him. I threw myself on the ground, pounded the earth, begged and screamed. I refused to believe what I had read. It didn't seem possible to die of starvation in the Leningrad I knew.

"Mama, what's the most frightening thing in the world?"

"Hunger, child," my mother told me when I was eleven.

Had she somehow foreseen her own death?

I hid out in an alleyway, where a drunkard started spouting nonsense at me.

"My mother's just died of hunger in Leningrad!" I told him in a weak voice.

"I'm sorry, I'm sorry..."

The drunk man stepped back. Devastated and frozen, I went home. The only person who could help me found my wild cries embarrassing. I didn't want to go there but he was probably waiting.

Which hospital had my sisters been sent to? What was happening to them?

Erik gathered his courage and asked his acquaintances from the Central Committee to send an inquiry. The reply came immediately. My sisters were in Hospital Number 4 on Obvodny Canal, both in grave condition. Once again I applied to the political administration office, asking for permission to go to Leningrad in order to bring my sisters here. They denied me for a second time.

I sent telegrams and letters to the hospital director in Leningrad. He wrote back that my sisters had had a blood transfusion but their condition was still critical.

In Leningrad, where people were dying of hunger, some still found a way to donate their blood...

I went straight to a blood donation center. From then on, I gave five hundred grams of blood every month, for which I'd get a package of food, including butter. I melted the butter and stored it in clay pots, determined to use it to restore my sisters' health when I saw them. The hospital director knew that the inquiry about my sisters came through special government channels and promised to send them to Frunze with an escort as soon as possible.

But that never happened. The old director was dispatched to the front and the new one didn't answer my letters. I entreated my few remaining friends in Leningrad not to abandon my sisters and to keep me updated on their condition.

Then I received a telegram which nearly destroyed my last bits of sanity. It read:

MAMA VALYA IN HOSPITAL

Did this mean my mother was alive? Where was Renochka?

Into the post office walked Yakhontov. When he saw me, he took the telegram straight to the postmaster. The telegraph officer made inquiries regarding the route of the telegram, which, apparently, had passed through many points. During the war, telegrams from Leningrad were sent to Central Asia via Siberia. At each readdressing point the content of the telegram was confirmed, and it wasn't until we reached the initial telegraph office in Leningrad that things became clear: the censor had assumed that "MAMA" was the addressee and had excised "RENOCHKA DEAD" from the text. The original message ran:

MAMA RENOCHKA DEAD VALYA IN HOSPITAL

Renochka was dead too… The youngest and sweetest, who always did whatever she could for others.

I didn't cry this time. Life had savagely disposed of our family.

Many years later Valechka told me how our youngest sister had lain in the bed next to hers, whimpering as she died: "Valechka, it hurts so much! I'm dying, help me! Help me!"

My middle sister survived. She was released from the hospital and dragged herself home. Our apartment had been ransacked. She went to the neighbor's, who explained, "Your relatives came and took everything. I've sold the rest. I thought you were going to die."

Exhausted, Valechka hardly made it to an orphanage, where she begged them to take her in. Starvation had so weakened her that she was unable to walk.

For a while I lost touch with her again. Then I received a horrific letter, written from Uglich, where her orphanage had been evacuated; to get there, they had traveled along the waterways of the Mariinsky Canal System. My fourteen-year-old sister wrote artlessly and inconsolably about what was consuming her: how once, after redeeming the food coupons and receiving bread for the whole family, she was climbing the stairs to our fourth-floor apartment on legs so swollen from hunger she could barely move. She pinched off one piece after another from the family's ration, until she had eaten it all.

I was the only one left who could warm her soul. I begged the director of the orphanage to send my sister to me. He told me to send money to pay for an escort to accompany my sister, which I did without delay. I was expecting her any day.

IN THE FALL OF 1942 I insisted that Erik apply to the Medical Institute to become a certified doctor.

"Only if you apply with me. We have to do everything together: study together, work at the same hospital," he said.

Apart from Erik's irreversible "together," there was nothing else to win back from the war and exile, from the fate that had annihilated my family.

Overcoming my fear of anatomy, I passed the entrance examinations and was admitted to the Medical Institute that had been evacuated to Frunze from Kharkov. Erik enrolled as a fourth-year student.

Most of my new classmates had just finished high school and I was "the oldest." In anatomy class the girls held perfumed handkerchiefs over their noses, but I tried to do without them. Erik managed to obtain atlases and reference books from the public library. I did well in all subjects and became absorbed in studies. I enjoyed staying after lectures to help others clarify things they did not understand. One of the students, whom I often helped with Latin and Anatomy, was a Kirghiz boy named Chingiz. Soon I became the best student in our class. I longed to be called upon by the teachers. It seemed like I was the obvious choice to receive the Stalin Scholarship. I was in great need of the stipend, since I was enrolled full-time and had to give up my work in the theater.

It wasn't easy to cope with the housework during the war. There was neither firewood nor coal. When it grew dark I would furtively wedge an axe into a someone else's wooden fence and wrench out a board or two to feed our *burzhuyka* stove for the night. Sometimes I gathered a sufficient amount of old clothes and other rubbish, soaked them in a puddle of fuel oil, and used them to heat the stove. The rags roared hoarsely and angrily, flaring up quickly.

Barbara Ionovna visited us often, "to swill down some coffee," as she put it. She asked us to store whatever remained of her belongings. She treated me with a particular respect.

In January 1943 the reading period for our exams began. Erik and I were both making good progress. I was only worried about the last examination: it was time for me to donate blood again. It was out of the question not to go to the donation center or even to postpone the appointment. After the procedure I felt extremely weak and my head was spinning.

Erik picked me up and we walked home together.

As usual, I melted the butter from the donation package, except now I was saving it only for Valechka. To help her recover became my goal in life. I set aside a small part of the donor's food package so that Erik and I could celebrate the end of exams. I heated our stove with fuel oil and baked pancakes, the likes of which, in those days, most people could only dream of. Erik brought out a pair of shoes he had bought for me as a present:

"Try them on. They're for you. If you weren't here with me… Thank you for everything!"

We sat together in front of the stove. It was still hot. Most of all I just wanted to sleep.

As I was making the bed, I thought I heard steps outside the window.

"Did you hear that? Can you go look what it is?" I asked Erik.

"...Yes, it's the wind. That's all."

"...There it is again."

"You're too tired. Tomorrow the break begins. You'll be able to rest."

To sleep in... that would be so wonderful! After the exams, the blood donations and all my misfortune and grief, I felt ill.

"Sleep now, sleep," Erik kept saying. "I won't wake you up in the morning. All right?"

"All right," I answered, dreamily.

Chapter 4

It was January 30, 1943, and the annual winter break was about to begin.

Half asleep, I guiltily mumbled to Erik that I was going to stay in bed.

He walked out to the kitchen, quietly closing the door behind him. Drowsily I heard his soft steps, the tinkle of the metal wand against the sides of the half-empty water tank, the creak of the sideboard door. The sounds were muffled. I snuggled into the thought: "He loves me, he takes care of me."

Erik drank a cup of tea and came back to the room for his briefcase. Already in his coat, he leaned over and kissed me. I murmured something back without tearing myself away from my warm slumber.

Only as he was leaving the room did I half-open my eyes. The backlight from the kitchen imprinted his silhouette on my visual memory, but as the door closed behind him I turned to the wall and fell into a deep sleep, unaware that, at that very moment, Erik was walking out of my life forever.

It was around nine when I finally managed to get up. Barbara Ionovna said she'd drop in that morning and I needed to go to the market before then. I tried on the new shoes Erik had given me. They fit well. I put galoshes over them and hurried to the market.

The frost was less biting by now. Mornings were damp and foggy, and the days sunny and warm as in spring. The market was quite far away and the new shoes were hurting my feet, so on the way back I walked slowly, breathing in the cool, fresh air flowing down from the Ala-Tau Mountains.

About a block and a half from our house I saw a woman in a karakul fur coat and hat coming out through our gate.

"Finally," my heart leapt with joy, "they've brought Valechka!"

In spite of my sore feet I hurried toward the woman, stopping her with a shout.

"Are you looking for Petkevich?"

The woman nodded. I passed her and flung the gate wide open. Valechka was not there.

"Where are you from? Uglich? Leningrad? Come in! Let me hang up your coat. Please, sit down."

But the woman didn't sit down.

"I'm here for you," she said in a flat tone, "The Director of the Institute wants to see you immediately."

The first thought that flashed through my mind was that something had happened to Erik, but then I remembered I was in the running for the Stalin Scholarship. Of course: it must be something to do with the scholarship.

"All right," I said, "but my mother-in-law is about to arrive. I'll wait for her and then come. And look: I've just got this blister on my foot!"

The woman strutted up to the china cabinet, found a piece of cardboard on one of the shelves, folded it four times and handed it to me.

"Put this under your heel and let's go. He's waiting for you."

"What a strange woman!" I thought to myself, putting the cardboard into my shoe.

"Well, how's that?"

"Better. Thank you."

I scribbled a note to Erik: *Called to institute. Back soon.* For some reason I didn't write a word to Barbara Ionovna.

I followed the stranger. I was limping and the woman attempted to take me by the arm. Instinctively I withdrew. I had only to put on a different pair of shoes, but in my agitation the thought hadn't occurred to me.

We walked half a block down the street in silence.

A car was parked on the side of the road. I'd noticed it when I first saw the woman, but then I was burning to know if they had brought my little sister and had hurried on without looking to see who was sitting inside.

All of a sudden, the woman stopped, thrust open the car door, and growled:

"Over here!"

Men in NKVD uniforms were sitting inside. Everything in me became tangled and hard.

"Why didn't you tell me straightaway?!" I heard myself ask.

"It's better like this."

I looked back. Like a silent gunshot, the street flashed momentarily with the warmth of early spring. I saw lonely passers-by wrapped in their own thoughts. The blind street neither understands nor cares! The door closed behind me with a click.

The car rolled down the street toward the center of town before pulling up in front of the NKVD headquarters, which took up a whole block. Two of the men got out. The third stayed inside, waiting as I got out first. I was directed to the main entrance where a guard kept duty at a wooden barrier.

"Passport!"

Intuition is shrewder than intellect. As I gave up my passport I sensed there was no way out of this place for me. I was already on the other side of reason.

I was led through corridors. Men and women in military uniforms were rushing about with files tucked under their arms. Typewriters clattered behind closed doors. A semaphore light flickered at the end of the corridor. Uniforms, top boots, leather belts. This was the organization I had never been able to think about without fear! Now I was seeing it from the inside.

The officer accompanying me pushed open one of the many doors. It was a narrow office, with one barred window overlooking the courtyard. He pointed to a chair by the door and told me to sit down. Rummaging about in his desk drawers, he grabbed something and walked out.

I was alone. My thoughts were spinning on their own axis, like wounded birds, unable to take wing. What about Erik? He'll come home for lunch and find my note. He'll start worrying and rush to look for me... but where? None of it seemed to have anything to do with me! I couldn't drag my mind into that room.

An hour passed. Then another. And still I sat alone. Should I simply walk out? Go up to the barrier where I left my passport and say "I'm not needed here anymore"? But I didn't waste much time on this idea as I didn't even dare stand up. I had the feeling there were hundreds of eyes in the room.

Exhaustion, hunger, torment and confusion now blended into one ghastly mixture. I was suffocating. To get away, out to the street, anywhere! Just out of here, now, this instant! Tears began streaming. My head was on fire.

At that very moment the officer returned.

"I have to go," I said in a trembling voice. "My husband will be worried. I'll come back later, if you need me."

"You'll wait here as long as we need you to," the officer said firmly. As he turned to leave, he added: "It's good for husbands to worry a bit sometimes."

He kept coming and going over and over again.

My dwindling patience was fermenting into revolt. At one moment I would pretend to be brave, at another, overwhelmed with rage, I would lose control over myself. The need to escape these walls was driving me to distraction. At the apogee of exhaustion I grasped, not just with my mind but with my entire being, that this was only the beginning. I suddenly knew that from this moment on there would be much, much more for me to endure. This understanding came as a revelation, brutal and cold: things would only get worse, endlessly. Something inhuman had entered my life forever, never to leave, and I was unable to endure, could not tolerate it. My last bit of courage abandoned me.

I had already been detained for ten hours. My wristwatch was showing 9 p.m. when the officer finally positioned himself at the desk and started the interrogation:

Last name?

First name, patronymic?

Year of birth?

Education?

Name of father, mother?

Siblings?

Husband?

The form was filled out. I thought he would get straight to the point, but he simply got up and walked out again.

Night fell. Beyond the walls of the tiny room the typewriters stopped clattering and the battery of footsteps died away to silence.

Only at 1 a.m. did the officer enter the room in such a way that I understood: this time he would be staying for longer. He ordered me to sit closer, directly across the desk from him. Raising his eyes from his notes and enunciating his words clearly, he said:

"Petkevich! You are under arrest!"

I wanted to crash to the floor, to undo what I had just heard. There was a physical need to get away from the feeling of being alive. I only wanted to sleep, or if nothing else that there might be silence.

My first interrogation began. The interrogator produced the arrest warrant, then settled himself comfortably behind the desk and prepared to work.

"So, Petkevich, tell us about your counterrevolutionary activity. Everything. The whole truth."

Did I really have to answer? I couldn't do a thing. I couldn't even hear his voice.

"I'm not involved in any counterrevolutionary activity. You are mistaken."

"We are never mistaken. It is better if you tell us everything yourself. Now!"

"But I've nothing to tell."

"You can start by telling us exactly what your mission was when the Leningrad center sent you to Frunze. What did you smuggle here? Who's your contact in Frunze? Who was giving you orders in Leningrad, before you came here?"

I had anticipated a conversation like this but had not bothered to prepare for it, to reshape my mind, because I felt no need to defend myself. My life was transparent. I had nothing to hide and felt I could sort out any misunderstanding. But now, faced with this monstrous, inconceivable assortment of allegations I began to question my own decision to join Erik in exile and start living here. Did these questions really refer to *me?*

"Give me your handbag," the interrogator commanded. "Take off your watch. Put it on the desk."

Something stirred inside me. Surrender my handbag with all my personal effects? My scissors, letters and the powder compact, engraved *For dear Tomochka from David?* I may have just been robbed of my whole life, but I was not going to give up my handbag.

I sat motionless.

The interrogator rose, leaned over the desk and deftly seized the bag. So he wouldn't have to touch me, I took the watch off myself.

"What did you smuggle back to Leningrad from Frunze when you left so suddenly in the spring?" the interrogator asked, bringing me back to the procedure. This was how the NKVD interpreted my desperate rush home to see Mama after I quarreled with Erik and my mother-in-law. I answered that I knew nothing of any centers, that no one had instructed me to do anything and that I hadn't smuggled anything anywhere.

"Which secret service were you working for? What kind of sabotage were you planning here?"

Questions were thrown at me like rocks, shocking and idiotic, devoid of rationality. There was no more air, no way out of this net of fabrications. The tireless interrogator kept writing down my answers in the record. All faith in common sense and truth abandoned me.

Trying to bring some sobriety to the room, I repeated:

"You are mistaking me for someone else."

"No, Petkevich, we are not mistaking you for anyone. You have to understand: the only thing that can get you out of here is a voluntary confession."

He pursued the same line of inquiry: which secret service, what mission?

All of a sudden he broke off the interrogation. In an apologetic voice, as if trying to correct an inexcusable negligence, he exclaimed:

"You're hungry, aren't you? You haven't eaten anything since this morning!"

He made a phone call and ordered the duty guard to bring two portions of the main course. Beef Stroganoff appeared on the desk. In the middle of the night, in the office of an NKVD official, it seemed like a meal from hell. If stubbornness is a sign of life, I was alive, because I knew I would not be touching that food, no matter what.

He ate the meal by himself and resumed the interrogation. I had nothing to answer apart from "I don't know," "No," and "I've never heard of such a thing." He tried to appeal to my reason: first, "to tell nothing but the truth"; second, "to eat in spite of everything." Then he asked: "How much did they pay you?"

The incessant questioning suddenly stopped again. The interrogator called the guard:

"Take the prisoner to her cell!"

I'd heard all about the prison cells of 1937.

"Straight ahead, to your left, right, down, left."

A door squeaked and a patch of starry sky glittered overhead before disappearing again. A few more steps down, and I found myself in the NKVD inner prison. More guards. Doors and bolts unlocked and slammed shut. A long corridor with countless doors on both sides and dim electric bulbs hanging from the ceiling. Again, keys were clanking. So much metal! I'd heard the cells were so overcrowded there was no place to lie down. How many people would be here, and what would they be like?

One of the doors unlocked. It was pitch-dark in there, an abysmal hole. I looked back. The duty guard and the interrogator were still standing behind me. The interrogator handed me my hat, which for some reason he had held on to.

I stepped inside. The door closed behind me.

My one desire was to lie down. I fumbled about, feeling the wall and the floor. The cell was empty. Apart from the walls and cement floor there was nothing. For a while I stood leaning against the wall, then slid to the floor. I was shivering. My insides were stinging. I stood up and slid down again like a sack. I heard my dull scream: "Erik! Where are you, my Erik? I want to go home! Why am I here?" Like a wild beast, freed from all inhibitions, I started banging my head against the wall. I wanted to destroy this mechanism that registered the whole hopelessness of my situation. I wasn't appealing to justice. It was already clear there was none. I was calling instead for some supernatural power to carry me away from this unbearable reality.

In the space of that one endless day, January 30, 1943, I embraced the most brutal side of existence; I understood how they tormented my father and what pain he must have gone through.

During the night I found the hat the interrogator had given back to me. Inside it was a piece of bread that had been served with the Beef Stroganoff.

MORNING DECLARED ITSELF with the flickering of a putrid yellow bulb hanging from the ceiling. The cell was even more frightening in the light. The stone walls were covered with splashes and stains of unknown origin; they screamed with names and inscriptions etched with spoon handles and fingernails.

The prison was resuming its daily life. Countless feet shuffled past the door. Somebody was coughing convulsively, iron dishes clattered. The peep-hole opened several times. Eyes were watching me.

"The night bucket is in the corner," a voice announced through the slot.

I knew what the bucket in the corner was for. Shivering from cold, I crumpled my coat and sat on the bucket, my back to the door.

The slot in the door opened again. I was given a bowl of slop and a piece of bread.

Time was now marked by the different prison sounds. The guard would shove a bowl with food through the slot. Every now and then a cell door would open, and I'd hear: "Step out." I was expecting to be called too, but night fell, and still nothing happened.

The lockup was under the stairs. People in steel-soled top boots ran up and down, the noise bombarding my head. It seemed something only had to move a bit more and I would lose my mind altogether and all pain would disappear, but nothing could overcome the despair that gripped my whole being, like a plague.

I was kept in the lockup for three days.

Finally, on the fourth day, the door opened.

"Step out. Straight ahead, to the right, up…"

I trudged along the corridor until I found myself in front of a door. I was in the prison courtyard. Everything spun around and flew off somewhere, plunging me into a vortex. When I came to and struggled back to my feet, I saw a camera on a tripod. A tag with a four digit number was hung around my neck.

"Turn in profile! Now face front!"

I was taken to another room where a woman about my own age, in an NKVD uniform, deftly daubed my fingertips with a sticky substance and pressed them onto a piece of paper.

The way back through the corridor was longer. We passed the lockup without stopping. The three-day ordeal was over. The guard unlocked a cell door at a different bend of the corridor. There were people inside! I rejoiced, as if life on earth was just beginning.

They were all women and appeared friendly. They seemed to meld into one face, one breast onto which I just wanted to collapse.

"Don't cry!"

"Let her cry!"

"Leave her alone!"

"Come over here. Here's your bed."

"Oh, dear, but I know you! I often saw you in the town with your husband. Such a beautiful couple!"

"Have you just come from the outside? How is it there?"

"What are you here for, anyway?"

"Don't lie down, that is forbidden during the day. You're only allowed to sit."

After the three days of torment my head fell onto the pillow by itself.

The peephole opened.

"Hey, you! Get up! Or you want to go back to the punishment cell?"

Once again I had the premonition: "This is going to be an eternal ordeal, eternal exhaustion. Get used to it."

There were ten beds with mattresses and pillows thinly stuffed with straw, each with a patched faded blanket. Beside the door stood one night bucket for everyone to share. Embarrassment and shame would have to be forgotten.

The cell was in the basement. The windows, level with the courtyard asphalt, were covered with bars and screens which shut out the sky. A wooden shelf held mugs, bowls and a laundry basin, all made of aluminum. On one of the walls hung the Rules of Conduct for Inmates in the NKVD Inner Prison, a text of some fifty paragraphs that was supposed to govern our daily routine: wake up, carry out the night bucket, walk around the courtyard, interrogations, interrogations, interrogations, eat, a little sleep at the beginning of the night and then the night interrogations. The cells were searched while we were out and when we returned there were personal searches, strange hands feeling all over our bodies. Meanwhile, the guards could scrutinize us through the peephole as much as they pleased.

Prison life was conducted on two levels: upstairs—interrogations; down in the basement—the cell, our home.

I was summoned for interrogation without delay. It was a different room but the same interrogator. Later I would recognize him to be in his mid-thirties, a little taller than average, blonde, with a simple but not stupid face and slightly protuberant eyes, but for now I could only see him as the personification of Evil.

"Have you thought it over? You have to understand, Petkevich, it's useless to try to fool us. What kind of mission did the Leningrad center send you on to Frunze?"

"I know nothing about any Leningrad center. I came to Frunze to be with my husband," I answered again, hoping he'd finally believe me.

"I see you've decided to be stubborn, have you? We know everything. Do you get that? *Do you?* Answer right now: which secret service are you working for?"

He kept asking the same question, over and over again.

One of the interrogations was led by the "karakul" woman who had arrested me.

"You're still young. It's not too late to become a new person. Why don't you confess everything? Then we'll help you choose the right track in life."

Confronted with my silence, she started yelling:

"Just look at her! We've had others like you. Forget you have a character!"

She was burning with desire to reduce me to some raw material she could twist and mold as she pleased. I couldn't understand why she hated me so much.

"Forget you are a woman! Yes, yes, you'll have to forget that!" she raged.

Then the first interrogator jumped in:

"So, let's get back to the mission the center assigned you. Whom did it concern? What was it exactly? I want names."

He wouldn't believe that my departure from Leningrad was voluntary; he refused to believe in any personal motives. My answers, "I don't know," "There was no such thing," or "It didn't concern anyone," only made him angrier. Losing his temper, he yelled:

"You do know! There was such a thing! Names!"

Then he asked me something really extraordinary.

"You said you wanted Hitler to invade the Soviet Union, didn't you? What then?"

The question hit on a fresh wound. He knew my mother and sister had just died in Leningrad; it was the war, the siege and Hitler that killed them. Why in the world would I be rooting for Hitler? Who or what did they think I was?

"I've never said anything of the sort. I don't want that. I couldn't!"

"You said it, Petkevich. You wanted it."

Even after a dozen interrogations I still couldn't ascertain what the main charge against me was. I was being accused of everything, but none of it made any sense.

I was growing less and less interested in the process of this "investigation," becoming preoccupied instead with thoughts of Erik. I wanted to snatch a moment to ask about him. Had they informed him of my arrest? What was happening to him?

Eventually I gathered up the courage.

"Tell me, what's happening to my husband? Have you told him where I am?"

With unexpected anger, the interrogator answered:

"You should worry about yourself, not him. That would be more appropriate."

Until now it hadn't even occurred to me that Erik could also be in prison. The thought shot through me like a bullet: Could they have taken both of us? No! Not possible!

INTERROGATIONS usually took place at night. Two or three times we would be pulled from our beds, but no matter how worn out these nightly sessions might have left us, we still had to get up early every morning at the same time and it was strictly forbidden to catch up on sleep during the day.

Women of contrasting character and style were crammed together in our cell. Olechka Kruzhko, whose bed was on my right-hand side, was a draftswoman. She was twenty-six and had two children. In a whisper she described how happy her family life had been: how in the evening she would tuck her children into bed and lull them to sleep. She described the crisply starched, dazzling white bedsheets. Only the green eye of the radio would illumine the bedroom and as music played softly she and her husband would exchange impressions of their day. Olechka laughed and cried as she remembered this. She had been accused of telling jokes that "undermined the foundations of the Soviet regime," but her investigation was going smoothly and she had no doubts she would be released. I found Olechka's optimism an incomprehensible psychological mystery, but it was nonetheless uplifting.

An elderly doctor, Aleksandra Vasilyevna, had a retiring nature. She didn't talk much about herself and reacted calmly to outer provocations. When a guard yelled at her, she would simply say: "He must have slept badly." When someone complained of hunger, she'd say: "Imagine what it must be like at the front!" Her husband and son were both conscripted to the front on the same day. That morning, bidding them farewell, she had thrown her arms around their necks and cried at the top of her voice: "I won't let you go! These bloodsuckers! Stalin and Ribbentrop were photographed together!"

She was accused of "counterrevolutionary propaganda and agitation" and didn't believe she'd be released.

Two Kirghiz girls, both nineteen, stuck together, keeping apart from the rest. One had passed herself off as the wife of a Hero of the Soviet Union so she could enjoy the attendant privileges, but her ruse was soon discovered. The other was also caught in some shady enterprise.

The most silent of us all, the Georgian Tamara, suddenly had a fit of hysterics. She howled unrestrainedly and wildly, throwing herself at the door and hammering on it with all her might:

"Take me to the interrogator immediately, or I'll tell everyone I'm the daughter of Ordzhonikidze!"

She did in fact look like Ordzhonikidze.

"But why were you arrested anyway? Why are they keeping you here?" we all clamored at once.

"For nothing! They've been trying to make me work for them, but I refused. They said they'd let me go if I consented. But I won't keep silent any longer!"

In the corner was Polina's bed. She was a nurse by profession. Even though she was already forty she would become enraged when someone addressed her by both her first name and patronymic. Tall and attractive, roguish and vulgar, Polina liked to be "naughty." Sometimes she would sing in a hoarse drunkard's voice or spring onto her bed and throw her skinny and no longer young legs into a high Can-Can, or perform "The Cygnet Dance" from *Swan Lake*. She told bawdy stories to cheer us up.

"Once, this girlfriend of mine and I were walking in the street when all of a sudden we saw this little window into a shoemaker's shop. The shop was in a cellar, the little window was open and there were a few shoemakers sitting there, working. So straightaway I lifted up my dress, dropped my underpants and shoved my splendid buttocks right through the window. The cobblers must have thought they were dreaming! They had to let go of their needles and readjust their glasses. Then one of them grabbed an awl and made for the window… I hardly had time to save my ass!"

Polina spoke merrily about her case:

"My boyfriend was in General Anders's army, but the Germans caught him. So, he was captured by them, and I was captured by us!"

She would return from her interrogations as if she had been out on a date: full of vim and vigor, with sparkling eyes. She talked about her interrogator with a suggestive grin on her face.

"You're the only one among us, Polina, who won't waste her life in a camp," Aleksandra Vasilyevna once said.

"That's true! If only I could get to the camp sooner, where there are more men! And, pray to God that you end up somewhere nearby—I'll make sure you don't go to waste either!" answered Polina, bursting with laughter.

Vera Nikolaevna Sarantseva was about twenty years older than me. Her bright blue eyes and intelligent face often changed expressions, mirroring her thoughts and moods. A lawyer by training, Vera Nikolaevna was fluent in several languages. She was educated, well-read and categorical in her judgments. Independent, rational and calm, she was light-years ahead of me.

In a letter to an aunt, she had written that "hikes" were very popular in Frunze. The censor maintained that she had written "kikes," and she was accused of anti-Semitism. There were other charges as well, even more absurd. Vera Nikolaevna never doubted she would be set free, but unlike Olechka Kruzhko she relied not on the investigator's mercy but on her own ability to defend herself properly, along legal lines. I immediately felt drawn to her. Her steady and vital self-understanding, her dignity and thorough knowledge of the law were captivating. While she was in prison Vera Nikolaevna discovered her mother had also been arrested. She was much more concerned for her mother than for herself and was afraid that her mother's impulsiveness might harm them both. Vera Nikolaevna was the only one in our cell who received food parcels and she'd beg the guard to take most of the food to her mother.

There was one consolation in prison: the library. And what a library it was! It consisted of books confiscated from prisoners, with the owners' names blacked out with a thick line of ink. Vera Nikolaevna and I avidly read Tolstoy, Stendhal, Zweig and many others, and afterward we would discuss what we had read.

"I suddenly remembered who you remind me of: Vetrova!" she once told me. "Do you recall her portrait in the Peter and Paul Fortress? She poured lamp oil over herself and burned herself alive."

No, I didn't remember. But I suddenly understood the level of despair that must have driven the historical Vetrova to such an extreme.

Vera Nikolaevna resembled a member of the People's Will revolutionary party. Sometimes she would pace up and down the cell, singing. I had never met her before but she touched off a vague memory... In the main street of Frunze was a house where Chopin and Rachmaninoff were often heard wafting from the window, and whenever I passed it I would slow down to soak in the music. Behind the window I could discern a cherry lampshade and a round table like the one at the Anisovs'.

"You lived at 7 Dzerzhinsky Street, didn't you?" I asked Vera Nikolaevna.

"That's right," she exclaimed in amazement.

This friendship, formed in the cell of the inner prison, was to help me withstand the months of investigation and much more besides. It accompanied me through my entire life.

Many women knew their interrogators' names, and sometimes they would describe their appearance and mimic the way they talked. The descriptions were so detailed that once I managed to recognize one of the six officers present at one of my interrogations.

They sat around in armchairs, and some of them started asking me questions of their own, interrupting my interrogator, while others were smoking and didn't say a word.

After they had discussed my "counterrevolutionary activity," they didn't mind having a chat.

"Well, Petkevich, who's your favorite writer? Balzac? Really?"

Uneducated and completely uncultured, they appeared quite content with themselves and their lives. The ongoing war was none of their business. They conducted their own war, here.

ON SUNDAYS the duty guard came to the cell with parcels. Naturally, I longed to hear my name called. Depending on what was in the parcel, I might at least have some information about what was happening to Erik. And then one Sunday… my name *was* called.

The duty guard brought in a small package and three clay pots that I had used for saving lard for Valechka. In the package I found some of my underwear, my horn comb and a few other small items.

The package was full of necessary and useful things but seemed lifeless. I felt especially oppressed by the clay pots. How would my sister interpret my silence? Only now did I understand why I had been denied permission to visit my family in Leningrad: obviously, as I was filling out my application they were compiling my arrest warrant.

In spite of everything the parcel cheered me up a little. I put a scoop of lard into everybody's bowl with our gruel. Warm golden nubbins of fat floated on the surface of the gray slop.

As I approached Vera Nikolaevna, she pulled her bowl away and protested:

"No! Keep it for yourself! Who knows how many years you'll have to serve."

She wouldn't relent, so I threw her portion into the night bucket.

"What a character you have!" she said in outrage, supported by a general grumble of disapproval.

Character? Which the "karakul" woman had ordered me to forget about? But I had no character whatsoever! My passivity during the investigation, my confusion and spiritual bankruptcy frightened me. It seemed there was nothing inside me but fear and pain.

"Did you get the package?" the interrogator asked in a formal tone.

"Do you know who brought it? My husband? My mother-in-law?"

"I did!" he answered.

"You?"

"Just yesterday we searched your house and I packed together everything I thought you might need."

Now I hated him even more—for his "I packed together everything," for the compassionate gesture of bringing me the lard.

They did a search only now? And what about Barbara Ionovna's belongings? The interrogator did not take long to relieve me of that worry.

"We knew her things were there. She got them back... Where and when did you meet Serebryakov?" he said, unexpectedly changing the subject.

"Who?" I asked, not immediately realizing who he was talking about.

"Are you trying to evade the question again? Yes, Serebryakov! Don't you remember?"

"I knew a Serebryakov, but that was back in Leningrad." Suddenly I heard myself ask: "Tell me: who is he? I could never figure out who he was."

The interrogator didn't answer or repeat the question but suddenly became interested in my life in Leningrad.

"What can you tell us about Nikolay G.? About Raya? Liza?"

What could I say about my friends? I loved them with boundless trust and devotion.

"In Leningrad, when you gathered in G.'s apartment, you read unauthorized poems by Akhmatova and Esenin. Not by Mayakovsky, by the way, not by Demyan Bedny, but by decadents. Then you held anti-Soviet discussions. Who usually started them?"

Easily summoning up information about my Leningrad friends, the interrogator mentioned the names of the two Kirills, Nina, Roksana...

Unable to keep up with the flow of accusations, I was stunned: what did our innocent gatherings and poetry readings have to do with anything? All this seemed to have taken place so long ago that it now hibernated deep in the substrata of my memory. Our meetings were something no one except us could have known about. Why was he asking about them now?

"We didn't hold anti-Soviet discussions," I replied.

"You did hold anti-Soviet discussions. We know everything, Petkevich!"

'We know everything'... This insistent refrain suddenly expanded to take on its full meaning. The papers on the interrogator's desk were full of information about us all. He would go so far as to ask who told such-and-such a joke on such-and-such a night. "You said the prizes for the piano competition were awarded unfairly... You said the system of education was not properly thought through... Clearly, you had nothing but scorn for the Soviet regime!"

Viewing my own past through the prism of others' denunciations led me to madness. Reckoning with an exterior, "authorized" version of my life, I developed some double vision, soon recognizing neither myself nor any of the distant facts. When the full power and authority of your country's officials conspire in the distortion, you get blinded and lose the natural, unmediated ability to perceive things in your own way. Before long, even the most harmless conversations take on the appearance of crimes, and most frightening of all, you too begin regarding them as such.

"Incidentally, Petkevich, did you know we've been planning to arrest you since Leningrad?"

My university, work, laughter and cozy chats with friends: all these suddenly appeared to me as mere illusions. It seemed to me everything was decaying, collapsing in on itself, suffocating me. This savage feeling took hold of me in defiance of all common sense and logic. So, yes: apparently, I did know, and yes, that was precisely what I had hoped to escape by leaving Leningrad and coming to Frunze!

"Where is my husband?" I heard myself ask with sudden energy.

"Under arrest. Same day as you, early in the morning."

As if he'd just made some casual remark about the weather, the interrogator went straight on with his questions, but they hardly reached my ears. I couldn't concentrate on anything else but Erik, who I felt sure wouldn't survive arrest, let alone prison.

"I'd like to give half of the lard to my husband," I pleaded.

"No, I won't allow it," he answered bluntly.

"Please!"

"No!"

"Why?"

"Because your mother-in-law brings parcels to him and doesn't bring any to you."

"It doesn't matter. Please, let me."

"The scoundrel will do without the lard. Enough!"

Were Erik and I sharing the same case, or were we facing different charges? Did Barbara Ionovna blame me for everything? In those years people would often say, "She suffered for her husband," or "He ended up in prison because of his wife" and look no further for an explanation. "After all," I thought to myself, "the whole investigation now seems focused on Leningrad. He has almost stopped asking me about Frunze, so Barbara Ionovna must be right. Both of us really were arrested because of me."

INTERROGATIONS followed one after another. Citing both real and false sources, the interrogator forced me through a variety of hoops that seemed to have no discernible pattern. I was found guilty of every crime under the sun. After he claimed they could have arrested me back in Leningrad, something else followed:

"We were going to arrest the two of you in Tashkent."

That must've been during Erik's "illegal" assignment, when we were admiring the landscape and narrow streets of Central Asia. I felt completely dispirited: had there never been a time when I was not pursued and shadowed?

The questions now became supplemented with informal "appendages."

"Why did you come here?" he asked suddenly.

"You just said you were going to arrest me back in Leningrad? So what difference does it make?"

"We *were* going to. But we didn't!"

The interrogator paused and offered me tea, saying he happened to have a bun and some sugar.

Then he added matter-of-factly: "Illusions, illusions and nothing but."

Having "uncovered" my Leningrad past, the interrogator turned back to the subject of war.

"After promoting his rise to power, what were you planning to do under Hitler?"

"Why are you asking me that? I've never said anything like that. I couldn't possibly support Hitler."

"Yes, Petkevich. You certainly said you wanted him to invade."

"Who did I say this to? Tell me, who?"

"To Muralova."

It was the first time I'd ever heard that name.

"Who's Muralova?"

"You don't know?" The interrogator grabbed some documents from his desk and read: "I, Muralova, cleaned floors for the landlady who rented to Petkevich. It was there that I heard Petkevich saying: 'If only Hitler would come soon, life would be easier.'"

Lots more followed, all on the same level.

Indeed there was some woman who came to clean floors for our landlady, but apart from the usual pleasantries I'd had no contact with her whatsoever. Who could've forced her to write these ravings?

"Let me speak to this Muralova. Let her confirm in my presence that I really said this."

"That'll happen too," the interrogator assured me.

Then he took another direction, a much more difficult one than mere accusations.

"Tell us, what did H. say when she visited your mother-in-law?"

"I was hardly ever at my mother-in-law's and I never joined in such conversations."

"We are interested in H.'s anti-Soviet statements. It's important. You have to remember."

"I don't remember."

"I'll remind you. During one of her visits, H. recounted that Stalin allegedly destroyed Lenin's last will and testament. Do you recall that conversation? Then she said that Stalin took revenge on Krupskaya. Is that correct?"

"I never heard anything like that."

"Then tell us, which of you is the liar: you or your husband? He says both of you took part in this conversation."

"I can't remember."

"Haven't you sworn to tell only the truth? Where has your revered truth disappeared to?"

A moment comes when you realize that "the simple truth" is anything but; before you know what has happened it has turned into a denunciation, and you—a denunciator.

As the investigation progressed it became clear that I was also being charged with anti-Semitism: allegedly, I had said to someone at the post office, "Hey, Yid! Stand in line!" No matter that this kind of language and way of thinking were totally alien to me, I still had to prove that the accusation was an absurd fabrication.

Eventually, the absurdities were knocked together into paragraphs and the interrogator read out the charges. There were three of them: a connection to the Leningrad terrorist center, counterrevolutionary propaganda and anti-Semitism.

Unlike Vera Nikolaevna, I had no understanding of legal matters. I never considered filing an appeal or even asking for a clarification of my charges. I knew it didn't matter how many charges there were: one was enough to deprive me of freedom. Erik's arrest showed how the mechanism functioned: both our fathers were imprisoned in 1937. Erik was an exile, I came to exile. We were both potential enemies of the regime. Alleged or real—a mere detail.

By now I could scarcely keep myself going. I felt utterly displaced. I no longer had a home or family. Erik was in prison and Barbara Ionovna had disowned me. Only sleep afforded me the power to carry on, but because of the countless interrogations even that was scarce.

Sometimes our heavy prison sleep would be eclipsed by bloodcurdling, animal-like howls. The screams always came from the same concrete dungeon. A prisoner was being tortured. He could have been guilty or not: what difference did that make? Others' cries of pain reverberated within us not just for an hour or a day, but for a lifetime. Prisoners under investigation, we would be thrown out of our beds in the Central Asian hinterland, shuddering at the sound of this deathly, nerve-gripping horror.

It suddenly seemed as if all the preceding interrogations, designed as they were to accommodate preformulated charges, were only the beginning, a threshold to something even more inhuman, and that far greater dangers and ordeals lay ahead.

IN 1937, prisoners under investigation would be seated opposite their interrogators. Sometimes a prisoner would become so enraged by the ridiculous accusations that he would grab an ink pot or a paperweight from the desk and hurl it at his torturer. In light of such events, the prisoner's chair was soon moved closer to the door.

That's where I sat before the next interrogation, waiting to be bombarded with a new set of questions. The interrogator was reviewing the record and remained silent for a long while.

"It's not really allowed," he said suddenly, "but I'll turn on the radio. Enjoy. Have a rest. I won't question you today."

Unlike the cell, the office was warm and bright. Bit by bit, I relaxed. I noticed that the top of the interrogator's desk was black glass. Outside the window the sky was dark. On the radio they were playing Tchaikovsky's *Swan Lake.* The music seemed discordant, almost hostile, belonging to a different world, but the momentary peace I'd been granted was lulling me to sleep. Without noticing, I became withdrawn, as though I was vanishing somewhere far from earth.

Meanwhile the interrogator kept pacing back and forth between the bookcase and his desk. I didn't pay any attention to him, until suddenly he was standing right next to me.

"What beautiful hair you have, Tamara!"

It was worse than any blow for which I might have been prepared. I didn't know how to defend myself against this. When he kneeled before me, I sprang to my feet.

"Don't be afraid of me," he was saying. "I love you, Tamara!"

His unbelievable, terrifying words filled me with panic. I didn't know what to do, but even more alarming was my own coldhearted logic, which allowed me quickly to respond:

"And have you felt this way for long?"

"Yes, a long time," he answered. "I know you… You are pure and innocent. I know all about your life. I know you better than you know yourself. I know the kind of life you led in Leningrad, how hard up you were there. I know about your sisters, your mother, about your years here in Frunze. Don't you remember me? I came to see you at the Medical Institute. I came to your class… in civilian clothes, of course. Once, you looked at me intently. Then we came to your house. There were several of us. One of us joked: 'We've come to arrest you'… You turned so terribly pale then!"

He went on and on. The whole world was cracking apart. I couldn't bear it any longer.

"Get someone to take me back to the cell!"

Stricken by panic and dismay, eventually I saw a way out, if only a narrow one, when my cellmates told me that a prisoner had the right to ask for another interrogator.

No sooner had I been brought in for the next interrogation than I blurted out:

"I want my case forwarded to another interrogator, or I'll contact the warden."

"I think you are right to tell this to me first," the interrogator replied, "rather than the warden. Do you know what will happen to you if I pass your case to someone else? They'll hustle you off to serve the full fifteen years."

"So be it. Whatever term they give me, it's all the same."

"To whom? It's not the same to *me*. I am not giving up the hope that you'll walk out of here free. Let these thoughts about another interrogator go. For me you are just a prisoner under investigation, nothing more," he kept cajoling.

But there was something else behind the idea of changing interrogators than just the need to escape his protestations of love. I thought a different interrogator might be nicer to Erik, and also that my own interrogations might be shorter and more definite. Hostility is easier to bear when it is distinct and clear and so, though I feared falling into the clutches of any of the six interrogators who had asked whether I liked Balzac, I kept insisting, "Give me another interrogator!"

"Do try to understand: it might be fatal for you."

"Fatal? Why?"

"Read this." The interrogator handed me a stack of paper.

On the first page, in typewritten text it said: "Petkevich praised Hitler's war machinery. She said she was dreaming of him invading our country... She said she hated the Soviet regime..." and so on. There was too much there for me to memorize. It could no longer have been Muralova who had written this. It had to be someone else.

Before I had time to read through even one-tenth of it, the interrogator snatched the sheets away and tore them into bits.

The charges against me in connection with the "center," the terrorist missions, sabotage and support of Hitler all stemmed from the first political label pinned on me back in Leningrad: "This girl cannot have good feelings toward the Soviet regime." But if the investigator could have broken through the fetters of protocol in the way that he had and admit, "I know you are innocent"—even if only once, and perhaps unintentionally—then what was this struggle, this mortal combat between interrogator and prisoner, all about?

"It was customary among your Leningrad friends to use expressions like 'enthusiast of the plow,'" the interrogator addressed me. "Who did that refer to? Who did you call by that name?"

Young and callow as we were, we happily bandied around this phrase: in those days, it was a common way of describing someone considered uncouth and uncultivated. The matter had absolutely no legal implications in my case, but the interrogator asked the question with particular vigor, as if such cutting remarks were offensive to him personally. Here, in his office, the phrase suddenly acquired an air of dark social malice.

I was falling into the trap of equating personal ethical weakness with legal guilt; at that moment it appeared to me preferable to be guilty of at least something than to be endlessly entangled in a relentless battle with absurdity. Instead of answering the question intelligibly, I blushed with shame. I felt as if I had been caught sinning against the cherished concept of equality and, by the same laws of absurdity that now took precedence, I was already calculating the probable length of my sentence.

IN THE MORNINGS the cellmates would share their dreams, looking for premonitions. Olechka Kruzhko dreamed of her home and the crisply starched bed linen. Everyone agreed this foretold freedom and—unbelievably—soon afterward she learned she was to be released.

Excited and talkative as she prepared to go home, she vowed that as long as we remained in the inner prison she would bring parcels to each of us, and especially to me.

"Anyhow," she said, "should you need anything at all, you can always get a message to me through the doctor."

I found it astonishing that my cellmate could have had special contacts with prison staff, let alone the doctor, a silent, disinterested woman who hardly paid us any attention on the rare occasions that we actually saw her.

Olechka was told to hurry up. Everyone was shaken up, and we all shed a few tears. She kissed us all and left.

Her release made a strong impression on everyone. For some reason, Vera Nikolaevna was the only one who did not share the joyful mood.

Refusing to succumb to apathy, Vera Nikolaevna kept up her spirits by pacing up and down the cell for hours on end. She taught me her favorite French proverbs and coached me in perfect pronunciation. Intelligent, courageous and dignified, in everyday life she would often appear touching and helpless.

I was constantly thinking about Erik. If the duty guard asked, "Who wants to clean the floors for an extra portion of food?" I would immediately volunteer—not for the promise of food but for the chance to hear Erik's voice behind a cell door and maybe even give him a sign. But the doors were iron-clad and it was hard to tell the difference between a groan and a roar from behind them. I scrubbed the concrete floors, and as I emptied the bucket in the courtyard I'd gulp down an extra portion of air, nothing more.

IT WAS THE MIDDLE OF MARCH. A month and a half of investigations lay behind me.

"Ah, Princess Tarakanova has arrived! Do please be seated!" The interrogator attempted a joke. "Do you recall the painting? By Flavitsky, I think."

Straightaway he steadied himself again, becoming formal, cold and obstinate.

"So, you were saying you wanted Hitler to come."

"I didn't want Hitler to come."

"Yes, you did, and you said so."

"No, I didn't. And I didn't say it."

"You did."

His tone was peremptory. I knew he would never give in. The sense of reality quickly started to melt down, and mental weariness descended into physical exhaustion and indifference.

"Could anyone possibly want Hitler to come?" I still tried to object.

"You said it. You wanted it."

It suddenly felt cowardly, not courageous, to be doggedly maintaining my innocence.

"I wanted it! I said it!" I shouted out.

"You wanted what? You said what?" The interrogator grew incredulous.

"I said: 'I want Hitler to come!'"

"But you did *not* want it. And you did *not* say that," he said somberly.

He sounded sincerely reproachful, while just a moment ago he was deaf to my denials. With quiet seriousness he said:

"The way I have conducted this interrogation is not the worst way, Tamara Vladislavovna. Another interrogator would've done things quite differently. Understand this and don't forget: in all circumstances, night and day, your answer must always be the same: 'No, I didn't say that!' Understand?"

The interrogator was teaching me the rules of the battle. But why?

That same night I was summoned a second time.

Once again the interrogator adopted a razor-sharp tone as he leveled a new charge against me.

"It says here you claimed that in '37 prisoners were tortured."

"Yes, *that* I did claim."

"But it's a lie!"

For the very first time since my interrogations began, something inside me straightened up.

"It's not a lie! It's the truth! A friend of ours who was released in '38 got a 'bracelet' from an interrogator stubbing out cigarettes on his wrist—I saw it with my own eyes. I also saw another person who had his ribs smashed during interrogations. Prisoners *were* tortured in '37. It's true. And I said so!"

"Lies! Dirty slander! There was no torture," the interrogator roared.

"Yes, there was! There was!" I insisted.

I managed to turn the interrogator's lesson in battle rules to my own advantage. My newfound fervor and sense of independence had triumphed!

The interrogator jumped to his feet and stepped right up to me, but I wasn't afraid of him. He stared straight into my eyes, then stretched open his lips and ran his finger over a row of metal teeth.

"Do you see these? All these teeth," he said slowly, "were smashed out in '37… but… *it never happened!*"

Back in the cell, I was utterly bewildered. Why '37? How on earth did he dare say that out loud?

ON MARCH 29, 1943, I turned twenty-three. It was a Sunday. The cell door opened and the duty guard announced: "Parcels!"

Among others, my name was called.

I rejoiced to think that Barbara Ionovna had finally relented. Inside the package was garlic, onions, boiled eggs and a bun. Something obscure, I recall, perplexed me, but I shrugged off the feeling without bothering to identify it. I shared the treats with everyone.

Interrogators never worked on Sundays, but nevertheless I was summoned. The offices were empty and the corridors resonated louder than usual.

"Did you receive the parcel?" he asked.

"Yes. Thank you for allowing it."

"Happy birthday. My mother also conveys her congratulations. It was she who sent you the parcel."

I went numb. This had to be nonsense! Did it mean Barbara Ionovna had not been here to visit me? I realized that in fact it was he who bought the bun and the boiled eggs at the prison food stall. I could hardly hold back tears.

With cruel indifference he went straight on with the interrogation, taking up the topic of Leningrad.

"What can you say about Nikolay G.?"

I remembered Kolya G. fondly. I assumed he was fighting at the front.

"Kolya? He's a kind, decent and romantic person."

"Romantic! When will you finally learn to see things realistically? Why do you always have to hide behind illusions?"

Unable to get me to speak, he handed me a sheet of paper, which read: *Interrogation record of Nikolay Grigorievich G., sentenced to 10 years under Article 58 (2). 1941.*

Kolya testified that my mother and I had regularly held anti-Soviet conversations and dragged him into them. He claimed that my mother and I were opposed to the Soviet regime and that we had led him astray.

Everything grew dark before my eyes. Kolya would never have said this without being beaten and coerced!

Once again the interrogator held forth about my "illusions" and "inability to see the world soberly." I tried to filter his words in my mind to make them less painful, but the news about Kolya was too hard a blow. Yet there was something even worse to come.

The interrogator asked if I had any requests. Since it was my birthday, he said, he was ready to grant any wish.

"Let me see my husband!" I whispered in agitation.

"What for?" he asked frostily.

What could I answer? Why, just to see him, to find out what happened to him, to feel myself needed, to make sure that neither arrest nor prison could separate us…

Once again the interrogator rummaged through the files, dug something out and handed me another sheet of paper folded in half and covered in handwriting.

I took it with anguish and dread.

On the form of the prison protocol, in his own handwriting, Erik recounted his affair with one of the exiled women in Frunze. The protocol said: "My relations with Anna F. continued after I married Petkevich."

I couldn't read it to the end. Anna F… Yes, I remembered her: Barbara Ionovna had insisted we pay her a visit once. When we arrived, the woman hardly glanced at me before walking out to the kitchen, where she began sobbing convulsively. Barbara Ionovna explained that it had something to do with her son…

A couple of recent absences of Erik's had haunted me. His explanations at the time didn't quite add up, and I was troubled by the feeling that he was deceiving me. Now the answer lay in my hands. This was something far worse than arrest and prison. Now I knew how it felt!

It would have made sense back then to assume the confession was faked, but alas, I had no doubt it was true. I could not claim: "I don't believe it: I know my husband!"

Social or political upheavals were beyond my full comprehension, but now it appeared that I didn't even understand personal matters. I failed to understand even the fact that Erik had been unfaithful. I must have failed to be lovable; his infidelity must have been the result of some defect of mine.

Next time he summoned me, the interrogator mentioned casually:

"You wanted to see your husband? You'll see him today."

I was led into a large room, where a few people were already sitting. Among them I saw Erik, unshaven and pale, his face twitching convulsively. He lifted himself up laboriously and said something to me. As if blind and deaf, I could neither understand him nor distinguish my own words. We were seeing each other again for the first time after two and a half months since the day of our arrest. I could see he was suffering, but apart from pity, I felt nothing.

When my name was called out, I answered mechanically. I was pointed to a seat at a table. An interrogator I had never seen before asked me the standard set of biographical questions and made me aware that false testimony would be punished according to Article such-and-such. He started asking me what kinds of anti-Soviet conversations the woman named H. had held in my presence, and in particular whether I heard her call Stalin a "bloodsucker." I recognized the woman sitting across from me as a friend of Barbara Ionovna.

I answered I had never heard such words from H.

The interrogator turned to Erik:

"Do you confirm that H. made such statements?"

"No," he answered.

"We have your evidence here in which you testify that H. did revile Stalin."

"I never heard it," said Erik, fending off the accusation.

Unbending, supercilious and pale, H. sat on her chair with downcast eyes. She seemed full of disdain for the interrogator, for Erik and for me, as if this proud, embittered woman held the whole world responsible for what she was going through.

What was this all about? A confrontation? Or perhaps just a kind of performance supposed to unmask Erik and H.?

I was the first to be led away.

Had I seen Erik? Yes and no. What had I managed to learn? Only that he was worn out.

I NEVER CRIED at interrogations, except once.

The interrogator asked me again if I had any requests.

"No," I replied.

"Not even one?"

"No."

"It doesn't need to be about the investigation," he insisted. "Perhaps there is something I could do for you personally?"

"I don't need anything."

"I've been collecting your mail from the post office. Wouldn't you like some news about your sister?"

I flinched.

He opened the desk drawer and pulled out letters, unsealed and folded in small triangles.

Valechka wrote: *Why do you never write to me, Tamusya? When are you coming to take me away from here?*

I cried violently, inconsolably.

Perhaps the sight of my grief had an effect on the interrogator, but his words brought me immediately back to my senses:

"If everything goes the way I expect, you'll see your sister soon. But if the worst happens, I won't abandon her. My mother is a good, kind person. She'll take Valechka in."

It wasn't the first time he would stun me by saying or doing something that overstepped all limits. Inside the walls of this appalling place, his idyllic promises, so casually made, sounded blasphemous. But I could not simply ignore such remarks. I had to rely on intuition to compensate for my inexperience.

"In a day or two a man will come to see you. Be prepared to talk to him," he said.

I feared that man with a hitherto unknown intensity.

I was called back later that same day. The interrogator said he had more letters for me and particularly wanted me to know what Roksana had written. Her letter began: *My dear! My extraordinary one!*

She lengthily expounded on how lonely she felt and how empty her life was without me.

"She loves you, doesn't she? How she loves you!" the interrogator repeated emphatically.

"Yes," I replied simply. "She is my friend."

He swiveled oddly in his chair, keeping silent and staring at me intently. I couldn't tell if it was with pity or curiosity. Suddenly he rose from behind his desk and advanced slowly toward me, unbuttoning his pants.

In blind panic I leaped from my chair to the door, grabbing the handle and tearing it open. As he swung it back, the door bashed me on the cheekbone before slamming shut. Quickly regaining control over himself, the interrogator moved to the window. He stood there with his back to me, leaning against the open shutter frame.

I couldn't stop shuddering with revulsion. He broke the stony silence to telephone for the guard.

Back in the cell, the women took one look at my face and assumed I'd been beaten.

"No," I told them. "The guard accidentally bumped me against the doorframe."

I WASN'T SUMMONED for the next two days. Indeed, I couldn't imagine how the interrogator would continue questioning me. When the summons did come, I found it difficult to even look at him. I could not tell whether he had carefully rehearsed for this meeting or if he was in the grip of genuine remorse.

"Forgive me, Tamara! You must accept my apology! To make it up to you, I'm going to give you the chance to have me put in prison for at least fifteen years. Though it's all nonsense, of course! I trust you. Sit down."

He opened the safe and drew out a file.

I didn't want any more surprises. I didn't want to learn anything new!

"Quickly, read this! You have to know it all!" he commanded passionately.

The file was marked "Dossier." On the first page appeared the names of two agents: "Diamond" and "Nord." Next came the personal questionnaire of Diamond, whose *bona fide* name was... Roksana Aleksandrovna Srogovich.

The file contained Agent Diamond's finely detailed reports on everyone who had ever come to our apartment in Leningrad. There were statements of who said what, and when. The dossier revealed the exact words used by Mama and me to express our opinions, and exactly how we reacted to this or that particular news or event. Dates, times and circumstances were all listed in clinical detail.

From morning to morning, week to week and year to year, our lives had been spied upon, dissected and analyzed.

The sky seemed to cave in. I flung the file away from me without bothering to see who Agent Nord was. I begged to be taken back to the cell.

As if through a microscope, our family had been observed by the NKVD, but what could they have discovered? That I said my father was innocent? That I refused to take back my Komsomol card after being expelled by the forest of hands raised against me? That I said prisoners were tortured in 1937? And what could they possibly have learned from my poor mother—she who dug trenches defending her native city and died there of hunger? We were ordinary people, left destitute after my father's arrest. My God! What could they have found interesting about us?

They had stolen our lives. They had labeled everything, interpreted everything. They spared no expense employing people to record every word I had uttered since the age of seventeen! And who was this "They"? Our own government, the ruling authority!

There was nowhere to turn. No private life, no action or move remained for me. Everything had been X-rayed, disclosed, turned into reports and tossed onto the trade-fair counters of the NKVD for consumption. In place of a normal life, there was only a baffling mechanism, some wild tentacled monster that gorged itself on people's destinies. The concepts of time and space, good and evil ceased to exist: I felt nothing but sharp pain, loathing and dullness.

Poisoned by the nightmare that had enveloped me, having succumbed to cowardly weakness, I didn't bother to see what the second informer's questionnaire contained and, missing my chance, condemned myself to a punishment of never knowing.

POLINA'S AND VERA NIKOLAEVNA'S investigations were over. All that remained was to sign off on their cases. Then they had to face the trial. After the verdict, they would be taken to the city prison and from there transported to a camp.

Someone said that cells in the city prison were overcrowded, that thieves were locked up together with political prisoners, that beatings and rapes were commonplace, that lives were lost over card games. Thoughts of the future made me grow numb.

The months of interrogations showed how profoundly the state had scrutinized not so much my "counterrevolutionary" life but rather my private one.

Now, when the interrogator cautioned, "They will acquit you, but only if you take my advice," I pricked up my ears.

"Olga Kruzhko," he continued, "your former cellmate: hasn't she gone free?"

Quick as lightning, I remembered the interrogator's recent admonition: "Be prepared to talk to that man." The hints were now laid bare. Olechka Kruzhko, who so desperately missed her cozy home, had gone free as an informer. That was how the interrogator intended to close my case as well.

Three months of nightly interrogations had exhausted me beyond measure. Only in the mysterious, dark recesses of sleep did the waters of life continue to flow. But sleep would be ripped asunder by a harsh, scraping din. It called: "Petkevich! Petkevich!" It was my very own name, which I had long ceased regarding as mine. All over again, I had to rejoin the material world, reinhabit my body, stand up and shove the nameless, formless energy that sleep had scattered back into what was referred to as "Petkevich." After regaining this hateful biographical label, I had to climb the staircase to the interrogations.

An unfamiliar man in civilian clothes sat in the office at the interrogator's desk. The interrogator was standing behind him, leaning on the windowsill.

I innately understood that this man was the one I'd been promised to talk to.

Just as on my first day in prison, he was monotonously asking: first name, last name, where, what..., as if everything was starting again from the very beginning.

"You said in '37 prisoners were tortured, did you not?" he asked, his voice growing sterner.

"I did."

"That the German army, unlike ours, is well-equipped?"

"I did."

"That you wanted Hitler to come?"

"Yes."

Behind the man's back, I saw my interrogator clutch his head in consternation and frantically signal me to stop, to come to my senses. But no! His panic only urged me on.

Bit by bit, my mind became clear. I was finally setting myself free, and better still—in front of witnesses.

"Yes!" I answered to every question. "I said this! I did!"

Let everything shatter! For the first time behind these walls, I felt good, because I suddenly sensed inner freedom; it was inviting me to taste life again.

"Take her away!" the man in civilian clothes commanded.

Next day, the interrogator told me that the man was the prosecutor. He said that with my own hands I had ruined everything that had been so difficult to arrange. But a different kind of insight was telling me that everything had already been ruined long before and there was nothing I could have done about it.

IN A FEW DAYS they announced that my trial would take place the next morning.

God knows why, but on the eve of my trial I was elated. The coming day was destined to bring me a chance to see Erik and to learn the judges' decision.

I laundered my clothes, washed my hair.

In the morning my cellmates administered a sort of extreme unction.

"No, no, you should wear the gray dress... Comb your hair back, just like you had it a week ago... No, not like that. Here, let me do it... Once they see you, they'll smile and let you go... So long! God bless you!"

I kissed everyone in turn.

I was led out to the prison courtyard.

It was May, and the spring air tasted of youth. A silky breeze caressed everything it touched. Guards were milling about in the yard. The prison warden, a gray-haired, mustached front-line officer with medals on his tunic, was also there. Seeing me, he broke into a smile.

"Well," he said, "I am almost sure they'll let you go. And you, do you yourself believe you'll be released?"

"No, not really," I mumbled, instead of blurting out the words fluttering in my breast: "Yes, I want to believe!"

The warden seemed disappointed.

It wasn't until I was led out of the NKVD inner prison's gates that I realized I was being escorted by four guards wielding rifles, two in front and two behind. Why so many? The question occupied me for a moment, but then I saw the street, trees with sticky leaves, speeding cars, sunlight, people. The escort turned into a fine web of metal, barely significant in this ocean of fresh air, all-encompassing freedom and fragrance.

A sunny, balmy day was reverberating around me. But when I saw a long line of people stretching alongside a large building with a sign saying *NAN*—"bread" in the Kirghiz language—I remembered there was a war on. I recalled the ration coupons: cardboard forms with square boxes indicating the month and day. The breadline, this concrete sign of war, crowded out the beautiful spring day.

As I was led down the street, passers-by were glancing back at me: a state prisoner was being escorted! I saw a familiar face… It looked at me briefly and turned away: "See nothing, know nothing." This was all too familiar. I saw a professor from the Medical Institute, the one who used to be proud of me as a student. He seemed to be taking long strides to try to head me off, but when he recognized me, he became confused and turned away.

I was paraded down the main street of the town. It was a little more than half a kilometer from the prison to the courthouse.

Boys of ten or twelve were playing at the roadside. Seeing the procession, they stopped their game. The words of one of them cut deep into my heart:

"Let her go!"

But no sooner could I take in this unexpected cry, a child's generous gift, than the words of another boy cut in:

"Shoot the lousy swine!"

The street splashed all its "humaneness" right into my face. The boys playing by the road were left behind, but their words would remain with me for the rest of my life. How much truth there was between "let her go" and "lousy swine"! There was no longer any unified measure of life. Life was split and would remain so for generations.

Since early morning I had been thinking, "I'm going to see Barbara Ionovna. She'll be standing outside the courthouse. She'll shout: 'Tamara, I've hired an attorney for you!' She won't be able to hold back, and she'll weep. I'll tell her: 'Don't cry, Mother,' expressing everything with that one word, 'Mother.' After all, she'd come to make peace with me before the arrest, had asked me to forgive her but then she must have gotten scared."

I didn't have the slightest doubt that Barbara Ionovna would be there that day. It was only difficult to think about Erik, as if we were not just going to face the trial together but also going on a date.

A small crowd of people had gathered near the district court. I was trying to find Barbara Ionovna but couldn't spot her anywhere. A few faces looked familiar. It took me a while to understand that they were my fellow students from the Institute. There were about seven of them. My classmate Chinghiz stood at the front of the group. Why were they here? I had completely forgotten about them. We had studied together for such a short time. It seemed almost impossible that they had inquired about me and come to the trial—whether out of curiosity mixed with fear or courage mixed with dismay. I hadn't been thinking about them, but they had come nevertheless.

Chinghiz was asking the guards if he could hand me a package. They inspected it before giving him permission.

"This is for you, for you!" The Kirghiz boy squeezed my elbow and swiftly handed me the package.

I recognized the familiar combination—400 grams of butter, some bread and some sugar—at once: in exchange for the food Chinghiz had donated his blood.

I never met Chinghiz again. I know nothing about him and now even his last name escapes me. Neither does he know that, to this day, I still get a lump in my throat whenever I think of him. His gift opened up a different kind of reckoning of the good and evil in my life.

I WAS LED into an empty courtroom. The judges' desk, a barrier, defendants' bench… I was seated on one of the chairs, guards on either side of me.

A short man hastily entered the room.

"I'm Attorney Baran… the public defender."

The law required that. if no private attorney had been hired for the prisoner, the court acting on the prisoner's behalf appointed a public defender, without whom the procedure could not take place. But it was all a game. 1943.

"How do you feel?" Baran asked. "I feel quite good. I think we'll be all right. Your case doesn't have *corpus delicti,* legally speaking."

To clarify some details, he asked me a couple of questions. Then Erik was led in. Immediately his presence became the most important thing for me, much more important than the trial itself. Neither the guards who accompanied him nor those who stood by my side said anything or made any move to stop him when he dashed toward me.

"When?"

"Eight in the morning. I'd barely walked into the consulting room and taken off my coat. And you?"

"Eleven, as soon as I came back from the market. A woman in a karakul overcoat was waiting for me by the gate. She said the director of the Institute wanted to see me. I wrote you a note and put it under the stone."

"Don't trust them!"

I didn't ask Erik the most essential questions, the ones about Anna F., about why he himself, he who hated them… and, most important, how he dared… I couldn't. I didn't want to. Even without me asking, Erik was looking at me intently as if trying to ascertain whether I blamed him or not.

Erik was weak but surprisingly calm. He comported himself with courage, and I took comfort in it.

An attorney approached him. Barbara Ionovna had hired a defense counsel, but only for him.

We were ordered to the defendants' bench.

No members of the public were permitted into the courtroom. But "my" public, Chinghiz, had climbed up a branch of a poplar outside the window, from where he was able to watch what was going on inside.

"Court is in session. All rise."

People with dull, indifferent faces entered the room and took their seats.

I was overcome with a relentless chill. Erik gripped my hand tightly and whispered: "Stay calm."

I answered the questions: last name, first name. I heard Erik answer them too. I was asked:

"You are charged with counterrevolutionary agitation. Do you plead guilty?"

"No."

They addressed Erik:

"You are charged with… Do you plead guilty?"

"No."

The judge smiled at us in an almost encouraging and friendly way. The people sitting behind the desk exchanged glances.

Drawing of a Christmas tree in one of Central Camp's barracks. Knyazh-Pogost, the Komi Republic. 1943–1950 (unidentified artist).

(above) Knyazh-Pogost House of Culture. 1945–1953.

(right) Aleksandr Osipovich Gavronsky before his arrest. 1932.

Olga Petrovna Ulitskaya, the wife of Aleksandr Osipovich Gavronsky.

Aleksandr Osipovich Gavronsky after his release. Vesely Kut. 1954.

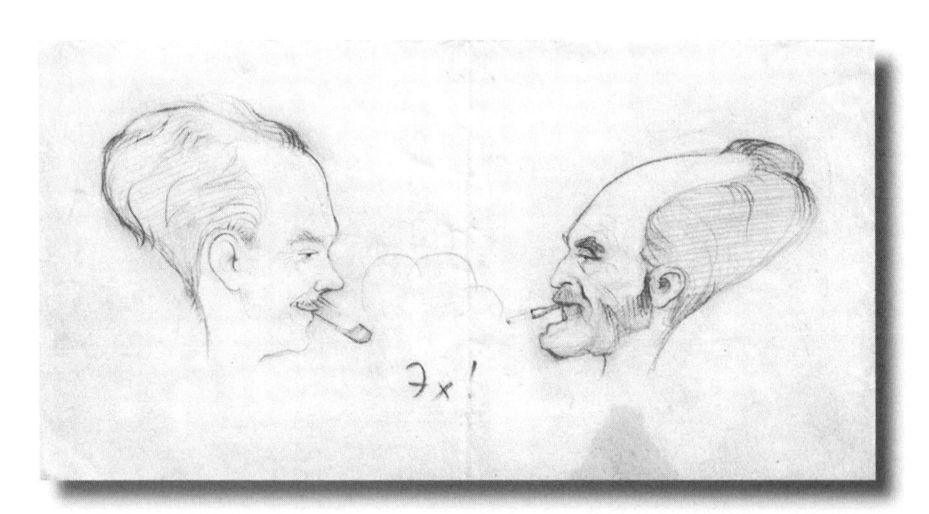

One of the poems Aleksandr Osipovich Gavronsky sent to Tamara Petkevich in the camps. Drawing by Boris Starchikov (undated). Translation:

Have a look, the best of pairs!
Really a different breed!
They get along, no moans or swears,
Without fighting, sans affairs,
We all should pay them heed.

Have a look, how both of these
Are as happy as you please,
How they're able not to notice
When life is far from swell.

Like two brothers, thrown together,
They'll know happiness forever
And afterwards—in hell.

Посмотри, – какие двое!
Не найти таких!
Жить без воплей, стонов, воя,
Без скандалов, брани, боя
Ты учись у них.

Посмотри, как оба эти
Веселятся словно дети,
Как умеют не заметить
Всякую беду!

Потому-то эти оба
Будут счастливы до гроба
И затем – в аду

Н.

Tamara Petkevich's son with his father.

Tamara Tsulukidze, after her release, with her son Sandik. 1947.

Wanda Razumovskaya, after her release, with her daughter Kira. 1947.

(left) Hella Frisher after her release.

(below) Olga Petrovna Tarasova before her arrest. 1919.

(above) Semyon (Senya) Erukhimovich after his release. 1952.

(right) Nikolay Teslik (Kolya). 1948.

Tamara Tsulukidze after her release, in exile, with Ales Osipovich Palchevsky. Krasnoyarsk region. 1951–1952.

Dmitry Karayanidi after his release. 1952.

Boris Maevsky after his release.

"Witness Muralova, do you confirm that Petkevich expressed anti-Soviet thoughts?"

"Yes."

"What precisely did she say?"

"That the regime was no good."

"More precisely."

"I don't know."

"What else did she say?"

"I don't remember."

Mixing up her words, shifting from foot to foot, this woman who used to wash floors for our landlady was now giving her idiotic testimony. There were no other witnesses in my case.

With Erik the situation grew even more ridiculous.

"Witness Vorobtsov, what do you remember of P.'s anti-Soviet conversations?"

"He wouldn't go to the *subbotnik* and refused to help build the Grand Canal of Chuysk."

"How did he explain his refusal?"

"He said: 'How am I supposed to operate on the patients after a *subbotnik?* I have to take care of my hands. I can't afford to roughen them with a shovel.'"

"Perhaps, he was right, eh?" one of the judges interjected. "Would you yourself allow a surgeon who had just put his shovel away to operate on you?"

"God, no!" Vorobtsov answered with relief.

"P. was right then, wasn't he?" said the judge, pleased with himself.

As Attorney Baran spoke in my defense, he kept placing great emphasis on *corpus delicti,* drawing the judge's attention to the fact that the semiliterate witness Muralova was unable to remember a single conversation with the defendant that could be deemed reprehensible. He tried to convince the court that the charge of anti-Semitism was ungrounded, since I had many Jewish friends and also that expressions such as "kike" or "Yid" weren't typical of me.

Erik's defense lawyer waffled indefinitely.

The course of the trial was spoiled by the speech of the prosecutor. He let forth a stream of furious invective, claiming that Erik and I were traitors, renegades, enemies, anti-Soviet and antisocial elements who should be cleansed from the earth… Summing up, he demanded that we both be deprived of freedom for fifteen years.

One of the judges addressed Erik:

"You are allowed the right of a final plea."

He declined. Then they asked me.

"Send me to the front!" I asked.

The judges retired to confer. Erik and I were taken to a nearby room.

It was over three months prior to this moment that people, invested with diabolical powers, had come to our home, dragged us away from each other, put us in prison and shattered our lives. They now gave us ten minutes to talk. Awaiting the verdict, there was nothing else left for us to do but vow fidelity to each other.

"If they sentence me, will you wait for me? I love you, I love you! Trust me!" Erik was babbling.

I was looking intently at him. In spite of everything, in those pressing moments his words still retained some life.

"Having examined the case..." the judge read the standard introduction in a routine manner, "Under Article 58, Section 2, and Article 59, Section 7 (anti-Semitism), Erik P. is sentenced to ten years of deprivation of freedom, five years of deprivation of civil rights with property confiscation...

"...Under Article 58–10, Section 2, Petkevich, Tamara Vladislavovna, is sentenced to seven years of deprivation of freedom and three years of deprivation of civil rights with property confiscation. Petkevich is cleared of the charge relating to Article 59, Section 7..."

Seven years! It was as if the verdict was read out by someone else, not by the judge who just an hour ago was carrying out the trial.

We were given a typewritten copy of the verdict—a hardly legible document, the last copy of poor quality carbon paper. They told us we had seventy-two hours to appeal the verdict to the higher court. The possibility of an appeal being heard was nil, of course.

"Say good-bye," they told us.

And we did.

On the way back to the prison I saw neither spring nor sunshine.

AFTER THE TRIAL it was prohibited to return to the old cell, so I was put into a small office with a barred window. There was nothing even resembling a bed.

I thought of Vera Nikolaevna: did she also spend the night after her trial here? Or maybe she was already free by now?

It was impossible to remain conscious of the journey from prison to court and back to prison, to give meaning to the verdict and to the imprisonment that loomed ahead. My mind mechanically ticked out: seven years... seven years… Ten for Erik… What for? Who had constructed these awful weights that dragged down people's lives?

On the filthy desk in this office, next to the verdict, lay Chinghiz's donor ration. At the institute I had only helped this Kirghiz boy with Latin and anatomy, nothing more. His precious gift made me feel warmer.

I no longer thought about whether to forgive Erik. My mind was filled with raw fear: seven and ten years of camps!

Late at night a guard threw in a thin blanket and a dirty pillow.

I put the chairs together and lay down on this makeshift bed to nourish myself on unconsciousness. My sleep was heavy and black, like a thick layer of damp soil weighing down on me.

Again I heard the clanging and rattling of metal. Bolts were being opened. Into the office ran my interrogator. I sat up, frightened. Raising my head felt like lifting a stone. He was unrecognizable. His hair was uncombed and his feverish eyes were red.

"I thought you might've hanged yourself!" he blurted out.

Confronted with this gloating sentiment of a stranger, I burst out defiantly: "Not at all!"

There were many more insulting and spiteful things I wanted to say to humiliate him so he'd go away immediately.

"I didn't expect such a sentence. I was sure you'd be freed…"

He told me I had to appeal against the verdict. He walked up to the barred window.

"The apricot trees will bloom here seven times without you. The eighth time… Do you have any requests?"

I felt sorry about the photographs that must have been seized during the search: pictures of my parents, of Renochka and Valechka shyly smiling, and many others.

"Look after the photographs."

"I will!"

Racked with fear of the general prison, I couldn't get back to sleep. The inexorable horror was drawing closer. I asked myself: why hadn't I really hanged myself, as the experienced interrogator was expecting?

No, during that particular night the thought hadn't occurred to me. I wasn't yet capable of imagining all that would follow.

EARLY THE NEXT MORNING they came to take me to the city prison. I sobbed and begged to be allowed to stay. The warden attempted to console me, promising he'd try to keep me out of a general cell.

A Black Maria was waiting in the prison yard.

As it jolted along the cobblestone road, I peered through a small chink, out of which I could see the familiar streets of Frunze. Soon I saw the gray building with barbed wire along the tops of its walls—the city prison.

Three guards stood by the entrance, discussing something. My attention was caught by the sight of inmates carrying tubs of food. A masculine glance thrown at me made me shudder. Another guard came out from inside the building holding a gray cotton blanket.

I was told to climb onto the porch. He shook out the blanket and threw it over my head. He stood behind me clutching the corners, and ordered:

"Walk! Straight ahead! Down! Left!"

Without the slightest resistance, unable to see anything from under the blanket, I did as I was told. Shifting from foot to foot in the darkness, I expected that any second a trapdoor would open under me and I would fall into an abyss.

Only gradually did I make out a buzz of voices, a crowd of people surrounding me on both sides. Still wrapped in the blanket, I made way from this agitated mass into a narrow corridor.

"Straight ahead! Faster!" the guard barked.

All around me was guffawing, swearing and obscenities. Then there was a threshold, and the door slammed shut behind me. The noise grew less distinct. The blanket was removed. I was in a bathhouse.

Half dead, my aged heart slowly returned to its place. The guard told me to wash up.

"I'll come back in ten minutes. And put the latch on the door. There are men out there."

With stiff hands I threw the latch. It was cold in the bathhouse. Wooden washtubs lay upside down on the benches. Not even bothering to undress, I sat on a bench trying to stop the shivering.

"Hey, you! Open up!" I heard them banging on the door.

They were trying to lift the latch from the other side.

The phrase "it cannot happen" was once and for all made meaningless. I knew that from now on anything could happen. I sat on the wooden bench, staring vacantly at the shaking metal latch on the door. The swinish yelling men were about to burst into the bathhouse. I should have jumped to my feet but I couldn't make a move.

There was a slot in the wall through which I could see the prison courtyard. Blinded, my body sticky with horror, I crawled up to the wall and tried to scream, but something seemed to grip my throat. I realized I was screaming only after I heard my own voice.

I heard someone bellow from behind the door:

"Clear the path! Now!"

The cursing fell into silence.

"Open up. It's the guard."

I believed the voice behind the door. With my last bits of strength, I threw off the latch and fell unconscious. The guard poured cold water over me to bring me back to my senses.

Still wet but without the blanket over my head, I dragged myself through the corridors. I was led across the courtyard to a different wing of the building, where I was seated on a chair. They left me there for a long time.

"Take her to cell 106!" I finally heard.

My only hope was that the warden had kept his promise to keep me away from the general cell. How I clutched at it!

The guard unlocked one of the doors, and I saw a narrow cell with two metal beds along the walls. A young woman was standing in the middle combing her hair. Something told me she belonged to a species of humans I had never encountered before.

"What article are you?" she asked, before guessing correctly the answer to her own question.

"And you, Miss?" I asked her.

"Miss?" she snorted. "Your 'Miss' was just brought here a half hour ago from death row. Here is 'Miss'!"

"Is this my bed?"

"Yours."

Twenty-seven years old, she was astonishingly beautiful, of average height, with alluring gray eyes, tender skin and a gentle oval face. Her hair was splendid. But her voice was shrill and raspy, her gaze—dull and lifeless.

For a while she looked at me narrowly, then said wolfishly:

"What a dear little thing!"

Trying to keep up the conversation, I asked if she had appealed her verdict.

"Grandpa Kalinin had mercy on me: he commuted my death by firing squad to ten years."

I looked around the cell. There was a barred window high above, just below the ceiling, with a rusty metal grate on the outer side. The grate was attached from the bottom and only a thin sliver of sunlight got through. The walls were damp and shabby.

I was ready to drop from weakness. Thank God here they didn't prohibit lying down in the daytime.

Sounds and smells here were stronger and more pungent than in the inner prison, and the bowls and spoons were older.

IN EVERYDAY LIFE my cellmate Valya turned out to be sociable and easy-going. She would comment aloud on my behavior: "Always keeping silent! Always thinking! You've got to stop that, or you'll go round the bend." She seemed to pay no attention to the fact that she herself would also keep silent for hours on end.

Her story was: She grew up as a street urchin and was adopted by a gang of criminals. From about the age of eight, she acted as the gang's lookout. And so it went on. She married early: by age sixteen she already had a son. She loved her husband, who was the gang leader, but soon he got nabbed and was thrown in prison. Before long she was caught too. She served her time and was released. Meanwhile, her son was being raised by her sister. The three of them started living together. And now she'd "gotten into a mess" again.

Her prolonged stay on death row had forced Valya to be utterly frank. The gang she belonged to carried out "political" murders. When a high-ranking military official on the gang's hit list would come to town, it was Valya's "job" to go out on a date with him or invite him for supper to a prearranged address, where they would be waiting. Valya would have to participate in the murder. The victims' documents would then be used for "political purposes." Exactly what those purposes were, Valya didn't know. She couldn't even keep such terms as "espionage" and "blackmail" straight in her mind.

Once, after looking into Valya's eyes, I noticed a lifeless white dot shimmering within. After that I would be able to recognize murderers by their eyes. Like most people of this type, Valya felt the urge to recount the most crucial moment in full detail. Whenever she would start to describe the splashes of blood, I usually tried to turn a deaf ear, but once I had the desire to hear Valya's confession through to the end.

"I don't give a damn if I'm shot or if I serve ten years," she said. "If I want to live at all, it's only for one reason: to see my son Shurka again. He's given me such a riddle to solve!"

The case for which Valya had been sentenced to death was a major one. The gang had already bumped off several men and, contrary to the usual routine, this time she happened to be the one who kept hold of the victims' documents. According to her story, she put the documents in a small box and placed it on a shelf in the closet. There were two rooms in her apartment. Valya, her son and her sister were sitting at the table drinking tea when the doorbell rang. NKVD people walked in. They produced a warrant and began the search. Valya realized that nothing could be done, that this meant the end for her.

She stayed at the table, not even bothering to look when they proceeded to search the closet. "I just sat there, with my back to them, counting," she was telling me. "Here, they've finished with the bottom shelf, there is nothing there, to hell with that! Now they'll move on to the second shelf, grab the box, open it… and…" But the moment passed. She turned around and didn't see the box—neither in their hands nor on the closet shelf. She was feverishly trying to remember where she could have put it. By that time, they had already finished searching the second room. The box wasn't found.

They arrested Valya anyway. When her sister visited her in prison, she managed to tell her: "As soon as they rang the doorbell, you see, Shurka grabbed the box, climbed the drainpipe up to the roof and ran away. He says no one will ever find out where the box is!"

"What bugs me," Valya was saying, "is how he could have known that his mother's death was contained in that box. After all, he didn't know anything about it—I never gave myself away. So how did he know? There's nothing I want more than to see him!"

I thought about the boy too. His astuteness must have come from the depth of his nature. I tried to explain this to Valya. She listened.

ABOVE US was a solitary confinement cell, from where a man's voice, always singing the same primitive soulful tune, could be heard. The entire prison was listening to this strong, beautiful voice singing about a father guarding his son, about how, doomed to remain on opposite sides of the prison wall, they were unable to help each other, about how the father fired at his son when he tried to escape.

Edgy days in the city prison passed in fits and starts. After the daytime meal we would be taken for a walk in a "pen." It was a four-square-meter enclosure isolated from the adjacent squares with a brick wall about three meters high. Instead of a roof, there was the sky. The floor was the ground. These "pens" clung to each other along the perimeter of the prison yard. Here inmates from less populated cells were brought for a walk, locked up from the outside so they couldn't communicate with each other. Inmates from large cells were taken to the prison courtyard itself.

In matters of routine prison order and procedures, Valya was an expert.

"You wanna to see your Erik?" she asked me once. "Quickly, let's dig a peephole under the wall. I have to see my Kostya too."

She'd never told me about Kostya before. Only two small cushions, which she somehow managed to smuggle into the prison, had the inscriptions: "Good night, Kostya!" and "Beloved Kostya."

Valya didn't see her Kostya through the peephole we'd dug with our combs. She moved aside so that I could have a look. I lay on the ground. There were forty or so men circling the perimeter of the yard, one behind the other. Among them I spied Erik! His hands behind his back, he was trudging with that same hesitancy that always gave me a pang of sadness. "How far away you are, Erik!" I thought without making a sound.

Back in the cell, I sobbed for a long time.

After the lights went out, someone's whisper crept into my sleep. "Petkevich..."

Was it a hallucination? No! The whisper repeated itself again. Someone was calling me through the hatch in the cell door. I jumped to my feet.

"Here, your husband passed this over to you," said the duty guard, shoving a hunk of bread through the hatch.

Valya waited until I calmed down.

"You love him?" she asked.

"Yes."

"Listen to what I'm gonna tell you," she said. "When they call you for the transport, look around. If Erik isn't there, start a brawl: insult the guard, spit in his face, make him angry, so he'll refuse to take you. Got it? I'm not going anywhere without my Zoyka, even if they kill me."

"Who is Zoyka?" I asked.

Valya sat up in her bed.

"All right. Listen. There's something you have to know. My Kostya is actually Zoyka. Get it? She's my husband."

Valya told me about her love for this woman, probably also a criminal.

"Listen and try to understand. It happened in the cell, when I was locked up for the first time. We were sleeping next to each other; she started putting the moves on me. I was married at that time, I loved my husband. But *this* was totally different! Since meeting Zoyka I've completely lost interest in men. It's wrong. I know it's wrong, but I can't do anything about it."

Valya went into details about this aberrant world.

"If you could only know how jealous she gets!" she complained. "You never think anything like that's going to happen to you, do you? But it very well might, especially if you end up in a women's camp! You're cute. As soon as you see a woman wearing pants and speaking in a deep voice, with short hair—stand back!"

After her lessons, Valya would fall asleep, but for me the interrogator's words "I thought you might've hanged yourself!" became more meaningful. The camp was a den of madness, violence, guile and blood. Thoughts of suicide were driving me crazy.

Another of Valya's admonitions was the "commandment" not to work.

"Mind you, don't work!" she'd say. "They'll wear you out. You'll grow old overnight. You'll fall sick. Who'll need you? Don't be stupid. Refuse once and for all!"

It was from Valya that I first heard about *otkazchiki,* criminals who refused to work in the camps, and that it was because the political prisoners worked like dogs that they were regarded as rotten scum. According to Valya's thinking, they had to keep and feed her in the camp no matter what. But at that time I was still far from understanding the ideology behind her stance.

A WEEK OR SO LATER, in the middle of the night, the duty guard came for Valya.

"With your things!" he ordered.

Rejoicing, Valya quickly packed together her belongings. As she said good-bye to me, she casually added:

"I pity you. You're a good little thing, but..." she tapped her forehead, "you're a bit crazy."

Two hours later she was brought back to the cell with a black eye.

"Zoyka wasn't there!" she blurted out. "We'll wait..."

The next night they came for me. The same words—"Petkevich! With your things!"—made my heart shrink in anguish.

"Don't you dare get transferred without Erik!" I heard Valya say. "That'd be stupid! You'll ruin your own life! Ah, I know I'm just wasting my breath on you."

"Good-bye, Valya! Thank you!"

Only women were gathered for the transfer. Most gazed around blankly, me too. I realized the majority were 58-ers, which made me feel better. Someone said the transport was going to a women's camp but no one knew the place's name. We were searched. Our hair was cut. Handbags and any other things still in our possession had to be left in so-called storage. We knew we'd never get them back.

The night was long and agonizing. Was Erik still asleep somewhere in the prison? Or had he already been carted off on another transport before me?

I was awaiting my journey to the camp, to an unknown world, dangerous and hostile

Chapter 5

The night before the transport none of us slept.

In the morning rations were handed out: five hundred grams of bread and two spoiled herring each. The sun was already shining in the prison yard, but still we had not been lined up.

Someone found out our destination was the Djangi-Djir women's camp.

"Any idea how far it is from Frunze?"

"About fifty or sixty kilometers."

"What are we riding in?"

"Riding? What, you don't feel like walking?"

The reason for the delay finally became clear when a woman was brought out of the punishment block. She staggered and squinted in the light. Her swollen face, full of bruises, was blue and yellow.

The young baby-faced transport commander shouted out in a piercing voice:

"Everyone look over here! This scarecrow tried to escape! She'll get what's coming to her later. Now she's going to lead the lot of you the way she ran. If we have to walk an extra hundred *versts*, you've only got her to thank. Is that clear? I said, is that clear?"

The woman, indifferent to her surroundings, was placed at the head of the column.

We were counted. The squad, ten rows of women, four abreast, surrounded by guards and dogs, was ready to set off. The young commander yelled: "Try to run and we shoot! Three steps to the right or left counts as an attempt to escape! Understand? I repeat: three steps to the right, three to the left, and you get a bullet."

The prison gates opened and we marched out through the streets.

At one end of the town was the house with our abandoned room, at the other end my mother-in-law, Lina and the three-year-old wide-eyed Tatochka were still in their beds.

On and on we walked, without exchanging a word. Only the youthful commander continued to yell at the poor stumbling woman who was forcing herself along in front of the column.

Until about ten o'clock the walking was fairly easy. Gradually, though, everything we had found so pleasant after three months locked in a cell—air, wind, sun—became a punishment. The light blue sky turned dark and heavy, pitilessly pouring its molten lava over our heads. Each step forward in the constant wind stirred up sand that got into our mouths, eyes and hair.

We soon passed the limits of our endurance, but we were not allowed to stop, not for a single moment. One fell, then another. The guards shouted, "Stand up or we shoot!" Those unable to get up were heaved onto one of the wooden carts at the rear of the column.

I don't know how many *versts* we walked before our first break, when we were finally permitted to crawl under the carts on which the sunstroked women lay covered by sacks. We dug into our bread and spoiled herring, and since we were not allowed anything to drink, we turned away when the guards unscrewed their flasks and poured wonderful silver water down their throats.

Our faces were already burned by the sun, our eyes reduced to slits.

"What I got was a Pole," laughed the commander, "but she'll be a Mongol by the time we get there!"

And we set off again in the scorching sun.

I didn't know how much I could handle and what would prove beyond me. "Forget you're a woman!" the lady in the karakul coat had advised me. Now I had to forget I was a human being, too. It was to keep my mind from this frightening thought that I dragged myself on and on, driven by a crazed, preternatural stubbornness.

I was the youngest in the transport; beside me walked all old women. Each of us was forcing herself to the limit. If one fell, she made no sound or complaint. Here you immediately realized you were alone.

WE SKIRTED AROUND the settlement of Djangi-Djir until it lay behind us to the left. Ahead of us loomed two large barracks and some outhouses surrounded by rows of barbed wire. It was the camp. A watchtower stood at each corner. Guards carrying machine guns were walking back and forth. But it was something else that sent a chill creeping through me, freezing my blood in its veins. There, behind the barbed wire, standing motionless in the blazing heat of the day was a row of creatures, distantly reminiscent of human beings.

Who were they? Or *what?*

Everything—exhaustion, pain—receded before the fact that this sight could actually be real. We drew closer, and now we could clearly see: yes, these were indeed human beings. There were about ten of them, skeletons of different sizes covered with brown parchment-like skin, naked to the waist, with shaved heads and pendulous withered breasts. Their only clothing was some pathetic dirty underwear, and their shinbones were a hollow circle of emptiness. Women! All the suffering I had experienced up to that moment was child's play, a bluff, a sham! This was the real thing, the truth, the first letter in the alphabet of human suffering. I trembled, but whether from compassion for these relics of humanity or from horror, I could not tell.

After we passed through the camp gates it became impossible to avoid these parchment-covered skeletons. Walking past, we were amazed to hear intelligible human speech:

"Are you from the outside? What's it like out there?"

"We don't know. We've been in prison for six months."

We were sorted out and allocated our barracks. I was sent to the workers' barracks, with two tiers of plank beds lined along the walls. There was no one in there except the barracks orderly. Everyone else was at work in the fields. The women, who seemed to me mere shadows, followed me in. Three came up and touched me with their bony fingers.

"I have a daughter like you on the outside," said one.

I reminded others of a granddaughter or a sister. Some stood motionless at a distance, numb with detachment, and gazed at the newcomers.

How many borders, how many limits had they already stepped over?

Many of them were classified as invalids and deemed unfit for work by a commission of doctors. They were due for release but nevertheless remained in the camp and were still working, sitting on their plank beds in the invalids' barracks and making yarn on a spindle.

Beyond the barbed wire stretched the endless steppe. The wind whipped up the sand. The world was thick with stifling heat, sand, watchtowers, inconceivable cruelty.

I made up my mind to quit, to drop out, to take my own life. There was neither panic nor despair in this categorical feeling. The decision came completely naturally. Death at this point seemed more worthwhile than life. I considered the means. There was neither poison, nor razorblades, nor water.

The camp manufactured rope. I left the barracks and wandered around until I found a solid piece. Now I had to decide where. The toilet was a pit dug in a corner of the camp enclosed by a low reed fence; it was in full view of the sentry guards. The beams that supported the barracks roof crossed over at one corner and jutted out. That could be of use. But the place was easily seen from two watchtowers. So I had only to wait until it was dark, and then… Only a couple of hours to wait! The interrogator knew what he was saying when he told me, "I thought you'd hanged yourself."

I went back to the barracks, the first barracks of my first camp where, finding consolation in my resolution, I waited for nightfall.

Noise tore me from numbness. The barracks were filled with workers coming back to their plank beds. Several hours must have passed. It was already evening.

"We've got newcomers. A transport?"

Just one question. No one was interested in anyone or anything else.

These women too were painfully thin and burned dark brown by the sun, their arms and legs covered in wounds and striped with green tincture. Some tumbled down on their plank beds, others got busy cooking something. They heated the stove, whose pipe led straight out through the window. Several women crowded around it. Four squatted before the stove and tossed turtles into the fire, which they were lucky to catch in the steppe. When the shells began to glow, they pulled the turtles from the fire with pokers and hurled them heftily to the floor. The shell broke and revealed a lump of baked flesh. From that they made "French" soup.

A woman in the corner had something white, red and slippery in her hands. As the rest exclaimed "Look what a fat one you've got!" she scratched out intestines and entrails from it. With the ferocity of a starving animal she tore into what turned out to be a gopher. The catching of the little animal was fervently discussed. Envy of the lucky huntress was coupled with praise for the guard who let her catch the creature.

I stared at the women as they prepared their additional rations, letting my gaze travel from one to the other. One wore a floral-patterned red dress that caught my attention. I had to make a strenuous effort to remember exactly what it was. Suddenly it came to me: I had seen this dress in the prison cell! Vera Nikolaevna had begged the guard to give it to her mother…

I hurried over to the thin woman with crew-cut hair who sat with her back to me, and touched her on the shoulder. She turned around. I knew the eyes. But the face… Yes, it was her, Vera Nikolaevna. Only a month and a half had passed, and I could hardly recognize her. My heart opened up and tears flowed.

"Don't take it so hard, my friend," she consoled me. "We'll survive this too. What luck that we've met again! Come, I'll introduce you to my mother. She's also here."

I was stunned by Maria Silvestrovna's thinness and her composure. Such equanimity, so aloof from the barracks reality, was only possible because her daughter was here with her.

"So you weren't released, Vera Nikolaevna?"

"Not yet, but I will be."

"How many years did you get?"

The sentence was exactly the same as for Erik and me: her mother got ten years, Vera Nikolaevna seven.

For me, this camp reunion was a sign. I didn't tell her what I had planned, and for today death was postponed.

Vera Nikolaevna persuaded her neighbor to make room, and I took a place near her on the plank bed. We had been given gray pillow slips filled with straw and torn half blankets. The light bulb that hung from the ceiling cast a glow that scarcely reached the head of the beds.

"Sleep now," said Vera Nikolaevna, cutting short further conversation. "Tomorrow you'll be sent out to work too. It's real hard labor here, you'll need all your strength. I'll try to persuade the work distributor to put you in our brigade. Get some sleep."

At five in the morning the wake-up call sounded: a loud bang against a metal rail that hung by the gates of the camp. Clambering silently from the plank bed, I had to make every effort to shake off sleep, as did all the women. Camp life had begun.

The orderlies brought in a zinc bucket with a murky brownish liquid they called coffee. Bread rations were distributed. Their weight depended on our work output of the previous day. After breakfast there was a roll call and checks; then we were assembled in brigades and marched off to work.

The brigade I joined collected mown hemp stalks in the field and put them together in sheaves. There was no escape from the pitiless baking sun. How desperately we wished it would disappear behind the horizon.

Several eternities passed until the midday break. Lunch was brought to the field: water soup with occasional kernels of corn. It was called *balanda.* The second course was watery corn porridge.

The workday continued till sundown. It was so hard to withstand that it seemed I wouldn't survive a second one. The only thought was how to escape the sun. I tore the lining from my coat, constructed a kerchief with a peak and tied it to my head.

Both from my own exhaustion and from what others revealed to me I learned that several principles ruled the camp—keep our stomachs empty, keep us out of sorts, punish us by not giving us bread and prevent us from thinking.

"BETTER THAT NO ONE KNOWS of our friendship, so don't tell anyone," said Vera Nikolaevna one day.

"Why?" I asked.

"The camp doesn't tolerate things like that."

In a few days a transfer was announced. Vera's and my names were on the list, but not her mother's. Vera was outraged:

"That's inhuman! How can you separate me from my old mother? Don't you know my appeal is being heard in the Supreme Soviet? I'll soon be released!"

Her outburst produced a reaction none of us could expect. No sooner had the list been read off to the end than it was announced that my name was there by mistake and that I was going to stay.

Vera was right: friendship among prisoners irritated the commanders; it was against the very spirit of the camp.

The transport was for Nizhny Tagil.

"Stand firm, Mother, take care of yourself and look after Tamara," whispered Vera, saying good-bye.

Maria Silvestrovna and I stood at the barbed wire fence, following the departing women with our eyes. I was going to say something to console her when, no longer trying to suppress tears and pointing at the group of officers, she suddenly uttered:

"One of them must've really liked you!"

It wasn't hard to realize that she said that out of intolerable pain, and so I didn't say anything back.

After Vera left with the transport, some door inside me slammed shut. Overcome with indifference, I proved incapable of any contact with anyone.

A *SOVKHOZ* IN DJANGI-DJIR collected hemp stalks and produced fibers, which were used as the raw material for rope and sacking needed at the front. Production output was credited to the *sovkhoz,* while the actual work was done by prisoners.

We worked in the fields, but there was also a factory housed in a large enclosed barn with three looms. There was a system of turning steel shafts working over each other into which hemp stalks were fed. From there the fibers came onto a grating with large teeth that the hemp was sifted through. Finally, heaps of airy fibers could be collected from the machine.

The curse of this work was the millions of tiny needles created by the breaking up of the hemp. They stuck in every pore of your body and itched endlessly. You couldn't shake them out of your clothing or find any way of getting rid of them. You could only put up with the torture day and night.

The most difficult task at the factory was feeding the stalks into the loom. The stems had to be sorted into rows and then shoved into the shafts. The machines would roar and rattle, veiling the building with a haze of dust and needles and making it virtually impossible to see the woman who collected the fiber from the other side. Through the roar, a sudden animal-like shriek would sometimes be heard. Exhausted from her twelve-hour shift, one of those feeding the machine had got her hand, or both hands, caught up in a noose of tangled hemp. The whole arm was pulled into the whirling steel shafts and there was no time to stop the machine. Help always came too late and the woman lost her arm, the blood gushed forth and most often she died not long after.

A huge quantity of crude Deccan hemp was stored in artificial reservoirs, where it would lie soaking for two or three months. A thick white layer of seething worms appeared on the surface of the water. A wooden jetty was then put across the reservoir, onto which the hemp was laid and thrashed with a wooden bat. The result was a dazzling white fiber that looked like silk. This prehistoric method was called "wet thrashing." Whoever worked on this job became covered in cuts and wounds. Their emaciated bodies were eaten away by the worms and the stinking water. The stench of the reservoir and a thicket of white worms not only had an appalling effect on people's hands and legs but also left deep sores on their psyche. Women would try to avoid this work by getting in with both the work distributor and the brigade leader.

Our work distributor, Marina Ventslavskaya, was a beautiful Polish woman who still bore traces of her former prosperous life. The foreman, Mikhaylovsky, was also Polish, and the only man in this all-women's camp. Both were prisoners. Even though I never asked them for anything, it seemed it was they who saved me from "wet thrashing," which I feared as much as anyone else did.

On the next transport my name was again called out. I was sent to the office. Ten prisoners were already there, all Polish. Both Mikhaylovsky and Marina were leaving with this "Polish" transport. But with me everything became clear right away: my questionnaire said I was born in Russia. As I had never been to Poland, I was a "fictitious" Pole, so I was sent back to the barracks.

Soon I was moved from the field brigade to the factory, where I had to feed the machine. The factory operated around the clock, and we all longed for the night shift because it brought some relief from the intolerable heat.

Every once in a while the hemp would not be delivered on time. The machines would stop, work would halt, and for some minutes we would be allowed to go outside and lie down on the compressed bales of fiber ready to be taken away. During these moments of respite I was haunted by inexplicable associations. The roar of the looms conjured up the rumble of trains at the Vitebsk Railway Station, from which my mother and I used to set off for Byelorussia to spend the summer. Each time I reached the factory, I relived the same kind of dismay I used to feel back then. During the rare moments of rest, I was carried away to the Rostov household in Tolstoy's *War and Peace:* I was Natasha hiding behind the flower bed! The radiance of that scene descended on me, and it became my secret refuge from everyday reality.

I was deaf and blind to camp life, but the camp did not let one out of its grasp. The guards were all different. Some were rather tolerant, but most of them were monsters. One was especially terrifying—young and cold, as if made of steel. Women said he had recently killed a prisoner after raping her, and that she was not the first and certainly not the last. People called him Beast.

One night, he was sitting on the bales of fiber above us, holding his machine gun upright. His face was lit by the moon. I gazed up at him, without a thought in mind, but the next moment, for God knows what reason, I heard myself ask:

"How many people have you killed?"

What made me say that? Everyone turned around and held their breath. Beast was neither embarrassed nor angry: "If I shoot you, that makes five," came the answer.

A few minutes later the hemp arrived. Before getting back to work, some women headed off to the toilet, which was about thirty meters away. I was about to follow them when one of the prisoners touched me on the elbow: "Don't go. He'll say you tried to escape."

Beast was also the guard who escorted us to work.

Heavy rains had soaked the ground and the road was muddy. We were trying to step around a huge puddle when he raised his machine gun:

"Stay in your lines or I shoot!"

As we started crossing the puddle, wading up to our knees in muddy water, he ordered:

"Sit down!"

At first we didn't believe it, but he bellowed, snorting with rage:

"I said sit! Or I shoot!"

And we sat down...

WHEN AFTER ABOUT TWO MONTHS I saw my reflection in a glass door at the medical unit, I didn't immediately realize it was me. I hadn't noticed myself turning into a skeleton. It was almost impossible to recognize anything familiar in what that mirror revealed.

We were always hungry, and the prisoners made different use of their daily bread rations. Some, like me, ate it all in the morning. Others divided it into three or more pieces and stretched these out over the whole day, which was probably a better idea, for it meant having something to chew on after work. When I came back from the factory, I would lie down immediately to stave off the pangs of gnawing hunger with sleep.

I had a high fever and was let off work. Apart from the orderly I was alone in the barracks. Lying on my plank bed, I noticed a hunk of bread, about 200 grams, on my neighbor's bed. No matter which way I turned, I couldn't get it out of my mind. The desire to eat was unbearable. Then, staring straight at the bread, I forced myself to keep saying: "That's someone else's bread, not mine. If I lay my hands on it, I am a thief. I will do without, I will be patient, I will never steal. I will be patient..." The bread still loomed insistently and mockingly before my eyes and stirred my memory: "Mama... My sisters... The siege... They were always hungry." But eventually I managed to vanquish the suffocating agony of hunger. I knew I had escaped disgrace.

Many in the camp received parcels and money. With the money you could buy the buttermilk that the locals brought to the camp gates. When Vera was still there, she would let me taste it. It seemed I had never drunk anything so delicious.

The only person I continued to wait for was my mother-in-law, Barbara Ionovna. Every day I would peer through the barbed wire hoping to see her on the other side with a whole loaf of bread.

I received no mail until suddenly, after about three months, I got several letters from Erik, one after the other. I feasted my eyes on the triangular envelopes, the handwriting and my name. He wrote he was doing well, working as a doctor in a camp that was closer to Frunze than Djangi-Djir. His letters didn't show any trace of apathy or depression. I wondered if perhaps he didn't want to distress me and wasn't telling me the whole truth. He was just as passionate as before: "My one and only! I love you, I think about you, I dream of you. I can't live without you!"

I tried to get a grasp on his every word, rereading the letters again and again. There was a lot written there, but his words were more like some external music than a direct call of one living soul to another. Answering his letters, I chose to keep the same kind of tone and not to describe the camp where I was.

THE BARRACKS was heavily populated with foreigners, mostly German and French. They were quiet and self-restrained and didn't stand out in any way. "If I'da been a hooker back home," joked one, "they wudden'a brung me to this camp." Two of these women have remained in my memory clearer than the rest: Kraft and Schaap. Both of them were sentenced for espionage, but it wasn't clear who they actually worked for. All their stories about the "undercover work" were reduced to romantic love adventures. They were extremely emaciated, but their femininity was so powerful it showed through, even here, in these conditions. As invalids they were not sent to work, so during the daytime they stayed in the barracks and crocheted skirts and bonnets out of hemp fibers with homemade needles. They adorned their bonnets with gardens of cotton flowers, which they decorated and painted with green tincture from the medical unit. Wearing those same coquettish bonnets, they went to the dump in the corner of the camp and rummaged through it from top to bottom. They spent hours there, quietly and diligently sorting out everything useable. They gnawed on bones thrown away by the guards, plucked goosefoot and other herbs, and survived on nettle soup. But they loved to talk about their outfits and fancy receptions from the old days.

A fervent dispute once arose in our barracks: who in the camp was better off—those who arrived here still young, or those in their declining years.

"Naturally the young!" some said. "They sit out their term, and when they get out, they still have so many years ahead!"

"No!" others objected. "We, the older ones, at least have some memories, some life behind us we can turn to. But the young? They haven't lived yet, and who knows if they'll ever get the chance."

I thought to myself, "You really do have it easier, you can find solace in the undergrowth of your biographies, you have had time to make Fate your own, but I have nothing to creep away into." Life, however, declared such polemics purely scholastic, for pain was the same for everyone, young or old.

Unexpectedly Maria Silvestrovna was summoned to the Second Department. She thought it had to do with some news from her daughter and asked me to go with her. But the paper they laid in front of her was her husband's claim for divorce. He figured it hopeless to wait for his sixty-year-old wife sentenced to ten years to be released, and in the meantime had met another woman whom he now wanted to marry. Terrified, I looked at Maria Silvestrovna, thinking she would drop dead on the spot. But she signed the paper straight off and left the room ostentatiously upright and unbending, with dry eyes. All her youth was crossed out at once, and indeed her whole life too.

Along with the invalids, she was soon sent to another camp.

I WAS ORDERED to the office of the camp's new technical supervisor. He was an unattractive man but had an intelligent face. People said he used to work as an engineer at a large factory. He told me he had appointed me leader of the field brigade that collected hemp. The position meant I had to be active and keep the brigade on the move, as well as maintain discipline—all things I knew nothing about, nor wanted to.

"I don't think I'm the right person," I protested with fear.

He cut me off: "Here you're not asked, you're ordered."

I couldn't imagine my further life in the camp, not even as far as the next day. And now the camp held me responsible for fulfilling the norm and, what's more, for the daily bread rations of nine women, none of whom had ever done any physical labor.

The brigade "drove" hemp fibers. To earn 600 grams of bread, by the end of the day we had to put 750 kilos of fiber onto the scales, light fiber, which so quickly became weightless in the drying sun.

At the end of my first day as the brigade leader, the scales stopped at 450 kilograms, which equaled a 450 gram bread ration. The foreigners remarked, "That willn't do! We'll have to chit like everyone else."

Cheating like everyone else meant that someone had to take on another duty: to run to the dirty irrigation ditch that flowed about 100 meters away, fetch a bucket of water, dip in a twig broom and sprinkle water on the fibers that came out of the loom until their weight would add up to 750 kilos.

The practice was a novelty, certainly not possible at the factory, and one could only guess how the guard would react. The old guard understood everything at once but kept silent. Different people came to collect the hemp from the factory, but no one ever questioned the document stating it was 750 kilograms. Some of them would even give me a wink, as if to say "Well, that's how it is!"

I was the youngest in the brigade, so it fell on me to run from the truck on which the hemp was loaded to the ditch and back. It was fifty degrees

Celsius; my legs were giving way, at times darkness would settle in before my eyes. It seemed, one more step and I'd collapse dead. And so it went, day in and day out.

Two weeks later, just as we were in the middle of dampening the hemp, the old guard called out to us. I turned around and saw our technical supervisor Portnov galloping on his horse in our direction. It was too late to throw away the bucket and the broom. I was caught red-handed. Portnov pulled up the horse alongside me.

"I could expect this from anyone else, but not from you!" he said without dismounting.

He rode on, but I stood still, nailed to the spot. I would have gladly sunk into the earth from shame, such a familiar burning feeling! I could have begged, "Please understand: it's only to keep ourselves alive!" But wasn't that obvious?

The women were alarmed and puzzled by what would happen next. Downcast, we dragged ourselves back to the camp. After work, all brigade leaders had to attend a meeting to get bread ration authorizations. I walked in, feeling as if I were going to be pilloried. Waiting for the supervisor to accuse me of cheating in front of everyone, I consoled myself only with the fact that at least I would be demoted from the position, which would relieve my soul and ease my life. But without saying a word he signed the bread permit.

What were we supposed to do the next day? Hunger was our Scylla, conscience was my Charybdis, and we were caught in between.

I received the bread for my brigade. The next day we continued to sprinkle the hemp to get at least 500 grams of bread.

At the end of the shift the brigade orderly had to crawl through a narrow slit under the loom and, lying on her back, extract the hemp fibers from the teeth of the machine. In this steel frame one could not move. To switch on the machine while it was being cleaned meant to cripple or kill the person lying underneath.

My turn came to be on duty. I was lying under the machine when I suddenly heard a deafening roar. The loom started; my hand was reeled into the gear. I lost consciousness. When I came to, all was quiet. The women pulled me out. My fingers were badly injured, my right hand bleeding profusely.

Only one woman from our brigade could turn on the machine—Yulya Eckert. Her hateful look followed me everywhere. She had been among those frightening parchment shadows that we first saw when we came to the camp. By now, she was the only one of them still alive. She managed to survive and worked in the brigade, but her strength was visibly melting away. Yulya was looking for someone to take revenge on. I was the brigade leader, and though my ribs, too, jutted out from starvation in her eyes I was luckier than she was.

I finally managed to stop the bleeding. I was expecting to hear words of sympathy; instead, Margarita Frantseva approached me and said, "You shouldn't be angry with her, Tamara." I knew that myself. Ours was a shared misery. But still…

Trying to escape stuffiness and hordes of bedbugs, we would often leave the barracks and sleep on the ground. After the incident, Yulya had softened and tried to get closer to me. A couple of days later, when we woke up in the morning, we found Yulya dead. How right were the women who had more pity for her than for me!

ONE DAY there was no bread delivery to the camp, then two days, then three. Twice a day we were given only a bowl of thin *balanda*. The camp commandant issued an instruction not to send people to work.

We couldn't fall asleep. The barracks doors were wide open. The steppe resonated in the distance. The commandant's voice was heard through the open doors. He was in his office, talking over the phone to the town officials: "…Five days and no bread! The camp isn't working! I can't let people starve behind the barbed wire… If you don't ship bread tomorrow, I'll open the gates and set them all free, everyone who's still able to stand on their feet! Let them all go wherever they want…"

The commandant was young and we hardly ever saw him in the zone. I remembered one night, while inspecting the camp, he called on our barracks with a female graduate of the Medical Institute who worked here as a doctor. The young woman wore a pink dress; he was wearing his uniform. I peered out at them from my corner on the upper bunk. I thought I was dreaming it. They were so young, and it was obvious they were happy together. I blessed them in my mind.

Soon the bread was delivered, and we started to work again, until everything grew dark before our eyes.

We went to work in tattered bras and filthy, faded knickers. The rest of the clothes some of us might still have retained were burnt by the sun. My "sun-dress," which I cut out from the lining of my coat, was living out the rest of its days. The absurd look of our brigade was only made stranger by the French and German speech mixed into our Russian, and by the armed guard accompanying us to work.

On our way back to the zone, completely exhausted, we had to pass through the settlement. The locals stood watching, shaking their heads. Compassionate souls couldn't bear the view and every now and then would throw each of us a cucumber.

Once a private car pulled up by the elm tree behind the camp gates, the only tree in the entire settlement. The women became agitated, trying to guess which of them was about to have a visitor. A ridiculous thought occurred to me: it must be my interrogator!

I looked at the car once again. It was really him. I saw his face behind the windshield. His intent look followed the half-naked brigade passing in front of him, but he recognized no one. I could muster no feelings of anger or hatred toward him.

Every now and then commissions would arrive from the city. Each time we had to line up and answer their questions.

"Any complaints? Bedbugs? Lice?"

We stood in silence. I can't remember anyone ever mentioning that bedbugs and lice swarmed over the barracks and our clothing. Nothing would make any difference.

During one such inspection I heard the voice of a civilian woman from a group of officials standing nearby:

"Which one is Petkevich?"

Strange eyes scrutinized me with undue familiarity. Under her gaze I felt what I really was: neglected, scraggy, infinitely far off from the world to which that woman belonged. I almost thought that maybe someone from the Medical Institute had sent her to find out about me, but it was too far from being true.

Much later I found out that the woman was the director of the medical unit in the camp where Erik worked. She was curious to see me, his wife, whose place she had now taken. But ignorance spared me back then.

One day I was notified that somebody had sent me money. I could hardly believe the news: I had waited in vain for so long. I turned in the direction of the town and thanked Barbara Ionovna for not forsaking me. "I knew you were thinking about me," I whispered into the wind. And then a letter came. Barbara Ionovna asked how I was doing and described how difficult things were for her.

Letters from Erik came sporadically. Sometimes he wrote in torrents, sometimes there would be a long pause. I found bitter explanations for this: when he didn't write, he was fine, and when he did, it was because he felt lonely. He never complained about his life. He had a successful practice as a doctor and shared with me how many prisoners and civilians he had already operated on, including the camp commandant himself.

BREAD WAS DELIVERED irregularly: "It's war!" was the only explanation. It became more and more difficult to get up and go to work, hunger and filth made it harder to breathe, the hemp needles constantly stung our bodies. Life was drying up. Had someone asked me what wellspring of life-hope I found to sustain me, I wouldn't have known what to say. But then, despite life's logic, I would remember the moonlit nights of the steppe, the strange feeling of being close to some godly spheres. The steppe and those nights were a temple of sorts. During night shifts we would find ourselves in the heart of the Asiatic landscape. It was filled with the rustling of sands, grasses, the droning of cicadas. At one moment hunger carried you off into unconsciousness; at another it elevated you, and you felt as if you were ascending into the universe. The earth lovingly beckoned the resonant moonlight down to her, nourishing herself from it, bathing in it, absorbing it. I saw the height of these nights and understood: it's grand and inaccessible, but it exists. After work, falling asleep in the barracks, I dreamed at least once of overcoming the exhaustion, of breaking through slumber and entering the kingdom of these great nights.

Every time I shuffled back to the zone after the day's shift I would sit on the ground, leaning against the barracks wall, and gaze without any thought or feeling through the barbed wire into the steppe expanse. I watched the glaring air vibrate and settle itself for the night. I clearly saw bizarre silhouettes of houses and roofs in the distance. They piled on top of each other, and the sight of a hazy reddish city was thrilling. It was the Fata Morgana of the steppe, an inconceivable mystery.

One evening after work, the technical supervisor came into the barracks. We were all lying motionless on the planks, trying to conserve our last bits of energy.

"Who wants to go work at the *sovkhoz*? They need to build a new vegetable storehouse. They'll feed you."

After a pause, about seven women agreed to go.

"What about you?" he turned to me.

I knew this meant a chance to survive, but it was so hard to force myself to move. I sensed I was personally marked by some sign of life, and overcoming the desire to stay put, I crawled down from the boards.

It was seven o'clock in the evening and the heat had backed down. At the farm they explained that first we had to make the bricks. We dug a pit and kneaded clay. Some fetched water, others dug out the foundation. We worked at our own pace, without any norms to fulfil, no guards watching over us. We could hear children's voices, the peaceful rattle of buckets and milk churns. A woman had just milked her cow and was coming back to her house; a baby started crying; the lights went out in one of the clay huts. Ordinary human life! Was there still such a thing in the world?

The members of the *sovkhoz* were pleased with our work, and it was already dark by the time they invited us to sit down at a table under a canopy in the yard. Each of us received 200 grams of bread. Some people brought salt, watermelons and cucumbers. We had long since forgotten such things.

In the morning there was the usual wake-up call and work in the field. "Will they come and call us again in the evening?"

The collective farm workers got used to us. Each of us now had her own patron who would slip a rotten potato or even a piece of melon into our hands. Once they even treated us to macaroni; completely unbelievable was the invitation to use their *banya*. It was ages since we last washed: there was no water in the camp for that purpose. The only thing you could do was to steam your rags and get rid of the vermin for a short while.

I knew there were interesting people around me but could find neither the energy nor the desire to talk to them. One person, however, managed to break through my silence. It was our orderly, Evgenia Karlovna, a thrifty and obliging old woman. She didn't go to work but instead kept our barracks tidy as much as was possible without water. Once, while I was at work, she replaced the straw in my pillow with hay so that I would lie more softly. Another day she saved some hot water for me. When I returned from work to the barracks, she would greet me with a joyful cry: "Finally!" Her attention came out of nowhere, for no good reason, and it felt strange to know that someone was waiting for me in the barracks, that someone cared about how much bread I had managed to earn. In the depth of my heart I felt guilty for not being responsive enough.

Evgenia Karlovna told me about her family drama. She worshipped her daughter and loved her husband. "One evening I was sitting at home waiting for my husband to come back from work. I had wrapped his dinner in a blanket to keep it warm. It was already very late when he finally came and stood in the doorway. He locked the door and said: 'Sit down. I have to tell you something. I have syphilis.'" As she was telling me her story, she wept as much as she must have wept back then. I pitied her.

In November a new transport was put together, with my name on the list. I was afraid of the journey, of the new place and the criminals. I wrapped my woolen jacket and shoes in my overcoat without lining and was ready to go when the work distributor approached me and said that the technical supervisor wanted to see me in his office.

After the incident with the moistened hemp fibers I only saw him when he sanctioned the bread rations or called us to work in the *sovkhoz*. He had never spoken to me, and of course, I didn't dare speak to him myself.

When I came in, Portnov looked tired and gloomy. He offered me a seat and came straight to the point:

"You're being sent off with the transport because I insisted."

I didn't know what to say.

"You've got to be more careful choosing friends. Do you know what I'm talking about? Someone from the NKVD was interested in you. Your friend Evgenia Karlovna informs him in full detail about everything you've shared with her. Believe me, the best thing for you now is to go somewhere else. I only wish you well. And don't make the same mistakes again!"

The guards outside were already lining up those leaving with the transport. I stood up and thanked Portnov.

"Wait," he said.

He went behind the partition and came back with a pair of woolen socks.

"It's winter. I don't know where you'll wind up. Take these. They're my extra pair. God bless you!"

He came closer, put the socks in my hands and kissed me on the forehead, looking at me with warmth and kindness.

"If only everything could turn out well for you, you dear girl!"

I wept bitterly and painfully, pressing the socks to my breast.

Evgenia Karlovna was among those who came to say good-bye.

THE TRANSPORT set off into the night.

As on the first journey, the coils of tumbleweed swept over the steppe. The escort was lenient. The watchdogs barked, but later even they became quiet. The wind abated and the stars came out. The twinkling dome of the sky seemed cool and comforting. Our footsteps swished in the sand.

We put a great distance behind us. The turmoil in my soul had grown into humility. As I walked I kept thinking of the man who had once caught me cheating but now decided to protect me. I was thinking of the woolen socks he had just given to me, of the donor ration that Chinghiz had given me at the courthouse, about the intricate blend of Good and Evil, of the need to grasp it all together, of my own inability to do so.

To think about Erik was especially hard. He had written that an NKVD officer didn't know how to thank him for the successful surgery, that the commandant of his camp was ready to do anything for him after he had saved him from appendicitis. I thought, if they're all so eager to help him, why doesn't he ask to transfer me to his camp, or at least somewhere else where conditions would be better? But right away I reproached myself, repeating: "No! I don't need anything from anyone! I'll get through this on my own!" I knew I was condemned to go through the dark thickness of misery by myself.

On that night transport from Djangi-Djir, a strange fancy or, perhaps, a distant hope arose in me: someday I'll tell all this to someone in such a way that at the moment I myself wasn't able to understand; maybe to a child, or perhaps to a man who would listen to me. Maybe to other people, too, but I will definitely speak of what I had seen and lived through. It was both the smallest and the greatest feeling of all, like the first aspiration of one's soul, making everything else in the world seem less significant.

The sand got into our shoes and rubbed wounds on our feet. It was impossible to imagine what the end of the journey would feel like. Nothing existed anymore except exhaustion.

Many people plodded along in those times either to the front or to the camps, with their souls deeply plunged into similar wells of desperation. The former worlds were breaking apart, new faiths were being born. Never had I felt God as close as I did then.

From two camps that lay on our way more prisoners were added to our column.

It wasn't until the following evening that we finally reached Frunze.

It seemed that at the last moment we would turn away, walk around the town without even seeing it. But our way to the prison lay along one of the town's main streets. Townspeople stepped aside and stood by the curb, giving way to our column.

It was hard once again to be in town, to see normal life, to know that a couple of blocks away, in Barbara Ionovna's house her family was now sitting down at a table to have dinner or just to chat.

All of a sudden I saw one of my former classmates from the Medical Institute. She was walking in our direction, arm in arm with a young man. Over her shoulders was the same white boa she had always worn for lectures. My heart hammered violently. She would now recognize me and… Will she call me or maybe even try to come closer? Will she at least be surprised to see me? We were already walking almost alongside each other… She glanced at our column. For a moment our eyes met, but she didn't recognize me, didn't show any interest in the procession. I came to my senses: my God, how was she supposed to recognize me? I was just part of a ragged crowd driven by escort guards. Free people could see us only as a faceless mass, bizarre and uncomfortably out of place.

IN THE MORNING the warder of the town prison walked into the cell, yelling, "You're going to the storehouse to sort out potatoes! *Bytoviki*—step out!" Only a few volunteered, so when he turned to the 58-ers, I made up my mind to go.

The most incredible things happen in prison and war.

After we walked several blocks, we came to the street where my mother-in-law lived. I could already see her house. There still was a chance we could make a turn to the left or to the right and leave the street behind; we could still walk through the upper or lower part of the town. But no, we were walking directly toward Barbara Ionovna's house.

Until that moment I didn't know the pain that was frozen inside me. I trembled and shook with sobs. I used to live here! There was the garden where Erik called me to see the apple trees, the same garden where I used to hide to calm down when we quarreled. Now I was being led past under guard without the right to stop and walk inside…

"Shhh! Quiet! Calm yourself!" begged the women and held tight to my elbows.

In front of the house squatted Tatochka, digging in the sand with a shovel.

"Tatochka, run and tell your grandma, Tamara is here!" the women called hastily to the little girl.

The girl stood up, looked seriously at the strange-looking women and said trustingly: "Our Tamara is gone!"

At that moment I saw Lina in the window, nursing her second child. The women waved to her and signaled at me, but we had already left the house behind.

When Tatochka nevertheless relayed the message, "The aunties said Tamara is being led by," Lina understood what the matter was. Half an hour later her head appeared above the fence of the storehouse where we were brought to sort potatoes. She approached and handed me a hunk of bread.

"Tomorrow we'll bring you a parcel to the prison," she said.

Her voice was cold. I realized again with clarity: I was erased from the life of this family once and for all. It was me whom they blamed for everything that had happened. I waited for the promised parcel, but in vain.

THE NEXT MORNING the transport was assembled. When we were lined up, eight abreast, I could see neither the head nor the tail of the column. The escort was reinforced, and the dogs growled and barked and tugged restlessly at their leashes. It was the first time I had been in such a large transport.

We were given the same shoes made of hemp, but this time we had to take a cobblestone road.

Suddenly, from one of the lower streets of the town, I saw Barbara Ionovna running in our direction. Her gray hair was uncombed. She threw back her head and yelled, "Ta-ma-ra! Ta-ma-ra!" That scream went deep into my heart, turning everything in it upside down. My bond with life was restored! I was so tired of living without warmth that when I heard Barbara Ionovna's voice I wanted to fall down, to crouch by the roadside, to let the column pass on and utter just one word to her: Thank you!

She tried to break through the crowd but the guard shoved her roughly aside with his rifle. She staggered and stayed standing at the side of the road, following us with her eyes.

I don't remember how many *versts* we walked. The cobbles quickly wore through the soles of my shoes, turning them into rags. Many were already walking barefoot. When we came to a halt I remembered Portnov's gift, but it was too late; the socks couldn't help anymore. The pain was unbearable. No one paid attention to our groans. The guards, vigilant and wary of escapees, drove us on and on without stopping. The transport had to reach its destination before nightfall.

We were only some hundred meters away from the Novotroitsk camp when I lost consciousness. I don't know who dragged me in through the gate.

It was a huge barracks, with rows of double plank beds lined up along the walls. I noticed it was filled with both women and men. A night bucket, one for everybody, was brought in and put by the door. The door was locked from the inside.

Next to me on the plank bed sat a young woman. She wept, and her feet were bleeding too.

"Fifty-eight?" she asked me.

"Yes. What's your name?"

"Sonya Blyakher, also fifty-eight."

We sat together, wrapped in one coat, shivering from cold and pain. There was tumult and cursing. Not everyone was exhausted! The criminals immediately grasped the situation.

"Get ready! Let's get your grub!"

There were many Kirghiz women on our transport who received sacks of food from their relatives living nearby. About eight men went after them, tearing at their possessions. The women screamed, bit and clutched onto their sacks. The "chevaliers" became enraged. They ripped the resisting women from their plank beds and dragged them into the middle of the barracks. The sacks were kicked aside. They stripped one, two, five Kirghiz women, hurled them on the floor and raped them. A heap of bodies was formed. More and more joined in. Something bestial overtook them and spread on to the others. Women's screams were drowned out by coarse laughing and inhuman panting…

Sonya collapsed in a strange, soundless hysteria. She dug into me with her fingernails. We crawled into the darkest corner, only wishing to turn into nothing, to dust, to smoke, so that no one could see us, so that we wouldn't see or hear anything. But I saw… Five men were coming toward us from the opposite end of the barracks. What should we do? Beg them? Scream? Appeal to their consciences? No! Kill! Kill them and ourselves!

The barracks door remained locked, though some tried to hammer on it and call for help…

The five men came closer and closer. Finally they were upon us and… sat on the plank bed.

There was nothing except the quick feeling that they came to protect us.

"Article?" asked one, turning his face to us.

"Fifty-eight," I exhaled.

"Where from?"

"Sonya—from Moldavanka. Myself—from Djangi-Djir. You?"

"Tokmak."

"Then you must know my husband!"

"What's his name?"

"Erik."

"That's our doctor! You're his wife? That's right! We've seen your photograph. You look like… almost like in that picture. He was also supposed to be on this transport. But he was kept back there by… well, anyway, he was kept there. You might've met here…"

The conversation became a support. I could finally take a breath. Providence had, at least for today, spared me from that which was worse than death.

THE DOOR WAS OPENED in the morning. Names were read out and the barracks were emptied. The "night masters" also left. Sonya and I stayed inside. We weren't able to walk anyway. Silence fell and we plunged into sleep.

It would've taken me a long time to come back to my senses after that night, but from the bunk above I heard a conversation between two men. They spoke in muted voices.

"How long have you been in the Party?"

"Since 1918."

"So how did you survive '37?"

"I don't know myself. And you?"

"Since 1920."

"Tell me, do you understand what's going on?"

"What's there to understand? The NKVD receives orders: so many railroads have to be built in Komi or in the East, so much lead has to be mined. So they find free manpower, like you and me, like the others..."

"Don't talk nonsense. There has to be another reason."

"It's not nonsense, brother, it's a fact."

"Does He himself know?"

"Of course! How would He not know? What do you think?"

"It's crazy."

"There you are!"

I saw them again later, when we went on the transport. They were both in their fifties, their faces furrowed with wrinkles. Communists since 1918 and 1920! One wore a sailor's shirt under his jacket. They, too, lived through the night of mass rape, common night bucket for men and women, foul cries of hatred and sinister laughter. Which of their historical remembrances would they add that night to? In any case, they hadn't stood up for anyone.

Nothing could erase their dialogue from my memory. There was something monstrous in their exchange of hypotheses. They spoke of Stalin as if he were the leader of a gang. The madness and impossible vigor of the five-year plans was directly related to arbitrary arrests and ten-year sentences by the NKVD, who turned those they didn't like into mere work stock. I tried to shove off the incredible conjectures that the intentional transformation of a great many people into cattle for the benefit of others was what the new society was about. The society my father and mother had fought for!

Over the next month and a half I went from one *sovkhoz* in Kirghizia to another, on five different transports. The fields were all under the snow. We harvested frozen cabbages with cleavers, tore turnips from the ground, loaded stone-heavy white beets onto flat wagons.

In one camp I met Polina, my cellmate from the NKVD inner prison. She was just as undaunted and cheerful as before. She told me about her "hero," in whom she had found the love of her life. In the evening she introduced us. It was one of the five men who had saved Sonya and me in the Novotroitsk camp. Now I saw him as a kind and retiring man, although the aftertaste of the circumstances in which we had first seen each other was embarrassing. I suffered because I didn't manage to find the right words to express what I felt toward him, which extended beyond gratitude. Apparently it was he who had taken the initiative to come to our help that night.

In my short life there had already formed a group of people, whom I scarcely knew, who had given me the right to consider this world suitable for living. Thanks to Chinghiz, to the technical supervisor Portnov, and to those five men in the barracks, I once again found faith in humanity.

THE BELOVODSK CAMP, where I came to stay for a long time, lay by the Tien Shan Mountains. Whether Belovodsk itself was a settlement or a small town I never found out. The camp was divided into a male and a female zone. All the facilities—the kitchen, the bathhouse, the medical unit and the administration office—were in the men's zone, which also had five living barracks. The women's zone consisted of only one elongated building with tiny mica windows.

We arrived on a cold, grim day. It was raining. The barracks was dug into the earth; water and mud flowed in. Climbing down to the floor from the plank bed, one stood ankle-deep in mud.

The local old-timers huddled on the upper bunks, evaluating every newcomer who descended over the slippery steps into the barracks. In Djangi-Djir there had been only politicals, but here the camp was run by the criminals.

"What a dear little thing! Look at that!" one of them pointed at me.

A kerosene lamp burned inside the dark dirty barracks. The air was thick with intricate cursing. I found a place on the upper bunk. There were no mattresses or pillows. I put my bundle with my shoes and woolen sweater under my head. Every time I thought of exchanging that sweater for bread back in Djangi-Djir, the women stopped me, warning me about the winter cold.

It was still dark when someone woke me up. I saw a gang of petty thieves crowding on the lower bunks, as was prescribed by the criminal ordinance. With hideous grimaces and contortions, they looked like swamp creatures. They danced on a plank that was laid on the floor, parading the items they had just stolen from the newcomers. One of them wore my shoes; another was dressed in my woolen sweater.

In the morning I saw that several bunks were disassembled at the end of the barracks; six or eight real beds stood in their place, each covered with a feather mattress and a couple of fluffy pillows. Alongside the beds stood a cast-iron stove, which dried the surrounding floorboards. The privileged members of the barracks lived there. Whatever the "biggies" ordered was carried out on the spot by their obsequious "maids."

A woman with a broad worn-out face approached and told me in a hoarse voice that she was the brigade leader and that I had been attached to her brigade. Her name was Anya Fyodorova. The brigade had to dig a foundation pit for the sugar factory evacuated here from Kharkov.

We worked down in the pit. Steel gangplanks leading upward were laid along the bottoms of each of the pit's levels. The clay soil clung to the wheels of the barrows and our pathetic footwear. It took an enormous amount of energy to push a wheelbarrow laden with earth to the top. The norms were high. We had to strain every nerve to earn a six- or seven-hundred-gram bread ration.

A hundred meters away the criminals sat in a circle and played cards. Their stakes were not only money but also human lives. By the end of the day, whoever lost the game had to kill the person he'd been playing for. The victim would be stabbed and quickly buried. Relying on the guards' protection was useless. The guards and the criminals got along very well. To keep the number of prisoners correct upon return to the camp, it was said that the guards would dig out the stabbed corpse, shoot the dead body and hand it in, announcing that the man had attempted an escape.

Everybody who was digging the earth knew that at any moment the gruesome lottery could turn him into a corpse. There was nothing left for the fear-laden consciousness other than to get by with bravado: life or death—nothing worth thinking about!

I'd already been in the camp for two weeks. Bread rations were distributed by the brigade leaders. One day, after all the large pieces had been taken, Anya Fyodorova looked straight into my eyes and gave me four hundred grams of bread instead of the seven hundred I had earned. I had only one moment to protest. I had to establish myself once and for all at any price! But I let that moment pass by, losing far more than I could realize then.

I knew that in exchange for her own safety Anya had to give the bread taken away from us to the "biggies," the actual bosses of the stinking lodgings. It was commonplace to steal and to barter, to lash out and be friends again, to rule and lay down the law. I heard the curses but didn't take them in. I saw how the women adjusted to each other and to their life in the barracks. Many who had never let a filthy word pass their lips were now quickly mastering the jargon, submitting to the spirit of the camp. As I instinctively held myself away from the vicious crowd, I was only becoming a target of open hostility.

I was happy to be transferred to another brigade, which had to clear stones from an area where railroad tracks would be laid, leading to a factory being built nearby. The stones were sixteen to twenty kilograms each and we had to load them onto a flat wagon and push it to the unloading place. My new brigade consisted of robust criminals, and I made every effort not to lag behind. My heart skipped a beat in dreadful apprehension when one of them got worked up:

"Look at our dear little thing! Well done! Look how she hauls ass! She can push the wagon on her own!"

I had to come up with some witty rejoinder, but I said nothing. Once again the moment found me tongue-tied. I kept pushing the wagon loaded with heavy stones, a guard standing on top of it. He looked past me as if he saw nothing. The women roared and cursed:

"Go, bitch! Push, push! Come on, bitch, push!"

The sinister entertainment urged them on.

"Kick 'er in the ass till she pushes faster!"

They had taken their hands off the wagon and were now walking behind me. I pushed the wagon another couple of meters and sank to the ground.

The brigade took a short break to smoke. It seemed the criminals forgot about me. But I knew all too well that this was not the end.

According to a decree passed during the war, it was a serious offense to leave work without permission or to be late for work. The machines at the factories were usually operated by fifteen- or sixteen-year-olds, mainly girls. Many couldn't stand the hard work and ran away. They would be sentenced to five years and sent to the camps. They were known as "Decree girls." Their parents often visited them, bringing them food, which the criminals immediately stole. The girls would weep and beg the criminals to return their parcels, but were only laughed at.

I was lying on my plank bed semiconscious as usual, when a brawl started in the barracks. A girl was weeping because someone had stolen her parcel. Nothing special, but the girl turned out to be a smart one; she quickly figured out what to do. She went to the far end of the barracks and complained to the bosses. They accepted her complaint and the show began. "We'll find your parcel!" they promised. Naked females, armed with wood planks broken off the beds, went to "restore law and order" in front of everyone's eyes.

The thief would be beaten with the edge of a plank until her bones cracked. Then the sack of bones would be carried away.

"It's her!" shrieked one of the women, pointing in my direction. "She stole it!"

They moved toward me, taking up their positions in a circle to beat up the thief so that the entire barracks could see.

A deadly chill tore through me from heart to stomach. Paralyzed, I was frozen on my bunk. So this is what my end is going to be like, I thought.

"There's the parcel!" suddenly someone else called from below.

The "judges" reluctantly turned around. They dragged out the sack from under the lower bunk and took it with them to their hideout in the far corner of the barracks to devour the food. The "Decree girl" followed her rescuers to feast with them.

I lay on my bunk, falling in and out of consciousness. The horror didn't let me go. I had almost experienced death again, just like in the city prison when, covered with a blanket, I was led through the corridors. I was nearly killed as a thief. That was the edge, the outer limit…

Every morning, before going to work, when we were assembled and counted and told that anyone who tried to escape would be shot on the spot, the foreman walked around our column with his special springy step. He wore a canvas overcoat with a hood and held a notebook in his hand. With his clear dark eyes he appraised everyone, evaluating our working capacity and instructing the brigade leaders. He was a Bulgarian named Khristofor Rodionovich Ergiev.

One day he called me out from the column:

"You're going to Baturin's brigade," he said.

Then, in a loud voice, he addressed Baturin:

"Baturin, you're taking this girl!"

"In my brigade it's work!" the brigade leader protested.

"So, she'll work."

"We carry bricks!" Baturin said to me.

"I'll carry bricks," I promised.

Grisha Baturin was a thorough brigade leader, "with principles," as he said himself; a cunning little man with a thin feminine voice, nimble and kind. No one argued with him, and the bread was divided fairly. His brigade, mostly men and a few women, worked on the construction site of the future factory. It was called a "cordon zone" because, instead of breathing down our neck, the guards here encircled a huge territory, where several brigades worked at the same time. Here I could actually fulfill the meager norm to sustain my life.

IN BELOVODSK there was a sacred patch of land, where on their way back from work the prisoners would look to see if a relative stood waiting with a loaf of bread. Nearly every night I dreamed that Barbara Ionovna came and brought the longed-for loaf. To wait for her became an obsession.

Unlike Djangi-Djir, the Belovodsk camp stood near the railroad, but bread was delivered here just as irregularly, and once none came for several days in a row. The local camp commandant didn't yell into the phone receiver that he would set the hungry prisoners free; we were sent to work as usual.

On the third day, long before reveille, I was awakened by shuffling and whispers:

"We're not going to work then... No one works today!"

Several women set out to nail shut the barracks door from the inside. It was inconceivable where they got a hammer and nails, since the barracks was searched daily.

"Are we all in?" asked the ringleaders.

There were women in the barracks whom I had underestimated, no matter that they were criminals. People rebelled, they tried to protest—a real strike! It seemed everyone breathed to the same rhythm; even at the far corner of the barracks, with its feather beds and fluffy pillows, it became quiet.

The ones by the little mica window reported, "The men went out... assembled... they're looking at our barracks... waiting for us to come out. Exchanging glances... they understand something's going on..."

We held our breath when they whispered:

"It's over! The work distributor and the warden are coming!"

There was hammering against the barracks door from the outside, but the door didn't give way. They realized it was nailed up.

"Open up! You hear? You'll regret this! Open up now!"

"We won't open until you give us bread!" called the women. "We're not going to work without bread!"

From the observation point by the window the women reported:

"They're going back to the men's zone... The men have already left for work."

And then:

"They're coming back... With axes and crowbars!"

The spirit of the strike in the bawdy barracks transformed and mobilized both the strong and the weak. Everyone was ready to fight.

The door gave way under the blows of axes. In a moment it creaked and fell into splinters. The camp administration walked in.

"Who is the ringleader? Step forward!"

It wasn't hard to imagine what would happen next. The first batch, six women, was taken to the Third Department, then another six. Then the guards came back to the barracks and led the women who had nailed up the door to the punishment cells.

"Cheap whores!" they cursed as they were leaving.

The unity that had formed just two hours ago was now trampled under the same old lashing fear. But faith in people capable of resistance, albeit of a most pathetic type, had nevertheless returned to me.

When the men came back from work, shamed, furious and hungry, tumult broke out in their zone. We could hear screams, and soon warning shots rang out from the watchtowers. The men didn't calm down until the nightfall.

The next day bread was delivered, but I could no longer stand on my feet.

THE INFIRMARY I was brought to was overfilled. On the trestle-beds, jammed up against each other, were emaciated men and women with white-yellow-greenish faces. The medical barracks was dug into the earth. The meager ration, not to mention the lack of real medicine, wouldn't help anyone to recover. One might only hope to sleep a bit and rest from work. It was cold, and the thin gray blanket, which I pulled up to my chin, didn't make it any warmer.

Next to me lay the skinny woman who had once stolen my skirt but then protected me from the frightful beating. I wanted to ask her why she had done so, but I knew she would only snarl back at me. For her, it was easier to act out of pity than to explain where the feeling came from.

It was March. There came a nipping frost.

On my fourth day in the infirmary, already late at night, a transport arrived from Belovodsk. The prisoners wore ragged clothes, totally unfit for the weather. People with frostbitten hands, feet and faces were dragged in, many of them unconscious.

One face seemed familiar. It took me some time to realize it was Portnov, the technical supervisor from Djangi-Djir. He was too weak to open his eyes. What had happened to him over these three months? Why was he put on a transport? That moment I wished only one thing: to find a piece of bread and a cup of sweet tea to give to him. How abominable the powerlessness of a pauper!

An old Uzbek man occupied the bed beside me. He was always asking for water, as was the neighbor on my right. A few nights I managed to overcome exhaustion, get to my feet and pour some water into their mouths. But once, when I woke up in the middle of the night, on both sides of me lay corpses. They were put on stretchers and carried away.

Portnov tossed about in his trestle-bed. I sat on the edge of my bed, desperately trying to come up with something. I couldn't stay in this deadly cellar any longer, but the thought of having to go back to work in that cold made my blood chill. It was hopeless to wait for help. I had to pull my last bits of strength together and try to earn a bigger ration. If I made eight hundred grams of bread, I could keep five hundred for myself and bring another three hundred to Portnov. No, six hundred for myself and two for Portnov... Whether out of mere delirium or some trace of my will to live, I came to a firm decision: I would help Portnov, a man in trouble, just as he had helped me a few months ago. At my own request I was discharged from the infirmary.

In order to earn a record ration, one had to carry as many as fifteen bricks from the warehouse to the worksite at a time. I managed to pick up seven and counted the steps. Not a single unnecessary move; only the bricks and the steps. "It's only hard on the first day. Then I'll have my fill of bread and it'll be easier," I urged myself.

The way led across the tracks of a narrow-gauge railway. The most difficult part was to cross the tracks, holding the bricks. I stumbled over the rails and fell to the ground with my entire load. I lay on the ground completely indifferent, not even trying to get up, looking up at the blue sky...

Someone stood beside me. I saw top boots, then the flap of a canvas overcoat. The stranger squatted in front of me.

"How old are you?" he asked.

"Twenty-three."

"What's your term?"

"Seven years," I answered mechanically, lying across the rails.

"Article?"

"Fifty-eight."

"I see... Will you agree to work as a standardizer at the factory? Let me help you up. Let's go see your brigade leader. Where is he?"

The man helped me to my feet. I didn't believe a word he said.

Apparently, the administration of the construction had asked the camp chiefs to transfer a few specialists to the site. They would even pay the camp fifteen and a half rubles a day per every skilled worker. Both sides benefited from such trade, since it didn't require any concessions to the camp regime. Prisoners and free workers mingled together on the construction site anyway. But what did I have to do with all that? I wasn't a specialist.

The man's name was Vasily Ivanovich Lukash. A native of Kharkov, he was hired to work here as the chief engineer. After he talked to the brigade leader, Baturin went to the camp commandant and told him about the offer. Soon I was transferred to the factory.

Lukash introduced me to the chief standardizer, who showed me around the metalworks and the machine shop, explained the work procedures, and instructed me on what the various components were used for. They asked me to perform a couple of tasks and, in the end, were satisfied with my results.

I thought of Vasily Lukash as my guardian angel. My life changed from the ground up. In the morning I would leave the camp with everyone else, but then I'd go straight to the office. Rain, snow and wind were now always behind the window. I was acquiring a new profession, never mind what kind.

IN THE OFFICE there was a loudspeaker. The employees gathered here to listen to the synopses of the Information Bureau. Letters from relatives fighting at the front were read, as well as names of soldiers and officers killed in the battles. The war was now as real for me as for everybody else in the country.

In 1944, even those men who had an exemption were drafted into the army, including my guardian angel Lukash. I was embarrassed to remind him of myself. But one day he saw me at the factory and approached me himself.

"I'm leaving for the front. I asked my assistant to keep you on the job. Don't worry, everything will be all right."

In my inner paralysis I couldn't find the right words to thank him; I couldn't tell him what was really in my heart: Come back safe, you good man!

Soon call-up papers came for his assistant as well, but he didn't forget to pass Lukash's request on to his successor.

I didn't mind the long workday. It only depressed me when in the evening I had to go back to the camp.

Once I was in the forge when the siren sounded for midday break. Everyone left, but I stayed inside and sat down in a dark corner to eat my ration.

Outside two men were speaking:

"Who is her husband?" asked one.

Their conversation brought to memory my first morning in Belovodsk, when before sending us to work, the work distributor called out: "Who is

Petkevich?" I made a step forward. "Let's go," he said mysteriously. "Your man is waiting for you in the zone."

My heart ached. Fearing that Erik wouldn't recognize me, I followed the work distributor. "Right there!" he pointed to the corner of the barracks. A man I'd never seen before was standing there. "And the one who wanted to see me, where is he?" I asked.

"It's me," said the man. "I saw you arrived yesterday with a transport. You don't remember me?" Now I recognized him: it was one of the men who protected me in the Novotroitsk camp. "My name is Pyotr Gordeev. Back then I didn't get the chance to introduce myself. Remember?"

"Of course, I remember… But why did the work distributor… Why did you call yourself my husband?"

"So what? I only wanted to help. What a character you've got!" he continued, "I'm not some gangster, I'm a construction engineer! It's true, I wanted to help. Now at least they'll know you have someone, they won't have their designs on you…" The engineer Pyotr Gordeev, an experienced prisoner, kept saying something else, but I didn't hear. Offended and perplexed, I was trying to understand his logic.

Now, sitting inside the forge, I heard him answer someone's question about my husband:

"He is a doctor, Erik Andreevich. We were in the same camp. He lives with the director of the medical unit. She really arranged everything for him: sausage as much as he can eat, she even brings him champagne to the zone."

"Sausage and champagne…" I kept repeating, "Sausage and champagne…" The next moment I couldn't breathe. A sharp pain pinned me to the wall. I realized I had become completely alone, like a tiny patch of land with the last vestiges of the harvest burnt down.

IT WAS HARD to imagine what impression an awkward type like me made in the factory office. Apart from myself, in the room worked two accountants, a clerk and a family evacuated from Leningrad, a mother and her two daughters. The elder, Nirsa, was about my age. Before the war she had studied at the conservatory. She was very pretty and we got along quite well. The free workers, who were suspicious and hostile toward me at first, now became friendlier, too.

One day Nirsa brought me a red rose. The gift startled me. It was like calling off the quarantine in which I felt I had separated myself from others for so long.

There was another person, Alfred Richardovich P., a silent and imposing old man with a neat white beard. Every once in a while he would stop by the factory office, sit down on a stool in front of me and look at me for a long time.

"Aren't you scared of him?" Nirsa once asked me in a whisper.

I wasn't. Some peace descended on me when this old man was near. Perhaps it was merely the beauty of his age that cured and calmed me. I must have reminded him of someone. Sometimes I felt that despite the almost fifty-year age difference we yearned for the same thing, something that was gone forever.

Once Alfred Richardovich came to see me during the afternoon mealtime with dried apricots and a half-liter bottle of molasses. "My children sent me this luxury. Would you share it with me?" he asked ceremoniously, almost timidly.

There were many Poles in Belovodsk at the time. They said they had been "offered" Soviet citizenship, and when they refused, they were arrested and sent to the camps. Since I was the only one who had Polish roots, though I didn't speak their language, they accepted me as one of their own and called me "Pani Tamara." The Poles didn't take the camp seriously; they regarded it only as a tool to make them scared. They firmly believed that their government would rescue them. "By Christmas we'll all be at home!" they assured each other. And after Christmas passed, they smiled: "Then by Easter!" After Easter they said: "Then by the November holidays for sure!" They stuck together and never lost their sense of humor.

For the first time in a very long while I smiled when a member of a visiting commission asked one of the Poles who knew Russian what kind of work he performed:

"I work as a locomotive," he replied.

"I don't understand," said the inspector in an irritated voice. "Please be so kind to explain."

The Pole didn't seem to be embarrassed at all and explained ironically:

"I pull a wagon loaded with stones. In place of a locomotive. *Ta-ak!*"

Another Pole, by the name of Henrik, spoke decent Russian too. In Poland he had been in charge of a forestry, which was very much in keeping with his appearance. A big good-natured bumpkin, he looked like a bear and often offered to help me.

"Do you also believe you'll be released soon?" I once asked him.

"It can't be otherwise, *nie mozhno!*" he broke into a smile.

It was beyond me to understand where their optimism came from. We Russians ate whatever was dished out to us, but the Poles rebelled: "Either you give us more, or we're not working." The Poles were allowed to buy cornmeal in the factory canteen. Not us.

When I heard them laugh and joke, I thought it was I who really understood camp life, not they. I thought the Poles were light-minded and even silly. No one would ever let them go! But I was wrong. They understood everything perfectly. Behind them they had the experience of living on the outside as free people. But what was there to rely on from my life?

MY WORK as a standardizer in the cozy office ended just as suddenly as it began. As part of the campaign to tighten the regime, an order was passed to dismiss prisoners working at the factory. Grisha Baturin encouraged me to return to his brigade, which was now working in the quarry. We had to pickaxe gravel, load it onto the wagons and haul it to the factory "in place of locomotives."

In the evening, after work, the shouts from the watchtowers would stop, the orderlies would take away the empty food vats and one could find a little time for oneself. The workers would drag themselves outside the barracks, sit leaning against the walls and doze. I too leaned against the barracks wall, stretching out my legs. The earth, warmed by the day's sunlight, soothed the exhausted body, relieved the gnawing pain. The sky would grow dark, an ocean of fresh air above. One could gaze out across the steppe endlessly. Somehow it substituted for thinking. The earth smoked and smelled of distant steppe fires.

"A transport is coming!" someone called.

Immediately a crowd started to form by the gates.

A new transport could mean the most incredible encounters. A prosecutor or interrogator could come across their former victims whom they had not so long ago thrown in prison. The camp inhabitants would immediately find out and wait to see how the relationships between the two developed. One would expect a dramatic outcome, but time did its work. Shared suffering would often make the interrogator try to justify himself before his former victim, whose desire to take revenge would also abate and lose meaning. Sometimes, of course, the camp administration had to intervene and send one of the two to a different camp.

On that spring evening the Poles were passionately greeting the new transport, meeting their compatriots and friends. Tearing their kepi from their heads, they threw them into the air.

As soon as the transport passed through the camp gate, one of the new arrivals was taken straight to the punishment block.

Next morning Henrik whispered to me:

"Yesterday they brought Beniusz, Pani Tamara. That's bad."

"Who is he, then?"

"Oh, Beniusz, he is a man of great wit! He is a little bit my friend too."

For the Poles, Beniusz wasn't just an absolute authority in their political disputes; he always knew how to cut short ordinary brawls and fights. Three days later I saw him at the factory with Henrik, wearing the same military jacket and kepi as most Poles did. He was a slim man of about forty.

"I've already heard a lot about you, Pani Tamara. I'm Juzef," he said in Russian.

Like all the Poles, he regarded the camp merely as a temporary matter. The true character of that man hid behind his sarcastic humor. He joked and teased me but, at the same time, was attentive and kind.

"How're you going to manage in Warsaw if you don't speak Polish?" he laughed. "And how did Pani end up here? She didn't show up to a May Day parade? Or maybe Pani Tamara is a real saboteur?"

All prisoners carried their eating bowls to work, tying them with a rope to their belts, which we wore over our quilted jackets. Both Henrik and Beniusz had neat military bowls made of steel. I was ashamed of my rusty tin can and always walked away to eat on my own so that they couldn't see me. Beniusz figured this out. He proposed we eat together, go to work together and come back to the zone together. "Let's be in the same *kolkhoz,* as you people say," he suggested. Whenever Beniusz managed to get an extra portion of corn porridge, no matter how hard I tried to refuse, he put some into each of our three bowls.

One day, a pipe burst in the completed area of the factory. We were all ordered to bale out the water. We were soaked to the bone. Although it was already spring, the temperature outside was below zero. We hastily lined up to get back to the barracks, our clothes frozen as stiff as tree bark. We were counted once, twice, again and again.

"Escape!" a whisper passed through the rows. "Some daredevil decided to give it a try."

Additional guards came. They were searching the factory, the pipes, the boilers and every corner. It was clear we would be kept outside until they found the fugitive. Shivering, we shifted from one foot to the other, hopping on the spot. The men boxed with each other to keep warm.

It became dark. The sky filled with stars. Henrik came up to me. "Look over there, that's my favourite star, the Vega. When we're free again… Promise to think of me when you see that star!"

Again the guards combed through the territory but couldn't find the fugitive. We were completely stiff when they finally led us back to the zone. I looked for Beniusz but didn't see him anywhere. When I finally spotted him, I waved but he didn't respond. The next morning, when we assembled for work, he didn't stand by me.

He came to see me only in the evening.

"I'm going to stop hanging around with Henrik. Yesterday I was jealous when I saw you two talking. I've never had that feeling before."

His words drove out the foulness of the camp. But the sight of the shot escapee who lay in front of the gate, his legs in the ditch, his young face turned toward us, immediately brought me back to reality. Nothing could block out the view of the stifled protest, of an executed man yearning for freedom.

EARLY IN THE MORNING, when we would arrive at the factory, there would usually be a couple of special minutes. The foothills of the Ala-Tau Mountains were covered in scarlet tulips. A brown mountain pass loomed behind, and then a quaint conglomeration of ice-capped peaks rose up in the distance. Shivering with the morning cold, I tried to catch the moment when the sun tainted them pink.

Baturin's brigade now worked on the stone-crushing machine at the factory site. One day I was carrying some bolts from the workshop. I decided to take a shortcut through a densely littered area, without paying attention to the caution signs. Suddenly I heard: "Halt!" The yell was decorated with curse words. I turned around. Not far ahead of me I saw a horse wildly thrashing in convulsion after treading on a bared electric cable. I stood still, not knowing what to do. I saw Beniusz running toward me, leaping over the cable. He took me in his arms and carried me out of the hazardous zone.

Back in the barracks, lying on my plank bed late at night, I tried to understand where the strange commotion that had been with me the whole day had come from. When Beniusz held me in his arms, pressing me close to himself, I felt, I remembered… that I had breasts, that I was a woman. The feeling was awkward and embarrassing. It didn't need to be. The karakul NKVD official had hammered into me: "Forget you're a woman!" How fluent they were in the grammar of annihilation! How absolute was their control over the destiny and the very nature of a human being! I really had forgotten.

It rained and rained. At work and in the barracks we were sunk in mud.

Somebody woke me up in the night.

"Step outside. Someone's calling you."

The rain thundered on the worn-out roof of the barracks. Dull light bulbs gleamed under the tin lids of street lamps. A dog ran back and forth along the length of the restricted area, rattling its chain and barking.

Someone was calling my name from the men's side of the camp. Behind the neutral zone and the double net of barbed wire I managed to discern a gaunt figure.

"It's me!" I heard Beniusz's voice through the rain. "They're taking me away. I came to say good-bye. I'm going free! Do you hear me?"

Free? My God! He doesn't understand anything! Doesn't he know that at night prisoners are taken away only to be shot?!

"I hear you, I hear..." I answered.

"You are so dear to me. I didn't think they'd take us away so suddenly. Good-bye! I wanted you to have my food bowl. Catch!"

The steel bowl flew over the wire and plopped into a puddle.

"Halt! Who's there?" the guard yelled from the watchtower. The beam of a searchlight swept along the wire.

"We might not see each other again... I kiss your hands. God save you!" said Beniusz hastily.

I pressed the dirty bowl to my breast and placed his words deep in my soul.

The first Polish division ever formed in the USSR was named for Tadeusz Kosciuszko. That night, a group of Poles from the Belovodsk camp were taken to the local enlistment office and were offered the opportunity to join that division. But they didn't consider it theirs. Though they had all asked to be sent to the front, Beniusz categorically declined; the rest refused after him. A few days later all the Poles were transported.

I was left perplexed by their unbending faith in their government, who they believed would never forsake them. The Poles refused to lose hope, nor would they taste humiliation. They didn't turn down their right to choose which army to serve in. I could never forget their gallantry or their ability to hide the ugliness of camp reality behind the words "God protect you!"

IN THE CAMP everything was as before: waking up, assembling single-file before setting off to work, struggling to earn the bread ration. But soon the brigade leader Grisha Baturin astounded me with a strange question. He glanced at me with his sly little eyes and mumbled in a thin voice:

"What I want to say... If I only knew how!"

"What is it, Grisha?" I asked in fear.

"You're educated, intelligent and so on... I came across a newspaper, and there was a story that crept into my soul. Would you read it aloud to everyone in the club?"

The idea seemed pure nonsense, but I took the newspaper. The story was called *The Wife,* by Elena Kononenko. It was about a soldier who was wounded at the front and lost both legs. From the hospital he wrote a letter to his wife: if she wanted to see him like this, he would come and wait for her at the train station. At the appointed time the woman rushed to the station, without feeling the ground beneath her feet. When she saw the torso of her husband, she stayed rooted to the spot. The man saw her horror and turned away. But the next moment the wife, full of compassion and pain, called his name, rushed to the crippled man and flung herself around his neck.

The story moved me. After reading it twice I was able to memorize the entire text. I had never read anything from the stage, but I told Grisha that I'd learned it all by heart.

"I knew it! At the concert Vasily will play the accordion first, and then it'll be your turn."

Stage fright had a stranglehold on me. The little club room was packed. The cries of the woman in the story became stronger than my own suffering. Later I would hear these cries at night. They revealed the depths of the war and the camps, where there was no way out other than turning one's soul inside out. As I recited the story, I saw tears in Baturin's eyes. The female criminal who had once saved me in the barracks cried too; so did the men, all the hungry and ragged workers, who filled the tiny hall.

I thanked Grisha, who had found a better use for me than the Soviet court. The attitude toward me changed, and I myself changed in a certain way too.

THE CAMP COMMANDANT who inspected our lineups for work suddenly stopped in front of me:

"A newcomer?" he asked.

"No," answered the Bulgarian foreman instead of me. "I told you about her before. She used to work at the factory as a standardizer."

"We need standardizers ourselves!" the commandant interrupted him, then turned to me and asked as if I was guilty of something: "Why haven't I seen you before?"

That same day I was given a job at the earthworks. The commandant's favor meant that now I had to set the bread ration for other prisoners like me.

When I entered the office for the first commission, my heart sank. At the table sat hardened criminals, crafty and tough men. They looked at me narrowly, trying to figure out what the strategy was in appointing me standardizer.

I measured pits and foundation trenches, but my metering results would always be a few times lower than what the brigade leaders indicated in their reports. Not so long ago I was doing the same thing, sprinkling hemp stalks in Djangi-Djir. With a heavy heart I conceded and agreed to sign the swindle, having declared to the hard-bitten jailbirds that they had to inform me about all such "additions." I was afraid, but I tried to do my best not to show any fear. Still, I dreamed of being sent back to the general works in Baturin's brigade.

When several days later an inspection came, everything seemed to have ended by itself. They ordered to send the standardizer Petkevich to the punishment block with a reduced bread ration. I rejoiced: they would finally dismiss me from the position! But they didn't.

It looked as though I took the entire blame on myself, and soon a piece of bread was smuggled for me into my cell.

When I returned to the barracks, one of the women started paying me special attention. In the evening she would offer to bring me my supper.

"No, Zhenya, thank you. I can go myself," I would protest.

"We gotta help each other, and stop your 'thank you' and 'myself.' You and I, we might end up on the same transport, after all. You're beautiful, but your clothing is good for nothing. Here, take this! And don't forget about me when somebody from the administration pays you some attention, all right?"

The vagaries of camp life were innumerable. A woman criminal sitting next to me grinned: "Let her go to hell! She steals from your ration while bringing it to you, and you guzzle it down and thank her!"

PORTNOV HAD COME DOWN with a bad case of tuberculosis and some time before was sent on a transport. A couple of times I'd managed to bring him a few pieces of bread.

From time to time people also offered me a dried crust of bread or some buttermilk, but I always refused. Though I no longer hoped to receive a letter from Erik, I still waited for Barbara Ionovna. Day after day I peered through the barbed wire at the spot before the camp gate.

On our way to work, someone's relatives would suddenly appear from behind a shed or out of a pile of logs. Aleksandr Iosifovich Klebanov's wife and sister were the most inventive. They would appear in the most unexpected places. Prisoners marching in a file tried to swap places to allow the lucky one to march on the side of the column so that he could exchange a few phrases with his family.

I was sitting by myself in a wooden shack, finishing my lunch, fishing out the last nubbins of corn porridge from the bottom of my bowl. I heard nothing except the clanging of my aluminum spoon against the tin. It wasn't until I finished eating that I raised my eyes and saw Klebanov standing in the doorway. I don't know how long he was watching me, but after that I always tried to avoid him.

One day at work I felt sick: I was very hungry. As soon as I reached the building of the workshop, I fainted. When I opened my eyes, I saw Aleksandr Iosifovich, holding a tea kettle where he had crumbled some bread.

"I only wish one thing," he said in an angry voice. "One of these days I'd like to meet your husband. I could tell him a few things."

His hot-tempered words flooded me with bitter warmth.

In the morning we found out that a transport for distant camps was being put together. This time my heart pounded especially hard. To go away, to stop waiting for letters from Erik that he didn't write anyway, to stop peering at the spot by the prison gate where I hoped to see Barbara Ionovna with a loaf of bread...

Amazed at my reawakened will, I planned to go to the work distributor and beg him to put me on the transport list. But when the next morning the foreman came to our barracks and read out the names for the transport, my name was already on the list. The thing was solved by itself.

Alongside the railroad tracks the guards had erected tents. In one of them they distributed some shabby clothes, and in another they searched us. I had kept the letters I received from Erik in Djangi-Djir. Before the female guard who conducted the search could do it, I tore them into small pieces myself. The wind picked the scraps. They whirled high into the air and settled on the Central Asian earth.

It was going to be a large transport. New batches of prisoners came from the neighboring camps. I looked to see if Erik was among them. But he had been spared.

A long train stood ready. We were loaded onto the filthy and putrid cattle cars.

Chapter 6

The transport was going north. The destination was kept secret.

No sooner had we been divided into groups and started boarding the train cars than our stamina and resourcefulness were put to the test. Within seconds the car occupants arranged themselves into a visible hierarchy. The top bunk by the little barred window was taken by Natasha Shatalova, a tall, black-eyed Armenian. Her cronies, all convicted of petty theft, settled nearby.

The escort guards ordered us to elect an elder and organize a duty roster for the night bucket. Natasha was elected. This was an apt choice, as even the guards were impressed by the beauty of this strong-willed woman. She spoke in a low mezzo-soprano voice and sang gypsy love songs. She had been imprisoned for theft during the war under the notorious Article 107.

Many thought ahead to the distant camps and imagined fertile lands, but for the time being we had to adjust to the transport and endure the journey.

In the middle of the car stood an iron stove, with a kettle on top and a few logs and a bucket of coal at its side. The floor, like the upper bunks, was covered in a thin layer of straw and served as the lower bunk. I found a spot in the corner on the floor, one of the worst. It was against the wall, and the cold made me shiver through the entire journey. Next to me sat the miserable Nelly, who never stopped babbling. She was imprisoned for petty theft but wanted us to believe she was a hardened prisoner, so she bragged about this being her second conviction and assured everyone that conditions would be much better in the North than back in Belovodsk. She held her sallow face in front of mine and boasted:

"See how fresh my skin is! I don't even need creams or make-up. I wash my face with urine!"

Some of the women were withdrawn and silent but most had rowdy, unpredictable tempers. Brawls were constantly flaring up and the bickering women had to be dragged apart. Only when the *burzhuyka* stove was heated would the women settle down, or else someone would start howling hysterically.

A burly woman, imprisoned for murder, needed to unburden her heart. She would go from one woman to another, sit down next to them and recount how she had grabbed the axe and swung it. More details followed, how the blood had splattered across the walls… She kept her nebulous eyes fixed on the listener, trapped in the wheel of a nightmare known only to herself. Whenever I awoke at night, I would see her sitting up, her empty eyes wide open, chained to her horror.

The train was a heap of misery and neuroses, twisted, sick imaginations and downright filth.

For several days we moved slowly on, making numerous stops, through Central Asia. Sometimes the train would be directed onto a side track where the engine was shunted and the car shoved roughly to and fro before the wheels once again clattered onward. So much iron, so much cold around us: rails, bolts and bars, the grip of Fate.

We traveled a week, eight days, nine days…

All of a sudden someone called from the upper bunk:

"Russia! We're in Russia! Look at the woods!"

We all took turns climbing to the upper bunk to peer through the little barred window.

But in a moment the clamour ceased and Natasha's loud whisper was heard:

"Look, girls, so many cars with wounded men!"

Once again everyone climbed to the upper bunk. At the sight of the military trains, the women fell silent.

One train with wounded soldiers rolled by us, then another. On the berths in the passenger cars lay crippled men with bandaged heads, arms and legs. These trains carried forth unconsciousness, resignation, screams and unrelenting pain: the bandaged, bloody misery of war.

A long stop lay ahead of us in Syzran. We were allowed to wash and the guards led us to town.

Yes, we were in Russia. How different from Central Asia it was! The leaves of poplar and birch trees rustled gently and a fresh wind ruffled our hair. Late May, still cool, fresh and resonant. Each cell of my body was suffused with a painful memory. How could I have lived without this all? The Volga glimmered in the distance. It was the first time I'd seen the great river.

We were taken to a real bathhouse. Water flowed from one, two, three taps. Its very availability was enough to drive you mad. For months we had been covered in dirt, and now we washed ourselves with the tiny pieces of soap we had each been given, rinsed ourselves and poured water over our bodies again and again until we grew weak with happiness. How strange it felt to be clean!

And again the cold, the rattling of wheels, the restless rhythm of a slow journey…

After Syzran our bread ration was delayed, and soon we didn't get any more at all. "There is no bread," they told us.

"You've no right to leave us without bread!" yelled Natasha.

Rifle butts slammed against the door from the outside. Natasha's charms no longer worked on the guards.

A military train, bound for the front, stopped on the track next to ours. At first the soldiers didn't realize what kind of "freight" our train was carrying. They leaned out of the windows and started teasing us:

"Hey there, cuties, where's the party?"

No one replied, but Natasha turned away from the cherished window, jumped to the floor and started pounding on the wall.

"We're starving! Where's our bread? Give us our bread!" she screamed in a fury fed on hunger.

Her explosive screams hammered on our nerves, caught on and spread to others. Soon our whole car was pounding and screaming, then the next, then a third. Hundreds of pounding fists could be heard from within twenty cars as the entire trainload thrashed against the walls and doors of these cells on wheels.

"Give us our bread! We're hungry! Bread! Bread!"

The screaming grew into a roar. We yelled not with our throats but with our empty stomachs in the wild hope that someone would protect us.

Outside the guards and officers ran back and forth. They were getting agitated and tried to calm us down. But it was too late! The prisoners were on the verge of shattering the train into splinters.

The men in the military train were watching. We could see them exchanging remarks with each other. They finally realized what kind of train was standing alongside theirs.

Several officers sprang out of the train and approached the escort commanders.

"These women are entitled to their rations. Give them their bread. Who holds the highest rank here?"

The transport commander obsequiously suggested to the officers that they follow him to his car for an explanation.

"Bring the documents here. Explain it all in their presence," an officer objected, his tone becoming openly hostile: "You have no right to starve people!"

At the sound of his insistent voice, our entire train grew silent again.

"Whose side are you taking, Comrade?" the escort commander tried to put the officer to shame: "Who do you think you are fighting for? *Criminals!*"

After a moment of dead silence we heard the outraged shout of our defender. The answer seemed startling:

"Who are we fighting for? For our mothers and wives who could be in that train!"

As if a pick-axe had broken through my callused soul, I lay motionless in my corner on the floor, holding my mouth shut so as not to allow a helpless and frightening howl: "Yes, yes, we are innocent! We've been tortured and we don't understand why!"

The transport commander was adamant. "You're making a little mistake, Comrade..."

But the front soldiers wouldn't back down. "Bring over the documents! And be quick about it! We're returning from hospitals to the front line and must be certain that everything is in order at home!"

The military train shuddered and moved off; the women exploded. From deep within them a mixture of feminine tenderness and obscenity broke forth:

"Hey, curly head, you can have me!" a voice cried out to her invisible defender. "Ah, you and I... we could..."

The equally candid replies of the departing soldiers were becoming less and less audible.

"Come back safe from the war, boys!" called the women.

And the trains rolled apart, each in its own direction. Theirs—toward war and bullets; ours—to a different hell.

The soldiers' efforts weren't in vain. They had seen that the daily ration of bread and soap was set in the accompanying documents. The guards had been profiteering by selling our rations in the markets of the towns where the train would stop.

"He's right, a hundred times right," proclaimed a woman, who till then had kept silent throughout the journey. "We do our time for a couple of plucked ears of corn or for cursing the war. Aren't we mothers to them? Are we not their sisters?"

Day after day rolled past, one after another, until twenty had rattled away. The train was now moving along a single-track rail.

"It looks like we'll be the ones to build the second track here!" said someone.

"Woods everywhere, no dwelling in sight whatsoever," came a voice from the upper bunk. "It's the taiga!"

We waited for nightfall, but it wouldn't descend. We were in for long white nights. Only when we were given our meager rations did we have an idea of what time of the day it was.

Twenty-three... Twenty-four... Natasha counted the days by carving notches in the wall with an aluminum spoon. On the twenty-fifth day the train slowed down and stopped.

Stillness, like at the bottom of a well. It was so quiet you could hear your ears ringing. The end of the world!

The doors were shoved open.

"Come out, get some air!" shouted the guards as the gangplanks were laid against the train.

Stumbling, dazed after the month-long journey, we crawled out and sat on the ground. Alongside the railway was a ditch and many dragged themselves to it to drink. The water was brown from peat. I remembered that when I was a child I saw tadpoles and bugs in similar peat bogs where my father used to work. I didn't drink.

At one of the next junctions several cars were uncoupled. The rest of the train moved on for about another hundred kilometers until finally we were ordered to get off. The station was called Svetik.

A group of local officials stood near the train. Amongst them was a woman in an NKVD uniform. With her bleached hair and mouth thick with lipstick she looked like a mannequin. She did not seem to fit into the whitewashed haze of the northern night, the depths of this forest or our own exhaustion. Pulling out files with our personal records she called out names, scrutinized us with an experienced eye, and divided us into two groups, *over there* and *over here.*

I heard my name called. For an instant my heart went cold, as if it grasped the importance of the moment. The woman nailed me with her leaden gaze and snarled: "Over there!" This instant of undisguised enmity, as well the appearance of the women "over there," made me realize that "over there" was far worse than "over here." What had the painted official managed to "discover" in me, covered with filth and staggering from nauseating weakness? What were her parameters for classifying people?

The sorting went on.

Natasha was also sent "over there," and she also let her head drop. Had she realized something, too?

But the petty thief Nelly and I were separated. During the journey she was constantly telling me, "Here, wrap yourself in my jacket while I sit by the stove. I can hear your teeth clatter… I hope they send us to the same camp… I feel like a human being when you're around." She was now standing in the group across from ours. With her chin pointed at the officer and her mouth rounded like a tube at one moment and grinning at another, she hurled silent curses at the NKVD woman.

We were lined up and counted. Surrounded by guards and dogs on all sides, the column set off. It was as if we hadn't crossed the entire country from south to north, as if we hadn't even changed camps.

We hobbled along for three kilometers or so, until we finally came to a stockade surrounded by barbed wire, with guards and watchtowers. At last, a place to live! The conditions didn't matter, as long as we had a roof over our heads.

Smoke curled over one of the roofs. Could it be that they were heating the bathhouse for us?

As we were led through the checkpoint we were told: "At five in the morning—off to work!"

We were taken straight to a barracks. Inside there were rows of plank beds for four people—two double beds above, two below—known as *vagonki.* The acrid smell of freshly cut wood suffused the air.

"Bedbugs everywhere!" someone cried in horror.

The vermin were countless. They fell on us like beasts of prey, eclipsing everything else: exhaustion after the month-long journey, our need for sleep, our desire to get warm. Some of the women grabbed their straw mattresses and tried to resettle outside the barracks in the open air but the cold soon drove them back inside.

At five in the morning a loud clanging against a length of rail woke us up: work!

The camp had the same name as the station: Svetik—"a small light." It was a misnomer. A thick wall of giant spruces made the place murderously dark. Dense bushes of willow-herb above human height grew beside the road which we were led along to work, threatening to devour everything around them.

In Svetik there was only one type of work: felling trees. I joined a brigade that cut up trunks. All day long we sawed. From the very beginning our hands were covered in blood blisters. Unbearable pain soon spread over our bodies, dulling our senses until we were frozen with stiffness, unable even to stand up straight. We sawed in pairs. In order not to let your partner down, you had to muster an inner strength you did not know you possessed.

Alongside us men felled trees. With an ear-splitting crack the falling trunks would hit the branches of neighboring trees as they crashed to the ground with an even more ferocious noise. At first, every time someone cried out *Tim-ber!* we would run out of the way of a falling tree, but as our energy dwindled we became increasingly calloused to the danger.

So it was, day after day. The deadening work sucked our blood, nerves and bones. It took less than a month to turn us into shambling zombies.

At night the stove in the barracks was heated and we dried our sopping foot wraps, pants and shoe covers. The air was thick with the stench of sweat and putrid fumes. We wanted to break away and take a breath of fresh air, but no sooner did we hit our plank beds than numbness overtook us, and in spite of the bugs, we fell into a deep sleep.

I wasn't aware of anyone around me, not a single face, not even the women who slept beside me. Not one of them remained in my memory. I couldn't grasp what was happening around me. The woods, two-handled saws, tree trunks, thoughts of bread—nothing existed outside of this unceasing cycle.

There are things one can talk about intelligibly, but it is hardly possible even to recall the horror of the camp.

Nominally, the camp was under civilian administration, but in reality it was run by prisoners. To live or not to live—this was something decided by the work distributor and the head of the KVCh, the Culture and Education Unit.

When our transport arrived, the work distributor was looking for a girl to make his "wife." The girl he chose was pretty. He had the privilege of having his own household and living in a separate shed next to the general barracks. For this he obediently paid off the camp authorities and strived to meet the figures they set up in the work plan. Complaints such as "I'm sick," "I have a fever," "My hands are one big blister," were taken by him as a personal insult. The hefty man with a massive red nose and sausage-like fingers raged and spat out dirty curses as he dragged the women who tried to plead for mercy down from their plank beds. Whoever tried to resist was thrown into a punishment cell and kept there on a three-hundred-gram ration, the rest of the bread being appropriated by the work distributor himself. His favorite saying was "The wolf is your friend," which sounded especially apt in the taiga.

Felling trees in the Komi Republic, I no longer perceived as absurd the conversation between two old Bolsheviks I'd overheard in the Novotroitsk transit camp. Whose slaves were we? To answer that murderously "simple" question you had to have some strength, time and lucidity of mind. How accurate the formula heard back in Djangi-Djir was: "One principle rules in the camp: to drive people on without allowing them to think or come to their senses, and keep their stomachs empty."

If I had any idea of what was going on in the camp, it was only through Natasha. She was protected by her countrymen, who held key positions. There was one Armenian in charge of bread rationing, which made him almighty; another worked at the clothing depot. Natasha tried to help me too, and once she asked if I would like to scrub the floor at the warehouse for an extra half-kilo of bread.

I zealously scrubbed the jagged floor boards and crawled under the shelves with camp jackets, boots and nails, but I failed to please the boss of the warehouse. He gave me the bread, but told Natasha he wasn't going to call me again.

Then Natasha fell in love.

The bathhouse was run by a seventy-five-year-old wrinkled woman with eyes like a boiled fish. People said she was carrying on an affair with a quiet young fellow fifty years her junior whose nickname was the Hairdresser. Together they made a strange pair, hardly resembling human beings. It was inconceivable how Natasha could fall in love with the sluggish Hairdresser! He shaved the guards, and they brought him a guitar from the outside. Natasha sang and he accompanied her. The real absurdity was that after being with Natasha, this sickly lad would run back to the old bathhouse attendant.

Natasha got the idea to stage a concert, which meant she and the Hairdresser could rehearse together after lights-out. "Who can dance? Who can do what?" Natasha kept asking around. Many volunteered. "Help me out!" she begged me. "If you agree to lead the concert, then it might come to something. Do this for me! Please!"

I gave in. I was too exhausted and indifferent to my surroundings to mention anything about the story I had recited in Belovodsk.

We put together a program. Natasha's show enjoyed tremendous success. They wouldn't let her off the stage. I took on the role of the master of ceremonies. To my own misfortune.

The next day I was summoned to the KVCh. The function of this administrative unit was more than vague: there were no newspapers, library, radio or cinema in the camp anyway. The head of the KVCh, Vasilyev, was a gloomy, sickly looking, thin and sinewy man, exempt from all other duties.

"Sit down, Comrade," he said, pointing to a chair.

The KVCh was housed in a small room with a table, two chairs and a stove. Behind the faded cotton curtain stood a bed. Vasilyev began by praising my role in the concert. He then asked my article, sentence and previous education. He introduced himself as the former second secretary of the Ukraine Komsomol Central Committee.

"I personally knew Postyshev and worked with Kosior," he said. "People were jealous. Someone wrote an anonymous letter against me, and I was slandered and put in prison. So now I'm suffering just like you."

He asked if felling trees was too hard for me and answered the question himself.

"It takes nothing for a person to freeze to death there! I'll give it some thought… I'll see if I can transfer you to work in the zone; I might arrange for you to work in the KVCh. We surely can launch some activity here together!"

He seemed lifeless, inanimate. I felt uncomfortable with his familiar tone, his calling me a "comrade" and offering "to launch some activity." It was hard to call the baring of his yellow horse teeth a smile, even though he tried to be nice.

Suddenly he stood up and grabbed me by my arms, panting and pulling me behind the curtain. Before my mind could grasp what was happening, I instinctively pushed him back with such an unexpected strength that he hit the side of the stove with the back of his head and crashed to the floor. I became paralyzed: I thought I had killed him. But in a few seconds he rose and growled:

"You'll rot! You'll be groveling at my feet begging for help… I'll see you rot!"

I don't remember how I made it back to the barracks.

The very idea of rape meant the ultimate limit, behind which there could be only death. The sharp sense of being cut out of life was my only clear sensation, and Vasilyev's vengeful promise "I'll see you rot!" became my daily reality. It meant nothing but death for me.

DAY AFTER DAY, week after week, one and the same thing: getting up at five in the morning, hastily drinking the wish-wash called tea with a small piece of bread, lining up in file four abreast. The boggy ground would groan underfoot as we were led through the forest to work in our brigades. With every step our feet squished in the mud. The only thing that changed was the tracts of forest. The saws became blunt, but we kept sawing the tree trunks, which seemed to be made of steel.

The wearing work and the constant proximity of an axe often confused people. Every now and then someone would chop off a finger or two—just to escape the unbearable labor and the swarms of mosquitoes, which stung right to the nerves. Those who had the courage to do this were called "self-choppers."

It was impossible to fulfill a norm that earned you more than five, or at best, six hundred grams of bread. The bread was leavened with oilcake and was hard as a rock. For lunch a "vitamin allowance" was given out in small scoops: a decoction of spruce and pine needles to prevent scurvy. Many, including myself, already had the disease. It began with purple spots over the legs and then grew into pus sores, then finally open ulcers.

One day after work I made up my mind to go to the medical unit. The attendant treated my wounds and dismissed me from work.

I didn't have any faith that the exemption would hold any weight in the camp and, especially, doubted that the foreman or the work distributor would have any mercy. When the next morning our barracks prepared to go to work, my heart sank from uncertainty, but I knew I was exempted and stayed on my plank bed.

As soon as the brigades were lined up and counted and the sick list was checked, the work distributor stormed into the barracks.

"Get up! Or do you want me to help you?" he roared as he approached.

Fearing his greasy hands, I crawled down as quickly as I could.

The KVCh director Vasilyev considered it his personal duty to see the brigades off to work every morning. Regardless of the weather, he always stood like a statue by the camp gates to make sure he knew who had been exempted.

In the evening the attendant from the medical unit said angrily:

"I'll never give you an exemption again! Vasilyev was so mad he was ready to finish me off."

He needn't have bothered saying this. Once Vasilyev had promised to take revenge, he preferred to do it behind your back, taking great pleasure in methodically annihilating you. The literal meaning of his threat was already quite evident: I could barely move my legs; they were like blocks of wood. My body began to rot.

Every morning, with the clang that resounded off the metal rail, I realized I had to go to work. I would crawl down from my bunk and drag myself to the camp gate. Apart from these simple tasks, nothing managed to catch my attention. Vasilyev's face embodied Evil. I was losing my grip on reality. Nothing beyond the camp gates existed for me, except my sister. Where was my little Valechka?

My namesake, Tamara Timofeecheva, a teacher of literature, Natasha and I were usually the last ones to return to the barracks after supper.

"Hold on!" Natasha said one evening, stopping in front of the barracks. "Do you understand that we're dying?"

Only then did I notice how much Natasha had changed. But I could no longer find the energy to ask what was going on with her.

"Let's swear that if any of us ever makes it to a different camp, she will try to pull the others along. Each of us, let's promise!" said Natasha.

For a moment something blazed up in my soul. She had thought it out well! We held hands and each, in turn, gave our vow.

"It's almost as good as that oath on Sparrow Hills!" Tamara Timofeecheva summed up.

ONE'S ABILITY to empathize completely faded away. The eyes saw how someone would sit wrapped in thought on her plank bed, rocking like a sleepwalker; how others would be hauled out at night to the bed of the work distributor, or the foreman, or the director of the KVCh; how on their return to the smoky barracks these women would stare vacantly at the feeble candlelight before finally turning to the wall to get some more sleep until the morning gong. Routine scenes of camp life, hardly arousing any emotion.

Only out-of-the-ordinary occurrences could make an impression, such as when someone failed to move out of the way of a falling tree, or was fatally stabbed in the zone or in the barracks or died after having his bones crushed in the punishment block.

Sometimes I shared the saw with an emaciated, sickly woman. In the barracks she would tell everyone about her two little daughters, seven and nine years old, left behind on their own.

"They'll be ruined, they'll die without me!" she kept repeating. "Don't you understand? How can they survive without me? How?"

Once after work we were lined up, about to return to the camp. The guards had already counted us at least ten times. A prisoner was missing. It was announced: "Escape!" The guards combed through the forest again and again. Perhaps someone had died? Or fallen unconscious? They didn't find anyone. Finally they discovered it was the mother of the two girls. Her desperate decision to escape seemed out of keeping with her frailness and timidity, but also a consequence of it.

Because the guards took the blame when a prisoner escaped, they grew mad with rage. The tightening of the regime took on the most unpredictable forms. If one now asked to go out into the woods to urinate, it would be under the direct supervision of a guard. This affected our psyche; the irritation grew stronger and stronger and needed an outlet. According to the logic of the camp, the one who escaped was the one to be blamed.

They searched for the woman for several days. Sentry posts had already been set up in the taiga, and now these were reinforced by guards hiding in dugouts. After about a week, in the middle of the day, three NKVD men emerged from the forest. An eerie-looking creature staggered in front of them. The din of axes and saws abated.

It was she. Shapeless shreds of what had once been clothing hung from her body. Her red face was swollen like a pancake. Mosquitoes had ravaged her, and she was bleeding. She managed a few more steps forward and then stood still, totally indifferent to her surroundings, flaps of skin sagging from her bones.

Neither compassion nor sympathy broke from the hearts of her fellow prisoners, only implacable rage. After a week under tightened regulations, they were ready to take revenge not on the guards but on one of their own, the unluckiest of all. Uncontrollable madness overtook them as chunks of wood and stones and hideous oaths rained down on the half-dead woman. Neither the NKVD men who tracked the fugitive down nor the guards who sat smoking nearby made the slightest effort to restrain the frenzied pack.

Suddenly the rage petered out, as swiftly as it had flared up. The first to come back to their senses made the others stop too. The woman lay on the ground. No one was allowed to approach her. What had she endured during the seven days she had roamed the taiga, gnawing on roots and berries, searching for a way out? Only God and she herself knew. Later, some said she'd been sentenced to yet another term; others reported she hadn't survived the investigation and died.

Thoughts of escape must have occurred to everyone. The fantasy tormented me too. Rebelling against reason, every cell of my body would shriek out for home. But the knowledge that there could be no escape from the NKVD would soon erase this idea from my head like chalk from a blackboard. In any case, where would I run?

A NEW FACE appeared in the camp. The doctor Pyotr Polikarpovich Shirochinsky was brought here with a small local transport as a "delinquent." Apparently, Svetik served as a punishment camp. With six years of his ten-year sentence already behind him, the old doctor still retained traces of his past gentility and posture. He looked completely out of place, which, as he confessed, was precisely why he was sent here: "Just the way I looked irritated the commandant in my previous camp." The same motif of "class hatred" determined everything.

Pyotr Polikarpovich's arrival for me was a sign of fate. He inspected the wounds on my legs and raised his eyes. "We must cure you at any price, child."

But when he issued me an exemption, the story repeated itself. Pyotr Polikarpovich released me from work and Vasilyev drove me back, no matter how fiercely the doctor protested.

One day Pyotr Polikarpovich asked me to stay in the medical unit. He put a bench under my inflamed feet and told me about himself and about the camps. I learned that our camp was called the Northern Railway Camp and that still farther to the north lay the camps of Ustvymsk, Abezinsk, Inta, Vorkuta and many others. He explained that the camps were subdivided into points, which in turn formed divisions. Our camp belonged to the Urdoma division. I was impressed to hear that there were the camps inhabited by the intelligentsia, almost without criminals.

Throughout his stories, he kept mentioning one name more than any other—Tamara Grigorievna Tsulukidze, a famous Georgian actress.

"She organized a puppet theater in the Protoka Camp," he said. "A wonderful actress and an exceptionally charming woman! It'd be great if you met! And, you know, I believe you *will* meet some day!"

The disgraced doctor was not only an open-hearted dreamer; he managed to achieve the impossible: I was transferred to a brigade that worked on the vegetable farm. Together with other emaciated women like me, I now did my best to fulfil the tasks of the agronomist Zaytsev.

During the midday break the brigade huddled together around the bonfire. We often saw Zaytsev with a young girl who had come to work in the North as a volunteer. The women said they were in love, but snarled: "They're asking for trouble! Right in front of the guards… They should at least hide somewhere to be more careful!" Had I known that later on fate would bring me face-to-face with the tragic outcome of this love, I would have paid more attention. A free person and a prisoner! That was illegal, punishable!

Vasilyev's pride was hurt when he found out I had been transferred from felling trees to the farm. A former functionary, he could do without anything but power. At his command I was now additionally assigned to the firefighters' brigade, which meant I had to make the rounds of the camp from midnight till 2 a.m. Like a windup doll, I slept from ten till midnight and then got up to go on fire duty.

Walking through the camp again and again, I had to guard the buildings from catching fire. The prisoners slept. The guard dogs barked. The sentries on the watchtowers changed. Behind the fence roared the gigantic gloomy spruce forest, dense as a wall. It seemed like I was living in a prehistoric time, as if there was nothing else in the entire world apart from dogs and guards.

AS SOON AS WE CAME BACK from work, they drove us on:

"Eat your supper quickly! Everyone's going to the medical unit for inspection!"

Women explained that a commission of doctors had come to examine us and send the sick to the infirmary.

When I arrived, a huge line had already formed outside the medical unit.

When my turn came, Pyotr Polikarpovich turned to the visiting doctors:

"She's the one I told you about."

A doctor with bright eyes and a lively attractive face smiled and told me to step behind the screen, take the bandages off my legs and undress. He examined my chest.

"It says in your file you studied foreign languages, then went to medical school. Is that right?"

He asked if I knew any English. I was so nervous all I could say was, "a little."

"Scurvy. Hospitalization," the doctor concluded when the examination was over.

Pyotr Polikarpovich looked satisfied. He closed his eyes and nodded. It seemed something right and fair was taking place, as if some strange play were being acted out in which I was merely a supernumerary. Hospitalization? Even the thought of it seemed unbelievable.

The camp became quiet. It was time for me to go on my night watch.

After I finished my first round, I was walking past the medical unit when the door creaked and two visiting doctors stumbled out onto the porch. One lit up a cigarette; the other started singing what must have been a popular war tune:

> The night is dark,
> Only bullets are whistling through the steppe,
> It's just wind that's whirring through the wires,
> The stars are twinkling dimly…

I leaned against the barracks wall and cried as I listened to the song.

One of the doctors jumped down from the porch and walked toward me:

"And here I am thinking, whose white kerchief is glinting over there? Are you allowed to be wandering around the camp so late?"

"I'm not wandering. I'm on duty. Fire duty."

"Fire duty? You should be lying in bed! You're seriously ill."

It was the same doctor who had insisted on my hospitalization.

Suddenly he held my hand and kissed it. Dear God! The world turned upside down. A free man was kissing my hand! I had grown unaccustomed to such things. I had completely forgotten who I was and what I was living for.

"Doctor P. wanted to take you to his infirmary, but I didn't let him. You'll move to Urdoma. We have electricity there, and books. We'll get you back on your feet, you'll be fine."

These humane and healing words, coming from a stranger, were hypnotic. But they were uttered by a free man to a prisoner, and the effect was also dumbfounding and painful. I held on to the barracks wall, afraid of losing consciousness, out of a newly burgeoning hope.

The next morning the doctors left and the camp resumed its habitual life.

"What is that doctor's name?" I asked Pyotr Polikarpovich.

"His name is Bakharev. You'll be all right! Consider you're already in the hospital," he assured me, obviously pleased with how things were turning out.

The prospect of going to the hospital, of breaking out of the camp, was driving me mad. I was dying to know when they would transfer me and whether I'd be able to last until then. Some said I'd have to wait a week, others said two or three, or even a month.

WHEN THE CAMP'S ECONOMIC PLANNER asked to talk to me, I became frightened. Rashid was a Crimean Tatar, also a 58-er. He introduced himself and asked if I knew him. The entire service personnel of the camp looked the same to me. I must have seen him somewhere, but I surely didn't know him.

Rashid had seen my name on the transport list for the hospital. He understood this was the only way for me to survive, but nevertheless, he didn't want me to leave for Urdoma. He told me he had long wanted to help me but had been powerless before Vasilyev; that I had no idea what it had taken for him and Pyotr Polikarpovich to transfer me from felling trees to the vegetable farm. He said he liked me because I was a "pure" person, which he, as a Tatar, valued greatly; he had never told me this, fearing I would take him for just another Vasilyev. Now he only wanted to warn me against going to Bakharev's hospital. "He won't leave you alone. He is a womanizer."

Why did he have to tell me all this? What was I supposed to do? Go to the authorities and say, "Strike my name off the list, I refuse to go to the infirmary. I want to stay in Svetik."?

Back in Belovodsk, Beniusz had reproached me for what he called "submissive determination." Now, as I realized my own inability to struggle for existence, at the edge of the abyss where life and death were so thinly separated, my resistance expressed itself in the desire to break away from this place at any price, where the threat to "see me rot" would some day come true.

It wasn't easy to ask Pyotr Polikarpovich about Bakharev.

"What difference does it make? Do you realize what awaits you here?" he answered angrily. "I know, I know what you're asking. Yes, people say things about him. But I've already explained everything to him about you. He won't dare. You have to get away from here as soon as possible. You're already an invalid!"

How I clung to that word: invalid! What made me even think Bakharev would be attracted to me? Where did Rashid get such an idea? I was a complete goner. The only thing left for me was to get out of the camp!

I held my breath when a couple of days later the work distributor came into the barracks and read out the names for the sick transport.

I wasn't on the list… But didn't I know it beforehand? Vasilyev wasn't done with me yet and he would get his way.

Tamara Timofeecheva was leaving with the transport. We said good-bye and she hobbled to the gate. With murderous attentiveness Vasilyev watched the people walking out of the camp.

The transport left. I sat down on a tree trunk. The wind beat against my back, creeping under the collar of my worn-out quilted jacket and robbing me of the last bits of warmth. Tomorrow, I thought, there will be the same stench from the foot-wraps, the night watch, the death-like abyss of sleep, and the breath of death itself.

Pyotr Polikarpovich begged the free workers to call the camp division to find out if something could still be done about my case. Later, he told me that Doctor Bakharev had made another attempt to get me out of Svetik. To do so he had had to destroy my personal record, which got him into trouble. Pyotr Polikarpovich's words hardly remained in my memory, for I felt it hopeless to believe in another chance. My existence was noted only on the registers of prisoners and, perhaps, in the compassionate souls of two or three people.

In a couple of weeks my strength petered out. I hardly noticed when someone came running into the barracks and called out to me:

"Quick! Grab your things and come to the checkpoint!"

All I managed to say to Natasha was:

"I remember our oath. But if we don't see each other again, I'll never forget you!"

Pyotr Polikarpovich repeated excitedly, "Well done, Bakharev! Well done!"

I wanted to tell him: "It's you who did this, dear doctor, it's you!" But I had no more energy.

"We'll meet again and you'll see, this will all seem like nothing but a revolting joke," he said.

The camp betrayed his optimism. We never saw each other again. A good man, Doctor Pyotr Polikarpovich Shirochinsky, died in the accursed Svetik camp.

I was still looking around, anticipating seeing Vasilyev and hearing him call me back. But the gate slammed shut behind me and the wooden stockade swallowed those left in the zone, separating them from me.

Doctor Bakharev somehow arranged a special escort to transport me to Urdoma. I couldn't help but think of him as a magician. The young guard was cheerful. Because I could hardly move my legs, he called me "granny," hurrying me onward so as not to miss the train.

As we climbed into the train car, the passengers perked up their ears. One of the women asked the guard if she could offer me some tea. He didn't mind. "Yes, Mother, go ahead." That crowded train revealed to me all the limitlessness of the Russian capacity for tenderheartedness and chaos.

From the Urdoma train station we walked about a kilometer along the tracks. The camp stood on a hill and could be easily seen. I could even count the buildings and outhouses that peeked up above the fence.

The guard led me to the checkpoint and handed me over. As I stepped into the zone, a woman came running out. Her dark eyes burned through me with hostility and suspicion. The guard and the checkpoint orderly exchanged glances. My joyful mood evaporated. It was not the first time a free woman had sized me up like a piece of merchandise.

THE CAMP LOOKED CLEAN. Neat pathways led from one building to another.

I was shown the way to the bathhouse. The newcomers who had arrived on a transport just a few minutes before me crowded the entrance.

In the anteroom, a young good-looking doctor, Evgeny Lvovich Petzgold, was examining the new arrivals. As soon as I walked in, Bakharev, who was the head physician of the Urdoma infirmary, came in too. He shot a glance at the patients and casually said to me: "Aha, you're finally here!" Then he quickly sorted out the patients' records into several piles and announced where each was going. I ended up among the surgical patients.

There was a free cot in a six-person ward. The pillow, the blanket and the clean linens perplexed me. There was something desperately sorrowful and insulting in the transition from ugliness to normality. In a year and a half of living in the barracks, I had only seen the dim light of oil lamps, but here a real light bulb was lit at night. I turned to the wall and lay motionless in the clean bed, devoid of any thoughts. Every time the door opened I coiled in fear that someone would see me and yell, "What is *she* doing here? Back to Svetik!"

I was ordered to stay in bed and was only to get up to have my bandages changed or to eat. I finally realized how sick I was. In Svetik I didn't have the time to examine my wounds. Now I saw that the ulcers on my legs went to the bone. My gums and my tongue were swollen; I suffered from a permanent inner chill.

It took me a while to understand anything about my new surroundings. Next door to the surgery ward stood a building where operations were performed. There was also a maternity ward for free workers. The infirmary barracks consisted of ten wards crammed full of people with broken bones, injuries, respiratory infections and various other illnesses and diseases. The dining hall and the kitchen were right in the barracks. The food was prepared by two nuns, Nura and Sasha, both serving ten-year sentences. Surgeries took place both during the day and at night. Someone or other would be released from the hospital and sent back to the general works in one of the nearby camps; new patients would be admitted in large batches or individually; the corpses would be carried to the morgue in a corner of the zone.

Gradually I got to know all the patients in my ward. The most sociable was Polina, who was cunning and kind. Polina, or Aunt Polya, had been sentenced for speculation. In a few weeks her sentence would run out and she was going to be released. This put her at the center of everybody's attention.

The day after I arrived in Urdoma, the same dark-haired woman whose gaze had scalded me at the checkpoint came into our ward.

"Who is she?" I asked the women after she left.

"The head nurse of the surgery," Aunt Polya replied. "These days she goes by Vera Petrovna, but she used to be just Verka. I was in the same camp with both of them, in Koryazhma."

"Both of whom?"

"She's our doctor's camp wife."

I was relieved to hear this.

"Was Doctor Bakharev also a prisoner?" I asked.

"Of course. What else? Since '37! He sat out his entire stretch."

"What for?"

"Something political," Aunt Polya replied. "Vera Petrovna was just a small-time crook. She worked as a cashier in some store and got caught embezzling money. They met in the camp. He was released before her, but then she came here too. A very practical woman, and dreadfully jealous!"

The energetic Vera Petrovna was the almighty boss in the surgery barracks. Women sewed and knitted for her in the wards and then invited her to try on a gown or a blouse, asking if she wished to have her new mittens patterned or plain. She paid back these women by allowing them to stay longer in the infirmary. Whether coming to the zone or going home, she always carried a heavy sack. The two nuns cooked lunch for her in the camp kitchen. They were also allowed to leave the camp to clean Vera Petrovna's house, wash the floors and do her laundry.

The second nurse in the surgical barracks was Bronya, a thick-legged, unattractive woman, also a '58-er. She spoke in a servile, sugary voice with Bakharev and Vera Petrovna but was haughty and arrogant with everybody else. Competent and punctual like a good clerk, she took care of all the subsidiary work in the barracks.

Every morning, a doctor would make his round of the wards, sometimes accompanied by a nurse. People said that some of the doctors in Urdoma used to work in the Kremlin before their arrest.

The infirmary was run by two directors: one was from the NKVD; the other, Bakharev, was the chief doctor, the real master of life inside the camp. They got on well with each other.

Bakharev was a gifted surgeon and gynecologist, as well as a responsible administrator. He kept everything under control and never overlooked even the tiniest detail. He had time both to talk to his patients and to pressure the local authorities for the necessary equipment and rare medication. He was cheerful and self-confident, and it seemed the possibilities that the camp offered were well aligned with his own plans and desires.

THE TREATMENT and the very atmosphere of the infirmary gradually got me back on my feet. Although far from being completely recovered, I could already walk about the barracks. I still remained withdrawn and apathetic and avoided talking to people. Indifference was self-protection, and self-restraint seemed to be the norm.

Bakharev remembered his promise and asked if he could bring me something to read. I refused: I wasn't yet ready to read books. But his attention was nearly terrifying, and every time he tried to approach me I'd feel uncomfortable. Standing in the corridor and talking to a patient, he would open the door to our ward and glance in my direction without interrupting his conversation, as if trying to make it clear where his real interests lay. He would take an official tone as he ordered me to do something: "Go to the staffroom and help Bronya roll up the laundered bandages!" Or, "Do you know Latin? Then go help Vera Petrovna renew the labels on the medicine bottles. She has lots of other things to take care of." Vera Petrovna would purse her lips and say dryly: "If that's his order, do it."

My humble efforts to establish a normal relationship with Vera Petrovna were nipped in the bud. She couldn't curb her stormy antipathy toward me and stressed it in every way she could. The doctor pretended he noticed nothing.

"Tamara Vladislavovna will sort out the patient records," he would tell her. "Show her how to do it."

Her hostility weighed heavily on me, and I was glad when one day Vera Petrovna asked me to go to the pharmacy to get the medications.

I threw my quilted jacket over my hospital gown and was ready to go.

The pharmacy was an outbuilding next to the infirmary barracks. A man with an aquiline nose and cheerful eyes opened the door. He introduced himself as Abram Matveevich. When I told him that Vera Petrovna sent me to get the medications, he let out a whistle:

"All right, come in! What a surprise, what a surprise!"

My arrival interrupted the conversation of several people who were sitting in the little entrance room of the pharmacy.

"Let's get acquainted," I was told. "Sit down."

An attractive young woman in a white smock introduced herself: "I'm Lena, a nurse in the third medical building." Two men made to stand up. One looked cold and sullen. The other said something stale and vulgar.

"What should we make of such an innovation?" asked Abram Matveevich, obviously hinting at something. "Our Vera, who never trusts anyone to deliver the medicine, now sends us a newcomer. She's a crafty woman, you can be sure!"

"Please give me the medicine. They're waiting at the infirmary," I said.

"Why don't you sit down," Lena said in a melancholic voice. "She sent you here so you could tarry with us for a while, isn't that true? Who knows, maybe one of our friends will woo you and get in ahead of Filipp."

Lena had correctly figured out Vera Petrovna's strategy. One of the men from the pharmacy, Semyon Nikolaevich, started visiting me in the infirmary barracks, though I asked him every time not to come again. Vera Petrovna encouraged his visits, which were becoming more and more frequent. I was afraid of the man in a shabby service jacket, completely bald, who had served for the state security in its early incarnation, the OGPU, and then for the NKVD. He had the burdensome habit of looking straight into your eyes.

"I see you think of me as some sort of plague, don't you? Too bad! I come to you as if to a confessor. Don't turn me out. My heart is heavy," begged Semyon Nikolaevich.

He was lavish with stories, and when he had finished, he asked:

"Scary stuff, huh?"

"Scary." I would agree. "You see, I'm a bad consoler."

"I don't need consolation. But if you turn me away, I'll be damned," he declared, and went straight on to his next confession.

"It was in the early '30s. We were mobilized to confiscate gold. Have you ever heard of this? We caught hundreds of those bastards. The floor in the room where the prisoners were kept was trimmed with iron plates and the door was reinforced from the outside. We'd start to grill the suspects, gradually turning up the heat. You should've seen how they started to dance! They screamed, yelled and immediately remembered where they hid the gold, how much was hidden… They'd tell everything. Of course, some were innocent. Once I came home extremely tired, you know. My wife started howling: 'I'm begging you, Semyon, let the wife of an arrested man talk to you.' The woman rushed straight out from another room and, bang, fell to her knees, trying to catch my hand to kiss it. I shooed them both away and kicked my wife out…"

It wasn't hard to imagine how this man, blind to the difference between ideology and mere sadism and with an unhealthy commitment to "service," tortured people. Recounting the tricks of the trade, only now did he try to understand what he'd actually been doing. As for me, I had to peer straight into the cruelties of life as they appeared in front of me, and I didn't dare protest.

After a lengthy treatment, Semyon Nikolaevich got better. When he found out he was to be transported to another camp, he begged the authorities to let him stay on, resisted his transfer and stormed around. When, despite all his efforts, he was nevertheless loaded onto the train car together with the rest of the transport, he slit his wrists. They managed to save him and sent him back to the infirmary. Deep in my heart, I was glad when the doctor who bumped into him in the hallway became outraged and yelled: "What makes you stick to this place? You got relatives here? Make sure I never see you in the surgical barracks again!" They'd been prisoners in the same camp and had once been friends.

IN THE CORNER of the surgical barracks, where people went to smoke, the ambulatory patients told each other stories of their lives and shared the details of their cases. Truth here was inseparable from legend. People extolled and exaggerated their pasts, but the eyes of the storyteller revealed anguish and subjugation. Here the patients also predicted the future and interpreted dreams.

I was reluctant to share my dream with anyone: I had dreamed I was perched somewhere very high; rivers flowed below, carving the earth into rectangles of different shapes; mountain ranges could be discerned; a town, leading its normal life, emerged. There, at this incredible height, the frameworks of a gigantic bridge across the vast expanse were installed. I had to make it to the other side. Step by step, I moved along the metal girders, holding onto what seemed to be the railing. Suddenly, when half of the distance was already behind me, I came to a precipice. Two or three fragments of the bridge were missing. There was nowhere else to step, nor did I have any more strength to grip the banisters. I was about to fall down into the abyss… when everything disappeared. There were no more feelings, no perception of what was happening. But then I suddenly found myself on the other side, which I thought I'd never be able to reach.

The dream was unusually gripping and real. What mystery hid in that void, when even the subconscious was disabled? In a way, the miracle in the dream was parallel to how my life turned out. Despite the arrest, the camps in Central Asia and Svetik, my life did not come to an end.

IT WAS TIME for Aunt Polya to be released. She came to say good-bye and brought me her wooden suitcase:

"This is for you. Keep it and remember Aunt Polya!"

"I don't need it, Aunt Polya, thank you. I don't even have anything to put in it."

"Don't go offending me. You've got many years ahead of you, you'll find something to put in it."

The broad-faced, big-boned and somewhat coarse woman looked at me sharply; at that moment she appeared very wise, and my heart shrank from her simple and unpretentious words:

"Our doctor, he has fallen in love with you. Be careful. Don't trust him too much; you're in a real fix."

My most palpable wish in those days was reduced to one thing: that my sincere gratitude to Filipp Yakovlevich Bakharev and my faith in his honesty would ward off his advances. Seriously sick, I was living on a different plane of existence, without feeling the need to restore myself or pull myself back together. Only time and silence could help me. But the aggressive spirit of the camp, as well as the doctor's impetuous personality, had its own cycles.

At the end of the day, I was called in for a medical examination. Bronya was on duty. There was no one else in the medical staff room except Bakharev.

"How are you feeling? Any complaints? Go behind the screen, I have to examine your breathing."

I feared they would release me from the infirmary, or something even worse…

For agreeing to admit that a sick person was actually sick, for his efforts to rescue me from Svetik—the doctor claimed his reward.

I was numb. My will and energy abandoned me…

After he left, I remained sitting on the trestle-bed, nailed down, unable to make a move.

Bronya walked in. She went up to the desk without looking in my direction, then threw a glance at me and muttered something in a condemnatory tone, as if it were her duty to annihilate me on behalf of all humankind. Two tears ran down her cheeks. Something trembled inside of me: Did she pity me?

"Life is a cruel thing," she said philosophically. "I respect Vera Petrovna. How I pity her!"

"Of course," I said to myself.

The condemnation of a strange woman was nothing compared to my own self-judgment. Up until now I'd found strength in personal virtue and dignity, but now what? Femininity could no longer serve me as a means of staying afloat.

THE NEXT DAY the doctor told me, "There is a post-op in Ward 5 in poor condition. Someone has to watch by him. Maybe you?"

I felt better when there was work. I spent three days by the dying patient's bedside.

Several weeks later a few of us were summoned to go before a commission that would determine whether to release us or to keep us in the infirmary. A group of recovering patients was being sent back to the general camps. Sometimes a prisoner was transported back to the same camp where he had worked before hospitalization. I was terribly afraid to think of such a future.

Behind the desk sat three doctors.

"Show your legs. Your tongue..."

"It seems a bit too early to release her," one of them admitted.

"We will!" Bakharev cut him short. Before his words could sink in, he turned to me: "You'll stay here to work in the infirmary's surgical unit. You'll move in with the nurses."

The doctor's decision seemed like a slip of the tongue.

The Medical Institute in Frunze had scarcely equipped me with any practical skills. I had to learn on the job.

In the mornings brief meetings were held at the infirmary, where the staff reported on the condition of critical patients and about everything that had happened during night shifts. Whether at those meetings or in the dissecting room, I always felt nervous among the old experienced doctors. I worked with limitless zeal, driven by the desire not to make a single mistake. I even remembered all the Latin terms and sometimes was able to help an older doctor remember how a nerve or a muscle was called. I felt less and less out of place.

Early in the morning, with my quilted jacket over my shoulders, I would run to the medical barracks and stay there until late at night. There was always plenty of work to do: giving out the medications, bandaging and feeding the patients, carrying out other procedures. Various new assignments kept coming in. As they said, it turned out I had "magic hands." I was happy when the patients willingly came to me to change their bandages; I treasured their requests to sit with them in their wards or help them read a letter from home.

In the other section of the barracks, next to the medical unit, lived the camp clerks, who were mainly women imprisoned in 1937. They were friendly with me, despite the fact that I belonged to a different generation of prisoners who hadn't experienced their nightmare. The women didn't talk much about the year '37, but whenever one did bring up those times, others would join in with their own additions and remarks.

It was they who had built the camps. Only the wild virginal taiga had been here to greet them. There was no railroad, and the guards drove them to their points of destinations on foot. They would hang a small plate with the name of the future camp on a pine tree, and the prisoners would start building the camp for themselves. They chopped trees, sawed and planed trunks, built huts for themselves and more solid lodgings and watchtowers for the guards. They dug wells, fed swarms of gnats and mosquitoes with their own blood and in the same place buried their fellow prisoners. The first ones to die were the "brains" of the country who pored over their scholarship before '37 and had no idea how to hold an axe or a saw. Various diseases, filth, cold and labor beyond human powers finished them off.

My hair stood on end from these stories. Hearing them from real people, I found their horror became, for me, inextricably linked to the history of the country I was living in, to all of mankind and to my own personal fate. I don't know how they managed, how they survived.

I was drawn by the sense of unity and wisdom that defined the relationships among these women. But even here conversation was a luxury: once finished with their work, they would rush back to their barracks to write a letter, drink a cup of watered-down tea and putter about their meager belongings.

Those lucky enough to get privileged jobs in the camp, unlike their fellow general workers, were called *pridurki*, "house-boys." This nickname reflected the common laborers' frustration with how things had turned out for them. Not all house-boys, however, kowtowed; many performed their duties with pride, honesty and devotion. The economists, planners and accountants who worked for the camp were also prisoners. They ensured the functioning of the entire camp, including the medical unit. What often determined one's position was not the professional qualifications but the general giftedness of a person. Journalists, engineers, teachers and scholars mastered whatever professional skill was in demand.

Everyone was fond of the sixty-year-old Matvey Ilyich, whom people called "the Kremlin worker." I never knew the origin of his nickname. In the camp he was in charge of food supply; in other words, he was responsible for receiving and distributing rations among both prisoners and free workers.

It was he who introduced me to the term "second-timer." The term applied to a substantial number of prisoners—those who stayed behind the barbed wire even after they had sat out their initial sentences. A postscript would appear in their files: *Await further instruction.* Without facing another trial, they would be given another term, retained in the camp, denied all privileges and made to work just as before. Matvey Ilyich, a cheerful man with bright blue eyes, was one of the "second-timers."

Later he told me about his wife, who died right after his arrest. His son was taken in by some distant relatives, who understood the situation in their own way: the arrest of the father meant he was an "Enemy of the People," but the child, of course, had nothing to do with it. The son graduated from an institute in Moscow with a degree in chemical engineering and decided to stay in the capital. The privilege had a price: he had to renounce his father officially.

For Matvey Ilyich, everything came together: he was summoned to the Second Department, where he was presented with the renunciation of his son, as well as the authorities' decree not to release him until "further instruction."

One day, not long after I started working in the surgery ward, he stopped by. "I couldn't resist meeting the girl they've been hiding here so cautiously."

I didn't adopt his playful tone and we stood there together, a bit awkwardly. But at that very moment we heard the voice of Filipp Yakovlevich walking into the barracks. My visitor's expression revealed an uncanny fear. In a boyish manner, he helplessly dashed aside and hid himself behind the door. I went white as a sheet and my heart leaped out of my chest, as always happened whenever the doctor unexpectedly showed up.

After the doctor took what he had come for and left, Matvey Ilyich emerged from hiding. Within seconds we'd learned a lot about each other and both burst out laughing.

"Are you afraid of him?" my guest asked.

"Not really," I attempted to assert.

Matvey Ilyich didn't try to expose me.

"Well, it looks like I got a scare. What an embarrassment for an old fool like me!"

In Matvey Ilyich, with his kind and boyish face, I forever gained a faithful defender.

"Stop by the boiler room when you get a chance," he once told me. "They're making you a pair of felt boots. You've got to try them on."

I held my breath: how was it possible that a strange man worried about keeping my feet dry? I had long since gotten used to wearing boots with holes in their soles; had accepted the dampness, hunger and cold with a senseless humility.

After making all sorts of excuses, I tried the boots on. The bootlegs were cut from patches of old blankets. When I wore them later on, I blessed Matvey Ilyich with my warmed heart.

More than once during my stay in Urdoma, he supplied me with an extra bread ration. One day, with a half-prankish, half-guilty smile, he casually held out a stick of butter to me.

"There is no butter in the prisoners' food allowance. As for the guards, they'll do without this little bit," he said, trying to hide his embarrassment.

Bronya was standing nearby; by now she had warmed up to me. She and I pinched off pieces of butter with our hands and, swallowing them, were amazed by the delicious taste.

My fear of Filipp Yakovlevich prevented me from telling him about the vow the three of us had sworn at Svetik. Tamara Timofeecheva had been brought to the infirmary, but I didn't know anything about Natasha. I shared the burden of our obligation with Matvey Ilyich, who asked the doctor to help my friend. Filipp Yakovlevich was disappointed with the fact I hadn't confided in him directly but nevertheless inquired about Natasha. She was in one of the camps in the same division. She was doing fine, so she deferred the offer to get transferred to Urdoma until things got worse.

Even after I moved to a different place, my friendship with Matvey Ilyich did not cease. We wrote each other letters, in one of which he told me he had met a good woman, grew attached to her and was happy. His happiness was brief: like Doctor Pyotr Polikarpovich Shirochinsky, Matvey Ilyich didn't make it to his release and died in the Urdoma camp. The woman he had written to me about buried him on a hill high above it. Later, whenever I'd pass that place, whether at night or during the day, I would lean up against the window in the train, trying to discern the cross she had affixed atop the grave of the kind man.

WINTER CAME. Light dry snow gave way to damp and fluffy flakes. They fell and fell, as if aiming to wrap all the camp buildings, all that was around, in their whiteness. Snowdrifts piled above human height, drowning out people's voices and blocking the view of the barbed wire. In the mornings, everyone worked together to clear paths.

It was a bright sunny morning and we were gathered outside after a meeting at the infirmary. Doctor Petzgold flung a snowball at me. I threw one at Lena, whom I had befriended since I first met her at the pharmacy. Then each of us threw one at Simon, an attendant from the sixth infirmary barracks. Filipp Yakovlevich followed us outside, but as a free worker he felt it improper to join our snowball fight. His eyes burning with indignation, he demanded that I immediately stop the game.

I was enjoying a happy period of revival, surrounded by a normal language environment. I was living in the nurses' dorms with only seven other women; the work was tolerable, and I was no longer tormented by hunger; I wore a white uniform and always had water and soap to wash my hands. In the barracks, firewood crackled in the stove; beyond the window there was crisp frost. Fire and ice: life was contained in these elements. Never before had I seen twilight so dark-blue, gray dawns so mysteriously and excitedly promising a new day, bread and life itself. At the foot of a hill outside the camp, trains puffed as they lumbered along the tracks. Their forced whistles seemed to be telling us that they were coping with the expanse.

In the evenings, the strains of a violin were heard. I wondered where they came from. Someone told me it was Simon.

"Is he a musician?" I asked.

"No, a journalist. He's from Moscow. A bachelor, with good principles."

"Where did he manage to get the violin from?"

"His friends sent it to him."

Simon was an ironic man. He used to say, "I know I'm not exactly handsome, but believe me, I'm not dumb..."

Once he came to see me during my shift with an idea to put together a concert, just like Natasha proposed a long time ago.

"Kapa Dogadaeva will perform a Spanish dance; I will play the violin; Pavel Ivanovich will play the spoons. They promised to bring an accordion from the outside for Sergey. What do you say?"

"I can't play any instrument."

"Then could you recite some fable? Please!"

Remembering the concert at Svetik, I was afraid to agree. Simon spent a lot of time persuading me until I gave in.

Once, back in Belovodsk, I had read Kononenko's *The Wife*. I felt that the heroine in the story was still speaking through me and had left certain things unsaid. The guards had taken the newspaper clipping away from me during one of the searches, but it turned out I still remembered it.

I was extremely afraid before the concert, but once onstage, I felt all the far-flung particles of my soul coalesce again. Many in the audience cried. I was honored and praised.

In Urdoma I also met Tanya Mironenko, who remained my friend for many years after. She was slim and reserved, with dark hair and green eyes, and unlike anyone else I knew. She worked at the lab together with Doctor S. and, as she herself confessed, was living through a happy time in her life.

Once, as I was about to give eyedrops to one of the patients and had already filled the dropper, a strange feeling stopped me and I moved the dropper away at the last moment. I took the bottle of eyedrops to the lab to show Tanya.

"Something is not right. I'm not sure what. The color seems a bit off."

"That's not the right medicine," Tanya confirmed after checking the bottle. "There could've been serious complications."

I was too bewildered to say anything. Tanya advised:

"Don't say a word to anyone, especially to her. Understand? Tell Vera Petrovna you broke the bottle by accident. You must look and speak as if you guessed nothing, all right?"

"But..."

"But what?"

Tanya's warning seemed odd, but I followed her advice.

The next time I came to the laboratory to pick up test results, I saw Vasilyev waiting by the door among other patients. In my eyes, this man from Svetik embodied all the camp's filth and turpitude.

When Tanya asked me what was wrong, I tried to explain what I could. On my way back I had to pass by Vasilyev again.

Tanya found out that Vasilyev had arrived at the infirmary as a patient. The tests he was waiting for revealed that he had an ulcer and a bad case of tuberculosis. He was sent off to a "tuberculosis camp," where he died a couple of months later.

I DIDN'T THINK about the future. Like most 58-ers, I didn't believe I would ever see freedom again. But I was still troubled by the thought that I'd never have a real profession. I was glad to hear the head physician address me at the next meeting:

"Tomorrow we are conducting an elective surgery. You'll need to attend. You must learn. Watch Vera Petrovna carefully while she handles the instruments."

I couldn't imagine, however, what the following day would bring.

I proceeded with the basic duties of a surgical dresser: washed my hands according to the procedure, carefully took out the doctor's smock from the box and helped him put it on.

The operating room, which was closed most weekdays, served as my examination room that morning. It was an outhouse with glass walls that overlooked an area of the zone with no barracks. The painted floors shone, and the air was fresh inside. As always, two other doctors were present during the surgery. The patient was rolled in on a cart.

I listened to the staccato commands of Filipp Yakovlevich: "Scalpel. Clutch. Pincers."

Vera Petrovna handed him the instruments.

Trying not to notice the blood and fighting off nausea, I stared at the instrument table. But my mind drifted and before I could grab onto the windowsill for support, I fainted. When I came to, the patient had already been carted out.

From behind a closed door, I heard Vera Petrovna's screams, dirty curses and threats:

"I don't want this bitch sticking around one minute longer! Get her ass out of the camp right now, or I'll find a way to throw you in prison together with her!"

As if in a fever, I stepped inside.

"I am begging you: send me away! Please, send me away from here!"

I never knew before how hopeless shame could be.

Several hours passed. I was lying on my bed in the barracks when Tanya came in.

"She's in the lab. She asked me to bring you over. She wants to talk to you."

I didn't want to go. I wanted to do at least something my way, not according to someone else's dictates. But I stood up and went.

The woman I was seeing before me bore no resemblance to the one who'd been shrieking and cursing just a few hours earlier. She started jabbering: if I were a good person, I would forget everything that happened, return to the medical barracks and catch up with work. She said she could have easily sent me to a punishment camp a long time ago, where I would have died. But she didn't. If I didn't want Filipp to kick her out, I had to forget everything and tell him that she and I had made up with each other. She knew he loved me, not her, but she could not imagine her life without him and was ready to be his housewife, wash his feet and do absolutely anything just to keep him near. She had calculated that I had another five years in the camp. During that time, Filipp would probably fall in love hundreds more times, and since she knew him better, everything now had to remain the way it was, because his momentary whim would pass, as it always did. Vera Petrovna asked if I understood at least that. She insisted again on pretending that nothing had happened, that everything was already forgotten.

"I hope you help me get transferred to another camp," was all I could say.

"So you want him to kick me out, right? What do you need that for? You know he'll never forgive me for this. I'm begging you: tell him we've made up."

Her reasons and methods of persuasion revealed an unknown strategy: she had jumbled everything up to such an extent that now I appeared to be the main misfortune in the lives of this unhappy couple.

"You will tell Filipp we've made up!" she insisted. "You have to do this for me."

No sooner did she leave the lab than Bronya came running to tell me that the doctor was looking for me and wanted to see me in the medical unit.

The room at the infirmary seemed empty, but then a tired voice was heard from the dark.

"Come in and sit down. Don't turn on the lights."

For a long time he kept silent; then asked:

"Should I tell you about Vera Petrovna?"

"What for?"

"You have to know. She is a total stranger to me."

"I don't have to know all this."

"And that I love you?" the voice continued. "That there is no one so dear to me? Today I understood it."

"Please, send me away from here."

"You really want that?"

"I do."

"Do you understand what may happen to you?"

"Yes."

"Well, you shouldn't worry. They can send you away whenever, anyway. I'm not going to do it myself."

His tone was unusually calm and serious. There was not a trace of the crudeness that would often betray the doctor's intentions. What was his real cast of mind? When was he genuine? He went on and on: only now did the beautiful world open up to him; until today he was living a terrible life, not bothering to think about its meaning; today he understood he loved for the first time.

I was devastated. My only desire was to leave immediately.

"You have nothing to say after everything you've heard from me? Do you still want to transfer?"

I didn't want to leave this camp, of course, but not because of him.

Nothing had changed by the next morning. I tried not to think about him, about her. Life seemed loathsome; I wanted to evaporate, to disappear.

I asked Bronya to cover me for a couple of hours at work, went to the third medical barracks and asked Lena if I could stay there for a short while. Lena gave me a cup of hot water to warm me up and left to hand out the medications.

Through the window I could see the administrative office, where free workers had to check in before their shift. I saw the chief doctor climbing up the ice-covered stairs onto the porch. His steps were heavy and slow; the collar of his overcoat was turned up. Usually so nimble, he could now barely move his feet. His labored movements were more suggestive than words. His was a plight I understood well: he was suffering.

I began to question my feelings toward him. He was my only defender. Had he not snatched me away from that camp in the woods, I would have long ago been thrown into a common grave. I rushed to find Lena to tell Filipp to come see me.

I saw him almost running. He knelt before me and kept thanking me.

I'd always been haunted by the affliction of uncertainty, but at that moment, despite common sense, I believed that he really loved me. It was odd and absurd, but that's how it was. I saw that this free man, irrepressible as he was, had the same yearnings and pitfalls as I did. Though I never forgot his summoning me behind the screen and the humiliation afterward, now I found myself bewildered by a feeling of compassion. Instead of finding a friend, or a defender, I only encountered inner turmoil.

I COULDN'T COMPLAIN of a lack of new impressions: the patients at the infirmary were constantly coming and going, and I would always find myself involved in the fates of a great many people, if only for a short while.

At the beginning of my night shift, I made a round of all the wards. Most of the patients were half asleep. I let the Kazakh orderly go to sleep too. Back in the staffroom, I turned on the lights, lay the patients' files on the table and set about writing new prescriptions. Suddenly someone jerked the door and, making a deft monkey-like movement, turned the key, locking the door from inside.

I was terrified to find myself face-to-face with the stranger. I had no idea what might have brought him to the staffroom. His eyes were jumping. It was one of the newcomers who had just been admitted to the infirmary.

"Nurse, give me some ether!"

"What for?" I heard myself ask.

"Where is it? Give it to me now!"

I had no clue that ether was an addictive drug.

"I don't have any," I mumbled.

"You do! Give it to me, or I'll kill you!"

He could have easily carried out his threat. He didn't look like a human being.

"The ether is kept in the operating room, and it's locked."

"Give me the key!"

"The key is with the doctor."

I was afraid. No one was around to help me. I didn't know exactly what I'd do at the next moment, but I was suddenly sure I wouldn't give him what he was asking for.

The man, with a morbid bluish pallor, stood by the door in his underclothes and kept demanding: "Give me the ether!"

"Here, all I have is alcohol. Drink it."

"No. I need ether. Give me the ether!"

Some latent power, capable of either crippling or fortifying a person at a moment of danger, was telling me to insist:

"There is no ether! You won't get it. Is that clear?"

The man fell to his knees. Stiffly and maliciously, he begged me: "I can't go without it, I'll die. Give me the ether!"

I tried to appeal to reason: "Go to sleep. I won't tell anyone. Otherwise, you'll go back to the general works again."

But the addict was deaf to my words. I kept talking to him just to gain time and finally managed to lead him off to his ward.

Back at the staffroom, I felt the familiar exhaustion, gray and heavy, weighing down on me.

A FREE WORKER arrived at one of the infirmary units in grave condition. Her fever was up to 42 degrees, and she was diagnosed with malaria. The tests weren't promising. Her case was discussed at the doctors' general meeting. Filipp ordered her to be transferred to the surgical ward. Taking over the shift, I approached her bed. Her face looked familiar: it was Zoya, the girl who used to visit the brigade leader Grisha Zaytsev in Svetik. They would spend hours together sitting by the bonfire.

Zoya was unconscious and came to only for a few moments.

"It's not malaria," said Filipp. "It's sepsis."

As soon as she opened her eyes, he leaned over and asked her:

"What did you do? Tell us, what did you do?"

"Nothing," she replied with her dry, cracked lips. "It's nothing."

The doctors conferred several times before they finally decided to perform intravenous alcohol injections and intramuscular salt solutions—there was no other medication. Zoya would lose consciousness over and over again. Delirious, she would mutter, "Grisha, look, so much water! The entire field is under water… Carrots, so many carrots… Help me… Don't swim, don't swim…"

A large lamp was brought in and put by Zoya's bedside. The doctors stood around. Leaning over her, Filipp would wait until she came to her senses again and kept asking her, "What did you do, tell us!" I couldn't understand what the doctors wanted from her, why they were tormenting her in vain.

Suddenly Zoya gained consciousness. She soberly looked around, spotted Bakharev and said in a disdainful, triumphant voice:

"I tricked you, doctor, nonetheless!"

"You tricked yourself," answered Bakharev, ordering to give her another dose of salt solution.

I was about to run the needle into her thigh when he cancelled his order.
"Don't. She needs nothing else." Her muscles no longer responded.

The autopsy revealed a horrifying picture: pus everywhere... She had performed an abortion on herself—with the help of a carrot. Her neighbor knew, but when she called the doctors, it was too late.

A young girl, she came to work in the North on an assignment after graduating from an agricultural institute. Here she met a chubby-faced prisoner and fell in love with him. Pregnant, she faced the choice: to have a child or to keep Grisha. Choosing the former meant condemning Grisha to a punishment camp. No one was around to ask for advice, only emaciated prisoners and guards' wives, who could denounce her. Without confiding in any one, the inexperienced Zoya did everything on her own.

It was not a doctor she was looking at with disdain at the moment of her inglorious death: her last words—"I tricked you nonetheless!"—were addressed to a faceless, overarching power.

It was already one o'clock in the morning when someone knocked on the window. Frightened, I turned off the lights. When I half-opened the curtain, I saw a man's face pressed against the window glass. The man was asking to be let in. Before I even saw him, I knew it had to be Grisha Zaytsev! How did he manage to get inside the camp? What would I tell him?

He didn't recognize me; he scarcely noticed anything at all. "Nurse, how did Zoya die? Tell me."

He was freezing. His teeth were chattering, and he could barely articulate his words. Handing him a cup of hot water, I tried to say something. But he interrupted me without listening:

"Please, take me to see her, for God's sake!"

"To see her where?"

"There... You know where."

Of course I knew. Hoping to see her alive, Grisha sneaked to the camp from the outside. Now he wanted at least to see her dead body.

"Take me there, nurse! I'm begging you, I need to see her!"

I found a kerosene lantern in the storeroom and took the huge key to the morgue off the wall. In the middle of the night, we set off for the small outhouse in the far corner of the zone that so many people had passed through. There on the table lay what had once been Zoya. Grisha grabbed her body and howled, pressing it to his chest: "Zoya, dear, what have they done to us? What have you done, Zoya! Do you hear me? It's me, it's me..."

Afraid that someone would hear his wails or see the light, I shook him on the shoulders: "Stop, Grisha, don't cry like this..." I pulled him away and led him out of the morgue by force. He stayed a little while at the infirmary, clasping his head, and left.

I often think: no one except me knows about Grisha, no one knows what has made him the way he is now. I witnessed a defining moment in a human being's life. Perhaps he has a family, and sometimes he must be unbearable to live with. I don't know where he is. And it probably doesn't occur to him that his and Zoya's fates have become part of my own. Although… someone must have let him in the camp! Some guard must have had mercy.

A BULKY MAN was brought to the infirmary with a broken hip. I took the scissors and carefully cut his wet cotton-wool pants to disentangle the injured part so that the doctors could examine him. Even Bakharev, who always knew how to calm down a patient, was for a long time unable to determine the nature of the fracture. The man screamed and wouldn't allow anybody to touch him. The doctor ordered us to prepare him for operation. Under anesthesia, the patient cursed up a storm, and his legs became flexible. Bakharev probed the huge lump in his thigh.

"The bone is fine. It's a callus from an old injury that's helped him fake a fracture."

It was the doctors' turn to start cursing. One of them went to see if the guard who had brought the malingerer was still here, in which case the man would be taken straight back to the camp and punished. I pitied the "patient": people said he arrived at the infirmary from sheer hell. He simulated a fracture just to get some rest, to regain strength. With bated breath I waited to hear what the doctor would say. Taking off his smock, he looked at me; he understood what I expected to hear; he dismissed the guard and took the man to a ward. Such understanding was deeper than any declaration.

The man, quiet and guilty, stayed at the infirmary for two weeks.

Filipp's constant favors were more than just help; whatever he did was always original and creative. Such was his initiative to organize medical courses for nurses. He gathered the doctors who worked at the infirmary to lecture and conduct practical training. He even persuaded the administration to accredit the training, which was a completely unbelievable achievement.

He put a lot of effort into trying to get me released before my term was due and, sure of a successful outcome, even found an attorney in Moscow and wrote to him about my case. These signs of love became the stronghold on which I stood. I came to believe in the exceptionality of his love and it made me feel safer. Everything suggested that was the only way he could express his feelings. The anxiety disappeared from his face when he saw me at work; he would press his cheek against my quilted jacket, which hung on the same hook as his overcoat. It seemed that the laws of the camp were so clear to him that he regarded them as some game of chance, in which he made his bets. "I know everything," he would say. "Just trust me!" There seemed to be no line between certitude and self-confidence for him.

Yet our idea of how people lived on the other side of barbed wire was just as vague as theirs about our life inside the camp. These were two worlds apart. Vera Petrovna would tell us how, when Filipp had to go some place or other, she would fry cutlets and boil potatoes for him to eat on the train; she would also equip him with a bottle "so that he doesn't get bored on the way." Her stories were impressive, but none of them seemed to have any relation to my own life.

From the city where she lived before her arrest, Vera Petrovna brought along most of her belongings. Her elderly mother and eight-year-old son from her first marriage joined her in Urdoma. The boy was told that in the North he would live with his father; that was how he referred to Filipp.

This handsome dark-eyed boy once came to the zone, calling, "Papa, let's go home!" As they walked away together, I followed them with my eyes. Filipp turned around and quickly came back. "I thought you'd feel better if I returned," he said. He knew how to move me.

We would often hear from the free workers about various "trophy" films they had seen.

"During all these years, you haven't once been to the cinema?" Filipp asked thoughtfully. "I'll work something out."

In spite of the regulations, he managed to get permission from someone or other, and one day about fifteen of us prisoners were taken to a club for free workers, two kilometers away from the camp. We walked silently in single file, afraid to say a word and hardly believing what was going on. The doctor and Vera Petrovna walked at some distance behind us. It seemed I was observing this absurd picture from the outside: our line, the guard with a rifle, the free couple following us in the rear.

The guards' wives became indignant at our appearance in their midst. Aware of their burning glances, we shuffled through the hall and sat in the back row. As soon as the lights in the hall went out, someone came in and called Bakharev: a new patient needed help at the infirmary, which meant that the doctor was unable to stay for the film.

The screen was improvised out of a bed sheet. We heard the whirring of the projector, and the next moment the title of a newsreel, *Leningrad,* appeared on the screen. A wild pain pinned me down to the spot. I dug my teeth into the sleeve of my jacket so as to stifle a moan. On the screen, the Neva flowed in my native prewar Leningrad; undamaged embankments and bridges were beautiful beyond measure. I realized I had forgotten the city in which I was born, in which Mama and Renochka were buried. The film stuck into my soul with thousands of sharp splinters: it testified to the existence of my city and the camp on the very same planet.

The American trophy film was called *The Hurricane.* The romantic story with a tragic end gripped our imaginations, which had for years been kept on a strict diet.

The next day, after the evening meal, I recounted the film to the patients, who gathered to listen in the largest ward of the surgical barracks. Their interest was insatiable, and they wouldn't calm down until late at night, demanding that I rehash the plot again and again from beginning to end. I told them about the love of Marama and Terangi, about how he was put in jail, escaped and was captured again, until he finally managed to run away and celebrate his wedding with Marama; how in the morning Marama woke up to see that the birds were flying away from the island; how a tornado started at nightfall; how the islanders rushed to their temple and, kissing the ground, prayed and pleaded for mercy, but the wind and the water smashed the walls of the people's last shelter, and the blossoming island was washed off the face of the earth.

Taking a pen and paper, I described the film for Filipp, scene after scene.

THE YEAR 1944 was coming to an end.

On December 31, Bronya was to take over the shift at the infirmary, but I told her I was not leaving the barracks before the patients got their medicine at the end of the day.

Nura, a nun who worked at the infirmary as a nurse, changed the linen in all the wards. As always happened during holidays, the patients lay in their beds sadder than usual. I knew who had to be approached with a kind word, whose pillow to straighten out and who was looking to share news from home.

I had started gathering alcohol for this occasion a long time ago. I poured a few drops of alcohol, instead of the regular medicine, into the measuring glasses and gave them to the patients. As the New Year's treats flowed down their throats, they would break into a smile and close their eyes, contented.

Matvey Ilyich got hold of some bread and butter and brought it to our medical dormitory. A small Christmas tree was delivered from Filipp. I decorated it with pieces of cotton wool, threw a few logs into the stove and sat by the fire. At around ten, the door suddenly opened and Filipp ran in, saying: "I couldn't leave without wishing you a Happy New Year! I will love you for the rest of my life." He and Vera Petrovna were going to celebrate the holiday at the club, together with the camp administration.

Lena was getting ready to go to the pharmacy and celebrate together with Abram; Tanya was leaving for the lab, where another doctor was waiting for her.

Everyone was gone. Without waiting till midnight, I went to bed.

Not long after, I was shaken from my sleep. On one side of my bed stood Lena, on the other—Abram. "Get up! Fifteen minutes till midnight. We even boiled some caramel. Come quick!"

I was touched: they remembered me, even though the two of them did not need my company.

Bright stars glittered in the icy expanse above the zone. Inside the pharmacy building, it was warm and cozy. We just hoped that the guards were also celebrating and wouldn't come to check on us.

"Happy 1945! To freedom! To the end of the war! To amnesty! Thank you, friends, for thinking about me."

By one in the morning I was back to the barracks. I had to replace Bronya at six.

On the first day of the new year, I was finishing my shift when an orderly came in, saying that the doctor wanted to see me.

The door of a small ward for free women was thrust open and out leaped Filipp, grabbing me by the hand and pulling me inside. The room was empty.

"Did you have fun celebrating?"

"Yes, Lena and Abram invited me to join them."

"I kept thinking about you all night, and you went to celebrate at the pharmacy!"

He grabbed me by the throat and started choking me with an iron grip.

Just as suddenly he came to his senses and jumped away. A moment later he was kneeling before me and begging for forgiveness, trying to kiss my hands.

I could no longer bear Filipp's suspicions, Vera Petrovna's shadowing me, the way my life was turning out here.

I went to see Bronya.

"Would you work the next shift for me. Tell the doctor I am not coming to work anymore. Let them send me away immediately. I can't stand this any longer!"

Bronya passed my words on to Filipp.

She and I were sitting at the dormitory when the door opened and Filipp appeared in the doorway. He was so drunk he couldn't stand on his feet and toppled face-down right onto my bed.

It was impossible to do anything in the camp without everybody finding out, especially for a free worker, and even more so for the chief doctor. The guards could walk in any minute, and it wasn't hard to imagine what would ensue. Bronya rushed about:

"Filipp Yakovlevich! Stand up! You can't stay here. I'll walk with you, please. Here, let me help you to your feet..."

Bakharev wouldn't move and just stammered: "I'll leave if she forgives me." And then: "I'll stand up if she returns to the infirmary barracks." He turned to me: "Forgive me right now, or I'll do something terrible. If you don't love me—I won't live!"

It was useless arguing with the drunken man. I just had to make sure he left the zone immediately. He begged for forgiveness, and I said I forgave him; he asked me to say I loved him, and I did.

Triumphant, he suddenly stood up from the table, on which just a minute ago his head was lying so helplessly. He had taken into account every detail and played out his scheme timely and expertly.

Turning out to be completely sober, Filipp was begging me to forgive his jealousy, madness and savagery. Lavish with words, he kept repeating he loved me and wouldn't let me go anywhere. He said he knew me better than I knew myself, that I was talented in everything in the world; that he recognized my achievements at work... As if his confession wasn't enough to express his feelings, Filipp blamed himself for being a womanizer, for putting a notch in his belt with each "victory," saying that only now did he realize how foul and vulgar his life had been.

MY PAST KEPT reminding me of itself. Recollections floated about my imagination like the debris of a ship that once used to have a destination, and sometimes a whole silhouette of the past would float up to the surface. "No one in the world knows where I am," I thought to myself, meaning Erik and Barbara Ionovna.

During one of these dark moments, I wrote Erik a short bitter letter. The answer came immediately. Erik's letter was long; repetitions sounded like incantations, but I didn't believe a single word of it. I didn't believe he had sent any petitions to the Gulag administration asking to have me sent back to Kirghizia; that he had tried to make special arrangements with his camp's authorities; that he had actually thought about us being together again. I expected honesty from him, which would rehabilitate at least a part of my past but found no trace of it. One thing was clear from his letter: he was in a bad way. His muddled words revealed nothing but helplessness, a need for support. I had to admit that his exhaustion and dismay were also my exhaustion and dismay, that his confusion would be the ultimate outcome of my life as well. Although our correspondence helped me maintain the connection between the past and the present, we were now merely remnants of a tumultuous period in our lives.

In the years to come, our correspondence would break off and resume again. Only five years later, in 1949 when it was already too late, Erik sent me a letter I was longing to receive back in 1944–1945.

> Tamara! My only friend, my greatest and most painful love! Here is what I want to tell you to start with: I am not the way I was back then. Now I am tormented; I can't understand how I could abandon you during those frightening days. The only thing that justifies me was that I could hardly make ends meet. I was inexperienced and stupid. Since I received the postcard you had written to me, after all my attempts to find you, I have tormented myself, thinking how abominably I acted toward you. I hid it all from you, pretending that nothing of the sort had ever happened, but my conscience requited me for this with so many sleepless nights full of torment… It's even good you didn't write back. Forgive me this, my dear! Forgive and have mercy on me. I have done a lot of good things for people, and I always think: it is just to pay off my sins before Tamara.
>
> I close my eyes and try to remember the past: you have always been with me. During the winter frosts in Belovodsk, when again and again I would read the words your hand had scribbled on a piece of thick cardboard from the shop you used to work at and where later, swallowing tears, I worked as well. When I felt especially awful, my lips whispered the dearest word, "Tamara," and I would feel better. Then, the impossible coal mines of the faraway Sulukta, where, standing up to my waist in water in an old mine deep under the ground, filthy and lice-ridden, I whispered your name and felt warmer. Then—Siberia, where I was terribly cold and just as terribly hungry. I came down with typhus and lung fever, followed by pyonephrosis, but nevertheless, tossing about in my bed, I kept repeating your name, which made everyone around me know that you, my wife, meant everything to me. So do understand me! Can I really be without you? Can I live, knowing that you may not be with me? Let all the hardships and miseries I have gone through tell you that I can't live without you.

> I love you infinitely. Try to understand and forgive me. I am not afraid of writing to you that if you abandon me, I will cease to exist… I will still have to sit out another three years after you get released, but in the end we can be together. Will we?

This letter came when everything had already become irrevocable. But when Erik wrote for the first time, I set out to write an answer.

I was sitting in the infirmary staff room. Filipp dropped by to get something. He was in a hurry: the administration wanted to see him.

"What are you writing?" he asked in passing.

"A letter to Erik."

"I see…"

After a brief moment of hesitation, he fetched a pen from out of his pocket and, seizing the letter, put his bold signature across the sheet of paper.

"I'll read it when I come back."

The door behind him slammed shut. I bluntly stared at his signature. Now I wouldn't have the chance to rewrite the letter, even if I wanted to. Filipp did not trust me. He trusted no one and wasn't embarrassed to reveal it.

A NEW TRANSPORT arrived at the Urdoma medical unit. Among the new arrivals was the wife of the writer Sergey Tretyakov. Her husband, a friend of Mayakovsky's, was shot in 1937; Olga Viktorovna was sentenced to ten years.

After she had recovered, she was allowed to stay on at the camp and work as an accountant. When I first met her, Olga Viktorovna was serving her seventh year. About forty-five years old, slim, of average height, with graying hair and glasses set on the bridge of her nose, she looked like an aging student. Remembering her past, she'd blossom, but she never let her strong individuality distort her recollections.

When the free workers had a day off, Olga Viktorovna would come to the staff room as soon as I was through handing out medications to the patients. Waiting by the window, I'd see her approaching slowly through the corridor of snowdrifts along the narrow path, carrying a small basket with two cozy cups and a coffee pot she had brought from home. Her daughter would occasionally send her a parcel with coffee. I heated up the *burzhuyka,* and our "ritual" would begin. "In the fall of nineteen-such-and-such," Olga Viktorovna would start her story, "Sergey and I arrived in Paris…" For her, Paris, Berlin and New York were real, terrestrial cities with museums, cathedrals, poets and writers they knew personally. For me, of course, they were terra incognita. I avidly listened to her stories about travel and adventure, but most of all I liked when she read poetry and talked about her husband or Mayakovsky.

I longed to find out the real reasons for Mayakovsky's death. His suicide and its motives had been ignored by our schoolteachers. It was a riddle I passionately wanted to solve. I tried to absorb their moods and yearnings, the very atmosphere of their gatherings. "One night," recounted Olga Viktorovna, "Osip had an argument with Volodya… I wanted Sergey to take his side, but he supported Osip… Volodya got agitated, then became silent, sat in a corner and took a cat on his knees…" Or, "That night, Lilya teased Volodya. He frowned and looked tormented, as though there was something he was trying hard to swallow…" The poet's pain resounded in my heart. The image of Mayakovsky as a rebellious tribune poet would miraculously merge with this new portrait of a man with such a gentle and vulnerable soul emerging from Olga Viktorovna's stories.

Sometimes she would just sit warming herself by the fire and ask me to tell her about myself. What could I say? My memory was bound up in a tight sheaf I hadn't unrolled in a long time. I didn't know what was still preserved and what had been forever ulcerated with betrayal. But I could recall one episode.

"I knew Yakhontov."

"Volodya? Good Lord, I knew him very well!" she exclaimed. "How brilliantly he recited his namesake, Mayakovsky! And Esenin. And Pushkin. He is a real master!"

I was glad I could tell her about meeting Yakhontov in Frunze, about his unforgettable staging of *Nastasya Filippovna,* about our strolls through the fog in Leningrad. Here it all seemed to be just a beautiful sad fantasy. And his fear! Having felt how stricken he was at the time, I thought: how strange that my memory of him was now revived precisely by that fear. I wondered what he would say if he knew where Olga Viktorovna and I ended up.

Our Sunday coffee ceremonies relieved us from the daily turmoil. Olga Viktorovna had numerous friends at different camps. Avoiding official mail, they managed to exchange letters and artwork through private channels. I was amazed to hear that here, in the camps, the wellsprings of art survived, for it seemed to me that prisoners were disunited, immured in their own miseries.

"I wish you could meet Boris Genrikhovich Kreitser from the Solvychegda camp. A very clever man, and a brilliant painter, too."

Olga Viktorovna kept on recommending her friends to me:

"Lev Adolfovich Fink works at Central Camp. A fervent, talented man."

She introduced me to her circle, just as Pyotr Polikarpovich had gotten me "acquainted" with Tamara Grigorievna Tsulukidze back at Svetik. Before I met them in person, I already knew a lot about these people and worshipped their genius.

Once Olga Viktorovna asked:

"Will you find time to read my friend's story? His name is Boris Shustov. It's called *Ruble.*"

I was happy and embarrassed when she handed me the text. I was discovering the spiritual element that fought for existence at some remote realm of camp life; the element I had longed to embrace, which would give me desire to live on.

"Have you read Romain Rolland's *The Enchanted Soul?*" she asked me one day and only shook her head when I replied I hadn't. "Too bad I don't have it here with me. But it's my 'gift' to you anyway: it is your type of book."

Olga Viktorovna would go back to her barracks, and the reality of camp life set in again.

One guard used to come for intravenous glucose infusions—a treatment for free workers only. The short, nimble man rolled up the sleeve of his soldier's shirt and, baring his skinny and anemic arm, excitedly recounted a story about two people I knew:

"The officer called and ordered me to nail the two bastards, to teach 'em a lesson for messing around in the camp. So I hid in the grass in the corner of the zone. The grass grows high there… I wait there and say to myself, 'Well, just show yourselves, I'll teach you!' At that moment the fellow comes out of the barracks and slips behind the boiler room. I look again, and see that the bitch flies out of her dorm and sneaks in the boiler room, too. I wait for as long as it takes, then crawl closer and, bang! I show up in front of them just at the right time. They were terrified! They both went white as ghosts and couldn't get a word out. Well done, eh?"

The guard roared with laughter, proud of his cunning. He was the embodiment of raw power, capable of anything.

"Why would you do that? Imagine yourself in their shoes…"

"What do I need to imagine myself in their shoes for? I'm not a fascist, not some kind of scum, like them. I'll tell you what: they should be shot right off the bat!"

His work, his way of dividing people into "scum" and those like himself, eventually took its toll on him: he shot himself in the head. There was something even he couldn't come to terms with.

No one ever talked to me openly about Filipp. Old-timers, who had been through hell and high water in the local camps, seemed to pity me. I couldn't have been mistaken: they wanted to protect me, without trying to teach or reprimanding me.

I was beginning to discern one of the greatest treasures of humankind: the "continental" unity of people sharing miseries and joys. I would recall the epigraph from John Donne to Hemingway's novel *For Whom the Bell Tolls,* "No man is an island, entire of itself; every man is a piece of the continent, a part of the main. If a clod be washed away by the sea, Europe is the less, as well as if a promontory were, as well as if a manor of thy friend's or of thine own were: any man's death diminishes me, because I am involved in mankind, and therefore never send to know for whom the bells tolls; it tolls for thee."

Once I overheard scraps of a conversation between Filipp and Simon, the attendant from the sixth barracks. I was struck by the intensity of their words, no less than by the desire of a stranger to intervene. I sensed an indistinct, heretofore unnoticed, stormy danger. My life, it seemed, was returning to normalcy, and I didn't pay much attention to anything else. Simon was scolding Filipp, who had once been his friend and was now his superior in the infirmary:

"...You're ruining her, Filipp. Basic decency requires that you leave her alone..."

"You don't understand. I love her. It's none of your business, anyway..."

When Simon came to talk to me in person, I felt even more confused.

"I can't forget your recital of the story *The Wife.* I have friends at the culture brigade. I could write to them about you."

Not knowing what exactly he wanted to save me from, I hid behind the indefinite, "I don't know..." but Simon wouldn't give up:

"Forgive me for meddling in your life, but I don't think you understand: you're under the sword of Damocles. Assume that, in his own way, he loves you. But he'll never leave Vera. They're cut from the same cloth. Just their income from abortions alone makes a much more solid tie than his feelings toward you. He is afraid of her, and he's right. Vera is mean and conniving; she won't back down till she wipes you out..."

Simon's words sounded like slander, money from abortions—sheer raving. What abortions, where? I was indignant, though I said nothing back. His characterization of Filipp and Vera hit a raw nerve. Naïve and inexperienced, I never perceived the Bakharevs as a family.

Nor could I imagine back then that a man who had knocked on the door of my life in such a rude manner would later become more than a graceful and heartfelt friend. I was far from knowing that the twists and turns of life would one day force me to remember every single word of that conversation.

THE APPROACHING ARRIVAL of TEC, a theater ensemble collective, was actively discussed in the camp; names of actors were mentioned. "Just wait, you'll see and hear for yourself!" I couldn't understand what TEC, or the culture brigade, was or what theater actors had to do with the camps.

They arrived late at night. The frost was so biting one had to run from barracks to barracks without stopping, so as not to freeze on the spot. I was on duty at the infirmary. It was a quiet evening, and I felt calm and peaceful. I washed my hands, and when I glanced at the fragment of mirror that hung on the wall I didn't immediately turn away as usual. No matter what people said, I never considered myself talented or beautiful. But now I liked the way I looked. I was twenty-four. For a moment, it seemed I was young and pretty.

I heard the front door slam. An unfamiliar elderly woman with cheery eyes stood on the threshold. She was wearing an ear-flap fur hat and a camp quilted jacket, around which a scrap of blanket was wound. She greeted me with an exclamation:

"Oh, what a princess we have here! Well, well… Who are you, sweetheart? A nurse? We'll take you with us away from here in no time! Sorry, I didn't even introduce myself. My name is Wanda Kazimirovna Mitskevich. I'm from TEC, the theater ensemble. And you are?"

Then she asked where to find the doctor.

Several minutes after Wanda Kazimirovna left, a real pilgrimage to the infirmary ensued. In perfectly timed intervals, the newly arrived actors popped in, turn by turn, just to ask the same question: "Would you please be so kind as to tell me where to find the doctor?"

I could perfectly imagine what a dressing-down awaited me for the "guest tour" that Wanda Kazimirovna organized. Indeed, the doctor came running immediately. He made arrangements to put up the actors and came back to reprimand me, saying that actors were frivolous people and demanding that I stay away from them.

Next evening TEC was giving a performance.

At supper, everyone was hurried: the mess-room had to be turned into a club. Benches were brought in and arranged in rows. The front of the room was turned into a stage. There was a buzz in the air: "Alliluev the tenor… Such a voice… And Slanskaya the soprano… Golovin, the baritone… Erukhimovich must have prepared something new…"

The sight of women dressing up for the prison-camp concert was, by itself, a new and contagious spectacle. I still had the old gauze kerchief tinted with iodine in the wooden briefcase from Aunt Polya, and I was already wearing the felt boots that Matvey Ilyich had sewn for me. I decided to go to the concert in my white gown, to look as if I had just come from duty. But my workmates protested and demanded that I have my pick from three different dresses. My head was spinning from the simple, long-forgotten pleasure of having matching attire.

The club was packed. People made room for others to sit, then grew quiet. Finally, the curtain, patched together out of gray blankets, trembled and parted, revealing a brightly colored backdrop that depicted the prairies. The orchestra started playing. My soul slipped and the music carried it away in an unexpected direction, tossing it from side to side and pulling tight the collar of my memory. In a moment, touched by the unspoken element of the music, the entire hall was sobbing. There were no radios in the camps. We had forgotten what music sounded like.

The characters of the operetta *Rose Marie,* dressed in exotic costumes, appeared on the stage. The aria of Jim the Miner seemed like a hallucination. The plot was gripping, revolving around the most unpretentious and melodramatic of all human feelings.

The second part of the performance included an acrobatic duet and dancers. The solos by Alliluev, Golovin and Slanskaya were the most impressive of all, as well as the humoresques by Erukhimovich. Losing all sense of time and place, we listened attentively and, without feeling ashamed in front of each other, laughed at one moment and cried at another, living through our own thoughts, anguish, desires and despair.

After the concert they announced a dancing party. The very word "dancing" sounded alien, if not criminal; it seemed we would be punished for it any minute. However, within seconds, the benches were stacked against the wall and a dancing circle was formed.

I saw Filipp staring at me, demanding silently that I leave. But I couldn't bring myself to go back to the barracks while the orchestra was playing a waltz. All I asked was just one dance. The desire to whirl like I used to in the dancing halls of Leningrad was so intense that it seemed I was soaring up, relieved of all weight by joy and delight.

There was no end to men inviting me to dance. The illustrious soloist Alliluev was already on his way. "I won't obey, I'll stay!" I wanted to whirl faster and faster, to take hold of the space surrounding me…

I forced myself to walk out of the club.

The lighted windows of the mess hall cast their light into the frosty night. The music trickled outside through the thin walls. Intoxicated, I waltzed around one barracks, then another. I wanted to take flight into the fathomless starry height, to turn into a witch, to saddle the silver slice of the moon looming above in the sky.

Returning to the barracks from the dancing party, some women immediately lay down and fell asleep, while others asked for a smoke and plunged into memories of their loves, homes and husbands; lying down with their eyes closed, they dreamed of something very personal.

The next day I was told that the director of TEC wanted to talk to me. My heart pounded.

"They say you did a splendid job reciting Kononenko's story *The Wife*. What do you think of working with us? We need an elocutionist. I don't think you'll regret it if you agree. The procedure is simple: I report to the head of the Political Department, they consider your case, and if your article isn't too bad, they issue a permit. What do you say?" Semyon Vladimirovich Erukhimovich was waiting for my answer.

I wanted to say, "My God, of course!" But the thought of Filipp held me back. How could I agree without asking him, the man I owed my life to? I felt that saying yes would be a betrayal, a line I could not cross.

"I have to think about it."

"All right," said Semyon Vladimirovich. "Though no one usually says that…"

The young director with a fetching smile didn't hurry me. Diplomatic and thorough, he asked me to tell him about myself. Before he left, he repeated:

"Make up your mind! It's a good company."

If only Filipp could let me go! If only he would say, "Go. You'll be better off this way." He knew that was what I needed to hear. But I realized he would never let me go of his own will. He wasn't that kind of man.

I avoided meeting the TEC director again, never giving him an answer.

IN ABOUT A MONTH, the permit nevertheless came for me from the Political Department.

"You sought this out! You asked them to take you on!" Filipp raged. He wouldn't believe me and didn't want to hear anything. But not to obey the Political Department was out of the question.

The day of my departure was set, and Filipp announced his incontestable plan to me: he would take me to Knyazh-Pogost, where the camp administration was stationed, about four hours away. There, he himself would call on the head of the medical unit and win me back, since there was a shortage of nurses in the camp. I don't know how he managed to get rid of the guard who was supposed to escort me, but Filipp took over the guard's duty and even got a hold of his revolver.

"I'll be waiting behind the door, and if I hear you say you want to be with TEC, I'll shoot you on the spot with this gun," he said to me.

"You won't have to shoot me," I answered, vowing my indebtedness to him. "I won't agree."

I was saying good-bye to my friends and my patients, who clung to the windows to see me off.

The guard saw me to the train station, then disappeared. My legs were no longer ravaged by scurvy, and I climbed the train car with ease. As if in a theater, I observed the carefree passengers in the train car: food and vodka were being unpacked from wicker baskets; some dozed peacefully on their berths while others chatted. But behind the window, next to the elongated washbasin dug into the earth, prisoners stood in line waiting for their turn to wash. They would eat their evening meal and return to their barracks overridden with bedbugs. Again watchtowers, the taiga and more and more camps along the way…

Hermann's aria from *The Queen of Spades* played on the radio. I always felt strange listening to it, frightened by the perception of life as a gamble.

We arrived in Knyazh-Pogost around one in the morning. The train halted for a few minutes and set off again, going further north, to Vorkuta. All of a sudden, panic overtook me. I realized I would never be able to lose touch with people or places I had grown tied to by the will of Fate. Filipp would now walk me to the unfamiliar camp, hand me over, and then… He didn't feel much better. It seemed beyond him to lead and leave me there. He couldn't make a move. Sticking his head into the corner of an outbuilding of the station, he pounded his fist on the wall and moaned:

"There is nothing I can do! Nothing!"

I froze with fear when he told me to wait and went to the wooden hut with the signboard *Lodging*.

I didn't ask what it took him to get a room so as not to take me straight to the camp. For a few hours we sat there in complete darkness, as if inside a lair, paralyzed with fear by which we were both condemned to counting off nervously the swelling, sultry minutes we had left before morning. There was not even the slightest illusion of freedom. Even such a reckless person as Filipp was utterly dispirited.

By the start of the workday we stood in front of the two-story building of the camp's Political Department. A guard who had been assigned to me was already waiting for us when we arrived.

"Prisoner Petkevich," he reported when we entered the waiting room.

"Oh, the one for TEC? Take her to the zone."

"Please, the thing is…" I started, "I wanted to ask you to let me stay at the Urdoma infirmary. I'm a nurse there…"

But I was interrupted and told I'd be able to lay out my requests when the head of the Political Department, who was away then, returned. Meanwhile I had to go to the camp.

The three of us walked in silence. A few steps away from the checkpoint, we stopped. Filipp and I had to say good-bye. He was pale.

"I'm going to see the head of the medical unit. I will always love you and I can't live without you. I'll do anything to get you back." He grinned. "I'll give him my golden cigarette case. Perhaps this should work better than any requests. I'll win you back. I will!"

Struck by the intensity of his grief and amazed by his cynical frankness—to trade a human being for a cigarette case—I stepped across the threshold of the camp's checkpoint. Filipp stayed on the outside behind the fence.

I was directed to the corner of the zone, where I'd find the TEC barracks.

It was pouring, and the snow was turning into slush. Avoiding stepping into puddles, I trotted off.

The zone was huge. Old-time barracks of darkened wood beams were densely packed together in rows. They all looked the same.

An elderly bearded man with a cane passed by.

"Do you know where the theater barracks is?" I asked.

"I do, ma'am!" the man said and looked at me with a welcoming curiosity, his eyes almost laughing. "I was just going there myself."

"Can I walk with you?"

"You can, ma'am!" he said in the same ironic tone. "Why the crying? Is it so necessary?"

"No… yes…"

Without saying another word to each other, we safely got to the barracks.

Inside, beds were lined up against the walls. In the middle of the incongruous building was a long table. The barracks were at the same time a living quarters for men from TEC and a rehearsal place.

In the far left corner, a shabby plush curtain roped off the directors' booth. In the right corner, parallel to that booth, a steel barrel, which served as a stove, lay on its side. Thick damp logs hissed from inside. The fire, receding at one moment and blazing up at another, was struggling to overtake the soggy wood.

Sitting on their beds, the men were finishing whatever they had to do in the morning before the rehearsal.

"Look who's here!" they greeted me.

A series of questions and invitations poured down on me:

"Sit closer to the fire! Let me help you to a cup of hot tea. Make yourself comfortable."

I instantly felt like I was visiting old friends. The young TEC director explained:

"It wasn't our idea to summon you. I understood you didn't want to leave Urdoma. The fact is that the head of the Political Department was looking through the files, noticed your photograph and put you on the list. So don't take it personally."

I wasn't the first, or the only, arrival. To beef up the troupe, about six people had been called in at that time. Among them was Dmitry Femistoklevich Karayanidi, a brilliant pianist and conductor, graduate of the Baku Conservatory, a charming man who had spent seven years in the general works before he arrived here. The rest had, essentially, nothing to do with the arts.

Held back by my promise to Filipp, I addressed the TEC director:

"Please tell the Political Department I am of no use to you. I really have to go back."

"You have to ask our stage director," he replied, pointing at the bearded man I had run into in the zone. "Though it looks like he's already figuring out what role to give you. Why don't you talk to him about this?"

The stage director, whose name was Aleksandr Osipovich Gavronsky, did not ask me questions. It seemed my request to be rejected from TEC only piqued his interest toward me. But both of the men promised neither to interfere nor to insist on my enrolment in TEC. The head of the Political Department was to arrive any day now. It was entirely up to him alone to decide.

I found myself surrounded by a special life, different from anything I had seen before. Instruments were being tuned, singers were warming up, dancers were stretching their legs. A strange muddle of sound reigned in the barracks, which somehow created a sense of comfort and harmony. It was a miracle to see American egg powder, macaroni and frozen fat in the food rations of TEC members. Everything had an imprint of uniqueness, and only captivity was shared with the rest of camp life.

On the second day of my stay at Central Camp, a woman came to the theater barracks. Her appearance struck me as not belonging to the camp at all. When I asked who she was, I heard the name, "Tamara Grigorievna Tsulukidze." She was the one whom Doctor Shirochinsky had spoken about with such admiration back in Svetik, adding, "I'm sure you *will* meet some day." I feasted my eyes on her, so refined and full of feminine charm, but I did not have enough courage to approach and talk to her.

Everyone here seemed talented, professional and interesting in his own way. As for myself, I felt like a transient guest. I couldn't escape the image of Filipp's worn-out face, his pleading eyes. I couldn't forget how he pounded his fist against the wall at the train station, repeating, "There's nothing I can do!"

Gradually, though, these feelings dissipated.

The stage director entered the barracks. He elegantly set his cane aside and, leaning on it slightly, raised his brow. Allowing a deliberately sorrowful sigh, he declared in a full voice so that everyone could hear:

"My sweetheart, you know, has totally flipped her lid!"

The jargon was so unexpected and out of keeping with his appearance that I grew bewildered. The next moment I burst out laughing, hee-hawing impetuously. It was the first time I'd laughed like that from the day of my arrest. I couldn't stop; it was as if some terrible burden fell from my shoulders. All the while Aleksandr Osipovich was looking at me archly.

That marked the beginning of our friendship.

THE HEAD of the Political Department, Shtanko, returned to the camp. He appeared on the threshold of the barracks, accompanied by a large suite of officials in durable pressed coats and creaky top boots. The new arrivals were asked to stand in the middle of the barracks. With his greatcoat across his shoulders, the "Citizen Chief" inspected the newcomers.

"What do you do?" Shtanko asked the woman who looked the oldest.

"I dance, and I sing, too," she answered.

"Well, well!" he grinned boldly.

"And you? You?" he asked everyone turn by turn.

I hid my hair under the kerchief and waited for my turn, trying to look calm and indifferent.

"Last name?"

I answered. Shtanko squinted, and I understood: he'd already been asked to dispatch me back.

"What can *you* please us with?"

"I can't do anything!" I replied bravely, pinned down by the chief's eyes.

"Can you sing at least?

"Sing? No, I can't."

"Dance?"

"No."

"Recite poetry? Play any instruments?"

"No, nothing at all."

He paused for a moment and concluded in an irritated tone:

"So you say. Well, if you can't do anything, then you'll have to learn! You're staying."

Taking advantage of the administration's visit, the TEC director bombarded Shtanko with requests. He reminded him of his promise to provide the actors with new costumes, allow new songs in the repertoire and so on.

Something spurred me on to approach the head of the Political Department:

"Citizen Chief, let me just go to Urdoma to get my things!"

Shtanko turned around:

"You've got so many things?" His laughing eyes looked at me with curiosity.

"Not too many, but..."

"But what? Need to see Bakharev?"

It was clear that Shtanko knew everything. I could only say yes.

"Give her an escort guard! Let her leave for three days, no more!" he ordered the camp commandant.

While everyone was surprised by Shtanko's "kingly" gesture, in an instant I had gained the reputation of being foolhardy. Even though in three days I had to be back, everything seemed to be turning out for me.

FROM THE SLOPES of the Urdoma camp anyone approaching could easily be seen.

I saw Filipp run wildly down the hill in the direction of the checkpoint; he seemed to have forgotten the basic prudence imposed by the regime of the camp.

"You came, you came back!" he kept repeating, crying, unashamed of his tears.

I reassured myself: "He loves me endlessly. How could I not have even tried to come?"

The same night, Tanya Mironenko, the most reserved and austere of all the nurses, told me:

"I knew, of course, he was keen on you, but I never imagined he would get so carried away, that he'd love you so much. Without you he's just a corpse."

Three days flew by.

I was surprised to see Filipp calm and even serene, given that we were parting forever. Soon, however, everything became clear:

"You're not going anywhere. Everything's been settled. You're staying to work here."

I doubted that such an authority as the head of the Political Department would ever change his mind but decided not to debase my trust with Filipp by asking who exactly gave permission for me to stay at Urdoma.

Working life got back to normal. I watched the patients while on duty, bandaged wounds, made injections and assisted with surgeries.

I couldn't wait to tell Olga Viktorovna about my meeting with Aleksandr Osipovich.

"You're not the only one he's produced such an impression on. There are dozens of people who are under his charm. He's a brilliant stage director, extremely clever and very sarcastic. One slipup, and you'll never hear the end of it."

About two weeks passed. One evening, after the day's shift, Filipp came running from outside the zone to say he had gotten an urgent message from Svetik: a man had been run over by a train and needed to be operated on. He asked me not to leave the medical barracks after my night shift and said he'd stop by as soon as he got back.

Filipp ran off. But when just half an hour later two officers came into the barracks, I grew numb with a heavy presentiment.

"You've got five minutes. Pack your things and report to the checkpoint!"

I went to the dorms to get my wooden suitcase.

Two guards with a dog were assigned to escort me. The German shepherd, held on a leash, rushed about and barked wildly. They were sending me to a punishment camp.

My memory hasn't retained whether we walked or drove or took a train.

Even the most hardened criminals and old-timers were afraid of the punishment camp. To wind up there, one had to commit a murder while already serving time. There they'd bring fugitives, or prisoners accused of organizing political riots or writing leaflets. Never was I more afraid, except on the night that the interrogator showed me the warrant for my arrest.

THE OMINOUS PUNISHMENT CAMP, which no inspection commission or TEC ever visited, was situated on the right bank of the Vychegda River. Fenced in by several rows of barbed wire, it was under reinforced guard, with many dogs. Before I saw the faces of the camp's inhabitants, I was terrified by the scowls of the guards.

I arrived after nightfall. The air in the overcrowded barracks was permeated with the putrid smell of foot wraps and shoe covers drying by the stove, a stench I recognized from my time in Svetik. By the stove, someone was cooking food they'd stolen from parcels or provisions taken from other prisoners. Nobody seemed to notice when I walked in. I found a free spot on an upper bunk. My imagination ran wild with frightening scenes: a group of criminals would approach and stab me with a knife, or pull me down to the floor and start beating me senseless... I couldn't control my fear, but finally I managed to fall asleep.

It was still dark when the familiar sound of a loud bang against a steel rail broke into my dreams: reveille.

Tired and gloomy women puttered about the barracks. Of course, not everyone got up. Some criminals "with principles" stayed in their beds. Their tenets were "not to work, not to become a sheep, not to let them turn you into a useless old woman that nobody needs." Even in this camp the work distributor didn't seem to care. He picked on women randomly, cursing at one, hitting another. A blow on the neck, a shriek... Such a familiar score!

I stole a glance at the prisoners walking toward the checkpoint. I knew by now that overt curiosity could immediately engender deadly hatred, so it was better not to look at all, to keep your eyes on the ground.

I was assigned to a brigade that dug trenches. The skills I gained back in Belovodsk came in handy, though by the middle of the day I ran out of energy. I knew I would have to overstep one limit after another. I kept digging the earth.

People talked about a recent revolt in the camp. Prisoners had rebelled because of reduced bread rations and demanded an outside inspection. The watchtowers turned their machine guns on the zone; the prisoners were ordered to quiet down. The guards opened fire on those who refused to disperse. About a dozen people were killed. They were taken away and buried in the forest. A feeling of despondency hung in the air.

Again everything was reduced to filth, cursing, fear, fighting for the work norm. Luckily, no one tried talking to me. In my dreams I saw only cubic meters of earth and a shovel breaking through the frozen layers of soil.

Filipp managed to get in touch with the local doctors who could help me, but when I was summoned to the medical unit, the attendant told me:

"We can't do much. It's beyond our power to exempt you from work. Everything's tightly controlled here. The only thing we can do is request that you be transferred to the workshops."

In the locksmith's workshop where I was transferred one had to whip up the norm just as anywhere else.

An intelligent-looking man approached me:

"My name is Miloslavsky, I'm from Moscow. Nice to make your acquaintance! What are *you* here for?"

It was hard for me to say why.

"What about you?" I asked.

"I dared write to the Gulag administration that the authorities pinch from the prisoners. Have you ever seen a fool like me?"

Miloslavsky gave me some advice: "Don't talk to anyone in your barracks. Don't even think about complaining: they'll give you another sentence. Many prisoners here are summoned to the Third Department and offered a chance to collaborate with the authorities. Pretend you don't understand. Don't go anywhere out of the barracks after work, not even to get water. Don't breathe, don't look. Don't see or hear anything."

About ten days after I was transferred to the workshops, a man from the medical unit came for me.

"Take this sack of linen to the disinfection chamber. Someone's waiting for you there."

My heart almost leapt out of my chest. It must have been Filipp! How did he manage to sneak into the punishment camp?

The bathhouse attendant silently pointed me in the direction of the chamber, where linen was loaded for thermal disinfection. I opened the small door leading inside. The wood-beam ceiling was low and there wasn't enough room to stand up straight. There on the floor sat Vera Petrovna.

"Quickly, sit down next to me. I have just a few minutes," she said.

She started in her peculiar chattering manner.

"First, I brought you a pair of boots. Filipp is worried you'll have nothing to wear when spring comes. Yes, I can see for myself: your feet are totally wet. Second, he is trying to arrange with the medical authorities that you be transferred to Mezhog. It's the largest medical settlement around. He has completely gone out of his mind. He's raving that you'll be killed here, or that something worse will happen. So he does one stupid thing after another. Here's a piece of paper: write to him that he should calm down. Well, I didn't want to tell you this. He wouldn't let me, but eventually you'll find out anyway… The thing is: Filipp is under investigation and he'll probably be put on trial."

She recounted what had happened:

"Filipp's summons to Svetik to operate on the man who was allegedly run over by the train was staged. They had to get Filipp out of the way while you were being sent off. He went there, saw there had been no accident, and immediately understood everything. He rushed back, burst into the infirmary and saw Khan-Dadash, an attendant from another barracks, sitting at your desk. He's the one who told Filipp that you'd been taken away to the punishment camp. Filipp felt sick, so they called me and Doctor R. In the morning, as luck would have it, the wife of one of the officers from the administration was brought in to give birth. Filipp was sick and couldn't get up. He could've kept silent at least, but no, he said: 'I'm not going anywhere! The officer didn't give a damn about Tamara and sent her away. Now, let his wife give birth however she wants to.' You know yourself how terrified Doctor R. is of childbirth. Everyone ran around looking for another doctor. Meanwhile, the officer's wife delivered the child in the staff room, with almost no assistance. The case has been passed on to the prosecutor. They'll never forgive Filipp for it, of course. They've had a grudge against him for a long time. Perhaps you don't know, but all in all he has paid them off for fifteen transfer orders that came for you. Now they'll remind him of everything!"

When she was through, Vera Petrovna left.

I was trying to grasp every fact of the news. It was hard to believe that Filipp refused to deliver the baby. There must have been something almost superhuman in him to say, "I'm not going anywhere!" It seemed incredible that he paid them off fifteen times for me. It turned out that my transfer to the punishment camp had already been planned for a long time. What was he going to do now, when those he had gotten along so well with turned against him? Filipp was under investigation, also a victim.

And again there was nothing but the shovel, the earth, the permanent need to look back, exhaustion, bitter dismay.

Soon I was called to the checkpoint "with my things." I no longer had any things, though, except the empty wooden suitcase. All my possessions—felt boots, gauze kerchief and the boots that Filipp sent to me—had been requisitioned by the local thieves.

An old man stood at the checkpoint waiting for the transfer.

"Doctor Fedosov," he introduced himself. "You going to Malinovskaya, too?"

I didn't understand.

"I mean, to Mezhog."

A separate camp was often associated here with the name of its commandant or doctor. "Sent to Vaganova" stood for a transfer to the tuberculosis camp in Protoka. "Ended up at Malinovskaya" meant that a prisoner had been dispatched to the psychiatric hospital.

"Don't be afraid," said my fellow traveler. "Mezhog isn't only a mental asylum."

The escort guard asked:

"Should we go straight across the river? The ice is still solid. Or would you rather walk the roundabout way, about five kilometers longer?"

Biting wind blowing at our backs drove us on. Rescued from the dreadful camp, we didn't even look back.

Spring was already on its way. I hadn't noticed its arrival. If only I could keep walking like this across the river for ever and ever!

THE MEZHOG CAMP consisted of a psychiatric hospital, children's quarters, an infirmary, a greenhouse and some work sites. There was one huge barracks for the medical staff and sawmill workers. Part of it was occupied with double bunk beds, while the rest of the living space was taken up by densely packed cots.

After the punishment camp, I felt especially withdrawn among the new people. Everything around me was onerous, disturbing and heavy.

It took some time before I understood: I was pregnant.

The need to come to terms with what had happened, to make a decision, drove me out of the crowded barracks to a secluded corner of the zone.

I was gnawed by doubts, my conscience was unclear. I realized I'd have to remain in the camps for another four years after the child was born. How would I manage? On the other hand, I knew that the little daughter of Mira Galpern, Aleksandr Osipovich Gavronsky's friend, *was* growing up in the camps. The girl was marvelous, and she would be a grown-up by the time of Mira's release.

My cot stood next to Agnessa Alikhanova, an agronomist. Every night, before falling asleep, she would take a photograph of her little boy out of the drawer and look at it for a long time. Her son was a beautiful Ossetian child: black-eyed and serene, wearing short trousers and a sailor's jacket.

The photograph was bewitching. Agnessa's need to look at her little boy was like an obsession and spread to me, too. To have a child, to hold a son or daughter in your arms seemed like sheer happiness.

Soon I would have no time for myself. Something greater than just a decision was looming in my future. If not now, when? Despite everything in the world, I would have the child! There would be a baby whom I could give all my heart to. I would never again be all alone in the world.

One evening in Mezhog, however, I nearly changed my mind. I was standing by the barracks window overlooking the camp's nursery. The chemical-crimson sky heralded a storm. The nursery windows were glowing like blood. The colors, aggressive and violent, cast their horrid light across the entire zone. It was a hellish sight: as if life had been turned into a sinister grimace, an arena where all living matter was abused and exterminated. The fact that little children, whom their parents had dared give life to, were living behind barbed wire was impossible to reconcile. What was I thinking? To have a baby would be insane and selfish!

But there was no chance for me to escape into a different world. I had to cope with my reality, for the sake of the future. "What is it with me?" I fought back my delusion. "I've gone so far into nowhere, and now the child is the only thing that can bring me back!" I believed that motherhood would help me break free from my inner imprisonment and would replace it with an everlasting connection to life.

I wrote to Filipp. Incredible as it was, things settled down with him and the threat of the trial receded. His response was full of supplications not to make any thoughtless decisions. He wrote that he would wait until I was released and promised to take care of me and the child.

No sooner did we come back from work than the work distributor entered the barracks and ordered me to follow him to the checkpoint with my things. Where were they going to transport me now? I wasn't even thinking of TEC (they must have forgotten about me a long time ago), but it turned out that's where the order had come from.

It was sheer nonsense to leave Mezhog now. In a few months I would have to return anyway, since this was the only place with a children's home.

Bogged down in doubt, I paced alongside the escort guard toward the train that would take me to Knyazh-Pogost.

Chapter 7

Central Camp was a separate unit of camps. Its chief commandant had the same power as the commandant of an entire division, which was comprised of not one but a number of different zones. Central Camp was the administrative base of the division, which explained its special status.

Many locals told me the stories of what they had been through before they came to work here, at the administrative center. In 1937–1938, tormented by lice and hunger, just like the women from Urdoma, they felled trees, laid railway tracks, loaded tank cars with oil when it was forty below zero with their bare hands and then tore the skin from their palms, frozen to the iron walls of the tanks.

It wasn't hard to understand what it meant, in these circumstances, for a prisoner to return to a profession he held in his previous life, or at least to a level of physical work he was capable of. Drawn exclusively by their will to create, people contributed ingenious ideas, projects or technical inventions to society at large. Some rationalization proposals authored by prisoners brought unheard-of profits, not only to the camp but to the whole country. A new practice of exploiting giftedness and creativity had been born: authorless, anonymous ingenuity. The precious resource of human talent was nationalized by the state.

In the middle of the century, our society lived on prison camp slave labor, at the same time embellishing its façade with one of the most attractive slogans in human history: "Freedom! Equality! Brotherhood!" Articles and sub-articles of the criminal code, arbitrarily devised, provided the state with an uninterrupted inflow of manpower, legitimizing the unpaid appropriation of the outcasts' intellect. The psyche of those lucky enough to escape this fate obsequiously reconciled the gap between the slogan and the intensely inculcated unfreedom, inequality and non-brotherhood.

In their daily lives, the camp authorities exploited the prisoners' skills in every way possible. When the commandant of the Northern Railway Camp Division, S. I. Shemina, had to be urgently operated upon, his subordinates panicked: "He must be sent to Moscow immediately. There's no one here to perform the surgery." But Shemina himself retorted:

"There *is* such a man here: Bernard Markovich Shargel!"

In return for the masterful operation, the surgeon from Odessa was exempted from a few months of his prison term.

The relationships between inmates and free workers sometimes took on grotesque forms. A guard might come to the zone in search of a helpful prisoner:

"Do you know anything special about the Second Congress of the Party?" he would ask.

"I know a bit. I was at the Congress as a delegate."

"Write it down for me. I have to deliver a report on the topic."

Political prisoners wrote such reports thoroughly and creatively. On the other side of the zone, the semiliterate guards would then recite the text, syllable by syllable, without bothering to think of its meaning.

Occasionally, even a sort of mutual sympathy would arise. But the line between the people and the Enemies of the People remained insurmountable.

EVERYTHING SURPRISED ME when I arrived at Central Camp: the electric lights of the settlement visible from the zone, a real bench by the mess hall, a recreation club. Most striking of all were the people who still retained those habits of unencumbered behavior I had grown completely unaccustomed to. I found myself surrounded by intelligent faces and remarkable women. Working under a roof gave many of them the chance to preserve their bearing and even coiffures. One parted her hair straight and tied it at the back, another would wear her hair in a braid wrap or style her bangs straight. The women with youthful faces, however, would most often have gray hair. After work, I observed them walking around the camp in sheepskin coats, the same type the camp administration would wear. I delighted in looking at them and tried to guess what kind of character each of them had.

In the barracks, people actually noticed each other. They cheered each other up with a warm word and could stir one's thoughts and soul, especially those of a fragile youth like me.

I arrived in Central Camp when TEC was on tour, giving concerts in the neighboring camps. They were expected back any day. I was given a place in the general barracks, and to my great surprise no one goaded me off to work in the morning. After the morning roll call, the orderly went out to get water. Except for myself, only one other woman stayed in. The pale northern sun touched timidly on my cheek, then slid down and lingered over the tucked blankets on the beds. I plunged into my personal problems.

"What are you brooding about?" the woman asked.

Afraid of disclosing the real reasons or seeming too outspoken, I said that my life was over, that all was lost, and so on. The woman burst out in short order with an avalanche of indignation:

"What do you mean life is over? How dare you say that all is lost?"

My words must have touched something deeply personal in her. She jumped out of bed and began to reprimand me, pacing around the barracks like a tigress:

"Who gave you the right—you, who are still so young—to write off these moments as being outside of your life? Yes, these very moments! What other life do you expect for yourself? How can you declare this one invalid? It's going on fourteen years since I was thrown behind the barbed wire! What other life do you think *I* should hope for? *This* is my life! It exists, and it's mine! You have no idea how many have perished, how many have not made it…"

Much united me later with the stormy and life-loving Wanda Georgievna Razumovskaya. But in our first meeting she fulminated, scolding me vehemently for what I'd said. My tears dried up. Her wrath was candid and enthusiastic, sweeping away all falsehood.

I had told myself many times, "No, this isn't really my life. My life will begin after I'm released, or at least not until my child is born." Some noxious embers inside of me had blazed up, and Wanda Georgievna's dressing-down helped to extinguish them.

AS SOON AS TEC CAME BACK, I was transferred from the general barracks to the theater dorms, with fourteen beds for the women from TEC and the puppet theater.

I was nervous with the thought that my incompetence as an actress would become evident, if not today than tomorrow. What would happen to me then? But as I settled into the new place, a feeling of peace, which went against all logic of my personal situation, came over me.

The very next morning, just like everyone else, I went to work at the theater barracks. On the sheet of paper that was pinned to the door there was an announcement:

Staging of Chekhov's The Anniversary

ROLE ASSIGNMENTS:
Shipuchin—G. L. Nevolsky
Shipuchina—T. V. Petkevich
Merchutkina—V. K. Mitskevich
Khirin—Ya. K. Stanislavsky

Directed by A. O. Gavronsky

I read and reread the announcement, trying to absorb it. One of life's unimaginable whims! That piece of paper was a document that vindicated my place in this new life. I grew cheerful and couldn't help repeating the names to myself: Gavronsky, Nevolsky, Stanislavsky, Mitskevich… Here was my name, not on a camp transfer list, but among famous actors!

The new life started with table-work rehearsals—a concept I wasn't familiar with yet. Everyone read his part line by line, and afterward we spoke about how we perceived our characters.

The stage director with sarcastic eyes sat across from me at the long, unfinished wooden table. He joked, mocked and teased the actors. I liked his precise manner of speaking, his words rushing forth like a river at high water. My festive mood did not desert me. In the morning, I would get up and go to rehearsals with a feeling of happiness.

Before long, the period of table work was over and we moved to the stage. Aleksandr Osipovich went through every mise-en-scène several times, each time refining and complementing it with a new shade. Before he could formulate what he expected from me, I answered him with a revised recitation of the phrase or with a different gesture, enchanted by his prompting. There was no time to consider where the impulse came from. An unfamiliar power, not entirely of my own making, whirled and carried me on.

Chekhov's Tatyana Alekseevna Shipuchina, the lighthearted, self-enamored creature: How did she manage to change my life so much?!

Every time Aleksandr Osipovich praised me, the blood in my veins flowed faster. I caught his corrections with a kind of super-hearing, with every cell of my being. I realized, if he stepped aside, everything would wilt and grow dim inside of me and "the emperor would be naked." Everyone who was close to Aleksandr Osipovich experienced the happiness of their own revival and development to their highest potential.

I had only three or four months before I'd be sent back to Mezhog. Meanwhile, each day brought the joyful promise of the next day's rehearsal, delight at the stage director's next subtle invention, and my own belief that I was capable of justifying his expectations.

ONE EARLY MORNING in May, someone's yell cut short my dreaming. Everyone jumped to their feet, wondering what was going on.

"The war is over! Victory! Peace! There's no more war, brothers!" Not two, not three, but ten, twenty people were yelling.

Beside ourselves with excitement, we ran out into the zone, burst into other barracks, hugged and shook each other and cried. Peace, peace! The frightening, the horrendous, was over. A question flashed through my mind like an explosion: Will they release us now? Of course they will! How is it going to happen? Amnesty? By a decree? Or will they simply open the gates of the zone and let us go? Will it be today? Tomorrow?

But the guards, of course, knew better: "What are these turncoats so happy about? Damn actors!"

The war had taken root in all of us. It kept one from utter despair: it was a disaster greater than imprisonment. The misery was shared by all. But on the day of the victory we were not allowed anywhere close to the festivities. We had to segregate ourselves from society, to plunge into a realistic understanding of things. Very soon we realized that the victory would not affect our fate. Even the second-timers, whose personal records clearly stated *Await Further Instruction,* and who were supposed to be imprisoned only until the end of the war, were nevertheless kept in. I was going to sit out my entire term, along with everybody else. It was just as true as the fact that Mama and Renochka would never come back again, even though the war was now over.

Meanwhile, amnesty was granted to "the people": the state granted freedom to thieves and murderers.

The head of the Political Department ordered the TEC director to organize a chorus. Anticipating the question of who would actually sing, he specified: "There are young and beautiful people in the collective. Get all the dancers and actors on stage. Let them sing!"

There were plenty of musicians in the collective who were assigned to be our teachers. I joined the rest in trying to hit the right note.

After the chorus rehearsals, stools would be arranged into rows, and the orchestra, the best of the theater collectives, would take over. The orchestra was conducted by Dmitry Femistoklevich Karayanidi, whose otherworldly talent was recognized even by the experienced musicians. It seemed to be a separate world that lived by its own rules and had its own language, often unintelligible to newcomers like me. For several hours before and after rehearsals, the trumpeter, the flutist and the saxophonist practiced on their own, huddling together in a cozy corner of the barracks.

The diligence of the TEC acrobats was striking as well. They were tireless and demanded much of themselves, keeping a rigid diet even in the camp. The more skilled professionals tried to teach elements of the craft to beginners. The atmosphere of the working barracks was engaging; the constant bustle actually made sense and softened one's heart.

In the evenings, we were led out of the zone to perform for the free workers at the local House of Culture or in a small club in the settlement. Our soloists, Makary Golovin, whose brother Dmitry was a famous singer at the Bolshoy Theater, and Sergey Alliluev, enjoyed the greatest success among the public. The wives and daughters of the camp officers shouted "Bravo!" much to the irritation of their husbands. The two singers were more than once sent off to a general camp for "amorous intrigues," which they were less responsible for than the enterprising free women. The women, though, would immediately rush to their aid, and the soloists were brought back to the orchestra.

In the camps, it wasn't customary to ask each other what one was in for, and Makary was no exception. It was rumored that the Golovins were somehow connected to the murder of Meyerhold's wife, the actress Zinaida Raikh. It was said that once, in a restaurant, Dmitry Golovin pulled out a cigarette case; the actors sitting next to him at the table recognized it as belonging to the Meyerhold family. Supposedly, this incident prompted an investigation. Most of us, however, considered this to be a fabrication, behind which was hidden a much baser political subtext.

At TEC, work, everyday life and personal relationships all fused into one. Ours was a life on wheels, and so we cooked for ourselves and ate in groups. Before leaving for a tour, we would be given dry rations. I was invited to join the "*kolkhoz*" made up of the TEC director Erukhimovich, Makary Golovin and the pinup Olya. Olya and I took turns cooking and we managed just fine. After club concerts for free workers, Senya, Makary and Olya often returned with a can of stewed pork or egg powder. One time Olechka managed to get hold of a few potatoes. As for me, for singing in the chorus I received small bouquets of northern flowers.

Jokes were an essential part of our life. If someone burned the *kasha* or spilled water on his musical scores, everyone else would abandon whatever they were doing at the moment. The thirty members of TEC would form a line, and each one, with affected concern, asked their unfortunate friend the same question: "I'm sorry, is something wrong?" And God forbid the person lose his temper or show a lack of humor.

Like TEC, the puppet theater also performed at the nearby camps. By pure coincidence both troupes were living together at Central Camp at the same time while working on their new programs. To this stroke of luck I owe my friendships with many people. Aleksandr Osipovich took a great interest in Tamara Tsulukidze's work on Andersen's *The Nightingale,* and, it seemed, in Tamara Grigorievna herself.

"You haven't seen the puppet theater yet? Don't wait too long. Today's their dress rehearsal," Aleksandr Osipovich informed me.

A painted screen stood on the stage. In a black velvet dress and high heels, Tamara Grigorievna entered and stood in front of it. Her manner of speaking was unhurried, her gestures sparing and elegant. The Georgian actress was irresistible.

She was the wife of the Georgian stage director A. V. Akhmeteli, whose tragic end Beria himself had a hand in. As for Tamara Grigorievna, she was sentenced to ten years.

Every person remembers the moment when their fate was decided. Tamara Grigorievna recalled how seven robust bestial interrogators rollicked and pushed each other off their chairs before reading out her sentence. "You were something," said one of them, "and now you're in pretty deep." Trying to sound educated, he added: "You had a role in Gorky's *The Lower Depths,* didn't you?"

Yes, she had indeed been "something": the beloved and loving wife of Akhmeteli, the tender mother of their son, Sandik, an actress who had tasted fame and was admired in her motherland.

Before ending up at the Northern Railway Camp Division, Tamara spent one year in solitary confinement in the prison in Yaroslavl, then went through various transports and camps. Was it "the depths"? Everyone had his own idea of that concept.

I was stunned by the puppets and the very existence of such a theater in the camps. Years later, Tamara told me that when she worked as a nurse at the tuberculosis camp in Protoka, a surgeon named Trofimenko came up with the idea of organizing a puppet theater and even got started on the puppets: he carved the head of a little boy out of a piece of wood. Bits of wool thread became the puppet boy's hair, buttons—his eyes. The little boy was called Styopka. He was placed on top of a cupboard at the local KVCh.

"We hadn't seen children for so many years," Tamara recounted wearily, "and all of a sudden, in the middle of our gray existence, there appeared the naughty and cunning face of Styopka. We couldn't tear ourselves away from him!"

She wrote a script. Someone constructed a partition. The composer V. A. Dasmanov wrote the music.

The camp administration heard about the new program and summoned them for a preview. Tamara's mother managed to sew a velvet dress and send it, together with a pair of shoes, to her daughter in the camp in time for the show.

The commandant S. I. Shemina liked the theater and the puppets. He issued an order to hire people to help Tamara create a show. He said, "Our kids are growing up to be hooligans, without any entertainment. So you'll be serving them and, incidentally, the camp too." The theater was transferred to Knyazh-Pogost.

The children's writer Nina Vladimirovna Gernet, a friend of Aleksandr Osipovich's, immediately responded to his request to help with the repertoire; she sent her own plays and a manual, *How to Make Puppets,* as well as a package with beads, silk and velvet scraps, glue and sequins. The children of the free workers impatiently awaited the arrival of the puppet theater.

It would require tremendous imagination to fathom what such a theater meant for the children of prisoners. Camp children didn't know what freedom was; they had never seen a cow or a chicken or daisies in the field. They knew only the guard dogs that patrolled the outside of the zone. When a puppet dog appeared on the stage as a character in one of the shows, the children burst into tears, and it was impossible to calm them down. The performance had to be stopped.

After one performance of *The Nightingale,* a boy about five years old ran up to Tamara and gingerly touched her dress with his index finger. When she leaned down to ask what was the matter, the boy lifted his eyes and said in a quiet and secret voice: "I love you, Aunty." He did not know Tamara's name or how she came up with the idea to create this remarkable theater in prison. But the songbird from the play stirred an unfamiliar feeling of joy and anguish in him and awakened the little boy's soul.

IN OUR CORNER of the barracks burned a little stove. We cooked on it and warmed ourselves nearby. Spellbound by the fire, Elena Gustavovna Frisher, a Czech Comintern communist whose job it was to sew the puppets, would sit for a long time next to the stove on a pile of firewood.

"My name is Hella!" she would correct everyone who called her by her name and patronymic.

She had a mop of curly black hair. The traits of her face and her entire appearance belonged to a different culture and indeed, it seemed, to a different time, as if she had just come off of the relief of a medieval coin. Her astonishing black eyes glared with irrepressibility.

"She's attempted suicide at least five times," women said. "When they were bringing us here on the boat, she jumped into the river. We barely saved her life."

Hella Frisher, née Glasova, was drawn into political activity by a friend. She met her husband in Vienna. He once worked as an engineer at a cable factory in Krakow, but when his bosses found out he was involved with a communist, he was fired. After he'd been out of work for a long time, they received an invitation to go to Argentina. Gottwald, the secretary general of the Communist Party of Czechoslovakia, intervened and offered them an opportunity to go to Moscow instead. To do so, Frisher had to join the Party. They left their son with Hella's sister in Prague and set off for the Soviet Union. In 1937, they were both arrested. Her husband was shot; Hella got ten years in the camps.

At first glance, the women in our barracks led quiet lives and were friendly with each other. No one tried to impose herself on another. But nevertheless there was always drama in the air.

One morning, Khava, a quiet and unpretentious girl, slept in when everyone else was already up on their feet. Her head drooped strangely off the pillow.

"Khava, wake up!" Mira Galpern shook her on the shoulder.

A note fell to the floor: *Don't blame anyone for my death.*

Someone ran to call a doctor. We could vaguely guess the reasons for what Khava had done. After her life was saved and she was released from the infirmary, Khava remained just as quiet and withdrawn. It wasn't until many years later that we realized what a brilliantly talented person we nearly lost forever.

This "box of women's bodies" was a vat, against whose walls beat the lava of passions, personal stories and pains.

IN 1945, ENTIRE TRAINLOADS of rags and other trophy junk arrived from Germany. Camp authorities divided bundles of fabric and clothes among themselves. By the order of the Political Department in the person of Shtanko, some of the stuff was allotted to TEC and the puppet theater.

A long dress was sewn especially for my role. I threw off my old military blouse, which had been darned at least three times, and tried on the magnificent silk garment. In this turn-of-the-century attire, I didn't immediately recognize myself. The poignant feeling of being young overwhelmed me.

The public at Central Camp was said to be just as sophisticated and hard to captivate as the beau monde of Moscow. People who used to frequent the Moscow Academic Art Theater, Tairov's and Meyerhold's theaters served their terms here.

The day of the premier of *The Anniversary* came.

As if through a dense fog, I heard the buzz of the hall filling up with people, someone announcing the play, calling the actors' names… The curtain rose and the performance began. Despite the fear that engulfed me before my entrance, the play went on. I was cheered up by the sound of approving laughter.

Aleksandr Osipovich rightly figured out what a keen, almost childlike need for laughter was felt by the people who'd been kept behind barbed wire for so long. He treated Chekhov's drama as a farce, but it wasn't all comic. A phantasmagoric agglomeration of foolishness, carelessness, blunt vigor and inflated falsehood set the stage for the absurdity inherent in the play.

The Anniversary enjoyed unconditional success, and I was among those who were praised that night.

I approached Aleksandr Osipovich with words of gratitude but could utter nothing worthwhile. How could I thank him for my rebirth, for the flash of heretofore unfamiliar powers and feelings, for the free expanse that unrolled before me? Only with veneration.

After the premier, one of the administrative employees, Ilya Evseevich, came to see me, saying, "The House of Lords is giving a dinner party today in honor of your debut."

"House of Lords" was what they called a section of the barracks partitioned off from the rest of the living area, where five "directors" and "deputies" had their beds. Among them was the intelligent and reserved Boris Markovich Kagner, an expert in literature and theater who worked as the head of the Planning Department in the camp administration. People said he was, and remained, a staunch Trotskyite. It was for this that an additional term was tacked onto his initial ten-year sentence.

The second lord was Nikolay Trofimovich Belonenko. He was from Leningrad and used to be a renowned engineer. He was imprisoned for "economic counterrevolution" and had already been in the camps for fifteen years. His rationalization suggestions brought huge profits to the camp.

Before his arrest, Ilya Evseevich used to be a journalist. Here, he served as the deputy to the head of the Finance Department of the Northern Railway Camp administration. He was friends with Olga Viktorovna Tretyakova, and it was through her that we got to know each other. She managed to pique his curiosity in me to such an extent that at one point he had arranged a special trip to Urdoma just to meet me; he arrived a day after I had already been sent to the punishment camp, but this "criminal circumstance" only doubled his curiosity.

When I first arrived at Central Camp, Ilya Evseevich walked into the TEC directors' office, his shabby leather overcoat rustling with each step, and asked to be introduced to me. After that, he would often stop by to chat in the evenings. His young eyes, kind and wistful, peered at me from under his horn-rimmed glasses. He fell in love with me, ardently and impulsively. Every morning, the gangling silhouette of the orderly would appear in the window of our barracks, and I would be given a letter or a poem from Ilya Evseevich.

Everyone tried to stay as late as possible in the rehearsal barracks. Some looked to play a game of chess, others to have a friendly chat. As for me, I stayed to listen to Aleksandr Osipovich's stories. He would reminisce about Aleksandr Moissi, an actor he considered one of the greatest, and his role as Osvald in Ibsen's *Ghosts.* Or else, he would infectiously describe the modern dance of Isadora Duncan. His ability to carry one away straight to the world of Chekhov's *The Cherry Orchard* as it was staged at the Moscow Art Theater was so powerful that it obliterated the border between dream and reality. But at the designated hour, the door would open and Sergeev, the lame warden would walk in, throw a steely glance and order us to disperse.

UNDER AN ORDER from TEC, Simon, the medical attendant who played the violin, arrived from the Urdoma infirmary. I had more friends now, but I didn't feel any better. He didn't speak much of Urdoma but still insisted that I break up with Filipp. Filipp wrote me often, and I replied to his every letter. Apart from him, not a single soul knew I was pregnant.

I shared with Filipp news of *The Anniversary*'s success and told him that I had met the stage director, Aleksandr Osipovich Gavronsky, whose magic made me feel liberated on stage. But Filipp became downright worried and even frightened by my letter. I could only imagine what it must have cost him to come to Central Camp immediately afterward.

He was unusually tender and attentive, and all his worries seemed to be reduced to just one question: "You haven't changed your mind, have you?"

I told him the truth—I hadn't. There was something indisputable, like a command from a higher realm, in the belief that only the birth of a child would enable me to start a new life.

Filipp calmed down and said he believed me. But the next moment he insisted that I introduce him to Gavronsky.

Aleksandr Osipovich already knew about Filipp, but it still seemed inappropriate to introduce Filipp to him out of the blue. The incompatibility of these two men was very obvious to me.

They looked at each other with curiosity.

After Aleksandr Osipovich left, Filipp said with an eerie note of dismay in his voice:

"He'll take you away from me."

There was not one iota of masculine jealousy in his words. He understood everything. But I couldn't help feeling awkward in front of Aleksandr Osipovich and feared his reaction.

In the evening, after he finished talking with someone, he turned to me:

"Well, Tamarochka, he is a lovely man." He paused for a moment and added: "And very touching, too."

Neither of these characteristics fitted Filipp, and I understood that the worst of my expectations had come true: Aleksandr Osipovich categorically disliked him.

Barely able to hold back the tears, I tried to console myself. Maybe Filipp really was touching? Maybe Aleksandr Osipovich had managed to see the very helplessness of the energetic, matter-of-fact man; that was, after all, what I had responded to in the first place.

But of course, the truth was simple: he didn't like Filipp.

As I rose to leave, Aleksandr Osipovich, sketching something on a scrap of paper, stopped me without lifting his pen and said:

"You know, Tamarochka, I'm grateful to him. He really did save you. And there is nothing you can do about this fact."

I stood motionless. Grateful? Could a man as sarcastic as him have meant such a thing seriously? Still, he was right: there was nothing I could do about that fact.

THE NORTHERN RAILWAY CAMP administration appeared to be a unified clan but in fact was far from being such. Everyone had his own story.

The head of the Political Department, the tall, handsome and robust Shtanko, was a "promoted" functionary. A man who enjoyed life, he looked after TEC and the puppet theater but couldn't make heads or tails of art. His ridiculous phrases were fertile ground for our numerous jokes and anecdotes.

His first deputy, Pavel Vasilyevich Bazhenov, was a railway engineer. The Party sent him to build the Northern Railway, but it wasn't until he came here that he was appointed to the Political Department.

The chief commandant of the entire Northern Railway Camp, Semyon Ivanovich Shemina, had a reputation as an educated and good-hearted man who recognized the humanity in each prisoner. In Shemina's case, his appointment amounted to punishment and exile: he had been a high-ranking military officer in Czechoslovakia before 1937, when his wife, a Pole, was arrested; after he refused to renounce her, he was sent to work here.

People said that once Shemina received a letter from the distinguished actor Nikolay Cherkasov, asking him to keep Aleksandr Osipovich in Central Camp in order to save him from the general works. Gavronsky was spared, but alas, cases like this were infrequent. Scores of children, husbands and wives wrote letters renouncing their loved ones, so that somewhere, in a faraway town, they wouldn't wind up getting fired from work or left without academic degrees. And here a renowned national actor pleaded for a stage director he only barely knew.

Someone had memorized the letter and passed it on for others to know it, too:

> One of the eminent figures of Soviet theater and cinema, A. O. Gavronsky, is serving time in your camp. I ask that you do your best to make sure the conditions of his life and work are favorable. After his term is over, this gifted stage director will go a long way in working for the benefit of our Soviet art.

Many years later, during one of my trips to Leningrad, I saw Cherkasov at the City Palace of Arts.

"May I speak with you briefly, Nikolay Konstantinovich?" I asked, approaching him.

Cherkasov held me by the arm, led me to a couch and sat down next to me. He was no longer in good health and was breathing heavily.

"I wanted to thank you for the letter you wrote to the commandant of the Northern Railway Camp about Gavronsky."

He livened up:

"That's right! I did write such a letter. Did it help? I didn't imagine it would, I didn't think so, but I wrote it nonetheless."

I told him that his letter had helped, and not only Aleksandr Osipovich, but all of us in the camp who knew that such a letter existed.

"Thank you, thank you!" Cherkasov repeated several times. "Honestly, I had very little hope."

As long as Shemina was the camp commandant, Aleksandr Osipovich had a writ of protection. However, it was the Third Department that had real control of the camp.

Once, a man from Gavronsky's barracks came running:

"Aleksandr Osipovich is not feeling well. He sent me to call you."

The bunks in the elongated men's barracks were closely pressed together. There were two less crowded sections partitioned off with wooden boards. Aleksandr Osipovich's trestle-bed was nestled behind one of these partitions. A makeshift desk pieced together of several boards stood next to his bed. He was lying under his blanket with his eyes closed. Scraps of paper were scattered on the floor.

"There was a search. They took everything he had written," a neighbor explained.

Aleksandr Osipovich half-opened his eyes. They were foggy with anguish. "Yes. They took away everything," he said distinctly, and his eyelids closed again.

I had no idea what to say. I could only sit silently next to him in the crowded barracks.

In prisons or camps deep in the woods, so-called shakedowns were constant; sharp objects were confiscated. But what happened here was different—more frightening than a theft or a robbery. Even in the zone, Aleksandr Osipovich had not abandoned his studies of philosophy and mathematics. The authorities took even that away from him.

Aleksandr Osipovich seemed to be sleeping when suddenly he uttered in a clear voice:

"The pawn. Move the pawn!"

I understood: the game was his way of fighting insufferable pain. Later, when Aleksandr Osipovich would tell me, "One needs a lot of power to endure his own powerlessness," I always remembered that gray day, the barracks, his semi-delirious condition, his method of resisting savagery.

On personal forms he would write: "Son of a capitalist." He was born in 1888, into the Vysotsky family, which was famous in Russia for their "Vysotsky" brand of tea. A saying once popular in Odessa ran: "Tea of Vysotsky, sugar of Brodsky, people of Trotsky." At his parents' factory, Aleksandr Osipovich organized readings of political literature, meetings and discussions. As an SR, a member of the Socialist-Revolutionary Party, he was arrested by the tsarist government and sentenced to death by firing squad but managed to flee abroad, where he lived for several years. Before returning to Russia, he graduated from the philosophy department of Marburg University, earned a degree in philology from the University of Geneva and studied at Jean-Jacques Rousseau Institute. He authored works on number theory and non-Euclidian geometry.

He had worked in theater since 1916. Over the course of a year, before 1917, he staged productions at the Zurich Theater and was the stage director of the Geneva Drama Theater, where the repertoire included *Twelfth Night, Inspector General, The Brothers Karamazov, Balaganchik, The Pillars of Society* and *The Death of Danton.* After the revolution, he continued working in theater in Russia, and in 1924 became the director of the Chaliapin State Theater Studio. The same year, Aleksandr Osipovich took an interest in cinema and directed several films. During the twenties, he held a number of high administrative positions in Moscow, where he collaborated with A. V. Lunacharsky. He then moved to Ukraine to work with the Ukraine Film Company, and there he partnered with A. P. Dovzhenko.

Aleksandr Osipovich was arrested in Moscow. When his wife went to Lubyanka for an explanation, the interrogator told her: "Your husband knew about the plot to assassinate Stalin." The accusation was completely ungrounded, without a single witness, yet Aleksandr Osipovich was exiled to Medvezhya Gora in Karelia. His wife followed him.

In 1937, the term of his exile ended. His wife had left a little earlier. No sooner did he arrive in Moscow than he was arrested again, right at the station. It was popular to arrest people on the trains and at train stations at that time. Another investigation followed, with a trial in absentia. Aleksandr Osipovich was given five years of camps and sent to the Komi Republic in the North.

He was supposed to be set free in 1942. A provocateur, one of his fellow prisoners, was "assigned" to him, and it was under her denunciation that Aleksandr Osipovich was thrown into the central isolation block, where he spent several torturous months awaiting death by firing squad. His case, however, did not "weigh" enough for capital punishment, and he was given a new, so-called camp term of ten years.

When I met him, he was sitting out his ninth year of both exile and imprisonment, and he had six more years ahead of him. In fact, he stayed in the camps much longer and there were many ordeals he had yet to face.

THE NIGHT BEFORE TEC was leaving for a tour, Ilya Evseevich came to say good-bye and asked me to step outside to talk. He wanted to know why I had been ignoring his letters. When I refused to explain, he became angry, tore the book he was holding into pieces and threw them to the ground. Indignant, I ran away, but an hour later one of the lords came to the barracks, calling me.

"Ilya isn't feeling well. Come. You're the only one who can calm him down."

Outraged by this nonsense, I tried to refuse, but after the neighbors begged me to go, I reluctantly agreed.

Ilya Evseevich lay on his bed, a wet towel on his forehead, looking pitiful. There was something hearth-like and peaceful, totally out of keeping with the camp, in this scene. He half-rose and thanked me for agreeing to come in spite of everything and, so he hoped, for having forgiven him. My animosity vanished, and before long we were chatting as if nothing had ever happened. I was thinking to myself that his ugly behavior by no means reflected his real nature and that I was right to make up with him, but suddenly our conversation took an unexpected turn; Ilya Evseevich asked keenly:

"Tell me one thing: you're pregnant, aren't you? Am I right?"

I was taken aback. Perhaps I wouldn't have been so flabbergasted had the question been posed by a woman, but I was shocked to hear it coming from a man so relatively distant. There was something "motherly" in his penetrating shrewdness, a trait he shared with the men I had known in Belovodsk.

"I am," I said.

"Let me take care of all the problems when the baby is born!"

"The child has a father," I snapped back.

Filipp's reputation for licentiousness gave good reason for such a conversation. Scarcely anyone believed that he loved me. So where did my own unconditional faith in the opposite come from? In the midst of the new events and impressions, I couldn't help thinking of my own life with fear and panic. It would appear to me imputed by some obscure power whose origins I did not know how to interpret. Granting me a reprieve at Central Camp, fate had loosened the leash for only a short while—just to let me taste people's attention, care and admiration. Ahead of me, however, as something predetermined and final, loomed the same austere life's dry ration I had already had a sufficient taste of.

THE MAIN TASK of TEC was to cater to the labor camps of the Northern Railway Camp Division. We did not have a train car of our own and had to catch passing civilian trains to get to the camps. The guards would crowd the passengers out of their compartments to prevent us from any contact with the free people. But the passengers would dash away from us without being forced to.

Station names flashed by: Vislyana, Yosser, Zheshard, Tobys, Irael, Madmas, Shezham, Mikun… Shabby station buildings looked peaceful and innocent. The camps stood many kilometers away from the railway.

From the station we would get to the camps on foot, every now and then meeting a filthy gray file of prisoners marching to or returning from work.

The barracks were overcrowded, and we would be lodged in the offices, the medical units and at the local clubs. Beds were scarce, and we often slept on the floor or on tables. In the mornings, we'd have a rehearsal and in the evenings there would be a concert.

The workers, returning to the camp from the forest or other work sites, would find out about our arrival. They'd hurry to wash and have supper and then crowd into the club or the mess hall, which in some camps doubled as a concert hall. The front rows would be reserved for the guards. The prisoners would take their seats behind them. At the start of the concert, everyone would grow silent.

I knew from my own experience: in godforsaken zones deep in the taiga, people whose lives were ruled by hunger and physical labor often forgot that music and song still existed on earth. Our concerts reminded them of poetry they had long forgotten; it proved to them that rhyme and meter existed, that there was a cycle to art and life, with a beginning and an end, and hence, please God, their lives could be saved.

The audience of prisoners, closely pressed against each other, retained one way to soothe their tormented souls: bitter tears. From the back of the stage, peeping through a hole in the side wings, I saw how impetuously tears streamed down the emaciated faces of men and women. Unable to tear myself away and wiping tears from my own face, I sacredly believed we needed each other. Only this faith could extinguish the burning guilt we felt toward the people in the audience since our conditions at TEC were immeasurably better than theirs.

Tears would be replaced with a smile when the dancing duet, and then the acrobats, entered the stage. When we put on *The Anniversary*, people's pent-up feelings would explode and bursts of laughter would thunder through the hall. Our nightly performances, which I awaited with sheer happiness, became the meaning of my life.

TEC actors had friends and acquaintances in every camp. Those who remained in the zone without ever getting beyond its gates, perceived us, who traveled along the road from camp to camp, almost as free people.

"What's new?" they would ask. "Heard anything about the amnesty? Tell us, what's it like on the outside?"

After our concert in Shezham, the hospitable Dr. Nusenboim invited us to his infirmary for dinner. A tongue of flame danced inside the oil lamp. Some of the patients asked for permission to sit with us; they sat quietly for a few hours, wrapped in blankets they had brought from their wards. The sense of reality abated and everything seemed like a dream. The doctor put a pan of potatoes fried in cod-liver oil onto the table. We unpacked our dry rations. Ardent questions and revelations ensued, and we chatted till morning.

More camps stretched ahead after Shezham. Everywhere we would meet interesting people of rare, and often peculiar, individualities, genuine gentlemen and rather eccentric types. A deferential kiss on the hand was like a password to the forsaken land of cordiality and affection, or just a gaze, or a cry, "I'm also from Leningrad!"

The camps were hidden in the taiga; they were dispersed across the tundra. We sank in bogs and mud, drove or dragged ourselves on foot, bent under the weight of our suitcases. We would finally halt for a day or two at a camp, give a concert, pack up and set off again. Traveling with TEC, I got to see the entire Northern Railway Camp system, stretching all the way to the Pechora River, where behind the barbed wire languished tens of thousands of prisoners whose fate I shared.

WE ARRIVED in Mikun early in the morning, and in the evening we performed *The Anniversary.*

After finishing the play, I descended a steep shabby stairway from the stage to the dressing room where the actors removed their makeup and costumes. Helping me down the stairs, our administrator whispered:

"Someone's waiting for you."

I saw an unfamiliar man standing across the room by the door. He was wearing a crude sackcloth shirt and had gray hair. I expected him to introduce himself, but he kept silent and only stretched out his hands as if trying to distance himself from me.

"Don't worry, Tamusya, don't worry, I beg you. It's me, Platon. It's nothing. Yes, yes, it's me," he mumbled in a broken voice.

Something forced its way through my memory when I heard the name and the voice, but it was beyond me to comprehend that in front of me stood a man from my previous, free life, Platon Romanovich.

"Don't worry, don't worry," I heard his voice as if in delirium, struggling to connect the disjointed fragments of my life. "I didn't believe it when I saw you on the stage. I thought my heart would break into pieces. *You* are in the camp? *You* are here? Wait, I can't..."

People surrounding us were also crying.

We went to the zone and sat down on a nearby tree stump.

"Tell me, how did you wind up here? I must be losing my mind."

He lovingly called me "Tamusya," and I, as before, called him Platon Romanovich.

"And you? You were at the front, right? The last letter I received from you was in Frunze, in early May, in '42."

"In September, our division was encircled. We were taken prisoner, and then were brought straight here."

"How many years did they give you?"

"No one gets less than ten."

Platon Romanovich was brought to the camps with one of the numerous transports carrying frontline soldiers unfortunate enough to have been taken prisoner by the Germans. After the war was over, all of them were sentenced to ten years under Article 58-1: Treason.

"How's your mother? How are your sisters?"

"Mama and Renochka died. I don't know where their graves are. Only Valechka is alive. She'd been evacuated from Leningrad with her orphanage; I don't know where she is now."

"Have you heard anything of your father?"

"No, nothing."

"Where's Erik? How is he?"

"In Central Asia, also in the camps. He got ten years. He writes sometimes."

"And?"

"He's by himself, I'm on my own."

"Alone?"

I told him everything. Seeing the horror in his face, I myself became terrified by everything that had happened. I didn't know why exactly he was crying: for me, for himself or for something bigger?

"And your decision, is it the right one? To have a child, here, now?"

"But where else? And when? Don't worry, I'll manage. I know I will."

"Do you remember my request, then? If it's a boy, call him Seryozha. I'll be his godfather."

We didn't reminisce about Leningrad, about how he'd come to meet me, about Yakhontov, Moscow, his imploring me not to go to Frunze and offering to marry me. He had the war and captivity behind him, suffering and gray hair. It was impossible to talk about everything at once.

He ran off to the barracks and came back with a package.

"Here, take this! You're the only person in the world whom I love. I couldn't even think of writing to you to say where I ended up, but now... It's fate! There are some warm clothes in here. I don't need them. You need them more. Here's some canned food from the parcel."

"No, I won't take it."

"Don't push me away, Tamusya. I only ask one thing of you: don't push me away!"

"Who sends you parcels?"

"Remember my red-haired friend, Simon? He sends them, though not under his own name—through other people. He works for the organs. If they find out he is in touch with me, he'll be in big trouble. Where can I write to you? Will you answer?"

"To Mezhog. Of course I will."

It was time for TEC to leave. He stood near our truck and asked my friends to watch over me. He held my hand and tried to smile. At the last moment, he said, "I have only one thing to say to you: I love you." I knew it to be true.

I cried, sitting in the tarpaulin-covered truck. It hurt to think of Platon Romanovich, of the life they had taken away from us. He was completely alone, digging a foundation pit in this camp, with no other prospects except the general works. I blamed myself for not having said enough.

IN THE MIDDLE of June, I felt something warm moving inside of me. I grew more and more detached from the outside world and plunged into thoughts about the child. I would tire quickly and could never get enough sleep. But my thoughts about the future were peaceful.

At one of the camps we crossed paths with the puppet theater. There was a free bed next to Tamara Tsulukidze's. Before going to sleep she took out some photographs.

"This is me and Sandik, my son... Here I am in the role of Amalia from Schiller's *The Robbers,* and here I'm acting in Shanshiashvili's *Anzor.* This is one of me with my husband..."

The pictures Tamara had held on to were consoling evidence of the love of a family, as well as an attestation of the incredible suffering they'd endured. Indeed, this woman had a happy past. It was impossible to imagine what she felt, thinking about her famous husband. Her southern homeland was far away; her son was being raised by other people.

The puppet theater was leaving for Urdoma.

"Could you pass a letter to Filipp Yakovlevich?" I asked her.

"Sure. I know him. He always gives us a warm welcome."

The shows of her theater melted the hearts of both prisoners and free workers. Apart from being an actress, Tamara Tsulukidze was an excellent organizer; people called her a "trainload of energy." When once the administrator of her theater stole food that had been allotted to the entire troupe, she slapped him in the face in front of everyone. Someone reported to the head of the Political Department that she beat the actors. He listened to the informer and replied: "There must be a reason!"

LIFE FLOWED into the camps like dirty water. Traveling with TEC, we met more and more soldiers and officers who had been first taken prisoner by the Germans and were then thrown in prison upon return to their motherland. Now an order came for us from the Political Department to deviate from our route and give a concert at a camp with German POWs. We hadn't even imagined that such camps existed.

From the station we walked on foot. One by one, we crossed the squeaky suspension bridge across a small river, the bridge swinging underfoot with every step. The road led deep into the taiga.

The camp's commandant politely requested that we not to bring any sharp objects, should we have any, into the zone.

The pathways in the camp were neatly swept and powdered with sand. The barracks weren't dug into the earth but stood on foundations. The windows were made of glass, not mica. The club where we were to perform was spacious.

The translator, a German, came to familiarize himself with the program. He asked, for example, "What is a *yamshchik?* Is it a coachman?"

When we came on stage, the local guards and their families had already taken their seats. It was time to start, but no one else entered the hall. It was clear that the German soldiers refused to come to the club. The guards bustled about, and soon lines of German prisoners were brought in by force. With impenetrable faces, they ceremoniously sat down on the benches. In this hostile and tense atmosphere, our show began.

Not a sound, not a single clap was heard. The guards in the audience applauded, but their sparse efforts sounded pathetic. We finished the concert in dead silence.

It was 1945. The war was over. Behind the barbed wire languished Russian political prisoners, many convicted of "praising German machinery," as well as the German POWs. We perceived them as invaders, as pure evil. What did they think of us? Hostility and hatred blinded us all.

After the concert, as if to apologize for the embarrassing situation, the high-ranking chief commandant invited us for dinner. The table had already been laid out. Sliced white bread, the likes of which we hadn't seen for many years, was piled high on the table. There were pots filled with buckwheat and, extraordinarily, next to them lay donuts stuffed with jam.

We stood in front of the table and could barely believe our eyes. Was this how the Germans were being fed? An insult gripped our throats.

"Sit down, please!" we were told.

Suddenly, Seryozha Alliluev, our tenor, yelled in an unusually high-pitched voice: "We're not going to eat that German grub! Let *them* gorge on it, if that's how you feed them." He spoke for all of us.

"Why German? This is our food. You have to understand: politics requires this."

Offended and stunned, we walked away from that place as fast as we could. Some cursed, others cried helplessly and bitterly along the way. The majority of us walked silently.

ON THE SAME TOUR across the camps of the Northern Division, we received another unusual assignment, this time to give a performance in the town of Yarensk, where we knew there were no camps or prisoners whatsoever.

The path meandered through rectangles of oat and barley fields. Cornflowers gleamed through the rye. Childhood memories—the Byelorussian fields and stubbles—swept over me.

"Do you know what this is?" I would ask my friends. "This is clover. And this one is vetch..."

The sun was high. Birds sang.

A series of unforeseen problems emerged when we got to the free town. They didn't know where to lodge our prisoner theater. It was impossible for us to stay in free people's houses. There were only two escort guards. Eventually, they ordered to put us up in a local hotel. But the guests, who had come to town on business, protested: "We won't live together with criminals. That's outrageous! They'll rob or kill us. Oh, they aren't thieves or murderers? Well, all the more so—we have no desire to be near these traitor bastards!"

After the first wave of indignation passed, the citizens calmed down and relented, though some of them left the hotel immediately.

The hotel seemed like paradise. There were real beds with blankets, sheets and pillows, finished hardwood floors, carpets, the cozy sound of creaking doors, a kettle with boiling water. How peaceful it was to look out the windows! Freedom smelled deliciously; it had its own sounds. The comfort that surrounded us prevented us from falling asleep. The escort guards sat in the hallway so that anyone who tried to leave his room could be easily spotted.

The public at Yarensk liked our performance so much that they asked the Political Department to keep us in town for a few more concerts. Permission was granted, and now we performed for money, before a full house.

One impression from Yarensk grips my soul to this day.

In the afternoons we would be led—under guard, though in quite a disorderly file—to the town's dining hall. Sleepy one-story houses lined the street, with curtains hanging from the windows and flowers on the sills. On one of the houses hung the sign: *Children's Home No. 7.* We saw a group of children, five or six years old, standing on the porch, enthusiastically and anxiously discussing something. Two women were instructing or explaining something to them. The children impatiently jostled each other, looking around. When we approached the orphanage, a flock of them rushed toward us and hastily pushed small paper packages into each of our hands. A muddle ensued, out of which children's voices were heard, "Take it, it's for you, for you!" Confused, we tried to hold the children in our arms, but they dashed headlong back to their porch.

Wrapped in each package, made of notebook paper covered in writing, there was a carrot and a couple of lumps of sugar.

A hoarse roar betrayed the chief escort guard. Unable to bear the scene, he was the first to burst into tears.

They must have prepared the children long in advance. What did they manage to instill in them, in those hungry years after the war, which made them willing to share their meager food rations with prisoners?

As we walked onward, choked by tears, we looked back and waved to the little stray souls whose kindness warmed us for many years ahead.

TO THE NORTH of us the land was densely populated with camps: Ust-vym, Ukhta, Abez, Inta, Vorkuta. It was the forest, the deposits of oil and coal that defined their production profiles. Each of these camps had their own culture brigade or theater collective.

It was considered "good manners" among the commandants of the northern camps to have a quality theater troupe. The head of the camp in Vorkuta, a man named Barabanov, was famous for filching talented actors from neighboring camps; he would issue orders through the Gulag, the main administration of camps, to have them sent over. People said that in

Vorkuta there was a real theater, with Tokarskaya, a famous actress of the time, playing the lead roles.

The concert brigade from Ukhta also had a good reputation. Indeed, about 80 percent of them were professional actors. The head of the brigade was Eggert, a well-known film actor. Many of the actors were from Harbin on the Chinese Eastern Railway: Grozdov, Savitskaya, Ryabykh-Ryabovsky and others.

Our TEC director, Senya Erukhimovich, was also from Harbin. He was proud to have seen these actors on stage there when he was a boy. It was he who told us the story of how cohorts of "Harbiners" wound up in the North.

When the Japanese entered Manchuria and formed Manchukuo with Puyi, the son of their last emperor, as its head, provocations and diversions ensued. The Japanese proposed to buy up part of the territory that belonged to the Soviet Union. The USSR agreed to negotiate, and in 1935 the deal was signed. The Soviet Consulate in Harbin appealed to the Soviet citizens living in Manchukuo to return to their homeland. Out of fifty thousand people, forty-eight thousand agreed. As the Chinese Eastern Railway workers were returning to Russia, they were greeted with slogans of welcome, flowers and tables laid with food throughout their way.

In 1937, a special paragraph appeared in the government's long list of articles used as pretexts for arresting people: "Persons who have ever been abroad are subject to isolation." That was how members of the forty-eight thousand who had decided to reunite with their countrymen wound up in the camps. Upon their arrest, it was alleged that before leaving China for the Soviet Union, they had been recruited by the Japanese intelligence. During the interrogations, most of them were made to admit that the mere fact of recruitment was already enough, for it was obvious that the only reason they couldn't accomplish more in their subversive mission was because they hadn't had the time.

There were samples as well, offered to those under investigation in a ready-made form, slightly adjusted to each individual case. For example, they'd been instructed to write the following: "Once, a man came to see me at my apartment. He asked me to collect information on the Red Army and told me to enter a university."—This clause was, in fact, inserted if the person had applied to a university upon his return to the USSR.—"In a certain amount of time, a messenger was supposed to come and give me a password, something like, 'How are your studies at the university?'" Those who refused, as well as those who did sign, were indiscriminately charged with counterrevolutionary activity and sent in prisoner cars to the northern camps for ten years.

Compared to our poor Northern Railway Camp, the camp of Ukhta seemed to be well equipped. Everything made sense here, and even the roads we drove on were less bumpy.

Pointed out to us were several houses that stood separately on the bank of a small lake; these houses made up the local "board of weights and measures," just like in Moscow. Here, however, the "board" consisted of specialists who also happened to be serving prison terms.

No less astonishing than the mysterious laboratories and large-scale construction sites was the land itself, which lavished natural riches upon its country. Some time ago, geologists had discovered massive oil deposits here, but before that they found radioactive water. The most valuable local resource, however, was the same as everywhere else: an endless supply of manpower.

Meanwhile, the head of the Northern Railway Camp Political Department had our TEC director study the documents held in the camp's archive.

"Why don't you compose something about the construction of the railway? Something worthwhile on the subject?"

The documents revealed the following: in 1922, in the Vorkuta region, a certain Popov, who was hunting in the tundra, tossed a stone into his campfire, and the stone burst into flames. The hunter repeated the action with another stone, to the same result. When he returned to his village, he told people about the miracle and showed them his discovery. They decided to send the stone to Lenin with a messenger. The scientists determined that it was anthracite, rich in oxygen content, which could be easily quarried because it lay on the surface. That same year, the People's Commissariat passed the decision to start explorations in the tundra. It took a long time to explore the large territory. And in order to mine coal, the old highway, built from wooden beams and running between Kotlas and Vorkuta, had to be turned into a railway.

According to the documents, it was as if the construction of the railway began only in 1940. In reality, everything started much earlier. The oldest of the northern camps was considered the one in Ukhta. In 1937, enormous batches of prisoners started being delivered there, and many new camps appeared, one after another. The first train, which ran along the new tracks from the Kotlas station to Kozhva in 1941, was also engineered by prisoner-operators. The authorities who had come to celebrate the occasion dispassionately watched the slave pioneers rejoice and cry after their first venturesome train run. A year later a bridge was built across the Pechora River. The prisoners also built depots, pump stations, railway buildings, warehouses, houses and the settlement itself. During the war, when Donbas in Ukraine was cut off from Leningrad, the northern towns of Ukhta and Vorkuta took over as the country's main stokehold.

Nothing of what had been done by the prisoners before 1940 was made public. The composition about the Northern Railway was ready, but the censors expurgated everything that related to prisoners and their labor. The truth, the essential facts—by the sweat of whose brow this railroad had been constructed—was altered as the authorities saw fit. It was replaced with an inflated story of the current five-year plan. The state would never acknowledge the role of prison camps in its history, denying their very existence.

Later, whenever I trekked a distance along these tracks after concerts with TEC, a chill crept over me from the depths of my consciousness. On moonlit nights, the steel rails glimmered deathlike, the ghosts came alive and Nekrasov's poem would haunt me:

> The tracks go straight and the mounds are narrow.
> Pillars and bridges grown all around.
> And alongside—Russian bones lie harrowed...
> How many, Vanya? Can we ever count?
> ...
> "Brethren! You reap what once we had sown,
> While we've been fated to stay here and rot...
> Do you still hear our cries in your souls,
> Do you remember or not?..."

Our trip to Ukhta was cut short by the order to return immediately to Central Camp to perform for the authorities, who had gathered there for a meeting. The passenger trains, running on schedule, had all departed, and the only way to get to Knyazh-Pogost was by freight train.

A long train of funnel-shaped hopper cars, filled to the brim with coal, pulled in to the station. I climbed up a cast-iron beam, trying to find support like everyone else. Amidst the wind and the speed, my head was spinning at the sight of the track ties flashing by underneath. My hands and legs were growing numb. It seemed as if all the signal posts flashed green as we approached, so that we wouldn't have a moment's respite; as if we were the subjects of some horrible wager over just how much tension a human body could withstand.

Many people from other camps were brought to the meeting where we were to perform. A day off was announced. Outside the club, a loudspeaker was installed and music was piped in.

Excited and uplifted, prisoners thronged the zone. Friends and acquaintances were looking for each other. The shining sun and the festive atmosphere concealed the camp's ugliness. On top of the roofs of the houses outside the zone, we saw scores of people watching what was going on inside. They looked stunned to see the prisoners strolling about freely.

It was an astonishing spectacle to see so many interesting, beautiful and intelligent people suddenly gathered together. They were not just part of society but rather a whole sociohistorical formation thrown behind the barbed wire, far from being homogeneous, and often quarrelsome among themselves from within, but all speaking one language.

"Who is David Vladimirovich Schwartz, the man you introduced me to?" I asked Aleksandr Osipovich.

"He's quite a remarkable individual. Ask him anything, he'll know it. He used to be an editor of the Great Soviet Encyclopedia. His sister, Esfir Vladimirovna, is also here…

"See that fellow? His name is Gorelik. He's a physicist and a mathematician. If you'd like, he'll calculate for you the distance to Saturn in no time; he'll instantly multiply a seven-digit number by any figure.

"Also, see that fellow who seems like he's just been upset by something? He's my neighbor. I'll ask him to give you his sonnets."

People unburdened their hearts in convivial conversations, plunged into recollections and warmed each other with fervent debates. They knew a great deal about life and humanity and were delicate enough not to touch on private subjects.

IN UKHTA I was shown the woman who had been assigned as a "provocateur" to Aleksandr Osipovich while she was at Central Camp. It was because of her denunciations that he'd gotten his second term. I took a close look at the woman and later on, when I told Aleksandr Osipovich, "She's not a human being!" he just kept silent. When I brought up the subject again, he said in a detached and peaceful voice:

"Sometimes, a fact alone isn't enough."

It wasn't the first time I'd witnessed the tolerance of a victim toward his informer. Such encounters were frequent. A feeling of protest and indignation would flare up but very soon fade away, as if divided by a certain X, the residue being more like bitterness than a vehement desire to fight.

"Investigation techniques have always taken advantage of the responsibility that the arrested person feels toward his relatives and friends," an acquaintance of mine from Central Camp explained. "At interrogations we were threatened: sign, or we will arrest your mother or daughter, shoot your wife." Anyone winding up between the millstones of the NKVD knew this mechanism all too well. But sometimes, a fact alone wasn't enough! I had yet to come to terms with this not-too-novel truth of our world. It was time for me to start thinking and understanding things differently, to reconsider my own feelings and the deeds of my former friends. God and the devil, morals and immorality ceased to be stark absolutes. Each of these concepts built up its own "anti-space" around them, which overlapped and penetrated each other. Ideas and principles were growing less and less clear-cut until they became an impassable thicket. At the time, I did not know yet, however, how to deal with such judgments superimposed over facts. I passed for an idealist and hated everything that engendered a double consciousness.

Near the mess hall, the club and the administration office at Central Camp there were patches of tilled soil where someone had planted tobacco. The sticky sweet scent of the unsightly quatrefoil flowers had a special power over me. Setting off to the theater barracks in the evenings, I would make a circle just to inhale the odor. The smell of tobacco became inseparable from my memories of Central Camp.

It wasn't until much later that the question crossed my mind: Where did those flowers come from? What ridiculousness it was to plant flowers inside the zone. I telephoned an old friend:

"Senya, do you remember the smell of tobacco at Central Camp in the evenings?"

"Why, of course!"

"Then tell me, for God's sake, who planted it? Whose hands, whose heart did it?"

"There was a woman, Infantyeva. She'd ask her relatives to send her seedlings in the parcels."

"Maybe you can tell me another thing, then? At the dinner at the House of Lords there was a bottle of sweet liquor with a handmade label..."

"Sure. Do you remember Brusser, the brewer from Gorky? He also received parcels, not with seedlings but with extracts and syrup. He cooked lemonade and liquor for the officers, and drew his own labels, too. The North was hard for him, and he'd always say, 'It grows dark before my eyes from these damn white nights.'"

ALTHOUGH I WAS ENJOYING the atmosphere of Central Camp, in my mind I had already bid farewell to this place. After one of my sad conversations with Aleksandr Osipovich, he invited me to his barracks. I sat down by his wooden desk. He took something out of his suitcase. "I wanted to introduce you to my wife, Olya," he said and held out a photograph. A beautiful, sorrowful face looked at me from the picture. She was wearing a winter coat with a fur collar and had short hair; her eyes revealed stiff pain.

"This is my wife. I call her Zulu. Some day, you'll meet her. You two will be good friends."

Here it was—the secret source of Aleksandr Osipovich's strength! They had been apart for more than ten years. I knew that all that time she supported him and sent him parcels and letters. I could not imagine back then that I would really meet her six years later and that she would become a very close and dear person to me.

"Thank you!" I said, returning the photograph. "We've been introduced."

Together with the picture, by accident, he also took out a letter. He thought for a moment and said:

"These are poems by Elena Blaginina, dedicated to my Olechka. She is her friend. Elena's husband is the poet Georgy Obolduev, who was arrested in '37. Would you like me to read you some of them?"

I only wished he would continue speaking, reciting poetry and introducing me to his friends. I felt that these poems from a lonely soul would give me strength to live. After he finished, I asked to copy them into my notebook.

THERE WAS A FIRE in the surrounding forest. The air smelled of smoke. We were sent to extinguish the fire and worked side by side with free people, including officers, for many hours. We dug trenches, smelled of smoke and were exhausted and covered in mud.

All of a sudden I found myself face-to-face with Shtanko, the head of the Political Department. I could tell that something was on his mind, but he said nothing. In a few minutes, however, our TEC director, embarrassed, came to me and reported:

"Shtanko asked me to talk you out of going to Mezhog. He wants you to get rid of the child."

I knew he was speaking with the interests of TEC in mind, but I was still outraged.

The puppet theater returned to Central Camp from tour. Tamara Tsulukidze brought me a letter from Filipp. He was worried about me and asked when they'd finally send me to Mezhog.

"He went to see me off," Tamara told me, "and spoke fervently about how he loves you. It didn't look like he was lying. He became dreadfully candid and told me he often runs out to the forest and looks off in the direction of Central Camp for a long time; he said he kneels there and almost prays for you. I'm not one for such histrionics, but that's how he is, isn't he? Do you believe him?"

"I do," I said.

"Then forgive me a hundred times!"

I knew Filipp's passion for putting on a show. I thought it was just his energy seeking an outlet. I was only slightly disturbed by it. "He loves me," I consoled myself, and I really believed him.

One day, a billboard next to the House of Culture appeared, announcing the arrival of a concert brigade from Moscow led by the famous composer Pokras. Taking advantage of the commandant's good mood, we asked for permission to go to the concert, under the pretext of learning the craft from the renowned actors. Shtanko agreed, provided that we sit in the orchestra pit so as not to be seen.

Pokras entered the stage to greet the audience. With a practiced nonchalance, he looked around the rows. When he noticed the faces looking up at him from the orchestra pit, surrounded by guards, he seemed puzzled. He paused for a moment and, without looking back to the hall, bowed not to the audience but to us.

The empathy he displayed in front of everybody gripped our throats like a spasm. We returned to the zone excited—not so much by the concert but by the audacity of the free actor, so daring by the standards of that time.

TEC WAS PREPARING to take to the road again. The camps of the southern unit of the division were on its route, which meant I could travel all the way to Mezhog together with TEC.

In the evening I stopped by the theater barracks. Everything seemed as usual. Dmitry Femistoklevich and Mahomet Uteshev, both from Baku, were debating the advantages of the Azerbaijani bathhouse. Olechka, who had joined their "*kolkhoz*" a long time ago, was cooking something on the stove. Some were writing letters, others played instruments or chatted. An apprehension suddenly crept through me at the thought that I was leaving TEC and Central Camp, that I was abandoning my friends, including Aleksandr Osipovich.

Not a single person around me approved of what I was doing, but they all had lives of their own, or families, behind them. What did I have? How else could I patch that breach in my soul through which the darkest gusts of the universe blew in?

I said good-bye to my friends from Central Camp.

In Mezhog, the entire TEC alighted from the train to see me off. They promised to write.

The guard and I set off. I looked back until the train passed out of sight.

— Chapter 8 —

The camp was six kilometers from the railroad. The fields and meadows gathered the warmth and tint of the dim sunlight, but the taiga forest allowed no sun into its thicket, letting the light touch only the top of the canopy. The birds were chirping. I tried to take as many gulps of freedom as I could before we arrived at the camp.

I was lodged in the same medical barracks I had lived in during my first stay here. The place looked almost the same, but the people had changed.

In the camps, the women with children were called "*mamkas*." There was much to this nickname: a recognition of some of their rights, a share of condescension and lenience, pity and disdain. As with everything else here, there were *mamkas* of all types: young and old, thieves and intellectuals, those married to their children's fathers, those without them. A father, of course, was always desirable, but it was the child that became the light of the women's lives. The women's determination to have a child in the camps was a solitary rebellion against a society that had gotten the hang of taking even that—the inalienable right of every woman—away from them. Only time could make clear who would win or be defeated in the fight for the power of life against cruelty. The conditions of this fight were hideously unequal.

In the bed beside mine lay a young nurse, Olechka Udres, who had just given birth to a weak baby girl. The baby's father, an older doctor in the same camp, dearly looked after both of them. But Olechka often cried, saying: "The baby has the eyes of a grown-up. It seems like she's saying good-bye to me…" Soon after the baby died.

The young and attractive Tonya paced around the barracks. The foreman with thick wet lips had gotten her pregnant. She lived with him, without crying or complaining, but her gaze revealed a strained question: "Is this all? And for what?"

A woman from my native Leningrad, proud and educated, was sometimes visited by her husband, a prisoner doing time at a different camp. They were both head over heels for their newborn girl, though the baby's health was very poor. This baby was their entire world; nobody and nothing else existed for them.

As soon as I moved to Mezhog, Filipp increased his attention toward me tenfold. He often wrote, and sent regards with everyone who was traveling to Mezhog. His parcels contained pieces of fabric, soap and even things like thread and tooth powder. His love protected me. Many told me how lucky I was to have somebody who loved me so much. I felt calm and peaceful.

I was assigned to work in the agricultural brigade. Early in the morning, at the sound of reveille, I would set out to the camp checkpoint, just like before. Whether I worked in the fields or in a greenhouse, most of the time I had to remain bent over. Returning to the zone extremely tired, I'd wash my hands and want only to lie down. But the older women instructed: "No, sweetheart, you have to move. Go take a walk around the zone." I would obey and set off to make my circles around the barracks. I hearkened to the women's advice on how to prepare myself for maternity.

My child kicked inside of me. I gasped for breath, but every day after work I forced myself to go for a walk. The doctors didn't like the way I looked. Filipp had asked the local chief doctor to petition for lighter working conditions on my behalf, but I resolved to work just like all the rest.

I wondered if it would be a boy or a girl. I felt something grand and beautiful drawing near.

UNEXPECTEDLY, I was summoned to the Second Department. It turned out that Vera Nikolaevna Sarantseva, my friend from the NKVD prison in Frunze and the Djangi-Djir camp, had been looking for me. My relatives hadn't been searching, but a friend had not given up on me! Indeed, there is some greatness in prison friendship.

We began writing to each other, and our correspondence carried on for thirty years.

Vera Nikolaevna had been released. Altogether, she was imprisoned for little more than a year. Of course, they did not have the right to transport her to Nizhny Tagil at the time. Her release decree followed her from station to station, though it was often misaddressed and delayed. Meanwhile, she languished in transit prisons. Freedom would not admit her overnight.

On her release, she was told that even though she had been rehabilitated, she still could not live in Frunze. Her assigned place of residence was

Kazalinsk, where she found it impossible to find a job. Vera Nikolaevna described in detail her hungry life, how she survived only by chance earnings and fed herself on watermelon rinds.

Her mother, Maria Silvestrovna, remained in the camps.

When, in spite of all the difficulties, Vera Nikolaevna's father obtained permission to register his daughter in his apartment, the first thing she did was to apply for a correspondence course at the department of philology at Moscow State University to study Spanish and Italian. She renounced her former career as a lawyer once and for all, since in those years the profession had shamefully disgraced and compromised itself.

Vera Nikolaevna visited Barbara Ionovna in Frunze. She told her how we first met and how we again came across each other in Djangi-Djir. I don't know what else she told her, but Barbara Ionovna started writing to me; her each letter was warmer and more cordial than the previous one. She asked me to forgive her for her injustice and hard-heartedness, wrote that I was a good person, certainly much closer and dearer to her than her own son, and even implored me to come live with her upon my release.

Olga Viktorovna Tretyakova was brought to Mezhog with a transport. We were beside ourselves with joy to see each other again. But once we were together, we were in for some difficult news.

One day, Olga Viktorovna ran into the barracks and, in a broken voice, cried from the threshold:

"Volodya Yakhontov is no more!"

I was terrified. The superstitious women in the barracks scolded Olga Viktorovna:

"How could you? She clasped her face with her hands! The child will have a birthmark!"

"He committed suicide," Olga Viktorovna cried. "Here, read this: '...threw himself down the stairwell from the seventh floor and left a note: *I'm flying to the stratosphere.*'"

How twisted his mind must have been! To crush himself against the floor, the big man that he was, with thick wheat-colored hair, gravitating to the musical spheres. The Petersburg fog, our walks around the Bronze Horseman, the round table at the Anisovs' in Frunze and the frying pan with stewed "military" onions, our outings to the town market for a pumpkin, his confession and his sacramental request: "Turn around, look who's walking behind me." What horrible torment did Vladimir Nikolaevich want to escape? What personal defeat did he hope to convert into death with such luxuriance, "flying to the stratosphere"?

DECEMBER CAME. I was exempted from work for two weeks before I was due.

The wind howled in the chimney. Snow whirled outside. Waking up, I would look through the window at the rows of the snow-topped barracks, at the snowdrifts and at the sky. I would comb my hair, put on a flannel dress Filipp had sent me and sit down with a needle to sew clothes for my baby. I cherished the approval of the women in my barracks, who said I "walked beautifully."

In the afternoon the barracks would empty. Everyone would leave for work. Only the nurses, who were sleeping after night duty, and the orderly, whom I helped to heat up the stove, would remain.

My thoughts and feelings were extremely acute. For some time I imagined I would die in labor; my life would end before it reached its climax, but I didn't know how to redirect it to the desired point. My only solace was to think of Filipp; I was sure he wouldn't let me die. However, I shared my feelings not with Filipp but with Aleksandr Osipovich. Filipp would tell me, "It's normal for anyone in your condition," but Aleksandr Osipovich, describing a similar case with his brother's wife, understood even that which was barely perceptible.

A few days before my baby was due, a new friendship arose. I met Serafima Iosifovna Rudova, who had also come to Mezhog as an expectant mother. She was older than me, but her perception of the world was youthful and optimistic. She was bearing her child with such ecstatic and light anticipation that she was radiant with happiness.

She was devoted to the man she had met in the camps, the talented physicist M. Koretz. Of all the families that originated in captivity, I never met a happier one. I suppose the joy with which Simochka awaited the birth of her child forever remained in the memories of those who knew her. Their wonderful daughter, Natasha, has imbibed it in full measure. Simochka expected to go into labor after me, but the weak Natasha was born earlier. It was Sima's limitless love that warmed the baby and nursed her to health. As for me, I was still taking my walks.

On December 7, the women in the barracks proclaimed that my strolls around the stove were uneasy and strained, wished me good luck and accompanied me to the infirmary. The doctors repeated what they'd said earlier: "Not good. The adverse effects of working in a bent-over position are obvious."

On the third day, my condition deteriorated. I saw the doctors discussing my case with confused looks. Gritting my teeth, I endured the pain.

Someone leaned over me: "Filipp Yakovlevich is worried. He calls every hour."

I heard other words as well: “Cesarean section.”

No longer aware of what was going on around me, I drifted in and out of consciousness, but the pain always brought me back to reality. I was puzzled why no one was helping me. I was dying. What were they waiting for?

There was a commotion and hesitation again. The doctors, afraid to disgrace themselves before their free colleagues, must have resolved to save both me and the child. Prestige was more important to them than my life.

I heard the low indignant voice of Malinovskaya, the head of the medical unit:

“Are you out of your mind? Don’t you see we’re losing her? Put her on the operating table immediately. Cesarean section!”

A cry of relief from someone else followed:

“Here he is! Filipp Yakovlevich, come, quick!”

Hardly believing my eyes, I saw Filipp’s face above me deep in concentration and heard his energetic orders:

“Syringe with pituitrin. Quinine in small doses. Another syringe.”

“Stay with us! Everything’s going to be fine. Do you hear me? Try to do what I tell you. Do you hear? Do you understand?” he pleaded.

I had waited so long for him; he had finally come. But what boundless pain!

Filipp lifted my head and gave me some water. More injections, and again his whisper, “Everything will be all right…”

I gave birth to a boy.

Filipp was holding the baby in his arms. In a fog, I realized: “I have a son. I’m alive. Filipp is near.”

“It’s time, Filipp Yakovlevich,” the nurses hurried him. “Someone might come and see you. Thank you. You have to go.”

Sliding down the slopes of consciousness and coming up to the surface again, I saw Filipp standing in the corner of the operating room crying. If I had the strength to express my feelings at that moment, it would have been a soulful supplication: “Don’t dare leave me now! Stay here, just once stay for as long as I need you. It’s the only way two people can ever get close.” But he was a free man and could not stay with a prisoner in a camp he wasn’t working at.

I was put in a tiny ward with pink walls and left alone. Everything receded.

That night I had a lifelike dream: I was here, in Mezhog. The door of my ward opened and Erik stumbled in. He looked miserable, and only I knew how bad he felt. He kneeled before my bed and buried his face in my bedsheets. His grief tore me to pieces: “I’m guilty before you, Erik. It’s up to you to be good or evil, but still I feel guilty. Maybe not before you, but before myself. I don't know. Don't cry, Erik, I beg you. Let me go. I have another life now."

When I woke up, I was disoriented for a long while. That night I bid farewell to Erik forever.

An amazing day was coming, a new and splendid life. I was waiting for them to bring me my son.

Filipp sent me a note: "I'm happy! Thank you! I'm yours for our entire lives. Name the boy Yury. God protect you both, my love!"

The son was given my last name. His patronymic was Filippovich. Under "Name of Father" there was a dash.

Because I had a difficult labor, I was kept in the infirmary longer. These few days were an illusion of a normal life. Next to me was my little ball of energy and instincts, whose eagerness and demands alternated with mysterious sleep. My soul felt broad and reawakened. I was no longer living in vain on this earth. I was proud of myself; I was happy.

THE DOCTORS, led by Aleksandra Petrovna Malinovskaya, were making their rounds. The door of my ward opened.

"Well, how is our courageous Tamara doing? I'll take her on. I need people like her at the medical unit," she said to someone.

It was thus, while still a patient, that I was appointed to work at the camp as a nurse.

On the day I was discharged from the infirmary, they took my son to the nursery. Every three hours I'd run there to feed him.

"Tamarochka, dear!" Simochka begged me, "My girl doesn't get enough breast milk."

Her brown-eyed daughter, Natasha, became my son's foster sister.

It was a hectic schedule. The first feeding was at six in the morning. Then off to work. Running to the nursery every three hours. The last feeding at midnight. Afterward, I could hope to catch a bit of sleep before everything started all over again. My mind was constantly preoccupied with worries about my child: "Is he dry? Is he crying? Hungry?"

The children were handed over to their mothers through a small window with blinds. In the spacious room, about fifteen nursing mothers would sit next to each other on a low bench. I had to learn to disengage from everyone around me.

From the constant cold and draughts I developed mastitis and a fever, but I still ran to the nursery through the blizzards and nipping frost.

My son was gaining weight. Born three and six-tenths kilograms, he already weighed five, and soon six. He started recognizing me and smiled with his toothless little mouth when I whispered to him the words we both needed to hear. Our shared world forced out everything else.

THE LOCAL AUTHORITIES created a medical unit in their camp to keep up the "horsepower" of the prisoners, all in order to maintain a higher rate of production output. Young, emaciated inmates were brought here to gain some energy, just to be sent off to especially hard work right after they'd be discharged. The majority of the patients were petty-crime convicts.

Aleksandra Petrovna brought me to one of the barracks.

"Tamara, you'll have forty daredevils to look after. Think of how to organize their lives. I'm sure you'll manage."

"On my own?"

"Of course."

I felt helpless and only wanted to sit on the floor in the empty barracks with forty trestle-beds and cry out: "I won't manage, don't you see? Alone? With forty unfamiliar prisoners? What must I be to them—a nurse or a teacher?"

In a couple of hours the medical barracks filled with forty males, adults and teenagers. Each of them was given clean underclothes. There were ten hospital cardigans to be shared among them. Looking at their faces, I thought I'd rather die than deal with them. In an alien voice I instructed:

"You—bring firewood. You—heat up the stove until it gets warm. You—go to the storeroom and get mugs and bowls for all. Bind brooms out of fir tree branches. What else?"

I ran about the barracks in search of books and tried to remember some poems by heart. I'd address the older patients:

"Perhaps you remember some film? Would you retell it to everybody? Oh yes, let's elect an elder."

The new arrivals were intoxicated by the joy of having a respite from work and the chance to restore their health. They wouldn't miss a chance to crash on their trestle-beds and catch some sleep. But, of course, the sick ration wasn't enough to satiate the young, hungry men. They always wanted sleep and spoke only about bread.

In the evenings, I read books to the patients. I'd ask each prisoner what bothered him. It appeared that, after all, I would manage. But it wasn't the first time a newly gained feeling of stability was annihilated by a blow so heavy it nearly knocked me off my feet.

On the fifth day, one of the patients came to me and said his blanket had been stolen. Another followed with the same complaint.

Who could I tell, and how? There was nothing to pay for the lost blankets with.

"Who stole the blankets?" I asked the patients, confused.

My question sunk in silence. It wasn't a problem to sell stolen goods or exchange them for bread in the camps.

In Mezhog, as everywhere else, there were criminals who stood on principle and refused to work for the state. In camps like this one, they were severely punished, often with another long prison term. To escape trial, they resorted to various means to fake an illness: they pierced their palms with a needle beneath the thumb and injected kerosene under the skin, inhaled sugar ground to dust into their lungs and so on.

At the end of the working day, the door of my staff room was thrust open. Two hardened thugs of the camp—Ivan, whose nickname was Bacillus, and one of his aids—walked in. They held their hands in their pockets.

"Our pal needs help. Not a word to anyone!"

"What happened?" I asked.

"Get your instruments. Let's go!"

I threw some clothes over my shoulders and followed them out of the staff room.

We came to a ladder, leaning against the wall, and climbed up to the attic. Their friend's arm was blue and swollen, thick as a log. Pus had developed after he injected kerosene under his skin. They understood as well as I did that he urgently needed a surgeon, but to show up before a doctor would certainly mean an additional sentence.

It was frightening to touch the swollen arm of the criminal. I took out a scalpel, made an incision, irrigated the wound with Rivanol and bandaged the arm.

Each morning, at the clang of the metal railing, the prisoners had to be lined up and counted. The next day, my "patient," supported on both sides by his friends, dragged himself down from the attic and made it on time to the roll call. Soon he got better.

Just as unexpectedly, Bacillus appeared in the barracks again. He hailed the patients with the voice of a guard:

"All rise!"

People knew him and were afraid of him no less than I was.

Moving from one patient to another, he looked narrowly into their eyes.

"You stole the blanket, bitch!" he stopped in front of one man. He walked to another: "And you. You have two hours to find the blankets. And God forbid anything else ever gets lost here again. You'll have to deal with me."

The blankets were returned. Nothing was ever stolen after that.

The thugs had calculated their gains with mathematical precision and thanked me in their own way.

THE NAME of the nursery director, Metryakova, instilled fear and respect in the inhabitants of the Mezhog camp. This robust and masculine pock-marked woman looked more like a constable than a doctor. She had a frightening philosophy: “If the baby survives, it is strong and healthy and should live; if it dies—that serves him right!” However, she kept the nursery in good order and spent a lot of time at work. The nursery attendants were perfectly drilled and afraid of her.

There were a number of lucky *mamkas* who worked at the nursery and, therefore, could always be near their children. For this privilege they paid the despotic director with absolute obedience.

My working barracks was about a hundred meters away from my son Yurik’s nursery. When it became warmer and the children were brought outside for fresh air, I recognized his cries among the hundreds of other children’s voices. I would dart off from work and run straight to the nursery, squeezing through a hole in the fence. Without fail, I always ran into Metryakova:

“What are you doing here at this hour?” she’d ask, blocking my way.

“My son is crying!”

“So what? Imagine that: ‘He’s crying!’ Let him cry.”

“He’s crying hard. I’m sure he’s in pain.”

“Perhaps. When the pain is over, he’ll stop.”

Nothing could move this Darwinist. She gave in neither to pleading nor to crying. No matter how hard I tried to find the right tone to speak to her, nothing ever came of it. Meeting her, I’d put on a foolish smile and address her respectfully, always thanking her, even when I had no reason to. Yet it was as if I did not exist.

I was nursing my son, holding him in my arms, when Metryakova came right up to me and, lifting the hem of her smock, boldly ran it across my cheek.

“Oh, it’s not make-up? I thought you painted your mug.”

I jumped to my feet. “What’s wrong with you?” I yelled. We stood face-to-face—I, with my child in my arms; she, as my ranking boss and a free worker. She grinned, waiting for me to say something first. I swallowed a lump of bitterness and said nothing.

Metryakova hated *mamkas*. In her eyes, they were all just a swarm of delinquents. She’d show up during the nursing hours and yell at one mother or another:

"How're you holding your child, you shithead? And you? What're you doing, bitch? You'd rather nurse a jackal, not a daughter! Look at that moron!"

And, indeed, there were enough morons among them.

"My little brat's got a snout just like his father," one criminal boasted. "His dad is the foreman, the best man there is."

When she named the nine-month-old boy's father, it turned out that he was also the father of a newborn girl, the daughter of another criminal. First the situation entertained the audience of nursing mothers, but the stream of curses wasn't enough to exhaust the two women's hatred and they started to fight. They pulled each other's hair and scratched one another. Covered in blood, each was trying to prove that the man was hers. In a fit of rage, the hardened female grabbed her infant son by the legs and started striking her rival on the head with his body…

The half-dead boy was narrowly saved. Metryakova ran in, yelling, "Let him die, I don't care!" Perhaps this time she was right.

I heard and saw everything, but I had my sanctuary; I pressed Yurik to my chest and walked away.

"Smile at me, my son, laugh for me!"

He'd laugh, and I'd feel happy. We had our own enormous world.

I embroidered his shirts and jackets with rabbits and suns, along with his initials. My son was the most charming of all the children! There were others more handsome than him, but he seemed the friendliest and the most tender.

RODION EVGENYEVICH MALAKHOV, who used to be a frontline soldier, was the administrative director of the camp's medical unit. A former scout, he had been punished for a military offense and sent to the NKVD forces to "educate" prisoners. Officials of this type radically changed life in the camps; they founded a system based on military principles: reveille, lights out, roll calls, mealtime and sleep—everything had to be done according to a perfectly timed schedule.

Wearing his short sheep-fur coat, the director would show up anywhere—in the barracks, at the mess hall, or at the checkpoint when the brigades were lined up before going to work. With his predatory flared nostrils and aquiline glance, Malakhov seemed to be the embodiment of physical health. He spoke in an abrupt and coarse tone. Though widely feared, he was also considered a fair and respectable man.

I had never spoken to him personally and had no idea why he summoned me to his office. A lamp with a tin lampshade shone on his desk.

"Tamara Vladislavovna? Come in, have a seat."

I felt a relief when he called me by my name and patronymic.

"How's your life here?"

"Good."

"Are you satisfied with your work?"

"Yes."

"How's everything in the barracks?"

"Everything's fine, thank you."

"What barracks are you living at?"

"The medical barracks."

"Would you like me to transfer you to the barracks for office workers?"

"No, thank you, I'm used to my current place."

"So you don't need anything?"

"Really, nothing."

"Do you know why I'm asking you all this? There's a man at the administrative center whom I've known for a long time, David Vladimirovich Schwartz. He sent me a letter. He's asked me to help you."

It wasn't difficult to figure out that it was my friends, and especially Aleksandr Osipovich, who'd talked to Dr. Schwartz for me.

"Feel free to stop by if you need something."

I rose to leave, but Malakhov stopped me:

"Since you have nothing to ask from me, I'll ask *you* to do something. Could you memorize Gorky's *Death and the Maiden* and recite it from the stage?"

"I'll try," I answered. When I recited Gorky's poem, Malakhov was content. The audience applauded and demanded an encore.

PRIVATELY, the prisoners called Aleksandra Petrovna Malinovskaya, the head of the medical unit, Catherine the Great. She was one of the most astonishing women I ever met, passionate and clever. People said she was "sinful," and perhaps they were right, but that wasn't her main trait. Before her arrest, she was a distinguished doctor. After she sat out her five-year sentence at the Northern Railway Camp, she stayed on to work. A little plump, of average height, with the corners of her mouth pointed slightly downward, the chief doctor always looked sarcastically aggrieved.

The local mental asylum, which served both free and incarcerated patients, was her brainchild.

When I was leaving Central Camp for Mezhog, Aleksandr Osipovich wrote a letter asking her to help me, though he warned me that Aleksandra

Petrovna didn't take well to women. She was, however, quite a rare person, he assured me. I never gave her the letter, but eventually this woman did so much for me that I nearly owe my life to her. Later we became good friends, but our relationship started in a funny way.

The caretaker at the infirmary was a stumpy, good-hearted Siberian man who looked like a pigeon-toed bear. Aleksandra Petrovna was attracted to him and, hoping to save him from a transport, hid him for a while in the mental asylum. Eventually Danila got fed up, climbed over the fence and escaped. He came to the infirmary and knocked on the window of my staff room, looking miserable and begging me to have pity on him.

"I ran away. It's hard there; I may as well go and hang myself."

The robust man was nearly crying. I understood him, as one serf understands another, as a sister understands her brother.

"What should I do?" he asked.

"Go back." I told him.

In the morning Aleksandra Petrovna came to my barracks, furious and frowning. I expected a snippy question from her, but after taking a look at each other there was no need for words. Legendary individual that she was, at that moment she had the look of a guilty child.

At the asylum there was an archive of the patients' medical records; the files provided a vivid picture of how the intricate world of the human psyche had been destroyed. Access to the archive was restricted, but legends circulated in abundance.

Hella Frisher, who had once been Aleksandra Petrovna's patient, told me the story of the most horrifying camp event she had witnessed.

A certain Totos Vartanyan, a wine merchant in Armenia, was caught stealing. He was put on trial and sent to the camps. He was said to have been depressed from the very beginning, and soon he was brought to the mental asylum in Mezhog. Vartanyan was a quiet madman, but around him were other, more violent patients. One of them, by the name of Voinov, a former NKVD official, had an eccentric principle: "A soldier who doesn't dream of becoming a general is a bad soldier." Working as an interrogator at Lubyanka, in the depth of his soul he dreamed of being employed in more serious operations than those he had to perform on a daily basis. He managed to achieve some results and would have gone farther had he himself not been eventually imprisoned and sent to the camps. The bloodiest page of our history had firmly projected itself onto the aggravated consciousness of this functionary. He was sent to the asylum as a violent patient. Wandering the corridors, he would issue decrees: "On such-and-such a date all the women of Moscow are to be arrested. The citizens of such-and-such a place are to be exiled. So-and-so is to be shot within twenty-four hours." He'd sign his decrees "Deputy for the People's Commissar of Internal Affairs of the USSR, Voinov." After issuing an edict, he would calm down for a while, but then he would notice: there were no shouts, there was no action, there were not enough tears. Voinov's clouded but energetic consciousness demanded satisfaction. Thoroughly and secretly, he was preparing to take action.

While the medical staff was changing shifts, he locked the door to the psychiatric ward, barricaded himself inside, and barked out: "Hack 'em up!" He had providently gotten hold of axes as a means to carry out his order. The quiet wine merchant Totos Vartanyan was appointed executioner. Together with a group of other patients, the meek Totos, who adored Malinovskaya and called her "mother" and "sweetheart," made for her office, armed with an axe. Several people had their arms and legs chopped off along the way. Streams of blood gushed everywhere.

At that moment Aleksandra Petrovna was in another department, one floor below. Hearing the heartrending cries, she and the rest of the staff rushed upstairs. They broke the door open and crushed the barricade. The first ones to burst through fell under the lunatics' axes.

Malinovskaya ran in and saw Voinov coming after her with axe in hand. Mikheevich, an elderly medical attendant, threw himself between the two and was killed on the spot. The next moment, Voinov raised the axe above his head, but Aleksandra Petrovna threw her hands in the air and screamed in a commanding voice: "Where's the verdict? When did the court confer?" Voinov stopped in his tracks and backed down in hesitation. The idea of a court procedure had been firmly hammered in his head.

"The sentence must be passed by the troika!" Aleksandra Petrovna advanced vehemently. "And you must lead the court session! I demand that the court be led by you!"

The most important thing was to gain time. All around was bloody chaos.

The "troika" was immediately convoked. Voinov began the trial. Aleksandra Petrovna started a dispute, demanding that they consider the fact that she had been looking after them, prescribing their medical treatment, and generally maintaining a good attitude toward her patients. The "troika" took her merits into account and condemned her to the "deprivation of one finger by means of an axe." Help came too late. She put her index finger onto the table, and the axe chopped it off.

Only then did the guards and the firefighters break the windows and aim their water hoses into the barracks.

"TAMARA VLADISLAVOVNA, wake up! I need to talk to you," someone shook me on the shoulder.

It was still dark and too early for reveille. I opened my eyes and saw Vera Petrovna standing by my bed.

"Where can we talk? I have very little time."

My heart ached. As I pulled my clothes on, I thought to myself. "What brought her here? How did she manage to sneak in?"

She explained that she came to Mezhog, with a prisoner who had given birth in Urdoma, just to meet with me, and now she had to hurry to catch the train back.

"How have you been? You look wonderful. How's your son? Everything's all right? I'm glad for you."

Then she got straight to the point:

"You must do something about this, Tamara Vladislavovna! Believe me—I'm defending your interests."

She handed me two sheets of paper covered in writing.

"Read it. Read, quickly!"

I recognized Filipp's handwriting: *Lyolya! After yesterday's date I can't think of anything but you...*

"Who's Lyolya?" I asked.

That was precisely the question Vera Petrovna expected.

"A transport came recently with many Polish women. There's a certain Lyolya among them; she's pretty but hideously fat. Filipp is having a fling with her. She's a vamp, a beast. Mean and cold. She's not like you—she doesn't respect or acknowledge anyone. She's using Filipp for her own benefit. You have to write to him, threaten that you're not going to put up with this. You two have a child, after all. He's a scoundrel! Just don't tell him I came to see you."

Her mission accomplished, Vera Petrovna left.

When I went to the nursery to feed Yurik, a nurse told me that early that morning, a free woman had come to look at my child.

Twenty-six years old, I failed to detect anything greater in Vera Petrovna's visit than merely a desire to breed strife between me and Filipp. Protecting Vera Petrovna's identity, I wrote to Filipp: "People say..." The accusatory energy of his reply, however, turned my entire question inside out, distorting the point beyond recognition. He had a natural gift to turn his own misdeeds into someone else's guilt. Apparently, the problem was not with him but with me since I dared believe what "people said."

THE CAMP had its own rhythm, schedule and problems. Wanda was right to tell me with indignation, "What other life are you expecting?" I stopped being stubborn: I realized more and more profoundly that no matter what my daily life was like, it was the only life I would have. Though I came to understand this, I didn't quite know yet how to internalize it.

At the daily meeting of the medical personnel, Aleksandra Petrovna told me:

"As of tomorrow, you'll be going into the kitchen to sample the food."

I was touched: behind her stern tone lay the desire to secure some additional calories for me.

I got up at four in the morning. Agitated, I entered the kitchen. The cook silently poured rich soup from a small pot on the stove into a bowl and set it before me on the table, next to the log book labeled: "Food Register." A sizeable hunk of meat lay at the bottom of the bowl. The "treat" was presented to me the way a master would throw a bone to his dog.

I had to sign off on the quality of the food in the log book. But the soup I'd just tried bore no resemblance to what the prisoners were fed on. Despite the fact that, of course, I needed additional food, I found myself unable to go to the kitchen every morning and accept the crumbs of charity from the special pot.

"How foolish of you, you blockhead!" Malinovskaya scolded me.

The majority of the nurses at the Mezhog infirmary were women from Harbin, between twenty-five and thirty years old. It was a choice selection: they were tall and beautiful, with slender legs and agile bodies. In the summer, they'd throw on their medical gowns without bothering about underclothes; they'd girdle themselves skillfully, walk challengingly, and cope with their duties at the infirmary deftly and with ease.

Once after my shift I dropped by one of the infirmary staff rooms. In the twilight, several young women were sitting next to each other on a cot chatting. They were telling each other ticklish anecdotes, giggling in low voices and ardently going on about the subject of men. "I make him wash my feet!" said one, laughing. "He doesn't mind. He washes them and then kisses them."

They didn't spare the men they were discussing of well-aimed characteristics. Their lighthearted, unconstrained intonations revealed homey warmth, alluring and comforting. I felt the desire to keep up the conversation, but it was as if something had gotten hold of my tongue. I knew my presence was a burden, and when I rose to leave no one stopped me or asked me to stay. It vexed me, but it was clear I didn't match their company.

On my way back I dropped in on Valya, a brisk, dark-eyed nurse I was friends with. She welcomed me warmly.

"Don't turn on the lights. Let's sit in the dark."

Twilight was always pleasant. It softened the tones and dissipated some of the ugliness of the zone. As we were chatting quietly, we noticed a man trying to crawl in through one of the windows.

"A thief," said Valya. "Be quiet."

Assuming it was empty, the man was aiming to sneak into the staff room.

"He'll touch on the crossbar, and I'll slash him on the fingers with a razor. You'll see: he'll immediately find the door to get his hand bandaged," Valya whispered decisively, reaching for the razor.

It wasn't hard to understand her thinking: one should always be on the offensive against foulness. But to slash a man with a razor? I stood up noisily. The thief ran away.

MY SON WAS NEAR, in his nursery barracks, but I wasn't allowed to visit him except during designated hours. Filipp was unfaithful. Loneliness was strangling me. I went back to my barracks and buried my face in my pillow. I tossed about, unable to find comfort.

"Tamarochka, I want to share this treat with you. Take it. I got a parcel from my daughter today." Olga Petrovna Tarasova, one of the infirmary nurses, was holding out a piece of dry cake.

I declined.

"Take it. I have some soy chocolates, too. Don't cry."

"I'm not crying. I am just feeling wretched. Why are the dogs so rabid today? Do you hear them?"

The German shepherds were barking viciously out by the checkpoint.

"You know, Tamarochka, one time I saw the most wonderful group of dogs."

"Where?"

"At the top of the Alps, by the pass to Italy. When I lived there, we went to visit the Saint Bernard Monastery. We approached its walls exactly at the hour when the famous St. Bernard dogs were being fed. Food bowls stood on the ground in two long rows in front of a shed, and every dog came to its own bowl. Then we heard the jingle of a little bell and the dogs started eating.

"During snowstorms and blizzards the dogs were let out. Each of them had a tiny keg of wine attached to their collars. They'd disperse in different directions in the mountains and canyons to rescue wayfarers who lost their way. The dogs dragged those who were too cold to move back to the monastery."

"Is that just a made-up story, Olga Petrovna?"

"No, Good Lord! It's the truth."

"What brought you there, to the Alps?"

Her eyes sparkled like those of Princess Maria from Tolstoy's novel. Olga Petrovna told me about the happy days she had spent with her husband in Switzerland and in Paris, where they attended music lectures at the Sorbonne delivered by Romain Rolland, accompanied by a pianist. My private despair gradually evaporated. I was being introduced to the spirit of human commonality that traveled across centuries, supporting and saving lives.

In Petersburg, Olga Petrovna graduated from the gymnasium named after the Duke of Oldenburg.

"Where was it situated?" I asked.

"On the Petrograd Side, on the corner of Bolshoy and Kamennoostrovsky Prospects."

"Incredible! That's my school, too! I studied there my first three grades, though by then the city was called Leningrad, and the gymnasium had become School No. 82."

Olga Petrovna dreamed of becoming a doctor, but she couldn't enter the institute until she was twenty-one. She left for Geneva, where she enrolled in a university to study medicine. Soon her sister Zeta, an active revolutionary and member of the Social-Democratic Party, came to live with her. Zeta, who believed that Russia was an agrarian country, supported the socialization of land and the people's fight against the tsarist regime. Olga Petrovna made up her mind to be a doctor in the provinces and, enthused with her sister's ideas, became a revolutionary too.

Olga Petrovna Tarasova, née Krasilnikova, was born in 1883. Her grandfather was the mayor of the town of Sevastopol. When, in 1900, famine broke out in the Kherson province, Olga Petrovna went there with a group of volunteers and organized a cafeteria in the village of Kurtovka. The local *zemstvo* supplied grain. Olga Petrovna baked bread and fed the starving peasants. But supplies were limited. She wrote a letter to her mother in Sevastopol, in which she described the disastrous condition of the people. Her mother showed the letter to naval officers who were renting a room from her. They, in turn, read it to the sailors onboard their ships. A general collection of money and clothes began. The officers' wives also responded. Food parcels, sacks of clothes and money started being shipped to Kurtovka.

In Geneva, where Olga Petrovna lived after she left Russia and picked up her revolutionary ideas, she learned the craft of a compositor at a printing house. Upon her return to Russia she was sent to Saratov, where she met her future husband, Boris, who served as an envoy for a revolutionary group.

Later the two of them were dispatched to a high-security printing house in the town of Penza, where messengers came from Moscow to take the pamphlets on taxes and various proclamations they printed back to the capital.

In 1910 the Penza police arrested both Olga Petrovna and Boris. During the search they found a typecase, which served as direct evidence against them.

The officer escorting Olga Petrovna to Petersburg introduced himself as Levental. "Don't you remember me?" he asked her. "We used to meet at get-togethers at the Karabchevskys'?"

In Petersburg, she was handed over to the police. They put her in a coach with blue curtains on the windows and took her to the Peter and Paul Fortress. There she spent nine months, after which she was exiled to the Arkhangelsk province, where she met Vera Figner, the famous revolutionary terrorist.

As for Olga Petrovna's husband, from the fortress he was exiled for seven years to Kolyma. The couple kept in constant correspondence until suddenly it broke off. Then she received a letter postmarked "Paris." Apparently, Boris had escaped. Olga Petrovna decided to chance an escape as well. One of the local exiles gave her a secret address in Warsaw and told her the password. From Warsaw she managed to get to France, where she reunited with her husband. They settled in the Latin Quarter in Paris.

Once in Paris, the wife of Yevno Azef, the famous founder of the Fighting Organization of the Socialist-Revolutionary Party, invited them for dinner. Azef produced an abominable impression on both of them. "He was tall and fat, with a thick golden chain that hung down to his belly. He had a coarse face and untrustworthy eyes. As my husband said, he was the kind of man you'd expect to involve himself in a conspiracy," Olga Petrovna narrated.

Through Azef's wife, she received the assignment to smuggle dynamite to Russia, which was how she saw her motherland again.

Only later did I manage to correlate the light and soft image of Olga Petrovna with her biography and understand what Nekrasov's lines meant to her, as well as what special meaning she imparted to them. Her eyes shone when she said she was happy "to have left the exultant and idly jabbering people for the side of those perishing for great love!" Having gone through nine months of imprisonment in Peter and Paul Fortress under the tsar, in '37 she was sentenced to ten years by the Soviet regime.

TEC ARRIVED in Mezhog earlier than was expected. I was in for a great surprise: together with the actors came Aleksandr Osipovich, who almost never traveled with the theater because of problems with his legs. My teacher's visit signaled his courage and keen interest in my life.

"Well, I felt I had to see your son!" he explained. His own son had died in exile in Karelia.

"Where is the baby?" everyone kept asking.

Some of my more daring friends sneaked into the nursery, avoiding Metryakova's defense lines. After much humiliation and supplication, I talked a nurse into letting me take my son to the staff room after Metryakova left the camp for the night.

My tender child grabbed Aleksandr Osipovich's beard with his tiny hands and, holding it tightly, produced a delightful and melodious babble.

"Are you complaining about your mother? Well, well. Tell me everything, that's what I came for, right?" Aleksandr Osipovich kept up the conversation.

Both seemed very pleased to meet each other.

Throughout TEC's visit I had to run back and forth from work to the nursery and only managed to find two or three hours altogether to talk with Aleksandr Osipovich. After TEC left, he sent me epistolary poems, which again proved to me that daily-life exhaustion could in fact be put to words with a smile and humor.

IN 1946 the contingent of the camps radically changed. The former duality of camp population—the criminals and political prisoners—was now replaced with a much greater diversity: traitors, members of General Vlasov's Russian Liberation Army, soldiers of the Organization of Ukrainian Nationalists whose leader was Stepan Bandera, and others. The war, the Nazi imprisonment, the partisan movement, as well as the Baltic resistance dumped myriads of people with unfamiliar ways of thinking and peculiar modes of behavior into the camps.

Inflamed dialogues of frontline soldiers who had fought for their motherland for three or four years, were taken prisoner by the Nazis and then thrown in prison upon their return home, were the hardest to witness. Their nerves were strained to the limit. They argued, screamed and almost fought with each other. But, at the same time, one kind word would often be enough to calm them down. They had a difficult time staying quiet after lights-out. They kept on going over the "mess" they had gone through, which sat deeply in their consciousness, recalling in heartbreaking tones the ignorant orders of the high-ranking officers, the ambitions and pretentiousness of the lower ranks, the cowardice or bravery of fellow soldiers dead or alive. They judged everything zealously and fervently and seemed to believe that by drawing other people's attention to the exuberant trials of war they would be able to prove their own innocence, rescue the truth and refute the infamous article, Treason.

Next to them were men of a different type, with sly eyes and a hunched bearing, who whisked timorously about the zone. In exchange for being exempted from work they were ready to kiss not only the guards' hands but also their top boots. It wasn't hard to recognize a particular social formation in their buttery and obsequious faces, which were in stark opposition to the resentful looks of the former soldiers. Many other broods were brought together in the camps, too.

From time to time I would hear a knock on the door of the staff room, and a smiling young man would walk in and take out a solid hunk of salted lard, wrapped in a clean white cloth, from under his shirt.

"Take it, sister! It's from my parcel."

They were from the Baltic. Offended by their conviction that they could easily bribe anyone, I would drive them out. They would wait a while, as if testing me, and then, sobered and reassured that I wasn't fooling around, they'd ask me cautiously to hide their prayer books or Bibles, which they'd managed to hold on to. A respectful relationship gradually took root between us.

Prisoners with criminal convictions were also different from their previous generation. Masha Golubeva, a former soldier, worked at the pharmacy. She was a buxom and agreeable simple woman who still wore her military blouse. She would jauntily dance the *barynya* and sing rollicking *chastushkas,* and just as loudly she would sometimes burst into tears. At the front she had had an affair with a lieutenant. Once, after he had been dispatched to the regiment staff, he came down on a motorcycle to visit her. She told him she was pregnant, but the lieutenant answered, "What do I need a child for? See you!" and started his motorcycle. Masha called to him from the porch but he never looked back. She took her revolver out of its holster and shot the departing lieutenant in the back, killing him on the spot. The court sentenced her to five years for murder.

SOME UNIMAGINABLE NEWS spread around the camp. A commission was coming to collect signatures for a government loan. Prisoners, who never received a single ruble and had no way of knowing on what basis their labor was converted into state profits, had to lend money to that state. People deprived of freedom, those who dreamed of bread at night and cherished the very idea of a "motherland," subscribed to the loan imposed on them by the government.

The prisoners were lined up. Without further ado, the functionaries ordered:

"Sign here. Put an amount. What? Shame on you! You've got to double it. They were right to throw you in prison if that's what you want to escape with! Are you begrudging money to your own country?"

My turn came. Like everyone else, I had to certify that I did not mind a reduced ration and tattered clothing; that I was willing to take part in yet another hypocritical enterprise of the regime. But I recalled how at the start of the war spurned clergymen, metropolitans and ordinary faithful handed over golden chains and other jewels or transferred sums of money to the Soviet Army to help build new aircraft. One type of feelings crossed out the other. I signed. People avoided looking into each other's eyes.

Soon other news came, no less incredible in its own way.

All of a sudden they started whitewashing the barracks. Bedbugs were being urgently exterminated. Lanes were being leveled. Visiting inspectors would turn over the tables, run a handkerchief under the bottom side and shake their heads reproachfully:

"What's wrong with you? There's dust all over!"

"What in the world is going on?" we asked.

"They say that a UN commission will be inspecting the camps."

At the sound of this abbreviation, the wind of the distant outer world wafted in. A semblance of hope stirred in our souls. People of other nations! A different social order! Could this possibly have any relation to us?

Everyone's favorite place at the infirmary barracks was by the gigantic oven, where people would gather to warm themselves up. The twenty-eight-year-old Neyman stood there, too. I had noticed a while ago that his eyes shone as if he knew something he wanted to share with me.

"Nurse, I'm telling this only to you. I will be freed soon. I got a letter. It says that the Jews have organized a community abroad. They're collecting money to get us released. I promise: I'll do anything to get you out of here, too. See, it's wonderful. Over there they petition for those of us who are stuck over here."

In a similar way, the Poles in Belovodsk believed that they would be rescued by their government. Neyman had faith that his people would save him. As for me, I wasn't even sure I could consider myself a legitimate inhabitant of the earth. No, I didn't share the faith of the charming red-haired Neyman.

"FILIPP YAKOVLEVICH has come! He's waiting for you at the nursery," someone called to me.

We were allowed into the precious little room where Yurik's cot stood.

Filipp took his son in his arms, looked at him and pressed him to his chest. "My baby, my little boy, my dear son!"

He was very excited. Turning his affected face to me, he said:

"I'm so grateful to you, Lyolya!"

I could only remind him of my name…

"It's all nonsense! You can't doubt for a single minute I have someone else in my life except you two. There're only three of us, that's all! Believe me! I'm begging you, believe and forgive me! How stupid… Forgive me."

For the hundredth time I was witnessing this metamorphosis. From being bombastic and fussy he became frank and artless so quickly there wasn't even enough time for the pain to scald me.

"Tell me you believe me!" he insisted.

"I believe you," I answered, closing my eyes.

"Thank you! You can take refuge in me. Rely on me, trust me in everything! I won't deceive you. I'm forty. I've dreamed of having a son so much. Only now have I finally found a family. Let's talk everything over."

There was never enough time to talk properly. His visits were illicit, the minutes he stayed were controlled by fear for ourselves, as well as for those who had let him into the zone. The main news he hurried to tell me was that he had finally broken up with Vera Petrovna and left Urdoma. He was living on his own, separating himself from her geographically, as well. He said that was how he was going to live from now on until I and our son, his family, would be able to join him. Of course that wasn't a short wait, but he hadn't given up petitioning for my release. He also said he was now working as the head of a large medical unit; that he was happy and loved me and his son the way no one had ever loved before.

A LETTER came from Vera Nikolaevna. She had managed to find my sister. Valechka was living in Moscow. I didn't know how to tell her that I was in the camp, that I had been tried and convicted. Unsure of what she was like now, how much she might be able to understand, I didn't know how to explain the reasons, but I couldn't wait to hear how her life had turned out, what was going on with her; I finally gathered my courage.

In her reply, Valechka wrote that after leaving the orphanage in Uglich she had been mobilized to build a gas pipeline near Moscow. She hadn't had the chance to finish school. She was living in a workers' dormitory and earning little. She couldn't understand what had happened to me and asked simple questions which had no answers.

I felt I ought to let her know about Yurochka and Filipp. I didn't want to hide it from her, but nevertheless I couldn't bring myself to put it down in any of my letters.

Filipp was leaving on vacation to the South, to Essentuki. He was going to pass through Moscow and asked for Valechka's address: "I want to meet her. She's your sister, after all." I hesitated and wouldn't give the address to him, but when he arrived in Moscow, Filipp found her himself and paid her a visit.

Though I still regarded her as a helpless teenager, my younger sister was already a nineteen-year-old, grown-up girl. The siege, the war, the orphanage and the construction work had shaped her accordingly. Her letter, in which she described her impression of Filipp, was striking.

> Forgive me, my dear,—*she wrote,*—but your second husband didn't produce a good impression on me. He might be a nice man—after all, I saw him only once. Try to understand me. I pity you, and I have a hard life myself, but I was struck to hear him say that you have a son. He told me about your life; that you wear a quilted jacket in the nipping frost. He told me what they feed you on there, and said that he loves you madly. But how can he take vacations to the resorts, to Sochi or Essentuki, while you work and suffer there in the camp? I'd rather he spent his money on something warm for you to wear.

It was painful to realize she had faced the hardships of war and those that followed it in such a merciless way on her own. But I was bewildered by the straightforwardness of her judgments and her perspective on life, which was puzzling above all because of the definite standards Valechka seemed to have, regardless of her own circumstances. As for me, with the baggage of knowledge and intuition that I had, I was far from having such expectations of fairness from life.

COLONEL VARSH, a man with bushy eyebrows and the stature of a tank, who was the new deputy to the chief commandant, came to Mezhog with one of the commissions. Holding his hands behind his back, he paced aloofly in front of his retinue. The inspectors, ready to rush in to answer his questions, respectfully kept their distance.

"They're coming here!" shouted my patients, looking through the window.

Everyone was ordered to line up

"It's pretty clean in here," Varsh admitted. "Everything looks smart. Any complaints?"

"None!" answered the patients unanimously.

"Why don't the other barracks look so cozy? Who's the nurse here?"

"Petkevich," the local authorities reported.

"You?" he asked me and then turned to the foreman: "Put her on the list."

It was a list of candidates being considered for early release.

The commission went on to inspect other sites of the camp.

I was late to feed Yurik. As soon as they left, I headed for the nursery—as usual, by climbing through the hole in the fence. I nursed my son and was holding him in my arms when the nursery attendants announced the commission was on its way.

Varsh saw me immediately.

"Whose child is that?" he asked.

"Mine."

He didn't say out loud what clearly showed through his face: he had made a mistake; I wasn't quite a model prisoner to be considered for early release.

"Cross her out!" he barked.

Foresight told me that merely striking me off the list wouldn't dissipate the colonel's anger. My only worry was not to incur graver consequences.

ALEKSANDRA PETROVNA was more demanding with me than with the rest of the nurses. When one batch of prisoners' time at the infirmary was up and a new transport was arriving for the next two-month term, she ordered:

"I'll put you on the commission to admit the new arrivals. This time we'll do it differently: we'll gather all the criminals in one barracks—the punishment barracks—so that the rest can live normally. It is not wise to have bandits all over the place."

"Who will you appoint to be a nurse there?" people asked her.

"Who? Petkevich, of course!"

I thought she was playing one of her eccentric tricks on me and didn't take it seriously, but Aleksandra Petrovna wasn't joking. My heart skipped a beat.

"Aleksandra Petrovna!" I implored. "I can't possibly be the nurse at the punishment barracks! I'm not capable of it."

"You'll be capable!" she cut me short. "You will."

She pretended she didn't notice my panic. I was morbidly scared of criminals, of their vicious sallow faces, putrid mouths crammed with gold caps, eyes that showed no reaction to anything human.

A long line of emaciated, overworked bodies stood in front of the table. Most of the men were covered in tattoos. Their chests, backs, bellies and arms were sheer picture galleries of mermaids, female visages, animals, names, various designs, as well as expressive aphorisms. Some seemed embarrassed by their embellishments, while others paid them no mind. At the moment, they only craved two months of rest and better food.

It was the turn of a pale, extremely gaunt criminal. I recognized him instantly.

"Your name?" asked Aleksandra Petrovna.

"What? You know me. I'm Lvov."

"Of course, the famous Lvov is paying us another visit! What should we do with you?"

"Let me stay at the infirmary!"

"Just to misbehave again? I don't know… It's up to Tamara Vladislavovna. If she admits you to the punishment barracks, then fine, you can hang around for a while. If not, I'll send you back right away."

She addressed me:

"So? Are you going to take him on?"

After Lvov, Lavnyaev stood next in line. I recognized him, too.

Of course, Aleksandra Petrovna was unaware of what had happened a few months earlier.

I'd been sitting in the barracks one evening, sewing some clothes for my son, when Lavnyaev walked in, holding a blue woolen sweater.

"Wanna buy it? Just thirty rubles."

I imagined how good the fluffy sweater would look on Yurik after I reknitted it for him. Filipp had just sent me thirty rubles and I had the money handy.

"All right," I agreed.

I wasn't aware of these common schemes. The moment I gave him the money and reached for the sweater, Lvov burst in and, aping genuine indignation, went after Lavnyaev.

"Damn it! You stole my sweater. Give it back, or I'll kill you!"

Lvov was supposed to grab the sweater from me, whereby both the money and the sweater would be in their hands. Yet something strange came upon me. I knew I was not going to return it. It grew dark before my eyes, but I yelled out, "I'm not giving it back to you!"

The most important thing was not to give in. The women in the barracks got scared: "Give it to him! What are you doing?"

Growing white with rage, the criminal came after me:

"I'll kill you!"

At that moment I hated him with all the power of my soul. Losing control over myself, I yelled back:

"Kill me! I'm not giving it back to you!"

I was afraid, but my feeling of hatred was stronger than fear. I rose up against the thug for all I had gone through: for the female criminals who raised the plank to beat me to death, for their foul curses, for their humiliating shrieks—"Bitch, push the wagon!"—for everything that had ever been stolen from me before, for my entire degrading life.

Outraged, Lvov kicked the plank bed with such force that everything fell down off it to the floor. Hysterically, he started tearing his shirt into pieces. But his animal-like intuition was telling him he was confronting another mass of rage whose charge was no less powerful than his own. Running out of the barracks, he was still yelling:

"Just wait, I'll get to you! I'll kill you!"

The women looked at me as if seeing me for the first time, struggling to reconcile the former quiet, polite image of me with what they'd just seen.

In the aftermath, when everything was calm again, I burned with shame. "How could I? What's going on with me?" Once, a long time ago, I had a similar feeling when I rose up against my father after he lost a wallet with public money.

All that had happened flashed through my mind now as I faced the two criminals during the medical inspection. I said I wasn't going to admit them. Aleksandra Petrovna, who wanted to fortify my authority, backed me up:

"Well, if Petkevich says no, you'll have to do without. I'm sending you back."

The issue was closed. I didn't feel right: unaware of the incident with the criminals, Aleksandra Petrovna could have understood everything wrong.

During the break, Lavnyaev called me behind the gigantic oven that stood in the middle of the barracks. Lvov was already waiting there.

"Nurse, take us in!" he said, with a note of threat and sincere supplication in his voice. "Everything's gonna be in order."

"Promise me."

"We promise."

I felt relieved by the fact that they addressed me first. I was almost grateful to these crooks who were involuntarily offering me their peace.

They stayed at the infirmary for two months and caused no trouble during all that time. Lvov had tuberculosis. In some way, they were also victims. I met them much later at a different camp. On the day of my release they honored me with a surprising gift: a cooking board, a wooden hammer and a scoop they made with their own hands.

It was hard to understand fully according to what principle the infirmary punishment barracks was populated. There were boys of eighteen and nineteen sentenced for various minor misdeeds during the war. Lvov and Lavnyaev, both thirty, were among the "old men."

There was a truly astonishing array of people.

The eighteen-year-old Seryozha Beketov, who had been drafted into the army in '44, was appointed a watchman at a bombed-out warehouse in Leipzig to look after grand pianos. Not having a shift-mate, he wasn't able to stay awake all the time, and the pianos were stolen. Seryozha was sentenced to seven years.

Viktor Lunev, the same age as Seryozha, was assigned to stand guard on a train car loaded with coffee, which, as it turned out, was to be sold on the black market. His commanders and their accomplices somehow managed to escape trial, but Viktor got seven years.

The boys were resentful and helpless. They were cheeky with the guards and resisted the camp regime. During one of their fights with the guards, an officer called them "Scum of the people!" They always remembered it. In their hoarse and spiteful hysterics, the boys shrieked that there was no kindness in the world, that all around were falsehood, "scumbags and swine." Moments later, however, their eyes would clear and they'd again be ready for chivalry and kind deeds.

When one of the officials of the Mezhog medical unit stopped by the staff room to lay out his feelings toward me and attempted to give his hands free rein, I pushed the door, which instantly opened, and a boy by the name of Yura Strakhov walked in, baring his teeth:

"I'll kill you, you rascal, if you dare touch her!"

The boy's protective outburst made me attached to him. I replaced his shirt, which he had already patched up three times, with a new one I'd sewn from a piece of gray coarse linen.

The "criminals" at the medical punishment barracks quickly arranged a roster and allotted duties among themselves. I talked Aleksandra Petrovna into letting them pick up extra work in the bread-cutting room, in the kitchen or in the boiler room. They greedily gobbled down anything that resembled food. We established trustful and even friendly relationships. The boys' eagerness to make this barracks their home, if only for two months, was captivating and infectious.

To heat the stove we received waterlogged firewood. The fire couldn't overpower the dampness, and there was nothing to chop the logs with. I managed to find a rusty axe at the camp dump. The boys fashioned a handle. Several of them stood on lookout as we began chopping the thick logs. However, the camp commandant saw us and called in guards to take the axe away.

"Who brought this?" the commandant asked.

"I did," I said.

Interrupting me, Viktor Lunev shouted:

"That's not true! I found it."

I was put in one punishment cell for three days, with only a three-hundred-gram ration, Viktor—in another. The boys waited for me to be let out to nurse my son and passed me some bread they'd saved for me.

Later I'd receive their heart-shaped letters that said, "You taught me the difference between black and white," or "Had I not met you, I would have died." For me, and for my son, these notes were of great importance.

Yet danger and savagery haunted me everywhere. Frightening criminals would arrive to the medical unit with a transport, changing places with the departing ones; a certain Kondratov once swore he would hack me to death with an axe. My son was the only hope, the only unquestionable aspiration I had, my present and my future. I pressed him to my chest and the world grew lighter. He laughed, and finally one day he uttered the sacred word, "Mama."

The day came when Yurik took his first step. His face took on a very serious expression and then brightened with a smile. He conceived of his step as his own creation, evaluated his achievement and looked very content with himself. Astonished, I whispered to him:

"One more! Here, come here to me!"

Looking into my eyes, he'd raise his little leg to make the next step and, laughing melodiously, topple over onto his back or right into my arms.

Returning to my barracks, I'd set about writing letters, diary entries of a sort, to my son; I promised him we'd climb trees together, have a grand piano and lots of music at home, help his father get things straightened out and so on. Filipp wrote me letters full of assurances that now, having lived by himself for half a year, he understood that his only dream in life was us and that he loved and was waiting for us.

A RUMOR SPREAD that a new transport for distant camps was being readied. Its destination was the Mariinsky camps in western Siberia.

To understand the meaning of transferring masses of people from one godforsaken place to another was impossible. No sooner would a transport from the North leave for Siberia than new batches of prisoners would be brought in from other faraway places.

Many *mamkas*, whose children no longer had to be breast-fed, were put on the transport list. Sobs and groans were heard around the camp.

This time I was relatively calm, hoping that the misfortune would pass me by. I knew Aleksandra Petrovna wouldn't give me away.

When a mother was carted off on the transport, her child was transferred to an orphanage for free children. How and where the mother could find her child years later was a mystery. An unimaginable bustle was going on in the barracks. One mother, a criminal, stripped herself naked and was running on the upper plank beds, cursing and swearing that she was pregnant again and that they had to let her stay. Five guards wrapped her tightly in a blanket and took her to the punishment block, from where her screams reached us for a long time afterward. No matter whose human cry it might be, it always turned the soul inside out.

I was administering intravenous injections when two of my patients walked in:

"Nurse, we were ordered to put you onto a stretcher and take you to the surgical barracks."

"What? That's not funny."

"Malinovskaya ordered us to bring you there immediately."

My blood turned cold, but I couldn't bring myself to join this bizarre game.

"I'll be there soon," I answered.

Aleksandra Petrovna came in first. In a pronouncedly strict voice she said:

"You don't fool around with what you have. Get onto the stretcher immediately and off you go to the surgical barracks!"

What could I possibly "have"? I understood that something extreme must have happened: I was on the transfer list. I got myself onto the stretcher.

The nurse on duty, Verochka Zhevnerovich, had already been warned. I was put in a medical ward and waited for Aleksandra Petrovna, but she wouldn't come. I knew she had lots of urgent things to sort out while the transport was being put together, but still…

When the transport was gone, Aleksandra Petrovna finally came to my ward, sat in front of me and explained that the camp's Third Department had received a telegram: *SEND MOTHER PETKEVICH MARIINSKY CAMPS LEAVE CHILD MEZHOG VARSH.*

"You'll have to stay here a bit longer," ordered Aleksandra Petrovna. "I'll discharge you in a few days."

I couldn't recover from the fear even after I was discharged from the surgical barracks and got to working again as usual. Whose idea was it to tear me away from my son? What did Varsh have to do with it?

Malinovskaya's willingness to resist Varsh by declaring me sick was a daring sign of her kindness toward me. I loved this woman and couldn't imagine how I could possibly thank her.

In the evening she came to the staff room. She had the same bitter wrinkle above her mouth, her eyes looking experienced and shrewd. She waited and then asked:

"Tamara, I'll now ask you a difficult question. Think. You don't have to answer right away. Could it be Bakharev?"

The question was not so much difficult as it was utterly horrific. Yet it had been asked. It existed.

The telegram could only have been the result of someone's deliberate and ardent efforts. I myself bluntly searched for a cause, too. No, Filipp couldn't have done it! What reasons could he possibly have? I rejected this frightening thought. To doubt Filipp meant to bring my life to a collapse. A thousand times—no! To believe Filipp's love and be true to myself was the only way to keep my heart going. I could try to explain everything by attributing the telegraph to Varsh's personal hostility toward me during his visit to Mezhog, but still, it didn't quite settle things in my mind.

THE YEAR 1946 was coming to an end. On December 12, it was Yurik's birthday, a real holiday. My son was one year old!

Metryakova relented and allowed me to stay with him on that day for as long as I wanted to. I nursed him, dressed him up and undressed him again, put him to sleep in his cot, taught him how to walk, and played with him.

Olga Petrovna congratulated me in the morning. A letter and wonderful gifts for Yurik came from Filipp. He called me his wife, the mother of our son. He swore he would never deceive me and wrote he was grateful to me for making his life happier. He hoped to manage to have both me and Yurik transferred some place closer and asked if I was truly committed to sharing my life with him, to staying with him through whatever may come. He supposed it would be better for Yurik to live with him till my release; they would both be waiting for me. "Be calm," he wrote. "There is no need to get alarmed and think what to do. I am being honest with you. We have agreed to be honest with each other, haven't we?"

It was a moonlit night. The sky was full of stars, and there was a biting December frost. Filipp's letter made my mood even more festive, although, of course, I was not going to part with my son.

On my way to the barracks I ran into the foreman, who had in fact been looking for me. He told me to see the new administrative director, who had personally brought Filipp through the camp's checkpoint.

"I couldn't miss my son's birthday!" Filipp greeted me cheerfully. "I simply got on the train and left. They'll manage without me, though there's a ton of work."

His arrival was a gift worthy of the day. Together we went back to the nursery. Yurik was asleep.

Filipp told me about his work. He looked especially uplifted and full of energy. He even began studying English and exercising. He seemed sure he had full control over the world around him; he was the master of his circumstances, and no one was capable of refusing any of his requests. Since he was living alone, he needed somebody to take care of him, so he was going to hire Olga Ivanovna, a woman I knew from the Urdoma infirmary, as a housemaid. He thought Olga Ivanovna fitted this role well: thrifty and practical, she was over sixty years old with no family, and since her release she'd been making her living as a maid for camp officials.

When I resisted Filipp's plan to take our son to live with him, he said he was going to ask the head of his camp's division to issue a special warrant to have me and Yurochka sent to the camp in Revazh. I did not mind being transferred provided that I and my son would be there together.

In general, his plans were vast. He had brothers who lived near Kursk. "I wrote them about you," he said. "They already love you and are waiting for us to visit. They're happy for me, the father. Once you get released, we'll go straight there, then to the south."

The story about the telegram from Varsh perplexed Filipp a great deal. It seemed he was solving some riddle for a few seconds and only then said, "No, it's nothing serious. Don't worry, it's really nothing." And at that moment it occurred to me: "How could I have missed this simple explanation? Of course, it was Vera Petrovna! She must have gone to talk to Varsh about me." I should've figured this out myself, but Filipp hadn't mentioned her name for more than half a year. His vow that he not only harbored no love for Vera Petrovna but in fact could hardly stand her, calling her "worthless and stupid," during all that time, only crowned the issue.

About three weeks passed. The warrant we were waiting for hadn't arrived. Filipp kept sending me alarmed letters with descriptions of how he went to meet the transports arriving from our camp division and how dispirited he was not to see us. "Have you changed your mind? How could you not even let me know, if that is the case?"

IN JANUARY another sinister rumor spread around the camp, which Aleksandra Petrovna confirmed: children older than one year would be sent to free orphanages and nurseries in the Komi Republic. This resolution had apparently been passed several months ago, and a special commission compiling the lists was going to arrive in Mezhog soon.

What might have seemed a humane idea of rescuing children from the camps was, in fact, monstrous. Who could have possibly come up with the plan to take them away from their mothers? Up until now, the little ones stayed at the medical unit until their parents were released.

Free orphanages had not just bad but truly ominous reputations. The enormously high percentage of handicapped or crippled children, often infected with tuberculosis, spoke for itself. Many did not know how to talk until they were four or five years old: pointing at an object, they'd just make dull noises, or at best could articulate separate syllables but not whole words. Everything inside me grew numb from the stories of underdeveloped children sick and covered with scabs.

All these thoughts came to mind later. At that time I simply could not help imagining Yurik being taken away to an unknown nursery, where he'd stretch his little hands out in vain for his mother, or look to the door for me and I'd never appear, or cry without me being there to soothe him.

I realized I was in a far better situation than many others. My son had a father who was willing to take him on and even begged to do so. But I was flustered nevertheless. I would feel safer sending my son to live with my sister, but she was too young and lived in a dormitory. I even toyed at the idea of finding Platon Romanovich's friends in Moscow. He regularly wrote to Mezhog and was worried about me. The most natural option—to give my son away to his father—I somehow put off as the last resort.

I instantly wrote to Filipp, asking him to hurry up with the warrant for our transfer, although the new resolution could now apply to the Revazh camp as well.

Aleksandra Petrovna abstained from giving advice. Only once did she let herself sum up the situation with a logical deduction:

"Bakharev will find a way to get the son out of the orphanage. To do so, he won't need you. Or you'll have to prove he is not Yury's father."

Beside myself, I finally told Filipp that he could take Yurik. It was my son's health, after all, that was my main concern. Filipp wrote that he'd come with Olga Ivanovna early enough before the general transfer of children began. I was all out of sorts from these extreme decisions. I thought, I'll make him promise me... I'll make him sign a written obligation... But that would mean hurting a person who loved me. I had no doubts about his feelings, and I couldn't be wrong. He loved me more than I loved him.

They came on a dark, frosty winter morning. Olga Ivanovna was allowed into the zone together with Filipp. I had imagined her face to be friendlier. I must have expected sympathy from this older woman. Filipp tried to calm me down: "She's kind and caring. The way she looks is not important." From Filipp I also expected some special words. I had three years—an eternity!—before I'd be released. Filipp's resourcefulness was my only aspiration: "He'll think of something. He'll find a way to bring my son over so that I can see him regularly."

Olga Ivanovna was packing my son's clothing into her suitcase. Helping, I threw ingratiating glances her way, saying, "Olga Ivanovna, be so kind... Please, I'm begging you..." My son, unaware of what was happening, was dangling his legs. I wrapped him in a cotton-wool blanket that Filipp had brought. He took Yurik in his arms.

I accompanied them to the checkpoint...

After they left, I set out to write Filipp a letter with many questions: about the journey, if Yurik had cried on the way, if he was eating well, where his crib stood, reminders to put the gray jacket over the white one, requesting that Olga Ivanovna take the boy outside often, and so on.

I started receiving his detailed reports. He described in length how Yurochka slept, what he was like when he woke up, what new words and sounds he mumbled. Responding to my anxiety about Olga Ivanovna, he wrote: "You said she must be kind, since I have chosen her. She always grumbles and is never satisfied with anything. That's just the way she is. But no matter what she does, there's no way of doing it better!"

Just a few days later, all children from Mezhog were sent to the various orphanages scattered around the Komi. Any lingering doubts about my decision disappeared at once. Of course, everything was in my boy's best interest. But I still missed him horribly. I could find no way to suppress or even control my yearning for him. My life was now fully dependent on letters from Filipp. I read to the very bottom of them, and even deeper.

Filipp's promise to get me transferred to his camp division still stood. I was awaiting the warrant.

AFTER MY "criminal" patients left, Aleksandra Petrovna announced:

"I'm transferring you to another job. You'll work as a nurse for the free workers, as well as for prisoners. You have enough skills for intravenous infusions."

"But I won't manage!" I pleaded with her again.

"I've heard that before. I know it by heart."

Medications for free workers came from a special fund. My mornings were allocated for free patients, the evenings—for the prisoners. People crowded in front of the entrance. Among them were guards and their wives. The officer who had thrown me into a punishment cell for bringing the axe was among those waiting his turn. Now he tried to crack jokes and sound witty.

The stout and healthy-looking agronomist Tselishchev aimed to be the last in line. He hoped to linger for a while and talk. But when he came in, he just sat silently and blankly stared into the distance. During the summer he would bring me posies of wildflowers. His presence vexed me but something prevented me from turning him out. Finally he said with a smile:

"It seems a wall has been erected all around me—in my thoughts as well as in my desires, in my entire life. I keep bumping into it. I thought you were exactly the person who'd understand."

I was taken aback: it was *my* image of the world, too! Of course I understood. Not that I wanted to, but that was a different matter. I was enclosed within all sorts of walls, which threatened one day to eclipse the sky.

The agronomist's confidence alarmed me: why would he disclose such an intimate feeling? Why would he, a free man who'd never lived in the camps or fought at the front, have such a frightening image of the world? It seemed he could end up at Aleksandra Petrovna's mental asylum any day. I was struck by how blurred the line between madness and normality was. I remembered Yakhontov. I became convinced that constant uncertainty in one's own mental steadiness was also a disease. Why was it never taken into account? I asked Aleksandra Petrovna:

"Do you think the agronomist is healthy? It looks like he doesn't feel well."

"There are so few who do..." she answered.

Aleksandra Petrovna had been inviting me to see the mental asylum for a long time, offering to show me her "children." I tried to put off the visit as long as I could: I wanted to turn my face to the sun, not to darkness. But once I agreed.

Behind a high fence there was a two-story wooden house, which looked different from the rest of the camp buildings not only because of the extra floor but also because, in the summer, it was decorated with flowerbeds. The patients diligently tended the flowers.

As Aleksandra Petrovna walked along the lane, the patients followed her with half-smiling eyes, drawling, "Ma-a-ma."

On her desk lay a pile of drawings of otherworldly creatures and plants, of tangled and twisted lines, or else—just mouths or noses.

Patients from the Baltic republics were especially numerous. Some of them cursed in Russian with a maniacal persistence; others looked detached and almost blissful, as if some wonderful music was being played into their ears and nothing could tear them away from it. Behind the wall, I could hear the attendants suppressing a man who was writhing and howling from some nightmarish visions. A toothless old woman with an unnaturally straight back, who imagined herself an English queen, paced nobly back and forth.

A violin hung on the wall in Aleksandra Petrovna's office.

"Do you play?" I asked her.

"No. It's for those who do."

I remembered Aleksandr Osipovich telling me, "Malinovskaya is a woman of great talents. She's written a series of stunning stories." I felt the urge to ask to read some of them. But the axiom, "Don't ask! Don't express interest!" weighed on me. My accursed fear of looking uncivil or discreet had robbed me of so many discoveries! There was only one question I couldn't help asking Aleksandra Petrovna.

"Why does one person survive a dozen catastrophes while another can't cope with even one small misfortune?"

"It depends on the person's psychiatric predispositions," she explained thriftily.

I thanked her in my mind. It meant I was healthy.

SOME CHANGES took place in the camp. Rodion Evgenyevich Malakhov was transferred to another camp division, and a new administrative director was appointed to his position. I knew the new director's wife, Asya Arsentyevna, from Urdoma, where she'd worked at the pharmacy.

I was summoned to the new administrative director's office. When I walked in, his wife was also there. As it had been in Urdoma, here Asya Arsentyevna also worked as a pharmacist. The director walked out, leaving us face-to-face.

"It was I who asked you to come. Sit down, Tamara. The conversation isn't going to be an easy one."

Something came over me when I heard her words and tears welled up in my eyes in anticipation.

"No, it won't work that way. You'll either be courageous, or we won't be able to talk at all," Asya Arsentyevna stipulated.

"I'll be courageous. I'm listening," I assured her.

"I couldn't bring myself to speak to you about this for a long time. I even consulted with my husband. We both like you and we don't want to be scoundrels to you. To make a long story short, you have to know: your son is being raised by Vera Petrovna."

"Olga Ivanovna…"

"Olga Ivanovna is their housemaid."

I became horrified by my own naïveté. In Urdoma, Simon had told me: "He is tied up with Vera through their common 'business' more than anything else could ever bind him to any one." Back in Svetik, the Crimean Tatar Rashid had told me the truth. In Knyazh-Pogost, Ilya Evseevich tried to make it clear to me. No one except myself trusted Filipp. Why did I believe him? Events of the recent past flashed through my mind like in a kaleidoscope: he rescued me from the hell of Svetik, he did so much when my son was born, and twice he virtually saved my life. So why was I always afraid of him? Why did my blood run cold every time he'd unexpectedly show up?

I wrote Filipp an incoherent and foolish letter. He responded:

> I came back after being away for ten days and went straight to town to get your letter from the post office. Large drops of cold sweat dripped off my face, and a chill spread through my body as I read it. You've written horrific things. What for? Could you really believe that Yury has been living with me as my tenant? Is that what you mean? And do you really suspect I've been carrying out my plans just to get rid of you? Is that what you wanted to say? You're crazy! You even write that I'm living in some sort of bliss with V.P. You're blind! You don't see that I've only been carrying out my own duty, my obligation. You're thoughtless. You don't understand that everything I've been doing is just for the sake of Yurik and you.
>
> Never have I loved you so fully and deeply, so devotedly and candidly, so eternally and with such joy, as I love you now. I think of you all the time! I passionately want to hold you, tired and racked, in my arms, which are always outstretched for you. I want you to tremble with joy and forget the whole world of misery and anxiety. I want to press you to my chest so that you might regain faith in people, faith in your own feelings, faith in your own self, and so that you could feel my love, my friendship and my protection. I want you to be proud of your happiness. If you love me, you have to believe me. Be faithful to me, genuinely faithful, to keep your conscience pure.

I dismissed his words. I needed to read just one phrase: that Vera Petrovna was nowhere near our son; that I'd been lied to. But he didn't write this. That was precisely what he brushed aside as an insignificant detail.

"Remember when Vera Petrovna was gone for a long time?" a nurse in Urdoma had once told me. "She went to a resort to take mud baths. She had many abortions when she was a prisoner. When she met Filipp, she wanted to keep him at any price, but she could no longer have children. The treatment she received didn't help either."

The meaning of Vera Petrovna's visit to Mezhog suddenly became clear. Before taking any further steps, she wanted to see my son. She liked him. She loved Filipp. With outstanding cunning, she worked systematically in attaching herself to him. My son became her main stake. But it was too late for my insight to make any difference.

I wondered whether I should stop writing to Filipp. But to live without knowing anything about my son meant not to live at all. I had to find a way to harness myself.

No longer fearing anything or having to lie, Filipp Yakovlevich didn't wait long to strike me with a lethal blow.

> I can't hide from you the fact that Vera Petrovna does not entrust him to anybody. She is with him every moment. Only when I come home and take him in my arms does she sometimes take a break for a short while, but the next moment she'd be back with him again. When he fell sick, she cried. She is frantically attached to him. She took two months off work just to be near him. She adores him. He is her life.

The letter ended with a postscript: "I love you, my dearest, my only wife!"

There was their house, a hundred *versts* away from my camp. In one of the rooms stood my son's bed, his little chair and table. It was warm inside, and the stove was burning. There they drank, ate and talked to each other. My son was producing his first words. He was caressed and looked after by a strange dark woman, a shrewd fox and a fighter.

That was the way he, the father of my son, wrote to me from freedom, "protecting" my son from me. I nearly ended up as a patient at Aleksandra Petrovna's asylum. I no longer wanted to feel anything...

It was 1947.

People who had built the camps in the impassable taiga—not just for themselves but also for those who would come to replace them—were preparing to be released. Those who survived imagined freedom as a chance to return to their interrupted former lives. They were busy writing letters to friends and relatives, mending their old clothes and sneaking peeks at themselves in the mirrors. The half-sane joy in their eyes was mixed with a deep-seated fear: somewhere, in the dens of secrecy and bureaucracy, the same anonymous power, driven by incongruous principles that only its own agents could know, randomly marked people's fates, capriciously determining whether or not to release them. Regardless of their term and sentence, and without an additional trial, some prisoners were kept behind, their release dates passing like so many grains in the wind. The entire cohort of prisoners from '37 was living as if under high voltage, yearning only to step over the threshold of the camp's checkpoint.

They had sustained themselves for ten years in various ways: some derived strength from the love for their families, others—from obstinacy. Those denied release wasted away within weeks, turning into decrepit wrecks.

When the first batch of prisoners got out, unexpected news spread around the camps: it was forbidden to settle in Leningrad, Moscow or any of the capitals of the many Soviet republics. At local police stations, all 58-ers were issued temporary IDs instead of a regular passport. These IDs were stamped with a "39," which in the language of passport regulations meant that they were restricted from living in a total of 39 cities throughout the country. The list also included ports and towns close to state borders. Former political prisoners were allowed to live only in areas at least 101 kilometers away from the specified centers. Thus, if a released prisoner and his family wished to reunite, the family members had to move to a provincial town or endure living in two homes, the family remaining in the capital and the released prisoner—101 kilometers away.

Painful questions that had grown like thorns into the prisoners' hearts over the years of their imprisonment would manifest themselves time and again. Not everyone knew that their family had fallen apart. Many came to understand this only now. They had long dreamed with bated breath of meeting with their children but disregarded just one thing: over the course of ten years, they had become old and vaguely familiar people for their daughters and sons, who could have been only two or three years old when their parents were sent away but were now in fifth or sixth grade at school. It wasn't rare that children, now living with new families, had no desire to recognize their real parents, who had served time in prisons and camps for some obscure crimes.

The return of prisoners to those who had, whether deliberately or by accident, betrayed them back in '37 was devastating. Each case and trial involved two or three "witnesses," and often more. The number of people who tainted themselves by bearing false witness was countless. In the meantime, many of them had become honored activists with high social and professional ranks. The returning prisoners presented a potential threat to their standing in the society: although they would rarely do so, the slandered could speak out against the monstrous testimonies of their former friends who were now eminent citizens.

What were these eminent citizens supposed to do? Repent and confess their cowardice, say they were forced to renounce their friends or, on the contrary, assert their own political rectitude? Few wished to have it out with one another.

After visiting their families, many of my friends returned to the North, which at the time was shocking and impossible to understand. Of course, the general picture of the '47 release consisted of a multitude of individual cases and fates, yet happy outcomes were rare exceptions.

Tamara Tsulukidze was released before anyone else I knew. Through a petition from the Political Department, for the selfless achievements of her puppet theater, she was exempted from seven months of her term. Once released, Tamara went to Tbilisi. All that time her son was being raised by her husband's relatives, the Mukhadze family. It was that unique case when the boy's consciousness had been fertilized with the idea that his wonderful mother was not guilty of anything and that he should await her the way one waits for a happy miracle to come true. Embracing Tamara Grigorievna, her fifteen-year-old son, Sandik, told her through unashamed tears: "I can finally say the dear word 'Mama' aloud!"

In Tbilisi, unable to resist the temptation, Tamara went to see a production at the Shota Rustaveli Theater. As soon as she appeared, people instantly recognized her, their beloved actress. A few men approached her and bowed. Another kneeled before her and kissed the hem of her dress. Yet all these signs of respect frightened her.

Tamara purchased a return ticket and flew back to the North. She accepted the offer of the Syktyvkar Philharmonic to organize a puppet theater in their town and moved there. She had a reason to live: life had preserved her son. Sandik only had to pass his exams in Tbilisi, after which he was going to join her in Syktyvkar. The mother and son counted the days until their reunion.

ON AN INCREDIBLY COLD DAY in December 1946, on the eve of her release, Wanda Razumovskaya came from Knyazh-Pogost to visit me in Mezhog. She stood in the doorway, wrapped in what looked like a tattered coachman's sheepskin greatcoat, puffs of cold air bursting into the barracks from behind her. She turned up the flap of her greatcoat and took out a small pot wrapped in several layers of rags and paper. It was a live primrose flower. She handed it to me, refusing to tell me where she got it and how she managed to bring it all the way here alive in such cold.

Wanda was preparing for freedom with excitement when suddenly she received an official denunciation from her son and a letter from her ex-husband. Her husband was categorically against her visiting their son. He wrote, "Forget about him! Think of his future. He has to live on, to make a career. Your arrival, your entire past will ruin him. Be a good mother."

Don't come! Don't cause trouble! Don't intrude! Don't hinder our smooth lives! These were all-too-frequent pleas to the released prisoners. Appealing to their conscience, their relatives would often add without embarrassment: "If you love your child!" Or: "If you are a true mother!" The release of their close ones was often perceived as a relapse of some plague.

Wanda's younger daughter was at an orphanage somewhere in the Vologda region. While still a prisoner, Wanda had been sending her dried crusts of bread. The girl waited impatiently for her mother to take her home, but Wanda did not have a home, nor any relatives. She decided to stay and work in the North. It wasn't until she found a job as a music teacher at one of the Knyazh-Pogost kindergartens that she went to get her child.

Later she described the savage and hungry life of the children in the

Vologda orphanage. When she arrived, she found her daughter rummaging through a garbage dump, searching for food. The girl not only had to be washed and scrubbed clean but also shaved to rid her of lice. Easily intimidated and underdeveloped, Kira longed for motherly warmth and tenderness. At one moment she'd be loving and obedient; at another she'd suddenly become aggressive or burst into wild hysterics. The mother and daughter started living together; their excruciating life fully reflected the crimes and humiliations of '37.

In '47, my father was also supposed to be released. What if he had survived the ten-year term and was set free? I imagined him coming back to Leningrad, searching in vain for traces of his family and having no one to turn to for help.

BEFORE LEAVING the zone after the day's work, Aleksandra Petrovna often dropped by the medical staff room where I worked. Then I'd set out to see her off to the checkpoint. When the frost was especially severe, the evening sky would be lit by the sprawling crimson patterns of aurora borealis; the heavens breathed out a formidable medley of colored clouds. The silent vitality of incomprehensible shades was depressing. Aleksandra Petrovna would go home, where her daughter and grandson were waiting for her, and I'd hurry through the blizzard along the icy pathways back to the barracks.

Aleksandra Petrovna, who had rescued me at some of the darkest moments of life, came to see me at one of the darkest moments of hers. Her face looked deathly pale. I didn't immediately dare ask her what had happened. I just made her lie down on my trestle-bed and covered her with a blanket. She lay prostrate, burying her face in my pillow. I couldn't believe it was she—my boss, a psychiatrist, a woman who had suppressed the bloody mutiny of madmen and put her hand under the axe.

"Tonight, while nursing, my daughter fell asleep and smothered her child. What should I do, Tamara?" she asked exigently, though nearly sapped of all vitality.

The news was shocking. I didn't know what to say.

"What should I do?" she asked me again in an even more demanding voice, then explained: "The thing is, the commission from Protoka, which will come to investigate the case, will be led by my mortal enemy. He'll do everything he can to put my daughter on trial."

Aleksandra Petrovna had to come up with some indisputable lie. She had already found a way to resolve the situation but just needed someone to confide in. Our conversation was beyond morals, definitely beyond any laws of God or jurisprudence, outside the boundaries of truth and falsehood. I understood at that moment what a burden it was for one person alone to take full responsibility onto her shoulders.

I thought, "Was it not she who ordered me to get onto a stretcher to save me from the transport that would separate me from my son?" I was grateful to her. Unsure of myself, I told her, "Yes, you should say it was asphyxia. You have to say it happened by accident!"

Aleksandra Petrovna managed to keep her daughter from going to trial. She was indeed a strong person who would respond to people's misfortune and burst into action where others would cowardly step aside. Many lives were saved by her frantic devotion to her profession, by her eagerness to cure, rescue and protect people.

Human nature is always broader and more vibrant than the law; but, dear God! how difficult, how lonely and frightening it was to be broader and vibrant! What a powerful lesson of resistance and combat it was when our lives were decided not by the law but by the troikas. Indeed, every man was his own highest judge.

"Can you do me a favor?" Aleksandra Petrovna once asked in an apologizing tone. "I love Gorky's story *The Khan and His Son.* Would you prepare to recite it? Please, do it for me."

I performed the story from stage in the camp, but that wasn't enough for her.

"I arranged it with the commandant: you'll be allowed to leave the zone. There's a general meeting of free workers at the club today. Please, recite the story to them!"

The club was filled with free people. A table for the presidium was hoisted onto the tiny stage. The meeting was declared open. Dull, vacuous words were spoken, about agenda, vigilance, the party of Lenin and Stalin, enemies of the people and so on.

My name was called and I started reading a story about a father and son who had fallen in love with the same woman; each unable to let the other have her, they decided to throw her off a cliff into the sea. The old khan said: "Everything is dead; only a woman's love is still alive. Whoever lacks it does not have a life; he is a beggar, and his days are pitiful." He couldn't endure the loss of his beloved and threw himself from the precipice, too.

Perhaps this legend was charged with a greater spectrum of genuine emotions than what had been going on at the club just before; perhaps that was why the people, who were indifferently raising their hands for something or other only a few minutes earlier, were now crying.

I HADN'T IMAGINED that Filipp would have the brazenness to visit me now, but Aleksandra Petrovna sent a messenger to tell me he was outside the zone.

Standing on the threshold of the staff room, he seemed unnaturally lively and was stretching out his arms to hug me.

"How is Yurochka? What's he like?" I asked.

"How absurd for a mother to have to ask such questions!" Filipp exclaimed bombastically. But the next moment he was already laughing and telling me: "If you could only see how he breaks his toys, what short work he makes of them, how he dashes to meet me when I come home from work! He gives us so much joy, so much happiness!"

I had no doubts he loved and pitied Vera Petrovna. Having put down her ingenious stake, she managed to demonstrate to Filipp how devotedly she could look after both him and my son, just for the sake of being near him, if only as his housemaid. For Filipp, it was a flattering discovery that glorified him in his own eyes.

I didn't clear myself of blame. I was guilty if only because I had failed to get out of the camp vortex on my own, and having believed Filipp, I'd naively created a heart-saving myth out of my inexperience. My old fear of him blocked my ability to unravel his scheme, but now I was afraid of him in a different way: my son and I were his hostages. I had to find an appropriate, delicate way to comport myself before him, blindly guessing about how to ingratiate myself to a force I had no control over.

Thoughts of the future—my son's, theirs and my own—paralyzed my heart and brain. By the time of my release, Yurik would be four. What place would they allot to me in his consciousness? For the next three years, this would be the only thing that mattered. I had to refrain from calling things by their names and keep up a friendly tone of conversation, no matter how forced and monstrous the subject might be. Despite everything, I still clung to the hope that my son's father retained at least some vestiges of humanity, convincing myself: "He knows how I wanted to have a child. He remembers the torment accompanying his birth. If he could feel mercy for Vera Petrovna, he should take pity on me, too."

Filipp shared his plans to go to the South with Vera Petrovna, her son and Yurik, to eat fresh fruit and bathe in the sea. Later, upon their return, he sent me some photographs of Yurik, in one of which my boy was sitting in the sand, squinting his little eyes in the sun; in another he was in a flower garden with a teddy bear in his hands. I could see that my boy felt happy, but peering into his little face I started banging my head against the walls: my son will forget me!

ANOTHER WAVE of regime-tightening swept through the camp. Searches increased, new transports for distant camps were being put together or prisoners were shuffled from one local camp to another. The administration of the Gulag recalled the head of the Northern Railway Camp, Shemina, whose place was now taken by Colonel Klyuchkin.

Taking advantage of Shemina's departure, the Third Department instantly dismissed Gavronsky from his position as TEC director and hastily transferred him from Central Camp to the Rakpas zone. Hella Frisher ended up on the same transport.

Fortunately, Aleksandr Osipovich survived the transfer better than one would expect. In the new camp, he got a job at the KVCh and, blissfully, was allowed a separate room apart from the general barracks. Though the room was so narrow it looked like a mere passage between walls, there he could have his own working space. He asked me not to worry about him and wrote that things there were quite all right. He could speak German to his heart's content with Hella and Ani Kolb and had other interesting people around him, too. He met new friends; among them was Ariadna Sergeevna Efron, the daughter of Marina Tsvetaeva. Aleksandr Osipovich was full of creative inspiration and started staging Chekhov's vaudevilles and stories by Mérimée for the Rakpas audience.

He also wrote about Boris Maevsky, "a man strikingly talented in every way," with whom he could talk about anything and whom he wished I would meet one day. Boris's name had been mentioned more than once in conversations with other people as well, especially in connection with a story that had become virtually sensational in the camps.

An actress from Moscow once came to seek an audience with Bazhenov, the deputy head of the Political Department, and offered to give a series of concerts for prisoners in the camps of the Northern Railway Division. Bazhenov was shrewd enough not to ask what impelled her to do so and gave permission for the concerts, which everybody adored. Only then did the actress ask him for permission to see her son, Boris Maevsky, whom she hadn't seen since he'd been sent to the camps straight from the front years before. Prisoners who attended her performance told how the tall, stately actress recited Gorky's *The Old Woman Izergil* from the tiny camp platform, while her son stood crying at the side of the stage behind a gray curtain.

In his letters, Aleksandr Osipovich often mentioned Motya, or "Moth," as he called her, a woman who used to be a translator before her arrest. When Ariadna Efron was transported to Siberia, Aleksandr Osipovich assigned main roles to Motya and was happy to have such a person to talk to.

I wasn't jealous, but the recurrent name—Motya, Moth—rubbed salt into my wounds. Feelings of homelessness and desolation were driving me mad. My only support gave way under my feet. I'd never stopped seeing the precious things of this world as stable, indivisible and singular: one mother, one child, one friend, one husband, one city that I loved. As for myself, in my twenty-seven years I hadn't become such a person for anyone. Not even for my son. I had to preserve my place as the matchless student of Aleksandr Osipovich! I clung to it like a drowning man.

I wrote Aleksandr Osipovich an unacceptable letter, in which I must have given vent to everything I wished to say, in actuality, to the father of my son. Aleksandr Osipovich heard my call and understood precisely this.

He pleaded to have me transferred to Rakpas and put his new friends in touch with me. I started receiving letters from Boris and Motya, but in light of all I'd experienced in the way of misfortune, these people seemed to me so very young.

My only way out was to return to TEC. Only then, traveling with the collective, would I be able to see my son from time to time. I wrote to Erukhimovich, the TEC director, as well as to his deputy, Georgy Lvovich Nevolsky. They responded that they'd be glad to have me back and would send an official request on my behalf.

By that time, much had changed in TEC. After seeing the new actors, Aleksandr Osipovich wrote that there were many gifted soloists, musicians and professional dramatists. "I was especially impressed by one actor," he wrote. "He's got an air of Oscar Wilde about him—extremely talented!"

The TEC stage director was also new—Boris Pavlovich Semyachkov, a graduate of the State Institute of Theater Art, and an ethnic Komi. People said he was a temperamental, creative and inquisitive man.

The changes in TEC scared me. I was apprehensive of the professional actors. Nor could I imagine TEC without Aleksandr Osipovich. I knew I wouldn't be able to meet their standards, but my zeal was just as strong as before, and I waited for the transfer warrant impatiently.

Meanwhile, there was reveille each morning, patients waking up and eating *kasha*, the clinking of aluminum spoons and bowls, the routine of the barracks. I sterilized syringes in boiling water, made infusions and injections and put cupping-glasses on the patients' backs.

I had just taken a sterilizer full of syringes out of the stove when a nurse from the neighboring barracks ran in, yelling:

"Something terrible has happened with Tamara Tsulukidze."

"What is it?"

"Her son was run over by a tram in Tbilisi!"

The sterilizer dropped out of my hands.

Fifteen-year-old Sandik, who'd waited for his mother to be released! What for? This was no longer social malice or political evil. It was something else—the wild carnage of Fate.

Some said that upon hearing the news, Tamara instantly forgot Russian and babbled incomprehensibly in Georgian.

She had no money to travel to Tbilisi. We all passed around a hat and the required sum was eventually gathered.

Many years later, I asked a relative of her family, Natella, about Sandik. She said he was a wonderful boy. Akhmeteli's sister, Ekaterina, and her husband, Mukhadze, a famous surgeon in Tbilisi, loved him as their own son and brought him up to become a humble, reasonable and good-hearted person. When his exams were over in the spring, they'd already bought him a ticket for Syktyvkar. The only thing left was to find somebody to accompany him. On his way home one afternoon, Sandik jumped onto a moving tramcar. The handle he grasped at tore off. He fell down on the rails and the wheels of the tram rolled over his leg. Help came too late. The boy bled to death.

For a long time we heard nothing of Tamara Grigorievna.

I WAS USED TO ERIK'S OUTBURSTS, when he would suddenly bombard me with letters complaining of his anguish and depression. These periods were brief, and when better days came he would fall silent again.

Barbara Ionovna wrote on a more regular basis. My ex-mother-in-law lived in poverty and isolation. She became like a mother to Tatochka, her granddaughter, when Tatochka's real mother started a new family. Tenderness, which had always been virtually absent from our relationship, started showing through with growing intensity. Yet one of Barbara Ionovna's letters drove me into a stupor.

She wrote that one night someone knocked on the door of her house. She didn't immediately recognize the man who walked in. It was my interrogator. He had decided to remind her of himself. He asked for a cup of tea and inquired where I was and if I was healthy. He said he'd been promoted and was leaving for Moscow, and that he stopped by to return some photographs he had confiscated during the search years ago. "It was Tamara Vladislavovna's last request," the shadowy man told Barbara Ionovna and handed her a weighty package.

The night after the trial was fresh in my memory: sleep interrupted by the sound of keys grinding in the door lock and the illicit appearance of the disheveled interrogator, who told me, "I thought you might've hanged yourself"; the idiotic dialogue: "Is there anything I can do for you?" and my answer, "You already did!" followed by my request, as if to apologize for my rude tone, to look after the photographs.

In conclusion, Barbara Ionovna wrote:

> I don't know what your and Erik's interrogator came for. You're smart, you have to understand: I'm tired of living in permanent fear. I'm afraid of every knock on my door, even of the sound of the door creaking, of everything. Forgive me, Tamara. After he left, I burned all your photographs. I kept only two, the ones where you're together with your whole family. Forgive me!

I could understand her panic—those years were filled with fear. Yet how was I supposed to come to terms with the fact that while the interrogator had preserved the photographs, my mother-in-law threw them into the fire?

ENIGMAS TO OURSELVES, we are shaped less by our own biographies than by the sacred matter from which we all descend. During the special time of recovery after a fresh round of pain, nature would offer me some new point of reference. Reference to what precisely, I could not say, but a blade of grass breaking through the soil, the forest beyond the camp, the ever-changing sky would appear new and slightly unfamiliar and I would start to hear and see the world in a different way.

Sometimes I would wake in the middle of the night, pull on my boots and venture out into the darkness. The chains of the tethered guard dogs clattered along the wire. The smell of freshly sawed tree trunks blended with the clammy fog. The plaintive wail of a distant locomotive echoed across the taiga's vast expanse, turning into a heart-rending cry for all the lonely and homeless souls.

I would sneak out of the medical barracks and run to the western side of the zone, fatally drawn to that border between freedom and captivity. Standing on a little hillock, peering through the wire fence, I could glimpse a bend in the Western Dvina River that flowed past the camp. The setting sun would imbue the sky with delicate tones that grew gloomier by the minute. I feasted my eyes on the water and stretched out my hands toward its freshness.

After rain, water droplets would hang in rows on the barbed wire. Searchlights from the watchtowers swept across the zone, illuminating the perfect little spheres as they succumbed to their own weight and plummeted down into puddles. The cold wind made me shiver but I stood in the slushy mud, listening to everything around me breathe and reverberate. Everything was pulsating with life, and I was part of it all. My soul stirred in response to these sparing signs of renewal, and I began once again to feel the world that existed beyond the confines of my individual destiny.

There was always someone or other in the camp who knew exactly the route of TEC. With faultless precision they'd say, "They're in Mikun now!" or "They've already passed Protoka!" or "Tomorrow they will be here!"

And the next day they came.

My heart pounded deafeningly. I was waiting to hear the words: "Come! Pack your things. The permit is ready for you to join us!"

Indeed, a few minutes later I heard the voices of Georgy Lvovich Nevolsky, the director, and Khmiel, the actor:

"Where's she hiding then? Ah! Don't you greet your friends? Come, everyone's waiting for you."

Not a word about a permit. Didn't they have one?

I walked with my friends through the familiar Mezhog zone, happy the theater was here. I trod on the hard frozen ground I'd had to traverse daily for the last two years or so. I felt that in the very next moment either a catastrophic disaster or a stroke of amazingly good fortune would befall me.

TEC was lodged in the bathhouse, as no other place could be found for them. Trestle-beds had been dragged in so that the actors could have something to sleep on. As we reached the bathhouse, Georgy gallantly pushed open the door for me.

A rectangle of sunlight was cast into the gloom, spotlighting a tall man crossing the hallway. I'd never seen him before. Apart from a beige quilted jacket draped over his shoulders, he was naked from the waist up. He was fervently debating with someone, but as the door opened he stopped and turned, breaking off from the discussion. He stood looking at me. Pinned to the spot, I stared back. The large dark-gray eyes of his swarthy handsome face displayed the kind of fervency and passion that, strangely, reflected my own current condition. The rectangle of sunlight seemed to illuminate only him.

As I crossed the threshold of the bathhouse, it seemed like time stopped, as if I was flying down a corridor to a place where neither camps nor chronology existed and where there was only the limitless power and freedom of feelings. Everything was transformed, unmasked and intransigent. Almost free, I was a prisoner again, for I already knew that this feeling would never abandon me.

"Please be acquainted," said a voice from the crowd, and the two of us shook hands.

Friends surrounded us. Assailed with questions, I answered as best I could. I kept looking at the faces of the people around me, mechanically asking them about themselves, but I was desperate to leave, to get away from everything except what was happening in my soul.

"It's time for me to go," I said.

Georgy Lvovich offered to accompany me. But then I heard *his* voice:

"May I come along too?"

I knew he would ask. I had willed it. With a mixture of joy and torment, I sensed: He is here! He is coming! He is with me! But is it still me?

Back in the barracks, I whirled around, boiling water and making tea, still under the spell of this sudden heart-swell. The entire universe now sat opposite me in the medical staff room, contained in just one man whom a few minutes earlier I hadn't even known.

The three of us sipped tea and chatted. Listening for the subtext of his every word, surrendering to his gaze, I could see that everything in him was just right: the right words, the right smile, the right folds of his lips and eyelids. To what prototype hiding deep in the subconscious was I comparing this man's visible, living lineaments? Something seemed to be pointing me toward a secret road that led to the furthest depths of reality, and I made up my mind to follow this road to its very end, no matter what might await me there.

I vaguely remembered the concert that the new troupe gave in the camp the next day, but it was without a doubt more refined than our amateurish performances. TEC now had an excellent singer, a splendid elocutionist and dancers. Then he, Nikolay Danilovich—tall, slim, handsome, elegant and professional—appeared on the stage. He recited Pushkin's poem *Count Nikulin.* As I tried to absorb every word he uttered, I suddenly realized it was he whom Aleksandr Osipovich had described in a letter as having "an air of Oscar Wilde about him."

After the concert, a dancing party was announced. Benches were pushed together. The orchestra began playing.

Everything ceased to exist except my anticipation of him, although, standing in a circle of friends, I animatedly kept "reviewing" their performances, as well as those by actors I didn't know.

He approached and requested my company for the first waltz.

Was that dance really happening in the zone, amid other prisoners, at the filthy and smoky camp club? Then why was there so much space, such a sweep of unleashed feelings? It was the first time I danced with such emotion, only now feeling the door to the beautiful world, heretofore shut, open wide.

The engine feeding the electricity broke down and the lights went out. Not willing to part, Nikolay and I sat backstage in a small storage room, in violation of camp rules. Merged by the twilight into a single indivisible soul, we talked in a half-voice. Someone quietly played the guitar and sang nearby.

It was pouring outside. The wind was wailing. Kolya accompanied me to the medical barracks. We walked through the zone at a forbidden, unhurried pace. I didn't know what was going to happen next. He stepped inside after me. Usually so uncertain and doubtful, at that moment I willed the camp rules out of existence. I was sure that nothing vulgar and petty would dare encroach upon these moments, and nothing did.

There was a melding of passion and inexperience. It promised nothing but perdition and salvation.

Trying to translate everything that preceded our meeting into a human language, we told each other:

"On the way here, I stood on the platform of the train car. The wind raged and tore at me, almost knocking me off my feet. I gulped the air. Anguish suffocated me and pushed me on… I was peering into darkness… I was waiting…"

"At night I would set out into the zone, into the cold and damp fumes of the taiga. I listened to the swelling earth and the ringing stars in the sky. I knew something incredible was going to happen…"

"Do you have anyone?" "A son. A sister. And you?"

"No one except my mother. Though I don't know where she is or if she's still alive."

"I also have a teacher—Aleksandr Osipovich Gavronsky."

"I know him. He is a beautiful man…"

The blunt clang of the steel rail at five in the morning. Clashing spheres of existence. I had to get back to my routine duties: handing out medications, bandaging patients and serving them their breakfast.

Through the window I caught a glimpse of Kolya sitting on a stump in front of the barracks.

"Go on about your business. I won't disturb you," he said as he walked into the staff room.

The three days that TEC stayed in Mezhog were full of oblivion, happiness and fear of our inevitable parting. How little and how completely I already knew him!

The best years of his life were spent studying at the studio of Yury Aleksandrovich Zavadsky in Moscow and in Rostov. Then came the war.

Almost the entire cohort of men imprisoned during or after the war were sentenced under the same Article 58-1: Treason. Under this frightening charge Kolya had been condemned to a firing squad, but after two months his sentence was commuted to ten years of camps. When he was arrested by the Soviets, they charged him with being taken prisoner by the Germans and working in a Nazi-occupied country since he'd worked in a theater in Poland.

"We have to be together. We'll work together. You have to make it back to TEC," he repeated dozens of times. His words contained hope. But the question about the permit had become mired in circumstances the TEC administrators could not explain. They sent one petition after another. The authorities of the Northern Railway Camp didn't react.

The gate of the checkpoint slammed shut behind Kolya. Again I remained alone in Mezhog, nourishing myself on wonderful remembrances. I didn't recognize myself. I was in love, for the first time, in captivity!

Correspondence in the camps fully depended on the free people traveling from one zone to another. In one of his letters, Kolya wrote:

> You will probably receive this letter on a memorable day of my life. You know it—for me, it was the border between life and death. It was on this day, in 1946, at noon, that they repealed my death sentence, and after spending 57 days in agonizing anticipation of the firing squad on death row, they transferred me to a general cell. Another life began from that hour. Remembering everything now, I can't bring myself to believe it all happened to me. Now I've met you, which means I discovered myself.

The letter was frightening. Indeed, I loved, and only love contained life. But why would it always be so full of torment?

Our hearts demanded to be together as soon as possible. Kolya communicated: "Today the TEC director spoke to the Political Department about you... The deputy director went again to talk to the authorities. He assured me..." But the permit just wouldn't come. Not pleading for freedom, we only wanted to be together, even if behind barbed wire. The intense energy of protest, capable of smiting everything in its way, drove prisoners to escape, landed them in isolation cells or flung them under bullets. This was called struggle, and now it had Kolya and me in its grip.

Strangely agitated as I was, I more and more often thought about my father. I remembered his obsession and fanaticism. Now I recognized myself in him, and him—in myself. Rethinking his precept of constant struggle, I realized that Father handed down a valuable gift to me. In the way I walked and felt, I noticed more than once the salutary traces of physical strength and health and thanked him for them. I struggled over the question: why did he have to damage it with his own hands? Why did he have to beat me as a child, forever instilling in me an accursed uncertainty that had failed me so many times?

During that time in Mezhog, after my motherhood and the newfound feeling for Kolya brought my heart back to life, I became horrified by my previous inability to register what my mother was feeling. I thought mercilessly, not with my brain but with my heart, about that which I had been ashamed of and previously tried to push aside: What measure of suffering, what impassability drove her to seek solace in wine after my father's arrest? More and more relentlessly, the image of her face, strained with shame and supplication after selling something or other from our household, would appear before me. I didn't rush to support her during those moments. Only now, as if shaken back to a waking life, did I fully grasp how my mother, unable to cope with the calamities of our century and stifled by inhumanity and the futility of her aspirations, was tormented. I recognized myself in this, too.

Penetrating deep into my parents' nature, into everything that had been done to my family, I felt like their mother. It didn't matter whether they were alive or dead.

A WOMAN FROM HARBIN, Lilya Gross, came running into the medical staff room. Her face shone:

"They've just reported over the intercom that TEC is coming! Go meet them!"

Four months had passed since I met Kolya.

The TEC administration still didn't bring a permit for me to join them. At Central Camp it was Ilya Evseevich who set out to take care of the problem, and the reason for the delay immediately became clear. It was the same deputy to the camp commandant, Colonel Varsh, who wouldn't sign the permit. Vera Petrovna's slander, her petition to send me to distant camps, were still fresh. Nor could Varsh forget that his own personal order to transfer me to the Mariinsky camps had remained unfulfilled.

I realized I would never be able to return to TEC. But I told Kolya: "Without Aleksandr Osipovich I won't be worth anything anyway."

"I'll help! We'll manage," he responded ardently. "You'll be back with TEC, believe me! We'll start working on Lermontov's *The Masquerade* as soon as you arrive." And he began reciting in half-voice:

Erroneously, maybe, we've been bound
By common fate. Your soul still so young,
You've heard just one first sound
Of life's great symphony...

...

But I love differently, I have waited,
Endured everything, learned and taken pains.
I often loved, more often still—I hated,
And there's much before me that remains.

As soon as TEC left, the staff room door thrust open and Aleksandra Petrovna walked in. In an austere voice she asked straightforwardly:

"With the actor—is it serious?"

"Very much so," I answered.

"You want to leave?"

"Yes," I said.

"Well, keep in mind that I won't let you go," she said in a tone she always took on at stern moments.

"Why?" I implored.

"Leave well enough alone," she answered resentfully.

I owed Aleksandra Petrovna a lot. What would have become of me without her? Perhaps I should have scourged myself for being ungrateful to her; but there was no longer any "well enough" without Kolya. I had discovered love, and Kolya and I had resolved to fight for it to the last.

In a few days, the work distributor drummed on the window of the staff room:

"Dance! Your permit for TEC has arrived!"

I could hardly believe it! But the next moment I remembered Aleksandra Petrovna's words. She could grant a pardon, but she could also inflict punishment.

Seeing her walking in the zone accompanied by her customary retinue—the doctors, the economist and the foreman—I grasped at one wild idea, which I'd only half-formed in my mind.

I dashed toward her.

Halting the people behind her with a flick of her hand, she stopped and shouted angrily:

"What else? What is it?"

"Your Majesty, Aleksandra Petrovna! Have mercy on me! Let God's servant Petkevich go to TEC!" I cried out, throwing myself to the ground and kneeling before her.

After "Her Majesty's" retinue interceded for me, she gave in.

"Begone! Out of my sight!" Aleksandra Petrovna finished playing out my scenario.

I was tearing myself from my son's birthplace, from his nursery, where I used to run every three hours to feed and talk to him, from the place where I had dreamed of our future together, from the path I walked along to the checkpoint to give my boy away to his father. It was here that I nearly went mad when Filipp renounced me. Here I inadvertently became an "educator" to many boys who were my patients at the punishment barracks of the infirmary and whom I longed to rescue from cynicism and frustration. Here I once grabbed the stalwart red-haired commandant by the collar when he started beating up one of the boys and threw him out of the barracks with my own hands. A man I loved, whom I now so passionately longed for, had also come here, to Mezhog, from his mysterious nowhere.

My farewell to Aleksandra Petrovna was a difficult one. We embraced each other. She said in a hoarse voice: "So you're abandoning me? This is what you get for giving your entire soul away."

The escort guard was waiting. This time, I was leaving Mezhog forever.

THE ASTRONOMICALLY DISTANT HAPPINESS was now converted into concrete kilometers separating Kolya and me.

The lame warder Sergeev, a Knyazh-Pogost old-timer, took my documents from the escort guard at the checkpoint and let me into the Central Camp zone.

TEC was away, touring in the northern parts of the camp division.

Behind the permit for me to return to TEC stood the efforts of many people. I went to see Ilya Evseevich. His strange confession, however, put me out of sorts.

"Don't thank me. I was just being selfish," he said. "I wanted to have you back on stage. But I have to tell you something: I read your letters to Nikolay Danilovich, as well as his letters to you. I handled the whole correspondence."

I could only ask, "Why?"

"I wanted to understand you. I know you'll hate me now, but I couldn't help it. Nor could I help, though, confessing this to you."

Even though I knew he did this out of "anguished love," it was still uncomfortable for me even to see him after that.

I was put up in a general barracks with the same *vagonki*-type rows of plank beds. The regal women imprisoned back in '37 were now replaced by a younger generation, among whom there were also many remarkable and attractive figures, Russians as well as foreigners.

"You'll feel more comfortable here!" one of my old acquaintances told me, complaisantly making room on the lower level of plank beds and taking a worse place for herself.

I was surprised. "Who in the world would give away such a good spot?" I thought to myself. The place, however, was vacated. The hubbub died down. Several curious gazes pointed toward me.

"Why don't you introduce yourselves?" said one of the spectators impatiently.

I saw an astonishingly beautiful woman, a bit plump but with the face of a Madonna, sitting in front of me across the aisle.

I held out my hand and said my name.

"Lyolya N." the beauty replied.

Here's what it was all about! That same Pole Filipp had gotten so enamored with that he once called me by her name. Her beauty was steady and natural. I couldn't help admiring her. We looked at each other with interest and took a liking to one another. To the great disappointment of the inhabitants of the barracks, nothing came out of the "confrontation of rivals" they had hoped to take in.

The arrogant Lyolya didn't wait long to raise the question about Filipp:

"Do you know that Bakharev loves you?"

I braced myself. She continued:

"Yes, he loves only you. These are the only things that distinguish him—that he's a good doctor and that he loves you. I don't think he can be of any use to you, though. You'll be released, get your son and that's it."

Counting the hours before TEC's return, I was in an elevated mood.

"May I stay for a while near a happy person like you?" asked one of the lords, Nikolay Trofimovich, as he sat down on a bench next to me.

Our friendship had been deepened by our shared participation in the fate of Boris Markovich Kagner or, rather, by our mutual dismay in the face of that fate. The old-timer Boris Markovich, who worked as the deputy head of the Northern Railway Camp Economic Department, was getting ready for release. Intelligent and tactful, he always lived somewhat apart from everyone else. The camp administration treated him with respect, as they well understood he was the brain of the camp's economy. "What's new in the world?" the camp commandant Klyuchkin would ask him earnestly. "Are you asking me?" Kagner would ask him back. "You, of course," Klyuchkin would reply. "You know everything better than any of us." Indeed, people like Kagner did seem to know everything better. But that was precisely why they were kept in the camps in the first place. When Kagner came to the Second Department on his release day, he was told that Moscow didn't approve of setting him free. He put his signature under the resolution: "Detain until further instruction." He became stooped overnight, his hair had gone gray and soon he was sent to the infirmary. Several days later he died, never seeing his family, who had stoically waited for him for ten years. Having heard of Kagner's death, Nikolay Trofimovich and I had sat silently for a long time on the porch of the infirmary.

TEC arrived late in the evening. Hearing the news, I couldn't immediately bring myself to my feet.

Kolya stood waiting at the entrance to the barracks, leaning against the side of a door that led out to the zone. The crowded barracks droned behind his back.

I felt intoxicated, expecting he'd run toward me. Instead, triumphant and ceremonial, Kolya stood still, looking at me as I approached.

I crossed a line that seemed somehow to be delineated from the rest of the world and walked into our invisible "home"—a space that now belonged only to the two of us. We couldn't bring ourselves to utter a single word. "Our altar the grassy earth outspread, and our priest the muttering wind…"

Chapter 10

The end of 1947 was marked by a slight weakening of the regime. Despite the particulars of some of the gifted prisoners' sentences, TEC had less trouble drawing them into the collective, and the directors had more luck petitioning on behalf of professional actors who were arriving on transports.

Along with other actors and musicians, TEC hired a splendid artist, Margarita Vent-Pichugina, who took on a dual role as costumier and stage technician. Her mother, a German, had married a Russian engineer and departed Germany in order to live with him in Russia. In 1926 Margarita went to study in Germany, where she married and eventually had four children. Twenty years later, in 1946, when Stalin, Churchill and Roosevelt signed an agreement to bring all the Russians back home, Margarita returned to her motherland, only to get a ten-year sentence under Article 58-1.

Margo was a remarkable woman. She always wore a thick cable sweater, around which she looped a thin leather belt. The knot of her hair was tucked up with netting on the back of her head. A mysterious smile never left her lips. She didn't speak much, and when she did, she never wasted words. Margo was like a sphinx. Many fell in love with her.

Her magic hands easily turned a piece of tin, broken glass or gauze into a *kokoshnik,* a purse, a crown, or any other kind of embellishment. She would dye fabric, sew dresses and decorate hems with elaborate patterns, and an article of magnificent clothing would be born out of nowhere, igniting the imagination of the female prisoners and arousing the envy of even the free workers. Margo's fantasies carried her away from the routine of camp life into the self-governing, untouchable world of creation, where a human being felt free and independent.

Once, marching down the road to one of the camps where we had to give a concert, we passed by a free woman walking with her children. Margo and

I followed her with our eyes for a long time. Margo's four children were in another country. In a sense, my son also lived "abroad." Perhaps it was at that moment that we became friends.

The gem of the troupe was the Armenian singer Inna Kurulyants, who had a beautiful mezzo-soprano voice. I don't know how she wound up in Romania, but she got her ten years for a "liaison with a Romanian officer." When Inna started to sing, I would drop everything and run to listen to her, no matter where I was or what I was doing. She was the one whom the audience most often applauded for an encore. A variegated flower of the wild, Inna wouldn't think twice before putting her fingers to her mouth and letting out with a shrill brigand-like whistle. Yet when she'd appear on stage in a long black-and-white dress sewn by Margo, she was a serene and charming young woman. In a voice of sharp honey, she would sing the words to a Spanish tune:

> Waves are splashing against rocky shores,
> Far away—the light of the moon.
> Muffled strokes of the silvery tide
> Speed up the blood in the veins.

When their terms were over, Senya Erukhimovich and Dmitry Karayanidi were released, but because of the notorious Regulation 39, both remained to work in the North—Senya as the director of TEC, and Dima as a pianist and conductor.

Senya's elderly mother and younger sister, Fira, came to visit him from Leningrad. After ten years of separation, they didn't want to part again; they came to live nearby, in Knyazh-Pogost. His mother brought Senya some of his clothes from their time in Harbin. He changed his quilted jacket for a durable winter coat with a beaver collar and put on his beaver pelt hat, which stirred the camp authorities' interest. Freedom especially suited Senya, who had always been an affable and smiling fellow but now seemed to be filled with an even greater joy, naively supposing that from now on life would bring nothing but pleasure and happiness.

To get an official approval for concert programs, which required a great deal of persistence and diplomacy, Senya would personally go to the Political Department.

"What's this nonsense?" the head of the Political Department would ask, poking his finger into the program. "What rubbish this song is, 'Wanders the Lonely Accordion...'"

"Why rubbish, Nikolay Vasilyevich? It's a good song, very melodious."

"Tell me: where in our Soviet villages have you ever seen a lonely accordionist? A crowd of *kolkhozniks* always accompanies him! Cross it out."

By hook or by crook, Senya would stubbornly fight for this or that song or performance.

"What's this thing called *Dawn* by Leoncavallo?" Shtanko asked him.

"Well, you know, it's about Aurora," Senya answered.

"Alright, we need a song about the Aurora. Keep it."

But when Shtanko heard the romance sung by Khmiel during the concert, he grew enraged:

"I didn't approve this! What's he singing?"

Senya explained to him what the song was about.

"What goddess of dawn are you talking about? There's only one 'Aurora,' the battleship. You've got to stop these tricks of yours!"

IT'S DIFFICULT TO REMEMBER whose idea it was to include Simonov's play *The Russian Question* into TEC's repertoire. In this play, a journalist by the name of Garry Smith decides to tell the American people the "truth" about Russia. The roles had been assigned:

Garry Smith—G. Bondarevsky
Guld—N. Teslik
Jessie—T. Petkevich

Directed by B. P. Semyachkov

The new stage director, it seemed, was happy to have me back in the troupe. "I pin great hopes on you!" Boris Pavlovich had said when we first met. Not knowing what difficulties this production would be fraught with, I was happy to have been assigned the role of Jessie.

Semyachkov used theatrical terminology I'd never heard before. The jargon of the State Institute of the Theatrical Arts frightened me. Boris Pavlovich would ask me to perform the simplest moves, which any professional actor was expected to handle easily, but I could manage none of them. I waited to be addressed in Aleksandr Osipovich's magical manner, but his language was unique and inimitable. Without it I could not take a single step. I was overwhelmed with despair and felt I was nothing more than a twenty-seven-year-old ignoramus who would never learn anything.

The stage director's friendliness was quickly replaced by overt disappointment. Once I overheard him speak to his deputy, Georgy Lvovich Nevolsky, in a puzzled voice, "There's really nothing she can do."

I could see that the rest of the actors waited patiently, but the more patient they were the more I withdrew into my own failure. I expected to be dismissed from TEC any day.

The concept of "public loneliness" had a concrete meaning in the camps. Though constantly surrounded by other people, one developed an invisible shell in which one's heart could be hidden.

"Let's try to rehearse together. I'll help you," Kolya begged me.

But, helpless and ashamed, I distanced myself from Kolya even more than from anyone else.

One day he found me in the far corner of the zone. I didn't want to see him and tried to turn him away. But he wouldn't back down.

"You have to tell me everything that is tormenting you. You mustn't keep silent! Tell me everything, I won't leave."

"Don't touch me. Leave me alone!" I shouted.

"You're wild! I am yours! I want us to deal with your problems together. Do you hear me? My heart beats for you alone! There is no 'you,' no 'me'—just us!"

He was saying words I'd always longed to hear but had forgotten how to believe. After all of the betrayals, I had grown used to enduring pain on my own and was calloused with distrust. Now, with Kolya standing beside me, it was painful and blissful all at once.

Kolya and I contrived to create a life for ourselves together, to share the innermost depths of our souls. He understood that Yurik was my permanent, unceasing pain. He'd try to comfort me, saying, "I've found out—we're going to Velsk soon. You'll see him. The time will come, you'll get him back." He told me about his mother, whom he had lost all trace of during the war. I vowed, at all costs, to find her after I was released.

Kolya was a born actor through and through. Physically fit and exquisitely handsome, he performed theatrical roles, recited poetry or prose, danced and pantomimed, all equally well. He had his own idols: Zavadsky, Mordvinov, Maretskaya, Abdulov.

"Remember the scene in the film *The Last Gypsy Encampment,* when Mordvinov walks through the rye field barely touching the crops? Then he spreads his arms, enveloping the crops, presses them to his chest and utters just one word, 'Bread!'? Mordvinov once told me it took him ages to master that one word, but then he got it," Kolya consoled me.

The three of us—Kolya, his friend Zhora Bondarevsky and I—often rehearsed together. Finally, Kolya's devotion, Zhora's sincere desire to help, as well as my own craving for professionalism untangled something inside of me.

"For Zavadsky, silence during rehearsals was sacred," Kolya reminisced.

Perhaps it was a similar "sacred silence" that reigned during one of our rehearsals. When I finished performing, I saw tears running down the cheeks of the stage director.

"Tamara! I have no words... Thank you."

From then on, my relationship with Boris Pavlovich was much warmer. Soon he gave me the role of the matchmaker in Chekhov's *A Happy Ending*, after which I played Ulita in Ostrovsky's *The Forest*. Rehearsals continued at their own pace.

One day, amid the measured hubbub of routine life, the barracks door opened, letting in the winter cold, and an unfamiliar man in a shabby overcoat entered.

"Hello, friends! Does anyone know where I can find Tamara Petkevich?" he asked in a cheery voice.

"That's me," I answered.

"I have a letter for you from Aleksandr Osipovich. My name is Boris Maevsky."

I looked with curiosity at the man I had corresponded with and about whom Aleksandr Osipovich had told me so much. He and Kolya exchanged greetings. They already knew each other from Rakpas, where TEC sometimes gave concerts.

"We're having dinner. Come join us," invited Kolya.

A suitcase covered by a clean cloth served as our table.

"Oh, you've got tea? That's good! The weather is something else today."

Boris looked over the barracks.

"It's nice in here. So tell me, what's new? What are you working on now?"

In a few minutes we were already talking like old friends.

Boris had the youthful face of a boy, but his eyes were rich with experience. He was intelligent, played the piano, wrote poetry and talked with ease about literature and music. Before the war he worked at the Central Theater of the Soviet Army in Moscow. Aleksandr Osipovich was right—he had many talents, perhaps too many. We discussed Ilya Ehrenburg's novel *The Storm*, which I recently happened to read. Boris and I began arguing, and I conceded. There was brilliance even in the way he handled the debate. Suddenly he said:

"I imagined you just like you are. But you're too beautiful. That's not necessary."

He was self-confident and comported himself with bravado, but somehow I sensed that inside he was just as homeless as the rest of us.

THE CAMP ADMINISTRATION finally allocated TEC two freight cars for traveling along the thousand-kilometer line between the zones of the division—one for the men, the other for the women.

We jolted along the railroad. At night, our cars would be coupled to a passing freight train or driven onto a dead-end siding. One jerk would be followed by another, even sharper. Suitcases with stage props fell down from the berths. The jolts resonated in our heads and got on our nerves, especially as we tried to fall asleep. It was as if the engineers of the trains that tugged us along didn't know that they were hauling not just coal and logs but also people.

The plywood walls of our TEC cars let the wind and frost inside. On the days when I was on duty, Kolya would come from the men's car to help me carry in buckets with ice, which we would then melt. We would break off chunks of coal from the great coal heaps scattered along the tracks, which we used for heating. I chopped kindling and lit the *burzhuyka* stove. The fire would start crackling. The steel stove gradually heated up, glowing and flickering red. TEC members scrambled down from their berths, throwing off layers of rags and clothes, curtains and pieces of scenery they had covered themselves with to keep warm. Men would leap out of their car to rub themselves briskly with snow while the guards watched.

Each of us would take his share of the props or equipment and head toward our destination on foot. We'd be put up in various tiny rooms and nooks of the camp's buildings, where we'd unpack our rags. I'd find an empty can and put a few branches of conifer in it to imitate coziness for the few days that we'd have to stay there.

At remote camps, we performed by the light of kerosene lamps or tallow candles; ascending the smoky semblance of a stage, we could barely see the audience on the benches. After the performance, prisoners would surround us and ask us to write down the lyrics of this or that song, or to take a letter home and drop it in a mailbox somewhere along our way. For Kolya and me, every such request was sacred.

Camp after camp, season after season—there were endless roads, luggage on our backs and concerts set to tears and laughter. Amid this ugly and beautiful world, we were together.

The Berezovy Zone, where Captain Silaev was the commandant, was the southernmost camp in the division. Some time ago Silaev had been a prisoner himself, convicted of petty theft. When the war started, he went to the front with one of the *shtrafbat* battalions, which were made up of prisoners, and even earned a few medals for outstanding service. After the war, he asked to be sent to work in the camp system.

Our concerts at that camp were always especially successful. We arrived on a day when the entire camp was swept up in a frantic, doomsday-like atmosphere. In the middle of the zone, huge vats filled with boiling water were hanging over fire pits; prisoners were bringing their trestle-beds and dipping them into the vats to get rid of the hordes of bedbugs.

For a while the Berezovy Camp became our base, a setting-off point for our tours around the taiga. One of our returns there coincided with the arrival of a commission of administrative officials. Silaev was waiting to meet both TEC and the commission at the local station. He wanted to accompany us personally to the camp deep in the taiga.

A small steam locomotive pulled two open train cars along the narrow-gauge railway. On one of the platforms there were chairs, taken from the guards' apartments, set up for the commission. We took the second platform. The locomotive puffed and panted, as if it wanted to let the taiga know of every *verst* it covered.

All of a sudden Captain Silaev noticed his loyal dog, Pegas, running alongside the rails, trying to catch up with the train. The track ran through a swampy and boggy area. Pegas raced alongside us, barking for us to take him on board, leaping back and forth from hillock to hillock, then running along the tracks again. We couldn't stand it any longer.

"Citizen Chief, stop the train! Let's get the dog!"

The officers on the other platform kept silent, reluctant to get involved in any sort of melodramatic nonsense. The captain's face was strained from fear for his dog, but with a swagger he said, "Don't worry. He'll make it!"

The dog tried hard, throwing his staggering paws up in the air. He no longer ran straight but in some intricate zigzag.

"Please, have pity!" we begged Silaev again.

For several more minutes the faithful dog kept jumping from peat hillock to track and back, eventually catching up with us and even outdistancing the train when suddenly we heard a heart-rending squeal beneath the wheels. The dog was no more.

Only then did the captain scream: "Stop the train!" He took the breathless dog in his arms and placed him onto the platform. His face looked pale.

He didn't let out a single word, nor did he shed a tear. He only yelled, "Come on! Let's go!" The officials would have considered Silaev a driveling fool had he shown pity for his dog.

A few days later the stuffed body of Pegas appeared in the captain's office. No one could forbid him to love his dog posthumously.

MOST EVERY CASE of escape I had heard of was a spontaneous impulse, rarely a thoroughly calculated plan.

Once a mother came to the camp to visit her eighteen-year-old girl. When she was granted permission to stay with her for two days outside the zone, she led her daughter on an escape through the taiga. The gap between her naïve wishful thinking and the reality of the law had a price: the mother was tried and put in prison, while her daughter received another term.

Early one morning we set out for the camp to rehearse our performance. The birds were chirping. We considered the forest our personal friend. But it was only the edge of the woods that seemed hospitable.

At the edge of a thicket I saw a cep mushroom. Looking closer, I saw more and more. Imagining what a delicious dinner we could all have that night, I asked the escort guards for permission to run farther into the forest to pick some more. I quickly filled the one basket that I had. "All right, enough! Come back!" Kolya shouted to me. But the brown caps were alluring. Every other mushroom looked sturdier and younger than the previous one. I put them into my kerchief.

Suddenly it became completely quiet. No chirping of birds, no shouts from Kolya were heard—just a wall of dead silence. I had lost my way. I dashed headlong to one side, then to another... Scratched all over by thorns, I frantically tore through the tree branches until I completely lost track of where I was.

I heard a crackle from the brushwood. When I turned to where the sound was coming from, the blood froze in my veins. In front of me, leaning on a tree, stood a creature of some sort, which I first took for a snag, staring at me with mad, cunning eyes. Looking closer, I saw it was a woman. She fixed her frightening gaze on me. I was too terrified to move, but then I started running, and I didn't stop or look back until all my strength was gone and I sank to the ground. The frightening woman hadn't followed me. I was being drawn into the despairing stillness, nearly going mad myself, thinking I'd never find my way out.

By virtue of instinct alone I managed to make out some unclear sound in the distance. I implored it to repeat itself. Another echo wafted through the thick wall of silence. I begged: "Save me! Repeat!" Everything ceased to exist except this feeble signal, which sounded remotely like the blows of a trumpet. My friends were helping me. Straining my ears to these mosquito-like sounds, I ran toward them, halting every few steps out of fear of losing their trace again. The sound became louder and louder until I finally saw the trumpeter, Volodya Kulikov, perched on top of some half-demolished grain elevator.

The TEC actors stood in a line, looking at me with disapproval as I emerged from the forest. Both the guards and my friends were scared. Kolya trembled. I could get a sentence for attempted escape, not to mention that the others would be in big trouble, too.

I told them about the creature. It must have been a fugitive prisoner who had lost her way and reason in the taiga. No one knew what to do. To go and find her meant turning her in to the guards. Nobody would dare do that, nor would we be able to secure permission to go to the forest again in the first place.

A short while after we left the Berezovy Camp and were standing next to our train cars at the Kotlas railway junction, waiting to depart, we saw a group of investigative officers approaching. They checked the documents with our escort guards and climbed onto our cars, peering into every corner and climbing under the berths, turning everything upside down. We were lined up and counted. It was clear that someone had escaped and they were looking for the fugitive.

"What? You haven't heard?" exclaimed a friend of ours from Knyazh-Pogost. "They're searching the entire division. All trains are being checked." He said it was Nikolay Trofimovich Belonenko, one of the lords.

"What are you talking about?" we all grumbled as one. "Belonenko is on an assignment in Berezovy! We just saw him there."

Indeed, Nikolay Trofimovich had seen us off when we left. We walked together through the forest, reciting poetry. Could he at that time have already been preparing his escape?

"I know he was there," the man replied. "They've searched for him. He's disappeared. But that's only half of the news. Do you remember the lame American who always walked on crutches? Well, he has escaped from the Central Camp's repair and engineering factory. They think they escaped together."

The news of the American escaping from Central Camp and Nikolay Trofimovich from a camp at least four hundred *versts* away was so incredible it took us a long time to digest it.

Details followed: the lights suddenly went out at the factory. While the guards were dealing with the outage and lining up prisoners, they discovered that one was missing. When the electricity was restored and the alarm sounded, they found the American's quilted jacket and crutches by the factory fence. Some reported seeing an automobile drive by, an unheard-of rarity in Knyazh-Pogost, and even assumed that an airplane was waiting for them somewhere nearby.

I couldn't bring myself to imagine that, like so many of those who had set out to escape before, Nikolay Trofimovich would be skewered with one of the long iron rods that the guards used to probe the cargo of the departing trains, or that his body would lie in the dirt by the camp's checkpoint. When a human skeleton, supposedly of a man torn to pieces by a bear, was later found in the woods near the Berezovy camp, it was just as terrifying to think that such a fate could befall him.

What did Nikolay Trofimovich think to himself as we sat together on the porch of the Central Camp's medical unit, silently mourning the death of Kagner? Could the thought of escape have come to him at that moment?

Whenever the idea of escape took hold of a prisoner, it was always like an all-consuming fire. Nikolay Trofimovich's determination was different. His decision seemed to have been thoroughly thought through. There was energy to his willfulness, precision to his thought, an urge to resist. He must have gone free. We all desperately needed such a legend of good fortune.

IT WASN'T UNTIL THE SUMMER of 1948 that we received an assignment to perform at Rakpas, the camp where Aleksandr Osipovich was staying. Much had changed in our lives in the long time that we hadn't seen each other. I desperately wanted Aleksandr Osipovich to like Kolya, who was not very sociable.

Aleksandr Osipovich lived in a tiny secluded room in the KVCh that looked more like a slit between walls, separated from the rest of the space by a veneer partition. A small table knocked together out of rough boards stood by the little window. His trestle-bed huddled in a dark corner. A pot of coffee, which his wife, Olga Petrovna Ulitskaya, regularly sent him from the outside, steamed victoriously on top of the small stove that heated his poor dwelling. Aleksandr Osipovich looked aged and unhealthy.

As always, a diverse cast of characters was crowded around him, coming and going, each requesting a few minutes of his time. The pretty, porcelain-faced Motya, the Moth, stood aside.

That night I appeared before Aleksandr Osipovich on stage disguised as the matchmaker from Chekhov's *A Happy Ending,* and then I recited a short story in the character of an old woman who worked at the railway.

"You surprised me," Aleksandr Osipovich concluded. "That was quite impressive."

As usual, he barraged me with questions—from Yurik to my health to the latest news from Mezhog. He gave me the magazine *Zvenya*—a collection of papers and documents on the history of literature, arts and nineteenth-century social thought—and directed my attention especially to an article about the reaction of Russian noblemen to the Decembrist uprising. The paper opened up a new level of tragedy in their lives to me: the fathers' attitude to their sons' deeds, the noblemen's ideas of honor, the sincere repentance of the Decembrists and their insistent request to talk to the tsar in person. I felt a powerful illusion of history coming to life, a lesson pertaining to everyone.

In one of our conversations, I referred to a term coined by Chernyshevsky and used it to sustain my argument. I spoke about the "new men" who were understood as an achievement of history. Aleksandr Osipovich grinned:

"Would you please explain to me then, what's new about these 'new men'?"

His irony induced a necessary amendment.

"It's true," I agreed. "Humankind, whether 'new' or 'old,' has lived and suffered in all times, capable or incapable of honor and dignity."

One night the guards didn't disperse us and we sat up in Aleksandr Osipovich's makeshift room till sunrise. It was a white night in June. He recited Chekhov's *Three Sisters,* reading the text in a way only he was capable of, supplementing Chekhov with his own modulations and our common burdens. Spellbound, we listened to the play as if for the first time.

A fresh morning breeze shook the slim trunks of young birches that had been planted at Rakpas, and I felt the same chill inside my soul.

Hella Frisher was also at Rakpas. I hadn't forgotten this foreign woman and her horrific fate. Aleksandr Osipovich discovered an unexpected talent in her as a writer. "A Russian writer," Hella would add, mispronouncing Russian words and laughing coarsely. She thought and wrote in German, and everyone who knew the language asserted that in translation her poems lost their charm.

When Aleksandr Osipovich once wrote to me that he was involved in a real romance with Hella, I didn't bother to translate it into the language of concrete reality.

Behind her exotic beauty lay a rebellious and passionate nature. She lived on impulse, soaring upward and falling down to earth again. Hella had her reasons for being the way she was: she was sitting out the last days of her term, but no one would ever let her return to her native Czechoslovakia. The Moscow Comintern no longer existed. All her Comintern friends had been liquidated in 1937. Except for Aleksandr Osipovich, she had no other spiritual support.

Fortunately, our Chinese friend Tsu ZinShan, who worked with Tamara Tsulukidze's puppet theater, was also getting released around the same time. Having made a rather strange decision to go neither to the center nor to the south of the country but to remain in the North, he got in touch with the Ust-Kolom Theater. They were looking for an artist, and once he got to the theater and was hired, he managed to have his friend, Jian Bao, join him there; he also secured an invitation for Hella to come and work as a costumier.

In Rakpas, Boris Maevsky spent a lot of time with us, too. He invited Kolya and me to his studio, full of stretched canvases and paintings on the walls. He worked tirelessly, fulfilling official as well as private orders from members of the camp administration.

Seeing us off, he held on to the side of our truck, stood on the wheel and, pulling himself up, said: "Kolya, you have to know: I love her." Kolya covered me with a tarp to protect me from the wind, sat close to me and embraced me tightly. Despite the long journey that lay ahead of us, my heart was full and content; I wasn't afraid of the wind or the cold.

We always felt better on the road than in Knyazh-Pogost, especially in the summer, and when the escort wasn't too rowdy. There was just us, the taiga and the tundra, the roads that would take me to my son and, later, lead me and Kolya to freedom.

We would roll open the door of the train car and sit on the edge, our legs dangling down. We would try to discern spots of red and black berries growing in the green moss on the curbs of the tracks as the train sped past. Reaching its destination, the locomotive would shunt and push our cars down to the dead-end siding along the old rusty rails overgrown with weed. We would sink in the stillness of the uninhabited station. After the concerts, waiting for our cars to be coupled to a passing train, we would light brushwood bonfires, the flames crackling and bursting upward to the sky.

Passenger trains rolled by at high speeds. Standing by the railway embankment with our heads thrown back, Kolya and I looked at the electric lights cleaving through the darkness. The orange caps of table lamps in the sleeper cars flashed by and sped away, heading toward Moscow. There was implacable sorrow in the uncomfortable mystery of the masters of our destiny who slept soundly in these cozy cars, in the tragedy of the woman who was perishing so bestially in the woods, sorrow too in ourselves, who stood next to the tracks waiting for the cattle cars to come carry us away further down the line.

VARIOUS ORDERS and resolutions pertaining to this or that limitation would catch up with us upon our return to Knyazh-Pogost. The camp did not tolerate calm and stability. Somewhere within the system lived the anonymous idea-monger who always came up with new means of terror.

An order was passed to transfer all the women at Central Camp over to the agricultural camp about three kilometers away from the main zone. After spending the day at Central Camp, we would be led there to sleep. The men now had to cook for themselves. As for us, we received dry rations since there was no stove at our new place.

That morning Kolya greeted me as usual. It wasn't until we sat down to have breakfast that he said:

"Promise you won't panic about what I'm about to tell you."

I already knew what would follow.

"Were you summoned?"

"Yes, tonight—after they led you away."

"What did they want?"

"They told me if I don't work for them, they'll separate us. Either way, I will lose you. But if I agree, I'll lose you forever. If I don't, time is on our side."

Kolya added:

"You know, the officer who spoke with me is my age. I asked him, 'You've no qualms about this? Are you really capable of separating us?' He cut me off. 'Don't be an idiot,' he told me. 'I should have done it a long time ago.'"

When in the evening the escort came to take us to our sleeping barracks, Kolya said in a whisper, whether asking a question or begging me:

"Will you… Will you pray tonight?"

We had never talked about God before. "It was there, in his cell on death row, that he addressed Him," I thought. As for me, I already prayed every day. "God, it will be fine if they send us to the general works, but please, only together! Don't separate us!" Every hour of our lives was spent in fear that one of us would be put on the transport list; we were afraid to think of the inevitable day when I'd be set free while Kolya would have to remain in the camps for five more years.

Kolya's summons to the Third Department was nothing more than an attempt by the authorities to recruit yet another squealer, since the order to send off everyone sentenced under Article 58-1 already lay on the camp commandant's desk.

No one touched me or came to see me. I was beside myself. Two people met each other amid the ugliness of the camp and were happy in spite of everything. People around them said, "Thank you for showing us it is possible."

After Kolya's departure, we wrote letters to each other daily. Between the blazing lines of his letters, I read his assurances that our "together" was unbreakable, that he was ready to endure anything to save it. He was attached to me "like an animal." The phrase was no metaphor in these bestial conditions. Our screams of protest didn't reach anyone's ears. Sadistically, they came and took us away from each other.

Kolya was sent to Rakpas. Since our last visit to that camp, TEC would travel there only once more.

Neither the journey nor our preparations remained in my memory. It was only the minute that I saw him and the hours we spent together that stayed with me.

During our visit, Aleksandr Osipovich told me:

"I understand why him. I understand it all, Tamarochka!"

Not knowing how to cope with despair, I only repeated:

"I won't be able to live without him. I can't!"

Not long ago Aleksandr Osipovich had written to me: "Think of your life. Instead of crippling you, it gave you the power, despite all evil, to become what you are today." Now, however, instead of the lofty words of consolation I'd gotten so used to, he uttered in a quiet and reserved voice:

"You can't endure it? Then you'll have to change yourself."

It was painful to bump into this unexpected formula. It was too harsh, too austere. I wasn't ready to accept it and could only guess intuitively how inevitable it was. I did away with the thought, "Yes, I will change, but not now. Now I only need to be near Kolya, nothing else."

THE CAMP AUTHORITIES saw how trite our concerts had become and decided to replace the TEC actors they'd just dismissed—those sentenced under Article 58-1—with prisoners convicted of real espionage. The logic behind such a decision was nothing but stunning.

Among the new members of TEC was a Czech woman, Elena N., who used to be a dancer and an acrobat at one of the cabarets in Prague. This sleek foreigner, invitingly attractive and pale-skinned, confirmed:

"Oh yes, I'm in for espionage."

She told us matter-of-factly about how a dentist drilled holes in her teeth to hide secret ciphers; how she'd hide top-secret reports in the spiked heels of her shoes or in her hair. She spoke of the human body as a sort of locker with numerous tiny boxes and cabinets to store secret information. But what surprised us most about her was the length of her term: six years. Six years for proven espionage! Without a "corpus delicti," I had gotten seven; Margo and Inna had ten. And Elena had only gotten six. Once, someone had the courage to raise this issue. Elena promptly replied:

"Why, I didn't work for just one side. I worked for your government, too."

Elena was permitted to bring three suitcases to the zone from the outside, and she kept them in the camp storeroom. She would occasionally bring something or other from her suitcases to the barracks to show off before the women. One day it was a stunning chiffon nightgown, which looked like a mirage of white smoke, another day—a low-neck blouse adorned with some magnificent pattern, or culottes. Like many others, I was seeing these items of luxury for the first time.

The women gasped, asked for permission to try them on, and quarreled with each other when they wanted to buy one. The lucky owner of a chic dress would strut back and forth about the barracks at the request of the rest. The plank beds would be turned into a gallery, and the middle of the barracks into a runway.

The resilient and beautiful Elena initiated those who listened to the sexual tricks she had used to entice men, spicing her stories with details.

The guards were enjoying more and more luck searching our barracks. They'd guess right away who exactly was hiding restricted objects, and where. Soon someone noticed that before leaving Central Camp for the night, Elena would sneak in good time into the investigation officer's room by the checkpoint.

To rid ourselves of the squealer was hopeless. Nothing could shame her, or the very arrangement of camp life, out of the usual pattern.

THE ADMINISTRATION of Central Camp conceived of a large-scale theatrical event in Knyazh-Pogost, and TEC was required to prepare an extensive program. The TEC directors grew bold and demanded, in turn, that the actors and musicians with Article 58-1 who had been sent off to Rakpas be brought back to ensure success of the concert. No one believed that the request would have any effect. But when the authorities needed to maintain a prestigious self-image and looked for amusement, everything became possible. Within a few hours they issued the order to bring back the actors, and a truck with escort guards set off for Rakpas. Life was returned to me and Kolya! The concert had an unheard-of success.

Unsure of the future, we started rehearsing new concert items at our own risk. Among the new shows were scenes from the *Bayadera* operetta, which Kolya had dreamed of staging for a long time. Indifferent to operetta, I declined to play the role of Marietta, claiming I'd never danced or sung on stage before. Arguing that staging the operetta would give everyone a chance to stay together for a while longer, Kolya demanded vocal and choreographic achievements of me. Overcoming my hesitation, I gave in and set out to memorize the words and moves. Margo concocted a costume for me. Eventually, as Kolya had predicted, *Bayadera* was very well received by the camp's authorities.

"All right, why don't you stage another operetta, a little more humorous and melodious?" they offered. "Get down to work!"

On the day of the premier, we celebrated Kolya's thirtieth birthday.

At one of the camps, we were lodged not in the barracks but in separate cottages, each with two apartments. We were surprised that prisoners could enjoy such living conditions, but I fell sick on the first morning and wasn't able to enjoy the rare comforts.

From the place where I lay on my bed I could see the front door and the entire corridor. I was waiting for Kolya. I knew he would come running as soon as he was done with his number.

In a short while I heard him come in. But seconds passed, and he didn't approach me. I opened my eyes and saw him standing in the doorway, still in his overcoat. It was so unnatural that I began to doubt whether it was really him, or whether I had a fever hallucination.

Finally, Kolya came closer.

"Something very strange just happened to me on the stage. I was reciting *Makar Chudra* when suddenly I forgot all the words. I couldn't even remember what the story was about. Someone from the orchestra prompted me, but I didn't hear. Then it came back to me and I finished."

I had never seen him like this before. "It happens," I thought to myself. Why was he so frightened? What was wrong?

Seemingly out of the blue, I recalled a difficult conversation I'd had with Khmiel, one of the TEC singers. He was an old man, grown wise with experience, but with his own oddities. Many avoided him. Once he told me, "If you don't want to lose Kolya forever, you have to abandon him." His words were so frightening I should have rather forgotten them at once. What did he mean, "To lose Kolya forever?" Even a single day without Kolya seemed impossible. I recoiled from Khmiel's foreboding and brushed it off as the venom of a panic-monger. However, as I remembered the incident now, lying in my bed, an uneasy feeling crept through me and lingered for a long time.

FINALLY THE TOWN where Yurik was living was put on our route. Our trip there had been postponed time after time because of some bureaucratic issues. I notified Bakharev of my arrival in a letter.

I asked Dmitry Karayanidi, the conductor of the TEC orchestra who had been released a while ago, to buy some toys for my son. He bought a large gray horse, as well as other presents, and loaded them onto our train car without bringing them into the zone.

I tried not to think about the circumstances accompanying my impending meeting with Yurik. My thoughts revolved around how I'd take him in my arms and press him to my chest, how he would reach out for me.

As soon as we arrived at the main camp of that division, Bakharev came to the zone and explained that because of his official position, it wouldn't be appropriate for him to bring his son to the camp personally; Yurik would be coming with Vera Petrovna. "There are too many eyes constantly watching," he told me.

After the concert, as the audience was leaving the hall, Vera Petrovna appeared holding Yurik in her arms. In the dim light of the club I saw my son as a shining little bastion of calm. I reached out my hands and called to him:

"Yurik! Yurochka!"

He looked at me and kept silent.

"Why don't you say 'Hello!'" Vera Petrovna urged him.

He was holding onto her neck with one of his little arms. As if playing with me, he glanced at me a few more times, smiled, then leaned back and embraced Vera Petrovna with his other arm, turning his back to everyone.

I kept on calling his name as calmly as I could. Without letting go of Vera Petrovna, my son scrutinized the people surrounding him, including myself, but wouldn't let me take him into my arms.

I knew it couldn't happen at once. I had to wait, to help him retrieve his memory of me. I had to be left alone with him. But it was precisely this most essential and simple need that turned out to be beyond my grasp.

"What a wild little creature you are!" Vera Petrovna rebuked him. "Look who is here. Look!"

She wouldn't say precisely what "who" meant. I caressed his back and his little arms. He said nothing.

"Say 'Hello!' Come on!" she kept prompting the child.

Having achieved nothing, vainly trying to persuade Yurik to talk, Vera Petrovna addressed him in a lighthearted tone, part of a game they'd apparently played many times before:

"Don't put me to shame! Show how you love your mother!"

Pressing himself against her even tighter, Yurik promptly showed how he loved "his mother." My strength was sapped by what just happened. Both my son and Vera Petrovna drifted out of my focus.

My TEC friends stepped aside, leaving the three of us alone. Again I reached out my hands to him and kept calling his name.

"He has grown, hasn't he?" Vera Petrovna said excitedly. "He likes dogs, you know."

My son gave me another cheerful look, almost without embarrassment, but soon he started acting up and asked to go home. As they were leaving, my son, supposedly a very warmhearted and tender boy, giving in to Vera Petrovna's expostulation, waved his little hand to me from a distance.

I was shaking just like I did at my trial back in Frunze. Hiding behind the stage curtain, I pressed myself against the cold wall. Though I'd imagined a similar scenario, what had happened was more sinister than anything I could ever conceive of. Sitting in the corner of the dilapidated stage, I knew for sure that the next moment a wave of ever greater and deadlier pain would swamp me. I wouldn't be able to withstand it; I would drown. Yet for some reason, the pain never arrived. It would only come later.

Kolya shook me on the shoulders. He demanded, "Cry, cry, for God's sake!" And he cried himself.

When I calmed down a little, I remembered that Vera Petrovna had told me in a surprisingly conciliatory tone that if I managed to talk a guard into taking me out of the zone tomorrow, she would bring Yurik to the outpatients' clinic at six in the evening, and I would be able to stay with him for a while.

In the office where Vera Petrovna brought me, the lights were switched off. A street lamp cast its light through the window.

This time Yurik immediately walked toward me and let me hold him. I could finally press him against me. I waited for Vera Petrovna to say, "I have to go, I'll be right back." But she wasn't going to leave.

I begged: "My little, mysterious son, I need to reach into your memory! You can't possibly have forgotten me!"

Yurik grew quiet. I felt that at any moment now our living bond would reawaken within him. That Vera Petrovna wouldn't stop talking caused almost physical pain. I knew she was jabbering deliberately just to obliterate the closeness between me and Yurik taking root in that room.

"No, this isn't necessary, we don't need it," she rejected my meager presents: the horse and the blanket I'd sewn for Yurik. "He has everything he needs. Our house is crammed with toys. No, no pastries—they are bad for him!"

Her blabbing sounded somewhat too agitated and excessive. I didn't think of the reasons for her nervousness. I was holding my boy in my arms while an escort guard was waiting for me in the corridor.

All of a sudden, Vera Petrovna exhaled some hysterical sound, jerked with the swiftness of a tornado and, sliding down the stool she was sitting on, kneeled right in front of me:

"Tamara Vladislavovna, let me have Yurik! You're young, you'll have more children. I can't have any. Let me have him!"

I could have imagined nothing of the sort.

"What are you talking about? You have a son. You have your own child!"

But she needed Filipp, and, therefore, my son, too.

Her madness threatened to draw me into a vortex of nightmare, yet something seemed to prevent me from making a wrong move. I hurried to pacify, to placate the dangerous force that had revealed itself to me in such an overt and cynical way. I had to reassure her I wasn't thinking of Filipp. I did everything I could to make her believe it.

I never told anyone about what happened at the outpatient clinic.

In about a week, when TEC had already moved on but was still not too far away, the Bakharevs sent me a message that Yurik had fallen sick with the measles and was running a high fever.

When he was ill in Mezhog, Yurik wagged his head, and the first experience of endurance would show through in his eyes. This image of him haunted me: my son was tossing about in his cot gasping for breath. The idea of returning grew stronger and stronger. I managed to persuade the commander to let me go and a guard agreed to escort me.

My arms and legs trembled as I approached Bakharev's wooden house. I knew that going there without permission was a mistake, but fear for Yurik could drive me much further than that.

Vera Petrovna opened the door.

"May I come in? How is he?"

"He's still not well. Go to the bedroom," she said angrily.

Yurochka was lying in a large bed and breathed heavily. Filipp, who was sitting in an armchair, rose:

"It's nothing too serious. He's better now. I've done everything that was needed. No need to panic."

Vera Petrovna's mother, who ran into the bedroom after me, measured me up and down with her ferocious eyes, and, recognizing who I was, started making a racket with aluminum basins and cursing loudly.

"It's no use to let prisoners into the house. Let her get her release first."

I knew from Vera Petrovna's own words that her old mother had long sworn to scald me with boiling water or to burn my eyes out with acid. Yet how blissful it was to hear her mention my release! It meant they'd been discussing it amongst themselves.

I kneeled down and put my head next to my son's on the pillow. He looked at me seriously and feverishly. I whispered something to him. Vera Petrovna—the hostess, the second mother—stood behind the bed.

When I turned my head to Filipp, I noticed a trace of smug self-satisfaction in his face. Of course: both of his women were suffering by his son's bedside.

ONCE WE WERE LED to perform at a camp we'd never been to before. We walked seven or eight kilometers deep into the forest along a barely visible path until we came to a zone surrounded by an old palisade of thick logs with barbed wire stretched above it.

After the concert, we weren't allowed to spend the night in the zone. It was a secret camp unit. The local commandants put our luggage on a sleigh and sent us off.

There was only woods and stillness around us. The moon flooded the snow with its light, making every snowflake sparkle. We were in the kingdom of a solemn winter night, as if in some parallel and truer world, where there was no need to waste words, where the creaking of one's own footsteps was a disturbing blasphemy, where everything was more godly and clearer than in our own lives.

Even after we came back to our barracks, no one turned the lights on. The bright moonlight cast through the window was enough. Dmitry, Inna, Kolya and I sat down for supper. We didn't know that the four of us would never gather together again.

The foreman entered the barracks with a transfer list. Nailed to the spot, we listened as he read out the names of those to be transported to the Tayshet camps.

When I caught my breath after realizing that neither Kolya nor I were on the list, it occurred to me that our soloist Inna was leaving forever. Dmitry, whose daughter just died, was now also losing Inna, whom he loved. Our Lithuanian singer Aldona Bludzhivaitite, the musician Mahomet Uteshev and many more dear friends were going away.

I looked at the strained face of Aldona, then caught Inna's confused glance. I took out my mittens, walked over to Aldona and handed them to her. She cried, just like I did when the technical supervisor from Djangi-Djir gave me a pair of woolen socks. She helplessly pressed herself to me and took off her amber necklace.

"Take it, it'll bring you luck. You mean a lot to me."

I gave Inna my warm kerchief. With tears in our eyes, we said good-bye.

Somewhere in the faraway Tayshet camps was Erik, performing his surgeries, as he wrote to me in a letter. I told his name to Inna and Aldona and scribbled a note: "Help my friends as I would help yours."

They rode off on a special train with all the signs of the "century of civilization": blinding searchlights installed on the roofs of the cattle cars, modern weapons, well-trained dogs that barked ferociously from the train platforms.

Not until many years later did I fully comprehend the simple truth: people's attitude to each other and to TEC in general was different. For those who had lived their "main" lives before they wound up in the camps, TEC was just a stroke of luck. For those who had no one waiting for them anywhere, TEC became their family. Each perceived the fates of the rest of this motley family as their own. Without love for my friends, without knowing the details of their lives, I would never have been able to understand my own life.

IT WAS THE SPRING OF 1949, the last year of my term. I was issued a pass that permitted me to move freely around the area without being escorted. The advantages of having such a permit were obvious. I could now walk from the agricultural zone to Central Camp on my own and no longer had to march back and forth under guard in a file of prisoners.

Once, after sunset, I dropped in to visit Wanda Razumovskaya. I couldn't wait to see her daughter Kira, whom she had taken from the orphanage.

"Come in!" Wanda answered when I knocked on the door.

As if shedding her camp skin, she stood before me completely naked, defiantly soaking up freedom through her pores. I should have told her she was gorgeous, but instead I grew embarrassed.

She bent down and pulled out a dish with cheap caramels from the drawer of an old desk.

"I have to hide the sweets. I'll never have enough for her!" Wanda artlessly explained the origins of the hiding place. "Kira gobbles up everything she can get her hands on."

I felt sorry for Kira, who unrestrainedly consumed any kind of food, unable to satisfy her appetite after the orphanage. My heart shrank with pity for Wanda too, who during the twelve years of her imprisonment had nearly forgotten how to be a mother. The entire settlement fixed its attention on her relationship with her daughter.

Once, Wanda's neighbor, the director of the local kindergarten, heard sobs coming from the shed in the courtyard. She approached and saw Kira lying on the logs. She took the girl to her place, and later read in Kira's diary: "Why isn't Mama my Mama anymore? She doesn't love me. I want her to love me." Wanda was furious and demanded that her daughter return home. Kira wouldn't go. Both of them suffered, and no one could help them.

Wanda, the lioness who had once rebuked me, "What other life do you expect for yourself? *This* is your life,"—of course, she wanted *hers* to be different. Fate hadn't granted her much in the way of female happiness, yet she did not want to resign herself to loneliness. All the men she knew turned out to be too shallow for her, and no one wished to plunge headlong into such a dramatic family life as hers. Wanda and her daughter inspired neither compassion nor pity in people, only gossip.

It wasn't easy for the released prisoners to adjust to freedom. This manifested itself in different, yet always dramatic, ways. At the train station of Knyazh-Pogost I once saw Olga Viktorovna Tretyakova, with whom I had spent many wonderful days in Urdoma and Mezhog. I was excited to see her and ran toward her. Casting a frightened and rather puzzled glance at me, she stepped back and pretended she didn't know me. For a prisoner to run to a free person was, indeed, inexcusable. Yet a freedom that didn't relieve people of permanent fear wasn't much different from prison.

KOLYA HAD BEEN saving money since they began paying us a few rubles a month two years before. For the day of my release, he wanted to buy me a coat. Next to some distant train station we found a small shop and asked the guard to take us there. Bales of fabric lay on the shelves. Kolya asked the vendor to take down one roll and inquired about the width of the cloth. Finally, pointing at a beautiful dark blue material, he said:

"This one is the best."

The coat was sewn by our tailor. Margo was the chief consultant.

The day of my release was swiftly approaching, though my heart didn't yet beat joyfully when I thought of freedom. Like an invalid who had lain in bed for several years in a plaster cast and had completely unlearned how to move, I panicked at the thought of the first steps I'd make on the outside. Things like finding a job and a place to live didn't worry me much. I convinced myself that if others could do it, so could I. My main thought was, of course, how to get my son back from the Bakharevs.

Although Aleksandr Osipovich's formula, "Sometimes, a fact alone isn't enough," had greatly surprised me when I first heard it, now I professed the same faith. Despite Barbara Ionovna's renunciation of me during the arrest, and despite the fact she had never visited me in Djangi-Djir or in Belovodsk, I believed that her heart ached when she thought of me. I was now receiving her letters full of repentance and torment. It was the same with Filipp. Despite everything he had done, I had faith that some rudiment of humanity would prevail over him when I got released, and he would give me my son back without a trial.

Once, as I walked along the tracks with TEC to one of the camps, I saw Filipp coming our way. The view bordered on a hallucination, yet it was him. His face revealed genuine joy, which he did not hesitate to express—as if, after a long period of seclusion, he decided to treat himself to a bit of merrymaking.

"I'm so happy to see you!" he exclaimed and kissed my hands in front of everyone. "I'm so happy!"

By the end of our concert, someone brought me a letter from Filipp. He called what had happened to him a tragedy and wrote that all the illnesses he had recently suffered stemmed from precisely his inner torment. He explained almost confidingly: "I've been so pressed down recently by the circumstances that I felt paralyzed and couldn't even bring myself to write you a letter. I thought of you constantly. I pity V.P., she is suffering both morally and physically, but it is you that I love."

I only paid attention to the tone of this letter. However, Filipp's main pledge, as I saw it, was contained in a letter he had written earlier: "If you're worried about the child, you shouldn't be. The boy is always yours, and even though I love him more than my own life, I will give him back to you upon your request at any time, even in ten years."

I revered that letter as my main support, as a divine document. I clung to it with all the power of faith I had left, although, after that faith had been profaned by Filipp, I had no right to trust his words more than I could trust him.

Some common sense prevailed over me after receiving a letter from Platon Romanovich, who had been sent off to the Far North, in which he managed to articulate what I'd been trying to hide from myself. No one would give me my son back amicably. I would have to take the case to court. But, not yet able to comprehend fully what the seven years of exclusion from the outer world had done to me, I grew torpid from the very thought of the law, lawyers and courts.

TWO MONTHS BEFORE MY RELEASE, we were sent to perform at a division of camps close to the Bakharevs. Filipp came to one of these camps to meet with me after a concert. I had imagined my "prerelease" conversation with him thousands of times and revisited earlier scenes of his tumultuous outbursts, his acting humane and dignified at other moments, his asking me about Kolya or mentioning his attachment to Vera Petrovna and Yurik.

Everyone left. We were alone in a small room of the KVCh at the back of the stage. Filipp took a newspaper from a shaky bookshelf, turned a few pages and put it back.

"You probably want to talk?"

"Of course," I answered, growing cold with the thought we were finally in for our definitive conversation. "You know I'm getting released soon, that I'll come to get my child."

"I suppose you're not going to do that straight off—at least not until you find a job and a place to live."

"That won't take long."

"We'll see."

I believed he would say something about my finding a job near Velsk so that he could see his son more often, but he seemed determined not to utter a single redundant sound. He waited for me to talk. It became very obvious: his silence had nothing to do with reticence but was rather the habit of a hunter waiting for his prey to make a false move. I tried to hold my ground on one foot like a heron, not knowing where to put the other.

In front of me sat a man completely alien to any of the earlier emotions we'd felt together. He was watching me with a hunter's cold eyes, trying to figure out exactly what danger I posed to him. Had I been drowning, I assumed, he would've cried but wouldn't have reached out a hand.

It turned out there was nothing to talk about. It was time to take action, or at least to prepare for one.

The idea that a mother had the right to her child sat deeply in people's consciousness. With the pass that I had, at the Kuloy railway junction where no one knew me, I decided to go to a legal advice office. "I'll tell them I'm a free worker if I have to," I thought.

I walked up the creaky wooden stairs of the settlement's council nearly fainting. In seven years, I'd grown unused to visiting any kind of official institutions. The lawyer heard me through, asked questions, specified details, thumbed through the code, citing the numbers of articles he was referring to. His conclusion came to the following: the best thing to do was to settle the issue by mutual agreement. If not, in cases like mine, the court would first of all have to defend the interests of the child, taking into account both the moral and financial means of the parties. From the point of view of the state, the child had to be raised in the conditions most favorable to him. The indisputable rights of the mother, as the lawyer spoke of them, appeared to be merely conventional, if not dubious.

"But isn't it true that the mother has all the rights?" I insisted.

"Of course, but only provided that she can ensure the normal development of the child. Do you have a place to live? Do you have a job? Then what are you worried about? Fill out the application. Get the required references."

What I heard meant that in order to match Filipp in a dispute over my child, my level of life after release had to be equal to his.

Freedom appeared hostile. I left that office completely crushed and sobbed with abandon standing by a heap of boxes piled by the side of the building.

Someone touched me on the shoulder:

"What happened? Come one, you shouldn't cry like that. Oh, is it you?"

I recognized the man. It was Rodion Evgenyevich Malakhov, the former commandant of the Mezhog camp.

"What's the matter? Tell me everything step by step."

I told him about my conversation with the lawyer.

"Why, he didn't tell you anything awful. Everything's fine. You'll work—you won't be able to get by without working anyway. Time will come and you'll have a place."

As it turned out in the course of the conversation, Malakhov was much better informed of my state of affairs than I could have expected him to be. He cherished no bright hopes as far as my case was concerned, and said:

"Here's what I'll tell you. You're a strong person, so please do as I say, all right? Listen to me. I have five hundred rubles on me. I'm giving the money to you. Don't be afraid. When things get better, you'll pay me back if you still want to. Now listen: wait till they take your son for a walk, grab him and catch the first plane. Don't let anybody know where you're going! Take the money!"

I had to explain to him that I hadn't been released yet and had another two months, that I could not accept the money from him and, most important, that I couldn't imagine stealing away my own son.

"Too bad. I wish you'd follow my advice."

There was much that had to occur before I could appreciate the farsighted advice of this generous man.

After Kolya heard my story about meeting the lawyer and Rodion Evgenyevich, he told me:

"Unfortunately, Malakhov is right. It's the only thing to do. You should have listened to him."

"What? To steal my own son, while having all rights to win him back legally? I don't even have his birth certificate. Yurik has my last name."

"You don't understand how dangerous the people you're dealing with are."

"And you? What about you? How am I going to run away without you? We've decided, haven't we, that I'll take Yurik and look for a job at Knyazh-Pogost!"

Neither Kolya nor I had an answer to this frightening question. Release meant freedom, Yurik and… separation from Kolya. Before I had time to say this again, Kolya repeated the more than strange phrase I had already heard from him many times:

"I told you: I will soon be on the other side of the zone!"

The words contained no real meaning. I could think of them as nothing but his desire to console me and categorically fought the assumption that the glory of Nikolay Trofimovich's escape, successful as people believed, had also stuck in Kolya's consciousness as a way out.

AS MY DAY OF RELEASE APPROACHED, I had more and more things to attend to. Deviating from the route that my pass permitted, I ran to all sorts of different places, trying to find a job at the administration, or at the outpatients' clinic or, if Senya Erukhimovich could still hire me, at the local branch of the Syktyvkar theater, where he now worked as an administrator. I had to find a place to live, too.

Unexpectedly, Georgy Lvovich Nevolsky said he wanted to talk to me:

"Tamara Vladislavovna, could you do me a big favor? I wanted to ask you to move in with Klava. She has a large room. She'll be glad to share it with you."

Georgy Lvovich wanted to help me as well as his pretty, slightly plump wife, Klava, who had taken to drink after her release. He thought she would be embarrassed to drink in my presence.

Ilya Evseevich asked me to visit him at the administration office.

"When you get your documents, fill out a statement that you're leaving the area and going to a place as far away from here as possible so that I can allot you more money for transportation." (The camp paid for a train ticket to the destination indicated in the prisoners' release documents.)

Twelve days were left until my release when TEC got an order to go north.

Growing numb with fear that the Second Department would forbid me to go with them, I climbed the TEC train car with everyone else. I was ready to endure anything for every day, every hour and every minute of being with Kolya. But a day passed, and still our cars hadn't been coupled to a train.

The Second Department remembered about me. Late in the evening of January 21, nine days before I was supposed to be set free, we heard the clatter of a rifle butt against the car door:

"Petkevich, you're ordered to return to the camp!"

That was it, the end.

Pulling my wooden suitcase down from the bunks, I began to say goodbye to my friends.

"Stand firm! Things will somehow get sorted out... Don't forget us..." I heard them say to me, not hiding their tears. "How are we going to manage without you? Come on, cheer up! It's freedom!"

The guards hurried me on.

Kolya and I got out of the car. Darkness. Nipping frost. Two guards with machine guns. Stars high above. Our sentences of different lengths were tearing our lives apart.

"All right, that's enough. Let's go!" one of the guards said.

We couldn't move away from each other. How could I make a step away from Kolya by my own volition, leaving him alone behind barbed wire for five years?

"Enough! Move it!"

...The guard and I had barely reached the bend of the road when I heard Kolya's inhuman scream:

"To-o-mi-i-i!"

His voice hung in midair; it tore through the ice and the frozen earth of the Komi.

The guards fell silent. Kolya and I dashed back to each other...

THE NINE DAYS that were left before my release I spent in sheer blindness at the agricultural camp.

Suddenly, reality reached my consciousness: I was getting released. I'd never be allowed back to the zone under any conditions again. I'd never again see Aleksandr Osipovich!

I dashed to the administration to ask for a permit to travel to Rakpas. They refused. I asked again and again until finally they contrived to send me to check on the condition of the ideological materials at the Rakpas "Red Corner."

A blizzard was raging. I stood on the road and waved until the driver of one of the passing trucks had pity on me and pulled over.

At the Rakpas checkpoint, the guards wouldn't let me enter the zone for a long time. "What kind of checkup is this? Who sent you?"

I managed to notify Boris I was here. He ran to the commander and convinced him to let me in.

Aleksandr Osipovich lay in the infirmary with pneumonia. I sat on the cot beside him in the gloomy, cold ward.

"Tamarochka, my Tamarochka has come!" he exclaimed in a weak voice. "You came to say good-bye."

Complaining of neither his health nor loneliness, he held my hand and kept repeating:

"Tamarochka has come to visit me. Thank you!"

Doctor Vladas Shimkunas came to remind me I'd promised not to stay long. But I had a lot to tell Aleksandr Osipovich—how dear he was to me, how I needed him, that it was thanks to him that I survived…

"We're not going to see each other again, Tamarochka. Don't interrupt me—we won't. Listen to my will. As soon as you can, my dear, the sooner the better, once you get a chance, go to Odessa, to Olechka. Introduce yourself, tell her about me. No one can do this except you. I know you'll like each other. That's all. I have no other requests."

I promised.

Boris ran into the infirmary:

"I'm waiting for you!"

I was indignant: What was he hurrying me for? Didn't he understand?

"Don't be angry with him," Aleksandr Osipovich said. "He feels horrible, too. Say good-bye to him like a friend, Tamarochka. That would be right."

Boris wanted to give me something as a keepsake.

"Would you like anything from here?" he asked, pointing with a sweeping gesture to a wall covered with paintings.

I looked around. "Yes. Vasnetsov's 'Alyonushka.'"

Boris grinned:

"Well, would you like me to throw 'Rooks' into the bargain—from me, personally"?

I couldn't bring myself to utter a single warm word to him. Boris said with irritation:

"You know, Tamara, you have no heart."

He was right—I had given it all to Kolya. I turned to leave. He followed me out.

"All right, don't be mad. I wish you to be happy on the outside."

Before leaving the zone, I dropped by to see Aleksandr Osipovich one more time.

The blizzard was still going strong. There were no trucks. Holding Boris's paintings under my arms, I forced my way through the snow in the direction of Knyazh-Pogost. Together with the snowstorm, I wailed about everything that had been, was and would be. I remembered meeting Tamara Tsulukidze after the death of her son. I had run into her by accident at the Knyazh-Pogost House of Culture. She looked completely wilted. I asked her meekly how she was. Lifting her shoulders slightly, she answered: "How am I? I hate myself for having stayed alive after Sandik." Her words and tone remained forever in my heart.

After about three kilometers, a dump truck drove out of the forest and picked me up.

IT WAS A GRAY GLOOMY MORNING, January 30, 1950. Seven years had passed since that morning in Frunze when the woman in a karakul coat appeared in front of the gate of our house.

The foreman came into the barracks.

"Go to the Second Department, fill out the paperwork."

The inspector leafed through my file, looking over my interrogation warrants pasted into the folder.

"They've given you quite a hard time," he admitted. In a fatherly voice, he continued, "So we're setting you free, right? Everything's fine. The only thing that isn't is that you've forgotten your husband. He's been showering us with letters. He asks that we send you to him. He wants you to be there to wait till he gets released. How many years? Oh, just three. We can do that. It's not a whole lot."

He handed me two petitions written by Erik's hand. In one of them Erik asked to issue me a waybill to Tayshet, where he worked. The other was addressed to the people's court:

> Regarding the case of my wife, T. V. Petkevich, on granting her permission to raise her son, I ask that my solicitation for satisfying her request is added to the file. On my part, I attest to the court that I will make every effort possible to adopt the child so that we can bring him up.
>
> September 7, 1949

Bewildered, I folded the certificate of release I was given, as well as the sheets from Erik. I handed my camp clothes over to the disinfection room. I stepped over the threshold of the checkpoint. With envy and ennui, the women I left behind in the barracks looked at me through the window as I walked away.

Chapter 11

First moments of freedom.

I walked about a hundred meters from the zone toward the settlement, put my suitcase onto the frozen ground and sat down on it in bewilderment. I waited for joy to rush forth, but I felt none. Inside the camp I had just left behind Kolya, Aleksandr Osipovich, my friends, seven years of life.

Dogs were barking in the settlement. The world looked flat and desolate.

I needed to find food and shelter before nightfall, and I had to obtain a temporary passport for three months.

Klava's house stood almost next to Central Camp, which for me was important. I dropped my suitcase off at her place and left to sort out my business.

My desires were basic and simple: to find a job in Knyazh-Pogost, to have four walls to call my own, to take my son as soon as possible and to see Kolya from time to time until his release.

I revisited the places where, only a month ago, they'd promised to find me work, but everywhere I was turned away. Some of my friends working in the camp administration were still pleading with the local officials at least to give me a temporary job; the motives behind the refusals were beyond comprehension.

Three years ago, in 1947, one could easily find work within the camp system. There was a need for people, and no one put any obstacles in the way of newly released prisoners. Since then, as it turned out, a secret directive had been issued that prohibited granting employment to ex-prisoners. Without citing this fact, the personnel departments all gave me the same answer: "There are no vacancies available. You're not needed here." The power of the newly passed injunction was greater than the mythical constitutional right to work.

The only chance I had left was Senya Erukhimovich's promise to arrange an audition for me at the newly initiated branch of the Syktyvkar theater.

I auditioned for the role of Mary Claire in Sobko's play *Behind the Second Front,* which earned me the consent of the director to join his troupe. I was given just a couple of hours to make a decision, and if I agreed, I had to be ready to leave for Ukhta with the rest of the actors as early as midnight.

Except for Simon, an old friend from Urdoma, I had no other close friends to ask for advice. He, as well as everyone else I knew, spoke with one accord: "This is your big chance, a stroke of great luck. Don't even think twice." Thus, that same evening I was hired as an employee of a free theater.

Everything happened rapidly. My fate was determined in less than twelve hours. The spirit of arbitrariness that reigned in the camps seemed to reign here as well. Without even staying overnight at Klava's, I found myself on the train again. Yet this time it was a passenger train, Moscow—Vorkuta, and I had my own berth. I comforted myself with the thought that at least we were going north, the same direction that TEC had recently gone, too.

The theater's repertoire consisted of only two plays: Schiller's *Intrigue and Love* and Sobko's *Behind the Second Front.* The troupe was mixed: two actors from Moscow, three or four people from the provincial towns.

I became friendly with Natasha S., a graduate of the Vakhtangov Theater Studio in Moscow, who played the heroine in Sobko's play. We went to the rehearsals, performances and the canteen together. Over the past seven years, I'd grown unaccustomed to forks and knives, and every now and then I'd catch Natasha's puzzled glance as I attempted to deal with a cutlet or some other entrée with the help of a spoon. She seemed especially shocked by my manners when other people joined us at the table.

The town of Ukhta received a good supply of food and commodities. There were dresses and gowns hanging in the stores, undergarments and high-heeled shoes displayed on the shelves. Natasha would briskly ask the store clerk, "Show me this one," or "Wrap that one for me." As for me, having nearly forgotten what money was, I'd spend my travel allowance buying up toys for Yurik and cigarettes and other small things for Kolya. I ran to the post office to send out the packages, and only then would I calm down. I'd use every opportunity to get in touch with TEC, or else Kolya, each time outdoing himself in resourcefulness, would call me up by phone. I dashed off long letters to him. His letters came daily. They were the only things that kept me going.

In the first few weeks the theater did well, but then the ticket sales decreased. The money was only enough to pay actors their travel allowances, and even that wasn't always the case.

One of our shows sold only twenty tickets. The theater managers consulted with each other and decided to cancel the performance. It was 8 p.m. and we were free to do as we pleased.

TEC's itinerary ran parallel to ours. While we were in Ukhta, they were in Izhma, only twelve *versts* away. At least freedom was good for something!

I dashed to the station. There were no more trains. The last bus had departed fifteen minutes prior. Yet I could no longer turn back.

"Where's the road to Izhma?" I asked the locals.

"It's dark already. All sorts of things happen here in the forest. There are wolves, too."

The frost was turning to ice. There wasn't a soul around. I would walk for a while along the road, then run, then walk again. I needed to reach the man who longed to be with me, who was ready to endure more than anyone had ever endured before, whose love knew no limits, who wanted to make the impossible possible, who promised to give me more than any human had ever given, whose love was so great it encompassed the entire universe.

At the Izhma junction, countless tracks crisscrossed each other, and hundreds of uncoupled freight cars crowded the area. I doubted I'd ever find the right one. There was one thing, however, that distinguished the TEC cars from all the rest: barred slots under the roof, illuminated from the inside. It was already late at night when I found them and knocked. A sleepy voice answered.

I identified myself. Inside the car people stirred and shouted for Kolya. The door rumbled open and I was pulled in. I was frozen. They boiled water for me. For several hours I could be with my old friends and the man I loved.

OUR FREE THEATER went farther north, to Abez deep in the tundra. The thin northern air made me weak and drowsy. The very idea of freedom, at these northern latitudes, was mitigated by the omnipresence of the camps. We gave concerts everywhere we could manage to sell tickets.

We arrived at Inta on the day of the elections for the Supreme Soviet. Tunes of bombastic marches wafted from the black loudspeakers that hung in the streets. The blizzard maliciously tore at the banners. Every now and then reindeer and dog sleds emerged from the snowy mist and glided to the polls. People in fur coats and high fur boots were arriving from their tents in faraway villages, jumping out from under the reindeer fells and solemnly ascending the stairs of the House of Culture to give their vote to whichever candidate they were told to support. As for me, deprived of three years of civil rights, I was not allowed to participate in this "democratic" ritual.

The next morning, a more authentic picture of the town revealed itself when a file of prisoners was led past the theater to work. The local camps were known as "special regimes." Each of the passing prisoners had a dirty white scrap of cloth with a four-digit number sewn onto their quilted jackets. The sight of numbers on people's backs stirred my memory: I recalled the man who came all the way from Magadan to Leningrad in '38 with news of my father. "I've never seen him," he told us. "We all just had numbers sewn onto our backs." That was how my father, too, was led to work. Mesmerized, I waited for the hour when another batch of prisoners would pass by.

One more impression of Inta stayed with me.

A famous tenor, a soloist of the Leningrad Mariinsky Theater, Nikolay Konstantinovich Pechkovsky, who had lived here until recently, had organized a sort of studio in the town. Many called themselves his disciples. After seeing two of their performances—Ostrovsky's *At a Busy Place* and Kalman's *Maritsa*—we asked the stage director, a man named Karpov, if we could meet with the actors. The troupe was made up of both free actors and prisoners. We were allowed to meet with them under guard and instructed not to make any personal contact with the prisoner actors.

We sat down on the chairs along the wall. The soloists of the Inta Theater sang romances and arias, accompanied by the prisoner M. on the piano. As he played, he kept looking intently at me and then let his gaze fall on the lid of his instrument. I understood that he was asking me to take something from under the piano's lid. But how could I approach him without the guards noticing? I persuaded Natasha to pretend that we were so overtaken by the music that we had to rush onto the stage. When I ran up to the instrument, my intuition turned out to be right: there was a letter.

As in all special regime camps, the prisoners here were deprived of the right to correspondence. The pianist knew I was from Leningrad and was asking me to deliver the letter to his sister personally whenever I got the chance. He specified that I should not send the letter by mail.

I had no idea, however, when I'd be in Leningrad or if I'd ever be there at all.

The whole undertaking with the new branch of the Syktyvkar Theater soon proved unprofitable. The administration had to dismiss some of the actors in the middle of our tour. When I was let go, I was offered a job as a propman, albeit for a much lesser wage, which I could supplement by taking onetime episodic roles.

For someone who had just a while ago felled trees and pick-axed stone quarries, what could be humiliating about the position of a propman? Yet I was exasperated by the prospect of life on the road with no creative satisfaction and a meager wage in return. I needed a home and a decent salary in order to get my son back.

No one seemed to share my discontent, however; not even Senya Erukhimovich.

"Don't you think I deserve something better as well?" he asked. "You think I belong here? Wait for a month and a half till we come to Knyazh-Pogost. Then you'll be able to look for another job, if you really believe you can find one."

After Kolya sent me a reproachful letter, I decided to stay with the theater.

We were almost at Vorkuta when our train changed direction and headed south. Again, TEC wasn't far away. I got permission to leave one day early, which meant that I could join the rest of the troupe when they'd pass by on the train.

I bought some vodka for the guards and small items like soap, cigarettes and combs for my friends, and purchased the ticket. No one except me got off the train at the deserted station of Chikshin. The train left. Near the siding, away from the main tracks, I found two uncoupled TEC cars, heavy padlocks hanging on the doors. TEC was at the camp giving a concert.

Hiding my bags underneath one of the cars, I headed toward the zone and managed to let my friends know I was here. Someone immediately brought me the keys.

I got onto the TEC car and heated the stove. The fire cast light on the plank beds and the belongings arranged on top of them. It was the same phantasmagoria, the same surreal world. I peered out the car through the snowstorm into the darkness. Finally I made out a familiar silhouette running in my direction. Kolya had gotten permission to leave the camp before all the rest. I dashed toward him, unsure of the world around us, or if anything else even existed at all.

SPRING WAS APPROACHING, and our tour was finally over. With stops along the way, we were returning to our base in Knyazh-Pogost.

On the train, Senya Erukhimovich came up to me with a man he'd run into.

"This is Doctor Sh. He wanted to meet you."

I knew the name: he was one of Filipp's closest friends.

"So this is what you're like..." said Sh., examining me with curiosity.

"And this is what *you're* like," I replied. I didn't know what to make of him, but I sensed he was a friendly and intelligent man.

Doctor Sh. suggested we go to one of the vacant compartments so that no one would interfere in our conversation. I listened to his story of how, after he was released three years ago, he arranged for his wife and daughter to come and live with him here. "But I love another woman, and I'm on my way to visit her now," he told me. "I'm happy only with her. I can't tell my wife. She waited for me for ten years. I don't know how I'm going to cope with all of this." I hoped he'd employ the same frankness when discussing Filipp, but he just pressed his face against the window and peered for a long time into the darkness. Then he said:

"The skeletons of these zones along the tracks don't tell you much, of course. I was here in the beginning, though. I built them. I remember everyone, those who are resting now in common graves, without a proper burial or cross. Some died of hunger, some of illness."

The doctor asked about me: if I had any relatives, where I was going to look for work.

Before saying good-bye he said, as if to cheer me up or clarify something:

"I'd love to help you in some way. But you have to be strong! There are a lot of snags. There are lawyers at Filipp's day and night."

There was nothing special in his slip of the tongue, yet it bore a hole into my consciousness. Homelessness, finding a job, the five remaining years of Kolya's term, the fact that I had nowhere to take my son, as well as the thought of a future court trial—all of this was driving me to the brink of madness. I didn't want to live anymore.

On my way back to Knyazh-Pogost, I made up my mind to visit Kolya for the last time.

When I knocked on the door of the TEC car, Kolya himself answered. He was sick and had stayed back while the rest of the actors were out giving a concert.

His throat was all bandaged up.

"Why didn't you tell me? Is it tonsillitis?" I asked him.

"What are you so worried about?" he tried to calm me. "It's nothing; my glands are just a bit swollen. It'll be better soon."

I made him take off the bandage.

It was a tumor!

"It doesn't hurt!" Kolya consoled me. "Look: I use two neckties to bandage my throat, they look like a ribbon; I enter the stage. Like that. No one notices anything."

Overtaken by dread, there, in Izhma, I ran from one doctor to the next, asking them to examine Kolya.

Their diagnoses were identical: tuberculosis of the glands. Kolya had to be treated with cod-liver oil and quartz-rays. I managed to find some oil, and Kolya's admirers from the free workers arranged for several sessions of quartz therapy. But could tuberculosis of the glands be cured in the camp? Everything became reduced to one thing—Kolya's illness.

One day I mustered my courage and went to Kolya.

"Let's end it all. I can't endure this suffering, this powerlessness, this pain anymore. Do you understand? It's just too much." I meant what I was saying.

"How many times they have already attempted to cut our lives short! Mine by the firing squad, yours—by hunger and humiliation. We must not finish it ourselves. We have no right to that. But we will be happy, certainly we will. Why don't you believe this anymore?"

And again Kolya uttered the unsettling words:

"I swear to you: I will soon be on the other side of the zone!"

On the eve of my thirtieth birthday, on March 29, 1950—the year of my good fortune, as my father had predicted—I stayed overnight with my prisoner friends, on the bed that used to be my own, near the beautiful Margo.

The first thing I saw in the morning was a portrait of me that Miller, one of the TEC artists, had painted from my photograph. The portrait was Kolya's present.

Logs chirred and hissed inside the little stove. My friends had prepared poems and drawings for me, and they treated me to tea. Something softened inside my soul. Of course, we thought, life could still be kind.

DIFFERENT CONJECTURES were made regarding the future of our theater: whether all of us would be dismissed outright or if the best actors would be merged with Syktyvkar's main troupe.

An official from Syktyvkar came to decide the theater's fate. A general meeting was scheduled to take place at the Knyazh-Pogost House of Culture.

I was changing my clothes in the makeup room when someone pulled the door open. Without apologizing or closing the door, a woman stood in the doorway, examining me from the threshold.

"What do you want?" I snapped, forgetting my manners. "Can't you see there's no one else but me in here."

When I went back up to the hall, I saw the woman sitting in the chairman's place. I could only grin to myself: there had been so many times when my fate was determined by such chance encounters.

Engulfed in my own problems, I was deaf and blind to the people around me. I didn't even notice the irritation that had accumulated among the troupe members over my frequent ventures to "places one had to avoid." In addition, I failed to produce a good impression as an actress. I was fired on account of cutbacks in the theater personnel.

What remained of the troupe was sent off on a tour again. Senya Erukhimovich left, too.

Tamara Petkevich. 1950s.

(left and above) Tamara Petkevich in various theatrical roles after her release. 1950s.

Again I dragged myself from one office in Knyazh-Pogost to another in search of work, and again I received rejections everywhere. The only position I turned down myself was that of an attendant at the public bathhouse, where they had promised to hire me without delay.

The money I had earned at the theater would last me a month at most.

I decided to go to Velsk to visit my son when, unexpectedly, Dmitry brought me a long letter from Kolya. In it, Kolya insisted on an idea that at first I thought preposterous.

"Since you're going to buy a ticket to Velsk anyway, you might as well pay a bit more and go to Leningrad for five days or so. You have to visit your sister. You can see a lawyer. Maybe one of your relatives will give you some useful advice. I'm begging you, go! You might have to wait a long time for another chance. Do it for me, for yourself!"

On another piece of paper, attached to the letter, were columns of numbers: the cost of a return ticket, expenses for food and so on. Kolya had calculated everything, down to the last ruble. "You'll manage. It'll be enough. I'll save some money by the time you come back. I'll go for all my medical tests while you're away. I promise."

In the midst of the disorder I lived in, such an idea simply could not have occurred to me. There was something dazzling, loving and wild in Kolya's suggestion. It was like being offered a gulp of holy water.

I already wanted to go, and though I didn't feel ready for such an inner upheaval, I thought that this might be precisely the impetus for me finally to throw off the chains that had bound me for so long.

I wrote to the Bakharevs, asking one of them to bring Yurik to the station to meet me. I also let them know that on my way back I'd make a stop at Velsk again. I sent a letter to Valechka in Leningrad, too.

By coincidence, Simon was going to Leningrad at the same time on business. Since his release three years ago, he had made use of the opportunities that freedom offered in an original way: he became a salesman for one of the local industries and traveled to the capitals with goods produced in the Komi Republic—a "commivoyageur," as he joked, "a voyageur from Komi." The main thing for him was to visit Moscow and Leningrad as often as possible, where he'd meet with old friends, go to the theaters and buy books to add to his splendid personal library. We set off together.

Arriving in Velsk, I saw my son through the window. I jumped down to the ground from the footboard and, stretching out my hands, ran to him. As if he could feel the enormity of my impulse, my four-year-old boy broke away from Vera Petrovna and dashed toward me, too. I twirled him in my arms, he laughed, and as long as the train stood at the station, we both believed we would be happy together in the future.

Seeing Simon, whom she knew back from Urdoma, Vera Petrovna pulled herself up and attempted a smile.

Of course, I wanted to take Yurochka with me to Leningrad and had even written to Filipp about this. He hailed me with a series of counterarguments, which I accepted, lacking any confidence about what my trip would be like, in the end.

WE HAD LEFT BEHIND Vologda and were already passing by Cherepovets. I peered out the window, hoping to see the Suda River, the river that, fifteen years ago, on a warm white night filled with the singing of nightingales, my family crossed together on a ferry while visiting Papa.

We were arriving in Leningrad early in the morning. The train slowed down. People waiting on the platform came into view. I saw Valechka: instead of a fourteen-year-old girl, she was now a beautiful, mature young woman. Struck by how we both had changed after nine years apart, unable to restrain ourselves, we sobbed. It was still hard for me to believe, even as I held her in my arms, that this grown-up person was once my skinny little Valechka.

The scene had an effect on Simon. He invited us for breakfast, but my sister had to hurry to work.

"You'll stay with Aunt Dunya. She's expecting you."

"What about you?"

"I live in a dormitory. There's no space."

Upon her return from the orphanage in Uglich, Valechka had sent numerous petitions asking the city authorities to give her back the room we used to own, but all her requests were denied.

As we were leaving the station, my heart leapt in anticipation of seeing the long arrow of Nevsky Prospect, the gilding of the Admiralty Spire, the symmetrical dignity of the buildings and streets. I had never imagined I'd see my hometown again.

Spring was in full swing, the sun was blinding.

"Let's have breakfast at the Eastern Café, by Hotel Evropeyskaya," Simon suggested.

I remembered the modest and elegant café.

"Order!" said Simon, handing me the menu.

"Sausages," I said mechanically.

My friend looked at me with reproach. The next moment he was telling the waiter, "Two hundred grams of sour-cream each, two pieces of toast with caviar, a salad, an egg and coffee for two."

I kept staring at the delicacies.

We exited the café and wandered over to the gorgeous Brodsky Street and to the Philharmonic. A man paced in our direction. When he saw Simon, they hugged each other.

"Mikhail Svetlov," the man introduced himself.

A young lady ran up to him:

"I need to talk to you!"

He turned to her and said sarcastically:

"Then try harder!"

I had completely forgotten such language existed. It seemed amusing, and so far off.

When I turned to go to Aunt Dunya's, Simon instructed me:

"Cross the street only at the crosswalks. If a policeman stops you, pay the fine right away, without any questions. No matter what, don't show him your passport. Say you forgot it at home, if he asks. Those caught in the city with a '39' stamp in their passports are immediately deported—and not in a passenger train, but in a prisoner wagon."

There was a popular joke at the time: "How are you?" one would ask a friend in the street. "Not bad, thanks," the other would answer, "Though my fever has jumped to 39."

AUNT DUNYA, whom we used to stay with in Byelorussia, the one who informed me in Frunze that Mama had died, didn't gasp in surprise when she saw me and barely asked any questions. As I followed her into the room, I didn't immediately understand why I felt so uneasy. But when I looked around, I saw our furniture! There were our table and chairs, and even the oilcloth with black ink stains, a memory of my little sisters diligently doing their homework. On the wall hung our mirror in the intricately ornate bronze frame, whose sharp edge had left me with a scar on my forehead.

The Leningrad of the siege had its own secrets and rights. I didn't dare touch upon them, although my heart ached from what I saw.

I was preparing myself for a confessional conversation with Valechka: I wanted to know how everything happened with Mama and Renochka. I waited to confide in my sister. But after meeting with her several times, I realized she was avoiding this subject, which would only stir up pain hibernating deep within her. I tried many ways to get close to her but was surprised by how difficult it was turning out to be.

My sister was a worker at the Mechanical Factory on the Obvodny Canal. The war, the siege and her illness hadn't allowed her even to finish school. I talked her into allowing me to see her dorms. The room she lived in was enormous, with beds for sixteen or eighteen girls. Some sat on their beds with their young men; others were eating or strumming their guitars.

Her roommates peered at us with curiosity.

"You look just the same! Where has your sister come from?"

"From far away. She works in the North," Valechka replied on my behalf. Fearing my obscure past, my sister must have kept secret the very fact I existed.

"Do you at least have a coat?" I tried to break through the wall between us.

"Don't talk nonsense, Tamusya. Of course, I do," she evaded my question.

"What about friends? Is there a young man?"

"Everybody has one, and so do I," she replied, avoiding any further candor even on this issue.

Only once did she open up to me, very briefly:

"Before she died, Mama tried to instill one thing in us: 'At any price, get in touch with Tomochka! I don't know how, but you must find her!'"

I was overridden with guilt for what happened to my family, and I'd apologized a thousand times in my mind for leaving them behind and going to Frunze. But it turned out there was no reason for us to speak about this. Another tragedy was taking shape, and I had to give it a name: my younger sister did not need me.

I didn't ask her to accompany me to our old apartment, where, the last time I'd been back, I heard Renochka laughing on her way home from school, and where Mama's body was thrown out onto the stairwell.

But I did ask my sister to come with me to the apartment we'd lived in on Vasilievsky Island.

A woman opened the door.

"We used to live here. Would you mind if we took a quick look around?"

"Come in, come in, girls! You're sisters, right? I can tell."

Inside everything was different. Amid the new furniture, however, there was our kingly oak-wood sideboard, which Mama decided to leave behind when she swapped this apartment for a smaller one.

"Our sideboard!" both of us exclaimed at once.

"Take it, my darlings! It means a lot to you," the woman offered.

Random kindness—a sign of postwar times.

"No, no, thank you! We have nowhere to put it anyway," we refused.

We asked if Father had come to look for us.

"No, no one came, no one asked."

For a few minutes we stood in the courtyard of our childhood.

"Remember when Yura Buchel once beat you up here, and I knocked him on the head with a log?"

We told each other more stories like this. And then I asked Valechka if she wanted to drop in at my school friend David's apartment.

We rang the doorbell. David's mother came to the door.

"Oh, God! Look who's here, look who has come, who's standing here in the doorway!" she cried.

She pulled us inside the apartment.

David was home, too. A young beautiful woman stood beside him.

"This is my wife, Lisa," David introduced her.

"What a day, what a holiday!" Sofya Zakharovna lamented. "Get the wine. We were just going to have dinner. And your mother... Your father... You had such beautiful parents! Oh, what a dreadful disaster, what grief..." she kept saying, shaking her head and bustling about to give us the warmest welcome she could.

David looked dismayed, as if embarrassed by something. He barely asked any questions.

After seeing our former home and my old friend's apartment, where everything, including the velvet curtain that divided one of the rooms in half, stood just as before, I couldn't control myself anymore and sobbed.

"Come visit us, please!" I heard behind my back as we turned to leave. "Tamarochka, Valechka, you are always welcome!"

NO ONE KNEW where Mama and Renochka had been buried. Nor was it known in what part of the vast country my father had perished, given that he never came back.

Not finding solace anywhere, I went to church. A great many grief-stricken people thronged to churches in 1950. I lit a candle for my family and kneeled, praying for higher powers to give me back my son, to have mercy on Kolya, to help me find shelter in life.

I longed to touch the stones of my tragic city with my heart, so limitless was my love for it. I sprawled across the marble stairs of St. Isaac's Cathedral, pressing myself against them.

Still trying to seep back into my past, I set out to visit my old dear friend Ninochka Izenberg. I remembered the house, but not the staircase—whether it was from the main entrance or from the courtyard.

Like David's mother, the mother of Nina, Nina Aleksandrovna, screamed when she saw me:

"My God, is that you, Tamara? Alive? From where?"

Ninochka held my hand and looked into my eyes. She was more than a friend—a rare, astonishing creature who had a natural gift to bring calm into people's hearts.

"So you stayed in Leningrad during the entire war?" I asked them.

"From beginning to end. We discarded bombs from the roofs, extinguished firebombs; we nearly starved to death. But we survived, miraculously," they recounted in turns.

Nothing could be compared to the siege, to the deaths of my mother and sister.

"How frightening the blockade must have been, I can't even imagine!"

"What can I say? It couldn't be worse than all you've been through..." Nina's mother replied. "I'll go down to the bakery; I want to get you your favorite 'Napoleon' and 'Buche' cakes."

A convulsion ran through my heart: someone remembered my favorite pastries!

Everything in Nina's cozy apartment was where it always used to be: the same lusterless lampshades on the wall lamps, the chandelier of pink glass above the round table, white chairs and armchairs, jardinières, bookshelves. I had imagined that during the siege all the books had been burned, all the glass objects broken. This home reminded me of a world that used to exist. On one of the shelves I saw my favorite antique edition of Vladimir Solovyov.

"What about *The Gorbatov Family?* Do you still have it? And Krzhizhanovskaya?"

"Yes, all in their places."

"Tell me about yourself, Ninochka."

"I'm married. But I'm getting divorced."

"Why? Who is he?"

"He's a chemist. There's no quick way to explain it. He's against the church, and Mama and I believe in God."

"Who else is still in Leningrad?"

"Liza is here. White Kirill was killed at the front, Nura was also killed."

"Nura?"

"Amosova. Oh, you didn't know her. She's my wartime friend."

I had exactly the same feeling: I wanted to speak of my friends from the

North as if they were Ninochka's friends, too.

"What about Borya Magarshak, Ilya Granovsky, Noy Levin—are they alive?" I wanted to know. "Is Asya Chizhikova still around?"

"I haven't seen them. I don't know. I saw Vladimir D. He's a military doctor now. He asked about you... Your hair is still the same. Your eyes have changed."

I had promised myself not to ask about Roksana and Nord, the ones who had denounced me. Maybe some time in the future, but not now. Yet in spite of myself, I found myself asking the question.

"Roksana's still here, the scarecrow!" Nina's mother replied. "I'd ask you about everything, but I'm afraid to cause you pain," she added.

"Ask! Don't be afraid. Now it's only the distant past that hurts. Everything else that happened... it's as if it happened to someone else, not to me.

With unexpected straightforwardness, Nina Aleksandrovna spoke up:

"Don't think I'm worming myself into your confidence, but they have ruined your life! Who are you now? Not a wife. Not a mother. You don't have a city or even a roof above your head. You weren't able to finish the institute. It's scary even to think about it! I can imagine how you hate them!"

I was ashamed to admit that at the moment I felt no hatred. It still lay deep at the bottom of the well. I hadn't had time yet to distance myself from what I'd been through for the hatred to surface. But I well knew that when all was said and done, a feeling much larger than hatred would sweep over me.

Everywhere in Leningrad I was greeted with warmth, love and memory. Aunt Maria cried as she rummaged through her things, looking for something to give me as a present. Hearing my voice in the phone receiver, my guardian artist Lily screamed:

"Where are you? I'll catch a taxi and come right away! Or you come. It was me who talked you into leaving for Frunze! It was my fault."

When she saw me, she choked up with tears.

"Had you not listened to me then, this nightmare would never have happened!"

I tried to dissuade her, but she kept on believing in her own guilt.

Other people's compassionate words not only moved me but also rejuvenated parts of my life. Liza, whom I found at the address that Nina had given me, cried bitterly and every now and then jumped to her feet:

"Have something to eat. Lie down! Have a rest. Take a bath. I'll sit with you. I need to have a good look at you." And then: "You know, Tomochka, when hunger broke out, there was only one question that kept my heart and brain going: how to get in touch with you, how to get to you, wherever you were. I couldn't think of anything else. Even after we'd been loaded onto the train to Birobidzhan, I still thought I'd jump out, change trains. I longed to see you, to endure this nightmare together with you."

People asked about the present only in passing, gladdened merely by the fact that I was alive. No one knew how to deal with me, how to reconcile themselves to the fact that I'd been arrested and imprisoned. The disasters of war were still fresh in their memories, and although sympathetic, they gravitated to recovery rather than to illness.

BEFORE I LEFT LENINGRAD, I still had to take the letter from the pianist in Inta to his sister. I was short of time. When I came in the afternoon, she wasn't home. Valechka and I went to her place for the second time around eleven at night. A neighbor opened up:

"M.? The room over there, the third one along the corridor."

I knocked on the door, but there was silence. I knocked again. No answer. We were turning to leave when a female voice exploded behind the door:

"Have you no shame? Why do you disturb people at home when it's time to go to sleep? Outrageous!"

"I'm sorry," I said. "I came in the afternoon, too. Can I talk to you for one minute?"

"Go away!" the woman yelled from behind the door. "Isn't it enough that you give me no peace at work? Now you've come to annoy me at home?"

Valechka was indignantly pulling me away by the sleeve: "Let's leave immediately! How can you?" But I could not leave. Pressing my lips to a slit in the door, I whispered:

"It's you who needs me!"

The woman, enraged, in a dressing gown hurriedly thrown over her shoulders, thrust the door open:

"And what do I need you for?" she hissed.

"I brought you a letter from your brother. He asked me to give it you in person."

She took a step back into her room.

"From whom?"

"From your brother, M."

"Quiet! For God's sake, quiet! Come here."

I turned to leave that apartment at once, but she grabbed me by the arm. Valechka was already waiting for me by the front door. The woman dashed to bring her back.

"Come back, I beg you!" she implored, then turned back to me: "Forgive me! Oh, God! I don't understand: where're you from?"

"From there."

"Why, you actually saw him?"

"I did."

"Alive? When?"

"A month ago."

"Is he emaciated? How was he dressed?"

"He was wearing a jacket. I don't remember what color."

"It can't be true! Is his head shaven?"

"No. He's got a head of hair."

"His hair? He still has it? Black? It's so magnificent!"

She covered her mouth with both hands so as not to burst out crying. She tore open the envelope and greedily consumed the lines scribbled by her brother's hand. She fell to her knees:

"Forgive me! What a welcome I gave you. I'll never be forgiven for this. I work at Smolny. Every day I have to admit thousands of visitors. All of them write petitions. They nose out my home address and come here. Try to understand! Forgive me."

I understood: at one end of her life there was Smolny and the Party, at the other—her brother, with a number sewn on the back of his camp jacket. It wasn't easy to live in between.

My sister and I walked in silence for a long time. Then, with an acute openness, she suddenly said:

"I have this feeling that you're a stranger! That some time ago you used to be my sister, but then something happened, and… well, that you died."

"Why, Valechka?" I asked, suppressing the pain.

"I don't know."

"Try to explain. It's important to me."

"I can't. You're from some different life. I don't understand you."

"Am I too gloomy? And everything around me is gloomy, is that it? I cry too much?"

"No. You're even trying to be cheerful, but I don't believe it."

"You don't believe what?"

"Well, you're somehow a stranger."

Everything grew cold inside me. I wanted to cry out, "Don't call me a stranger, my only sister! I'm close to you, I'm part of you."

Left without any support, Valechka had surmounted all of her misfortunes on her own. The name of her elder sister had become a vacant sound to her. She didn't know how before my arrest I tried to get her out of the orphanage, or what I had undertaken to try to bring her over to Frunze. She was right: I tried to pretend I didn't have a past. I was afraid to scare her off. But that only distanced us from each other.

The next day, a relative of ours told me: "You shouldn't take Valya along to all those places. Leave her soul alone. Don't burden us. Even your merrymaking is somehow always turned upside down."

Defending her, Aunt Dunya explained:

"You mustn't be angry. Her son was killed during the war. Her husband died suddenly of a heart attack. Her nerves are shot. She tells me, 'I can't look at those miserable sisters, I can't stand seeing them.'"

I longed to leave back for the North.

Only Valechka came to see me off at the station. Withdrawn into her thoughts for a long while, she couldn't hold back the question:

"So tell me: what were you in for?"

It was a normal question. After all, there had to be some reason for a person to go to prison for seven years. What could an answer like, "For nothing" mean to my sister? To her it would merely be a lie, my reluctance to be open.

She pitied me with all her confused heart:

"Take care of yourself. Come visit me, Tamusya!"

IN VELSK, I found an acquaintance of mine from Urdoma, who had offered to let me stay at her place and even to bring my son, so that we could be alone.

Filipp was away.

"He entrusted everything to me," Vera Petrovna informed me when we met.

Yurochka was hunched up and kept looking back at Vera Petrovna.

"Why did you buy all of these things for him? We don't need anything," she scolded me again.

"I'll be coming soon to take Yurik, Vera Petrovna!"

"You're not settled yet. Won't you feel bad? It'll be worse for the child at your place than at ours."

"Being with his mother can never be worse for a child!"

"Filipp told me not to get into any sort of discussions with you."

"You just said he entrusted everything to you."

"That's right—not to abandon Yurochka."

"Not to abandon him?"

"Not to leave him alone with you."

"What does that mean?"

"Ask Filipp yourself."

"I will take my son for a walk."

"No, Tamara Vladislavovna. That's improper. Everything's out in the open here. No need for unnecessary rumors. I'll be bringing him over. There's enough going on without that."

I couldn't bear her confident, proprietary tone. I refused to admit she had full rights over my son, or to feel that I owed her anything. But I was also afraid of a confrontation with her and Filipp.

I was tormented by shame that I'd proved so inept and confused when faced with freedom. Valechka's story about Mama's last words, "Try to get in touch with Tomochka," and Liza's confession, "There was only one question: how to get to you, wherever you were," kept coming back to me. Valya and Liza believed in me, but Vera Petrovna's argument, "You're not settled yet," reduced this belief to naught. As always, there was only one way out: to surpass both the circumstances and myself, to compress energy, to explode! Even a fish, knocking about wildly on a sheet of ice, sometimes manages to find its way back into the water.

IN KNYAZH-POGOST, I found out that Kolya had not been put in the infirmary, even though there was no visible improvement of his condition. TEC was away on tour.

Again, I searched for work. And again, "No vacancies."

Klava installed a trestle-bed for me in her little shack and gave me a blanket. Coming home from the hospital, where she was a nurse, she would swill vodka and tipsily sing melancholy songs. "I'm telling you, you won't find anything!" she would tell me over and over again. "Do you understand what we're living for?" she'd ask me the cheerful question.

She had taken her daughter from the orphanage. Although Klava was a kind person, she would lose control and beat her. Eventually, Klava poisoned herself and died.

In the evenings I'd visit Senya Erukhimovich's relatives. His sister was working at the town administration.

"Teach me to type, Fira! Maybe I'll find work as a typist."

"All right. Start!" And she'd put the typewriter before me.

Having nothing to eat, I maintained my pride: "No, I'm not hungry, thank you. Everything's fine."

Once, after yet another futile attempt to find a job in Knyazh-Pogost, I was on my way back to Klava's in a downcast mood. A couple I knew, a husband and wife, crossed the street and walked in my direction. They approached and handed me a loaf of bread.

"Take it, Tamara. You don't need to explain anything to us. We've been through it ourselves."

Only one of my efforts turned out to be successful. After besieging the information bureaus of various southern towns, I managed to find Kolya's mother. I got hold of her address in Kirovabad and triumphantly told Kolya. The son found his mother, the mother—her son. Darya Vasilyevna wrote me a letter:

> My dear daughter, Tamara! I received both of your letters, so dear to my life and my heart. First of all, I kiss you as Kolya's mother and, from now on, as your mother, too. I give my motherly blessing for your life together with Kolya and with me, if Fate has mercy on us and allows this to happen. Live well, love each other until your last days. God pitied us: Instead of sorrow, He sent us happiness, which is you, my dear daughter Tamara. I can't describe all the worries and anguish I have endured in the past ten years. I will only tell you that I looked for my son everywhere, and that you returned him to me. I am a mother again!

Darya Vasilyevna wanted to know how she could help Kolya. As for herself, she didn't have her own place and lived with a strange family. I forwarded Kolya her letters, whose artlessness moved me deeply, and begged him to respond as soon as possible. Kolya hesitated. I understood how he felt, having to burden his mother's soul with the news that he wasn't in exile, as I'd written to her, but in a camp.

THE REASONS BEHIND the persecution of ex-prisoners in 1950 were finally revealed, in full, in a most unprecedented way.

The main troupe of the Syktyvkar Theater arrived in Knyazh-Pogost to give a few concerts. They were staging Semyon Babaevsky's *Cavalier of the Golden Star.* Senya Erukhimovich invited me to go see the performance. After all, it was still a better way to spend time than watching Klava sit with her bottle. The show, however, was boring, and my mood was heavy. Promising Senya to stop by in the morning, I left after the first act. Senya stayed to watch the play to the end.

In the morning, arriving in the center of the settlement, where Senya's family lived, I saw his sister Fira running along the wood-boarded sidewalk. Her face was swollen, her hair tousled. She saw me and ran toward me.

"Quick, come to our place. They arrested Senya!"

"What's wrong with you, Fira! What're you talking about? Tell me intelligibly."

"After the concert, two men were waiting. He was arrested right in the street."

It was incredible, unthinkable. I couldn't help but ask the same enduring question, "What for?"

Senya's mother, half-insane, was shrieking: "My son! My boy, come home!"

An acquaintance who worked at the administration came running to their apartment and called me to come with him.

When we arrived, I was surrounded by former prisoners, released in '47. They were tearing me to pieces with questions.

"You went on tour together. Do you think he could've pocketed some ticket money? Did he say anything he shouldn't have? Try to remember! Maybe you noticed something?"

I couldn't console the agitated crowd. Their faces were gray and fallen. They desperately looked to each other for answers.

"What's there to understand?" one of them finally said in a heavy voice. "The second round of the '37 arrests has begun. And they started with the Jews."

I only wondered, "What do the Jews have to do with it?"

Fira sought permission to visit her brother. Taking the quilted jacket I used to wear in the camp, I went with her. Senya's explanations confirmed that which could only be attributed to the satanic psychosis of the regime.

"There are no new charges," he said. "The same ones I was arrested for in the first place. They take me for interrogations to Syktyvkar. I got a note from Tolubenko. He was there in another cell. He says he hadn't been pressed with any new charges either. They told us we'll be exiled to Siberia for life."

In Syktyvkar, they arrested Mira Galpern. Her husband, Aleksey Linkevich, followed soon after. In Kursk, they found Tamara Tsulukidze and rearrested her as well. Again, fear hovered above us for all twenty-four hours of each day. People were setting aside dried crusts of bread in anticipation.

No, it was not 1937. It was 1950. The arrests were not so brazen. They were no longer cutting people down in their heydays but merely finishing off those they hadn't yet completely annihilated. They were robbing the robbed, those who had no tears left to cry. Unlike 1937, people laughed, or at least tried to.

"O-la-la, it looks like we're safe for today!" a French friend of mine would repeat every evening.

Lev Frug, a witty man, joked:

"Are you trying to figure out their scheme? There is none. We'd do better to simply buy a ticket to Krasnoyarsk ourselves, turn up before the local bosses and say, 'Here we are!' At least that way we won't have to travel in the Stolypin prisoner cars."

HELLA FRISHER and our Chinese friend Shan came back after being fired from the theater in Ust-Kulom. Miraculously, Shan managed to find work at the Syktyvkar Puppet Theater. Tarno, a Romanian who used to work as a pharmacist at the Mikun railway clinic, arranged a job for Hella as a matron-nurse there. Both of them started thinking of a place for me, too. I relied on my "international connections," and one day they worked.

I was invited for an interview precisely at the moment when Kolya was being taken to the Central Camp infirmary. Mikun, where the clinic was situated, stood about a hundred kilometers away from Knyazh-Pogost. Though it seemed unthinkable to leave when Kolya needed me the most, in order to fight his illness he had to have a better diet, at the very least. I needed to earn money.

The chief doctor in Mikun promised to hire me as an attendant.

"The salary is three hundred rubles. I'm not offering you any lodging. In a couple of months I could try to transfer you to some better position."

I agreed.

Hella had found shelter with the Shpakov family, a husband and wife who occupied the larger room of a two-room apartment, while the second, smaller room was taken by a geologist. Hella slept in the kitchen on the floor, on the left-hand side. I was offered a mattress on the right.

Kolya could finally stop worrying about me. I wrote to him that I was working and living in warmth and comfort, and that now it was his health that was our main concern. Here, I told him, I could even find whatever medication he needed.

Indeed, the kind pharmacist, Tarno, promised to prescribe me anything we might need. As an employee of the railway clinic, I received a pass for free train travel, and on the eve of a day off I'd always speed to Knyazh-Pogost, spending the night at Klava's and hoping to pass some food and medications to Kolya through an old acquaintance, or at least to find out about his condition.

I reproached Kolya for not having answered his mother. He promised he would, but for some reason he kept putting it off. Then suddenly I got his letter, in which the truth stormed like a tornado.

> I feel very bad, Tomochka! I can't hide this from you. It's a pity you already told Mama that I'm alive. Perhaps there was no need to reopen her old wounds.

> Of what use can I be to her, already old, sick and lonely. She is a person who has lived all her life in hopeless poverty and daily misery. Forgive me, my dear, for this letter. I couldn't find enough strength to write it the way it is for a long time. But I must be honest with you. It's very hard for me now, not only today, but also yesterday, and the day before yesterday, too. The tumors are the same... Now there is a fever as well.

In Knyazh-Pogost, I found the address of the camp doctor. We didn't know each other, and she received me with hostility. Pleading with her to hear me through, I asked her to do everything she could, and couldn't, for Kolya, and to give me advice on what medications to bring. "He's only thirty-two! He's talented, kind, handsome; he's been through war. Our love defeated the camp itself! I found his mother. After ten years, the mother regained her son. He has to be put back on his feet, please!"

Gradually, the doctor thawed out.

"He's got tuberculosis of the glands. It's an unpleasant disease, but I could send him to a tuberculosis camp."

"No. That's not enough. We need a group of doctors," I answered, growing bolder.

In Knyazh-Pogost I believed I'd be able to persuade the best doctors there were to examine Kolushka.

"Please, allow me! I'll talk them into looking at him! Just give your permission and don't take it personally."

"All right," she nodded. "Anyway, they'll only confirm my diagnosis. And it won't be easy for them to get into the zone."

I understood that well. But there was Kolya, languishing behind the barbed wire. If he wrote to me, "I feel bad," it meant he was feeling insufferably horrible.

Among the stars of local medicine, Doctor Perelman was the only one I knew personally. I wasn't acquainted with Doctors Landa or Abraham. Dr. Landa, previously a famous professor, lived in a flea-pit dormitory together with Simon. In the evenings they played chess. Simon helped me persuade him. Other friends asked Doctor Abraham until he agreed, too.

At first, the Third Department of the Northern Railway Camp did not approve of showing the patient, who was a prisoner, to the free doctors. Yet the doctors pleaded, claiming it was a rare case and begging the commandants to make an exception.

After examining Kolya, they asked to repeat all the medical tests. Kolushka sensed he was no longer left to the mercy of fate alone and livened up. His letters became more confident: "I'm feeling better. The pain has receded. I'm improving. Only my fever is still high..."

I remembered how once Kolushka had forgotten the text while reciting the story from stage. He had never told me much about the German concentration camps, but once he mentioned in passing, "They exposed some of us to radiation."

I went to talk with each doctor separately, trying to make them say more.

"Wait for the test results. In a couple of weeks everything will be clear."

I was still holding out hope that Kolya would recover when a letter from Simon was delivered to Mikun by courier. Simon wrote that all the procedures were being properly carried out and that Doctor Perelman had seen Kolya today. He diagnosed Kolya with tubercular meningitis. Doctor Abraham was going to visit Kolya tomorrow. Yet Kolya's condition was very bad and Simon didn't know if Kolya would pull through. I had to stay strong.

I rushed to Knyazh-Pogost immediately and again went to speak with the doctors. Doctor Abraham, without dropping his eyes, said it was lymphogranuloma, while Doctor Landa diagnosed a worse condition: lymphosarcoma. "It was a crime to give him quartz therapy!" he added. Neither of them had much hope for Kolya.

But Kolya himself believed in recovery and passionately wanted to live.

I barely recall even being at work. I went to Knyazh-Pogost daily, bringing Kolushka medications and food.

The three infirmary barracks stood at the northern side of Central Camp. I'd asked Kolya in my letters to try to get transferred to the first barracks on the other side of the fence, which was directly behind Klava's house.

I would take a hammer and nails and, pretending I was doing some repairs, climb to the roof of the house and catch a glimpse of Kolya in his ward, through the window. I'd send him a note beforehand, and he'd wait for my appearances on the roof, which he called "sunrises." He'd come to the window, and sometimes he was even able to give me a sign to let me know how he was feeling. In a letter he would then specify:

> I was looking through the window, waiting for your dear face to show up. I thought your chimney was the third, but you appeared by the second. I can't see the second chimney from here—one of the fence boards, the one holding the lamp, is too high. So it wasn't until you showed up by the third chimney that I came to the window...

The guards in the watchtowers would yell: "Hey, climb down!" But Kolushka waited for "sunrises," and I'd climb back to the roof again. The more zealous guards pointed their machine guns at me and ordered me to climb down.

When it was raining, I couldn't always get a grip on the flimsy boards. I'd slide to the ground and climb back again. Gradually the guards got used to it and stopped noticing me. I'd nod my head in their direction to thank them.

Zhora Bondarevsky and Seryozha Alliluev, who had been dismissed from TEC after another wave of regime tightening, visited Kolushka in the zone. They kept consoling me: "He very much wants to recover! He'll get back on his feet."

But Kolya could no longer make it to the window.

Standing on the roof, peering over the fence into the windows of the infirmary barracks, I could hardly discern him waving his hands at me from his bed.

Kolya's camp doctor, Irina Grigorievna, now gave me permission to visit her at home at any time. One time when I went to talk to her, she started crying:

"He is a beautiful man! I didn't know a man can love as passionately as he loves you. When I came to check on him today, he asked me: 'What color are your shoes, doctor? Oh, when will I be able to buy shoes like these for my Tomik? I want her to click her heels like you do.'"

I puzzled over why he'd had to ask the doctor about the color of her shoes.

"He can't turn his head? Why?"

"It's the metastasis. He's become very nervous. It's frightening sometimes."

Life turned into sheer torment. I covered one page of a notebook after another, writing letters to Kolya. I composed fairy tales. I longed to transfuse my energy into him. I climbed to the roof time and again. I needed to be with him all the time, or at least to be constantly near Central Camp. I asked my acquaintances again to see if some job could be found for me in Knyazh-Pogost.

By the standards of the time, Ilya Evseevich's life had turned out better than most. He hadn't been rearrested. His wife and his two wonderful daughters had come to live with him. He was working at his old place. I knew he was looking for some work for me. When he suddenly called and told me to drop in at the administration, I ran there immediately.

"Tamara," he said. "What you're doing is inadmissible. You're maintaining contact with the camp. People tell the most incredible rumors about you. They say you even climb up on the roof there. How can you expect friends to petition on your behalf? Do you think I don't want to correspond with Aleksandr Osipovich? You know what he means to me. I would give up a lot just to have one game of chess with him! But we're all hanging by a thread. They can rearrest us any time. You have to understand this."

He kept talking, but I was suffocating.

The door to his office opened and Simon peeked in:

"Simon, Simon!" Ilya Evseevich spoke up. "Come in! Tell her yourself, bring her to reason. She must calm down. I'm telling her, but it's like talking to a wall. She simply doesn't know how to behave."

Simon's words cleaved the stifling air:

"Ilya, you're a scoundrel. Leave her alone. She's doing this because she can't do otherwise."

A minute ago it seemed that Ilya's logic wound itself into a noose that would have strangled me to death. Simon's rebuff returned breath to me. Indeed, during those dark days he was my most sensible friend.

"Take the key from my room, have a rest. You're completely exhausted, running back and forth. I'll find a place for myself, don't worry. Take some money, too. Not for yourself, for Nikolay!"

My brain was working in wild ways. I joined in a conspiracy with the dark, dim powers. At night, something would nudge me out of bed: "If you get up and make it to the forest barefoot, he'll live." I would get up and go. It wasn't until I carried out what I had ordered myself to do that I'd be able to find peace again for an hour or so.

Ilya Evseevich's scolding turned out to be helpful insofar as it plunged me back into reality. I suddenly grasped that instead of climbing up to the roof I must enter the zone, see Kolya and embrace him!

The very name of the head of the Third Department, Astakhov, gave everyone shivers. He was the one who sent people away on transports or to the punishment camps, sanctioned arrests and administered interrogations inside the camp. I had never had any personal contact with him, but I made up my mind to go and ask to be allowed through the checkpoint.

I rolled like a tsunami, ready to sweep everything on my way, toward the Third Department's one-story building with barred windows.

People attempted to talk me out of it: "You're crazy. Once you're in, he simply won't let you back out." Dmitry Karayanidi blocked my way: "Don't do this. They'll arrest you." But nothing could stop me.

"I need to see the commandant!"

"He's not in."

I waited outside the building until I finally saw him measuring his paces to his "headquarters."

"I need to talk to you."

"What's the matter?"

"I'll tell you when you admit me."

Without receiving an answer, I followed him in. He made a gesture to the guards to let me through. He sat at his desk, unhurriedly flipped through some papers and pointed me to the chair in front of him. I didn't let my eyes down under his metallic, annihilating gaze.

"What is it?"

"Give me permission to enter the camp to see a patient."

He looked at me again with his icy eyes.

"On what grounds?"

"We love each other. You know it."

"Do you understand what you're asking for?"

"Yes!"

He looked steadily into my eyes. I stubbornly gazed back at him. Without further words, he drew out a notebook and wrote me the permit.

No one believed me when, having bought food, I ran up to Central Camp's checkpoint. The steel-eyed warder Sergeev phoned the Third Department to double-check.

My friends were standing inside the zone, near the checkpoint, waiting for me. Without stopping or saying a single word to them, I headed to the infirmary barracks.

No sooner had I opened the door of Kolushka's ward than, without turning his head, he exclaimed in a broken voice:

"Is it you? I know it's you!"

And I saw him.

Metastatic tumors had paralyzed his arms and legs. They were scattered, like lifeless lumps, all over. But he was alive, overfilled with hope and almost happy!

Petrified, I tried to smile, talk and console him.

"I knew you'd come! I knew my Tomik wouldn't abandon me!" he said, fervent joy in his voice. "See? But I will recover. Sit here. I need to see you better."

All of a sudden, his vivacity converted itself into a sober, sharp question:

"Why aren't you crying?"

I didn't have the right to take this question to heart.

"They'll release you based on your health. I'll take you away from here," I whispered.

"Will you come again? Will you? Promise me!" His hands were holding mine with faith and passion.

My time was running out.

"Of course! I promise. Don't doubt that, my darling. I'll come!"

KOLUSHKA NO LONGER had the strength to write letters himself. Instead, I started receiving semiliterate notes written by a criminal, who was Kolya's neighbor at the infirmary.

> Tamara, I try to help him and often scold him because he doesn't eat anything and only drinks water. Can you tell him he should eat? Believe me, he dreams of you day and night. When you came to visit him, after you left he tore his hair and bit through his lip. I asked him not to be so put out. On Monday the doctors are meeting again to discuss his case. Good-bye. Regards! Mikhail.

I went to the Third Department again, though this time with less energy: now I knew the truth myself and could no longer find solace in assuming that others were just exaggerating Kolya's condition.

Astakhov, informed about Kolushka's health, didn't ask me a single question and signed a permit for the second visit.

Coming back from that meeting with Kolya, I wrote in my notebook:

> I won't be able to live on after you. My heart is turned off. I have no more power. Life is loathsome. When I see an emaciated, sick face, I pray that Fate leaves you if only like that. If only a cripple, it doesn't matter. If only your heart could beat near me. There was everything in our dreadful farewell on the day of my release, back in January: omen, despair...

In the end, Kolushka wrote a short letter to his mother. But what could I tell her now? Indeed, what had I done, having found her?!

Mikhail, Kolushka's neighbor at the infirmary, diligently sent daily reports:

> At 4 in the morning he asked to eat. We fed him: one tomato, one egg, 300 grams of milk and some butter. Believe me, Tamara, he never ate like that before. He is very kind. He gives me a peach, or something like that, but, I never allow myself to have anything of that. I know how you struggle to get these products. I pity you very much. You have so much worry, you spend your last kopeck. I'm asking you again: don't buy expensive foods. He still has several cubes of chocolate, 2 cans of condensed milk. He was raving all night long. He was asking you to come and was telling you different things—that he would kiss your feet and that you know how devoted he is to you. Tamara, today in the morning he asked us to help him sit up. Believe me, that

> has never happened before. He sat for about three minutes. I'm begging you, dear, you're still so young: don't worry. Respectfully, Mikhail.

In these letters, written by an eighteen-year-old criminal, as strange as it may have seemed, I found answers to all questions.

EARLY IN THE MORNING on June 27, I arrived in Knyazh-Pogost on a train from Mikun. In my pocket I had the third permit to visit Kolushka. I could wash his face and tuck in his blanket with my own hands.

A man and a woman, neither of whom I knew, approached me on the platform.

"Be strong, Tamara Vladislavovna, take heart. Your Kolya died today. Around five in the morning."

I was somewhere. I don't remember, I don't know where...

Suddenly a thought slashed through me: They will throw him, my Kolushka, into a common grave for prisoners! I won't know where. My mother was thrown out onto the staircase in Leningrad. Renochka's body was dumped somewhere else. My father, too, was tossed into a pit somewhere in Kolyma. Now Kolya? No, no, I cannot, I will not be able to withstand this...

I went to Central Camp to see the warder Sergeev. I found him at the checkpoint.

"If there is anything on this earth, if only the smallest, if there is anything anywhere at all..."

He didn't let me finish. He clenched his jaws, his voice quivered.

"Enough, enough! Go dig up a grave at the cemetery. Come at three in the morning. I'll give him to you."

At the town's cemetery I hired somebody to dig the grave.

By three o'clock, in the middle of a whitish June night, I was sitting on a pile of logs by the checkpoint at Central Camp.

Limping slightly, Sergeev walked out of the zone and headed toward me. I was afraid he'd changed his mind. He glanced at me and handed me a package—my letters to Kolushka. He had brought them out of the zone himself.

"Come get his things tomorrow," he said.

Amid the silence of the night, the gates of Central Camp's zone creaked open, and a horse pulling a bier stepped out. Kolushka's coffin, built by his prisoner friends, rested on the bier.

The horse halted. Sergeev stood still, too. Out walked another warder. I thrust myself to my knees by the bier.

"Here, you take the reins," the steel-eyed warder put them into my hands.

The road led through the settlement. People were standing about outside of several houses. They had known Kolushka and loved him. They crossed themselves and cried. I was grateful to those who stood, who came out of their houses that night.

Outside of the settlement, on the road leading to the cemetery, Dmitry walked restlessly back and forth. A few TEC actors ran away from the cars standing uncoupled at the train station. The guards were new to the camp and opened fire. The actors were brought back and punished.

I was bidding farewell to Kolushka.

That was how he kept his dreadful vow: "I will be on the other side of the zone sooner than you expect."

The grave was filled with earth.

Kolya was no more. And neither was time. I, also, ceased to be.

Dima remained. I asked him, ordered him, to leave me alone. I lay on the hillock. The earth was alive.

Then someone shook me on the shoulder:

"Enough. You'll come here tomorrow again. You can't stay here alone."

It was Sergeev. He'd come with a guard to take the horse, the bier and me back.

What prompted him to give Kolushka to me? Why did he allow me to bury him at the cemetery?

I have remembered you for many many years, steel-eyed, lame warder Sergeev. I bow before your heart of a man!

The wholeheartedness of people who felt and shared my pain helped me to stay alive.

Darya Vasilyevna wrote to me for a long time after. Then there were no more letters from her. My letters went unanswered.

Hella would find me at the cemetery, where she'd bring some canned food. She'd shake me:

"Eat something! Or I'll lie down right here and die. My dear Tomika, you don't want me to do that. For me it's easy. My son and sister are in another country, and I'll never see them again. My husband's been shot. And it is all my fault. How are we going to live on, Tomika? And why bother?"

Chapter 12

At the railway clinic in Mikun, where Hella and I worked, half of the employees were recent graduates of Leningrad medical institutes. The train from Leningrad to the Komi Republic took a little more than a day, and the young doctors would willingly come to work here on assignment, which made them eligible for housing warrants back in Leningrad.

To collect all the documents required by the court, and to be able to take back my son, I had to have at least nine square meters of registered living space. But, responding to my requests, the head of the clinic's therapy department, Denisenko, stated that it was not ex-prisoners but the young specialists from Leningrad who were given priority. "Funds are limited," Denisenko would add.

Yes, funds were limited, but my entire life now depended on having a room of my own. It was impossible to save anything from my pathetic salary toward renting a private room, as Hella and I were each paid only thirty-two rubles a month. I managed to obtain permission for a second job as an assistant in a laboratory, which brought me another thirty-two rubles.

A worker from the locomotive depot, who had recently built a house and lived there with his wife and five-year-old daughter, was looking for a tenant. I moved into an empty square room with two windows looking right out into the forest. I pieced together a bed by placing some rough boards on a frame made of thick logs. My old wooden suitcase, as usual, served as my table. For the first time in many years, I could lock the door and be alone.

Even the ill-boding whispering of the spruces behind the window ceased to seem frightening. "Here I'll put Yurik's bed. With a little time I'll be able to buy some linen and kitchenware. I'll start a new life."

But when my landlords found out I was an ex-prisoner, they grew hostile and ignored all my attempts at goodwill.

"Let me help you with the logs," I'd say to the man, seizing the other side of the two-handled saw. "I'll fetch you some water to fill up the barrel," I'd say at other times to his wife and hurry to grab the buckets. I'd cut logs and fetch water, but a piteous tenant like me was discomfiting for the wholesome couple.

"What's that you're writing all the time?" the woman asked me one day.

"Letters. Letters to my friends."

"So many? That doesn't sound right. It must be something else."

Their irritation grew stronger and stronger. Early one morning their five-year-old daughter came into my room.

"Come here, Katenka, let's draw our house and a squirrel," I called her.

Her thumb in her mouth, the girl stood still in the doorway, scrutinizing me with her eyes. Then she said:

"Go away! You're a beggar. We don't need no ha-ga-bonds!"

In the evening, her parents summed things up.

"Move out. We need the room. Our relatives are coming."

I moved back to the Shpakovs' kitchen, which Hella, grateful to have any shelter, still inhabited.

Whether at work or in daily life, our yearning to fit in was smashed to pieces by the firmly entrenched stigma: we were "has-beens," ex-prisoners. Most of our colleagues openly avoided us, and there were only a few young doctors who dared to be friendly.

We became especially close with the pediatrician Rita D., a woman with gleaming black eyes, who was the bravest and most life-loving of all. Yet soon I noticed that Rita stopped talking to another young doctor, the oculist Kalinina. When I asked if they had quarreled over something, after a moment of hesitation Rita answered:

"Yes, about you."

Dr. Kalinina had a brother who worked for the NKVD in Arkhangelsk, so she was better heeled in such matters than the rest, who claimed that the released prisoners were like everybody else.

"She—like everyone else?" Kalinina would exclaim, wagging her finger. "Never! She'll never be able to wash off that stain. She'll be a stranger forever."

The sinister prophecy of the cute ventriloquist had a lasting impression on the neophytes. Fences taller than those encircling the camps had been raised in the consciousness of the "non-has-beens." In everyday usage, people referred to it as an unspoken civil war.

It was beyond my power to convince the head of the therapy department to allocate me housing. Nor did I dare start looking for another job. Indiscriminately, I took any travel assignments in hopes of passing through Velsk, where I could embrace my son. I wrote letters to both of the Bakharevs, begging them to keep me informed. Vera Petrovna answered more regularly than Filipp. She said that Filipp had categorically prohibited her from writing to me but that she did write nevertheless. She kept promising to bring Yurik for a few hours when it got warmer, although "he," of course, wouldn't let her; she reassured me that my son would always be dressed and fed as long as she was near him. At times, I'd even manage to read out a measure of sincerity in her promises and, throwing our circumstances together in a slew of shared misfortune, pledged to myself: "I'll also let her see Yurik from time to time. She must've grown attached to him."

She never brought my son. It was up to me alone to figure out why Filipp wasn't allowing her to write to me.

After not hearing anything from him for a long while, I received a letter from Filipp, in which he wrote that sincere silence was worth more than a hundred false letters. He was about to go to Pechora, from where he'd send me a telegram so that we could meet at the station on his way back when the train made a stop in Mikun. The fact that he had written to me himself gave me another glimmer of hope for a peaceful outcome.

His telegram arrived in a few days, and I went to the station to meet him.

"I've decided to get off. There'll be another train in five hours," he explained. "Will you show me where you live?"

"I'm living with Hella. She's resting after night duty," I lied. "Let's go to the clinic."

When we arrived, there were several doctors he knew, including the bacteriologist Belik, my boss at the laboratory.

"How's Tamara Vladislavovna doing?" Filipp inquired.

Only trying to help me, Belik started praising me to Filipp:

"She promised me she could find a certain rare agent under the microscope, which I haven't been able to discover during my entire forty years of practice. Imagine: the other day, she calls me in and says, 'Look, I've found it!'"

Without a drop of irony in his tone, Filipp said coldly:

"Is that so? Her talents are simply frightening!"

I was bewildered: "What does he mean? Did Vera Petrovna tell him how I aroused joy in Yurik whenever I see him, that I'd managed to find work not only as a medical attendant but also as an assistant at the laboratory?" Then, suddenly, it occurred to me: Filipp was afraid of me, too. But this understanding didn't assuage my own fear of him. On the contrary, my fear only grew. When I told him before my release that I'd be back to take my son, his ambiguous answer, "We'll see," had perplexed me. Yet he knew what he was saying: he was able to foresee the longevity of Evil, to whose reign I owed my poverty, the fact that I was still living in somebody's kitchen under the permanent threat of being rearrested.

We sat down on a bench next to the clinic. It seemed that the air itself became tin-like in Filipp's presence. His words were one thing, himself—completely another. It was inconceivable that a while ago he used to be my protector.

"Tell me how you live," he turned his face to me.

"You mean, how well? Everything's fine at work. I have two jobs," I said as confidently as I could. "They're promising me a separate room soon. As soon as I have it, I'll come to take Yurik. I hope we can settle this by ourselves?"

"I know you'll come. But you don't have anywhere to bring him yet. He lacks nothing at my place now, neither food and care nor pleasures. He's gotten used to having it all. He is the meaning of my life. But I promised you once, and I can repeat it again: it's going to be fine."

"Do you talk to him about me? How do you explain everything to him? Does he ask about his mother at all?"

"He's too small for such questions. We shouldn't burden his soul for the time being."

"Of course not. But still, he must ask something from time to time. What do you tell him?"

"Calm down. Don't worry about anything."

"My life is insufferable without my son."

"I understand."

Between us was an insurmountable chasm, an open wound, and we were facing each other from two opposite sides of it, oscillating between war and peace.

The next moment, I heard myself ask what was perhaps the least appropriate of all questions; it was, however, but a desperate attempt to draw nearer to his true essence in some way.

"Tell me, what didn't I give you enough of?"

He swallowed and hesitated, but I pressed him for an answer.

"God, what a question! I didn't believe you'd love me."

Perhaps, just this once, what escaped Filipp's lips was a genuine and egotistical truth, so different from his customary bombastic speeches and tangled formulations.

He left. From his merry-go-round of frankness and evasiveness, I only wished to understand why he had come. To make sure I had no place of my own? To see if I was prepared to fight him in court? Then a thought flashed through my mind like the gleam of something I could not doubt: he had come to kill me.

ON THE TRAINS from Mikun to Knyazh-Pogost, I would meet the "splendid women of 1937" who had thrown off their quilted jackets three years ago. Their faces became rougher and lost their sheen by the year. Unable to afford a more luxurious present for a friend who was lucky enough to have been finally given a separate place to live, they'd often carry a steel dustpan, a bucket, a fire poker or another piece of hardware with them. We'd exchange questions: "So you're safe for now?" "Who else did they take?" "Any news from Tamara Tsulukidze? Has anyone heard from Erukhimovich?"

The Knyazh-Pogost cemetery constantly drew me to itself like a magnet. I'd go to Kolushka's grave whenever I had a day off. I put a fence around it, planted some flowers, installed a cross and a little bench inside the fence. I'd sit there for a long time and speak with him about everything in the world.

There had been a moment when I'd suggested to Kolya that we end our lives. He had talked me out of it, and now he was no more, while I lived on. I repented before him for this, trying to bury the memories of his secret plan to escape and of how quickly the flame in his heart had burned out.

On the way back from the cemetery, I'd visit my friends in Knyazh-Pogost. I always stopped by to see Fira.

"Any news from Senya?"

"You can't imagine where they dumped him. Novosibirsk region! Two hundred *versts* from the nearest station. He's working as a carpenter in a *kolkhoz*."

"What have you decided to do?"

"What's there to decide? He writes that as soon as he has a roof over his head, he'll call me and Mama, and we'll go. We can't let him perish there alone."

For those of us who had been forced by the official spheres of life into a cage of sorts, the entire world and all its human relationships had been turned upside down.

"Fira, I saw Tamara Vladislavovna run in!" It was Ilya Evseevich knocking on Fira's door. "I know she hates seeing me, but I have to talk to her. Ask her to step out."

He was standing by a tree in the yard. Depressed and candid, he repented: "Forgive me. Simon was right. I acted like a scoundrel." Toward the end of our conversation, it was no longer clear who the victim was and who suffered more—he who gravitated to official standards, or I who neglected them. We made up with each other. Our quarrel had been hard on me, too.

When Simon wasn't away, I often visited him. He'd greet me warmly:

"Oh, look who's come! Let's have tea. I have biscuits from Moscow. Here, enjoy—Shakespeare's sonnets, translated by Marshak… No, no, don't move, I'll prepare everything myself."

"Thanks for the poetry. I need it a lot! But what's this poster on the wall, anyway?"

I read: *Dear Citizen Thieves! Take anything you like. Please don't touch the books. S.K.*

Simon laughed:

"I always hang it on the wall when I leave for Moscow."

"Does it help?"

"It does, if you can imagine! They've taken my shirts but never touched the books."

"My friend, you are invincible!"

"No, dear, I am 'vincible,' very much so."

Simon successfully continued his voyages. Departing from Moscow to Knyazh-Pogost, he'd send me a telegram and I'd go out to meet him at the station in Mikun, where the train had a fifteen-minute stop. That was enough time for Simon to share the news from the capital and tell me a witty joke.

As usual, I was standing on the platform waiting for the Moscow express.

"I saw an amazing show about Pushkin at the Ermolova Theater. Yakut, such a miraculous actor, played the role of the poet," Simon was telling me. "I've finally managed to buy *Dangerous Liaisons,* a book I've been hunting for three years. And here is a little present for you," he said, handing me a miniature bottle of perfume.

When the locomotive was coupled and the train was about to move, Simon grew serious and smiled with confusion:

"You know, dear, it looks like I'm going straight into the wolf's jaws."

He said that his trip had been interrupted by a suspicious order to come back immediately. It smacked of a trap.

"What are you saying? Maybe you shouldn't go back then?"

"Where else would I go? What will be, will be," he said from the footboard of the car.

"Promise to send me a telegram! I'll be worried. I'll be waiting for the telegram!" I shouted as the train moved off.

Walking along the tracks, I kept thinking: "Will they arrest him?"

They did. As soon as he arrived in Knyazh-Pogost.

In all those years since Urdoma, Simon had been my loyal friend. He always warned me of approaching danger; he did not spare Filipp any blame, and he helped me live through the hardest times of Kolushka's illness; he was capable of laughing at anything that was worth it and never burdened anyone with outpourings of the heart.

They swept up everyone. The regime was afraid of its victims, whose growing numbers deprived it of comfort. The epileptic fit of a political tornado picked up the remaining ex-prisoners, raised them above the ground like fallen leaves, and carried them off to uninhabited tracts of the country.

HELLA AND I were finally issued authorization for an eleven-square-meter room.

"At least we'll sleep in our own beds till they arrest us," we cheered each other.

We began to establish our daily routine from scratch. We already had some plywood and a trestle; we bought a kettle and two mugs, converted a piece of gauze into a curtain. We had forgotten what it felt like to have enough to eat. We didn't remember what an entrée was. Our menu consisted of soup, bread and sweetened tea.

The idea that in the depths of one's soul pain was asleep was an illusion; it only ripened and swelled there. Only now, having found ourselves a measure of privacy, did we realize in full that the shared fate of one's private tragedy didn't abate. We comported ourselves normally in front of other people, but under our own roof we let ourselves go. We were simply sick.

Coming home from work, I'd go to the kitchen to heat up some tea and, walking back into the room, find Hella on her knees by the bed, her face buried in the pillow, sobbing violently. The tea would grow cold. Powerless to help each other, we could cope neither alone nor together.

Hella could live without personal belongings but not without her friends, especially Aleksandr Osipovich. She was stormy and unruly and had little patience. Her dictatorial, impetuous moods sometimes took on threatening forms, and it wasn't always easy to be with her. Each of us had our own divergent goals and eccentricities, and my independence was a hindrance to our relationship.

I loved Hella more than she loved me. I loved her the way she was. No one was as lonely as she, my poor Hella. No one here understood her outlandish beauty; no one told her how gorgeous she was.

In the evenings she would sometimes disappear. I'd find her on the platform of the shabby train station.

"Are you going somewhere, Helli?"

She'd answer me in German: "Gehen die Lieder nach Hause." The words were from Heine. They meant, "The songs are going home." Hella was deliriously dreaming of a journey to Prague.

"The time will come," I'd try to persuade her. "Now let's go back to that home of ours."

She'd exclaim: "My Czechoslovakia, my Prague!" and read poems by Jiři Wolker and letters of Julius Fuchik. She received dozens of books, which she sent to her friends, and when she ran out of copies, she'd rewrite the poems by hand. She took pride in everything that related to her motherland, though she cherished no hope of ever seeing it again.

"At least one of us ought to have some luck, Tomik!" she said. "Go and get Yurochka. I'm leaving for Syktyvkar. Shan and Boris Kreitser are already there. I'll stay with the Belovs. They are the only happy couple I know. Olga Viktorovna has been inviting me for a long time. We'll see what happens then. Don't indicate in the form that I'm also registered to live in this room. Let the court think it's all yours."

AT LAST, all the documents were ready to be submitted.

Preparing to leave for Velsk, I pictured my son, not as he was now, but as he had been when we were together back in Mezhog, a one-year-old boy in a gray sweater with a bunny rabbit sewn on the front.

I flew about the settlement, finding various useful objects to take back to my room.

The closer my meeting with the Bakharevs came, the foggier was my anticipation of how our conversation would turn out, what arguments I'd have to refute. But come what may, it had to be done. I had everything: freedom, a job, a room of my own. I decided not to telegram ahead that I was coming.

In Velsk, I went straight to the clinic where Vera Petrovna worked. I had resolved to talk to her first, relying on the fact that she was also a mother and would understand me.

She wasn't there. Someone told me she wasn't working at the clinic anymore.

I went to their house. An unfamiliar man opened the door.

"They've moved out," he said.

"Where?"

"I haven't been informed."

Where could they have possibly gone? Dumbstruck, I ran to see a friend.

"Where are they?"

"They haven't written you? They just upped and left one day."

"Left for where?"

"I don't know. Try to find Nikolay Nikolaevich. They were friends. Maybe Fedosov knows something?"

But those two just shook their heads and said they knew nothing.

Someone accompanied me to the local police precinct, where I was told: "They haven't registered their departure."

I ran somewhere else, but no one could clarify anything.

A group of people were gathered at Kapa's. From the chorus of voices I heard:

"He didn't want his son to have a mother who was a prisoner."

"But what about themselves: didn't they each sit out their own prison terms?"

"He got himself the right papers a long time ago."

"To take a child from his mother..."

"He bribed the whole court here. We all saw it. And she herself is such a tough broad..."

It seemed like any minute I would find a reasonable explanation. Somewhere, there must have been a letter that would give me a clue. If I believed for a moment that they stole my son, then life could not go on.

When I talked with Bakharev in Mikun, I had a feeling that he had come to kill me. What they had done was, in fact, akin to murder...

It wasn't until much later, when I managed to extricate myself from the traps of my drama, if only to a degree, that I understood in full measure how all the loathsomeness of the times had cast itself in the Bakharevs. Permissiveness. Lies. Stealing. The annihilation of the basic decency that people had been gathering over the centuries; indeed, the extermination of everything except for bestial egoism. While I was giving my energy away to fear, they were converting theirs into a faultless plot. I had trembled over their letters, cherishing them and hiding them again and again from camp searches, while they were bribing their way to false documents to save themselves from arrest. Face-to-face with what they had done, I felt I'd been cut off from the world not just for the seven years that I was in prison, but for an entire epoch. Yet, taking heart in how I'd managed to find Kolya's mother, I had no doubt I'd track down the Bakharevs as well. I stubbornly, ingloriously searched.

IN CHILDHOOD I dreamed of a breathing hieroglyph resembling two Cyrillic letters interlocking with each other; a different shape had haunted me in the years to follow: two steel rods, coiled around each other. These passionless constructions frightened me with their durability and bareness, inexhaustibility and lifelessness. "Look," my dream seemed to be telling me, "This is the line of your fate." But I couldn't bear looking at the iron designs.

There seemed to be no bridge that would carry me back to life, but I still firmly felt the need to perform my duties and maintain the love of my friends. When Kolya died, people heard my pain and their responsiveness was salutary. Now, a keen ear to my friends' miseries became my saving grace.

The Belov family, whom Hella had considered such a happy couple, got into a car accident on the very day of Hella's arrival. Olga Viktorovna died on the spot. Hella stayed to look after her crippled husband, Ivan Georgievich. She wrote me a frightening letter, describing everything that had happened, with a postscript: "Come! We're all shocked by what happened with Yurochka. We have to be together. There is 'a mighty handful' of us here. We're waiting for you."

I went to stay with them for several days. The inconsolable Ivan Georgievich said prophetically:

"I don't have a long time left. Olechka is waiting for me there. I know that, having lost Kolya and your son, you understand me as no one else can."

In Syktyvkar, I held long conversations with Shan.

"I'll only be able to live at home, in China. It's hard for me here."

"Do you believe you'll get back there some day?"

"I do! Don't be surprised: I really believe it!" he nodded.

I didn't question him or bring up my doubts.

Sometimes I wondered if we were even human beings, or something else. We were living through second arrests and exile, losing our motherlands and children, learning of "chemicals" used during interrogations, of radioactive testing in Nazi camps; despite all this, we kept up our individual lives engulfed in a foggy simplicity, striving after reason and warmth. The power of life asserted itself, and what each person was made of was always different from case to case.

A letter from the wonderful Margo became a distinct proof of what a person was capable of discovering within herself, of that matter which the very foundations of life were built on.

> My Good Tomik! Your letter arrived like a swallow in the cold of the winter, a swallow no one could expect.
>
> I arrived in Kyltovo firmly confident of finding work as a "houseboy," but

> I was immediately greeted by a dose of reality, just like in Central Camp. It was all due to my accursed article. My mood grew worse and worse. But work uplifted me. I found myself enraptured by collective, nameless labor. The Egyptian pyramids came to mind. There were moments when, as I stood on the edge of a field we had already "conquered," tears would well up and my heart would start beating faster in admiration before our crowd, before our common labor.
>
> Then I read in Stanislavsky's My Life in Art about discovering already well-known truths. He writes about physical freedom, economy of energy, and the lack of muscle exertion. I put his advice to use. For example: I'm handling a barrow loaded with clay. (I have twice as much in mine than any of my coworkers). It's only my chest muscles that are strained, my hands just guide the handles of the barrow lightly, and my legs move as if in a dance, easy and springy. I love my hands and my legs, which lightly move downhill and avoid slipping on the boards that are thrown over the babbling river. My entire body is resting, and it is only when it is absolutely necessary that I flex a muscle. This is the only way that I keep from getting tired, while my soul even glows with some sort of mischief. Do you understand, Tomik? Does anyone have to pity me? I am a pacesetter, I always achieve 130% of the norm. I need no bonfire to warm by or rest. In that way, I am free! My article is no longer a problem, damn it! Without any intrigues or favors, without any of what's required to get a "houseboy" job in the camp.
>
> Tomik! Do you understand how happy I am with the freedom that I gained on my own?"

After two months in prison and a series of interrogations, Simon was exiled to Pechora, where he tossed about in loneliness, like a bated animal. He wrote a letter in which he asked me to marry him, to consider all the pros and cons of such a proposition and not to write him any consolatory letters in case I decided against it, adding, at the same time, that he was waiting for me to let him know when I would arrive.

My friend was feeling awful. Instead of sending him a telegram, I went straight to the station and bought a ticket to Pechora—so that he could see with his own eyes and understand that my heart had frozen, that it might never be able to love again. Kolushka took it all with him.

At the time, I was receiving marriage proposals nearly every month. Through marriage, men hoped to escape the suffocating loneliness. When the skeptical F. arrived in Mikun from Knyazh-Pogost to ask for my hand, it was clear that even irony itself had given up. But it was different with Simon.

He stood waiting for me on the platform. Seeing a market-woman carrying a wooden box loaded with jars of withered northern flowers, he bought them all up and presented them to me. But when he looked into my eyes, he said:

"I understand everything, dear. Let's forget about it. And now—hello! Thanks for the pleasure of seeing you!"

He lived in a wooden hut. The wind beat against the wobbly shutters, whose hinges not merely creaked but groaned. In his small room, shelves hung on the walls, overloaded with books and files. There was also a portrait of me, enlarged from a photograph. He was cooking supper and making tea.

When we sat down to eat, Simon said:

"You know how Ilya and I always grappled with each other. He is in a grave state right now. So I ask you, please, be kind to him."

"Is he also here? Has he also been exiled?" I asked, shocked.

"Precisely."

Ilya Evseevich was already knocking on the door, reprimanding Simon:

"You're sitting here together, the two of you! Drinking tea! And what about me? Simon, why didn't you tell me which train she was arriving on? I don't trust you anymore!"

After Ilya was released from the camp, he spent his free vacations studying at the second university he had resolved to finish, and no sooner did he receive his diploma than he was rearrested and sent to exile. The intelligentsia was to be exterminated like an indigestible substance that the regime could not absorb.

Many inflamed words were spoken against violence, and there was that warmth of the soul we all equally longed for, in that meeting between the three of us in Pechora. Ilya cited passages from the Bible. We attempted to outline our supposed future, though it was hard to imagine it'd ever call on us again. Giving me Simon's room, the men went to Ilya's. The wind and the groaning shutters wouldn't let me fall asleep.

Both of them went to see me off at the station and presented me with the many kind words they'd devised in the loneliness of their exile. Guards were roving through the station. Again, someone had escaped. They skewered the heaps of anthracite loaded onto the hopper-cars with their steel rods.

Returning to Mikun, I received a telegram: *Don't worry dear you left more silent warmth than the warmth of words whatever the heart of a woman decides it is always right good-bye my dear friend Simon.*

As we linked the pain of one of us to the miseries of another, there was always a hope of acquiring a collective weight, of reaching a common mass that would enable us, together, to resist the evil that was pulling us off our conventional points of reference. We exalted each other in letters and, thereby, grew larger ourselves. We were becoming sisters and brothers, judges and priests, to each other. Piety toward each other's suffering helped to build up that special kind of relationship where there was no room for dishonesty. That was how we, who had been rubbed off the face of society, found it possible to preserve some sort of a life for ourselves. Grasping at the sky, we wandered about the earth, some for the sake of whatever was left of their lives, others—toward their deaths.

From the "Golden Taiga" in the far North, wrote a man who had loved me for many years—Platon Romanovich, a person from my previous life in Leningrad, whom I met again later in the camps. After being rearrested, he was sent to Yunashino, a settlement in the mines. His was an especially severe exile. He was living in the middle of the taiga, in a house surrounded by hills, with nine other workers. In the settlement there was a store, a school, a post office and several workshops; a river, now covered with ice, flowed through; once a month there was a film at the club, but after a full working day, having trekked eight kilometers there and back, few workers felt like walking another six to attend the screening. Platon Romanovich wanted to know who cut the firewood, heated the stove and fetched water for me. Raising my axe, I'd chop the wood more cheerfully thanks to the kind and caring words that reached out to me from the heart of this loving man.

There was loneliness and there were the feverish pages of his letters. And death, before long. Platon Romanovich died there, in the mines.

BORIS MAEVSKY, whose term would not end for another three years, was transferred to the camp in Mikun under a special warrant. An artist and sculptor, he had to create a design for the local House of Culture the railway administration was building. He was granted the right to walk freely from the zone to work.

At the time, there appeared heaps of translated books: the novels of Howard Fast, *The Seventh Cross* by Anna Seghers, Abrahams's *The Path of Thunder* and many others. Everything in these books seemed to be written about us, about the air we breathed in the twentieth century, about the shared pain and drama of mankind.

I was captivated by the truth of life revealed by the fearless foreign literature. Compared to our varnished Soviet novels, even the naturalism in these books was helpful beyond measure. With an inquisitive passion, I plunged myself into the new world that had opened up to me. It was a breakthrough, and it was Boris, who had given me the radio receiver that kept me company many nights with voices and music from foreign countries, who made this breakthrough happen.

"Have you read this? What do you think? Me too!" These were the routine words we would exchange every morning, meeting each other in the settlement on our way to work, I—from home, he—from the zone. It was as important to share our impressions from books, paintings and music as actually to read, see and listen to them, while to discuss them in a letter was even better, despite the fact that our interpretations rarely coincided and only revealed an organic difference between our personalities.

With his innate and all-consuming optimism, Boris did not hesitate to call the tragedy of our century accidental. History, according to him, was right. He had no doubt that the sociohistorical experience people had acquired would eventually lead them to "The City of the Sun," which was the dream of his much beloved Tommaso Campanella. Boris held this book in special esteem, for its author spent twenty-seven years in the dungeons of the Inquisition. The underlying idea of life, according to Boris, was spiritual unification among people. Hundreds of sheets were devoted to elaborating on this thought in his notebooks. The potential of each individual was the main thing; it, and only it, was what one had to orient himself to. Even in the camps, Boris remained a model Soviet romantic.

While I adhered to the past, it was the present that Boris revered. His phenomenal diligence and his remarkable talents reflected his natural need to respond to the events of the present day. Yet in his passion for the present day he felt lonely.

He'd expend great energy trying to make me his ally, to draw me into the things of the present. His efforts were contagious, and they did stir something in me. But even when I tried, nothing ever came out of it. Our relationship, insomuch as I could classify it, resembled a struggle. I was gripped by my own pain and misery, while Boris was convinced that I was just in the throes of an unforgivably long dream, which he strove to pull me out of. He was partly correct, of course, but he couldn't understand what had become of me after my son was taken away and Kolya, the only one for me, died.

> Never, never and never will I believe that the greatest happiness you're capable of was buried there with Kolya. Once upon a time, it was not me who came to Mezhog. That's all. A trick of time, nothing more. I was never afraid of your difficult nature, and it's not by hearsay that I know of it. And yet I hope it's temporary. Life didn't spoil you, you were spoiled by the worship of friends.

> My path is by all means an easier one. It's true I'm a coarse fortunate beggar with many foul habits. But no small fly in my honey can ever spoil my taste for life. As for you, you wish to live in a difficult way. So why don't you try to push aside your offense at my words about Kolya and look closer at your own life this year. It's simply absurd that I have to tell you what you really felt toward that gentle young man with a great talent.
>
> Every word that I say to you causes me pain as well. But who will tell this to you if not me? Forgive me. Your tragedies—they are but the age-long guilt felt by those who remain toward those who depart, a customary reverence of the heart before death, an inclination to the bitter depths of the soul, the poetry and mysticism of silence as a means of fighting life, fighting fate.

He yearned for warmth and simplicity, but whether he admitted it or not, my heart remained with Kolya. I told him not to rush me. My wounds had to heal in silence, with time, and time had always been what I lacked. I was tired of being attacked; I stiffened from forwardness.

We were coevals but, in a sense, belonged to different generations. I cherished Aleksandr Osipovich's explanations of where, for example, the sense of one's personal self-sufficiency stemmed from. Boris challenged this question as fundamentally wrong and tried to prove that a sense of "social self-sufficiency" was much more important than that of one's personal fulfillment. His letters were candid, fervent and current. It was tempting to feel part of the whole: the entire world was, indeed, supposed to belong to my generation, to us, even here.

I felt like two different people, corresponding with Aleksandr Osipovich and Boris, as if there were two languages, two measures of things. It surprised me that I was part of them both. I wrote to Aleksandr Osipovich in a relieved and simple manner. My letters to Boris were written by someone who could soar above her own burden if she would only give herself up to the momentary and shed the "eternal."

On a dark winter night, on one of the side streets of the settlement, Boris and I got into a particularly bad fight. He was on his way back to the zone, full of spiteful vengeance.

"You know, Aleksandr Osipovich and I used to give each other your letters to read!" he told me.

The sacred name of Aleksandr Osipovich, which had sustained me for so long, gave way. How could Boris dare encroach on that, how could he raise his hand against the only escape I had left?

"I don't believe you. It's a lie!"

"You need only illusions, your little cozy comfort of the soul? You don't like the truth, you don't want it?"

Two people, as if suddenly broken loose from their chains, were settling accounts with each other for all the universal evil they were entangled in. Standing on that side street in the nipping frost under the winking stars, we were hurling spiteful curses at each other from the depths of our barren hearts.

Powerless to get through to me, Boris threw himself to the ground and started pounding his fists against the crust of ice: "You're made of stone! You're impenetrable!" I ran away from him, thinking: "Out of here! It hurts! It's growing dark before my eyes."

When I calmed down, it became his pain that suddenly scalded me; it was his despair that lashed me. I rushed back to help him up, to explain to him that our torment was a shared one, that we needn't act as we had been. But when I got there, the street was deserted.

Boris was aware of his cruelty and never stopped explaining himself in his letters, neither then, nor later on. But what about Aleksandr Osipovich? Later he wrote to me that he returned my letters Boris had given him without discussing them, only muttering some general interjections. As for Boris, he was sure that Aleksandr Osipovich had read them.

Meanwhile, the emaciated and sick Aleksandr Osipovich was sent off on a transport to the Far North, to the special regime camps.

LENINGRAD REMAINED a constant temptation. The city was a different territory, both biographically and psychologically.

My travel assignments were not easy: one time, I would have to take the children of the railway workers to a sanatorium outside Leningrad, another —to deliver a patient in grave condition to a medical appointment. I didn't turn down any of them.

The sick children were especially difficult to travel with. I had to lift them to and from their berths, take them for walks whenever the train pulled into a large station, feed them and so on. Those who were older would run away and hide from me just as the train was about to depart. Sometimes sympathetic passengers helped me find the runaways, tried to convince the children to behave or offered to watch them so that I could have at least an hour of sleep.

Indeed, it gradually started seeming to me that, little by little, I was returning to the real present-day life of the country.

In Leningrad, the most important thing was to meet with Valechka. I liked everything in her: her smile, her gait. I believed I'd eventually be able to melt down the ice that had frozen in my sister's heart toward me.

During one of our conversations, Valechka softened and answered some of my questions:

"Yes. I'm in love with a certain young man."

"And he?"

"He loves me too."

"Who is he, Valechka? Does he live in Leningrad?"

"No. In Moscow."

"Are you going to get married?"

"No."

"Why?"

My sister fell silent.

"You didn't tell me where he works."

"He serves in the NKVD forces. Kremlin security."

That was the matter! All this time my sister had been suppressing bitterness and vexation! Or was it a more powerful feeling? The bride of an officer working for the Kremlin security had a sister who had spent seven years in the camps for political crimes! After surviving the siege and being mobilized from the orphanage to dig the gas pipeline, and currently having nothing more than a bed in the dormitory, my sister couldn't be happy on account of me.

I thought that perhaps Arkady, Valechka's young man, would give me some advice on how to withdraw myself from my sister's biography so as not to be a hindrance. I wrote to him.

He responded: "On your part, nothing can be done. I ask you, if you don't wish things to get worse, not to undertake anything. I might be able to get out of this mess myself."

When I arrived in Moscow, my sister's fiancé offered to meet on Sparrow Hills.

The slopes of the hills were littered with trash. We ascended further and further.

"Have a look at the city from here. Beautiful, isn't it?" said Arkady.

I liked this neat and handsome young man.

"So, what can be done with relatives like me?" I started, having prepared myself for a frank conversation.

"What's wrong with such relatives?" he parried. "You and Valyusha look alike!"

Arkady called my sister Valyusha, and spoke of Stalin as of a father.

"What do I need to do, Arkady?" I insisted. "Tell me. Should I go somewhere? Or should I just cease to exist?"

"Even if you died, it wouldn't change anything. We'd still have to indicate in the forms where Valyusha's father died, where he is buried; I'd still have to mention you."

"It's not really necessary to write where somebody is buried, is it?"

"It must be a long time since you've seen a questionnaire."

I still hoped for some concrete advice but all of a sudden the lieutenant said:

"Don't rack your brains over this. I'll quit, and that'll be it!"

"Quit? Quit what?" I was taken aback by the very possibility of such a simple solution, by the clarity of this man's soul.

"It won't be easy, but I'll quit this service. I love Valyusha."

My sister had met a genuine and whole-hearted man. Eventually, he did quit. They never acted against their conscience and lived honestly, which is perhaps why they were able to bring up two wonderful sons.

EACH TIME I ARRIVED in Leningrad, I'd avidly look forward to meeting my dear friend Ninochka, stormy and willful in her youth and levelheaded and calm now, a person who had found herself in faith.

"Help me come to terms with myself! There's something important that seems to escape me. We're not given brains for nothing, are we?"

"You have to understand, Tamusya: nothing depends on us."

"Nothing at all? Everything has been predetermined? Even the fact that they took away my son?"

"I know this isn't easy to accept. But we are given ordeals so that something inside of us changes. The ordeals show us the way."

Leafing through the Leningrad phone directory, I'd find familiar surnames, and once I ran across the name of the D. family who lived in an apartment above us in our house on the Karpovka. They had floors so polished they shone, a trapeze hanging in the doorway, a microscope on the desk. "Mama, may I go to Lyolya and Vova's?" "Don't stay too long…"

Vova and I saw each other later, when he was a medical student while I was studying foreign languages. He had predicted the career of a diplomat for me: "You'll be the second Kollontay!" We rode bikes during the white nights. As for Lyolya, I hadn't seen her since we moved out of our apartment.

It was her low voice that I heard over the phone:

"What a surprise! Tomka! Where are you? I want to see you! Where did you come from?"

How good that at least someone knew nothing of where I'd been!

"What about Vova? Is he in town?"

"Call him immediately. Write down his number. He lives on his own. You can't imagine how happy he'll be. Take his work number, too."

I called him at work.

"You? Incredible! I was thinking of you only yesterday!" he spoke in a deep voice. "Where are you? Tell me your address right now. I'll come as soon as I'm done with work, all right? Are you by yourself? I have to run to the surgery now."

"You are a surgeon?"

"I'll tell you everything when we meet. What's the address? I want to see you, do you understand?"

"I'm leaving. I'm calling you just before I'm off."

"To where?"

"To the North."

"The North? Why?"

"I live there. I'll see you next time I'm in town."

"No, no. Give me your address in the North then. Are you married? Then I'll come visit you!"

"I'll write you a letter."

"Wait. Don't hang up. I have to see you… Promise me you'll write!"

"You have my word."

I returned to Mikun and wrote him a letter. Vova replied. His letter excited me beyond measure. "Regards from my father, Mama and Lyolya…" They knew and remembered my entire family, all of us!

I imagined what our meeting would be like. For him, there had been the war, the academy where he worked, his research. He was a model ambassador for Today. What would he say if I gathered the courage and told him everything?

When I called him the next time I was in Leningrad, he suggested meeting at 7 p.m. on Leo Tolstoy Square, by the bus stop.

Leo Tolstoy Square! It meant so much in my life—my first school, the strange, mysterious building of the "Elita Cinema," subsequently renamed "Chisel" and then—"Arts."

Thick snow was falling. Vova stood waiting for me, dressed in a military greatcoat. Helping me to the arriving tram, he offered to go to his place.

He was a confident man. His outward appearance hadn't changed much.

He lived on Kamenny Island. The windows of his room overlooked one of the branches of the Neva.

"Come in. Wait, I'll turn on the lights. Give me your coat… Listen, it's damned incredible that you haven't changed at all."

"All right, all right. I'm all covered in snow."

"Snow suits you! You know what's most astonishing? That you're alive and I'm alive, and that today you and I met. Where should I offer you a seat? Here! Take this footstool too."

"I'm not that old yet, am I?"

"No, it's just for you to feel comfortable. Here, take the cushion too so that it's completely perfect."

"I can get used to this."

"Well, just wait! Let me look at you."

"You don't need to do that."

"Shh, don't say anything. I'll cook supper. You listen to the music, have a rest and get ready to tell me everything, step by step."

He would run off to the kitchen and come back, setting the table and glancing at me with his joyful eyes.

"It's almost ready. I want to surprise you!"

I remembered Vova as a little boy. Then—a youth. Now he was a mature man who wouldn't let me help him with supper. Why this lightness in my body? Where and when did I throw off the burden of grief and resentment I'd been carrying about on my shoulders?

"Dinner is served."

He shouldn't have said this. I wished only to prolong this delightful escape, to hide in silence and warmth. I wished it had taken him longer to cook supper while I rested the way I hadn't for ages.

"Tell me. Everything. Assume you're filling up a blank page," he demanded.

Without further hesitation, I blurted out:

"All right. First—three years of exile. Then—arrest. Prison. Seven years of camps. Now—again, practically an exile for over two years already. That's it. And you?"

There was a prolonged silence.

He rose slowly to his feet, took a throw-blanket out of the wardrobe, tenderly wrapped it over my shoulders and sat down on the footstool beside me.

"You—exile? You—prison? Camps? So many years? Tell me, tell me everything!"

"I'd rather not, Vova!"

"At least the most important."

"I told you already. And besides, the most important things, I couldn't tell you anyhow."

"Why were you put away?"

"What if I told you it was all for nothing? I wish you hadn't asked me that question. My heart was feeling so light until then."

"Forgive me. I'm an awkward, stupid blockhead. I'm sorry."

"What about you?"

"Me? Military Academy of Medicine. The Leningrad front. Ladoga. 'The Road of Life.' Surgeries, surgeries. Bombardments. Blood. I nearly drowned. I was wounded. I was unhappily married. Now I'm alone. I love surgery. I'm finishing my first scholarly publication. In the Medical Encyclopedia, there's a solid entry about your humble servant. You know, I am suddenly ashamed of all that…"

"No, don't be!"

"I'm telling the truth. You know, I always thought that the people who returned from *there* were invalids, people with extinguished eyes, resentful, embittered, cruel. But your eyes are shining! It's impossible to imagine that you've been through all of that."

"Is it true you can't believe it? That's so nice! It suddenly seems as if none of it ever happened, that I want to live on."

"Could you ever forget it all?"

"No. Without forgetting… Somehow, in a different way…"

In his room, there were remote-controlled appliances. I could turn on the lamp near the door, or switch on the radio, without even having to stand up.

"Did you do it yourself?"

"No, one of my patients did, after a difficult but successful operation. Would you like me to turn on the gramophone? My favorite record! Can you guess what it is?"

"No."

"Wait, wait! Everything that came out in all these years: films, concerts, music, books—did they all pass you by?"

"Except for some books. What's wrong?"

"I'm frightened."

"Of what?"

"I'm guilty before you."

"That's not true."

"It is. Would you understand if I told you I feel sorry we didn't go through all of that together?"

"Don't be blasphemous. You were in the war."

"Yes, but there's still something I didn't completely understand. Maybe *there* I could grasp it in full?"

"Do you feel like you have any accounts to settle with life?"

"I've never made them public. But I could tell them to you."

"I'm listening."

"No, no. But I want to tell you something else. I want you never, ever to leave."

"Yes, tell me, say it."

"It seems to me you also want it."

"Talk, talk. It won't happen anyway. So, talk."

"You are my joy. Today I heard again how my heart can beat."

A scrap of childhood and youth… My momentary presence here, in my native city, my motherland… The bygone and the present were merging together, finally.

We agreed to meet the next afternoon near the Bronze Horseman. It was cold but the Neva hadn't frozen yet. The November holidays were approaching. The city was decorating itself. Banners and garlands were hung in the streets. The ships sailed in.

"You are devilishly clever, madly rich. Don't scatter your thoughts, your words, your feelings so generously. Keep them."

"What for?"

"I don't know what for. But you're crazy… Do you remember this? It's the House of Scientists. Let's go in!"

We would run inside various buildings and run back into the snow again.

"For dinner, we'll go to the House of Writers…"

Vova chose the table himself.

"No, sit here, next to the window, so that you can see the Petersburg streetlights. Look how they sway in the wind."

We ran after a bus. People were glancing back at us.

I had two more days. Every free hour we spent together.

On November 6, we met near the Summer Garden, which was already buried under snow.

"Tomorrow I have to be on duty at the clinic. Will you come visit me there? The windows look out straight onto the Neva. We'll watch the fireworks."

On the night of November 7, a snowstorm broke out. I came to the clinic at the hour we agreed on. Vova, wearing a white smock, was coming down the staircase to the lobby.

His enormous office had marble windowsills and high windows through which the Neva could be seen.

He pointed me to an antique fretted armchair upholstered in leather.

"You're not mad at me for making you come to the clinic, are you?"

"No, I'm glad to see where you work. Everything is so luxurious here. And your white smock—you look so solemn in it."

"That's the way I wanted it," he said after a brief pause.

The next second I already knew there would be a painful, powerful blow. I wanted to shield myself, but instead I asked Vova:

"You wanted what?"

"What?"

"What was it that you wanted? What happened?"

"Just like that, at once?"

"Yes."

"Sit in that armchair. I'll sit here," he said. The distance between us was the width of the entire office. "I… Should I just tell you everything the way it is?"

"Of course."

"I can't see you anymore. I know myself. One more time, and I'm dead."

"Dead?"

"Exactly. I mean, I won't be able to give you up. I live as if in a fever—now, yesterday, today. I keep thinking of you. You understand, of course, that there'll be a choice: the Party, the clinic, my scholarship, everything I have acquired over my entire life, or—you."

…When had I heard similar words? Right after Father's arrest, but then it was Misha K., a student at the Marine Academy. I remembered my own words: "You've made the right choice, Misha. The Academy, of course!" and ran away. Though I was completely indifferent to him, it still hurt. That was in 1937. Now, it was 1952. Had nothing changed over all those years?

I repeated the same words:

"You've made the right choice!"

Everything was the way it should have been. The funniest thing was that I wanted nothing from my childhood friend. I'd simply confided in him, believing that in spite of everything the world had kept a place for me. I had lapsed into a reverie.

"You're so close. The entire world that I long for, everything I thirst for is embodied in you. That evening, these past few days, nothing else existed. But now the corners have become sharp again… No, wait! Don't leave!"

"Let me go!"

"Wait a minute. Can't we talk like old friends?"

"You've already said everything like an old friend. We've known each other since we were three, Vova!"

"So what should we do?"

"Nothing. That's the only way. I'm not angry with you, I swear. I understand. It's hard for me now not because it is you, but because it is life itself that has struck me a blow."

The wind bent and tore at me, blowing the handkerchief off my head as I walked across Liteyny Bridge. The fireworks were going off in commemoration of 1917.

THE MIKUN HOUSE OF CULTURE, decorated with Boris's paintings and sculptures, was finally opened. On its premises, the local administration decided to organize a musical and theatrical collective. The theater was headed by Anna Abramovna Berzin, the wife of Bruno Jasienski. Dmitry Karayanidi was invited from Knyazh-Pogost to lead the choir.

Dmitry and I were connected by years of mutual friendships: our singer Inna, he, Kolushka and I. He decided not to return to Baku, where he had lived before the arrest. His family life didn't last. If not for his shining, wide-open eyes and his ability to laugh at others' jokes, this swarthy and handsome man could be taken for a cold, closed person. I was glad when he started coming to Mikun more often. He was a first-rate pianist. Music was his primary passion, his favorite composers being Rachmaninoff and Chopin. After rehearsals, waiting for the train back to Knyazh-Pogost, he would often play for his own pleasure, and I would come to listen to these concerts without an audience. After them, the taiga, the settlement and the gloomy sky above looked differently.

On the day of the official opening of the House of Culture there was a concert. I hadn't been on stage for two years, and my legs gave way as I, barely conscious, recited Ghesler's ballad *Mother's Voice.* I read about how the son was killed by a bomb, and when the second son was born, the mother swore not to give him up to war, calling for other mothers to save their sons too. I heard the gripping silence settling in the hall. I was applauded and called back for an encore many times.

As I was leaving the stage, Dmitry stopped me.

"There is so much of the stage in you, so much fire!"

His deep voice and his eyes were telling me more than his words.

IN A FEW DAYS, I went to the post office to send a telegram congratulating Senya Erukhimovich on his birthday. A neighbor who happened to be there approached and whispered into my ear:

"Who are you writing to?"

We lived in the same building. Our apartments, though separated only by one wall, had different entrances.

"To my friend in exile."

Pursing her lips, she expressively dropped her eyes but the next moment raised them again and looked at the door, motioning for me to follow her outside. I stepped out onto the porch.

"Stop corresponding with your exiled friends!" she blurted out.

"Why?"

"You're an intelligent person. Break off with them immediately. Take my advice."

With an air of accomplished duty, she alighted from the porch and left.

I finished the telegram and mailed it to the faraway village in the Novosibirsk region. I stayed in the post office for a long time, not wanting to go anywhere, not even home.

It was obviously a warning. Again, I had that familiar, loathsome premonition…

The workday at the clinic was over and everyone had gone home. I was sitting in one of the consulting rooms, finishing my annual report.

The door suddenly opened, and a man walked in.

I had seen him every day as I walked through the settlement, either in his breeches and a white undershirt chopping firewood, or in his uniform, closing the gate to his yard as he left for work.

He thriftily pulled up a chair and took a seat.

"Tomorrow at eight you must present yourself at the MGB regional office—without your things, for the time being. No one should know about this."

He had already been gone a long time, but I still couldn't come to my senses. There was nothing I was afraid of with such panic as a summons to the MGB. "Afraid" was not the right word: I simply lost the ability to reason. The secret service was the source of all my misfortunes, of all my tragedies: Papa's arrest, family disasters, my friends' summonses and imprisonments, my own arrest, Kolushka's fate… I knew I'd been spared the worst of the camp horrors—the bloody corpses of fugitives, the bodies of raped female prisoners. And although it was not an arrest yet, the officer's dictate filled me with horror.

The local MGB was housed in a one-story building, like the rest of the houses in Mikun, except this one had bars on its windows.

An old, wrinkled officer sat at the desk, underneath the portrait of Stalin that hung on the wall.

"Make yourself comfortable… How's work? How's life?"

"Good."

"Right answer. How have your colleagues been treating you?"

"Fine."

"We know it. And how have we treated you?"

"I don't know."

"What kind of answer is that? How many times have you traveled to Leningrad? Have we ever prevented you from it? We could have, though, don't you think?"

"Definitely."

"There you are! So how have we been treating you? We've been treating you well. We trust you. But do we trust everyone? No-o, it's a rare person that we trust. Well, what about your friends in the Krasnoyarsk and the Novosibirsk regions, what do they write?"

"They live. They work."

"Obviously. Everyone works in our country. Everyone has to work. Do they miss you?"

"They do."

"What about your sister: were you satisfied with how you found her? How many years didn't you see her? What a meeting it must've been! It must've really touched your heart, right?"

"Right."

"And what a great reading you gave at the concert, about the mother. Good job! You're a real actress! My wife, she even shed a few tears, you know. And look how many friends you have. People like you. You receive so many letters."

In this way, briefly going over my life, they were reminding me: we know everything! No one can hide from us. Everything's under control. I knew the mechanism all too well from before.

"So it's settled: we've been treating you well. Don't you think you should repay us in kind? We also need to be helped. Do you understand?"

"No."

"What exactly's not clear to you? Every honest person should help us: give us a timely warning, let us know, if anything seems awry. There is no other way in our times. Nothing else works."

"If anything… I understand."

"Oh, no. Not like that. We always have someone to warn us, to let us know when there's occasion for it. We need to have timely information about the people you're in touch with—about the facts, their attitudes. That's what we need you to help us with."

"I can't do that."

"Don't be so hasty. Is this work too dirty for you? Would you rather have others do it?"

"I can't! Try to understand. I simply cannot."

"See how everything turns out with you? We welcome you warmly, and you're turning your back on us. That won't do. I'm telling you, it's not going to work that way."

The officer's friendly tone turned into irritation, and threats followed:

"You damn blue bloods! You're in for it!"

"What? In for what?"

"Oh, you can trust me on that! We have plenty of places deep in the woods, three hundred *versts* from the nearest railroad. Have you heard of them? There one's head starts thinking much faster. But it's usually too late. Think about it. I'll call you again soon."

The next time, the threats intensified. And again, he promised to repeat the summons.

At work I was nervous and didn't want to go home in the evenings.

When Boris asked me what was wrong and I told him I was sick, he didn't believe me. To hell with their demands to keep quiet! It was all the same. I told him about the summonses.

"Have they threatened you?"

"Yes, with exile, three hundred *versts* into the woods."

"And they'll do it. Don't you understand?"

"I wish I didn't."

Boris was afraid for me. The next morning, on his way to work, he handed me a letter in which he wrote that no man, no matter how cold he might be, was made of steel, and that, given all the passion with which I had fought for life in the past, I would definitely be able to arouse at least the slightest understanding in the officer, and that I should set this as my foremost goal during my next conversation with him.

Yet my intuition was more ruthless. I didn't rely on anyone's mercy and simply didn't believe in it. Had I not traversed the length and breadth of the path of hope only to burn my feet trying to reach Filipp's and Vera Petrovna's hearts? My naïve faith only turned into a feeling of guilt for the crime I committed against my son and against my own self. How banal and youthful it was to believe that merely with the fervency of one's feelings, the depravity and crookedness of society might be straightened out! There was a certain point beyond which people turned into beasts; I was familiar with that point.

The lights in Boris's workshop were on when I went up the stairway.

"What should I do? What?"

More articulately than in the letter, he formulated another option:

"We are not fools, Tamara. One month in the woods, in one of those wolves' lairs, can be an irreversible disaster. Of course you won't report on anyone! You'll work out a handful of neutral phrases; you'll play dumb. You can't allow them to just grab you. We can't go head-to-head with them. I know I'm saying rotten things, I understand! But you can't just surrender yourself to them for nothing. We'll think something out; we'll find a way..."

During my next summons, the officer pressed me with a series of reckonings, one following the other: I had to be grateful to the organs, and to them alone, for not having been rearrested and exiled like the rest, for having been allocated a living space, for being kept at work. The head of the local MGB was smashing me with "indisputable" arguments:

"Who're you talking with? With an enemy? A fascist? Who're you being offered to help? The power that protects you, that wants its people to live and work in joy!"

"But I can't talk to a person and denounce him afterward."

"We don't need denunciations! We ourselves won't allow anyone to defame Soviet citizens! There can be different kinds of conversations. We only need the objective truth."

"But I don't know anybody with anti-Soviet attitudes. I don't hang around with those types of people."

"Is that so? You should be more modest. If there are no anti-Soviets around, do Doctors' Plots appear out of the blue? Do you think you know everything about your girlfriend D.?"

"She doesn't do or say anything reprehensible."

"So go ahead and defend her."

"Against what?"

"Against your own anti-Soviet conversations with her."

"What? When?"

"Let me remind you. Which of you said that Lokshin was innocent? (Lokshin was an employee of the Mikun clinic who had recently been arrested.) You've been discussing it so fervently with her. So you're not quite one of us, it seems. Nothing could be easier than to press charges against you. What would you say to that?" he asked, bluntly changing his strategy.

"Press charges for what?"

"For the numerous statements you've made. For maintaining connections with prisoner Maevsky."

"What do you mean by connections?"

"I mean connections. Or is it me who runs to his workshop? And what does your correspondence with the exiles tell us about your own attitudes? Make your choice, Petkevich. You either lead an honest life such that we can trust you, or—well, we've no need for strangers, you know."

"I'm not a stranger," I parried, muddleheadedly and pathetically.

"Prove it. Prove it in action. Words are of no use to us. We can do without you, but it's unlikely that you can do without us. Do you prefer the forest? That'll fix you good. But there we won't let you slander our regime either."

I was only pretending, of course, that the filth and stench of the remote camps didn't frighten me; in fact, even my work at the clinic put me face-to-face every day with the fractures and mutilations, with everything that the wild power of "places deep in the woods" did to people. Crushed by the visceral fear of finding myself among thieves and thugs again, I clung to an illusion of a way out.

The officer went on:

"We're extending a hand to you. We want to help a young and energetic person like you to move on. It's up to you to prove if you're one of us or not."

Again I refused.

"Well, here is a pen and paper. Or you can go home and wait."

The fear of darkness and silence bore down on me. Faintheartedness won. I signed.

THE WORST WAS NOT HAPPENING, yet never did I feel so abominable and repulsive. Everything I used to hide behind now appeared as a sham.

After two days I wound up at the hospital. I lay on the bed, my face to the wall. When someone in the ward called my name, I didn't immediate realize it was the MGB officer: "Would you mind lending me a book to read? It's boring here."

I asked the doctor to discharge me immediately.

Like in solitary confinement, I spent several days behind the closed door of my room, asking myself difficult questions: Had I changed? Was I afraid of death? Did I still have any will left to live? Was I capable of confronting yet more horror in my life?

I was at a critical point. I had to decide who I really was, without anybody's help. Blindly, stumbling on fears great and small, facing Providence itself, without intermediaries or saints, comparing myself to the Roksanas and Nords of the world, I gradually managed to crawl out on all fours toward a point of light again. I couldn't tell whether I was making my way on my own or if I was guided by God, but I finally felt ready to shove off anything, to break through anything, so as not to give up any part of myself, so as not to yield in the slightest bit to the regime. I simply could not live the way MGB wanted me to.

I woke up in the middle of the night feeling more and more strength descending on me from somewhere. I jumped out of bed and whirled about the room, surrendering myself to this primordial dancing with no music, merging with the rhythms of the universe. Deftly spreading my hands to the sides, I was slashing and smashing my own fear, firmly knowing with every cell of my being what a person is born for, and why he is given a soul.

That night I overcame my fear and settled my score with it once and for all. It was my first and most important victory. Fear would still strangle and mow me down numerous times later, but its sticky and annihilating substance had been hammered down forever. Now I could have answered Nina's mother in Leningrad. I knew for sure what and whom I hated. I knew something else, too: in order not to become consumed by hatred, I had to consider death as an integral part of existence. I could not imagine what would happen tomorrow, but the feeling of freedom and orderliness gave me the right to raise my eyes again.

That same night, Dmitry Karayanidi came over uninvited, bringing a bottle of champagne and a can of conserved pineapples.

"What's the occasion, Dima? What is the party for?"

"No particular reason. May I?"

"Yesterday—no. Today—yes. I'm glad to see you, very much so!"

We talked. I told Dmitry they'd been dragging me to the MGB and wanted me to "help" them. Dmitry supported me with a few choice words:

"Don't be afraid of them, even if they threaten you with a revolver. And they can do that—they did it with me. But unless you yourself want to talk, they can't do anything. Stand firm."

"Where were you before, Dima?"

If only he knew what a hole I just crept out of, how torn everything inside me was and how good it felt in spite of everything to live on this earth, waiting for every dawn with a clean conscience.

He knew it. I was happy he was near, so close.

As he was leaving, he said unexpectedly, without raising his eyes:

"I'll never come again."

I didn't ask him to explain.

I WAS SUMMONED many more times, facing the same torrent of brutal threats in answer to my refusals.

"You'll ask for it yourself, but we're not going to listen! I'm giving you another week. We'll call you then."

The atmosphere at work grew more tense. I was no longer given any travel assignments. The annual report I had prepared suddenly disappeared. I couldn't find it anywhere and was officially reprimanded.

Late one evening, Anna Abramovna called me in and offered to have a talk outside:

"What's going on? The director of the House of Culture ordered me not to employ you in concerts or rehearsals anymore."

I told her I was being recruited.

"Rascals!" she said with indignation. "Watch out for them."

I found myself in complete isolation. Every day I expected an eviction notice or an arrest.

When I was finally summoned again, I saw that the leaders of the local MGB had changed. Behind the desk sat a new officer. It didn't take me long to realize that his predecessor had been much more lenient. Among the multitude of multicolored personal files, he found mine, a blue and bulky folder, and started leafing through it, nodding his head in agreement with the anonymous authors of those notes. I stared at his hands while I waited out the long silence. The dirty nails on the phalanxes of his fingers looked so wide and heavy it seemed each of them was crowned with a separate head. The essence of our society was firmly inscribed on his entire appearance. It wasn't hard to imagine the story of this man's "ascent." The portly and neat NKVD men, with their greenish gabardine greatcoats and their dogs on leashes, who roamed through towns back in '37, were now replaced by his type.

The conversation immediately took an unexpected and difficult turn:

"Bakharev: is he your husband?"

"No."

"But the son is his, right?"

"Yes."

"Then he's your husband. So why is he treating you like this?"

"He just is."

"That's a generous reply! You must be suffering without your son. That's all right—we'll find you your boy in no time. So, how're you going to continue on, Petkevich?"

"I live. I work."

"That's clear. We've spent enough time fiddling with you. Are you going to help us?"

"I told you already: I won't."

"If you prove yourself, we'll send you to study. You've studied English before, haven't you? We'll help you with that, too. Work will be more interesting, your life will be different."

"No! Let's not talk about it anymore. I told you clearly: I won't."

He let me go, giving me more time "to think it over."

The next time, losing control over himself, the new boss yelled:

"You think it's easy for us? You think I came here by my own will? That I'm not capable of anything else? The Party called me to take this position! The Party told me they needed me!"

He paced about his office.

"Of course, it's always easier to twiddle your thumbs!"

"I don't twiddle my thumbs. I work."

"I've heard that. This work of yours isn't enough. The world is more complex now. There's an enemy hiding behind every bush, waiting for us to slip up. Doesn't somebody have to stop them?"

The whole world, in his eyes, was a street fight. Everyone fought, wrestled, grabbed for each other's throats. He understood this. I didn't. He was a citizen of his country carrying out his duty and giving it all he had while some "brainless baronesses" like me were fooling around and spreading lies. Looking at me with barefaced hatred, he repeated:

"I'm appealing to your conscience, if you have any. Will you agree?"

"Haven't I served my time in the camps?"

"That's what we need: less suspicion!" he said in a pleased voice. "Types like you are precisely what we're interested in."

"No! I can't! I'm telling you again: I won't."

"Stop this 'I won't' of yours!" he snapped. I'm old enough to be your father. Do you understand who you're saying no to? To Stalin himself! There he is, standing on the rostrum on Red Square, just like during the war, addressing the people: Help! We need you! And you're going to tell him, 'I can't'? What would happen if everyone said that? You're being offered a life. You're being given the chance to be together with everyone else. It's your duty to respond to the faith that we have in you. You're being offered help with your son, after all. Are you at all human, or what?"

No, I wasn't human. I was but a progeny of pain. He did not have the right to talk to me as if I were some orphaned teenager; he did not have the right to promise to return my son in exchange for denunciations. Yet he wouldn't stop.

I couldn't take it anymore. I hated this man!

"Don't you dare go on! Stop!"

Yelling back at me, the officer slammed the door and walked out, leaving me alone in the office.

As I gradually calmed down, I thought: "It can't possibly be an ordinary recruiting. They need me to get to somebody in particular."

My folder—a complete, multiauthored "edition" of denunciations—lay open on the desk. Just as during my arrest in Frunze, I was being tested with loneliness. Behind my back, logs in the tiled stove were burning down to glaring charcoal. Wind slammed against the window. My room was only about fifteen houses away. If I could only lie down to bed and wake up in a different century, preferably in the previous one.

I flinched from a sudden knock on the window. I stood up, opened the door and called the officer.

He walked back in and opened the window.

"Who's this?"

"It's me, son, the school janitor," a buttery female voice reached from the outside. "There's that teacher, she's having her prisoner boyfriend visit her right now. They're in a classroom, sitting there in darkness. The third door down the hallway. If you send one of your men there on the quick, you'll catch them on the spot, for sure."

"All right, mother. Thanks."

The tricks of the trade, the most basic foundations of the society—conscientious representatives of the people in the roles of "mothers," and state functionaries as their "sons"!

"So?" the officer asked me abruptly.

"No use trying."

"I thought so."

He pressed a button under the desk and, just like in Frunze, a guard walked in immediately.

My legs barely obeyed me. My ears were ringing. A door to a small alcove was opened and closed behind my back.

I sat on the bench, then lay down, desiring to drop off, to feel nothing. Everyone—Semyon, Ilya, Tamara Tsulukidze, Simon, Mira, Aleksey—had gone through this. Their hearts must have been sinking like mine. Nothing depended on me any longer.

"So where should I take her?" I heard a voice from behind the door.

"Look in the dispatch papers."

"Should I call the escort?"

"Go ahead."

Then everything grew quiet. The hands of my watch were showing five in the morning when the keys rattled inside the padlock.

"Step out."

The guard pointed me to the office.

"Let's be done with it. Do you agree to cooperate?"

Did he, this heavy-handed boss, sit here the entire night? Or did he sleep his fill at home and just come back?

"No. Do whatever you've decided to do. That's all."

"Go. I'll call you again."

Not trusting him for a moment, I headed for the front door, my spine tingling in expectation.

Everything trembled inside me: they hadn't arrested me?

One branch of the road led to the settlement, the other to the woods. Dense milky fog rising from the marshland before the forest began to dissolve right in front of my eyes. I walked slowly, weighing my every step. It seemed like something eternally important was about to reveal itself to me, right now, in the midst of the melting fog in the Komi Republic.

NO SOONER HAD I OPENED THE DOOR to my apartment than Fanya, my neighbor who worked at the clinic's registry, darted out of her room, followed by a nurse, Anna Fyodorovna, who for some odd reason was visiting her at this early hour. Both were dead drunk. I could tell by looking at their clothes that they hadn't gone to sleep that night. I leaned against the doorpost, exhausted. Her face swollen from tears, the red-haired, freckled Fanya flew off back to her room and returned with a full glass of vodka, which they made me drink, pressing it to my mouth.

"I thought I'd never see you again. Forgive me! I'm foul, I'm a rascal!" Fanya wailed.

Of course! That's where their perfect accuracy of dates and hours stemmed from! She must have been appointed to spy on me a long time ago. That's why they lodged us together. How many of them had there been in my life? Serebryakov, Roksana, the other friend, Evgenia Karlovna in Djangi-Djir... Countless! And I almost wound up among them.

"All right, poor Fanya, don't cry."

At least she wasn't embarrassed to apologize.

The full glass of vodka didn't have any effect on me. My head remained clear.

I closed the door behind me. I had to think everything through to the end. Under no circumstances could I bear further summonses or the sight of the officer's fingers again, with their frightening yellow knobby nails. Passport? Yes, I had it. Work-log? I'd ask somebody to rescue it later. My belongings? I didn't need them!

I made up my mind to leave but didn't know where to go. Nor did I have any money.

Boris was to be let out of the zone at eight in the morning. I ran to meet him.

"They kept me all night under arrest, as if they were preparing me for a transport. I can't take it anymore! I'm leaving."

"Leave, leave!" Boris seconded me. "Money? I'll get you the money. Go to my mother's in Moscow. I'm sure you'll think something out together. Wait for me at the station, near the forest."

In a few hours Boris met me as promised. He handed me the money and rushed back to the camp.

"The train runs past the zone. I'll see you off from there. So long! See you in freedom! Go, don't delay!"

Everything happened like lightning. I cautiously asked an acquaintance, whom I happened to see in the street, to buy me the train ticket.

The train arrived. I climbed up the stairs of the car. I turned my face in the direction of Knyazh-Pogost:

"Forgive me, dear Kolushka! I couldn't come to say good-bye. Farewell, my only! Farewell..."

From the train the Mikun camp, perched right next to the station, looked like a neat blueprint: the square of the zone with watchtowers in the corners and rows of rectangular barracks inside. The prisoners had already been taken out for work; I knew that the lone figure standing between the barracks in the deserted zone was Boris. Bidding farewell to me, he raised both of his hands and outstretched them. The silhouette looked like a crucifix.

I was running away from the North. In fact, I was carrying out what the camp commandant Malakhov had advised me to do a long time ago, the only difference being that now I was leaving by myself, without my son in my arms.

The train was bound for Moscow. I desperately tried to think: then what?

FROM A POSTCARD I received from Aleksandr Osipovich while still in Mikun, I learned that in the special regime camps he was only allowed to write once every six months. Later, however, he was able to send a more detailed letter with a messenger. He asked me not to worry about him and to write as often as possible. Again, he told me about the interesting people that surrounded him, including mathematicians, an astronomer who believed in God and a metropolitan who had renounced Him. There was also the poet Yaroslav Smelyakov with a fifteen-year term. Aleksandr Osipovich asked me to visit Smelyakov's wife, Evdokia Vasilyevna, whenever I happened to be in Moscow, and to give her her husband's address in case she hadn't already gotten it.

I was tormented by the fact that I still hadn't kept my promise to visit Aleksandr Osipovich's wife, Olga Petrovna, in Odessa. Out of all moral obligations, this was my primary one. Not having enough courage to go straight there, I bought a ticket to Chernovtsy, where I had been invited a long time ago by a dentist, Anna Emelyanovna Borodina, who used to work at the Mikun clinic.

From Moscow, I sent a letter to the Shpakovs in Mikun, asking them to see that I was dismissed from work. I included a letter of attorney authorizing them to collect whatever was owed to me of my salary and to take my work-log, which I would need in order to find a job at a new place.

I arrived in Chernovtsy a week later. At the post office, I was given a letter from Moscow, from Boris's mother. She wrote that the Mikun MGB had reported me missing and wanted across the USSR and that from now on, in case my correspondence was under surveillance, the Shpakovs would refer to me as Rostislav.

Behind the traps set for me by the organs, there was a fit of unbridled and primitive vengeance: they had overlooked my departure!

I stayed in Anna Emelyanovna's apartment for five days, afraid to step outside. I didn't touch any food and couldn't sleep. But, unable to bear the self-confinement any longer, I recklessly set out for the cinema.

With the back of my head I felt someone's eyes watching me through the entire film, which I saw nothing of. When the film was over, I waited for the audience to leave the hall and, resigning myself to the end of it all, headed toward the exit.

A tall man was waiting for me in the courtyard of the cinema.

"Are you in a hurry?" he asked.

Not willing to show cowardice while being arrested, I bravely answered no.

"Then why don't we take a walk. I'll show you the town."

I thought, "What a slip of the tongue! He knows I'm not local. Now I can be sure of it."

"Thank you," I told him. "I've already seen everything here."

"Even the prison?" he asked with a smile.

"The prison? No, not yet."

I walked beside him.

He told me that his family had left for a resort, and thus, he was free in the evening.

It was no longer a drama but mere farce!

Only running out of air does a drowning man make a move to save himself. Realizing I was simply losing my mind, I made an irrevocable decision to catch the first train to Moscow to report myself straight to the Ministry of State Security, to find out right then and right there, at the cerebrum of this organization, what they wanted from me. I'd tell them I wasn't afraid of death and would commit suicide if they didn't leave me alone.

Naïve? Of course! But judging by the calm that descended on me at this idea, I understood there was no other way.

I was already on my way when a thought flashed through my mind: "Anything can happen, but just in case it all works out, when will I be in these parts again?" No longer hiding from the all-USSR search and submitting to a powerful inner impulse, I got off at the Razdelnaya station, where I switched trains and went to Odessa.

SOFTENED BY THE HEAT, dressed in gaudy *sarafans,* the suntanned and laughing women in the streets seemed strange to me; the life of the town appeared abnormal, as if I was incurably ill, while life here was shamelessly healthy.

I rode a rattling tram, typical of Odessa, to Pavlov Street where, in a ramshackle house, I found the apartment I was looking for.

Wanda Razumovskaya, who had once seen Olga Petrovna visiting Aleksandr Osipovich in the North, described her to me as a "lady of white gloves." Remembering this only now, I was embarrassed to think I wouldn't be able to keep up a high-mannered conversation. With a sinking heart, I pressed the doorbell.

It was a while before something inside the apartment clicked and the door opened. However, there was no one behind it. From somewhere above, a woman's voice asked:

"Who is it? Who are you looking for?"

Apparently, the door was opened from the second floor, by way of a pedal.

"I'm looking for Olga Petrovna," I said.

"She's in Kishinev at the moment," the voice answered. "She works there, with Moldova Film."

I had just passed Kishinev on my way here!

As I thanked the invisible woman and turned to leave, the voice from above called:

"You didn't say who is looking for her. What shall I tell her?"

"My name won't mean anything to her. She doesn't know me."

"Wait, wait a minute!"

I heard someone coming down, and in a moment an elderly woman with a kind face appeared before me.

"Still, who? I'm Elena Petrovna, Olga Petrovna's sister. Who are you?"

"Tell her Tamara Petkevich was looking for her."

"Who?!" the woman raised her eyebrows in surprise. "Tamara Petkevich? This is you? Could you really turn and leave, just like that? Who does such a thing?"

I was bewildered.

"Sasha wrote us so much about you!" Elena Petrovna shook her head. "We've been waiting for you! And you're going to leave... Come on in, immediately!"

I obeyed her imperative tone. Elena Petrovna kept giving orders:

"Put these shoes on. Come meet our mother. She is ninety-five. We call her Zayka. Sit down on the sofa. Just a minute, I'll feed you. I'll run a bath for you, but while it's being filled let me go down and send a telegram to Olushka. The post office is on the first floor of our building. Here's a book, some berries. Eat, have a rest."

It seemed that, in some miraculous way, I had finally made it home.

Olga Petrovna received the telegram and was back in Odessa that very evening. A shining person stood in the doorway. It was my first impression of her. Her entire appearance radiated light and warmth. A timid and kind-hearted woman, she did not seem to fit the description of a "lady of white gloves" that Wanda had given her.

There had been no letters from Aleksandr Osipovich for a long time. Nor did Olga Petrovna know if any of the parcels she had been sending him at the new address ever reached him, and one could not hope that the conditions in special regime camps would become milder in the future.

The sisters tried to persuade me to stay in Odessa as their guest, to have a rest and go to the beach. I didn't tell them about my circumstances and vaguely declined.

Under the pretext that it would be easier for Olga Petrovna to register my train ticket than it would be for me, she insisted that I let her handle my travel arrangements. But when we arrived at the station, the two sisters led me to one of the "international class" cars. Such a change after the cattle cars I'd been traveling on before!

"Believe me, this is more for our sake than for yours, so don't be embarrassed."

"Don't you think," Elena Petrovna turned to Olga Petrovna, pointing at me, "she's our little sister?"

On my way to my "final reckoning," I was departing with the feeling of having acquired a very special treasure: I became the "little sister" of Aleksandr Osipovich's wife and Elena Petrovna.

IN MOSCOW, on Kuznetsky Most, I took my turn in the line for the MGB waiting room.

I was going to make them explain why a person had no right to refuse to cooperate with the organs of state security, and what it was exactly that put me among the ranks of the especially dangerous criminals of the Soviet Union. All the knots had to be cut forever. It was a question of life and death in the most literal sense.

A high-ranking officer walking through the hall suddenly stopped near me and asked:

"What's your question? Come in… I'm listening."

As if in a delirium, I started telling him everything: how the MGB in Mikun persecuted me until I ended up in the hospital, about my refusals and the signature, about their threats to cart me off to the woods and to charge me with a criminal article, about their hypocritical promise to find my son, about the staged arrest at night, about the all-Union search and, eventually, about the fact that I was alone in the entire world and that if they didn't leave me in peace right then I would throw myself under the first tramcar I saw as soon as I left their headquarters.

Someone brought me a glass of water. When I calmed down, the officer told me to go to the waiting room until I was called.

I waited for a long time. They were making inquiries and double-checking the information. Finally, I was invited in again.

"Go wherever you'd like, except the restricted cities stipulated by Regulation 39. Settle down. Work. No one will bother you again. In case a conflict arises—here is our address and my name. Write to me. Should you feel a personal visit necessary, please come. Any other questions? Requests?"

"No!"

"That's all, then."

I trusted this man. He relieved my soul, unburdened it of the annihilating oppression.

I told myself I was simply lucky, that I'd happened to run into a man who had listened. The organ of state power, which had devoured an unimaginably large number of people, seemed to have satiated its appetite and promised not to touch me again. It was only now that I walked out of the zone and was set free!

It was unlikely, though, as I thought moments later, that my case was just an exception. Perhaps something had changed in the system, in the entire country? The thought was so agreeable there could be no better companion for walking around the streets of Moscow. Drunk with freedom, I roamed the streets, one leading into another, and then headed to the city's main telegraph office, Moscow-9.

Through the little window I was given a few letters, a telegram notification, as well as a money order for three hundred rubles, which I thought must have been a mistake since none of my penniless friends could ever send me such a huge sum of money.

Skimming through the text of the telegram, reading it again and again, I couldn't bring myself to grasp its meaning. It said: *Tamarochka Sasha returned all is well your letter received wiring three hundred love kisses Olya.*

Olga Petrovna? And Sasha—Aleksandr Osipovich? Released? Indeed, something must have changed somewhere.

I tried to compose a telegram in response but dropped it, half-written, and rushed to the railway station. With the money received from Olga Petrovna, I purchased a ticket to go back to Odessa, to the people I scarcely knew, but who were closest to me in this world.

IN ODESSA, I found neither Aleksandr Osipovich nor Olga Petrovna. Elena Petrovna told me that nearly the day after I left, her sister was summoned to the local office of State Security and asked if she was willing to take her husband, who had been released from the camp as an invalid, as her dependent, provided that he would settle 101 kilometers away from the city.

"Sasha is barely recognizable," Elena Petrovna shook her head. "He used to be so handsome! He isn't feeling well."

Of all the places situated 101 kilometers outside of Odessa, Olga Petrovna chose the settlement Vesely Kut, where she rented a room for Aleksandr Osipovich, and where I set out for immediately.

It was hard to imagine how he was going to live there by himself, in that Ukrainian village where there was no library, without the company of the philosopher Lev Karsavin, the poet Smelyakov and Ariadna Efron, without the rest of his friends. Nevertheless, his release was an extraordinary event beyond comprehension, and I only wished he could breathe freedom.

Olga Petrovna, loaded down with groceries, came to Vesely Kut the same evening. Late at night, when everyone was already asleep, she accompanied me to the house where I was going to spend the night. Dogs were barking as we walked past the small gardens. The settlement was flooded with moonlight. Gogol's *May Night* and *Terrible Vengeance* came to mind, and it seemed that this phantasmagoric glaring of the moon was just as handy for the crafty and whimsical devils to leap out of nowhere as darkness itself.

Olga Petrovna confided in me about the "diabolism" of the times:

"I remember that frightening meeting at the Kiev Film Studio, when people we had considered our friends rose one after another to slander and destroy Sasha. They accused him of making films that distorted Soviet reality, films that were alien to the proletariat. No one stood up to defend him, not a single person. At best, they kept silent."

It was the story about the beginning of her and Aleksandr Osipovich's life together, about how she, his assistant at the time, had knocked on his door, imagining how awful and lonely her "patron saint" felt after the crushing defeat at the meeting.

In 1934, their family, indeed their whole life was torn apart, the only reason being Aleksandr Osipovich's "alien" films. It was enough to keep the film director for twenty years in the camps.

All of a sudden, Olga Petrovna told me:

"Let's talk to each other like sisters. Call me Olya. Say it!"

Overcoming embarrassment, I repeated: "Olya!" I already loved her with all my heart.

Aleksandr Osipovich was glad to hear that I'd been invited to work at the theater.

"Now that's certainly something I can help you with."

"But dear Aleksandr Osipovich, the theater is so far away. It's in the Urals. Besides, no one will register my residence in a city like yours anyway."

"A good friend you are!" he said in disappointment. "We shouldn't be far from each other now."

I, too, was afraid of leaving, of going to the Ural Mountains all alone. I couldn't have guessed back then that Dmitry Femistoklevich Karayanidi, who had sworn in Mikun never to visit me again, would find me there, and that we would live together for seven kind and warm years.

After a year of our season in the Urals, we were invited to join the theater in one of the towns on the Volga. Later, Olya insisted that Dima and I move to Kishinev. It was ten years after my release that I finally moved, on my own, back to my native city of Leningrad.

Chapter 13

All those years, I was frantically searching for my son, sending countless inquiries to the information bureaus of large cities and small towns. Piles of replies came back saying nothing except "Not registered" or "Does not reside here." My friends would get in touch with their own acquaintances from the North and ask them if anyone had heard about Bakharev, and sometimes one or the other would report: "He's in Saratov," or "He's living in Kineshma." But I would receive the same answer from those towns: "Does not reside."

Only in 1956, when my son was already eleven, I received a postcard from Anna Abramovna Berzin, in which she told me where the Bakharevs were currently living.

A lawyer friend of mine, Nelly K., who had been offering help all through my long search, could finally put her expertise to real use.

I hastily collected all sorts of letters of support and references. Nelly left for the town where the Bakharevs lived. Telegrams from her started coming in one after another. She had almost finished all the necessary preparations and had even talked to Yurochka. He was doing well in school. She also spoke with Bakharev, who was frightened of having his parental authority with Yury undermined and therefore would not try to prevent his son from meeting me. Filipp was inclined to resolve the issue amicably and, as Nelly said, would probably propose marriage to me upon my arrival.

I had no faith in Filipp's assertions. He existed for me as a phantom of evil resourcefulness, nothing else.

BAKHAREV didn't wait for me to reach the airport building but ran out to the airfield, hoping to shield himself from a tide that seemed to be turning against him. He yelled above the sounds of the blizzard.

"We will register our marriage!"

Nelly had instructed me, "Answer yes to everything for the time being, all the rest—later." When Filipp stepped away, she quickly recounted:

"I came to see him in the clinic and waited till my turn came in line. He asked me, 'How can I help you," and when I told him I came from you, he turned dreadfully pale, clutched his head with his hands and canceled his consultation hours. He kept silent for a long time, then asked: 'What do you think, will she agree to marry me?' I saw Yurik. He's a good boy, very poorly dressed."

Bakharev ushered me to his car and offered to go to his clinic to talk.

People had warned me: "Emotions are inappropriate and even detrimental in these circumstances." Nevertheless, I lost my temper. "What have you done?!" I yelled at Filipp, who sank to his knees and crawled toward me on the ground. Beside myself with rage, I kicked him away.

I knew Bakharev would get even with me for this. Indeed, when I asked to see my son, he told me I'd have to wait until the next day.

"No! Today!" I insisted.

"All right," he conceded. "But under two conditions: First, I will introduce you as his aunt; second—no reminders of the past."

The room in the clinic where Bakharev brought my son was in a damp basement, with peeling walls.

"The farther from curious people, the better," he explained.

The young boy in a brown velveteen jacket with too-short sleeves looked around, perplexed.

"Yura, this is Aunt Tamara!" Bakharev said without explaining how I was related, where I was from, or anything else about me.

I asked my son questions, engulfed by the sole desire to awaken our "mutual memory" in him, to grope for a common nerve that couldn't possibly have disappeared between us:

"Do you like to play chess, Yurik? What is your favorite subject in school?"

Yurik was strained and tense and answered politely. The supplication hidden in my questions did not reach him. His memory and attention were distracted by something of the present and remained untouched.

My son seemed timid, as if there were no trace of boyish mischief or youthful curiosity in him. "Can I go, Papa? I have to do my homework."

"All right."

I had failed to arouse any recognition in my son, but I resisted the temptation to vent my frustration at this fact upon Bakharev. To win Yurik's trust and attention, there was a lot I still had to do. If only I could spend more time with him! "His memory of me is suppressed. It can't have disappeared," I consoled myself. "If not today, then tomorrow it will reawaken."

But I could no longer rely on "tomorrow." The next day Bakharev cut me off from seeing my son any further:

"I took him out of the town, to our relatives. Seeing him will bring nothing but harm to both of you."

"You either bring my son back this minute, or I'm taking the documents to court immediately!" was all I could manage to say.

"The court won't help you!" he parried.

"Then who will???"

Pressing his lips, Bakharev fell silent.

THE JUDGE, an attractive, bright-eyed woman about thirty, listened to me with distrust and bewilderment but accepted the documents nonetheless. My friends had sent dozens of letters to the court, each telling whatever they knew about the circumstances of Yurik's birth, how he grew up, how he was stolen and how I'd been looking for him for so long.

A hearing between me, Bakharev and three jury members was scheduled for the following day.

In answering the judge's questions, I had to speak about everything from the very beginning: the camp, the infirmary, the birth of my son, Bakharev's promises and subsequent trickery, my release and all that had followed. Resting their elbows on their knees and craning their heads intently, the three jurors sat silent and listened.

As I was recounting how the Bakharevs took Yurik and disappeared, the judge interrupted me and turned to my son's father:

"Filipp Yakovlevich, is this woman telling the truth?"

Expecting evasions and lies, I was surprised by his brief answer: "Yes," he said, failing to hide the emotions on his face. It seemed like only now was he actually contemplating what he had done.

The hearing resulted in the unanimous decision that my son be brought back to town and that I be allowed to see him. Bakharev didn't protest. His complaisance alarmed me.

"Tomorrow at three, come to our house," he told me when we went outside.

"Talk to Yurik before then. Explain everything. Tell him something like, the doctors didn't give me much time to live and I was sent far away to the mountains; that you didn't think I would survive and therefore concealed the truth from him."

I was ready for any kind of a dirty trick, such as finding my son gone when I'd arrive at the Bakharevs', but a much more frightening treachery was awaiting me.

No sooner did Nelly and I enter the room where Yurik, sitting at the dinner table, was doing his homework than Bakharev pointed at me and, blurted out:

"Yura! This is your mother!"

My son raised his eyes in horror and exhaled slightly:

"Why?"

Trying somehow to salvage the situation, I mumbled:

"Yurochka, it's nothing scary. Things like this happen. You will understand soon. Don't you remember me? You haven't forgotten that I used to come visit you in Velsk? I was bedridden for several years, but now I've recovered and come to you right away. We all love you..."

With his eyes down, not looking at anyone, he turned and walked out of the room.

In that way Bakharev had instantly managed to cause tumult inside my son's mind. For him I became a sign of trouble, and only his father could henceforth heal this wound, in his house, without the help of the troublesome "guest." Mathematical logic, the suddenness of the attack—I knew this tactic well.

THE MAIN CONDITION for further meetings with Yurik was that Vera Petrovna be present as well. There was nothing more perverted and unbearable than seeing my son in her presence. When I tried to protest, Bakharev only replied, "I won't allow it otherwise, and they have no authority over me here!"

Vera Petrovna would slam the door running in and out of the room, demonstrating her irritation. She followed us wherever we went.

"Do you understand, Yurik, why the hero of the film..." I leaned toward him in the cinema as we watched *Between Two Oceans.* "Oh, don't stuff his head with all that esotericism! He's too little for it," Vera Petrovna interfered. "Remember, Yurochka, how you bathed in a sea like that with your father?"

We were going to the planetarium. Vera Petrovna took her nephew Seryozha along, too. Riding the tram, the lively and smart boy would ask questions, but Yurik just stared out the window.

"You don't want to go? Just say so," she pushed him. "Why are you silent?"

But he did want to go, and he listened with interest to the story about Tom Sawyer that I told the boys along the way.

In the planetarium, amid the stars and planets rotating around us, I barely held myself back from grabbing my son, whose shoulders seemed so strained and unyielding, and pulling him tightly toward me.

It was all very draining. I went out to the planetarium garden. Nelly came running out after me.

"Just when you left, Yurik asked me: 'Where's Mama?'"

"It's not true, Nelly! He didn't say that!" I implored.

"I swear!"

The next time my son and I were left alone, I told him:

"Yurochka, we'll go to a very beautiful southern town, where everything is green!"

"What for? I don't want to."

"I love you very much. I've been without you for so long. It'll be good to be there together. You'll live there and go to school and you can come here whenever you like."

"No."

"Why, Yurik?"

"I don't want to."

No one had helped my son to form any idea of who I was. My son did not know me.

BAKHAREV had never adopted the boy legally. He knew I would've never agreed.

"How is it possible that in school your son is registered as Bakharev, while the last name on his birth certificate is Petkevich?" the judge asked me.

It was this legal question that disclosed the Bakharevs' fraud.

"You're in for hearing something quite sensational," the judge warned me the next time we met. "Here it is: you are not the real mother of Yury. It's Vera Petrovna who gave birth to him, not you."

On the table before me lay three forged copies of my son's birth certificate. Under "Mother" it was written: Vera Petrovna Bakhareva. Place of birth: an invented town, not Mezhog. Instead of the true birth date, December 12, 1945, there were three different dates in each of the copies, all with contradicting days, months and even years.

I trusted the judge. Unselfish and cordial, she considered my every feeling, but there was still something that seemed to cause her hesitation:

"I have to tell you: you came one year too late," she explained. "Only one year! The law has it that children over eleven decide for themselves which of their parents they want to live with. You understand yourself who your son will choose during the court hearing."

"Are you denying me the right to a hearing?"

"No, of course not. Much speaks to your advantage. But the court will have to take into account the wishes of the child."

Many times I had imagined my son in the courtroom, answering that question in front of strangers; I saw his lowered eyes and knew how his heart would freeze when, in the end, he'd point to the Bakharevs and say, "With them!" In the epicenter of the battle was my child's soul. I couldn't expose him to the court procedure; it was beyond me to fight for him in this way. He already had his own will. I was afraid to lose him.

"What about the fact that my son is being raised by people who have forged everything?"

"They will be made to answer for this, but it's a different issue. There's enough in their file for a whole different lawsuit, and some day such a suit will take place. But how can I help you now, except by offering my deepest sympathy? My heart turned inside out when I was reading your friends' letters."

"What do you suggest?"

"Recall the documents from the court. I'll even give you back all the letters. I don't want his attorney to touch them. By the way, Bakharev hired the best attorney there is. Try to sort it out with him amicably. Don't they have anything human left in them?"

The justice was able to cite many compelling articles and statutes, which in essence deprived me of any hope of getting my son back. I gave up the idea of a public trial.

NELLY'S VACATION ran out and she left. I stayed on by myself. Before long, I was already walking to Bakharev's house as a supplicant, playing the role they had devised for me.

In the middle of their gloomy apartment stood a large sideboard crammed with glassware.

"You don't have a single book at home," I observed.

"We don't have any today, tomorrow we can have a whole library," the host replied.

"Show me your photographs," I asked Yurik.

"Which ones?"

"Any photos with you."

In one of the pictures, Yurochka and his father were walking through a field to the river. In another—they stood near a calf, Yurochka stroking the animal… And here they were, squatting and feeding chickens; now they were sitting on a stool, the father fixing something, Yurochka, carefree, standing nearby…

As I was looking at those photographs, which told me the story of my son's life, while Vera Petrovna, in twinkling diamond earnings, whisked smartly about the apartment, I understood then and there that my son loved these people and everything that surrounded him here. He loved both of them together and separately. They loved him too. He had fused together with them. They were his primary and stable reality. All the mirages I'd held in my mind evaporated at once, and even the flow of time itself slowed down.

When, later on, someone told me, "Back in the North, Filipp even wanted you to take him to court," I looked at the man as though he were mad. "How could he want this?" I asked. "He did. Your son would have been awarded to you, and this would have given him the chance to get rid of Vera Petrovna, and would have taken the responsibility for that decision off his shoulders," the man explained.

Now Bakharev wasn't embarrassed to stoop to self-pity when he pointed his eyes at Vera Petrovna and said grievously:

"Don't you see who I've spent my whole life with?"

As I was leaving their house, he stood up:

"Let me walk you out."

Did he secretly harbor some feelings for me? No. From the dark corners of his soul came something I could only explain as moral and intellectual degradation:

"Do you understand at least, why I indicated that date as Yurik's birthday on his birth certificate? It's the anniversary of our first meeting, in Svetik."

In the moral coordinates of that man, I had been memorialized as but a date on a forged document.

THE COURT ISSUED A VERDICT: "Nullify the birth certificate as invalid." Although the suit had been brought not by me but by the prosecutor, the Bakharevs didn't spare a chance to add fuel to my son's unfavorable view of his mother. "A few days ago," wrote Vera Petrovna, "we received a notification from the prosecutor to come see him in court. Yura looked at the notice and said: 'It's Tamara Vladislavovna who wrote to him about it!' and frowned."

I never managed to reach through to my son's heart. All my attempts failed. I would go to the town where he lived and watch him growing up from a distance.

Bakharev died.

"Father left his coded notes," Yura told me much later during one of our meetings.

"Are you decoding them?"

"Yes, though it's not easy. He used an old key that was popular in the twenties."

"And you won't rest until you decipher them, will you?"

"No."

I don't know what Bakharev committed to paper, which "truth" he disclosed in his diary notes. But my son was filled with an insatiable interest toward his father and was indifferent to everything that related to me. His loyalty to Vera Petrovna, the woman who brought him up, left his heart undivided.

"You don't like them?!" he accused me once, half asking a question, half making a condemning statement.

"They took away my son!" was all I could say.

In Place of an Epilogue

I don't know what tormented Barbara Ionovna the most, but her supplication—"I want to see you! Have mercy on me: don't let me die without asking you for forgiveness!"—could not leave me indifferent. The past would not be put to rest easily.

She was living together with her elder son and her granddaughter Tatochka, who was already in the eighth grade in school, not far from Moscow.

It was around eight in the morning when I found the house outside the city where they were renting a room. Before I even finished asking the landlord if I'd come to the right address, Barbara Ionovna, completely gray-haired, ran out from behind the door and threw herself on her knees before me.

My ex-mother-in-law, aged and destitute, was sobbing, and soon we were sobbing together, about something greater than just what was mine, hers or ours. Pining away, she told me in detail how she lived and suffered after Erik and I were arrested.

"And your lot, too," she bemoaned, remembering herself. "There was so much that you had to live through."

She went on, complaining:

"Things never really straightened out between Erik and me. Our relationship never got back to normal. He came with his family to visit. His wife is a Ukrainian, they have two children. She's fat, though she seems kind—a real sergeant. She loves Erik and the children."

When I had applied for a passport, I'd innocently indicated Erik's name and the place of our marriage on the forms. I could blame no one except myself for the stamp attesting to my marriage. But Erik was shrewder: filling out his documents, he did not mention a word about being married to me. It didn't matter whether Barbara Ionovna and her son were at peace with each other or at odds, but she implored me:

"Don't make this fact public. He concealed the fact that you two were married. Now this new wife and his two children are listed in his passport."

Then she added in passing:

"He still believes he never would have been thrown in prison if he hadn't married you."

This cut me to the quick. Tatochka, who was sitting nearby, helped me withstand the blow:

"Auntie Tamara!" she whispered ardently, "Don't be upset. Don't regret anything, don't think about him..."

I was returning to the city by bus. It was pouring. The wind combed the rain dripping down the windows into parallel tracks, one outdistancing the other. I tried to convince myself to let nothing of what I'd heard of Erik stay in my mind, to let it trickle down together with this rain. After all, it was the same old betrayal, nothing more.

Several years later, instead of the spacious and comfortable apartment they used to own, Barbara Ionovna and Tatochka were issued a warrant for a nine-square-meter room in Leningrad. There was a time when every other Sunday they would come to my place for dinner. Barbara Ionovna, slim and poorly dressed, comported herself with her old dignity. She rarely smiled, but I looked forward to her visits and wanted to fill her life with at least a little joy. I understood her well in some ways.

In 1956–1957, after rehabilitation, one could file a claim for the property confiscated many years before. To do so, one had to submit a list of confiscated items, indicating their approximate value, which would then be collated with the corresponding documents from the person's personal file.

I filed my indemnity papers; the answer that came was startling: "No statement of confiscated property found in your file." It turned out that, despite the court's verdict, the interrogator had not confiscated our property and instead gave it all to Barbara Ionovna.

"You have to understand, Tamara: we had nothing to live on. I sold everything bit by bit," Barbara Ionovna told me.

She needn't have to explain. I knew the ways of hunger and poverty.

Barbara Ionovna died in Moscow. Erik, with whom she never reconciled, came to the funeral. Tatochka said that after spending several hours in a room with his mother's body, Erik emerged visibly aged and darkened. In the Leningrad Catholic church, Tatochka requested a service for her grandmother who had raised her.

THE NEED TO GET RID of the idiotic marriage stamp in my passport drove me from one office to another. Everywhere I was told the same thing: "Yes, it's really something... But we can't do much about it. Try consulting a lawyer."

The lawyer said:

"First your ex-husband has to divorce his current wife. Then he can start the proceedings to divorce you. After this, let him marry whoever he wants."

By the time I returned to Leningrad in 1959, Erik had already been living there for several years. I found his address and sent him a typewritten note: *Please call this phone number.* He called immediately.

"I have a request for you from Tamara Vladislavovna," I said into the phone receiver.

"Where is she?"

"In Leningrad."

"I suppose I'd rather meet with her in person than take a request through a third party."

"Well, that's possible. This is me."

A long pause followed.

"May I come immediately?"

"Tomorrow."

We arranged to meet the following evening near Lenfilm.

"Here we are, husband and wife, seventeen years later. Seventeen years from that morning... Is it really you, standing here like this, next to me? What have they done with us, Tamara? Can you give it a name?" Erik kept asking.

He used to be handsome, with his winning smile and half-sleepy mannerisms. Now he had grown stout. But he still adjusted his glasses with the same movement of his hands. The last time I had seen him was through the hole the jailbird Valya and I had dug underneath the wall in the courtyard of the Frunze prison.

"Shall we go to a café?" I asked.

"No, no—anywhere, just not around too many people."

"All right. I live close by. Let's go to my place."

We sat facing each other.

"Remember how you'd meet me in the alley from work, how once, running toward me, you fell down?"

"No, I don't."

"You fell. And when I used to remember it there, in the camps, my heart always ached, and I'd just long to help you to your feet... I didn't have the time to do it then: you stood up yourself. You always stood up without me later on too… And how you heated up the stove with rags soaked in black oil, how you baked the pancakes… Do you remember that?"

"Yes."

"Do you remember how I loved you?"

"Loved?"

"Yes. Only you. Always. Then and forever after."

"Enough, Erik. Don't. It wasn't that way at all."

"It was, it was! It's only thanks to you that I graduated from the Institute!"

"Are you happy now?"

"My happiness remained in that room with dirt floors, in Frunze."

"Fine, let it be so. You have children?"

"Two. And where's Yurik?"

"Not with me. I don't talk about it with anyone."

"How could you withstand all that?"

"Somehow."

"I wish they'd given me two sentences instead of giving one to you… I didn't know how you'd endure it."

"I also didn't think you'd manage, although you used to talk about how you'd show them if they only dared to touch me…"

"They did—and I did nothing to save you."

"You couldn't."

"I couldn't. That's why you stopped loving me. It's true, later on I performed a successful operation on the camp commandant. He could've reunited us there, in his camp, in no time. I cursed and scorned myself, but I just couldn't ask him."

"They would've separated us later anyway."

"Perhaps, but I still should have asked him! We lived so well, we never quarreled. And we could've kept on living like that up to now."

"We did quarrel, Erik."

"I don't remember! I don't! But I do remember us buying you the black velvet dress. How it suited you! When I wanted to feel better, I'd ask: 'If I could only dream of Tamara wearing the black dress!' And you would appear in my dream, but you'd be wearing a sackcloth, and I'd wake up with an aching heart."

"Don't, Erik."

"How I feared for you when you left to the North on the transport! When I was transferred to Belovodsk, you were no longer there. Since then I've become a different person. I learned what anger and revenge are."

"A human being certainly goes through that." "You think I've moved past these emotions?"

"I think so, yes. You have a family, children. Things like this make one softer."

"My wife sometimes has fits of hatred toward me."

"You're probably guilty of something from time to time. I doubt she's just a misanthrope."

"You mean you still wouldn't stick up for me?"

I cut him short.

"Here is what I wanted to talk to you about. There is a stamp from our marriage in my passport. Sheer nonsense. It's because of my own stupidity, of course..."

Fear flashed through his eyes. He kept silent for a few moments and said:

"You think I'll agree to divorce?"

There was no need to talk further. It became obvious he wasn't going to help me with anything. I glanced at my watch.

"Shall I go? Do you want me to leave?"

"Yes, it's time."

I shut the door behind him and lingered in the corridor for a while. Something like a groan reached me from the stairway. One floor down, Erik was crying on the landing. I went to him.

"Stop, Erik! Don't."

"Only now do I understand how thirsty I've been for your soul, for your intellect, for your eyes and voice. Why did they do this? What did they need us for? What should we do now?"

"Everything has been done, and not without a personal contribution, Erik. Calm down. Don't cry like this."

"I can't live without you. I didn't die then, so I will now..."

"It didn't happen then and of course it won't happen now. You're alive and everything is good with you. What you're feeling now is only temporary. It will pass."

He called me the very next day.

"I'm near your house. Step out. I need to tell you something."

He was walking toward me, smiling:

"Have you put a sweater on? Why are you coughing? Listen, you are very dear to me. You're my wife. I'm your husband. And I won't be anyone else to you in your life. I feel real when I'm near you. There's no one more beautiful..."

I smiled back:

"I'd pay dearly to see what's inside your head, Erik. What are you really like? I know one thing, though: you still don't account for what you say. I don't believe a single word of it. I haven't believed since those times. Are you just having fun? Aren't you ashamed?"

"I could be a different man. But you believed them," he said, in an accusing tone. "You gave me up to them. Why? I am filled with rage for how they crippled our life."

"What's underneath your rage, then?"

"Underneath it? There is no forgiveness there, either!"

We saw each other one more time, when he especially insisted. I was going to the cinema to see a new film.

"You know," he told me as we made our way there, "my daughter came up to me yesterday and asked: 'Papa, what's wrong? Has something happened?' She always knows what's in my heart. She's the closest person to me in the world."

"How old is she?"

"Nine."

"Already a big girl. It's good that you have such a friend."

Sitting next to me, he didn't look at the screen. Nor did I watch the film, trying as I was to work out what was going on inside him: here, the splash of his fantasies ran dry and his consciousness regained the ability to evaluate things soberly; he realized he had a good home and family and became frightened of losing it all over a mere outburst of emotions he had not quite gotten out of him in the past.

"I forgot... I've just remembered: I still have to stop by the institute."

He could have spared me the explanation. I knew he would rush to save himself from his own minute turbulence of the heart. I also understood he would never betray the family he had now. Fate allowed him this luxury. I tried to help him in my thoughts: "Go! And thank God that you have somewhere to go, now that you're rushing off like this."

I wished him no harm, though the pain still persisted. That was how we parted forever, never to meet or know anything about each other again, all the while living in the same city.

DURING ONE OF MY TRIPS to Moscow, I visited a friend from the North, at whose house gathered a group of elderly women, all prisoners of the '37 Generation.

They were excitedly discussing the latest Moscow news: all of them, the old Bolsheviks, had been invited to the representative offices of the Party, where they were told: "A special room has been allotted to you at the Lenin

Public Library, where you can sit and write your memoirs about your revolutionary activity, and about the camps too."

A genuine exultation reigned at the dinner table, stirred by the fact that they hadn't been discounted or disregarded by the state. They were glad that the state itself was encouraging them to tell their stories.

"What did you expect? That I should stay angry with the Party? If they had treated us that way, there must have been a reason for it!" spoke the most loud-voiced woman.

They kept repeating, turn by turn as well as in unison: "We're Leninites! The Old Guard! Bolsheviks who haven't betrayed the ideals of our youth! They confused us for the real enemies. They grabbed us by mistake! Yes, that's it, by mistake!"

These women were eager to brush aside their own, and others', suffering without even bothering to correlate their "bright ideals" with the fates of those who remained lying in common grave pits or under the ties of the far-off railways. They wanted only to reaffirm the political infallibility of the Party, to bring back their desired recognition, at any price. Their worldviews, frightening and loathsome, were motivated by the politicized, yet essentially biological, thrust for thoughtless existence.

Everything in me rebelled against their pathetic efforts to apply the theory of chance to one's individual life. Without saying good-bye, I left that house, never to come there again.

MY CHILDHOOD FRIEND died suddenly and incongruously in Leningrad. It wasn't because of the time we spent together as children, or because of our romantic meetings when we were seventeen, and not even because of our last encounter when we were thirty, that he remained part of the biography of my soul. It was because of something else, namely, his renunciation of me had seared guilty feelings into his heart, from which he never recovered.

Upon my return to Leningrad, I learned that everything had turned out well in his life. He loved his profession passionately, was a professor and a chair of his department at a university. He married for love and was raising two children. His difficult temper was the only thing that prevented him from leading a quiet life. He was excessively conceited, biting, and at times, at complete disarray, yet helpless too.

When he fell gravely ill, he asked me to visit him in the hospital.

"There is one true way of achieving things in the world: power. I have become self-assertive and immodest, and I will not tolerate anything that stands in my path," he declared.

I didn't believe his bravado.

"What path are you talking about?" I asked. "Your path to where? You have had a splendid career, after all."

"Punish me, beat me!" he didn't let me finish. "It's easier than living with this scratching shame in my heart. Speak, keep speaking! Really, what am I talking about? What way and what paths do I mean if all of them lead me nowhere but away from my true self? I feel the breath of such independence and strength from you! You are my romantic treasure! When I don't feel well, I tell myself a fairy tale about you."

Sometimes he would call me:

"I want to see you."

"What for?"

"I need to see you."

"But I don't need to see you!" I would grow angry.

"Then tell me you have a man who says tender things to you, who loves you, who doesn't let you feel lonely."

"What is it with you?"

"Tell me there is such a man. Swear!"

A few times he caught up with me unexpectedly on my way home from work. Once he looked completely dismayed.

"Just imagine: a graduate student whom I spent tons of energy on turned out to be a total lowlife. How do you like that?"

Another time his confusion was even greater:

"I just needed to see you. Tomorrow I have to operate on my own daughter. Do you understand?"

One day he called to tell me he'd been fired.

"Why? What happened?"

"Fired for being a Jew. I guess that's how it should be… You know, it's punishment for what I did to you."

He would deliberately refuse to settle scores with himself.

The doctors fought desperately for his life, but it all proved hopeless. His dismissal from work came as a fatal blow right to the heart. His beloved family grieved, and I too, very much.

I still remember him often. He was the only person in my life who had thought to ask: "Wait! During all the years you spent there, you didn't read, didn't watch any films, didn't listen to any music. You were deprived of everything that we had?" His piercing guess was medicinal at the time.

* * *

ALEKSANDR OSIPOVICH GAVRONSKY

In reality, life in Vesely Kut meant permanent exile for Aleksandr Osipovich. He had aged noticeably and it was difficult for him to walk. Yet whether in the fall, through impassable mud, or in winter, he would have to travel to the district center and register himself with the local authorities by the deadline. He did this faithfully until a local policeman volunteered to take Aleksandr Osipovich's documents to the town himself.

After I moved to Kishinev, I visited him often. There were low ceilings in his hut. Near the small window, which overlooked the garden, sat a man with the eyes of a sage. Behind the window in the yard there lay a giant pile of orange pumpkins.

"You call these pumpkins?" Aleksandr Osipovich smiled. "I thought they were watermelons. They were once so tasty, you know. I've been too embarrassed to ask the landlady for a taste."

In 1971, when he was no longer alive, I came across an issue of the magazine *Znamya,* with Yury Nagibin's autobiographical novel, *The Alleyways of My Childhood,* and read the following passage about Aleksandr Osipovich's mother, Vysotskaya:

> Evicted from her palazzos by the Revolution, the old Vysotskaya settled in our house, on the first floor, in a set of rooms whose windows overlooked a trash dump. The windows were at right angles to each other, and the resourceful old woman set up a small fence outside the house from one window to the other, whereby she managed not only to fence herself off from the dump but also to secure a small triangular patch of land, where she planted grass and flowers and even installed a tiny bench. She twined ivy and vine around the walls of the house between the two windows. And although the plot of land wasn't much larger than those gardens that Andersen's housewives would set up on their windowsills, the housing committee required Vysotskaya to make her garden available to the rest of the citizens residing in the house. The old woman agreed but hung up a sign that said: *Riding bicycles is categorically prohibited in this public garden.*

The mother was a capitalist, her son—a revolutionary who used to organize meetings of protest at the factory that his parents owned. But how similar were the ends of their lives spent in pens and enclosures!

Village children always crowded around Aleksandr Osipovich in Vesely Kut. He coached some of them in mathematics and helped others with German, or else played chess with them. He never stopped writing his sketches on philosophy and solving mathematical problems. The sheets of paper that Olechka brought him were all dappled with numbers. Mathematics and philosophy remained his passion despite the fact that there was no hope of ever publishing his works.

Olga came to Vesely Kut regularly, replenishing her husband's foodstuffs, especially coffee, and paying rent to the landlady. His dependence on his wife was taking a toll on Aleksandr Osipovich.

His friends from the North and those from his earlier life would also come to visit him, and the most frequent guest was Hella. We were all abominably poor and couldn't afford to make his squalid life here any better.

Visiting Aleksandr Osipovich, I always found myself drawn into an atmosphere of contagious ideas and inner reflection. I could ask him about the innermost secrets of life, as well as about God, in Whom he didn't believe. But most of all I would just listen. When evening came, a kerosene lamp would be lit in the hut, and the landlady would bring a jug of milk.

In 1956, Aleksandr Osipovich was rehabilitated.

With the certificate from the Military Board of the Supreme Soviet, which stated a "lack of corpus delicti" after all the terms he had served and which altogether cost him twenty-five years of life, Olya now had the right to take her husband to her home in Kishinev.

In total, they lived together but seven years, the rest of their lives having been spent in separation. After being apart for such a long time, the torment and bliss of their reunion was heartrending. Getting accustomed to normal life was a painful process, often insuperable and always dramatic.

I would tell Aleksandr Osipovich about new Italian films, such as *Roma ore 11* and *The Bicycle Thief,* which at the time struck our imagination. He would listen and say with grief:

"I've fallen hopelessly behind everything that is now happening in cinema. I could've been of some help to Olechka."

In the evenings, Olya would sit behind her small desk, writing scripts and editing others' work. In the mornings, after she'd leave for the studio, this place was occupied by Aleksandr Osipovich.

A documentary filmmaker, Olya traveled around Moldavia in winter cold or in the heat of summer, by train or by truck. I watched many of her films and reels about local cardiologists, small children, the leaders of the Moldovan underground, the villages spanning the hills in the reddish haze of the setting sun, where people made handicrafts, cultivated vineyards and danced. Her films, always warm and poetic, moved my soul with their humanity.

Trying to involve Aleksandr Osipovich in her work, she would ask him to listen to this or that script and take his advice, but once she became angry: "This doesn't touch you at all! You're not taking this seriously, Sashenka!"

It probably didn't touch him, indeed, and his attitude must really not have been serious enough. They saw the same reality with different eyes. Two loving people who once shared the same profession and worldview, if pressed to create two films about the same historical subject, now would probably treat the same theme in starkly opposite ways.

In order to sustain her family, Olya could not ignore the fact that her films needed to be ideologically impeccable. Honest and sincere, she did all she could to preserve at least some inner harmony with herself. The optimistic model of the world that was maintained in the art of the day remained her personal model as well, despite the fate of her husband.

She never asked me or Aleksandr Osipovich about anything that related to prison and the camps. She perceived our past as an extra-social, extra-political misery and instinctively kept away from judging the meaning and content of the historical tragedy.

As for Aleksandr Osipovich, his awareness of being helpless and useless was finishing him off. He was plunged into some truer, genuine world of perpetual values devoid of bustle and vanity. But there he existed alone.

Loving them both, I suffered for him. Seeing Olechka struggle to make ends meet, I was filled with deep sympathy for her solitary and inglorious fight for life. Theirs was a truly heartrending drama.

Aleksandr Osipovich was tired. He was tired of everything and everyone and was fatally ill.

The rehabilitation certificate gave Olya the opportunity to put him in a state hospital. After my rehearsals at the theater, I would now hurry there to be near him.

At that time Moldova Film started shooting the feature film *Ataman Kodr,* and Olya was offered the opportunity to direct it. After so many years of persecution on account of her husband, they finally acknowledged her right to shoot a full-length motion picture. Aleksandr Osipovich insisted: "You have to agree. That alone will help me recover." I also tried to persuade Olya, saying that I'd be spending my every free minute near Aleksandr Osipovich. In the end, Olya accepted the offer, provided that she would still take care of her husband in the hospital.

The shooting was on location, about fifty kilometers from Kishinev. Exhausted from work and the record heat of that particular July, Olya would hitchhike to arrive in the city by nightfall so that she could sit by her husband's sickbed. Aleksandr Osipovich would impatiently glance at the door:

"When is my Zulu coming, do you know?"

They were again—and perhaps like never before—united and indivisible. Aleksandr Osipovich's illness relieved him of his "dependent complex." Once the pain receded, he would become soft and astonishingly lucid with words.

The air in the hospital was stuffy. Wet bedsheets were hung in the doorways so that the patients could breathe more easily. Aleksandr Osipovich was alone in his ward. Walking quietly to his door, I heard his groaning. But as soon as I lifted the edge of the sheet, he converted his groaning into a tune. No one was supposed to know that he let himself give in to pain.

Once he said in a quiet voice:

"I'm going to die, Tamarochka. I'm tired. I understood only now how well I felt before the fits began. I wanted to give you Pasternak's *Safe Conduct* as a present, but I never did. Boris loved my sister. His poem "Marburg" is dedicated to her. We used to be friends a long time ago. What if you happen to meet him some day? Tell him about me."

From time to time Aleksandr Osipovich would lose consciousness. The injections brought relief after a while, and his cloudy eyes would gradually regain clarity. Realizing anew that I was sitting beside him, he said, as if continuing our old conversation about God:

"You know, it seems that there is something out there!"

What was revealed to him in those moments when his consciousness slipped away from his soul?

Olya saw how impatiently Aleksandr Osipovich waited for her visits. "I declined shooting the film," she announced. "No films. I want to be with Sasha all the time. All the rest is of no importance."

Resolute and loving, she would lean over him. An acute understanding pierced through me: I was witnessing their utmost and greatest tenderness, their love and gratitude to each other. Only they knew the torment of living apart, the suffering and final trepidation that swelled in their hearts now.

I understood Olya's need to be alone with her husband. She would tell me, "Thank you. Go now." But Aleksandr Osipovich would ask her to let me stay. I had to realize that the types of relationships we forged in the camps now belonged to the Past.

When my vacation came, I wanted to be of help, but Olya remained implacable.

"Leave, please. I don't need anyone's help."

I couldn't disobey her.

I incoherently explained to Aleksandr Osipovich that I had to leave for a tour with my acting troupe. But no sooner did Dima and I reach our destination than a telegram from Olya arrived: *Come back if you can it is frightening to leave him alone.*

We caught the first plane to Kishinev. By 11 p.m. I was already at the hospital's entrance, but the doctors did not let me in: "His wife is with him at the moment. Come tomorrow."

When I arrived at the hospital the next morning, Aleksandr Osipovich was no more. On a hot morning in July 1958, a crowd of people gathered outside the Moldova Film Studios in the southern city of Kishinev. There were few speeches and a lot of music. The locals knew Aleksandr Osipovich as Olga Petrovna's husband, a man who had spent many years in the camps.

Aleksandr Osipovich's grave is near the church at the Armenian cemetery of Kishinev. On the gray granite tombstone Olga Petrovna requested the following engraving:

1888–1958

ALEKSANDR OSIPOVICH GAVRONSKY

You loved people,
You helped them live,
You will always be with us,
Alive, unfailing and loved.

Yes, he loved people passionately. We were all but sketches reshaped by his hand. If one were to call, "Everyone! Send your letters from Aleksandr Osipovich!"—I think there would be several volumes.

A DISCIPLE and assistant of Aleksandr Osipovich and Olga Petrovna, Isidor Grigoryevich Vinokurov, once recalled the words of the playwright I. F. Popov: "The disaster was that Sasha considered himself a revolutionary while in fact he was a scholar."

The thought of the piles of sheets covered in his handwriting that remained in Vesely Kut gave me no rest. I offered to go there and bring Aleksandr Osipovich's papers. Olya was glad at my offer. "That's what I was just going to ask you. I have no strength to go there myself."

The train was arriving in Vesely Kut at night. An intelligent boy, Vitya Vrublyovsky, whom Aleksandr Osipovich used to speak particularly highly of, was meeting me at the station.

The August sky was spangled with stars. Their light induced one to silence.

In the morning, Vitya's mother, with a baby in her arms, came into the room. Two more little ones were holding on to the brim of her skirt.

Altogether, she had seven children. Her ten-year-old girl brought in a plate with cottage cheese, cucumbers and honey.

"Eat, dear, eat! No need to be bashful," the hostess said without a smile.

She leaned in the doorway, waiting for me to taste the food.

"Osipovich is gone. No more… Don't be shy, eat!" she kept repeating, wiping her tears.

I set out to the house in which Aleksandr Osipovich used to live. The landlady was fiddling with something in the garden.

"Hello!" I greeted her. "I came to take Aleksandr Osipovich's papers."

"I've gathered everything together and put it away. It's all in the attic."

The attic was neat but stuffy. In the corner, wrapped in a window curtain, lay Aleksandr Osipovich's belongings.

"But where are his papers?" I asked.

"The papers are here too. I've gathered everything. I haven't thrown a single sheet away."

I was looking through the neatly folded letters—from Olya, Hella, Tamara Tsulukidze, Nina Vladimirovna Gernet, me, and many, many more.

"There were sheets… not the letters. With numbers, lots of numbers!"

"There was nothing more. Everything's here."

"Please, try to remember. They were large sheets. Olga Petrovna would bring him these special sheets of paper…"

The landlady raised her shoulders to say she knew nothing. Only then did it occur to me to ask:

"Has anyone come here after Aleksandr Osipovich died?"

The attitude of strangers to our fates was nothing new to me: once they were told that somebody was an Enemy of the People, they tended to believe it. But there was something else, too: a glass of milk from an extended hand, a deep-hearted sigh, a compassionate glance.

Mira Galpern lived with a Komi family in Tentukovo. Her hosts would say, "What do you mean you won't sit at the table with us. We're no strangers. You're people, and we're people too."

In '37, in Yaroslavl, people were loaded onto trucks and taken outside of the city to be shot. The locals who lived on the outskirts reported, "They'd fire away there for a while but wouldn't bury them properly. So we'd wait for a few hours, then take a shovel and throw some earth over them so that the legs and hands didn't stick out, so that no one could see."

The landlady, a stern Ukrainian peasant, herself had been dekulakized.

Overcoming her fear, she told me as I was leaving:

"The policeman, the one who used to go to the center to register him, took something."

I remembered Aleksandr Osipovich's suffering when the guards took away his writings during a search in Knyazh-Pogost. Again, theft! Again, his works would accumulate dust somewhere, or else—come out under someone else's name.

AFTER ALEKSANDR OSIPOVICH'S DEATH, Olechka lived for another twenty years. Her ability to sympathize with any human being knew no limits. She could bring any ragamuffin to her home, feed him and give him ten rubles to get where he needed. Having given her life to Aleksandr Osipovich and sacrificed everything, she, a deep and sensible person, was afraid to think about her husband's fate; to do so would have devastated her.

Everybody needs to be loved, and I needed other people to believe in my love for them. Olechka gave me this, and I loved her with all my heart. When in 1976 I received a telegram from Olya saying she'd fallen ill, I took a vacation and went to Kishinev right away. After her surgery, I stayed with her in her ward. On the third night, I switched off the lights and looked out the powdery hospital window, through which bright moonlight illuminated the ward. Olya was breathing evenly and seemed to be sleeping. Lying quietly on the cot next to hers, I trembled when I suddenly heard her voice:

> It's darker than dark in the field.
> Someone cries out for help.
> What can I do?
> I'm tired and small myself.
> I'm deathly tired myself.
> How can I possibly help?

"Where's that from?" I asked her.

"Fyodor Sologub. Good, isn't it?"

"Oh God, yes!"

I went onto the balcony. In the distance—a ravine, the forest, hills; a horse-drawn wagon rattled by on the road below. A sullen peasant, wrapped in the warm moonlit night, was traveling somewhere.

Olechka wanted to live, and soon she felt better.

My days off were almost over. I decided I would take a few more when she'd have to have her second surgery. Upon my return to Leningrad, I called her daily, and Olechka wrote to me too. I almost believed she would recover, despite the doctors' pessimism. But when I called the hospital one day and asked a nurse to call Olya from her ward, the nurse told me: "The room is empty now."

The Moldova Film Studio erected a tombstone for Olechka out of the same granite as Aleksandr Osipovich's gray stone. They, who had lived so many years apart, are now next to each other, grave to grave.

ELENA GUSTAVOVNA FRISHER—HELLA

Hella came to Kishinev to visit Aleksandr Osipovich's grave together with Nina Vladimirovna Gernet. She circled the gravesite, sat down and sang Aleksandr Osipovich a lullaby in German, then whispered something. Nina Vladimirovna and I stood nearby and watched her.

After her release, she wasn't allowed to go back to her motherland.

"Day and night, I am back home in Prague, with those who buried me a long time ago. I am there to such an extent that I don't want to see anybody else, anybody who entered my life afterward, even though I've loved many of them and couldn't have survived without their love."

She was gnawed by guilt toward her sister, her son and her murdered husband. When it finally became possible to go to Czechoslovakia as a tourist, Hella didn't dare do so. "I've spent many nights thinking about it and decided not to. What does my sister, Lilly, who's considered me dead for thirty-seven years already, need me for now?"

After her rehabilitation, she received a room in Moscow. Her friends gave her some presents, including a TV and a radio. She suffered from insomnia, and at night she would tune in to the radio and keep tabs on all the persecutions, tank invasions and other events going on in the world.

It was her friendship with Nina Vladimirovna Gernet that brought Hella back to life. Nina Vladimirovna found her opportunities to translate Czech plays for Russian puppet theaters. Hella liked to accompany the troupes to the festivals. She would revive, become transformed and even coquettish. The charm of her biblical beauty caught the eyes of many, and her sharp and talented judgments often astonished the people around her. "All his life he has been his own best friend!" she would comment on somebody, or "Today I'd have traded an arm and a leg for another head." Or "I have several hearts, one of which is working well now," she would say, laughing. Her favorite saying was: "Many times in our lives it could never have been worse." But the festivities would finish and insomnia, anguish and gnawing loneliness would again attack Hella.

Two writers, Enna Mikhaylovna Alennik and Nina Vladimirovna Gernet, sat Hella down at a desk and pushed her to write about everything she'd seen and lived through. They personally edited what she put down, and eventually her text, with its peculiar tint of Hella's Czech accent, was approved and recognized by notable figures. Hella triumphed over herself even in this.

She was sixteen years older than me, but we were fatally related by the fire that burned inside both of us, leaving smoldering ashes, and those ashes, on which Hella's life glimmered, were ageless. She had experienced the collapse of her social ideas, love and motherhood. But when one day I received her letter, in which she wrote, "Come visit me, I want to introduce you to my young friends," every word of it was unlike the former Hella I knew, unlike any of her previous relationships. There were enough ardent ashes in her heart to engage in a triumphant romance with the younger generation, and for me it was a grandiose revelation that had to do not so much with a particular person but rather with humankind on the whole.

From the toasts proposed at Hella's seventy-fifth birthday, it became clear: her young friends understood her better than we did. For us, it was our shared pain that served as a bridge to Hella's soul. Her new friends, however, not only saw that she was lonely but could also discern her sense of humor and the very playfulness of her nature.

"I'll make it to eighty years old! Gratitude will help me!" Hella would promise. And she made it. But before her death she lost interest in nearly everything. When her new friends attempted to entertain her with a letter or story, she would listen to the end and then proclaim: "That's not interesting."

Her wonderful friends erected a monument to the lonely foreign woman in Moscow. On it, above her name, Elena Gustavovna—Hella Frisher, they engraved: *1904–1937–1984*. Much can be read in the additional date that came between the years of her birth and death.

TAMARA GRIGORIEVNA TSULUKIDZE

In 1951 a government directive signed by Molotov was sent out to all places of exile: "Former political prisoners to be employed only for physical work." This hateful document had a considerable influence on Tamara Tsulukidze's destiny. In the faraway village of the Krasnoyarsk region where she had been exiled, she was fired from her job at the local club, and the once splendid actress was assigned to work in a *kolkhoz* as a poultry-woman. In one of the photographs taken there, Tamara is sitting on the edge of a well and, her head thrust back, is looking at the sky; on another—she is holding a chicken as if she is talking to it.

We met again in Peredelkino, at the House of Writers, after all her ordeals, and fifteen years after my release. We ran into each other by chance and didn't immediately recognize one another, both of us having changed a lot. We talked for several hours and parted not merely as close friends but almost as relatives.

Upon her return from exile, Tamara performed in several roles at the Rustaveli Theater in Tbilisi, but soon after she moved to Minsk. The Byelorussian writer Ales Osipovich Palchevsky, who was equally lonely, helped Tamara survive the exile, and she married him. It was impossible not to fall in love with the handsome gray-haired Ales Osipovich. Before I even met him, I accepted him into my heart because of his pain, which I well knew myself: after his release, his son, already a grown-up person, refused to recognize Ales Osipovich as his father. Tamara, who had tragically lost her own son, Sandik, shared her husband's drama with all of her heart. "If you could only see the torment in his eyes during the rare meetings that he has with his son," she told me.

When, during one of my visits to Minsk, Tamara made herself comfortable in an armchair under a stand lamp and started reading from her future book *Just One Life,* in which she described the theatrical quest of Aleksandr Vasilyevich Akhmeteli, as well as her own fate as an actress and her short yet happy life with him as his wife, I saw how proud Ales Osipovich was of the literary gift that had awoken in her. It was the solicitous acceptance of each other's previous lives that revealed the meaning and power of Tamara's and Ales Palchevsky's marriage, of two people who had lost everything in the world.

In spite of the many obstacles on the way, her book nevertheless was born. The letters that streamed to her from readers, including the children and grandchildren of people with similar fates, gave Tamara much more than just a second or even a third wind and prolonged her life. These letters from her motherland were astonishing, unburdening as a confession, fervent and grateful. They came and came. She stored them with care, one next to another.

Her book, as well as the vast archival resources that she had collected for the theater's museum in Tbilisi, perpetuated her husband's name, Akhmeteli. As she was writing her memoir, she told me about yet another invention of the regime that had annihilated our lives:

"Remember the famous Armenian actor..." Tamara mentioned his name. "Imagine, he claims that he saw Sasha alive in 1946! That, apparently, he ran into him on a tram. He said: Sasha was wearing a pea coat; they embraced each other and Sasha told him that he was going to Leningrad to stage *Oedipus Rex*; he was going to stay with Chuvyachich but the actor said he made him go to his place, where he ran Sasha a bath and made his bed; according to him, Sasha slept for an entire day… Of course, he couldn't have made it all up by himself. He was forced to, he was made to spread these lies. But tell me, why? What for?"

There were other, more truthful versions of the last days of Akhmeteli's life, too. According to one of them, he was brought to Georgia from Moscow in shackles and led in the direction of Mtskheta. The escort guard whispered to him: "Run!" But Aleksandr Vasilyevich turned to the guard and said: "Will you shoot me in the back? Be brave, soldier! Shoot me like that!" Other people said that when he was thrown into a cell, bleeding and powerless, he could only utter: "I am Aleksandr Akhmeteli. Please tell everyone: I haven't betrayed a single person. Tomorrow they will shoot me."

It was beyond one's powers to think about this, yet it was impossible to disavow it either.

Tamara always longed to return to Georgia, yet she could no longer abandon Byelorussia, which she had also come to love. But when we went there together for a visit, she managed to fill my life with impressions of her beautiful country, where I had the chance to see the confluence of the Aragvi and Kura Rivers and the Pantheon in the mountains, to pay my respects to Nina Chavchavadze's memorial to Griboedov, to immerse myself in the ways of a Georgian household and national costumes. I became imbued and fell in love with the motherland of my rich-hearted friend.

Tamara Tsulukidze died in Minsk. Her remains were taken to her native land, to Tbilisi. Her urn rests next to her mother and her son, Sandik.

Like everyone else, I cried when I watched scenes from the last film footage shot in Tamara's apartment in Minsk. An ambulance stood ready on the street. Gasping for breath, Tamara hurried to tell the television reporters not about herself but about the last days of her friends from the theater in the camp.

The Theater Society of Tbilisi held a gathering in memory of A. V. Akhmeteli and T. G. Tsulukidze. The hall was packed: Georgia revered her famous countrymen. In the middle of the program, I heard a recording of Tamara's magical voice, in one of the roles she played in the '30s, and I understood: a ruined talent—that's where such pain came from!

They had pulled the scaffolding from underneath the actress who had known the grand stage. She was allowed too little space for her artistic talent, reduced to reciting poetry in small gatherings, proposing toasts to friends and inventing little surprises for her dear ones. Her only appearance in public during the last years of her life was at the anniversary of the Rustaveli Theater, when she presented its stage director, Robert Sturua, with A. V. Akhmeteli's rehearsal hand-bell and fascinated the audience with her refined and elegant speech.

AS EARLY AS 1952, I received a stunning letter from Shan: "Dear Tamarochka! Today, on December 16, at 11 a.m., I was informed that I can go back to China. I am reborn. I wanted to share my joy with you. I want to see you for another, final time." He wanted to know if the train for Beijing passed through the town in the Urals where I was working at that time. But unfortunately, the railroad that led to China was hundreds of *versts* away to the south.

At home he was appointed editor in chief of the illustrated magazine *China.* He traveled a lot and wrote that he was happy. Our correspondence broke off during the Great Proletarian Cultural Revolution—yet another historical upheaval, which robbed Shan's life of six years. Only twenty years later, thanks to one of Hella's young friends, Rita, did we find each other again.

* * *

I couldn't escape the implacable need to go to the North one more time to visit Kolushka's grave. There was one event that prompted me to undertake the trip.

A neighbor, hearing me open the door to my apartment, came out onto the landing.

"There's somebody sitting at my place. She's waiting for you. She says she's come from far away."

A woman I didn't recognize rose to greet me as I walked into my neighbor's.

"You don't remember me? I'm Kira, the daughter of Wanda Georgievna Razumovskaya."

I remembered her being twelve years old! She was now thirty-five.

Several years back, as I was walking down Nevsky Prospect, my eyes had caught a glimpse of a woman passing in the opposite direction. I thought, "How splendid she is!" and a jolt ran through my heart. We both looked back at the same time.

"Wanda?"

"Tamara! I've looked for you everywhere!"

A year before Wanda had been diagnosed with cancer. One of her kidneys had to be removed. Spectacular and temperamental, she zealously fought the illness.

After finishing a pedagogical school in Gorky, Kira went back to live with her mother. I took a great interest in their relationship. I couldn't forget how they used to quarrel, what convulsive torment their fights caused each of them.

"Kira turned out to be not such a bad daughter," Wanda had told me then. "But she's completely undeveloped and very stubborn. I can't even awaken the woman in her. She doesn't care about coiffures or dresses. She has no self-respect."

"So she never got married?"

"God, who in the world would marry my wretched daughter!"

After Wanda left, we kept corresponding. Then I received a letter from Kira: "Mama is in grave condition. She can't get up. She asks for oranges, but we don't have oranges here."

I sent them a parcel with oranges and lemons. Kira thanked me, but before long she wrote to me again—this time to say that Wanda had passed away.

And now Kira was in Leningrad.

I took my dear guest to the bathroom. "Take a shower after your journey while I cook something," I told her and showed her how the faucets worked. "Turn it to the right if you want hot water, to the left for cold." As I was bustling about the apartment and setting the table, I suddenly realized that I couldn't hear water running in the bathroom. I knocked on the door and asked if everything was all right.

The thirty-five-year-old woman stood in the bathtub, naked and shivering, arms folded across her breasts.

"I don't know, I can't make it work..."

"Why didn't you call me?"

"I didn't want to disturb you. You're busy."

How painfully familiar was this feeling of intimidation in a person who had always huddled precariously on the edges of life!

"What's wrong, Kironka! It's all right, child..."

In the evening, I tried to ask her more questions: "Did you get along with Mama? Was it good living together?"

Kira didn't cry; choked with tears, she let out a dismal wail:

"I'm so guilty for what I did to her, I'm so guilty!"

"Bless you, no! What can you be guilty of, Kironka?"

"Mama wanted me so much to be smart! She wished that I read more and continued with my studies, but I didn't want to, I couldn't. She was ashamed of me before everyone. She was so educated, so beautiful; she played the piano..."

That was how life could turn out! Ashamed of their own imperfections and unaware of who was to blame in this world, "wretched" children felt guilt before their beautiful mothers.

Kira's detailed stories about her life in the orphanage, about the refuse bins she had rummaged through in search of additional sustenance, about the other orphans, stronger and fouler than her, who would beat her up and take away whatever she'd manage to find... her heartrending and inconsolable fits of hysterics... all of that made me act. I found her a job as a teacher at one of the kindergartens. She loved children. But after thinking it over for a while, she refused.

"What about Mama's grave?"

"You'll visit her grave whenever you have a vacation."

"No. Mama will be angry if I leave that place. I can't."

I SET OUT FOR KNYAZH-POGOST in 1972, at the end of August.

On the train, I shared a compartment with a teacher from Ukhta, her five-year-old daughter and a clerk from the Knyazh-Pogost district committee. These people, with pathetic imaginations, considerably aggravated my journey. They went on about the political prisoners, with whom the lands we were passing used to teem, as if they were some plague; they lamented the fact that some of these prisoners had stayed to live in the area after their release. With a sinking heart I asked them who built the railway.

They didn't know.

"Some recruits were brought in to build it... But maybe prisoners too."

I peered through the window at the slogans along the railway tracks, laid out in stone on the embankments: *COMMUNISM—OUR GOAL! PEACE TO THE WORLD! FULFILL AND OVER-FULFILL!* As the train passed through the stations, I saw neat stacks of tree trunks and logs piled together to be transported; construction cranes blended harmoniously with the landscape. The billboards for one timber industry enterprise or another, indeed, warded off any thoughts of those who had unloaded cargo with their bare hands, sawed tree trunks, built everything and died here.

Running across the bridges, the train lumbered and groaned. The rivers had dried up, and emptiness resonated underneath. Wood beams stuck in the sandy bottoms of the rivers reminded me of the former tree-felling sites.

Forest and peat fires raged everywhere in the country that year. Fires near Moscow were extinguished, but not here. Even the areas of the forest just beyond the train windows could no longer be seen through the smoke. As the train moved on, I was plunging into an ominous hazy thickness.

My entry into the Past began from Velsk… The memories that surfaced were colorless. Vera Petrovna's words, "Yurochka, show how you love your mother"; the plan that she and Filipp devised… It was too late to fix anything. I lived my life without my son. I didn't see him grow up or hear him call me "Mama."

Kuloy… Here, the camp commandant Malakhov, a kind man who bore a resemblance to a strong bird of prey, tried to instill in my foolish head the idea that I should wait for my son to be led for a walk, grab him and catch the first plane without letting anyone know.

Kotlas. Here, traveling with TEC, Kolushka and I would wait to change trains. Exhaustion would knock us off our feet and we'd fall asleep cuddling on the dirty and defiled floor of the station.

Svetik… Frost would take hold of us to the bone here. Felling trees. Scurvy. Vasilyev's vindictive promise, "I'll see you rot!"

Passing through Urdoma, I tried to make out the cross on Matvey Ilyich's grave but couldn't see it…

Mezhog, where my son was born, stood a distance from the railway, and I could only discern the road that led there. Could it really have been me who brought, with my own hands, my baby boy, wrapped in a blanket, to the checkpoint and entrusted him to his father? The train was passing through Mikun. Here, my plagued consciousness had won itself back from the fear of the MGB, indeed from the fear that my entire life had been lived in.

Knyazh-Pogost… I couldn't help, one last time, setting my foot down on the soil that enveloped Kolushka.

Kira led me along the dusty road to her house. The cemetery was on the right, one and a half kilometers away from the settlement. I felt a magnetic pull between myself and that point on earth… It required me to be there right now, but it was already a dark night.

On the walls in Kira's apartment hung photographs of Wanda. An old piano stood in the corner. There was a wardrobe and stacks of cardboard boxes piled up to the ceiling. Above one of the plugs there was a scrap of paper stuck behind the wiring with "Instructions to Oneself" written in Wanda's hand: *1) Cultivation of will. 2) Daily exercises…* There were other points on that sheet as well, but I choked up… I couldn't read any further.

On the table in Kira's kitchen there was a row of three-liter jars with marinated pickles, tomatoes and juice—the customary groceries sold at the local store or at any other store like this in the remote parts of the country. My old friend's destitute daughter had purchased these dainties to give me a "royal" welcome…

I went to the cemetery in the morning, taking with me the blue paint I'd brought from Leningrad to paint the fence, and a hammer and nails to fix the bench.

There, not far from the entrance, on the left… A few meters more…

Everything was clean and well tended around Kolushka's grave, with only the cross slightly leaning to one side. I saw a dozen or so tiny northern pine trees that had sprouted through the soil here.

All was quiet. Smoke wafted from the forest. The dry, rough boards of the fence greedily absorbed the oil paint.

I waited—for either unbearable pain, or a sense of calm. Neither of them came. I was on a threshold, behind which there was a screen thick with the twenty-two years I had been away.

I called to mind everything: Kolushka's radiant kindness, earnestness, artistry and love. I stayed at his grave for a long time, but within these hours the Past wouldn't speak to me. It didn't admit me into its depths. Kolushka was angry with me for living on without him—much like Wanda would be angry with Kira had she decided to stay in Leningrad.

It was to Sergeev, the steel-eyed warder whom I recalled forever with a warm heart, that I owed thanks for the fact that Kolushka's grave existed on this earth. I wanted to find him or at least find out where he lived. In the settlement, I took my chances by popping in at every house and asking people, describing how he looked.

"I think I know him," one of the locals said finally. "He worked here for a long time as a shoemaker. Then he left to live in the Ukraine, or to some other place."

"What was his first name?"

"Name? I don't know. It wasn't customary to know names. We called him Senior Warder Sergeev."

I headed to the place where Central Camp used to be situated. There were no watchtowers or fences anymore. Only the deserted outhouse of the checkpoint marked the boundaries of what used to be the camp. Next to the ruins of the barracks, darkened and half-sunken to the ground, new cottages had been built. Pigs grunted and chickens cackled, roaming through the new buildings and the remnants of the barracks.

Right here, behind the barbed wire, used to be the "brain center." That tragic continent had sunk, and instead this new one, unaware of the old one's squalor, cruelty and filth, floated to the surface.

I plodded on toward Kira's house through the settlement.

Leaning her elbow against a low fence, a prune-like woman was standing outside a shabby wooden house. Some trait of her face seemed familiar. I slowed down and said hello.

"Hello, Tamara," she answered in a dim, indifferent voice.

I recognized this old woman as Vera Busygina, a worker from the Chinese Eastern Railway, who once used to be a beautiful girl.

"You've come to visit Kolushka?" she asked me, as if it had only been a week, and not twenty-two years, since I'd last come, as usual, to the cemetery from Mikun.

All that had been plugged up inside of me broke through. I finally gave vent to the feelings I'd been striving for with such anguish. The past grabbed hold of me and started pulling me into itself, trying to suck me in. But there were no kind mirrors in there, and the reflections only grimaced and frightened me. The untwisted energy that I had dared touch on, in the hopes of rescuing some gratifying remembrances, started striking me shattering blows, demanding that I make way if I wanted to escape self-destruction. But I kept stubbornly asking the old acquaintance of mine:

"The Moth? Yes, she's alive," Vera replied. "Sh.? No, he hung himself. Bronya? She poisoned herself a while ago. I.M. is in Nalchik, doing just fine. Who? Oh, no, she died already ten years ago..."

It was hopeless to resist the onslaught of vindictive powers. I wouldn't be able to withstand their attack if I didn't catch the first train and leave this place immediately.

At Kira's, seven or eight ex-prisoners who had remained to live here were waiting for me. Among them was Anatoly Kutsenko, the kind man who had been looking after Kolushka's grave.

All tickets to Leningrad were sold out. But the North was driving me away. I bought a ticket to Moscow.

There was no more Kolushka in the North.

I dreamed of him rarely, five or six times during all these years. The last time he appeared he seemed especially depressed. "I have to go now, forever," he told me. And, without waking up, I understood that it was only now that he was leaving me, this time for good. I didn't know where, although I knew that it was final, and that beyond the borders of life everything moved and changed according to even more rigid and inexorable laws.

GLOSSARY

Anders Army—a Polish regiment, headed by General Wladislaw Anders, formed in 1941, following the German invasion of the Soviet Union and Stalin's invalidation of the Soviet-German partition of Poland. Many Polish POWs were released from prisons and camps in order to join in the war effort, Anders among them.

Article 107—one of the *bytovye* ("everyday life") criminal offenses, for example, theft of state property during the war ("state property" included ears of corn on collective farms' lands).

Aurora—the Aurora Cruiser became a symbol of the Bolshevik Revolution when, on October 25, 1917, its crew fired a blank shot to signal the assault on the Winter Palace in St. Petersburg.

balanda—prison soup.

banya—a Russian bathhouse.

barynya (fem. of *barin*, "landowner")—a traditional Russian dance.

Bolshoy Dom (literally, "big house")—the unofficial name of the Secret Service headquarters in Leningrad, situated on Liteyny Prospect, which also included the investigation prison on neighboring Shpalernaya Street.

Bronze Horseman—the statue, by E. M. Falconet, of the Russian emperor Peter the Great in St. Petersburg, erected in 1782 on the Neva embankment; also the name of Aleksandr Pushkin's famous poem (1833), which solidified the symbolic meaning of the statue in Russian society, literature and culture.

burzhuyka—a portable metal stove, popular in Russia around the time of World War II, with the pipe reaching outside through the window; often placed in the middle of a room (or a train car, etc.).

bytoviki (from *byt*, "everyday life")—a category of prisoners convicted of nonpolitical crimes; unlike political prisoners, the Enemies of the People, they were considered by the authorities to be "socially close" (*sotsialno blizkie*), which earned them shorter terms and a privileged position in the camps.

chastushka—a traditional Russian poetic form (trochaic quatrain), usually humorous or satirical, often put to music; bears a resemblance to limericks.

collectivization—the policy of the Soviet government during the late 1920s and early 1930s to deprive peasants of their land and property for the benefit of collective farms (*kolkhoz*); it caused a wave of famine in the countryside, especially in 1932–1934.

dacha—a country house, usually of wood, used primarily in the summer.

Day of Ivan Kupala—the day of St. John the Baptist, July 7 (June 24, Old Style), celebrated in Russian Orthodoxy, especially by the youth; it involves many rites connected with water as an element of fertility and purification.

Decembrist—on December 14 (December 26, New Style), 1825, in Senate Square in St. Petersburg, an uprising took place to protest Nicolas I's assumption of the throne. The uprising was suppressed, and many rebels were sent into exile in Siberia, followed by their wives (hence, "Decembrist's wife").

dekulakization—a campaign launched by the Soviet authorities in 1929–1932 against well-off peasants (*kulaks*), who were regarded as class enemies; it was accompanied by collectivization.

densification—a literal translation of the Russian *uplotnenie*, which in the 1920 and 1930s was used to refer to the state-authorized process of forcing the owners of large apartments in the cities to "share" their living quarters with people arriving in the capitals from the countryside, whereby many private residencies were turned into communal apartments.

desyatina—a Russian unit of area used until 1918, equal to 2.75 acres (1.1 hectares, or 11 square meters).

Doctors' Plot—an alleged conspiracy of several prominent Kremlin doctors who were accused of poisoning and killing leaders of the state. The campaign, launched in 1952, ended with Stalin's death in 1953; since the majority of the accused doctors were Jewish, it triggered a strong wave of anti-Semitism.

58-ers—political prisoners prosecuted under one of the numerous paragraphs of notorious Article 58 of the Soviet Criminal Code.

Frunze—the name of the capital of Kirghizia in 1926–1991 (in honor of the Bolshevik leader Mikhail Frunze), now renamed Bishkek.

Gulag—an acronym for *Glavnoe Upravlenie Lagerey* (Chief Administration of Camps), a body of government that administered the system of hard-labor camps and prisons throughout the Soviet Union.

kazakin—a traditional dress, usually trimmed with silver or gold lace; a shorter version of the caftan.

kishlak—a rural settlement in Central Asia.

kokoshnik—a traditional headdress, often embroidered with jewelry, for women and girls.

kolkhoz (from *kollektivnoe khozyaystvo,* "a collective farm")—this form of state-owned agricultural economic unit, dating back to the earliest years of Soviet rule, became much more widespread during collectivization (1932–1934), bringing private farming and landowning in the Soviet Union to utter extinction.

kommunalka—a communal apartment (see **densification**).

Komsomol (from *Komunisticheskiy soyuz molodyozhi,* "Communist Union of Youth")—established in 1918, it served as the youth wing of the Communist Party of the Soviet Union (for ages 14–28).

kopeck—Russian unit of currency equal to 1/100th of a ruble.

Kresty Prison—the famous prison on the Neva embankment, almost across the river from Bolshoy Dom, unofficially known by this name (literally, "The Crosses") because it consists of two cross-shaped buildings.

kulak (literally, "a fist")—the class of relatively wealthy peasants, or independent farmers, before the Bolshevik Revolutionary and in early Soviet Russia (see **dekulakization**).

KVCh (from *kulturno-vospitatelnaya chast*, "Cultural and Educational Unit")—an administrative unit of a labor camp that oversaw the political education of prisoners, stage performances, etc.

Mannerheim line—a fortification on the Karelian Isthmus, which guarded Finland against the Soviet invasion during the Finno-Russian War in the winter of 1939–1940; named after Field Marshal C. G. E. Mannerheim.

Mariinsky Canal System (also known as Volga-Baltic Waterway)—a network of rivers and canals, approximately 685 miles (1,100 kilometers) long, connecting St. Petersburg and the Baltic Sea with the Volga River and the interior towns of the country, including Uglich; the main canals were built in the 1930s.

MGB (from *ministerstvo gosudarstvennoy bezopasnosti*, "Ministry of State Security")—the name of the Soviet secret police from 1946 to 1953.

nie mozhno—Polish, "not possible."

NKVD (from *narodny komissariat vnutrennikh del*, "People's Commissariat for Internal Affairs")—the name of the Soviet secret police from 1934 to 1946.

OGPU (from *obyedinennoe gosudarstvennoe politicheskoe upravlenie*, "Unified State Political Administration")—the name of the Soviet secret police from 1923 to 1934.

otkazchiki (from *otkaz*, "refusal")—criminal prisoners, usually of a high authority in the underground world, who refused to work in the camps so as not to cooperate with the regime, which was strictly prohibited by their code of honor.

People's Commissariat (from *sovnarkom: sovet narodnykh kommissarov*, "Council of People's Commissars")—the ruling government body in Soviet Russia after the revolution, subdivided into various People's Commissariats, for example, in charge of foreign affairs (original Commissar—Leon Trotsky), education (Anatoly Lunacharsky), etc.

Petrograd—in 1914, at the start of World War I, St. Petersburg was renamed Petrograd (a Slavic cognate for the initial German name). In 1924, following Lenin's death, Petrograd became Leningrad and retained this name until 1991 when, with the collapse of the Soviet Union, the city's original name was restored.

Political Department—an administrative unit of a camp division that held exclusive control over political matters in every individual camp it governed and that was itself subordinate only to the Operative Department (same as the Third Department); it reported directly to the Gulag administration in Moscow and not to the local camp division's commandant.

pridurki—a category of prisoners doing "privileged" jobs in the camps, for example in the kitchen, the bathhouse, etc.

red corner—traditionally, in a Russian Orthodox household, the corner where an icon is displayed. In Soviet Russia, when religious practices were outlawed, it euphemistically came to denote a room or any space where political materials would be held, such as portraits of the leaders, Soviet banners, editions of Lenin and Karl Marx, etc.

Road of Life—a road across the frozen Lake Ladoga, which provided the only access to the city of Leningrad during the winter months of the siege, 1941–1944.

ruble—the Russian unit of currency.

Second Congress of the Party—took place in Brussels and London in July

1903; it proclaimed Marxism as the official doctrine of the Bolshevik Party and stipulated the triumph of the Bolsheviks over the Mensheviks, who were branded as opportunists.

Shpalernaya—the first Russian investigation prison, initially called the House of Preliminary Detention. It was the place of confinement of numerous political figures under investigation both before and, especially, after the revolution.

shtrafbat (from *shtrafnoy batalyon*, "punishment battalion")—from July 25, 1942, regiments of the Red Army comprised of prisoners let out of the camps and sent to fight Nazi Germany; at the front they faced especially harsh conditions, took part in the most dangerous operations and received the most meager supply of food, clothing and equipment.

Siege of Leningrad—the blockade of Leningrad by the German army, which lasted almost 900 days (September 8, 1941–January 27, 1944), when the city was almost completely cut off from all supplies and ravaged by severe cold, hunger and destruction.

Smolny—a palace in St. Petersburg (erected in 1808) that initially housed the Smolny Institute for Noble Maidens. During the October Revolution Lenin chose it as his residency, and since then until 1991 it served as the headquarters of the Leningrad Party apparatus.

Solovki—the Solovetsky Islands, located in the White Sea, housed a Russian Orthodox monastery from the fifteenth century. In 1923 it became the site of the first Soviet labor camp, and in 1937 a prison (liquidated in 1939).

sovkhoz (from *sovetskoe khozyaystvo*)—literally, "a Soviet farm."

Sparrow Hills—in 1827, Alexander Herzen (1812–1870) and Nikolay Ogarev (1813–1877), both of whom later became progressive Russian writers and thinkers, pledged to each other "not to rest until their country was free." That oath became Russia's symbol of the struggle for the freedom of the people.

Stolypin car—special type of rail car for transporting prisoners, named after Pyotr Stolypin, the prime minister of Russia during the reign of Nicolas II, who engineered the mass relocation of peasants as part of his agrarian reforms.

subbotnik (from *subbota*, "Saturday")—a day of volunteer work in the Soviet Union (mainly cleaning the streets, collecting recyclable materials, etc.).

Summer Garden—a park in the historical center of St. Petersburg, laid out in 1725.

Third Department—investigation department; the most influential unit of camp administration.

troika—a triumvirate of representatives of the organs, which during Stalin's era passed sentences *in absentia* to speed up the prosecution procedure.

vareniki—a variety of stuffed dumplings in Ukrainian and Russian cuisine.

verst—a Russian unit of distance equal to 0.66 miles (1.07 kilometers).

Vlasov army—a regiment of former Soviet soldiers and officers who, often after being taken prisoner by the Germans, defected to the German side and fought the Red Army with General Vlasov's Russian Liberation Army (ROA); extradited to the Soviets by the Allies, most of them were sent to the camps with terms of ten, fifteen, and twnety-five years, while others were shot.

yamshchik—a coachman, or anyone who delivers goods or passengers by horse-pulled transport.

zemstvo—a form of local government during the rule of Alexander II, abolished after the October Revolution of 1917.

INDEX